THE PSYCHOLOGY OF CRIMINAL AND VIOLENT BEHAVIOUR

THE PSYCHOLOGY OF CRIMINAL AND VIOLENT BEHAVIOUR

David R. Lyon and Andrew Welsh

OXFORD
UNIVERSITY PRESS

OXFORD
UNIVERSITY PRESS

Oxford University Press is a department of the University of Oxford.
It furthers the University's objective of excellence in research, scholarship,
and education by publishing worldwide. Oxford is a registered trade mark of
Oxford University Press in the UK and in certain other countries.

Published in Canada by
Oxford University Press
8 Sampson Mews, Suite 204,
Don Mills, Ontario M3C 0H5 Canada

www.oupcanada.com

Library and Archives Canada Cataloguing in Publication
Lyon, David R. (David Robert), 1966–, author
The psychology of criminal and violent behaviour / Dave Lyon
and Andrew Welsh.

Includes bibliographical references and index.
ISBN 978–0–19–901008–0 (paperback)

1. Criminal psychology—Textbooks. 2. Criminal behavior—
Textbooks. I. Welsh, Andrew, 1974–, author II. Title.

HV6080.L96 2016   364.3   C2016-905044-0

Cover image: monkeman/Getty Images

Oxford University Press is committed to our environment.
Wherever possible, our books are printed on paper which comes from
responsible sources.

Printed and bound in Canada

6 7 8 — 22 21 20

Contents

7 | Learning   146

8 | Social Cognition   173

Researching Criminal and Violent Behaviour Boxes

Preface

The Psychology of Criminal and Violent Behaviour has been in the works since the two of us worked together at Kwantlen Polytechnic University. In our early years of teaching courses on the psychology of crime, we relied on existing textbooks. The challenge we faced was finding one that explained the major theories of interest at a level appropriate for our audience without delving into laws and legal procedures that did not apply. Later, we switched to individual articles from the published literature, which proved to be a good way of getting the content we desired. The disadvantage was that each article was written independently and the package as a whole lacked integration and consistency. In the end, we decided that the best approach was to write our own textbook.

Our goal is to show students how psychological theories can help us understand offending behaviour. It explores common psychological theories and explains their application to criminal and violent behaviour. This text is a theories book. As such, it avoids detailed discussions of criminal law—specific laws differ from jurisdiction to jurisdiction, but theories transcend political and legal boundaries. We also include statistics only when they are relevant to the theoretical explanations being presented or highlight common patterns. Our focus is on encouraging the reader to understand each psychological theory presented and its connection to criminal and violent behaviour.

Ultimately, we hope that students find this textbook accessible and engaging. We included numerous real-life case studies so that readers can immerse themselves in the subject matter and grasp the respective theory's potential application to the world around us. We have also provided a variety of research boxes in each chapter to give readers an opportunity to examine studies and research questions in greater depth. The text's marginal definitions, chapter summaries, review questions, and additional readings reinforce main concepts and encourage further investigation.

Acknowledgements

We are both indebted to the staff at Oxford University Press. In particular, we would like thank Dave Ward for his belief in the value of this project, as well as Tamara Capar, Janna Green, and Ella Mazur for their never-ending assistance and patience. We and the press would also like to acknowledge the constructive feedback we received from the anonymous reviewers and the following: Dick Day, McMaster University; Denise Iacobucci, Camosun College; Janelle Jackiw, University of Regina and Lethbridge College; A. Ross Keele, University of Saskatchewan; Hilary Kim Morden, Simon Fraser University; Giselle Patrick, University of Saskatchewan, Amy Prevost, University of the Fraser Valley; Heather L. Price, University of Regina; Paul Valliant, Laurentian University; and Uzma Williams, MacEwan University. As faculty members with full teaching workloads and research programs, we understand the time and commitment involved with reviewing this kind of project. Your feedback and suggestions were greatly appreciated and led to valuable developments in the writing process.

David R. Lyon

I would like to thank the faculty and staff at Kwantlen Polytechnic University for their generous assistance and support. I would also like to acknowledge my friends and colleagues from the Forensic Psychology Program at Simon Fraser University, particularly Steve Hart and Randy Kropp. I appreciate their willingness over the years to offer ideas and share insights on crime and violence. Thanks also to the endless love and support of my wife, Tami, and our children, Graeme and Rebecca, both of whom quite literally grew up alongside this book. Finally, I would like to dedicate this book to my late father, Don, who heard about it for long enough but never saw it published. I wish I had written faster.

Andrew Welsh

I would like to extend my sincerest thanks to my colleagues in the Departments of Criminology and Psychology at Wilfrid Laurier University, who supported me while writing this textbook. Whether it was having informal conversations in hallways or proofreading chapters, your willingness to help and support this project has not been forgotten. Many thanks to Alanna Crowder, who listened patiently while I wrestled with the many challenges of writing a book of this magnitude. It would never have been finished without your support.

1

Introduction

Learning Objectives

At the end of this chapter, you should be able to:

- explain what criminal behaviour is and identify some of the factors that influence how crimes are defined;

- define violence and explain some approaches to distinguishing different forms of violent behaviour;

- distinguish sociology and psychology and explain their relative emphasis in the study of criminal and violent behaviour;

- recognize the characteristics of a "good" scientific theory of criminal and violent behaviour; and

- identify the three basic research designs and outline their relative strengths and weaknesses.

CASE STUDIES

- **Manhattan, New York**—Jordan Belfort, the subject of the Oscar-nominated film *The Wolf of Wall Street*, pled guilty in 1999 to securities fraud and money laundering. Belfort and a number of his friends founded the brokerage firm Stratton Oakmont, which operated a boiler room that pushed penny stocks and defrauded clients out of millions of dollars. In his memoir, Belfort (2007) describes an excessive lifestyle of greed, lavish parties, and drugs.

- **Abbotsford, British Columbia**—Christopher Long received a four-month conditional sentence in 2013 for hacking into singer Carly Rae Jepsen's personal computer and social media accounts. Long downloaded a number of Jepsen's personal files, including photographs of a personal and sensitive nature and, possibly, nude images. Long admitted posting an inappropriate photo and comment on one of Jepsen's social media accounts, making it appear as though the singer had made the post (Hager, 2013; Lawrence, 2013).

- **Lionsville, Indiana**—Jared Fogle, a spokesperson for Subway restaurants, was sentenced to 15 years imprisonment in connection with charges for possessing child pornography and having sex with minors. Prosecutors alleged that he received pornographic images from the former director of Jared's Foundation, a charity Fogle established to raise awareness of childhood obesity, and procured young female prostitutes while on foundation and Subway business trips ("Jared Fogle, ex-Subway Pitchman," 2015).

- **Los Angeles, California**—Chris Brown pled guilty to assaulting his then-girlfriend and fellow singer, Rihanna, in 2009. Reports claimed that he repeatedly bit and punched her and choked her so hard that she had difficulty breathing; photos emerging after the incident showed her with a battered and swollen face. During a subsequent television interview, Rihanna said that the assault occurred after she confronted Brown about a text message from another girl. She explained that, when the argument escalated to physical blows, she used her feet to fend him off. Brown was sentenced to five years probation and 1,400 hours of community service for the crime (Duke, 2009; Rodriguez, 2009).

- **Oslo, Norway**—On 22 July 2011 Anders Breivik detonated a car bomb in central Oslo before driving 30 kilometres to the island of Utøya, where the Workers' Youth League was meeting. Attired in a blue uniform that resembled a police officer's and armed with an automatic weapon, Breivik calmly walked around the camp and shot everyone he came across (Ahlander & Moskwa, 2011). He killed 69 people before he was apprehended. It was later learned that he hoped his attack would start a "pre-emptive war" to end what he perceived was the colonization of Europe by Muslims (Raynor, Bingham, & Whitehead, 2011, p. B.2). His lawyer explained that Breivik did not feel his actions were reprehensible and believed that one day he would be thanked for his efforts.

The public's fascination with crime is long-standing. Just as we tend to rubberneck as we pass a car accident, we seem to be simultaneously captivated and horrified by the accounts of people who violate our most cherished social boundaries. Yet criminal and violent behaviour should be more than idle curiosity because it has widespread and profoundly damaging impacts. Victimization surveys from Canada, the United States, and England conservatively estimate that between 1 and 2 people in every 10 are criminally victimized each year (Chaplin, Flately, & Smith, 2011; Suavé & Hung, 2008; Truman & Langton, 2015). While the level of violent victimization is lower, it is not trivial. Surveys reveal that roughly one-quarter to one-third of all criminal victimization experiences involve violence (Chaplin et al., 2011; Perreault & Brennan, 2010; Truman & Langton, 2015). There is also mounting evidence that crime, especially violent crime, takes an enormous emotional, psychological, physical, and economic toll on its victims (AuCoin & Beauchamp, 2007; Chester, 2001; Lindert, 2015; Monnat & Chandler, 2015; Nicolaidis & Liebschutz, 2009; Warshaw, Brashler, & Gil, 2009).

The costs of crime are borne not only by the victims and their families but also by society, which must shoulder the expenses associated with law enforcement, prosecution services, the courts, and the correctional system. The Canadian taxpayers' tab for these services was estimated at over $15 billion in 2008, equivalent to almost $450 for every resident (Zhang, 2008). The 2007 figures for the United States were $228 billion, or about $750 per person (Kyckelhahn, 2011). Clearly, crime carries a tremendous financial burden along with the human cost to personal health and well-being.

While there can be little doubt that crime and violence are serious societal issues, much less certainty exists over how best to tackle these problems. Developing a deeper understanding of the factors contributing to criminal and violent behaviour, however, is a promising way forward. The more we know about the root causes of these behaviours, the better we will become at designing strategies to prevent and reduce offending. The goal of this book is to contribute to this process. It introduces major psychological theories and illustrates how they can give us insight into criminal and violent behaviour. With any luck, it will spark your interest and motivate you to contribute to this important field.

What Is Criminal Behaviour?

The title of this book clearly sets out its subject—the study of why people commit crime and violence. But before we can study or understand a phenomenon, we need to know what it means, how to recognize it, and what sets it apart from other, similar phenomena. At the outset of this chapter, we described several incidents involving a wide array of different behaviours, from fraud to murder. Many of the behaviours appear to be premeditated and carefully thought out, but they could also be spontaneous. The perpetrator and victim were usually in close proximity, except for one case involving remotely situated parties. Some of the people involved in the incidents had pre-existing relationships, while others did not know each other. Despite the diversity of these cases, nearly everyone would agree that they involve criminal behaviour. What, then, do these activities have in common that distinguishes them from non-criminal behaviour?

At the risk of stating the obvious, the key is that all these behaviours are crimes under the law. **Criminal behaviour**, then, is any act (or omission) that is a crime. Without delving into legal nuance, criminal law usually requires a high degree of knowledge and intention on the part of the perpetrator. Accidents and mistakes are not typically crimes. Suppose you mistakenly pick up the wrong sports bag after practice. You have not committed theft because you did not know the bag belonged to someone else and had no intention of taking another person's property. Once you realize your mistake, however, you must return the bag to its rightful owner immediately. If you keep it, you are intentionally depriving the true owner of his or her property and therefore committing theft.

Even if one accepts our definition of criminal behaviour, there is still room for debate over whether or not a crime has been committed. Some scholars claim that, from a purely legalistic standpoint, only the courts can make such a determination. For example, Paul Tappan (1947) maintained that social scientists should consider someone a criminal only if he or she was pronounced guilty by a court. He expressly argued against making any presumptions in this regard on the basis of arrests, charges, or anything else short of a conviction. Regardless of the merit or legal correctness of this approach, it is not in

criminal behaviour An act or omission that is legally defined as a crime.

keeping with the goals of this text. It overlooks the large majority of criminal behaviour that never comes to the attention of criminal justice system officials yet may be just as damaging and therefore worth understanding and preventing (see Perreault & Brennan, 2010; Truman & Langton, 2015). For this reason, we will focus on behaviours that satisfy the legal definition of a crime, irrespective of criminal justice system outcome.

The Social Construction of Crime

social construction of crime
The process of defining crime is social and political in nature and consequently the definitions of crime embody human values and moral beliefs about right and wrong.

consensus theory of crime
The theory that crime is defined in a manner that is broadly agreed upon by the members of society.

conflict theory of crime
The theory that crime is determined by the powerful and wealthy members of society, who define it in ways that promote and maintain their position of dominance.

Crime is a **social construction**—people decide what behaviours to criminalize and how those crimes will be defined. Although this topic is beyond the scope of this text, it is important to recognize that the process of constructing crime is socio-political in nature. Opinion is divided, however, over whether this process is primarily characterized by **consensus**, involving widespread agreement among the members of society on what behaviours should be crimes, or by **conflict**, whereby the powerful and wealthy elite define crimes in ways that maintain their dominant position over weaker members of society.

The social construction of crime is important for our purposes because it affects the behaviours we are interested in studying and understanding. As a socially constructed phenomenon, crimes are defined in ways that embody human values and beliefs; people tend to create laws that reflect their sense of right and wrong. Moreover, just as human values about right and wrong vary as a function of time and geography, so do the definitions of crime. Stalking is a good example. It is abundantly clear from descriptive accounts in classic literary works, early clinical reports, and the popular media that people have engaged in stalking throughout human history (Meloy, 1999; Mullen, Pathé, & Purcell, 2001). Yet it was only after the highly publicized stalking and murder of Rebecca Schaefer by Robert Bardo in 1989 (see the case study on next page) that specific criminal laws targeting this behaviour began to appear in North America and other Western countries (Mullen et al., 2001). As Meloy (1999) aptly noted, stalking is "an old behaviour" but "a new crime" (p. 85).

Definitions of crime also vary with the legal jurisdiction. Prostitution, assisted suicide, polygamy, and recreational marijuana use are legally permissible in some jurisdictions but crimes in others. In short, something that is a crime in one place or at one time may be legal in a different place or at a different time.

You may feel that reading on is fruitless given the apparent uncertainty over what behaviours are criminal and what it is we are trying to understand. If so, do not despair! John Hagan (1991) argues that a relationship exists between the perceived harm of a particular behaviour and the extent to which people agree that it should be criminalized. The lowest level of agreement concerns behaviours considered fairly harmless. Among the more controversial criminal offences are so-called victimless crimes, such as prostitution, that involve consenting adult participants and arguably lack a readily identifiable victim (Walsh & Ellis, 2007). The divergence of opinion that surrounds less serious behaviours means that their legal status is less certain and more susceptible to change. By comparison, there is widespread support for criminal laws that address behaviours deemed more serious in nature. For example, murder, sexual assault, and theft are almost universally regarded as crimes.

This difference was demonstrated empirically by Newman (1976), who surveyed people from six different cultures for their opinions about the legal status of various behaviours. If the act in question caused serious, non-consensual harm to others (e.g. robbery, incest, or

CASE STUDY

Robert Bardo

Los Angeles, California—After a brief modelling career and small parts in commercials, Rebecca Schaeffer landed a starring role in the TV sitcom *My Sister Sam* in 1986. During the run of the show, she came to the attention of Robert John Bardo. He was a lonely and socially awkward young man who found her youthful and innocent onscreen persona attractive. Bardo began writing her fan letters and, when his request for an autographed photo was granted, he took it as a sign of her interest in him. Bardo's letters eventually escalated into several failed efforts to meet Schaeffer on the set of her show (Saunders, 1998; Stone, 2007).

Following the cancellation of *My Sister Sam* in 1988, Schaeffer tried to break into feature films. She had a small part in the movie *Scenes from the Class Struggle in Beverly Hills*, which she hoped would lead to more

Photo 1.1 Robert Bardo appears at his arraignment proceeding for the killing of Rebecca Schaeffer.

Bettman/Getty Images

serious, adult roles. The film includes a sexually suggestive scene, which outraged Bardo. He felt that it was a betrayal of her wholesome image, and he became increasingly hostile in his letters, referring to her as "Miss Nudity 2-shoes" (Saunders, 1998, p. 27).

Bardo grew convinced that he had to stop Schaeffer from turning into an "adult fornicating screen whore" (Saunders, 1998, p. 27). He hired a private detective agency, which tracked down her address. When Bardo showed up at the actress's apartment on 18 July 1989, Schaeffer spoke with him briefly before asking him to leave. He did so, but he returned soon afterwards and shot her when she opened the door.

In the aftermath of Schaeffer's death, California enacted the first official anti-stalking law in the United States (Saunders, 1998). Bardo is currently serving a life sentence in a California prison. He was stabbed several times by another inmate in 2007 but survived his injuries ("Killer of Actress Stabbed," 2007).

theft), the number of respondents indicating that it should be a crime was uniformly high (94 per cent) across all represented cultures. On the other hand, the level of survey respondents who believed that less harmful, consensual acts involving adults (e.g. drug-taking) should be crimes was lower and more variable across the different cultures. These findings add credence to Hagan's (1991) assertion about the connection between the perceived harm of a behaviour and whether it is viewed as a crime. In addition, the general view that serious behaviours should be illegal shows that these acts form a relatively stable group of "core crimes" (Walsh & Ellis, 2007, p. 8). This book is primarily interested in this group of serious offences.

Violent Behaviour

While this book canvasses theories of criminal behaviour generally, it emphasizes violent behaviour. **Violence** is an intentional act of threatened, attempted, or actual physical harm directed against a non-consenting person (Webster, Douglas, Eaves, & Hart, 1997). Encompassed within this broad definition is a narrower subset of behaviours that involve **physical violence**, which is confined to intentional acts causing physical insult or injury to

violence An intentional act of threatened, attempted, or actual physical harm directed against a non-consenting person.

physical violence An intentional act that causes physical insult or injury, regardless of how minor, to another non-consenting person.

another non-consenting person. Punching, kicking, strangling, striking with a weapon, stabbing, and shooting are all examples of physically violent behaviour. These are often the sorts of behaviours that people immediately think of when they hear the word *violence*, but keep in mind that the definition adopted here covers much more than just physical violence. It also includes explicit statements (e.g. "I'm going to beat you up") and actions threatening physical harm (e.g. pointing a loaded gun at someone). Attempts to harm others, such as driving a car into a crowd of people, also fall within the definition, even if everyone scrambles safely out of the way (Webster et al., 1997). Such a broad conceptualization implicitly recognizes that violent actions not involving physical harm can still be damaging. This idea is consistent with a growing body of evidence showing that chronic threatening and other fear-inducing behaviours can have a profoundly negative impact on the health and emotional well-being of victims (e.g. Davis & Mechanic, 2009; Wilson, Douglas, & Lyon, 2011).

The diverse nature of violent behaviour complicates efforts to study and understand it. One approach for dealing with this challenge is to differentiate violence along one or more dimensions so that a smaller group of more homogenous behaviours can be studied (see generally Hart, 1998a). For example, violence is sometimes differentiated according to the nature or severity of the behaviour and thus classified as sexual violence, stalking, homicide, and so forth. Alternatively, different forms of violence may be identified using the victims' characteristics, as in the case of child abuse and spousal assault, or on the basis of the context in which it occurs, such as workplace and school violence. Violence can also be distinguished according to the perpetrator's apparent motivation. For instance, the classification system developed by the Behavioral Sciences Unit of the Federal Bureau of Investigation divides murder into one of four main categories, depending on whether the killing was primarily precipitated by a desire for monetary gain or status (criminal enterprise homicide), an underlying emotional conflict between the parties (personal cause homicide), a sexual purpose (sexual homicide), or membership in a group that supports murder (group cause homicide; Douglas, Burgess, Burgess, & Ressler, 2013).

Motivation is also the main distinction separating instrumental from reactive violence. Instrumental violence is goal oriented; it is used to gain an identifiable objective such as money, material goods, sexual gratification, or power. It is usually associated with premeditated acts that are carried out in an unemotional fashion against victims who have little or no prior relationship with the perpetrator. The mass murder perpetrated by Anders Breivik, described at the beginning of this chapter, is an example of instrumental violence. The act was perpetrated to achieve Breivik's disturbing desire to start an ethnic war. Instrumental violence is sometimes called predatory violence because, in many respects, the perpetrator and victim resemble a hunter and its prey.

Reactive violence usually occurs in response to an extreme frustration, a perceived insult, or an act of aggression. This type of violence has no goal except to cause pain or harm to the victim. It normally involves spontaneous acts of violence committed during periods when emotions, such as anger or alarm, are running high. Reactive violence is commonly directed at victims known to the perpetrator, including romantic partners, family members, friends, or colleagues. Chris Brown's assault of Rihanna is an example of reactive violence. Brown appeared to have no objective beyond lashing out and hurting his girlfriend because he was infuriated at being confronted by her. As we shall see in later chapters, the distinctive nature of instrumental and reactive violence (summarized in Table 1.1) has prompted speculation that these acts probably result from different underlying factors and mechanisms.

Table 1.1 Summary of instrumental and reactive violence

	Instrumental Violence	Reactive Violence
Definition	Violence committed to achieve an identifiable goal	Violence committed in response to frustration or a perceived insult, provocation, or attack
Planning	Associated with planned acts of violence	Associated with spontaneous acts of violence
Emotional arousal	Associated with an absence of emotional arousal	Associated with the presence of high emotional arousal
Relationship to victim	Associated with victims who are strangers or have distant existing relationships with the perpetrator	Associated with victims who have close existing relationships with the perpetrator

Theoretical Perspectives

A logical place to start a discussion of theoretical perspectives relating to criminal behaviour is to look briefly at the discipline of criminology, which is dedicated to the study of crime and criminal behaviour (Conklin, 2013; Siegel & McCormick, 2003). It is multidisciplinary in nature, drawing on a large number of diverse fields, including biology, geography, anthropology, law, sociology, and psychology. That said, it has traditionally been dominated by sociology and psychology (Wortley, 2011).

Sociology is the study of human behaviour in social groups and society at large (Scott, Schwartz, & VanderPlaat, 2000). Hence, it is primarily concerned with the influence of social groups and society on criminal behaviour and the construction of crime. Viewed through the lens of sociology, criminal behaviour is generally seen as a relatively common human response to particular social conditions. The focus is largely on factors external to the individual and related to the nature of the society, social group, or context in which people are situated (Bohm & Vogel, 2011). For instance, social structure—that is, the manner in which society is organized and stratified into groups or classes of people—figures prominently in many sociological theories (Walsh & Ellis, 2007). Sociological theorists want to know why criminal and violent behaviour is more prevalent among particular segments of society, such as the young, the poor, and certain ethno-cultural groups (e.g. Aboriginal Canadians or African Americans). They are also interested in explaining variations in criminal and violent behaviour across societies. For example, why is Canada's homicide rate lower than the United States' but higher than Japan's (Akers & Sellers, 2013)? Large-scale theories that use society as a whole or broad groups within society as the unit of analysis are sometimes classified as **macro theories** (Walsh & Ellis, 2007).

macro theory A large-scale theory that explains phenomena at a societal or broad group level.

Psychology takes a somewhat different perspective on criminal behaviour. Most introductory psychology textbooks define the field as the study of behaviour and mental processes. Criminal psychology, therefore, focuses on the mental processes and behaviour of individuals who engage in crime and violence (Bartol & Bartol, 2012). In contrast to sociology's emphasis on external social conditions, psychology centres on individually based factors (Bohm & Vogel, 2011). These factors are things that could be considered internal to a person, such as his or her biology, brain functioning, emotions, thought processes, and personality, or things that pertain to his or her individual experiences, such as family upbringing, or to immediate circumstances, such as being embroiled in a verbal argument

micro theory A small-scale theory that explains phenomena at an individual level.

(Wortley, 2011). The goal of psychological theorists is to explain the conduct of individuals rather than broad groups within society or society at large. Given this unit of analysis, these theories are often described as **micro theories** (Walsh & Ellis, 2007).

Despite the seemingly complementary nature of these two perspectives, psychology has often found itself pushed to the margins of mainstream criminology in favour of sociology. While the relevance and contributions of the latter are not in doubt, it is unlikely that sociology alone can ever provide a full explanation of criminal and violent behaviour. For example, some sociological and feminist circles claim that spousal assault is produced by society's patriarchal structure and values, which promote male dominance and the subjugation of women (Dutton, 1995a). Yet this cannot be the complete explanation because, even in the most patriarchal societies, only some men act violently toward their partners. The intent here is not to dismiss the possible roles of patriarchy or other social and structural factors in spousal assault but merely to point out that psychology can shed light on why some individuals exposed to these social values commit spousal assault while others do not.

In addition, society and the legal system have created a very real demand for psychological perspectives on criminal and violent offending. Legal decision-makers frequently confront issues that must be determined, either wholly or partly, on the basis of whether someone is likely to offend (Lyon, Hart, & Webster, 2001). This issue is central to many decisions in the criminal justice system relating to, for instance, bail, sentencing, correctional placement, and parole. The same type of issue arises in the civil context with decisions concerning employment, child custody, immigration, and civil commitment. Decision-makers are obliged to resolve these matters as they relate to a particular case. They are not concerned with everyone in society or even the individual's broader social group. They must decide if the person before them is likely to offend. As we noted earlier, the psychological approach is well-suited to addressing questions about individuals. Moreover, the demand for psychological theories and research to address these issues is unlikely to diminish any time soon given the heightened concerns that have emerged over security and violence during the past two decades.

Scientific Theories

theory A set of interconnected statements that explain the relationship between two or more events.

We all hold informal or working theories even if we do not think of them in these terms. Have you ever attributed a child's misbehaviour to lax parenting? Have you ever assumed that someone who performed badly on an exam has poor study habits? Though rudimentary, these conclusions are based on **theories**, sets of interconnected statements that explain the relationship between two or more events (Curran & Renzetti, 2001; Williams & McShane, 2010). Each example satisfies the definition of a theory by explaining the association between two events: parenting style and child behaviour and study habits and academic performance, respectively.

The informal theories we develop in our everyday lives are often based on nothing more than anecdotal observations and our subjective impressions of the world around us (Curran & Renzetti, 2001). This is what sets informal theories apart from scientific ones. Scientific theories must be both testable and empirically validated; their major statements or propositions must be subjected to the scientific method to determine if the evidence supports them (Akers & Sellers, 2013). Very generally, this process requires conducting systematic observations of the phenomena of interest (Curran & Renzetti, 2001). We will examine some of the major methodological approaches researchers use to evaluate psychological theories a little later in this chapter.

A theory must not only be scientifically testable and valid but also have good explanatory power. This term refers to a theory's ability to provide a full and precise account of the phenomenon of interest, which in our case is criminal behaviour (Bohm & Vogel, 2011). From a psychological perspective, theories should be able to explain both inter-individual and intra-individual differences in offending (Andrews & Bonta, 2006). **Inter-individual differences** are those that exist between or among people. Consider the results of the Philadelphia Birth Cohort study, which is discussed in the "Researching Criminal and Violent Behaviour" ("Researching") box below. The study found that only 6 per cent of the nearly 10,000 participants were responsible for more than 50 per cent of the offences committed by the entire cohort (Wolfgang, Figlio, & Sellin, 1972/1987). Other researchers also report finding that a disproportionately large number of offences are committed by a small group of offenders (see Farrington, 1997; Guttridge, Gabrielli, Mednick, & Van Dusen, 1983). A good theory should be able to account for these inter-individual variations in criminal behaviour and explain why most people rarely or never commit a crime, but a few people become persistent offenders.

Intra-individual differences reflect variations within the same person. Think about your own behaviour. You probably act differently at home than you do at school, at work, or when you are with your friends. Behaviour also changes over time, something acknowledged in many of our everyday sayings: "the terrible twos," "troublesome teen years," or "mid-life crisis." An individual's offending behaviour can vary in the same fashion. Take a look at the **age–crime curves** displayed in Figures 1.1 and 1.2. These figures show that crime rates vary depending on age and that the highest rates are concentrated at relatively young ages. This robust pattern appears throughout history and across cultures

inter-individual differences Variations that exist between two or more individuals.

intra-individual differences Variations occurring within the same person.

age–crime curve The distribution of criminal behaviour over the lifespan, which consistently shows that crime rates rise sharply throughout adolescence, peak in early adulthood, and taper off during middle and old age.

Researching Criminal and Violent Behaviour

The Philadelphia Birth Cohort Study

Wolfgang, Figlio, and Sellin (1987) studied a cohort of males who were born in 1945 and resided in Philadelphia for at least the eight-year period spanning their tenth and eighteenth birthdays. Using military draft and school registration records, they identified 9,945 participants. To evaluate delinquency, the researchers reviewed official police records. They found that 35 per cent of the participants were delinquents, as defined by the presence of at least one documented police contact. Collectively, the delinquents were responsible for more than 10,000 documented offences. Further analyses revealed that these offences were not evenly distributed. The researchers identified a relatively small group of delinquents who committed five or more offences. This group of chronic offenders made up only 6 per cent

of the birth cohort, but they were responsible for 52 per cent of all the offences committed.

A remarkably similar pattern emerged when the criminal behaviour of the same birth cohort was examined in adulthood. Wolfgang (1983) randomly selected 10 per cent of the original sample and then checked to see which of them had police records at age 30. Just under half this subsample (47 per cent) had an arrest documented in police records. Once again, it was possible to identify a small number of persistent offenders who accounted for a disproportionately large number of the offences committed as an adult. Specifically, only 15 per cent of the subsample had five or more arrests as an adult, but this group incurred 53 per cent of all the adult offences.

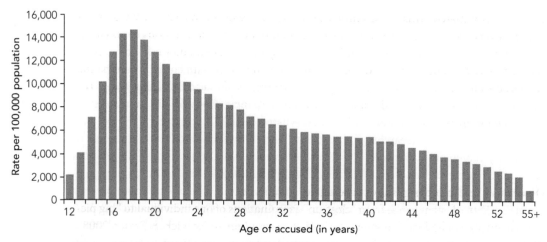

Figure 1.1 Age–Crime curve for Canada, 2011.

Source: Brennan, S. (2012). *Police-reported crime statistics in Canada, 2011.* Ottawa, ON: Canadian Centre for Justice Statistics, Statistics Canada, p. 19.

(Gottfredson & Hirschi, 1983). For example, a visual inspection of Canada's and the Netherlands' age–crime curves reveals the two are virtually indistinguishable.

Although the age–crime curve is based on the data of many people, it suggests the likelihood that committing crime fluctuates over the lifespan. In addition to explaining why some people are more likely to commit crime than others, a comprehensive theory should also help us understand why people are more likely to engage in criminal behaviour in certain contexts and at certain times in their lives.

Researching Criminal and Violent Behaviour

Research is an integral part of theory development. Psychological theories of criminal and violent behaviour are sometimes inspired by intriguing findings uncovered by research. As previously mentioned, a theory needs to be scientifically tested to see if it

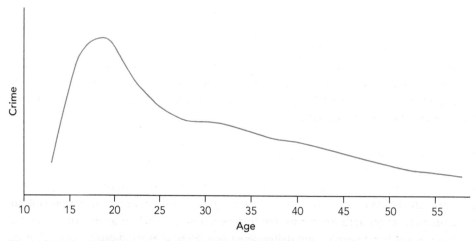

Figure 1.2 Age–Crime curve for native Dutch people in the Netherlands, 2005

Source: Jennissen, R. (2014). On the deviant age–crime curve of Afro-Caribbean populations: The case of Antilleans living in the Netherlands. *American Journal of Criminal Justice, 39,* 571–594. R. Jennissen, Copyright © 2014, Southern Criminal Justice Association. With permission of Springer.

can be substantiated. This book summarizes research relevant to each theory present-ed, and every chapter includes boxes providing more detailed descriptions of classic or ground-breaking studies in an area. To appreciate what these studies can and cannot reasonably tell us about criminal and violent behaviour, it is important to understand the basic elements of research design and methodology. The next section outlines the descriptive, correlational, and experimental study designs that you will encounter in this book (Stangor, 2011).

Descriptive Research Designs

Descriptive research designs give investigators information about individual factors or variables. These designs range from "close up" examinations of one individual to "big pic-ture" overviews of a broad group of people (Bernstein, Cramer, Fenwick, & Fraser, 2008). An in-depth examination of a single person is called a **case study**. Psychology has a long tradition of using case studies—much of Freud's theory of psychoanalysis, for instance, was based on case studies of his patients (Stangor, 2011). This approach has also been used to develop insight into criminal behaviour. The classic example is Edwin Suther-land's (1937) *The Professional Thief*; others include Carl Klockars's (1974) *The Professional Fence*, about a stolen goods dealer, and William Chambliss's (1972) *Boxman: A Profession-al Thief's Journey*, which recounts the exploits of a professional safecracker.

case study An in-depth examination or observation of a single individual.

Case studies provide a rich source of information that can be extremely valuable for studying novel, unusual, or complex behaviours in real-life contexts (Bernstein et al., 2008). Case studies are used throughout this book to illustrate how different theories can make sense of an individual's crimes. The main limitation of case studies is that there is rarely any way to verify scientifically whether suppositions regarding the causes of some-one's behaviour are correct and, even if they are, the extent to which they explain the behaviour of other offenders (Gazzaniga & Heatherton, 2006).

Descriptive research with groups is often conducted using surveys, interviews, nat-uralistic observations, and (particular to the realm of criminal behaviour) police crime data. As with case studies, descriptive research with groups can easily examine variables of interest as they occur naturally in real life (Gazzaniga & Heatherton, 2006). It has the added advantage of moving beyond a single individual and providing insight into the ex-tent that members of a group express common thoughts, emotions, behaviours, or other characteristics. For example, we might learn that most murderers, at least those identified by police, were under the influence of alcohol at the time of the killing. The chief limitation of descriptive research is that it provides no information about the interrelationships of different variables (Stangor, 2011).

Correlational Research Designs

Correlational research examines the relationships between two or more variables (Stan-gor, 2011). Once the pattern of relationships among variables is understood, it is possible to make predictions about future events. For instance, some research suggests that an inverse relationship exists between IQ and delinquency (e.g. Hirschi & Hindelang, 1977). That is, higher IQs are associated with lower rates of delinquency and lower IQs with higher rates. This knowledge allows us to predict that someone who displays lower intellectual perfor-mance is more likely to engage in delinquent behaviour.

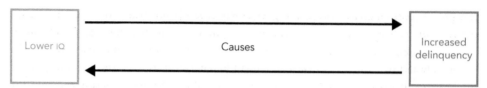

Figure 1.3 Directionality: Which way does the relationship go?

One of the challenges of correlational studies is determining the directionality of the relationship. In other words, do lower intellectual performances lead to delinquent behaviour or does leading a delinquent lifestyle lead to lower intellectual performance (Ellis & Walsh, 2003; see Figure 1.3)? One way to resolve questions of directionality is to employ **longitudinal research designs**, which repeatedly measure the same study participants at different times. For example, researchers might measure each participant's level of delinquent behaviour and intellectual performance at 8, 11, 14, and 17 years of age. The Philadelphia Birth Cohort Study, discussed earlier, is a longitudinal study. We will encounter several other longitudinal studies examples at various places in this book, especially in our discussion of developmental pathways in Chapter 4. Despite their value, longitudinal designs are used relatively infrequently because they tend to be expensive and time-consuming.

Another problem with correlational studies, and one that cannot be resolved using longitudinal designs, is the issue of so-called third variables (Gazzaniga & Heatherton, 2006). A **third variable** is an extraneous factor related to the variables under investigation (Cozby, 2007; Goodwin & Goodwin, 2013). It can create the appearance of a link between the study variables that actually exists only because each is independently connected to the third variable. For example, IQ and delinquency might be correlated simply because of the connection both variables have with socio-economic status (SES). Low SES could lead to increased delinquency (due to the influence of impoverished living conditions, antisocial peers, or living in high-risk neighbourhoods) and to lower IQs (due to restricted educational opportunities, limited resources, and more limited parental support). As a result, when SES is low, IQ scores decrease and crime goes up. Conversely, when SES

longitudinal research design A research design that involves making several observations of the same study participants over a period of time, sometimes many years.

third variable An extraneous and uncontrolled factor that may be responsible for changes occurring in a study variable.

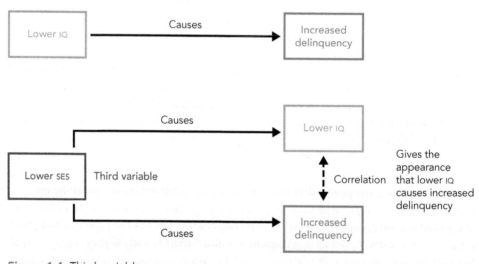

Figure 1.4 Third variables.

Source: Adapted from Baron, R. A., Earhard, B., & Ozier, M. (1998). *Psychology* (2nd Canadian ed.). Scarborough, ON: Prentice-Hall, p. 25.

is high, IQ scores increase and crime goes down. If SES is not taken into account, we get the false impression that IQ and offending are connected. Before moving on we should note that studies examining this issue report that SES cannot fully account for the IQ–delinquency relationship, although properly assessing its impact is complicated (e.g. Mears & Cochran, 2013). Relationships that can be explained on the basis of a third variable are sometimes called spurious because they are not genuine. Questions over third variables and directionality have led to the well-known axiom that correlations do not prove causation.

Classic Experimental Designs

Many of the challenges associated with correlational studies are addressed by experimental designs. A true experiment requires three essential elements: random assignment of the study participants; an experimental group; and a control, or comparison, group (Siegel & McCormick, 2003). **Random assignment** means that every participant has an equal chance of being in every one of the study groups (Hagan, 2005). This procedure is intended to ensure that the groups are roughly equivalent at the beginning of the study and that any differences observed later on are caused by the experimental condition (Baron, Earhard, & Ozier, 1998). Participants assigned to the **experimental group** are exposed to a stimulus or experimental variable that the investigators believe will produce some observable effect or response (Hagan, 2005). Participants assigned to the **control group** are not exposed to this variable. This group serves as a baseline against which the experimental group's behaviour can be compared (Goodwin & Goodwin, 2013).

The real strength of using an experimental design is that it permits **causal inferences**. If everything but the application of the experimental variable is held constant between the two groups, we can logically infer that the variable caused any subsequent behavioural (or other) change observed in the experimental group. By illuminating causal factors, experimental designs help to uncover why people behave the way they do, which is what we are ultimately striving to find (Baron et al., 1998).

The principal challenge of experimental designs is trying to control all the extraneous factors that might otherwise prevent us from drawing causal inferences. A laboratory may be preferred because it provides tight control over the research environment. The drawback is that laboratory studies often appear contrived and the results may not reflect what happens in real life.

Regardless of whether an experiment takes place in a laboratory or the field, there are practical and ethical constraints on what researchers can do. For example, we could not use a true experimental design to determine whether head injuries contribute to criminal and violent offending. Even if consenting participants for such a study could be found, it would be highly unethical. When random assignment is not possible, researchers sometimes utilize **quasi-experimental designs**. In our example, they might compare a group of people with pre-existing head injuries with a control group of people who are injury-free to see if the groups differ with respect to criminal behaviour. The difficulty with quasi-experimental designs is that the study groups may be non-equivalent in other respects beyond the experimental variable. Perhaps participants in the experimental group have a much greater tendency to engage in sensation-seeking and risky behaviour, which led to their head injury. In this scenario, any behavioural difference found between the two groups could be attributable to either the sensation-seeking or the head injury. To minimize this type of problem and ensure as much group equivalency as possible, the

random assignment The assignment of participants to different study conditions on the basis of chance.

experimental group The study participants who are exposed to the variable or condition under investigation.

control group The study participants who are not exposed to the variable or condition under investigation and are used for comparison purposes.

causal inference A logical conclusion made when experimental results show that one variable is responsible for changing another.

quasi-experimental group A research design that incorporates some of the features of a true experiment.

participants in both groups are often matched on major characteristics that the researchers believe could influence the results. Matching the participants on sensation-seeking behaviour will increase the likelihood that any difference detected between the two groups is attributable to the presence or absence of a head injury.

As this discussion shows, each research design has particular advantages and disadvantages, which are summarized in Table 1.2.

Meta-Analyses

meta-analysis A method of data analysis that involves combining the results of many studies on a particular subject to generate a statistical estimate of the overall magnitude of their findings.

The past couple of decades has witnessed an explosion in the use of meta-analyses to summarize the research in an area. A **meta-analysis**, also known as a quantitative review, combines the results of existing studies to produce a statistical estimate of the average effect reported. As such, this method can be particularly useful for making sense of conflicting results from a large number of studies (Stangor, 2011). It is as if the researcher conducted one big study instead of a series of smaller, independent investigations. Meta-analyses may be contrasted to the qualitative approach of the traditional narrative review, which relies on the reviewer's judgments to assess the general research findings in an area (Cozby, 2007; Hagan, 2005).

The value of a meta-analysis rests on having clear inclusion criteria outlining which studies are to be included and conducting a systematic search to locate as many published and unpublished studies as possible that satisfy these criteria (Stangor, 2011). Although meta-analyses pool studies employing different designs and methods of collecting data, reviewers typically treat these study characteristics as variables that are coded and subsequently entered into the analyses. This approach allows the reviewers to see what, if any, impact these characteristics have on the results. Reviewers can analyze other variables to see if they influence or moderate the size of the relationship.

For example, a recent meta-analysis by van Langen and colleagues (2014) examined the link between empathy and offending in 38 studies involving a combined total of more than 6,600 participants. Their analysis revealed that, across all the studies, empathy

Table 1.2 Features, strengths, and weaknesses of different research designs

Design	Features	Strengths	Weaknesses
Descriptive	Describes individual variables	Easy to undertake in real-life settings	Does not allow predictions Does not allow causal inferences
Correlational	Describes relationships between two or more variables	Easy to undertake in real-life settings Predictions are possible	Does not allow causal inferences
Experimental	Evaluates the effect of one variable on other variables	Causal inferences are possible Provides explanations of phenomena	Tend to be contrived and not reflective of real-life situations More difficult to undertake due to ethical and legal limitations

Sources: Adapted from Bernstein, D., Cramer, K. M., Fenwick, K. D., & Fraser, I. (2008). *Psychology* (1st Canadian ed.). Boston, MA: Houghton Mifflin, p. 44; Stangor, C. (2011). *Research methods for the behavioural sciences* (4th ed.). Belmont, CA: Wadsworth, p. 20.

exhibited a small to moderate connection to offending. Specifically, offenders displayed lower levels of empathy (defined as the ability to understand others' emotions) than did non-offenders. Interestingly, the strength of this relationship varied depending on the instrument used to measure empathy, indicating that some instruments worked better than others, at least in relation to offending. Stronger associations were also detected for male and juvenile offenders. In short, a meta-analytic review is a powerful way to summarize and understand the significance of research findings, which is why these reviews are incorporated throughout this book.

A Final Word on Research

The importance of any empirical finding hinges, to a great degree, on the extent to which it can be replicated. Isolated or highly inconsistent research findings should always be viewed with a healthy dose of skepticism because they could be due to chance or the peculiarities of the particular study. One recent project, which replicated a hundred different studies published in three leading psychological journals, serves as a strong caveat (Open Science Collaboration, 2015). Overall, the strength of the findings in the replication studies shrank by half compared to the findings reported in the original studies. Furthermore, 97 per cent of the original studies reported statistically significant results, but only 39 per cent of the replication studies were statistically significant.

The apparent failure to replicate original study results is not unique to psychology and can be caused by many factors that have nothing to do with the psychological process under investigation (Maxwell, Lau, & Howard, 2015). The important point to remember is that confidence in the reliability and robustness of any scientific finding grows with replication, preferably by different groups of researchers using different research designs, data gathering methodologies, and participant samples.

Organization of This Book

The topics of this book are sequenced so that the general principles and theories introduced in the earlier chapters can be applied to explain some of the specific behaviours addressed in the later chapters. Chapter 2 offers our first full look at psychological theories of criminal behaviour. We start by distinguishing between the fields of behavioural genetics and evolutionary psychology. We explore the role of behavioural genetics on criminal and violent behaviour and discuss how the diathesis–stress and differential susceptibility models explain gene–environment interactions. Evolutionary theory is used to examine cheating behaviour in society and explain sex differences in crime and the age–crime curve.

Chapter 3 overviews the structure of the brain and discusses how dysfunctions associated with specific areas may contribute to criminal and violent behaviour. We consider the part that various neurotransmitters and hormones play in the development of this behaviour. The chapter also examines several psychophysiological correlates of crime and violence, including those among the functioning of the autonomic nervous system, sensation-seeking, and high-risk behaviour.

Chapter 4 focuses on life-course factors or variables that contribute to the development of chronic criminal behaviour, such as early behavioural and dispositional difficulties; family-related factors, such as parental monitoring and disciplinary practices;

and various factors related to peer relationships. The similarities and differences between adolescent-limited and life-course persistent (or chronic) offenders are a major topic of discussion.

Chapter 5 examines how personality—our stable way of responding to and interacting with the surrounding environment—may influence criminal behaviour. As part of this discussion, we review the psychodynamic and trait perspectives on personality and crime, emphasizing attachment theory, impulsivity, and Eysenck's theory of personality. Finally, we introduce the concept of personality disorders and discuss two disorders that are particularly relevant to criminality: antisocial personality disorder and narcissistic personality disorder.

Following this general discussion of personality and crime, Chapter 6 shifts focus to psychopathy, a specific personality disorder. In this chapter, we describe the major symptoms of this construct before turning to a more detailed examination of how they may promote criminal and violent behaviour. We also identify and discuss various theories that attempt to explain the link between psychopathy and criminal and violent behaviour.

Chapter 7 reviews the major types of learning, including classical conditioning, operant conditioning, and observational learning, and outlines how they might explain the development and maintenance of criminal and violent behaviour. We also explore how these learning theories can provide insight into the relative success or failure of the punishments imposed in the criminal justice system. The chapter concludes with an examination of Akers's differential association-reinforcement theory, which integrates many principles of learning.

Chapter 8 examines how cognitions—thoughts, attitudes, beliefs, and values—influence the way people behave. It begins with an overview of Kohlberg's stages of moral development and proceeds to an examination of moral disengagement theory. Later, we discuss how affect and cognition interact in different ways to produce violent behaviour. The chapter concludes with a review of the general aggression model (GAM).

Mental health and substance abuse are two of the most significant issues or problems that confront anyone working with offenders in the criminal justice system. Chapter 9 discusses possible explanations for the general relationship of major mental disorder to crime. The chapter finishes by looking at how different mental disorders and specific symptoms are empirically and theoretically linked to violence.

Chapter 10 begins with an overview of the major classes of psychoactive substances and their effects. We explore the primary connections between substance use and crime, including how different intoxication and withdrawal effects may promote criminal and violent behaviour. The chapter ends with a focus on the most misused substance in Western society, alcohol, and outlines three possible explanations for the demonstrated link between this psychoactive substance and offending.

The next two chapters narrow in on specific theoretical explanations of particular forms of violence. Chapter 11 focuses on homicide. The first section of the chapter uses some of the theories discussed elsewhere in the book to explain homicides involving non-family members. Next, it examines homicides committed against family members. The chapter concludes by discussing multiple murders and reviewing various theories that have been advanced to explain serial and mass murder.

Chapter 12 addresses non-lethal forms of interpersonal violence (i.e. violent interactions involving two or more individuals, whether they be known to one another or strangers). The first half of the chapter addresses stalking, intimate partner violence, and some of the psychological processes contributing to these behaviours. The latter half is concerned with sexual violence. We describe the scope and nature of sexual violence before overviewing several theories that explain this behaviour, such as sexual deviance, learning, and cognition.

The final chapter, Chapter 13, looks at what psychology has to offer in terms of managing offenders and reducing future acts of criminal and violent behaviour. Two areas where psychology is indispensable are offender risk assessments and effective offender treatment. This chapter overviews four main risk assessment methods and highlights the strengths and weaknesses of each one. The discussion of offender treatment strategies identifies the essential elements of successful programs and outlines steps that can be taken to ensure programs are well-designed and delivered as intended.

Summary

1. Criminal behaviour is an intentional act or omission that violates criminal law. Generally, only intentional behaviours (and not mere accidents) constitute crimes. Because crime is defined through a socio-political process, it varies across historical periods and legal jurisdictions. Despite these differences, there still exists widespread agreement that behaviours involving serious harms such as violence should be crimes.

2. Violence may be broadly defined as an intentional and non-consensual act of threatened, attempted, or actual physical harm against another person. Such a definition encompasses a wide and diverse array of behaviours. In an effort to identify subsets of more homogenous behaviours, violence is often differentiated along one or more dimensions. The nature of the behaviours, severity of the harm inflicted, characteristics of the victims, and underlying motivation of the perpetrator are commonly used to identify different forms of violence. Sometimes a distinction is made between instrumental and reactive violence. Instrumental, or predatory, violence is perpetrated to achieve some identifiable goal or objective, such as money, material goods, sex, status, or power. By contrast, reactive violence is an extreme emotional response to a frustrating event or a perceived insult or provocation. It is theorized that different factors and psychological mechanisms are responsible for these different types of violence.

3. Criminology is the study of crime and criminal behaviour. Although criminology draws on a wide range of disciplines, it traditionally has been dominated by sociology and psychology. The sociological perspective focuses on the influence of social groups and society on criminal behaviour and the construction of crime and therefore emphasizes factors external to the individual. The psychological perspective focuses on the mental processes and behaviour of the individuals who engage in crime and therefore emphasizes individually based factors. As a result, psychology is uniquely suited to address many of the issues that arise in specific cases of criminal behaviour.

4. A scientific theory is a set of interconnected statements that explain the relationship between two or more events and that can be empirically tested. A good theory of criminal behaviour must be able to account for both inter-individual and intra-individual differences. That is, it must be able to explain why some individuals commit crime while others do not, as well as why specific offenders commit crime in some contexts and at some times in their lives but not others.

5. Research of any behavioural phenomenon, including criminal and violent behaviour, utilizes one of three basic designs. Descriptive research designs generate information

about an individual factor or variable without addressing its association to any other variable. Correlational research designs examine relationships between two or more variables. Once the relationship between variables is understood, it becomes possible to make predictions. Only experimental research designs permit inferences about causation, the logical conclusion that one variable is responsible for changes in another. Experimental designs require three essential elements: random assignment of the study participants, an experimental group, and a control or comparison group.

Review Questions

1. Discuss what is meant by the statement "Criminal behaviour is socially constructed."
2. Define instrumental and reactive violence and describe their respective characteristics. Review the following case studies and identify whether each one exemplifies instrumental or reactive violence:
   a. Aileen Wuornos (Chapter 5)
   b. Shia LaBeouf (Chapter 10)
3. Distinguish sociology and psychology and explain the unique contribution that the latter can make to our understanding of criminal and violent behaviour.
4. Distinguish inter-individual and intra-individual differences in criminal behaviour.
5. Identify the three basic research designs and highlight the strengths and weaknesses of each one. Review the following "Researching" boxes and identify whether each study exemplifies a correlational or experimental research design:
   a. "Moral Disengagement in Action" (Chapter 8)
   b. "Intoxication, Self-Awareness, and Aggression" (Chapter 10)

2

Genetics and Evolution

Learning Objectives

At the end of this chapter, you should be able to:

- describe the methodologies of twin and adoption studies and explain what this research says about heredity's influence on criminal and violent behaviour;

- explain what molecular studies reveal about genetic influences on offending behaviour and identify the major biological systems implicated by this research;

- discuss how genetics and environment interact to impact offending behaviour and outline two models that could account for this interaction;

- examine the evolutionary advantage of selfishness and why altruistic acts directed at genetic relatives represent a special form of selfishness;

- explore how cooperation among people enables some individuals to cheat and summarize two broad sets of theories regarding cheating behaviour; and

- explain evolutionary theories that account for sex differences in the rate of offending behaviour and for the shape of the age–crime curve.

CASE STUDY

Jeffrey Landrigan

Phoenix, Arizona—Jeffrey Landrigan had a difficult start to life. His biological father disappeared when he was a newborn and his biological mother, who used drugs and alcohol during her pregnancy, abandoned him at a daycare before he was a year old. Things looked brighter for him when he was adopted by the Landrigans, a relatively affluent and stable family living in Oklahoma. But Landrigan was a restless toddler and proved to be a handful for his new family. As he grew older, his restlessness gave way to increasingly severe—and occasionally violent—outbursts. By the time he was a teenager, he was abusing drugs and alcohol and committing acts of delinquency, which eventually landed him in the youth correctional system (Kiefer, 2010). As an adult, matters only got worse. One evening, Landrigan stabbed and killed a childhood friend who threatened to beat him up. He explained his actions by stating, "I don't take that shit off nobody" (Mangino, 2014, p. 146). He was convicted of second-degree murder and sentenced to 20 years in prison.

After escaping from prison by slipping away from his work crew, Landrigan headed to Arizona to locate his biological mother. Not long afterward, he was arrested in Phoenix for murdering Chester Dyer (Kiefer, 2010). Landrigan was convicted of first-degree murder and sentenced to death; he was executed on 26 October 2010.

Photo 2.1   Although he was raised by a loving family, Jeffrey Landrigan lived a life of crime, just as his biological father had. Landrigan's case raises questions about the role of genetics in criminal and violent behaviour.

Perhaps the most remarkable thing about this case is that, during one of his stints in prison, Landrigan learned from another inmate that he bore an uncanny resemblance to another prisoner. The inmate was referring to Darrel Hill, who turned out to be Landrigan's biological father. Hill was on death row in Arkansas and, just like his son, he had a drug problem, supported himself through crime, killed two people, and escaped from prison. The family's history of crime was not confined to these two generations: Landrigan's grandfather was also a career criminal and drug addict who, decades earlier, had been shot dead by police following a botched robbery attempt.

Source (except where otherwise noted): Malone, D., & Swindle, H. (2013). *America's condemned: Death row inmates in their own words.* Riverside, NJ: Andrews McMeel Publishing.

Introduction

evolutionary psychology The field of study concerned with understanding how natural selection shapes and influences mental processes and behaviour.

behavioural genetics The field of study concerned with understanding the influence of genetics on the expression of characteristics and behaviours within a population.

You may not be surprised to learn that on appeal, Landrigan's legal counsel argued, unsuccessfully, that he was "genetically predisposed to land on death row" (Malone & Swindle, 2013, p. 117). The idea that our ancestors shaped more than just our physical form animates behavioural genetics and evolutionary psychology. Although genes play a role in both of these fields, each is distinct. **Evolutionary psychology** studies how psychological mechanisms that evolved over many generations influence modern mental processes and behaviours and explains why these characteristics exist in the population today (Duntley & Buss, 2004; Quinsey, Skilling, Lalumière, & Craig, 2003). **Behavioural genetics** examines the degree to which our behavioural traits are genetically influenced (Plomin, DeFries, McClearn, & McGuffin, 2008). We can illustrate the distinction using aggression as an example: evolutionary psychology seeks to understand the advantage that aggression gave our ancestors and why it became widespread in the population, whereas behavioural genetics is concerned with uncovering the genetic basis behind why some people are more aggressive than others. This chapter reviews major theories and research from both fields to see what they can tell us about criminal and violent behaviour.

Behavioural Genetics

Overview of Genetics

Found in nearly every cell of the human body, **chromosomes** contain our biological blueprint, or plans. There are 46 chromosomes, which are arranged in 23 pairs. Each chromosome consists of a long, tightly coiled strand of **deoxyribonucleic acid (DNA)**. Each DNA strand is made up of thousands of **genes**—these small segments contain the detailed instructions that direct production of the different building blocks, or proteins, that make up our bodies and allow us to live (Carey, 2003). The paired nature of chromosomes means that every gene on one chromosome has a matching partner on the other. In fact, most genes exist in only a single form; therefore, both genes in the pair are duplicates and are the same for everyone (Plomin et al., 2008).

A small proportion of genes come in multiple forms. Known as **polymorphisms**, these genes account for the genetic variations that exist among people. Alternative forms of the same gene are called **alleles** (Plomin et al., 2008). For example, the gene that codes blood type is a polymorphism; its alleles are A, B, and O. Remember, genes are in pairs, so depending on the combination of alleles possessed, a person could be AA, AB, AO, BB, BO, or OO. Although some traits such as blood type are determined by a single pair of genes, things are seldom this straightforward. More often, a trait is **polygenic** and determined by the collective operation of multiple sets of genes (Richards & Hawley, 2011).

We inherit our chromosomes and therefore our genes from our parents. One of each pair comes from our mother (through her egg) and the other from our father (through his sperm; Plomin et al., 2008). This is why people often appear to be a mix of their parents—in essence, they were "constructed" from a combination of the genes inherited from both. The reason children of the same parents do not all look alike is that chromosomes are randomly distributed in the egg and sperm. With 23 chromosome pairs, there are literally millions of possible combinations for a zygote (a fertilized egg). Siblings nevertheless have, on average, approximately half of their genes in common. Which part of a chromosome pair a child receives from his or her parents is random, but probability indicates siblings will receive the same one about half the time. Because 99.9 per cent of human DNA is exactly the same for everyone, the notion that siblings share half their genetic material is true for only the remaining 0.1 per cent (Raine, 1993).

Familial Transmission of Crime

The argument advanced in the Landrigan appeal may be relatively novel in law, but the observation that crime seems to run in families is not new. In the 1880s Richard Dugdale (1887/1970) documented the presence of poverty and antisocial behaviour running through multiple generations of a family, identified under the pseudonym Juke, in upstate New York. Dugdale noted that cases of prostitution, pauperism, and criminality were concentrated in one line of the Juke family. More recent and methodologically rigorous studies

chromosome A microscopic structure that contains DNA.

deoxyribonucleic acid (DNA) A long, coiled, threadlike strand consisting of small segments known as genes, which constitute the blueprints of life.

gene A small segment of DNA that constitutes the biological instructions for a certain characteristic or part of the body.

polymorphism A gene that exists in more than one form.

allele An alternative form of a gene that exists in more than one form.

polygenic A trait or characteristic that is under the influence of multiple genes.

echo these general observations. For example, an analysis of data from a nationally representative sample of American youths found that over 50 per cent of all the arrests reported for the entire sample were attributed to only 5 per cent of the families and all the arrests could be attributed to 25 per cent of the families (Beaver, 2013; see also Frisell, Lichtenstein, & Långström, 2011). Studies also show that criminal offending in one generation of a family is associated with an increased risk in succeeding generations (Bijleveld & Wijkman, 2009; Putkonen, Ryynanen, Eronen, & Tiihonen, 2007).

The meaning of these findings is less certain. Evidence that crime runs in families could indicate the transmission of genetic influences from one generation to the next. On the other hand, it could be a sign of social transmission resulting from such circumstances as poverty, lack of education, and poor role models, which continue to be experienced by subsequent generations. In an effort to disentangle these effects, researchers have conducted heritability studies, which examine offending among known relatives to determine the importance of genetics for explaining individual differences in criminal behaviour (Carey, 2003). These investigations have typically been conducted on two groups: twins and adoptees.

Twin Studies

monozygotic twins Twins that develop from a single fertilized egg that, for unknown reasons, has split; also known as identical twins because the offspring are genetically identical.

Twin studies capitalize on the fact that twins can be monozygotic or dizygotic. **Monozygotic twins**, or identical twins as they are more commonly known, develop from a single fertilized egg that, for reasons not entirely understood, splits in half. Derived from one origin, the two resulting zygotes contain exactly the same genetic material. This is why monozygotic twins are always the same sex and look so similar. It is believed that the notorious Kray brothers, discussed in the following case study, were monozygotic twins. **Dizygotic twins**, or fraternal twins, are the result of two independently fertilized zygotes. This happens when two eggs, instead of the usual one, are released by the female at the same time and each is fertilized by different sperm. Dizygotic twins are no more or less genetically similar than siblings born apart from one another. They share about half their genetic material and may be different sexes. The development of both types of twins is shown in Figure 2.1.

dizygotic twins Twins that develop from two eggs that are independently fertilized by different sperm and consequently vary genetically from one another; also known as fraternal twins.

Twin studies look for evidence of a genetic influence on offending by assessing the relative relationships of monozygotic and dizygotic twins to criminal behaviour. If there is a stronger association for the former, genetics probably influence criminal behaviour, but if the association is about the same for the two types, it suggests that genetics have little or no sway. One way to measure the strength of the associations is to calculate **concordance rates**, which express the level of agreement as a percentage. A concordance rate of 60 per cent means that, if one twin has a history of criminal behaviour, there is a 60 per cent chance that the other twin does as well.

concordance rate The percentage of two individuals, usually twins, who match one another with respect to the presence of a particular characteristic or condition.

Ishikawa and Raine (2002) summarized concordance rates for twin studies examining adult criminal behaviour (see Table 2.1). Their work revealed that the rate for monozygotic twins across all the studies was double that of dizygotic twins. Furthermore, the rate was at least 1.5 times higher even after they removed potentially problematic studies involving small sample sizes, unreliable methods for determining whether participants were monozygotic or dizygotic, or results that might have been politically driven because they were obtained in Germany during the 1930s (Ishikawa & Raine, 2002).

Investigations of violent criminal behaviour among monozygotic and dizygotic twins are limited to a single study by Cloninger and Gottesman (1987). Although the concordance rate was higher for the monozygotic twins, a statistical test for heritability performed by Carey (1994) proved to be nonsignificant. It has been speculated that the latter

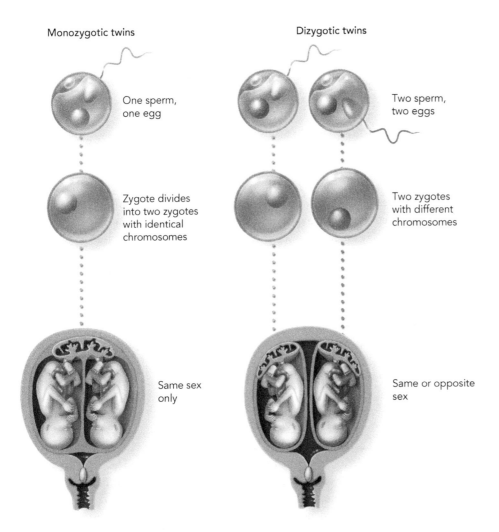

Figure 2.1 The development of monozygotic and dizygotic twins.
Source: Sophie Jacopin / Science Source

result might be a function of the generally low base rates of criminally violent behaviour, which makes detecting a statistically significant relationship difficult even if one exists (Carey & Goldman, 1997). Evidence supports this position. A meta-analysis of 24 studies that used different personality measures of aggressive behaviour, which is much more prevalent than criminally violent behaviour, reported a strong overall genetic effect (Miles & Carey, 1997).

A fundamental assumption of the twin study methodology is that environmental influences on behaviour are the same for both types of twins, but this may not be true (Carey & Goldman, 1997). It has been suggested that the concordance rate is higher with monozygotic twins because they receive more homogenous treatment than do dizygotic twins (Raine, 1993). You have probably seen identical twins who were dressed in matching outfits, enrolled in the same childhood activities, or given the same toys. There are also indications that monozygotic twins spend a larger proportion of their time together and socialize in the same circle of friends, which contributes to greater behavioural imitation than occurs among dizygotic twins (Carey, 1992).

Table 2.1 Concordance rates for criminal behaviour among monozygotic and dizygotic twins

Study	Location	Sex	Monozygotic Twins		Dizygotic Twins	
			Concordance %	N[1]	Concordance %	N
Lange (1929)	Bavaria	Male	77	13	12	17
Legras (1932)	Netherlands	Male	100	4	0	5
Rosanoff et al. (1934)	United States	Male	76	38	22	23
		Female	26	7	25	4
Kranze (1935)	Prussia	Male	66	32	54	43
Stumpfl (1936)	Germany	Male	60	15	37	19
		Female	67	3	0	2
Borgstrom (1939)	Finland	Male	75	4	40	5
Slater (1953)	England	Male	50	2	30	10
Yoshimasu (1961)	Japan	Male	61	28	11	18
Dalgaard & Kringlen (1976)	Norway	Male	26	31	15	54
Carey (1992)	Denmark	Male	34	73	18	146
		Female	20	15	7	28
Coid et al. (1993)	United Kingdom	Both	24	92	21	109
Total			**44**	**357**	**22**	**483**

Note
1. N = Number of participants.
Source: Republished with permission of Kluwer Academic Publishers, from *The Neurobiology of Criminal Behavior*, 5, Series: Neurobiological foundation of aberrant behaviors, J. Glicksohn, 2002; permission conveyed through Copyright Clearance Center, Inc.

CASE STUDY

The Kray Brothers

Reginald ("Reggie") and Ronald ("Ronnie") Kray were born 10 minutes apart on 24 October 1933. They lived together with their parents and older brother, Charlie, in a cramped house in London's impoverished East End. They were raised primarily by their mother, who cared deeply for both of them. Their father, who had deserted from the military at the beginning of World War II, spent most of his time trying to evade authorities and therefore was rarely at home.

As youngsters, the twins were inseparable and never far from trouble. Their first formal run-in with the law occurred at age 12, when they were convicted of firing a pellet gun in public. As teenagers, they were arrested for severely beating another youth and for assaulting a police officer. They were

Photo 2.2 Reginald (left) and Ronald Kray enjoy a cup of tea after undergoing 36 hours of police questioning regarding the murder of another gangster, George Cornell.

William Lovelace/Stringer/Getty Images

conscripted into the military at age 18 but deserted, just as their father had done years earlier, after assaulting the corporal in charge. Their antics earned them dishonourable discharges and nine-month prison sentences.

Shortly after their release, the Krays met a key figure in one of London's organized crime rings, became involved in the protection racket, and quickly became significant players in the city's underworld. When some of the more established gangs imploded as a result of criminal prosecutions, defections, and departures, the Krays filled the void. Reggie, the older twin, was more calculated and businesslike in his approach to crime; Ronnie was seen as unpredictable and prone to violence, behaviour that might have been a consequence of his schizophrenia, a useful tool to get what he wanted, or a bit of both. Throughout much of the 1950s and 1960s, the Krays and their gang, The Firm, controlled organized crime in east London. Their stakes in several extremely popular clubs and casinos, together with their American mob connections, brought them into contact with many A-list celebrities. The twins' public profile grew so large that they became household names.

Their luck ended in 1968, however, when they were convicted of killing two minor gangsters and sentenced to 30 years each. Reggie served his sentence in a variety of prisons while Ronnie spent the bulk of his time confined to Broadmoor, a secure psychiatric facility, until his death in 1995. In a fitting summary of the brothers' relationship, the wreath that Reggie laid at the funeral read "To the other half of me" (Chapter 20, para. 15). He died five years later, not long after his release from prison.

Source: Fry, C. (2011). *The Krays: A violent business: The definitive inside story of Britain's most notorious brothers in crime.* Edinburgh, Scotland: Mainstream Publishing.

The counter to this criticism lies in studies of monozygotic twins who were raised apart. These studies are quite rare and are limited to small sample sizes. The largest looked at 32 pairs of twins separated soon after birth (Grove et al., 1990). The investigators found that the twins exhibited a significant positive relationship for self-reported antisocial behaviour, despite being raised in different home environments and apart from one another's influence. Carey and Goldman (1997) concluded that, when the evidence is considered as a whole, the weaknesses associated with twin studies are not serious enough to discount their positive results.

Adoption Studies

Adoption studies help to separate the effects of genetics and the environment. Children who are adopted have the genes but not the environment of their birth parents and the environment but not the genes of their adoptive parents (DiLalla, 2000). Genetics are assumed to affect criminal behaviour if adoptees with criminal birth parents are more likely to engage in crime than are adoptees with non-criminal birth parents. A classic example of this type of study is the investigation of Danish adoptees carried out by Mednick, Gabrielli, and Hutchings (1983, 1984), reviewed in the "Researching" box on next page. They found that criminal convictions were significantly more common among adoptees born to a parent with a criminal history than adoptees born to parents without a criminal history.

Other adoption studies report the same general results. Carey and Goldman (1997) reviewed the investigations carried out with six groups of adopted children in the United States and Scandinavia and concluded that there was evidence of a genetic effect for antisocial and criminal behaviour in all but one group. In this group, the evidence was mixed. No link was initially detected between biological parents and their adoptive children for general crime unconnected to alcohol abuse, although subsequent analyses revealed a genetic tie to minor criminality among non-alcoholic offenders (Bohman, 1978; Bohman,

Cloninger, Sigvardsson, & von Knorring, 1982). Interestingly, like the twin studies reviewed previously, adoption studies have generally failed to discover a genetic component to violent behaviour (e.g. Bohman et al., 1982; Mednick et al., 1984).

Researching Criminal and Violent Behaviour

The Danish Adoption Study

Mednick, Gabrielli, and Hutchings (1983, 1984) looked at the possibility of a link between heredity and crime by analyzing a cohort of 14,000 people who were adopted in Denmark between 1927 and 1947. Nearly all the adoptees were placed in new homes before reaching the age of two. The investigators assessed criminal behaviour by searching the official court records kept for people 16 years and older. In most cases, they had sufficient information to check the histories of the children, birth parents, and adoptive parents. Adoptees were considered to have behaved criminally if they had at least one documented conviction. Parents were considered criminal if either the mother or father had a criminal conviction on record.

Using this information, Mednick and colleagues employed a 2 × 2 research design that put the adoptees into one of four groups based on the criminal history of their birth and adoptive parents (see Table 2.2). Due to the small number of female adoptees with criminal convictions, the researchers focused their analyses on the behaviour of the males. As shown in Table 2.3, they found that the prevalence of criminal behaviour among adopted sons was lowest when neither hereditary nor environmental criminal influences were present, intermediary when one influence was present, and highest when both were present.

Table 2.2 The 2 × 2 research design based on the criminal history of the birth parents and adoptive parents

		Birth parents	
		Criminal	**Non-criminal**
Adoptive parents	**Criminal**	Effects of Heredity + Environment	Effect of environment only
	Non-criminal	Effect of heredity only	No effects of heredity or environment

Source: Adapted from Mednick, S. A., Gabrielli, W. F., & Hutchings, B. (1983). Genetic influences in criminal behavior: Evidence from an adoption cohort. In K. T. Van Dusen & S. A. Mednick (Eds.), *Prospective studies of crime and delinquency* (pp. 39–56). Hingham, MA: Kluwer-Nijhoff Publishing.

Table 2.3 Percentage of adopted sons with a criminal conviction by parents' criminal history

		Birth parents	
		Criminal	**Non-criminal**
Adoptive parents	**Criminal**	24.5% $n = 143$	14.7% $n = 204$
	Non-criminal	20.0% $n = 1226$	13.5% $n = 2492$

Source: Adapted from Mednick, S. A., Gabrielli, W. F., & Hutchings, B. (1983). Genetic influences in criminal behavior: Evidence from an adoption cohort. In K. T. Van Dusen & S. A. Mednick (Eds.), *Prospective studies of crime and delinquency* (pp. 39–56). Hingham, MA: Kluwer-Nijhoff Publishing.

Molecular Genetics

Evidence of Single Gene Effects

Heritability studies help to quantify the influence of genetics on antisocial and criminal behaviour, but they cannot tell us which genes are involved. Recent advances in DNA research, however, have enabled scientists to work at the molecular level to identify these genes. One of the earliest developments on this front was sparked by a Dutch woman seeking genetic counselling. The woman came from a large family with numerous male members who exhibited mild mental retardation and impulsive aggressive behaviour, including incidents of arson, assault, and sexual violence (Brunner, Nelen, Breakefield, Ropers, & van Oost, 1993; Brunner, Nelen, van Zandvoort, et al., 1993). Further research of the extended family uncovered at least 14 afflicted males across 4 generations. Environmental explanations were ruled out by the presence of so many individuals from different branches of the family tree, from different parts of the country, and from different historical periods (Brunner, 1996). In addition, no female members of the family appeared to be affected, although an analysis indicated some of them might be genetic carriers.

These clues suggested that the syndrome might be linked to the sex chromosomes, which determine whether a person is male or female (Brunner, Nelen, van Zandvoort, et al., 1993). These chromosomes come in two forms that are visibly different from one another at the microscopic level: a longer X chromosome and a shorter Y chromosome (Richards & Hawley, 2011). Females have two X chromosomes and are described genetically as XX; males have one X and one Y chromosome and are described genetically as XY. Brunner and colleagues (1993) analyzed the DNA of 24 of the woman's family members and identified a defect in a gene located on the X chromosome. Because females have two X chromosomes, this defective gene's impact is masked by the non-defective gene. Males carrying the defect are not so lucky. They have only one X chromosome and thus nothing to prevent the defect from being expressed.

Additional testing eventually determined that the genetic defect was connected to a complete deficiency of active monoamine oxidase A (MAOA), an enzyme responsible for the breakdown of several **neurotransmitters**. A more complete discussion of the nature and role of neurotransmitters, including hypotheses regarding offending behaviour, is in Chapter 3. For now it will suffice to say that neurotransmitters are electrochemical compounds that facilitate communication between brain cells. Inactive or ineffective MAOA could alter neurotransmitter levels, something that Brunner and colleagues confirmed with further testing of the affected men. Given the central role of neurotransmitters in brain functioning, it is not difficult to imagine that abnormal levels might adversely impact behaviour. Nevertheless, this particular genetic defect has yet to be detected in another family, so it is hardly capable of explaining the crime and violence observed in society at large (Brunner, 1996).

neurotransmitters Electrochemical messengers that transmit information or impulses from neuron to neuron.

Brunner and colleagues' discovery generated a great deal of interest in the possibility of other genetic ties between MAOA and antisocial behaviours. There are various alleles for MAOA, generally classified as either low or high activity (Craig & Halton, 2009). Researchers have been curious about whether individuals carrying the low-activity forms might be at increased risk of antisocial behaviour compared to people with high-activity forms. Examining MAOA levels has produced mixed findings so far, with some studies reporting a positive association with aggression (Haberstick et al., 2014; Manuck, Flory, Ferrell, Mann, & Muldoon, 2000; Reif et al., 2007) and others reporting null effects (Caspi et al., 2002; Huizinga et al., 2006).

Perhaps unsurprisingly, much of the other research in this area focuses on neurotransmitters as the suspects most worthy of investigation. These studies typically look at the genes involved in producing, transporting, and breaking down neurotransmitters to see if they exhibit a relationship to various forms of antisocial behaviour (Morley & Hall, 2006). Numerous studies have linked several gene variants involving serotonin and dopamine—two of the more extensively researched neurotransmitters—to problem behaviours and offending at different stages across the lifespan (Beitchman et al., 2006; Guo, Roettger, & Shih, 2007; Haberstick, Smolen, & Hewitt, 2006; Hohmann et al., 2009; Retz et al., 2004). Unfortunately, the results to date have been quite inconsistent, and subsequent efforts to replicate the initial findings have failed as often as they have succeeded (Craig & Halton, 2009).

Evidence of Multiple Gene Effects

The lack of consistent results on the genetics of offending may be a function of focusing on individual genes (Craig & Halton, 2009). The notion that there is a single gene responsible for criminal behaviour has been widely rejected for a long time (Beaver, 2009; Fishbein, 2001; Raine, 1993; Rowe, 1996; Walsh, 2002). It is much more likely that any genetic influence is polygenic in nature and involves the combined effects of many genes (Plomin et al., 2008). A single gene may raise the risk of offending behaviour, but any effect is bound to be very small and hard to detect amid the complex interaction of different alleles and environmental factors (Craig & Halton, 2009). A study by Grigorenko and colleagues (2010) highlights the potential danger of studying genes on an individual basis. These investigators studied incarcerated adolescents and matched controls to see if they differed with respect to 12 allele variations of 4 different genes involved in dopamine function. No differences were detected for any of the individual alleles—if the researchers had stopped here, they would have reported that the two groups were genetically indistinguishable. It was only when they analyzed various combinations of these alleles that they determined the two groups were genetically different from one another.

It seems that people who show a propensity for offending probably possess several genes that collectively elevate their risk for this behaviour or, as Diana Fishbein (2001) says, they are "genetically loaded" (p. 30). In one recent study, Barnes and Jacobs (2013) analyzed the DNA of more than a thousand participants and counted the number of alleles relating to three dopamine polymorphisms associated with an increased risk of antisocial behaviour. Remember that humans possess two copies of each gene so the total number of possible risk alleles carried by each participant ranged from zero to six. The researchers noted a significant positive relationship between the number of risk alleles and scores on a scale reflecting the frequency and severity of self-disclosed violence. In other words, people with higher genetic loadings of "risky" alleles reported engaging in more serious violence.

Genetics and the Environment

Nature versus Nurture

One issue that never seems to disappear is whether human behaviour is primarily determined by biology or environment—the so-called nature versus nurture debate. Our discussion so far has concentrated on the nature side of this debate, that is, the role of genetics in offending behaviour. But it would be foolhardy to deny the influence of environment. One only needs to recall the twin studies reviewed earlier for evidence. Although the concordance rates of monozygotic twins were higher than those for dizygotic twins, they were far from

100 per cent, which is a good indicator that something other than heredity alone must be operating. That "something" is a wide array of social forces usually labelled the environment.

Meta-analyses performed by Miles and Carey (1997) and Rhee and Waldman (2007) provide additional evidence that biology and environment are jointly involved in offending behaviour. Both sets of investigators pooled a large number of twin and adoption studies to calculate the relative influence of heredity and environment on antisocial and aggressive behaviour. They estimated that heredity explains about 40 per cent of the individual variation observed in these behaviours among the population and environmental factors account for the rest. Neither study addressed crime or violence per se, but there is no reason to suspect the results would be markedly different. Two important and related points can be drawn from these results. First, both genetics and the environment are influential. Second, environmental effects are the stronger force. As these results and many others make plain, the nature–nurture debate cannot be decided in favour of one side or the other. Instead, offending behaviour is best viewed as the result of nature plus nurture (Fishbein, 2001).

Gene-Environment Interactions

Not only do both genetics and the environment play a role in offending behaviour, but it also appears that each influences the effect of the other. This gene–environment interaction has been observed in numerous adoption and twin studies (e.g. Cadoret, Cain, & Crowe, 1983; Cadoret, Yates, Troughton, Woodworth, & Stewart, 1995; Cloninger, Sigvardsson, Bohman, & von Knorring, 1982). With the development of molecular genetics, researchers have begun to look for interactions between the environment and specific genes. One of the earliest efforts in this regard was undertaken by Avshalom Caspi and colleagues (2002), who looked at the polymorphism governing MAOA activity among males in a longitudinal study of children in New Zealand. The researchers failed to find any differences in the severity of antisocial behaviour based on genetics alone, but further analyses revealed a significant interaction between the genetic makeup of participants and whether they were abused during childhood.

Specifically, low-activity MAOA allele carriers who suffered maltreatment as children engaged in significantly more antisocial and violent behaviour than low-activity MAOA allele carriers who were not abused (see Figure 2.2). In fact, the low-activity MAOA carriers subjected to maltreatment comprised only 12 per cent of the sample, but they accounted for 44 per cent of all the violent convictions. These results suggest that low activity somehow renders an individual more vulnerable to the harmful effects of abuse. Subsequent efforts to replicate this finding have met with mixed success, indicating that the nature of this gene–environment interaction is probably more complex than it appears on the basis of Caspi and colleagues' results (Foley et al., 2004; Haberstick et al., 2014; Kim-Cohen et al., 2006; Nilsson et al., 2006; Young et al., 2005).

Research is beginning to uncover interactions between other environmental factors and genes. Several investigations linking problem behaviours to various genes governing aspects of dopamine and serotonin function report that these relationships are significantly altered by adverse experiences connected to family, neighbourhood, and peers (e.g. Bakermans-Kranenburg & van Ijzendoorn, 2006; Beaver, Gibson, DeLisi, Vaughn, & Wright, 2012; Guo, Roettger, & Cai, 2008; Reif et al., 2007; Vaughn, DeLisi, Beaver, & Wright, 2009). Gene–environment interactions could also explain some of the inconsistencies in the research previously noted. An interaction indicates that genetics has a stronger or weaker influence on offending behaviour depending on environmental

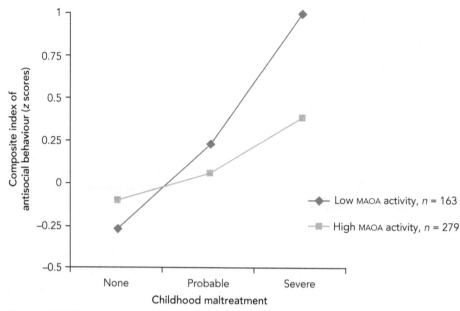

Figure 2.2 The interaction of MAOA activity level and childhood maltreatment on a composite measure of antisocial behaviour.

Source: Caspi, A., McClay, J., Moffitt, T. E., Mill, J., Martin, J., Craig, I. W., Taylor, A., & Poulton, R. (2002). Role of genotype in the cycle of violence in maltreated children. *Science, 297*, 851–854. Reprinted with permission from AAAS.

conditions. This raises the very real possibility that some studies failed to detect an association between genes and offending because they did not take the environment into account (Moffitt, 2005). The good news is that, by paying attention to the interaction of genes and the environment, future studies may yield more consistent and interpretable results.

Models of Gene–Environment Interactions

Several models have been advanced to explain how gene–environment interactions give rise to offending behaviour. One possibility is the diathesis–stress model, which has long guided thinking in this area. Another possibility is the relatively new differential susceptibility model, which takes a fresh view of the existing data. We will briefly discuss both models in this section. For more comprehensive reviews of these and other models, consult Shanahan and Boardman (2009) and Boardman and colleagues (2014).

Diathesis–Stress Model

The diathesis–stress model has dominated thinking about the interaction of genes and environment and the genesis of psychopathology for more than half a century. A **diathesis** is a predisposition to develop a psychopathological condition or disordered state (Ingram & Luxton, 2005; Zuckerman, 1999). In short, it is a vulnerability factor. There has been convincing evidence for some time that a variety of conditions, such as schizophrenia, have an inherited component or predisposition. The presence of a diathesis alone, however, cannot explain cases like the Krays, where the condition develops in only one identical twin (Zuckerman, 1999).

diathesis A genetic vulnerability or predisposition to develop a psychopathological condition.

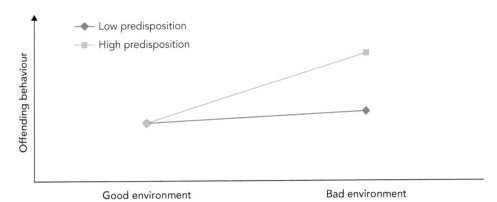

Figure 2.3 Diathesis–stress model.

The diathesis–stress model offers a possible solution to these perplexing cases. The essence of the model is that the genetic endowment people inherit increases or decreases their vulnerability for developing certain disorders. The onset of the disorder, if it occurs, is triggered by exposure to stressful events or adverse conditions. Hence, the combination of the diathesis and the stress produces the disorder. Not everyone exposed to the triggering event will develop the disorder. Individuals with the diathesis are the most vulnerable and run the greatest risk of manifesting the condition, whereas individuals who do not have the diathesis are unlikely to manifest it. People who manage to avoid the triggering conditions altogether generally do not develop the disorder regardless of their level of vulnerability (Zuckerman, 1999). Thus, the diathesis–stress model views disorder as the consequence of personal characteristics interacting with environmental conditions. It also accounts for why exposure to the same environment might lead to disorder in certain people but not others.

Figure 2.3 illustrates the application of the diasthesis–stress model to criminal and violent behaviour. One of the most consistent findings to emerge from the adoptions studies discussed earlier is that the highest rates of offending are found when unfavourable genetic backgrounds are coupled with "negative" environments (Cadoret et al., 1983; Cadoret et al., 1995; Cloninger et al., 1982). Findings from some molecular genetic studies also support the diathesis–stress model. For instance, research by Beaver et al. (2012) found that males carrying two alleles related to the neurotransmitter dopamine posed a significantly elevated risk of violent delinquency compared to non-carriers but only when they were situated in disadvantaged neighbourhoods characterized by a high proportion of single-parent families, unemployment, public assistance recipients, and so forth (Beaver et al., 2012). Using the model to interpret these findings, the dopamine-related risk alleles appear to constitute a diathesis that predisposes carriers to violent behaviour. So long as they grow up in positive environments, they are no more likely to engage in violence than non-carriers, but the combination of the diathesis and adverse neighbourhood conditions substantially increases their risk of violent delinquency.

The Differential Susceptibility Model

Ellis, Boyce, Belsky, Bakermans-Kranenburg, and van Ijzendoorn (2011) recently presented an alternative to the diathesis–stress model. It summarizes two closely connected but independently developed theories: Boyce and colleagues' biological sensitivity to context theory

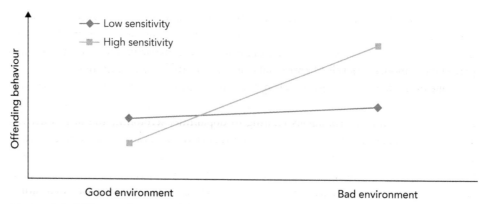

Figure 2.4 Differential susceptibility model.

(Boyce & Ellis, 2005; Ellis, Essex, & Boyce, 2005) and the differential susceptibility theory articulated by Belsky and colleagues (Belsky, 2005; Belsky, Bakermans-Kranenburg, & Ijzendoorn, 2007). For convenience, the generalized version of these two models described here is referred to as the differential susceptibility model.

This model's central premise is that individuals exhibit gene-based differences in their sensitivity or reactivity to the environment (Ellis et al., 2011). The crucial aspect, and what distinguishes differential susceptibility from diathesis–stress, is the idea that people are environmentally sensitive to both adverse and favourable conditions. The difference may seem subtle, but the implications are quite profound. The model predicts that individuals with the greatest sensitivity will suffer the worst outcomes in the most adverse conditions, but they will also enjoy the best outcomes in favourable conditions. Put another way, they are the most strongly affected by the environment "for better *and* for worse" (Ellis et al., 2011, p. 14; emphasis in original). The diathesis–stress model, by comparison, assumes that people differ in their vulnerability only to adverse environments and everyone reacts more or less the same to harmless or favourable environments.

Underlying the differential susceptibility model is the evolutionary view that environmental sensitivity is advantageous because it makes us attentive and responsive to our surroundings, a point that will be touched on later when the evolutionary theory of conditional adaptation is discussed (Ellis et al., 2011). The precise mechanism that might be responsible for this differential sensitivity is unclear, but Belsky and Pluess (2009) suggest that it may be a function of varying thresholds for experiencing pleasure and displeasure, which make people more or less responsive to rewards and punishment. Figure 2.4 presents a graphical representation of the differential susceptibility model as it relates to offending behaviour.

Proponents of the model suggest that previous research has always been viewed through the lens of the diathesis–stress paradigm, which may have led to the results being misinterpreted (Belsky & Pluess, 2009). Genes previously identified as elevating the risk of offending behaviour might actually have been amplifying environmental sensitivity, effectively raising the risk in some conditions (bad environments) but lowering it in others (good environments). With this in mind, Belsky and Pluess (2009) reviewed existing research on gene–environment interactions to see if the results were capable of supporting the differential susceptibility model. In particular, they looked for indications that people carrying so-called risk alleles gained the most benefit from positive environments, something that is not predicted by the diathesis–stress model. Their review located a substantial number of findings that fit the differential susceptibility model, including Caspi and colleagues' (2002) study. A glance back at Figure 2.2 reveals that the individuals who possessed the risk alleles relating to MAOA activity exhibited the most serious antisocial behaviour when they were subjected to abuse but the least serious antisocial behaviour in the more benign environment. Individuals with the non-risk variants of the allele displayed more moderate levels of antisocial behaviour in these two conditions.

One of the few studies investigating the model's utility for explaining antisocial behaviour was undertaken by Simons and colleagues (2012). They examined how the interaction between known risk alleles relating to dopamine, serotonin, and MAOA activity and environmental conditions impacted self-reported aggression in a sample of African-American teens. The findings matched the crossover pattern predicted for the model, which is displayed in Figure 2.4. Participants carrying the largest number of risk alleles reported the most severe aggression for the entire sample but only when they were situated in harsh, discriminatory, and crime-ridden environments. In more positive environments, they were the least aggressive. By comparison, participants with the fewest risk alleles reported less extreme reactions in both conditions: they were not as aggressive in negative environments or as peaceable in positive ones.

Further analyses revealed that the gene–environment interaction was mediated by participant attitudes concerning the code of the street—beliefs that value toughness and the use of force to gain and maintain respect. Based on their findings, the researchers concluded that individuals heavily loaded with risk alleles displayed increased sensitivity to the social environment. When these highly sensitive individuals lived in adverse environments, they readily adopted the street code assumed to prevail there. These hostile attitudes, in turn, promoted their extremely aggressive behaviour. These same individuals were equally sensitive to positive environments, but prosocial values dominated here. As a result, they showed the greatest rejection of the street code and, consequently, the lowest level of aggression. Individuals who were relatively insensitive to their social environment as a result of their genetic makeup did not strongly adopt or reject the street code and therefore engaged in more moderate levels of aggressive behaviour.

Putting It All Together: Genetic Predispositions and Behavioural Destiny

The diathesis–stress and differential susceptibility models share the view that some individuals are predisposed to offending due to their genetics. But predisposition is not destiny. Both theory and research suggest that human behaviour is highly influenced by the environment—accordingly, people who enjoy healthy, caring, and nurturing living conditions offend at relatively low rates regardless of their genetic predisposition. The differential susceptibility model is particularly encouraging because it theorizes that the people most at risk of severe criminal and violent behaviour in adverse environments exhibit the least risk in favourable environments.

In addition, epigenetic research indicates that genes may not be as static and fixed as once thought. The word *epigenetics* refers to alterations in gene activity that occur in the absence of changes to the DNA sequence (Richards & Hawley, 2011). It posits that environmental conditions can increase or decrease the level of gene activity without changing the nature of those activities (Walsh, 2009). The environmental conditions surrounding early life may be especially crucial with respect to modifying the level of gene activity (Tremblay, 2015). For example, laboratory research with rats revealed that the mother's care or neglect during infancy impacts the gene activity of her young and, in turn, affects the behaviours they displayed later on (Weaver et al., 2004). A more recent study of male

epigenetics Processes that raise or lower gene activity level without altering the genetic sequence.

prisoners suggested that MAOA dysregulation found among some offenders may be due to epigenetic processes (Checknita et al., 2015). Indeed, Tremblay (2015) speculates that epigenetic mechanisms could be responsible for the gene–environment interaction Caspi and colleagues (2002) observed for MAOA. Thus, the more we learn about genetic influences on behaviour, the more it confirms the environment's central role.

Evolution

Overview of Natural Selection and the Principles of Evolution

Over 150 years have passed since Charles Darwin (1859/1964) penned *On the Origin of Species by Means of Natural Selection*, which laid the foundations for our present-day understanding of evolution. Darwin was keen to unravel how organisms evolve and why they seem so well-suited to their environment (Buss, 2012). At the core of his ideas is **natural selection**, the differential survival and reproduction of individual members of a species (Trivers, 1985). In non-technical terms, this means that some members of a species are more likely than others to live and produce offspring.

You have probably heard the maxim "survival of the fittest" and already know which members of a species are most likely to live and reproduce. Unfortunately, this expression is often misinterpreted to mean that only the strongest survive. It actually refers to those individuals who, by virtue of their characteristics, are best matched or most compatible with their environments and therefore have the greatest chance of surviving and reproducing (Tibbetts, 2003). Such individuals may or may not be the strongest members of the species. They may be particularly well-suited to their environment due to their height (e.g. the giraffe's tall neck allows it to access food sources out of reach of many other species), speed (the cheetah's quickness enables it to run down its prey), colour (the chameleon's ability to change colour helps it to hide from potential predators), or another quality (Walsh, 2002). Thus, it is probably better to think in terms of survival of the "best suited" or the "most environmentally advantageous."

So how does natural selection account for evolutionary change? All members of a species vary in their traits. Those who possess a more favourable variation are better able to survive and reproduce in their environment. Consequently, they leave behind more offspring, who inherit the same characteristic and are also more likely to survive, reproduce, and pass on the variation. With each successive generation, the proportion of the population with the successful trait expands. If the process continues long enough, it will eventually lead to a wholesale change in the population such that all, or nearly all members share the variation (Buss, 2012). In this sense, nature "selects" trait variations that are conducive to survival and reproduction within the environment, hence the term *natural selection* (Walsh & Ellis, 2007).

A characteristic that is shaped through the process of natural selection and improves a species' ability to survive and reproduce is called an adaptation (Buss, 2012; Crawford, 1998a; Quinsey, 2002). Adaptations are usually associated with morphological (i.e. form and structure) or physiological changes, but evolutionary psychologists argue that natural selection is also capable of producing psychological adaptations. Kanazawa (2003) points to human taste preferences as one example of an evolved psychological adaptation. The search for food was a constant struggle for our ancestors, and individuals who spent a lot of time and effort acquiring low-calorie foods risked starving to death. People with

natural selection The differential survival and reproduction of individual members of a species and the resulting increase or decrease of the inheritable characteristics associated with those individuals within a population.

a strong liking for sweet and fatty foods had an edge in this environment. Their preference for these calorie-rich foods meant that they were better nourished, lived longer, and produced a greater number of healthier children. Their children inherited the same taste preference, which has passed from generation to generation so that now nearly everyone is psychologically adapted to like these foods.

The human preference for sweet and fatty foods provides a useful illustration of two further evolutionary principles (Kanazawa, 2003). First, adaptations are the result of natural selection forces operating at a particular time in our ancestral history, or what is termed the **environment of evolutionary adaptiveness (EEA)** (Crawford, 1998b). Each adaptation has its own EEA corresponding to the ancestral period during which it arose. If changing conditions create a mismatch between the EEA and the current environment, the adaptation may no longer be helpful and might even be harmful (Crawford, 1998b). Let's return to our example. Liking sweet and fatty foods was adaptive in the EEA when food was scarce, but this condition no longer exists in most Western societies, where people are surrounded by food everywhere they turn—from grocery stores to restaurants, food carts, and vending machines (Kanazawa, 2003). In an environment where food is abundant, our fondness for sweet and fatty things is leading to health problems such as diabetes, obesity, and cardiovascular disease (Buss, 2012; Kanazawa, 2003). What was adaptive in the EEA has become maladaptive in today's environment.

Lastly, it is important to understand that evolution is not a consciously chosen course of action (Kanazawa, 2003; Walsh, 2002). Nobody ever ate a bag of potato chips because they thought it would maximize their chances of passing their genes on to future generations. People eat chips and other fatty snacks because they taste good (Kanazawa, 2003). It just so happened that people with this taste preference in the EEA were more likely to survive and, as a result, the trait eventually came to dominate.

> **environment of evolutionary adaptiveness (EEA)** The set of conditions that existed during ancestral times and to which the human body and brain adapted.

Selfish and Antisocial Behaviours

Evolutionary psychologists claim that selfishness and other antisocial traits are adaptive and normal (Raine, 1993; Tibbetts, 2003; Walsh, 2002). Selfishness in this context may be defined as acting in ways that increase the chances of your own survival and reproductive success at the cost of someone else's (Dawkins, 2006; Trivers, 1985). The evolutionary benefit of being selfish is not difficult to grasp. Those who place their own needs first are the most likely to survive and to pass this trait on to another generation (Tibbetts, 2003). Selfishness, according to evolutionary theorists, is an innate and universally held trait produced by natural selection (Dawkins, 2006; Walsh, 2002).

The tendency to act in a selfish manner has advantages in terms of self-preservation; however, it also leads to decidedly antisocial behaviour (Raine, 1993; Tibbetts, 2003). A good example is the two-spotted astyanax, a small freshwater schooling fish native to Brazil. Research shows that these fish will deliberately chase and attack another member from their own school when exposed to a predator (Goulart & Young, 2013). This is an effective strategy because it diverts the predator's attention and therefore increases the attacker's chances of survival. The attacker's behaviour is also extremely selfish, as it comes at the expense of the wounded fish, which is rendered more vulnerable and is likely to be eaten.

Antisocial traits such as selfishness, aggressiveness, and impulsiveness presumably have conferred a similar evolutionary advantage on humans (Raine, 1993; Walsh, 2002). Admittedly, these traits sometimes give rise to behaviours that are criminalized and put people in prison, but keep in mind that adaptations are expected to be advantageous only in the EEA (Kanazawa & Still, 2000; Walsh, 2002). The advent of the criminal justice system and correctional institutions are relatively recent phenomena in human history, far removed from the EEA where these traits and associated behaviours are thought to have developed. The fact that something is maladaptive now has no bearing on whether or not it was adaptive at one time.

Altruistic Behaviour and Inclusive Fitness

The helpful and cooperative nature of most human interactions presents a greater evolutionary mystery. From a theoretical standpoint, behaviour that helps others does not make sense because it offers no obvious survival or reproductive advantage to the individual providing the assistance. Indeed, selfless behaviours such as sharing food, raising someone else's young, or protecting another person from harm can be risky. Evolutionary theorists refer to this type of behaviour as altruistic (West, Griffin, & Gardner, 2007). The mystery of altruism was solved, at least in part, by the ground-breaking work of William Hamilton (1964), who recognized that reproductive success is really a function of all the offspring produced by an individual in combination with those close relatives who share common genetic material (Walsh, 2002). This concept is called **inclusive fitness**. By acting altruistically in ways that aid the survival of relatives, individuals are actually increasing the odds that their own genetic material will successfully pass to subsequent generations through their shared genes. Because the altruists who perform these acts are indirectly enhancing the survival of their own genes, they are engaging in a "special kind of selfishness" (Crawford, 1998a, p. 13).

inclusive fitness The reproductive success of both the individual and his or her close genetic relatives.

Inclusive fitness provides a useful framework for understanding the self-sacrificing behaviour of family members. For example, grenade ants will split open their abdomens and spill a sticky substance onto intruders in a suicidal act of defence to protect the rest of their genetic relatives in the colony (Alcock, 2013). Altruistic behaviour is expected to be proportionate to the recipient's degree of genetic relatedness; an individual is more likely to help his or her children and siblings than more distant genetic relatives such as nieces or nephews. Daly and Wilson (1988a) went one step further, claiming that parents will expend more effort caring for, and be less abusive to, their genetic children than to genetically unrelated children. Their research showed that children were many times more likely to be killed by step-parents than by genetic parents. See the "Researching" box on their theory, which they dubbed the "Cinderella effect."

Researching Criminal and Violent Behaviour

The Cinderella Effect

Have you ever noticed the prominence of stepmothers in fairy tales? "Cinderella," "Snow White," and "Hansel and Gretel," to name just a few, all include cruel and neglectful stepmothers. According to Daly and Wilson (1998), wicked step-parents are a common feature of folklore across different cultures. The researchers argue that the presence of these characters is no coincidence; they claim that evolution lies beneath the step-parents' harsh and abusive behaviour portrayed in many fables.

Broadly speaking, evolutionary theory is built on the premise that natural selection favours structures and processes that improve survival and reproductive success. Daly and Wilson (1998) reason that parents are inclined to invest more heavily in related than unrelated children because the former contributes to their genetic representation in the population. The psychological mechanism behind this differential behaviour has yet to be determined; however, these researchers speculate that, as a result of natural selection, parents form stronger emotional bonds and greater commitments to their own children than to someone else's. For example, Cinderella's stepmother lovingly devotes all her time and energy to her own children's success but abuses her stepdaughter.

To evaluate their predictions, Daly and Wilson (1988a, 1988b) analyzed data regarding child abuse among families in Canada, the United States, and the United Kingdom. They found an unequal distribution of fatal and non-fatal child abuse, consistent with evolutionary theory. Specifically, the risk of being killed by a step-parent was much greater than being killed by a genetic parent (see Figure 2.5 for the Canadian results).

This finding carries several caveats. First, a careful examination of the figure reveals that the child homicide rate in stepfamilies for the highest-risk age group (i.e. 0–2 years of age) is roughly 600 per 1,000,000 parent–child pairs. So, while the risk of child homicide is higher among stepfamilies than genetic families, the vast majority of step-parents do not kill their stepchildren. Second, this finding is not uniform across the research (Temrin, Buchmayer, & Enquist, 2000). Finally, Daly and Wilson's research is correlational in nature, so we cannot rule out other explanations for the results. Nevertheless, evolutionary psychologists rightly point out that theoretical and empirical developments in their field uncovered the elevated risk of homicide surrounding stepchildren.

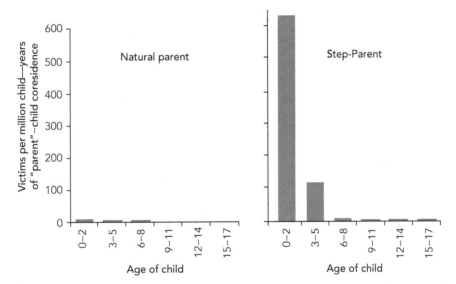

Figure 2.5 The risk of being killed by a step-parent versus a natural parent in relation to the child's age, Canada, 1974–1983.

Source: Republished with permission of Transaction Aldine, from *Homicide*, M. Daly & M. Wilson, volume, 1988; permission conveyed through Copyright Clearance Center, Inc.

Cooperative Behaviour

Inclusive fitness may shed light on altruistic behaviour among genetic relations, but it does not account for why people help friends or strangers. Robert Trivers (1971) theorized that helping individuals will be adaptive even in the absence of a genetic relationship, provided the recipient returns the favour. That is to say, I will help you now on the understanding that you will repay me with assistance later. Trivers (1971) argued that there is an evolutionary advantage gained by helping behaviour that forms part of a wider tit-for-tat social exchange.

Vampire bats are a popular example (e.g. Buss, 2012; Raine, 1993; Trivers, 1985). They feed at night on the blood of large mammals, such as horses and cows, but anywhere between 7 and 30 per cent of the colony are unsuccessful and return to the roost hungry on any given night (Wilkinson, 1990). Those bats that managed to feed are reliably observed regurgitating blood for the unsuccessful bats to eat so they do not starve. Moreover, this sharing behaviour does not depend on a genetic connection between the two bats (Wilkinson, 1990). The potential benefit of this social interaction is that the bat giving up a meal one night may be the recipient of a donated meal another night. Chimpanzees exhibit a similar system of reciprocity. They tend to share food with an individual who groomed them earlier that day (de Waal, 1989). Cooperative behaviour that produces mutual benefits in this manner is known as **reciprocal cooperation** (West et al., 2007).

reciprocal cooperation
An evolutionary adaptive behaviour that involves providing a non-related individual a benefit on the basis that he or she will return the favour and thereby increase survival and reproductive success.

Cheating Behaviour

The obvious difficulty with reciprocal cooperation is that the strategy is vulnerable to exploitation. Some individuals will engage in **cheating behaviour** by accepting benefits from others without reciprocating (Trivers, 1985). You may have encountered cheating behaviour first-hand if you ever helped someone move, loaned your lecture notes to a classmate, or given someone a ride in your car only to discover later that the person was unwilling to return the favour. Ellis and Walsh (1997) suggest that what modern society identifies as criminal or antisocial behaviour is an extreme form of cheating that causes serious harm to others. Over the past few decades, numerous theories have sprung up to explain the evolution of criminal behaviour, which Rowe (2002) broadly divides into alternative strategy and conditional adaptation theories. Each group is briefly described in the next two sections (for more comprehensive reviews of the individual theories, consult Ellis [1998] and Walsh [2009]).

cheating behaviour Accepting a benefit from another without reciprocating the favour.

Alternative Strategy Theories

Alternative strategy theories presume that criminal behaviour is connected to a person's reproductive tactics (e.g. Harpending & Draper, 1988; Mealey, 1995; Rowe, 1996). It is recognized that, within the natural world, organisms vary in the parental investment they make in their offspring (e.g. Trivers, 1972). Organisms that display high **parenting effort** expend a large proportion of their time and energy feeding, protecting, and training their young. By investing heavily in their offspring, these parents ensure a large percentage survive to maturity. The trade-off is that they can produce and rear only a relatively small number of offspring over their lifetime. This strategy is common among mammals.

parenting effort The time, energy, and resources dedicated to supporting one's mate and raising one's offspring.

Organisms at the low end of the parenting effort spectrum tend to focus on mating. They produce a large number of offspring but put little or no time and energy into raising their young. A few offspring usually survive because of the sheer number produced. Without parental support, however, most perish. Mosquitoes and salmon typify the high **mating effort** approach. They lay thousands of eggs but die long before their young even enter the world.

mating effort The time, energy, and resources dedicated to having sex with others.

Although humans exhibit high parenting effort, alternative reproduction theories assume that some degree of individual variation exists (Fishbein, 2001; Rowe, 2002). Some people are more oriented toward parenting effort while others, at least in a relative sense, concentrate on mating. It is further theorized that the relative emphasis an individual places on a reproductive strategy is related to genetic-based differences in the traits they exhibit (Fishbein, 2001). Rowe (1996, 2002) has identified numerous traits that facilitate mating effort. For example, a strong sexual drive and sensation-seeking are helpful for pursuing new sexual partners. In addition, weak emotional bonds to others and a lack of remorse enable the individual to break off old relationships without hesitation and quickly move on to the next sexual partner. Deceitful and aggressive tendencies may be useful for cajoling and coercing potential partners into sexual relationships. On the other hand, empathy, conscientiousness, and strong emotional bonds to others (especially one's children) lend themselves to parenting effort (Walsh, 2009).

Note that the traits associated with parenting effort encourage prosocial behaviour whereas those associated with mating effort promote law-breaking (Harpending & Draper, 1988). This is the key element shared by all alternative strategy theories of crime—the more people display traits that maximize mating effort, the more likely they are to behave criminally. As support for these theories, proponents usually point to empirical evidence showing a link between offending behaviour and various aspects of sexual behaviour that might be considered indicative of high mating effort, such as numerous sexual partners and early onset of sexual behaviour (e.g. Charles & Egan, 2005; Stouthamer-Loeber & Wei, 1998).

Conditional Adaptation Theories

The second group of theories views criminal behaviour as an evolved conditional adaptation, an evolved mechanism that detects and responds differently depending on the features present in the environment (Boyce & Ellis, 2005; Rowe, 2002; Walsh, 2002). Unlike alternative strategy theories, the present group contends that the behavioural strategy people adopt is triggered by their environmental conditions (Belsky, 2000; Cohen & Machalek, 1988; Rowe, 2002). Genetic influences are considered secondary to the environmental situation encountered (Belsky, 2000; Cohen & Machalek, 1988; Vila, 1994). Conditional adaptation theories differ from one another in terms of the timing and nature of the triggering events.

One version of conditional adaptation theories speculates that exposure to harsh, rejecting, and unstable home environments during the first five to seven years of life is critical (Belsky, Steinberg, & Draper, 1991; Belsky, 2000). Children who experience such conditions during this period of their lives consciously or unconsciously develop a sense that life, and relationships in particular, is insecure. As a consequence, they reach puberty and initiate sexual activity earlier than other children and generally exhibit behaviour reminiscent of a mating effort reproductive strategy. Conversely, stable home environments during the same period presumably produce a response consistent with a parenting effort reproductive strategy. Whichever strategy is adopted, children tend to maintain it throughout their lives.

Another version of conditional adaptation proposes that criminal behaviour is simply a useful strategy for obtaining resources (Cohen & Machalek, 1988; Vila, 1994). According to these theories, any organized and productive society creates a natural opportunity for some individuals to expropriate the things they want (Cohen & Machalek, 1988, 1994). Criminal behaviour is viewed as a relatively normal strategy that some members of every society can be expected to adopt. No particular time period is considered more or less critical for determining whether an individual will behave antisocially (Fishbein, 2001). Instead, individuals shift back and forth between cooperative and antisocial behaviour, depending on resource availability and, importantly, the strategies employed by others in the population. As discussed in the next section, there are natural limits to the proportion of people in a society who can engage in cheating. Finally, criminally expropriative strategies are thought to evolve over time, although this evolution is a function of cultural, not genetic, transmission. Behaviours that prove to be successful are selectively retained and shared from person to person so that they proliferate throughout the population; those that prove unsuccessful are repeated less often and eventually fall into disuse (Vila, 1994).

Constraints on Cheating and Criminal Behaviour

Despite the obvious gains that can be made by cheating and exploiting others, there are good reasons why this behaviour does not dominate human social interactions. The fact is that people do not give endlessly to individuals who renege on their social obligations. Most of us retaliate by withholding further cooperation. You may be able to think of individuals whom you will no longer help because they never reciprocate your assistance. Humans are not unique in this regard. Cooperative vampire bats stop sharing meals with non-reciprocating bats, and chimpanzees with food react aggressively when they are approached by other troop members who do not share consistently (de Waal, 1989; Wilkinson, 1990).

Thus, the short-term gains realized by cheaters often come at the long-term expense of bad reputations and diminished prospects for future cooperation (Walsh, 2009). These consequences mean that anyone resorting to this tactic more than occasionally must find new cooperators who are naïve to their history—something that is difficult in small, close-knit communities (Harpending & Draper, 1988; Walsh, 2009). The need to keep ahead of their reputation and the law explains why fraudsters such as Christopher Rocancourt tend to move frequently. As you read the case study on Rocancourt, think about how alternative strategy and conditional adaptation theories could apply to his behaviour.

CASE STUDY

Christopher Rocancourt

Paris, France—Christopher Rocancourt grew up in very humble surroundings in northwestern France. His father left him at an orphanage when he was a child, his mother having abandoned the family years earlier (Burrough, 2007). He was adopted three years later, but was unhappy with his new family and ran away several times before leaving for good at the age of 18. He moved to Paris, where he began his career as a con artist.

Most of his early attempts were feeble, but Rocancourt managed a major score when he forged the deed to an apartment building and sold it to an unwitting buyer for $1.4 million (Taibbi, 2006). He went on to pose as a member of the wealthy Rockefeller family, a son of actress Sophia Loren, a nephew of filmmaker Dino De Laurentiis and of designer Oscar de la Renta, and the son of a French countess (Burrough, 2007; Leung, 2003). Using these ruses to cheat people out of their money, he left a trail of unpaid bills and empty wallets everywhere he went, from Paris to Los Angeles, the Hamptons, and Vancouver (Leung, 2003). Rocancourt's cheating extended to his personal life—during his second marriage, he maintained a relationship with another woman (Burrough, 2007; Taibbi, 2006).

Rocancourt's modus operandi was remarkably simple. He posed as a person of wealth, flashed large wads of cash, and paid for lavish dinners. Fooled by the charade, countless victims handed over substantial amounts of money, expensive cars, clothes, and so forth, all on the understanding that Rocancourt was borrowing the items or making investments on their behalf. As soon as they realized what was happening, he would move on (Burrough, 2007; Leung, 2003; Taibbi, 2006).

When authorities eventually caught up with Rocancourt, he denied being a thief. He explained:

It's like I say to you, "Let me borrow your tie right now." Well, you say, "Okay, that is my tie. I'll let you borrow it." But today, I don't give back your tie.

Photo 2.3 Christopher Rocancourt converses with his lawyer during his sentencing hearing in March 2004. Photo: Robert Gauthier/Los Angeles Times/Getty Images

I broke a promise, yeah? That makes me a thief[?] . . . I did borrow it, but that doesn't mean I'm a thief. I didn't grab it. I didn't take it. I didn't steal it. (Leung, 2003)

After pleading guilty to fraud and other charges filed in Los Angeles and New York, Rocancourt was ordered to pay damages to his victims and to serve five years in prison. In an interview following his release in 2007, he admitted to being a con man and estimated that he bilked his victims of over $40 million. Although he maintains this chapter of his life is closed, he does not express any sympathy for the "stupid" people he ripped off (Taibbi, 2006).

The pursuit of cheating is further constrained because it is **frequency dependent**; its success depends on the strategy adopted by the rest of the population (Mealey, 1995; Barrett Dunbar, & Lycett, 2002). Cheating works only if there are other people in the population who choose to cooperate and therefore are available to be "suckered." If the proportion of cheats grows too large, the strategy becomes unprofitable because, as Wiebe (2012) observes, "If everyone cheated, soon nobody would cooperate" (p. 350). On the other hand, this strategy may be highly profitable when the proportion of cheats remains low and the proportion of cooperators is high.

> **frequency-dependent strategy** In evolutionary theory, a behavioural pattern that produces relatively greater success when its use within a population is rare and relatively lower success when its use within a population is common.

Sex Differences

Reproductive strategies lie at the heart of evolutionary explanations for the large sex differences observed in criminal and violent behaviour. Men's and women's different reproductive roles are thought to influence the reproductive strategies employed by each sex. Crucial to evolutionary theory is the reproductive capacity of ancestral males and females (Buss, 2012; Quinsey, 2002). The quantity of offspring that human males produced was primarily limited by the number of female partners with whom they mated (Quinsey, 2002). Furthermore, the male investment in reproduction is extremely small (Buss, 2012). The reproductive window for human females is much smaller due to the length of each pregnancy and menopause (Campbell, 2009; Quinsey, 2002). In addition, women's parental investment is extremely high because of gestation (i.e. pregnancy) and lactation (i.e. breastfeeding; Buss, 2012).

Trivers (1972) used the concept of parental investment to advance two propositions concerning sexual selection. The sex making the larger parental investment is choosier about mates, and the sex making the smaller parental investment will be more competitive for mates. Observations of animals exhibiting sex-role reversal bear these predictions out. For instance, the male pipefish offers a brood pouch where the female's eggs are nourished for several weeks. In this species, males make the greater contribution to parenting and do the choosing, whereas females make the smaller contribution and do the competing (Alcock, 2013). In any event, the theoretical implication for humans is clear. Ancestrally, women exercised more care over their mate choices while men generally engaged in **intrasexual competition** for sexual partners. The low parental investment made by men allowed them to pursue other mates, which led them to compete with one another (Rowe, 2002). The relatively greater size and strength of males compared to females is seen as an evolutionary consequence of this constant competition for female partners (Daly & Wilson, 1988a).

intrasexual competition
Rivalry among the members of one sex, usually for mates or resources.

Evolutionary theorists speculate that intrasexual competition for mates accounts for the higher level of criminal and violent behaviour among males. Because women can afford to be choosy, they will look for partners who can contribute to child-rearing and enhance their offspring's survival prospects (Campbell, 2009; Kanazawa, 2008). Accordingly, women will prefer men with status, power, and resources (Campbell, 2009). It appears that these evolutionary preferences still linger today because men of high wealth and status report more sexual relations than those without (Pérusse, 1993). Men try to cater to these preferences and thus attach a great deal of importance to acquiring and maintaining them.

Daly and Wilson (1988a) believe that this situation explains why relatively trivial affronts can quickly escalate into serious or lethal violence between males. Evolutionary theory tells us that it is costly to lose one's status and reputation, and so men are psychologically resistant to backing down in the face of insults, jostling, and minor disputes. Violence not only helps to preserve one's reputation, but it also serves to deter other potential rivals (Daly & Wilson, 1988a; Kanazawa, 2003). The end result is that minor altercations are much more likely to culminate in violence among men than women. Using similar logic, Kanazawa (2005, 2008) speculates that the evolutionary preference of females for partners with resources motivates men to acquire material resources through whatever legitimate or, if need be, illegitimate means available. Men's stronger desire for material wealth is the reason that most perpetrators of property-related crimes, such as robbery and theft, are men. These unconscious psychological mechanisms could also explain the dynamics of many street gangs: males join for the status, material goods, and women that membership brings and females are attracted to their status and wealth (Palmer & Tilley, 1995).

Anne Campbell (1999, 2002, 2009) took a different approach to explaining sex differences in criminal behaviour. Instead of addressing why men commit so much crime, she asked why women are responsible for so little. The answer, she believes, lies in the fact that the mother's presence is much more critical to offspring survival than the father's. The young depend exclusively on their mother for gestation and lactation. Mothers also typically assume the principal role in nurturing and protecting children throughout their development. Men cannot be counted on because they engage in dicey sexual and aggressive behaviour (Campbell, 2009). The importance of the mother "staying alive" has led to an evolutionary adaptive psychological mechanism that, in situations involving risk of bodily harm, causes women to experience fear at a lower threshold than men (Campbell, 1999). As a consequence, women are more risk-averse and less apt to engage in potentially dangerous conduct, which accounts for the reduced involvement of women in crime overall and particularly in relation to riskier violent crimes (Campbell, 2009).

Sex differences are not only noticeable in the prevalence of crime but also the nature of the offences perpetrated. Campbell (2002) characterizes the motivations of female and male offenders in sharply different terms that can be summarized as need versus hedonism. Women tend to commit low-value property crime out of economic need and as a way to provide for their children (Campbell, 2002). Conversely, men are much more likely to use crime and violence to enhance their status on the street and support lavish lifestyles filled with cars, flashy clothes, drugs, and women. This latter description is consistent with the theoretical expectations concerning male intrasexual competition.

Age–Crime Curve

Intrasexual competition has been used by Kanazawa (2003; Kanazawa & Still, 2000) to explain the age–crime curve. As discussed in Chapter 1, this curve is characterized by a low crime rate during early childhood, a steep rise and peak in young adulthood, and a gradual decline across the rest of the lifespan. These major shifts correspond loosely to periods of male psychosexual development that might be labelled pre-puberty, post-puberty, and fatherhood (see Figure 2.6). During the initial, or pre-puberty, period, males are sexually immature and incapable of reproducing, giving them no reason to compete for female attention. The absence of intrasexual competition removes the need for aggression or other, criminalized behaviours.

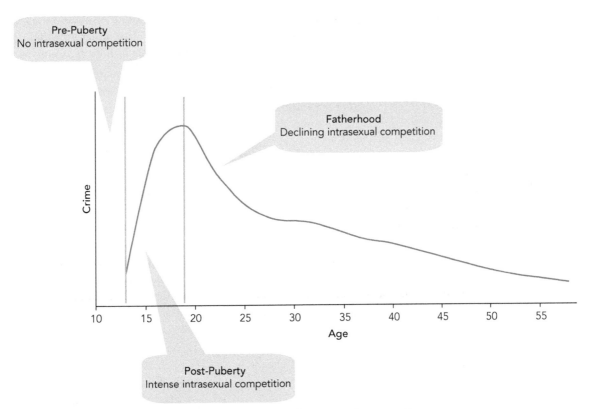

Figure 2.6 Age–Crime curve and different phases of intrasexual competition.

This situation shifts dramatically as males go through puberty, usually sometime during their early teens. Once males become sexually mature, intense competition emerges among them as they vie for females. We have discussed that status and material wealth are now important and that males frequently employ tactics such as violence and theft to gain and maintain an edge over potential rivals. According to evolutionary theory, this accounts for the sharp rise in the crime rates seen during the teenage years and into early adulthood (Kanazawa, 2003; Kanazawa & Still, 2000).

From an evolutionary perspective, engaging in intrasexual competition is initially advantageous for males because it can lead to reproduction. There is also no associated cost because males have nothing to lose. The birth of the first child, however, shifts the relative balance between these benefits and costs. A child means that the benefit of continued reproductive efforts is diminished because the father's genes have already been passed to the next generation (Kanazawa, 2003). In addition, there is a potential cost associated with continued competition because the father may be injured or even killed, thereby reducing the support and protection available for his offspring. Even if continued competition does not result in physical harm, it still requires attention and energy that might be better put toward raising offspring. This high cost of continued competition is vividly illustrated in walruses, which are known to roll over and accidentally kill their own young in the course of fighting with rival males. The combination of diminishing returns and rising costs tips the balance in favour of males abandoning further intrasexual competition following the birth of their first child. In the absence of this competition, their criminal behaviour begins to decline (Kanazawa, 2003; Kanazawa & Still, 2000).

Some speculate that the psychological mechanism responsible for the varying intensity of male intrasexual competition over the lifespan involves testosterone (Kanazawa, 2003; Kanazawa & Still, 2000). High testosterone is linked to dominance and aggressive behaviour (Archer, 2006; Mazur & Booth, 1998). Testosterone levels increase during adolescence, when intrasexual competition is on the rise. Recent research also shows that a man's testosterone levels drop after his first child is born. This decrease could explain why fathers lose interest in continuing the competition for mates, leading crime rates to fall (Kanazawa, 2003; Kanazawa & Still, 2000; Kuzawa, Gettler, Muller, McDade, & Feranil, 2009).

Kanazawa's (2003; Kanazawa & Still, 2000) account of the age–crime curve is exclusive to males, but the factors for females may not be entirely different. Although evolutionary theorists generally believe that intrasexual competition for mates is a predominantly male phenomenon, Campbell (2002) posits that females will compete when desirable males are in short supply—most likely when there is a wide discrepancy among men in the resources they can contribute to raising offspring, such as areas with high unemployment. In these conditions, females may be willing to fight to secure and retain higher-status, wealthier males. The general shape of the age–crime curve for females mirrors the curve for males, with two notable differences. First, the shape of the curve is flatter, which is consistent with evolutionary arguments that the level of crime and violence for females is lower. Second, the curve peaks at a slightly younger age, something Campbell (2002) attributes to the fact that females reach sexual maturity earlier.

Summary

1. Heredity's influence on the expression of antisocial traits and offending behaviour has been traditionally evaluated with twin and adoption studies. The former investigate

whether the members of each twin pair match with respect to offending behaviour. Heredity is implicated if the concordance rate among monozygotic twins, who are genetically identical to one another, is higher than the concordance rate of dizygotic twins, who share only some genes. Adoption studies assess the degree to which the offending behaviour of adopted children and their parents is related. A relationship between the offending behaviour of adopted children and their biological parents indicates a hereditary influence, whereas a relationship between adopted children and their adoptive parents indicates an environmental influence. In general, twin and adoption studies confirm that some individual variation in offending behaviour seen in the population is attributable to genetics.

2. Researchers have begun working to identify specific genes that may contribute to offending behaviour. Most molecular genetic studies focus on genes linked to the production, transportation, and breakdown of different neurotransmitters, especially dopamine and serotonin. The results suggest that the tendency to engage in criminal or violent behaviour is polygenic in nature and therefore reflects the combined effect of many genes. Individuals with the greatest vulnerability for offending probably possess multiple risky alleles.

3. Research reveals that offending is not only influenced by genetics but also by the environment. These two influences appear to interact with one another such that the impact of environmental conditions on criminal behaviour varies according to an individual's genetic makeup. The diathesis–stress model offers one possible explanation of this interaction, namely, that people vary in their genetic vulnerability for offending. It is only when genetically vulnerable individuals are in adverse environmental conditions that offending behaviour is likely to occur. Other individuals are unlikely to offend regardless of the environmental conditions. The differential susceptibility model is an alternative explanation. According to this model, people vary in their genetic sensitivity to the environment. Genetically sensitive individuals flourish when the environment is good and therefore display the least amount of offending, but they struggle and offend the most when the environment is poor. Less sensitive individuals exhibit moderate responses in both environments. The key distinction between the models is that differential susceptibility assumes that people differ in their reactions to both poor and favourable environments whereas diathesis–stress assumes that they differ only in their reactions to poor environments.

4. According to evolutionary psychology, selfishness is a universal trait because, during ancestral times, people who acted in their own self-interests were more likely to survive. Nowadays, this trait can lead to behaviours that are deemed criminal. From an evolutionary perspective, altruistic behaviour directed toward genetic relatives is a special form of selfishness because it increases the chances that the altruistic person's own genetic material will be passed on to the next generation by virtue of their shared genes.

5. Cooperative behaviour with genetic strangers makes evolutionary sense if it is part of a reciprocal social exchange, whereby one party lends assistance to another on the understanding that the favour will be returned in the future. The presence of willing cooperators allows some individuals to engage in cheating behaviour and accept benefits from others without ever reciprocating. Alternative strategy theories assume that cheating is a function of genetically based differences in traits, such as sensation-seeking, weak emotional bonds, and lack of remorse, which are advantageous

for pursuing an alternative reproductive strategy that emphasizes mating with many partners. By comparison, conditional adaptation theories suggest that cheating is an evolved psychological mechanism possessed by everyone and is a natural response to harsh, unstable, or underresourced environments.

6.   Evolutionary theory hypothesizes that the gap between the rates of male and female criminal offending is attributable to different psychological mechanisms that have evolved for each sex. Males typically engage in intrasexual competition for female mates. To make themselves attractive, males have developed an evolved psychological desire for status, power, and material resources, which may lead them to use antisocial and violent behaviours to acquire and protect these things. Intrasexual competition is greatest during adolescence and early adulthood, which is why the age–crime curve peaks at this point in the lifespan. A different psychological mechanism operates in women. Human offspring are highly dependent on their mothers for survival; thus, females developed a much lower threshold for experiencing fear. As a result, women tend to avoid dangerous activities that could jeopardize their future ability to care for their young, including many behaviours that are considered criminal.

Review Questions

1.   Explain the nature-versus-nurture debate as it relates to offending behaviour.
2.   Describe the diathesis–stress and differential susceptibility models and explain the emergence of criminal behaviour based on each.
3.   Compare and contrast the parenting effort and mating effort reproductive strategies and discuss which one is linked to criminal behaviour and why.
4.   Review the case study of Christopher Rocancourt. Explain his behaviour using alternative strategy theories and conditional adaptation theories.
5.   Discuss an evolutionary theory that accounts for the wide gap in the rates of criminal behaviour for men and women.
6.   Describe an evolutionary theory that explains the age–crime curve for men or women.

Additional Readings

Anderson, G. S. (2007). *Biological influences on criminal behavior*. Boca Raton, FL: CRC Press.

Buss, D. M. (2012). *Evolutionary psychology: The new science of the mind* (4th ed.). Boston, MA: Allyn and Bacon.

Carey, G., & Goldman, D. (1997). The genetics of antisocial behavior. In D. M. Stoff, J. Breiling, & J. D. Maser (Eds.), *Handbook of antisocial behavior* (pp. 243–254). New York, NY: Wiley.

Daly, M., & Wilson, M. (1988). *Homicide*. Hawthorne, NY: Aldine de Gruyter.

Quinsey, V. L. (2002). Evolutionary theory and criminal behaviour. *Legal and Criminological Psychology, 7*, 1–13.

Walsh, A., & Beaver, K. M. (2009). *Biosocial criminology: New directions in theory and research*. New York, NY: Routledge.

3

Biology

Learning Objectives

At the end of this chapter, you should be able to:

- identify and describe the brain's basic structures and their roles in emotional and behavioural processes;

- explore how dysfunctions associated with specific areas of the brain may contribute to criminal and violent behaviour;

- explain how hemispheric asymmetry or dysfunction, particularly deficits in the lateralization of language, might be related to criminal and violent behaviour;

- describe the roles that various neurotransmitters may play in criminal and violent behaviour;

- identify two main types of hormones and discuss their involvement in the development of criminal and violent behaviour; and

- discuss how low autonomic nervous system functioning is potentially linked to higher levels of stimulation-seeking and risk-taking and lower levels of empathy among offenders.

CASE STUDY

Chris Benoit

Fayetteville, Georgia—Chris Benoit was a popular professional wrestler who had trained with the legendary Hart family and maintained an illustrious career for over 20 years. From his humble beginnings in Calgary's Stampede Wrestling in 1985, he went on to wrestle in Japan and for several large national wrestling promotions (McKeown & Karp, 2008; "WWE Canadian wrestler," 2007). In 2000 Benoit joined World Wrestling Entertainment (WWE), the largest and most internationally recognizable wrestling entertainer; he won the WWE World Heavyweight Championship in 2004. Just three years later, however, Benoit's successes were eclipsed by tragedy.

On 25 June 2007, police were informed that Benoit had missed several WWE appearances. They arrived at his home in Fayetteville, Georgia, to discover the bodies of Benoit; his wife, Nancy; and their seven-year-old son, Daniel. The police determined that Benoit had strangled his wife and smothered his son to death, placed a Bible by the bodies, and then hanged himself from his weight equipment. Initial speculation about the causes of the murder-suicide focused on steroid use. The professional wrestling world certainly had problems with steroids in the past, and prescription anabolic steroids were found in the Benoit residence (McKeown & Karp, 2008; "WWE Canadian wrestler," 2007).

Subsequent investigations looked at Beniot's brain. After his career was cut short by a serious concussion, former WWE wrestler Chris Nowinski developed an interest in the adverse effects of concussions in professional sports. He obtained permission from Benoit's father to have neurologists examine his son's brain. The results were shocking. According to Dr Julian Bailes, the neurologist who conducted the tests, Benoit's brain showed evidence of extensive damage

Photo 3.1 Chris Benoit celebrates winning the Triple Threat match at Wrestlemania XX.

from multiple concussions and resembled the brain of an 85-year-old Alzheimer's patient. Bailes and his colleague, Dr Bennett Omalu, concluded that the damage produced a form of dementia that resulted in bizarre changes in Benoit's behaviour (McKeown & Karp, 2008;"WWE Canadian wrestler," 2007).

Bailes and Omalu had observed similar findings in the brains of retired National Football League (NFL) players who had suffered multiple concussions. Across studies of NFL retirees with concussions—including Terry Long and Andre Waters—the researchers noted an advanced onset of dementia-related symptoms and other structural changes in the brain. Both Long and Waters had multiple concussions and committed suicide following retirement (Guskiewicz et al., 2005; Omalu et al., 2005). Both had struggled with depression in the months leading up to their suicides, but neither had a prior history of depression or mental illness.

Could the bizarre behaviour and violent outburst that so tragically ended the lives of Benoit and his family have stemmed from his concussions? Did these blows to the head fundamentally damage particular brain structures or alter the proper functioning of his brain?

Introduction

neuropsychology The study of the brain, its functions, and its role in behaviours and psychological processes.

Neuropsychology is the study of the brain, its functions, and its role in behaviours and psychological processes. In forensic neuropsychology, clinicians and researchers are interested in, for example, how specific brain structures generate behavioural responses to perceived threats in the surrounding environment. This interest might focus specifically on impulsivity and aggressive or violent behaviour. A forensic neuropsychologist is curious about the brain's part in the experience of emotions, particularly how brain dysfunction might contribute to feelings of hostility or anger.

The Structure of the Brain

Just as we would not expect a car to run without an engine or a computer to perform without an operating system, we can't expect the human body to work without a brain. Our experiences and interpretations of the world around us, our thoughts and choices, and our behavioural responses are all governed by the brain. The complexity of human behaviour and experience is clearly reflected in the brain's architecture. Like a well-oiled machine, specific tasks and functions are delegated to specific areas, allowing us to function effectively in our day-to-day lives.

The largest area of the brain, and the area that governs our most complex functions, is the forebrain. It contains the **limbic system**, an important component in our discussion of the neuropsychology of criminal behaviour. As its name implies, the limbic system is not a specific brain structure but a loosely connected network of structures located along the border of the brain's cerebral cortex and subcortical areas. No consensus exists about which particular brain structures comprise the limbic system, but most neuropsychology textbooks include the amygdala, hippocampus, and parts of the thalamus and hypothalamus. Most notably, the limbic system plays a role in motivational, emotional, and memory processes.

limbic system An intricately connected system of brain structures responsible for primal emotional drives, including fear, aggression, hunger, and sexual arousal.

The part of the forebrain that contributes to our most distinctly human qualities is the cerebrum, which accounts for the vast majority of all the brain cells in the human central nervous system. Not surprisingly, then, our abstract thinking occurs in this area. The thin, grey, outer layer of our cerebrum is referred to as the cerebral cortex; it is folded into numerous grooves or convolutions, which allow a large surface to fit within the volume of our skull.

Our cerebrum is divided into the left and right hemispheres. A series of dense nerve fibres called the corpus callosum connect the hemispheres and allow information to be exchanged between each half of the brain. Although the cerebral hemispheres are structurally similar, research shows that they are lateralized—each is responsible for specific, independent functions. For instance, language functions are largely lateralized to the left hemisphere, while spatial abilities appear to be lateralized to the right. As you read this section, be aware that we are simplifying the nature and extent of **lateralization** for the purposes of this text and that neuropsychologists continue to debate the extent to which particular functions are localized to one hemisphere or the other.

lateralization The localization or specialization of particular processes or functions (e.g. language, spatial skills) to a particular hemisphere of the brain.

Each cerebral hemisphere consists of four parts, or lobes, that are to some extent responsible for different processes (see Figure 3.1). Three of these lobes (the occipital, parietal, and temporal) are located at the posterior of the brain and govern a range of functions, including the integration of auditory, sensory, and visual information. The functions of the **frontal lobes** are of greater interest in the study of criminal behaviour. These lobes are the largest in the cerebral cortex and play a role in several higher-order functions such as planning, decision-making, and aspects of personality. Although some tasks are localized to particular lobes, functions overlap across various regions.

frontal lobes The largest lobes in the cerebral cortex, which govern higher-order thinking, decision-making functions, and aspects of personality.

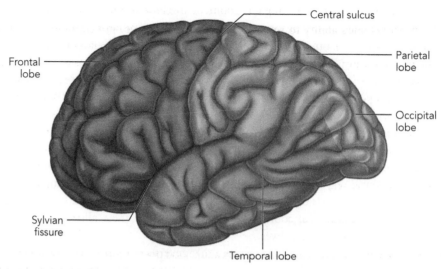

Figure 3.1 The four lobes of the brain
Source: Adapted from CC-BY_2.0 RobinH via Wiki

Brain Injury and Criminal Behaviour: General Evidence

The tragedies of the Benoit murder-suicide and the suicides of Terry Long and Andre Waters share a common link—a history of multiple concussions. But can a serious blow to the head change how a person thinks, feels, and behaves? **Organic brain syndrome (OBS)** is a general term referring to diseases, usually not psychiatric disorders, that cause decreases in mental functioning (Martell, 2007). A variety of physical conditions can result in organic brain dysfunction, including head trauma or injury, degenerative diseases such as Parkinson's, strokes, acute infections, or low levels of oxygen to the brain. A body of research has found some ties between general organic brain dysfunction and emotional and behavioural changes, including violent behaviour. A study by Martell (1992) detected multiple signs of brain dysfunction in 66 per cent of American forensic psychiatric patients. Interestingly, he also found that patients with a past diagnosis or history suggesting organic brain dysfunction were more likely to have a violent criminal history.

Head traumas or injuries resulting in a loss of consciousness are one possible cause of organic brain dysfunction. Numerous studies have observed that, following such an injury, people demonstrate marked changes in personality and behaviour, including aggressiveness, irritability, impulsiveness, and poor temper control (Kim, 2002; Lezak & O'Brien, 1988). Serious forms of traumatic brain injury have been found among criminal populations (Ferguson, Pickelsimer, Corrigan, Bogner, & Wald, 2012; Shiroma, Ferguson, & Pickelsimer, 2010). For example, Lewis, Pincus, Feldman, Jackson, and Bard (1986) conducted neuropsychological examinations of 15 death row inmates and discovered that all had a history of serious head trauma. A history of head injuries has also been identified among seriously violent subgroups of spousal assaulters (Rosenbaum & Hoge, 1989; Walling, Meehan, Marshall, Holtzworth-Munroe, & Taft, 2012).

Further support for a relationship between brain damage or dysfunction and aggression comes from studies employing **neuropsychological tests**, which are designed to measure cognitive or motor functions that are believed to be linked to specific brain

organic brain syndrome (OBS) A general term referring to diseases, usually not psychiatric disorders, that result in decreased mental functioning. Numerous physical conditions can result in organic brain dysfunction, including head trauma or injury, degenerative diseases, strokes, acute infections, or low levels of oxygen to the brain.

neuropsychological tests Tests or tasks designed to measure cognitive or motor functions that are believed to be linked to specific brain structures. Poor performance on these tests provides an indirect indication that an area of the brain may be damaged and malfunctioning.

structures (Durand, Barlow, & Stewart, 2008). A continuous performance task, for example, measures one's ability to selectively maintain attention on a continuous activity or stimuli. Poor performance on neuropsychological tests provides an indirect indication that an area of the brain may be damaged and malfunctioning (Hawkins & Trobst, 2000; Hodgins, 2002). To date, several studies have found a significant association between lowered performance on a variety of these tests and aggressive behaviour (Bryant, Scott, Golden, & Tori, 1984; Giancola & Zeichner, 1994; Lau, Pihl, & Peterson, 1995). A study of boys in Montreal found that patterns of stable aggression were correlated with poor performances on neuropsychological tests measuring executive functioning, which generally refers to higher-order thinking skills such as logic (Seguin, Pihl, Haden, Tremblay, & Boulerice, 1995). We will discuss these skills in greater detail later in the chapter.

Brain Plasticity and Early Head Injury

It was once believed that injuries sustained in adulthood posed more serious consequences than those in childhood because the brain was fully developed and "hardwired," thereby minimizing the possibility of any substantive rehabilitation (Andrews, Rose, & Johnson, 1998; Kolb, Gibb, & Gorny, 2001). Our knowledge about brain development and vulnerability has changed remarkably over the years and now challenges this conventional wisdom. We know that the brain is not fully developed at birth; structures and links, or neural connections, between brain regions are still developing. We refer to this dynamic state as **brain plasticity**, or "the brain's ability to change structure and function" (Kolb & Whishaw, 1998, p. 144). Plasticity of the brain does not cease in childhood—our brain is capable of regeneration across the lifespan. Nevertheless, there are limitations to brain plasticity, with the greatest regenerative potential observed in childhood, after which it slowly declines.

brain plasticity The brain's ability to change structure and function and to develop new neural connections.

Our current knowledge about the course of brain development raises serious concerns about the impact of head injuries in early childhood. The foundation for many critical neuropsychological and neurocognitive functions is laid in early childhood (Loeber & Farrington, 2000). For example, the most significant activity regarding neural connection development occurs over the first several years of life (Huttenlocher & Dabholkar, 1997). A growing body of research demonstrates that suffering a serious brain injury as a child can have devastating effects on emotional and behavioural problems in adulthood. Important to the purposes of this book, research indicates that early neuropsychological problems are predictive of persistent delinquency in adolescence (Moffitt, Lynam, & Silva, 1994). Other studies of children with early onset brain injury report that later criminal behaviour is relatively stable and increases in frequency as the child ages (Anderson, Damasio, Tranel, & Damasio, 2000; Tranel & Eslinger, 2000).

Specific Brain Regions and Criminal Behaviour

Brain Imaging and Criminal Behaviour

To this point, we have discussed the general effects of head injuries, with little focus on particular areas of the brain or specific deficits and their link to criminal behaviour. Advances in neuropsychology have given us the opportunity to examine brain structure and function closely, using a variety of relatively non-invasive approaches. Specific brain imaging techniques include the computerized tomography (CT) scan, magnetic resonance imaging (MRI), functional magnetic resonance (fMRI), and single proton emission computerized positron emission tomography (PET) An imaging technique that involves injecting the body with a radioactive substance to locate diseases and to evaluate organ function. Procedurally, the patient is injected and performs a task known to activate particular regions of the brain so that the scan, which measures blood flow, can provide an indication of the organ's activity.

tomography (SPECT; Roth, Koven, & Pendergrass, 2008). Another technique, **positron emission tomography (PET)**, allows neuropsychologists to observe the "working" brain in action. Procedurally, a radioactive substance is injected into the body and the patient performs a task that is known to activate particular regions of the brain. The scanning device detects the radioactive substance, which is used to measure the rate of blood flow in the brain and thereby provides an indication of brain activity.

Numerous brain imaging studies report a relationship between functional and structural deficits and criminal and/or aggressive behaviour (Hoptman & Antonius, 2011; Kumari et al., 2006; Kumari et al., 2009; Soyka, 2011; Wahlund & Kristiansson, 2009). Raine and Buchsbaum's (1996) review of 14 brain imaging studies on aggressive behaviour highlighted an interesting finding. Many of the studies seemed to suggest some specificity or localization of brain dysfunction among aggressive individuals; importantly, the source of brain dysfunction differed for various offender groups. Several studies observed dysfunctions in the temporal lobes of sex offenders, particularly among pedophiles and those committing incest (Hucker et al., 1986; Hucker et al., 1988; Langevin, Wortzman, Dickey, Wright, & Handy, 1988; Wright, Nobrega, Langevin, & Wortzman, 1990). Other studies found frontal lobe dysfunctions among violent offenders and sadistic sexual assaulters (Hendricks et al., 1988; Raine et al., 1994; Volkow & Tancredi, 1987). Based on these findings, Raine and Buchsbaum (1996) hypothesized that the nature of brain dysfunction exists along a continuum, with progressively more serious forms of violence associated with dysfunctions localized in the frontal lobes and less physically violent forms of sexual offending, such as incest and pedophilia, localized in the temporal lobes.

Bufkin and Luttrell (2005) reviewed the findings of 17 studies on brain imaging and aggression. They arrived at three major conclusions. First, brain imaging research shows that a specific area of the frontal lobe, the **prefrontal cortex**, plays an important part in aggressive behaviour. Second, temporal lobe dysfunction—particularly in the subcortical area, including the limbic system—contributes to aggressive behaviour. Finally, the likelihood of aggression, especially if it is impulsive, depends on a complex balance between the prefrontal cortex and the subcortical structures located on the left side of the temporal lobe. The premise that emerges from these findings, which is important to understand moving forward, is the varying nature of the contributions that different areas of the brain make to criminality.

prefrontal cortex The part of the brain located in the anterior region of the frontal lobe and which governs higher-ordering thinking, or executive control functions, and aspects of personality.

The Frontal Lobes and Criminal Behaviour

Hawkins and Trobst (2000) provide an excellent, succinct summary of the role of the frontal lobe and the deficits associated with damage in this region of the brain. Briefly, it is critical to higher-order thinking and decision-making functions, including directing and maintaining our attention, integrating internal and external information, generating intentions and plans, and initiating, monitoring, and adapting our behaviour. These activities are particularly important for our social behaviour (Grafman et al., 1996).

Numerous studies demonstrate that frontal lobe dysfunction contributes to criminal behaviour (see Bryant et al., 1984; Gornstein, 1982; Giancola & Zeichner, 1994; Golden, Jackson, Peterson-Rohne, & Gontkovsky, 1996; Hawkins & Trobst, 2000; Raine, 1993). For example, Yeudall and Fromm-Auch (1979) compared 86 violent criminals and 79 nonviolent adult participants on a series of neuropsychological tests. These tests revealed signs of increased frontal lobe dysfunction among the former group but not the latter. However, research has not uniformly found a strong relationship between frontal lobe dysfunction and aggression. Virkkunen, Nuutila, and Huuskol (1976) found no increase in criminality or aggressive behaviour in a follow-up of more than 500 World War II Finnish soldiers with frontal or temporal lobe damage. Hare (1984) also failed to observe any differences in neuropsychological test performance between a group of offenders considered to be at higher risk for aggressive behaviour, psychopathic offenders, and other offenders. Why do such discrepancies appear? Perhaps generalized frontal lobe damage does not alter behaviour, emotions, or mood. Findings from the Vietnam Head Injury Study, for instance, suggest that individuals with injuries to specific areas of the frontal lobes exhibit aggressive behaviour. Methodological differences among studies could also account, at least in part, for the lack of general consensus in the empirical research.

Despite some divergent findings, there is sufficient evidence to conclude that difficulties in the frontal lobes are relevant to criminal and violent behaviour. The next question to explore is why frontal lobe damage contributes to this type of conduct. Hawkins and Trobst (2000) identified seven common symptoms associated with frontal lobe dysfunction, which generally reflect problems with either personality and emotions or behavioural production and management. Personality and emotional problems may include apathy and emotional lability. Apathy refers to deficiencies in motivation such as an individual lacking emotion or enthusiasm about things in general. Frontal lobe damage, for example, may result in a loss of interest in social interaction or a lack of concern regarding the consequences of one's actions. **Emotional lability** refers to emotional instability, wherein an individual's mood may swing wildly for no apparent reason.

Hawkins and Trobst (2000) also identified deficiencies in the following areas of behavioural production and management: anticipating, planning, and sequencing; initiating behaviour; monitoring behaviour; altering or stopping behaviour; and employing abstract reasoning. Frontal lobe damage can result in problems with determining the effective order of behaviours and the likely consequences of pursuing a particular course of action. As Grafman and colleagues (1996) have noted, these deficits may lead to difficulties in social situations, where the ability to monitor our behaviour, anticipate consequences, and interpret responses to our actions prompt us to inhibit or alter our behaviour. Imagine you begin to tell a racy joke at a party full of your older relatives. The concerned expressions on their faces might signal to you that the joke is inappropriate; in response, you might decide to change the subject or stop talking. In the absence of these abilities, you would proceed and perhaps offend your audience.

The symptoms outlined by Hawkins and Trobst (2000; see also Table 3.1) may contribute to aggressive behaviour in at least four ways. Frontal lobe damage may impair an individual's ability to control impulses and inhibit inappropriate behaviours. Most people know that physically striking someone has legal consequences and they will inhibit an initial impulse to act in this manner. Individuals with frontal lobe dysfunction, however, often find it more difficult to restrain such urges. Frontal lobe damage also reduces the ability to anticipate the consequences of one's actions and to select adaptive responses in different social situations. During a conflict, for example, an individual with frontal lobe dysfunction may not be able to effectively generate alternatives to aggression. In addition, frontal lobe damage is characterized by rigidity or a failure to adapt responses to one's context, which can lead to problems because no single behavioural strategy works across all settings. For instance, you probably do not interact with your parents the same way you would with your professors, peers, or employers. We routinely adapt our behaviour to fit our environments,

emotional lability An emotional instability, wherein an individual's mood or emotional expressions can change rapidly without warning.

Table 3.1 Summary of frontal lobe dysfunction

Common Symptoms and Deficits	Contributions to Violence
Personality and emotion • Apathy • Emotional lability **Behavioural production and management** • Difficulty anticipating, planning, and sequencing behaviours • Difficulty inhibiting behaviour • Difficulty monitoring behaviour • Difficulty shifting or adapting behaviour • Poor abstract reasoning	**Poor inhibitory control** • Emotional reactions to events are exaggerated and, due to poor inhibitory control, frequently precipitate inappropriate behavioral responses. **Poor planning abilities** • Difficulties planning and adjusting behaviour mean responses often prove to be ineffective and a source of frustration that leads to inappropriate behavioural reactions. **Behavioural rigidity** • Inflexible and persistent responding means violence may continue to be inflicted long after the victim has stopped resisting. **Interpersonal inappropriateness** • Poor self-monitoring and interpersonal insensitivity may provoke social ridicule or angry reactions from others.

Source: Adapted from *Aggression and Violent Behavior*, 5(2), K. A. Hawkins and K. K. Trobst. Frontal lobe dysfunction and aggression: Conceptual issues and research findings, 147–157, Copyright (2000), with permission from Elsevier.

but frontal lobe damage may impair this ability. Finally, individuals with frontal lobe damage may overreact to minor provocations or fail to display an appropriate emotional response in other social situations. Their emotions may switch rapidly with little warning, perhaps provoking others around them and triggering interpersonal conflicts.

The Prefrontal Cortex and Executive Control Functions

Neuropsychological research on criminality and aggression has implicated the prefrontal cortex, which is located at the anterior region of the frontal lobe, above the forehead. Our distinctly human qualities are believed to reside in the prefrontal cortex—not surprisingly, this area of the brain is much larger in humans than in other mammals (Shimamura, 1996). The prefrontal cortex is similar to complex highway systems that pass through large urban centres. It is highly interconnected with other areas of the brain, receiving incoming information from the brain stem and the limbic system in the temporal lobes.

If a person's prefrontal cortex is damaged, subsequent changes to **executive control functions** (ECF) and personality—the two aspects of human functioning believed to be governed by this area of the brain—may partly account for his or her criminal behaviour. Hoaken, Allaby, and Earle (2007) offer a good overview of the importance of ECF for human social behaviour:

> Executive functioning allows humans to respond to situations in a flexible manner, to create and adapt plans, and to base their behaviour on internally held ideas rather than being governed exclusively by external stimuli. (p. 413)

executive control functions (ECF) Housed in the prefontal cortex, a variety of higher-order cognitive skills that include decision-making, planning and predicting, focusing attention, understanding abstraction and logic, and exercising social control.

CASE STUDY

Phineas Gage

Cavendish, VT—Phineas Gage's story is a cornerstone in neuropsychological research that offers an excellent starting point for understanding the complex connection among the brain, personality, and behaviour. On 13 September 1848 Gage was supervising a railroad crew that was blasting rocks from an area where the track was to be laid. The process involved drilling a hole into the rock, filling it with gunpowder, covering the gunpowder with sand to prevent an explosion, and packing it down with an iron tamping rod. While preparing one drilled hole, the crew were momentarily distracted. Believing that one of his assistants had already poured sand into the hole, Gage dropped the iron rod, which sparked and ignited the blasting powder. The resulting explosion sent the 3.5 foot bar hurtling from the hole. It struck Gage beneath his left eye, passed through his skull and frontal lobe, and exited just above the hairline on his forehead.

Amazingly, Gage not only survived the accident but also showed significant physical recovery over time. By all accounts, he was still an able-bodied man who showed no reduction in movement, speech, or intelligence. But he underwent a bizarre transformation in personality

Photo 3.2 Phineas Gage holds the tamping rod that caused his injuries.

and behaviour. Prior to his accident, Gage was known as a hard-working, responsible, and generally affable individual. In the aftermath of the accident, he became abrasive and difficult. Dr John Harlow (1868), his personal physician, described Gage's personality and behaviour as follows: "A child in his intellectual capacity and manifestations, he has the animal passions of a strong man. . . . His mind was radically changed, so decidedly that his friends and acquaintances said he was 'no longer Gage'" (as cited in Neylan, 1999, p. 280). Phineas Gage died in 1860 (Damasio, Grabowski, Frank, Galaburda, & Damasio, 1994; Harlow, 1999).

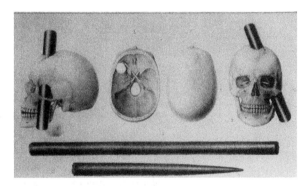

Photo 3.3 This lithograph shows the injury to Phineas Gage's brain. Photo: US National Library of Medicine

The case of Phineas Gage (see the case study) illustrates how damage to the prefrontal cortex may significantly alter personality and behaviour.

Since the case of Phineas Gage, a number of influential studies have been conducted on prefrontal damage in humans and its relationship to criminal and violent behaviour. In a comparison of the brain activity among 41 murderers and 41 non-murders, Raine and colleagues (1994) noted that the latter group showed high levels of prefrontal cortex activity when asked to perform a task designed to activate this area of the brain. Comparatively, the murderers showed lower activity levels while performing the same task. The researchers pointed out that this lack of activation was observed in only the prefrontal cortex.

A subsequent study by Raine and colleagues (1998) classified murderers as either predatory or reactive depending on whether the murder they committed involved instrumental or reactive violence (described in Chapter 1). Using a procedure similar to their earlier study, the researchers found that the reactive murderers had low levels of activation in the prefrontal cortex and, interestingly, the predatory murderers evidenced relatively normal levels. They also found that both groups had very high function in subcortical areas of the brain, where emotional regulation is believed to be governed. Several other studies have observed reduced prefrontal functioning in violent, antisocial persons (Amen, Stubblefield, Carmichael, & Thistead, 1996; Deckel, Hesselbrock, & Bauer, 1996; Lapierre, Braun, & Hodgins, 1995; Raine et al., 1994) and reduced prefrontal grey matter in antisocial personality disordered individuals living in the community (Raine, Lencz, Bihrle, LaCasse, & Colletti, 2000). However, researchers caution that a great deal about the relationship between prefrontal functioning and aggression remains unclear (Perez, 2012).

A number of theories have accounted for the association between poor prefrontal functioning—specifically ECF deficits—and aggressive behaviour. Some researchers suggest that problems with the prefrontal cortex result in difficulties with behavioural inhibition. In other words, when the prefrontal cortex underperforms, people have problems controlling inappropriate responses (Barratt, 1994; Blair, 2001). Thus, the problems with behavioural inhibition and impulse control previously noted in our discussion of frontal lobe damage may be localized to the prefrontal cortex. This particular problem is sometimes referred to as **disinhibition syndrome**, which is characterized by the inability to exercise control over emotional responses or to consider alternative, socially acceptable responses in stressful situations (Giancola, 1995; Starkstein & Robinson, 1997).

disinhibition syndrome An inability to exercise mental control over emotional responses or to consider alternative, socially acceptable responses in stressful situations.

Temporal Lobe and Limbic System Damage

Along with localizing dysfunction in the frontal lobe and, more specifically, the prefrontal cortex, researchers have also cited abnormalities in temporal lobe functioning as an important contributor to criminal and aggressive behaviour (Fabian, 2010; Flor-Henry, 2003; Raine, 1993). Evidence of structural abnormalities in the temporal lobes has been observed, for example, among mental health patients with a history of violence (Fabian, 2010). The temporal lobes, located on both sides of the brain, have been implicated in **episodic dyscontrol syndrome** (EDS), a pattern of recurrent outbursts of uncontrollable and unprovoked rage that are generally uncharacteristic for the individual (Monroe, 1970). These outbursts can occur in the context of other disorders, including substance abuse problems, dementia, and **temporal lobe epilepsy**. The *Diagnostic and Statistical Manual of Mental Disorders* (*DSM-5*; discussed in more detail in Chapter 9) classifies EDS as an impulse control disorder and calls it intermittent explosive disorder (IED). The *DSM* describes IED as involving several discrete episodes of failing to resist aggressive impulses, which result in serious assaultive acts or destruction of property (American Psychiatric Association, 2013).

episodic dyscontrol syndrome (EDS) A pattern of recurrent, generally uncharacteristic outbursts of uncontrollable and unprovoked rage.

temporal lobe epilepsy A neurological disorder that originates in the temporal lobes and is characterized by uncontrollable seizures stemming from abnormal electrical activity in the brain.

The Limbic System and Subcortical Structures

A number of researchers have noted the important role of emotional regulation in the genesis of aggressive behaviour (Davidson, Putnam, & Larson, 2000). Logically, our ability to control emotions, particularly negative ones such as anger or fear, should influence expressions of aggression. The limbic system, introduced earlier in this chapter, and its subcortical structures are central to any discussion of emotions and aggression.

Early associations between the limbic system and aggression were based on observations of patients with rabies (Eichelman, 1983). Since this time, researchers have identified specific structures within the limbic system that appear to be involved in criminal and aggressive behaviour. One such structure is the **amygdala**, an almond-shaped subcortical structure located in the medial margin of the temporal lobes (see Figure 3.2). The amygdala processes emotional information from the environment and plays a role in somatic memory, or memory for physiological states that we have experienced during particular events. The sensation of embarrassment or discomfort you may have experienced when disciplined as a child is an aspect of your somatic memory recorded by your amygdala. We can see, then, that the amygdala also plays a part in learning and memory as it relates to emotion. In addition to extracting emotional information from the environment, it is essential to the process of learning and remembering that future misbehaviour may lead to feelings of discomfort (Kiehl, 2006; LeDoux, 1996; Raine, Buchsbaum, & LaCasse, 1997).

The earliest links between the amygdala and aggression were reported in Heinrich Kluver's and Paul Bucy's descriptions of monkeys in the late 1930s. Specifically, the researchers noticed that monkeys with parts of their temporal lobes removed were extremely tame and docile. Subsequent studies found reductions in aggressive behaviours when the amygdala was selectively removed (Raine, 1993). Studies involving both animals and humans have found that amygdala stimulation increases aggressive behaviours, but electrically inhibiting or removing the amygdala decreases aggression

amygdala An almond-shaped subcortical structure that is part of the limbic system, which processes emotional information in the environment, and plays a role in somatic or emotional memory.

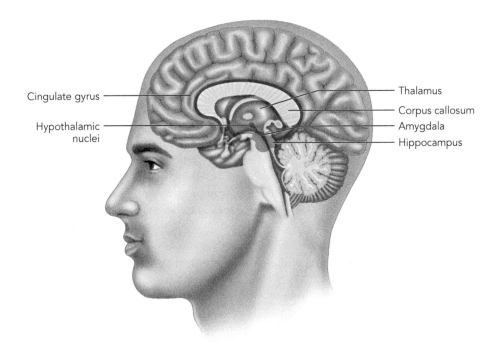

Figure 3.2 The limbic system and amygdala

Source: Adapted from CC-BY-2.0 from Anatomy & Physiology, Connexions Web site. http://cnx.org/content/col11496/1.6/, Jun 19, 2013.

(Coccaro, Sripada, Yanowitch, & Phan, 2011; Decoster, Herbert, Meyerhoff, & Potegal, 1996; Ferris, Herbert, Myerhoff, Potegal, & Skaredoff, 2006; Potegal, Ferris, Herbert, Myerhoff, & Skaredoff, 1996; Tranel, 2000). Brain imaging studies of affective, impulsive murderers show abnormally high levels of subcortical functioning in the amygdala (Raine et al., 1998). Recent research has shown a connection among amygdala dysfunction, lower amygdala volume, and reactive and/or impulsive forms of violence (Osumi et al., 2012; Pardini, Raine, Erickson, & Loeber, 2013).

The limbic system's role in emotional regulation is apparent in the body's **fight-or-flight response**, which readies a person to either flee from danger or respond with defensive violence. Emotional information about potential threats, such as fear, is sent to the amygdala, which triggers a response. Earlier in this chapter, we discussed Raine and

fight-or-flight response
The body's automatic physiological response to anxiety- or fear-inducing situations, which readies a person to flee from danger or respond with aggression to protect one's self.

CASE STUDY

Charles Whitman

Austin, Texas—By all outward appearances, Charles Whitman was an "all-American boy." He took an interest in the piano at a young age, was involved in the Eagle Scouts, and played baseball in high school before enlisting in the Marines. Yet Whitman's stint as a soldier ended poorly; he was court-martialled and demoted in rank for gambling, possessing a personal firearm on base, and threatening another Marine. While a student at the University of Texas at Austin, he began to experience mounting personal problems and depression. He visited the campus psychiatrist early in 1966, to whom he related his frustration over his parents' divorce and the stress of work and school. The psychiatrist noted that Whitman was overly hostile and had made numerous references to his violent impulses, even admitting that he had hit his wife on at least two occasions. Ominously, Whitman also described having the urge to shoot people with a deer rifle.

Shortly after midnight on 1 August 1966, Whitman killed his mother. After returning home, he murdered his wife, stabbing her five times while

Photo 3.4   Charles Whitman, shown here in his University of Texas yearbook photo, carried out what is considered by many to be the first mass shooting in the United States. Photo: Bettman/Getty Images

she slept, and then took several weapons—including a sawed-off shotgun and a high-powered hunting rifle—to the observation deck of the university's Clock Tower. Beginning at 11:48 a.m., Whitman spent the next 90 minutes firing randomly at people on the university grounds, killing 14 and wounding an additional 38. He was eventually shot and killed by the Austin police. An autopsy revealed that Whitman had a cancerous tumour in the hypothalamus region of his brain, which may have been pressing against the amygdala ("The Madman," 1966).

Before his death, Whitman wrote a note that included the following statements:

I do not quite understand what it is that compels me to type this letter.
Perhaps it is to leave some vague reason for the actions I have recently performed. I do not really understand myself these days. I am supposed to be an average reasonable and intelligent young man. However, lately (I cannot recall when it started) I have been a victim of many unusual and irrational thoughts ("The Madman," 1966).

colleagues' (1994, 1998) findings of higher subcortical activity in samples of murderers. It has been proposed that some reactive aggression stems from the amygdala's emotional regulation of fear responses in the fight-or-flight system (Blair, 2001; Siegel, Roeling, Gregg, & Kruk, 1999).

Remember that the amygdala is also implicated in somatic memory. During the fight-or-flight response, the amygdala processes information perceived as threats at an emotional level. Over time, we learn to associate certain events as dangerous or threatening, and this information is stored in the amygdala. When we encounter these same events or situations again, our amygdala immediately triggers a fight-or-flight response. According to one line of reasoning, we do not always respond with aggression because we are socialized to perceive this reaction as inappropriate. At an emotional level, we learn that aggressive responses can produce negative affects; for example, when you hurt another person and they express their pain verbally or non-verbally, you likely experience guilt and empathy for the victim. This emotional feedback is registered and stored in your amygdala and, if you encounter similar future circumstances, these negative emotions are recalled. Emotions, such as empathy, are particularly important for socialization (Blair, 2001).

James Blair (1995) has referred to this process as the **violence inhibition mechanism (VIM)**, a biological system and part of the fight-or-flight response. The presence of distress cues activate the VIM, which in turn triggers inhibitory emotional responses from the amygdala. The workings of the VIM can be observed in the animal world. For instance, a dog will often show submission to larger, more aggressive dogs by rolling onto its back, exposing its vulnerable belly and throat. The aggressor will recognize this cue and cease its attack on the smaller dog. Blair argues that a similar VIM exists in human beings and that certain violent offenders, such as psychopaths, have VIM deficiencies.

According to Blair, facial expressions such as fear or sadness should act as non-verbal cues of submission during aggressive acts. These cues should activate the VIM and bring about a cessation of aggressive behaviour. Violent and aggressive individuals, however, may not process emotional information the same way as other people and, as a result, emotional cues may not trigger the VIM. Research has shown that criminal psychopaths may exhibit deficiencies at recognizing emotional expressions in faces (Hoaken et al., 2007). Other studies have found that criminal psychopaths show lower activity in the amygdala during tasks that involve emotional processing (Kiehl, Hare, McDonald, & Brink, 1999; Kiehl et al., 2001; Muller, Wagner, Lange, & Taschler, 2003).

> **violence inhibition mechanism** (VIM) A biological system, and part of the fight-or-flight response, that is activated by distress signals and subsequently triggers inhibitory emotional responses from the amygdala.

Putting It All Together: The Prefrontal Cortex and Limbic System

The functioning of both the frontal lobe, particularly the prefrontal cortex, and subcortical structures associated with the limbic system in the temporal lobes may contribute to criminal behaviour. The prefrontal cortex, which governs personality and executive control functions, has extensive neural connections with other areas of the brain, including the limbic system. The limbic system is part of the "emotional brain" and integrates sensory information. In particular, the amygdala plays a role in somatic memory and is responsible for generating critical emotional drives linked to the fight-or-flight response.

Amygdala dysfunctions may cause individuals to misinterpret cues in the environment. For example, an individual with poor amygdala functioning may misinterpret ambiguous social cues as threats, thereby triggering strong aggressive emotional impulses. Subcortical structures, including the amygdala, generate negative emotions. In most cases, the prefrontal cortex will inhibit or suppress negative emotional responses if they are deemed inappropriate for the situation. Individuals with poor prefrontal cortex functioning, however, may be unable to inhibit their negative emotions and, consequently, be at greater risk of acting impulsively (Bufkin & Luttrell, 2005; Potegal, 2012).

Lateralized Hemispheric Dysfunction

The coordination of information across the brain's two hemispheres is asymmetrical. Contralateral pathways and connections to our cerebral hemispheres crisscross our body. That is, the left hemisphere communicates with and controls the right side, and the right hemisphere communicates with and controls the left side. Generally, information is communicated through these contralateral pathways. This functional asymmetry goes unnoticed because the corpus callosum allows the two hemispheres to share and integrate information into a meaningful whole. This hemispheric specialization is referred to as lateralization, a term defined earlier in the chapter.

Hemispheric specialization and its part in criminal behaviour have received a significant amount of attention. Much of this research has focused on a particular group of offenders, labelled psychopaths. Criminal psychopaths are characterized as highly impulsive individuals who demonstrate a deficiency in emotional experiences, including a lack of remorse or empathy. We will discuss psychopathy in more detail in Chapter 6. The psychiatrist Pierre Flor-Henry (2003) was the first to suggest the possibility that some violent individuals, including psychopaths, may suffer from left-hemisphere damage. Robert Hare (1998) has further posited that the callousness and remorselessness characteristics of some aggressive individuals reflect an imbalance in the functions governed by the two cerebral hemispheres. Theories of hemispheric dysfunction focus on deficits in left-hemisphere activation among violent individuals in two general areas: processing and comprehending language and processing emotional facial expressions (Hare, 1998; Hare & Connolly, 1987; Hare & McPherson, 1984a; Kosson, 1998). Hare (1998) has referred to this imbalance as **hemispheric asymmetry**.

hemispheric asymmetry
The asymmetrical distribution or lateralization of particular functions, such as language and verbal skills, to one hemisphere of the brain.

We have discussed that some violent offenders have demonstrated problems processing affective or emotional verbal information (Lorenz & Newman, 2002; Williamson, Harpur, & Hare, 1991). The meaning of many words operates at different levels. The lexical meaning of the word *snake*, for instance, describes a particular reptile. But the word may also have an emotional meaning, possibly referring to a cold-blooded, underhanded individual. Williamson and colleagues (1991) found that a sample of criminal psychopaths understood the lexical meaning but not the expressive connotation of emotionally charged words. Why would this reduced understanding be relevant to criminal or aggressive behaviour? Emotional processing could be related to the experience of empathy and, as such, be tied to behavioural inhibition. Individuals who recognize and understand emotion may be more likely to experience guilt and exercise restraint when deciding whether to commit a criminal or violent act.

Studies employing neuropsychological tests of hemispheric dysfunctions among violent offenders have produced mixed findings. Several studies have found that a disproportionate number demonstrate left-hemisphere dysfunction (Nachshon, 1983; Nachshon & Denno, 1987; Pillmann et al., 1999). Recent research has reported structural asymmetry in the frontal lobes and prefrontal cortexes of violent offenders (Keune et al., 2012) and aggressive adolescents (Visser et al., 2013).

Two other approaches to investigating hemispheric lateralization's role in violent behaviour have been employed. A great deal of research has been dedicated to examining how performance on measures of intelligence relate to violence. These tests, such as the Weschler Intelligence Scale for Children, include scales that measure both performance intelligence (e.g. psychomotor skills, non-verbal reasoning) and verbal intelligence (e.g. vocabulary, verbal reasoning skills). To date, research has shown that the relationship between intelligence and delinquency is largely accounted for by lowered verbal intelligence rather than performance intelligence (Quay, 1987; Lynam, Moffitt, & Stouthamer-Loeber, 1993; Moffitt, 1990; Moffitt, Lynam, & Silva, 1994). Poor verbal skills are associated with early-onset and persistent antisocial behaviour (White, Moffitt, & Silva, 1989). Deficits linked to verbal intelligence have also been related to left-hemisphere dysfunction. The second approach to studying hemispheric lateralization among criminal and/or violent offenders—dichotic listening—is described in the following "Researching" box.

Researching Criminal and Violent Behaviour

Dichotic Listening in Psychopaths

To test the hypothesis that criminal psychopaths exhibit an unbalanced hemispheric asymmetry, Hare and McPherson (1984a) used a verbal dichotic listening task to study selective auditory attention among a group of prisoners. A dichotic listening task presents a person with two different auditory messages at the same time, one to each ear. The participant's task is to tell the investigator which message he or she heard or recalls. Remember that, although auditory information arriving at each ear travels to both hemispheres, the connections to the opposite hemisphere are stronger. We should then expect that an auditory message presented to the right ear should be registered in the left hemisphere and vice versa. Because the left hemisphere specializes in verbal functions, it is generally expected that individuals who possess normally functioning brains will show greater recall for auditory messages presented to the right ear.

Hare and McPherson (1984a) divided their sample of prisoners into three groups based on the extent that they exhibited traits of psychopathy—high, low, and mixed. They then presented the inmates with the dichotic listening task, using pairs of one-syllable words (see Figure 3.3). Inmates low in psychopathy showed much greater recall for words presented to the right ear (normal lateralization). Inmates high in psychopathy

did not show such pronounced differences between the recall of words presented to each ear. The findings seem to suggest that psychopaths, a group of offenders posing a higher risk for violence, show reduced lateralization for verbal information. Other studies in this area also report that psychopathic offenders are less lateralized for language (Hare & Connolly, 1987; Raine, O'Brien, Smiley, Scerbo, & Chan, 1990).

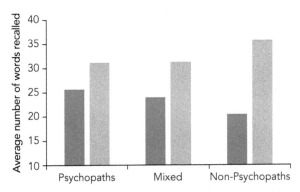

Figure 3.3 Performance in a dichotic listening task by group

Source: Copyright © 1984 by the American Psychological Association. Adapted with permission. R.D. Hare & L.M. McPherson, (1984). Psychopathy and perceptual asymmetry during verbal dichotic listening. *Journal of Abnormal Psychology*, 93, 141–149. The use of APA information does not imply endorsement by APA.

Left-Handedness and Reduced Lateralization

Approximately 10 per cent of the world's population is left-handed. Some people reason that left-handedness indicates left-hemisphere dysfunction and reduced lateralization for language functions. From this perspective, one might predict that left-handedness should be disproportionately observed among criminal or violent populations. Certainly, there have been some infamous left-handed criminals, including William Bonney (aka Billy the Kid) and Albert DeSalvo (The Boston Strangler). In fact, the technical terms for left-handedness, *sinistral* or *sinistrality*, are derived from the word *sinister*, a Latin term meaning "left." But other famous left-handed people, including Albert Einstein, Jimi Hendrix, Barack Obama, and Lady Gaga, are not criminals.

In their prospective study of 265 Danish children, Gabrielli and Mednick (1980) found that left-handedness observed at the age of 11 years was related to delinquency at age 17. Other, subsequent studies have also noted a preponderance of left-handedness among antisocial populations, lending some support to the theory (Ellis & Ames, 1989; Grace, 1987; Porac & Coren, 1981). Bogaert (2001) examined the frequency of left-handedness and ambidexterity in a sample of 8,000 men with a history of criminal behaviour and/or sexual offending and a non-criminal control sample. The results revealed that the frequency of non-right-handedness was higher among criminals and pedophiles than the controls, but the magnitude was quite small. Other studies have failed to find any relationship between left-handedness and criminality (Feehan, Stanton, McGee, Silva, & Moffitt, 1990; Hare & Forth, 1985; Yeudall, Fromm-Auch, & Davis, 1982).

The majority of research findings observe a higher frequency of left-handedness among criminal populations, suggesting that antisocial individuals may be characterized by reduced lateralization for language. Are left-handed people more sinister? Obviously, the existing research does not even remotely suggest that they are more antisocial or criminally inclined. Left-handedness is merely considered an observable indicator of possible left-hemisphere dysfunction; it is not a causal factor. The weak nature of the connection between handedness and criminality may arise because the former is not always an accurate sign of language lateralization. According to Raine (1993), in comparison to right-handed individuals, left-handed people are not clearly lateralized for language processes. The majority of left-handed people have language lateralized to their left hemisphere; only 15 per cent are lateralized for language in the right hemisphere and a further 15 per cent do not exhibit lateralization at all. In the latter case, language functions are represented fairly equally in both hemispheres.

Putting It All Together: The Findings on Lateralization

Research generally supports the theory that hemispheric dysfunction, particularly deficits in language lateralization, is related to antisocial and aggressive behaviour. This idea raises an important question: Why would problems with language be relevant to criminality? Raine (1993) has suggested that reduced lateralization for language may result in problems with both verbal comprehension and communication skills. Koenig and Linden (2004) have discussed how some violent crimes, such as homicide, are the culmination of arguments over relatively trivial misunderstandings. It is not difficult to see how problems with language comprehension and communication could lead to fatal misunderstandings in social interactions. People with poor verbal skills may become increasingly frustrated when they cannot successfully communicate their ideas and feelings to people around them and may lash out verbally or physically, provoking aggressive responses. Poor verbal comprehension may also result in misunderstandings or situations in which individuals perceive insults or provocative acts where none actually exist.

Neurochemistry and Criminality

The human body contains two communication systems that play an important role in transmitting information and regulating bodily functions and that are relevant to our discussion of neuropsychological factors underlying criminal behaviour. The **nervous system** is the comprehensive network of nerve cells—neurons, tissue, and organs—that regulates and coordinates all the body's activities. Our nervous system is composed of the central nervous system, which consists of the brain and spinal cord, and the peripheral nervous system, which is a complex network of nerves that joins the central nervous system to the different parts of the body. Our second communication system, the **endocrine system**, is a network of glands that secretes hormones into the bloodstream, regulating several essential functions.

nervous system The comprehensive network of nerve cells—or neurons, tissue, and organs—that regulates and coordinates all the body's activities.

endocrine system A network of glands that secretes hormones into the bloodstream, regulating several essential functions, including growth, metabolism, and sexual development.

Neurotransmitters

The communication and transmission of information across the nervous system's intricate network of neurons is achieved through neurotransmitters. Many different types of neurotransmitters are involved in this fast-acting neural highway and influence a multitude of behavioural and psychological processes, including emotions, mood, hunger, and sleep. An imbalance in the activity levels of some neurotransmitters has been linked to criminal behaviour. In fact, a large body of research examining this topic has accumulated over the years (Ferguson & Beaver, 2009; Fishbein, 2001; Perez, 2012; Potegal, 2012). This section focuses on some major findings regarding three neurotransmitters: dopamine, norepinephrine, and serotonin.

Dopamine

Dopamine is a major neurotransmitter that operates like a biochemical switch, activating other neurotransmitter systems. In addition, dopamine is involved in approach-oriented, or exploratory, behaviours and pleasure-seeking actions (Durand et al., 2008; Fishbein, 2001). The neuropsychological literature has generally associated overproduction of dopamine or excessive dopaminergic activity with aggressive behaviour. As will be discussed in Chapter 9, conditions such as schizophrenia are connected to an increased risk for criminal behaviour. Links between excessive dopamine activity and schizophrenia have led some researchers to suggest that this neurotransmitter is implicated in aggression. Amphetamine usage, which stimulates dopamine activity and is related to aggression, can produce symptoms similar to those observed among schizophrenic patients (Lavine, 1997). Drugs that decrease or block the effects of dopamine have also been found to reduce aggressive behaviour among psychotic patients (Brinkley, Beitman, & Friedel, 1979; Eichelman, 1986; Yesavage, 1984) and persons with mental retardation (Brasic, Barnett, Zelhof, & Tarpley, 2001). Other studies have observed a correlation among psychosis, aggression, and elevated dopamine levels among people with Alzheimer's disease (Holmes et al., 2001; Sweet et al., 1998).

dopamine A major neurotransmitter that operates like a biochemical switch, activating other neurotransmitter systems. Dopamine is also involved in approach-oriented, or exploratory, behaviours and pleasure-seeking actions.

Dopamine's potential relationship to aggression may be best understood by discussing this neurotransmitter's role in motivated or approach-oriented behaviours. Fishbein (2001), a renowned behavioural neuroscientist, has provided an excellent overview of this subject. She posits that dopamine activity increases in response to environmental cues of useful or pleasurable outcomes, such as food or an attractive partner. The release of dopamine triggers motivated behaviours; that is, as dopamine levels increase, we engage in behaviours designed to obtain rewards in our environments. Motivated behaviours can also include retaliatory or defensive responses in situations where we observe cues that have a perceived tie to threats. Fishbein (2001) argues that, when dopamine is overproduced, motivated behaviours may be initiated even without an appropriate cue or stimulus in our environment. Theoretically, then, aggressive and retaliatory behaviour may still be initiated in the absence of a legitimate threat.

Norepinephrine

norepinephrine A neurotransmitter and a hormone that is synthesized from dopamine and plays a role in a number of functions governed in the autonomic nervous system, including the fight-or-flight response.

Another neurotransmitter implicated in aggressive behaviour is **norepinephrine**—a neurotransmitter and a hormone synthesized from dopamine that plays a role in many functions governed in the **autonomic nervous system**, including the fight-or-flight response (Durand et al., 2008; Fishbein, 2001). In her review of the literature on neurotransmitters and aggression, Fishbein (2001) notes that, while some studies have failed to observe a relationship between norepinephrine and aggression (e.g. Bioulac, Benezech, Renaud, Noel, & Roche, 1980; Linnoila et al., 1983), most studies suggest that a link exists. Much of the evidence comes from studies examining the effects of drugs that increase norepinephrine levels (Lavine, 1997; Rampling, 1978). Numerous studies have demonstrated that drugs inhibiting norepinephrine activity successfully reduce aggression (Eichelman, 1986; Elliot, 1977; Lavine, 1997; Ratey et al., 1986). Beta blockers, which are drugs that block the action of various neurochemicals including norepinephrine, have been used with cardiac patients to lower their heart rate and blood pressure. These drugs are also sometimes used to reduce anxiety levels. In one study, beta blockers were shown to effectively reduce aggressive outbursts among individuals with autism (Ratey et al., 1987).

autonomic nervous system (ANS) The part of the peripheral nervous system that is responsible for regulating automatic or involuntary functions, including the fight-or-flight response.

Serotonin

serotonin A neurotransmitter that plays a role in several emotional and behavioural processes, including mood, appetite, and sleep regulation and behavioural inhibition.

The neurotransmitter **serotonin**, or 5-hydrotryptamine (5-HT), plays a role in several emotional and behavioural processes including mood, appetite, sleep regulation, and behavioural inhibition. Abnormally low levels of serotonin have been empirically linked with a variety of negative outcomes among humans, including suicide, mood and personality disorders (e.g. antisocial personality disorder), impulsive violent behaviour, and alcoholism (Coccaro et al., 1989; Moss, Yao, & Panzak, 1990). The connection between low serotonergic activity and impulsive aggression and/or violence among adult and youth offenders is a fairly robust finding in the literature (Bioulac et al., 1980; Coccaro & Murphy, 1991; Coccaro, Bergeman, & McClearn, 1993; Fishbein, 2001; Kruesi et al., 1990; Kruesi et al., 1992; Linnoila et al., 1983; Moss et al., 1990; Muhlbauer, 1985; Schalling, 1993; Soubrie, 1986; Virkkunen & Linnoila, 1993a, 1993b). Drugs that increase neurotransmitter levels also shed light on the relationship between serotonergic activity and aggression. Specifically, drugs that increase serotonergic activity have been found to decrease aggressive behavioural responding in a variety of groups (Brizer, 1988; Dale, 1980; Sheard, 1975; Sheard, Marini, Bridges, & Wagner, 1976; Siassi, 1982).

Putting It All Together: Neurotransmitters and Aggression

Meta-analyses generally confirm that neurochemical activity, especially involving serotonin, plays a role in criminal and violent behaviour (e.g. Scerbo & Raine, as reported in Raine, 1993). At this point, it is important to note that the existing research does not tell us that neurotransmitters cause aggressive behaviour. The evidence seems to suggest that abnormally low levels of serotonin, for example, are related to negative mood and impulsive patterns of behaviour. Fishbein (2001) believes that serotonin is involved in moderating one's ability to control behaviour (discussed in more detail in the next section) and mood states. Thus, a neurotransmitter such as serotonin may influence our ability to control impulses, as well as our tolerance for aversive external stimuli (Coccaro, 1989; Fishbein, 2001).

Work by neuropsychologist Jeffrey Gray (1981, 1987) provides us with an interesting theoretical framework for understanding how the balance of neurotransmitters may influence criminal behaviour. Gray proposed that learning and behaviour are functions of two interacting biological systems. The **behavioural activation system (BAS)** is responsible for activating behaviours in response to rewards and non-punishment in the environment. The **behavioural inhibition system (BIS)** inhibits behaviours in response to signals of aversive stimuli, such as punishment. According to Gray (1987), these two systems have a neurological basis and their functioning is tied to neurotransmitter systems. The BAS involves dopamine brain systems, and the BIS serotonin brain systems.

Don Fowles (1988) used Gray's theoretical framework to explain criminal and violent behaviour. He argued that underactivation of the BIS, which is related to low serotonin and norepinephrine levels, results in an impulsive behavioural style that increases the risk for antisocial and aggressive behaviour. Lower BIS functioning might be evident among individuals who fail to learn from punishment and show little anxiety in response to aversive stimuli. These individuals would likely engage in persistent criminal behaviour, despite censure and punishment.

behavioural activation system (BAS) A biological system that triggers emotional responses in the amygdala and activates behaviours in response to rewards and non-punishment.

behavioural inhibition system (BIS) A biological system that triggers emotional responses in the amygdala and activates behaviours in response to aversive stimuli, such as punishment.

Hormones

Another area that has received a great deal of attention regarding criminality is the role of various hormones. **Hormones** are chemical messengers that participate in the regulation of several vital bodily functions, including growth, metabolism, and sexual development. In contrast to the nervous system, the endocrine system is a slow-acting messenger system that produces diffuse and long-lasting changes in the human body. The endocrine system contains several glands—the hypothalamus, thyroid, adrenals, and the reproductive glands. The pituitary gland is the master gland; it regulates the release of hormones into the bloodstream in response to signals from the hypothalamus. The two categories of hormones relevant to our discussion are the sex and stress hormones.

hormones Chemical messengers secreted by the endocrine system that play a role in the regulation of several vital bodily functions, including growth, metabolism, and sexual development.

Sex Hormones

Sex hormones are responsible for the regulation of reproduction and the development of male and female sexual characteristics. The most commonly studied sex hormone in forensic psychology is **testosterone**, an androgen responsible for the development of male sex characteristics. Testosterone is produced in the male testes, the female ovaries, and

testosterone An androgen, or male sex hormone, that is responsible for the development of male sex characteristics.

the adrenal cortex of both genders. It has an androgenic, or masculinizing, effect on the human body, and levels of testosterone are naturally higher in men. Criminological literature has long illustrated a link between males and criminal behaviour (Hartnagel, 2004). As such, many people have inferred that a relationship exists between testosterone levels and aggression. Nonetheless, few relationships are empirically straightforward.

Studies examining testosterone levels and aggressive behaviour in animals paint a fairly consistent picture—testosterone is correlated with increased aggressiveness (Archer, 1991; Harding, 1983; Rada, Kellner, & Winslow, 1976). This association becomes less clear when the focus shifts to human beings. Early correlational studies of testosterone and questionnaire-based measures of aggression reported either non-significant or weak relationships (Rubin, 1987). Across three small-scale meta-analyses of existing research, Archer (1991) affirmed these earlier findings, reporting a relatively weak positive relationship. Other correlational studies have found positive correlations between aggression and elevated levels of testosterone among violent male offenders (Banks & Dabbs, 1996), conduct disordered youth (van Goozen, Matthys, Cohen-Kettenis, Thijssen, & van Engeland, 1998), and violent male alcoholics (Virkkunen, Goldman, & Linnoila, 1996). In addition, the administration of testosterone to male subjects in a laboratory setting can increase subsequent aggressive behaviour relative to aggression levels demonstrated by male subjects in a placebo condition (Kouri, Lukas, Pope, & Oliva, 1995).

Although it is produced at much lower levels in women, testosterone is still present. In fact, some evidence of testosterone's role in female aggressiveness exists (Dabbs & Hargrove, 1997; Fishbein, 1992). For instance, one study reported significant links among higher testosterone levels, increased self-reported levels of aggressive traits, and decreased prosocial traits among both men and women (Harris, Rushton, Hampson, & Jackson, 1996). Several studies have reported higher levels of testosterone among female adult offenders and delinquents with a history of violence relative to non-violent female offenders (Banks & Dabbs, 1996; Dabbs, Ruback, Frady, Hopper, & Sgoutas, 1988). Females' exposure to high levels of androgens in the prenatal and early postnatal periods has also been observed to correlate with higher levels of aggressiveness on later measures (Berenbaum & Resnick, 1997).

Associations between aggressiveness and high levels of testosterone have also been observed in other groups. Some research has found higher rates of aggressive behaviour among people afflicted with **congenital adrenal hyperplasia**—a disorder of the adrenal gland that can result in insufficient levels of certain hormones, such as cortisol, and excessive production of androgens (Berenbaum & Resnick, 1997). In a study of sexual violence, Studer, Aylwin, and Reddon (2005) examined the levels of serum testosterone among a sample of 501 convicted male sexual offenders enrolled in an institutional psychotherapy treatment program. The researchers observed elevated testosterone among offenders responsible for the most serious levels of sexual violence and reported a positive correlation between testosterone levels and sexual recidivism. Interestingly, treatment had an ameliorating impact on testosterone's part in sexual violence. Among those sex offenders who completed a treatment program, the levels were no longer predictive of sexual recidivism, highlighting the complementary role of environmental factors in the development of criminal behaviour.

Some inconsistencies apparent in the research findings can be attributed to methodological differences in the studies. One of the most potentially influential methodological issues is how testosterone levels are measured. Testosterone is not consistently released

congenital adrenal hyperplasia A disorder of the adrenal gland that can result in a failure to produce sufficient levels of certain hormones, such as cortisol, and excessive production of androgens.

into the bloodstream, so levels fluctuate markedly (Mazur & Booth, 1998). Moreover, testosterone release is affected by circadian rhythms, with levels higher in the morning and lower but more stable levels in the afternoon (Book, Starzyk, & Quinsey, 2001). Studies not only measure testosterone levels using different techniques, but they also often take measurements at different intervals during the day, something that could account for some of the variability observed in research findings.

Keep in mind that the testosterone–aggressiveness connection is bound to be complex and influenced by a number of factors. For instance, higher levels of testosterone may be correlated with only certain forms of aggression. Evidence has emerged that testosterone plays a role in a type of non-physical aggression known as **social dominance**, or behaviours designed to achieve higher ranking or hierarchical status in social or peer groups. Rowe, Maughan, Worthman, Costello, and Angold (2004) failed to find any link between testosterone and physical aggression among a group of conduct disordered boys, yet elevated levels of testosterone were associated with social dominance behaviours among these same youth. Perhaps even more interesting was that high levels of testosterone were linked to leadership behaviours among a control sample of non-delinquent boys.

In summary, there appears to be some relationship between testosterone and aggressive behaviour, although it is neither consistently observed nor empirically strong. The correlational nature of most of the research also raises concerns about directionality, an issue discussed in Chapter 1. Some researchers have pointed out that testosterone's effects on behaviour depend on context or environmental demands (Rubinow & Schmidt, 1996). Archer (2006) recommends the **challenge hypothesis** as an explanation. It proposes that male testosterone levels will rise in contexts that challenge reproductive success or mating. According to this hypothesis, the stronger relationship between testosterone levels and aggression among 13- to 20-year-olds might reflect the greater efforts this demographic puts toward mating. Theoretically, as men age and become more likely to get married, have children, and settle down, the need for increased aggression to compete for mating resources diminishes (Book et al., 2001). Some empirical support for the challenge hypothesis exists. For example, testosterone increases have been observed in anticipation of competition (Suay et al., 1999) and following a victory in competitive interactions, even in chess games (Mazur, Booth, & Dabbs, 1992). As described in Chapter 2, testosterone levels also appear to vary with changes in family status (Kuzawa et al., 2009).

Stress Hormones

Although studied less frequently than sex hormones and testosterone, there is nevertheless a considerable body of research investigating the possible roles of stress hormones in criminal and violent behaviour. Stress hormones are released into the blood stream by the pituitary and adrenal glands in response to stress signals from the hypothalamus. The most frequently studied stress hormone in the context of criminal behaviour is cortisol, which is produced by the adrenal glands (Raine, 1993).

Two major and conflicting research findings are of interest to our discussion of cortisol. First, some studies have observed abnormally high levels of cortisol among conduct disordered and depressed individuals (Susman & Ponirakis, 1997). In cases of increased cortisol activity, individuals may have a lower threshold for tolerating frustration or stress in their environments and, as such, may be more likely to react violently to minor provocations. Second, numerous studies report a link between low levels of cortisol

social dominance A form of non-physical aggression that is characterized by behaviours designed to achieve higher rankings or hierarchical status in social peer groups.

challenge hypothesis A theory that attempts to account for observed relationships between testosterone levels and aggression. The hypothesis proposes that males' testosterone levels will rise in situations that challenge reproductive success or mating.

and aggressive behaviour. For example, several studies found reduced cortisol activity among psychopathic offenders (Cima, Smeets, & Jelicic, 2008), conduct disordered children (Lahey & McBurnett, 1992, as cited by Raine, 1993; McBurnett et al., 1991), and violent adult and youth (McBurnett, Lahey, Rathouz, & Loeber, 2000; Susman, Dorn, & Chrousos, 1991; Tennes & Kreye, 1985; Virkkunen, 1985). In a study of college students, O'Leary, Loney, and Eckel (2007) administered a self-report test of psychopathy and took measures of cortisol levels following induced stress. Male participants high in psychopathic personality traits showed low levels of cortisol when stress was induced, while males low in psychopathic traits showed the expected increase in cortisol levels when exposed to stress. This effect was not observed among female college students.

High cortisol activity may reduce some individuals' ability to effectively deal with stress and provocation, thus increasing their likelihood of aggression. On the other hand, individuals with low cortisol activity may not experience any stress or anxiety at all. As we will discuss shortly, the experience of anxiety is important for socialization. We experience anxiety when we do something wrong or when we hurt another person. The absence of anxiety in these types of situations can be construed as an absence of conscience. One does not feel anxious; therefore, one does not feel bad. This may be one reason why psychopathy is related to violent behaviour.

Psychophysiology and Crime

Stimulation-seeking, high levels of risk-taking, and low levels of empathy have been frequently identified as risk factors for some subgroups of offenders, particularly criminal psychopaths (see Chapter 5; e.g. Patrick, 2006; Raine, 2013). To date, a large body of research has found a relationship between various psychophysiological correlates and criminal and violent behaviour. This area of research has focused on the functioning or reactivity of our autonomic nervous system (ANS).

psychophysiology The study of the relationship between the underlying physical and chemical functions of living organisms and their psychological states.

Psychophysiology refers to the study of the relationship between the underlying physical and chemical functions of living organisms, like humans, and their psychological states. Previously in this chapter, we defined the nervous system as the comprehensive network of nerve cells that regulates and coordinates all the body's activities (see Figure 3.4). Remember, it is divided into the central nervous system and the peripheral nervous system. The ANS is further subdivided into the somatic and autonomic nervous systems. The latter is balanced by two subsystems known as the sympathetic and parasympathetic nervous systems. The sympathetic nervous system (SNS) prepares the body for fight or flight by activating certain internal functions, such as heart rate, while the parasympathetic nervous system (PNS) reduces these internal functions when fear or a threat subsides.

As part of the fight-or-flight response, the ANS assists with regulating responses to perceived threats or dangers in the environment. Imagine an argument that escalates to a point where you are shoved violently by an aggressor or a time when the car you are driving spins dangerously out of control. Your cortex perceives these potential threats or dangers and communicates with other parts of the brain, including the limbic system. The limbic system and its associated subcortical structures trigger certain internal responses to prepare for a fight-or-flight response. For example, as we previously mentioned, the hypothalamus will trigger the release of stress hormones. Similarly, the ANS will activate

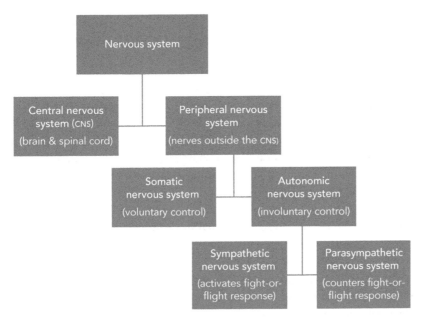

Figure 3.4 Divisions of the nervous system

several internal responses, including increases in your heart rate, blood pressure, and electrical conductance in your skin. (Have you ever experienced the feeling of your arm hair standing on end?)

A premise of psychophysiological theories of criminal and violent behaviour is that some individuals have an underresponsive ANS that reduces their reactivity to the external environment. Threatening or fear-inducing situations do not trigger the ANS in some violent offenders, such as psychopaths. As a result, they do not experience sufficient levels of fear to inhibit their behaviour; they take risks or engage in dangerous or harmful behaviours that normally elicit aversive feelings or sensations in most individuals. Similarly, expressions of fear or pain from victims, which normally elicit guilt or empathy, fail to elicit an appropriate autonomic response. Psychologist David Lykken (1957) referred to this situation as **avoidance learning**, a process whereby individuals learn behaviours, or learn to refrain from certain behaviours, in response to aversive stimuli.

Hans Eysenck (1991, 1997) also argued that the acquisition of prosocial behaviour is the result of a fear conditioning process that involves an interaction between the environment and the nervous system (see Chapter 7). Take the example of parental discipline and punishment. Parents correcting or disciplining their child aim to eliminate antisocial or negative behaviours and encourage the development of prosocial behaviours. From a psychophysiological perspective, punishment should trigger a response from the ANS, thereby eliciting an aversive feeling. To avoid this feeling in the future, a child must either engage in the behaviour without getting caught or stop engaging in the behaviour. Lykken (1957) initially studied avoidance learning, or fear conditioning, using a unique experimental procedure called the avoidance learning task (see the "Researching" box).

avoidance learning A process whereby individuals learn to initiate or inhibit certain behaviours in response to aversive stimuli.

Researching Criminal and Violent Behaviour

The Avoidance Learning Task

David Lykken (1957) investigated whether psychopathic offenders displayed unusually low levels of anxiety compared to non-psychopathic offenders and controls drawn from secondary and post-secondary schools. In one of the study's experimental components, participants were presented with an audible buzzer that sounded at intervals of approximately 20 to 60 seconds. Two different buzzer sounds were possible: one was always followed by an electrical shock delivered to the participant's hand and the other was not. Lykken expected that participants would quickly learn which buzzer sound warned of the impending shock and would become temporarily anxious in anticipation of it. To assess anxiety, Lykken monitored the galvanic skin response (GSR), or skin conductance, of each participant.

Consistent with predictions, the GSRs produced in anticipation of the shock were significantly lower among the psychopaths than among the student controls. In other words, the prospect of an electrical shock caused little anxiety for the psychopaths. This finding is often cited as evidence that psychopaths display poor anxiety conditioning or poor conditionability (see Chapter 7).

Another interesting component of the study was an avoidance learning task. Lykken hypothesized that psychopaths find it difficult to avoid repeating their past mistakes because they feel so little anxiety or fear about the negative consequences of making an error. As a test of avoidance learning, participants were given 20 opportunities to navigate their way through a mental maze. At each choice point, participants had to select one of four possible paths. One path was the correct way forward. Two of the three incorrect paths were dead ends. The remaining incorrect path not only prevented further progress in the maze, but it also delivered a mild electrical shock. The key was to quickly learn which path led to punishment and to avoid it on future attempts through the maze.

Scores for each participant were based on the punished errors committed relative to unpunished errors such that higher scores reflected better avoidance learning. Figure 3.5 displays the average scores for the three groups of participants. As expected, the psychopaths exhibited the worst avoidance learning performance, followed by the non-psychopathic offenders. The control group of students displayed the best avoidance learning performance.

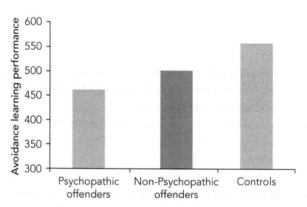

Figure 3.5 Average avoidance learning performance score by group

Source: Copyright © 1957 by the American Psychological Association. Adapted with permission. D.T. Lykken. (1957). "A study of anxiety in the sociopathic personality." *The Journal of Abnormal and Social Psychology*, 55(1), 6–10. The use of APA information does not imply endorsement by APA.

Several studies looking at the relationship of fear conditioning responses to offending behaviour report findings in line with the low autonomic functioning theory (e.g. Gao, Tuvblad, Schell, Baker, & Raine, 2015). Generally, two indicators of low autonomic functioning have been used in studies examining the link between criminal and violent behaviour and autonomic reactivity: skin conductance and heart rate.

Skin Conductance

Galvinic skin response (GSR), or **skin conductance**, measures changes in the skin's resistance to electrical currents and is considered a direct indicator of ANS functioning and an indirect indicator of emotional state. According to psychophysiological theories of crime, low levels of skin conductance are consistent with poor fear conditioning and, as a result, should be predictive of high stimulation-seeking and low levels of empathy—precursors to criminal and violent behaviour. For instance, a recent study recorded conditioning responses for nearly 1,800 children recruited at age three (Gao, Raine, Venables, Dawson, & Mednick, 2010). The conditioning responses were assessed by measuring the skin conductance of participants, who were repeatedly presented with a stimulus sound followed by an unpleasant noise.

Twenty years later, the researchers reviewed official records and found that 137 participants from the original sample had at least one criminal conviction. Each of these known offenders was matched with two non-offenders from the sample for age, gender, ethnicity, and social adversity. Remember, if offenders are difficult to condition, the connection they make between the stimulus and the noise will be weak; as a consequence, they will exhibit low anxiety levels and relatively small skin conductance responses. This is precisely what the researchers found. What makes the results so striking is that a low conditioning response evident at age 3 proved to be significantly related to criminal behaviour committed much later in life (Gao et al., 2010).

Heart Rate

Many studies have found a link between low levels of resting heart rate and several measures of criminal and violent behaviour (e.g. Jennings, Piquero, & Farrington, 2013; Raine, Venables, & Medick, 1997). In one interesting experimental study with introductory criminology students, Armstrong and Boutwell (2012) found that those with measured lower resting rates indicated that they were more likely to engage in a hypothetical crime and less likely to express anticipating guilt if they engaged in the offence. A recent meta-analysis of 45 existing studies reported that measures of low resting heart rate were consistent and robust predictors of criminal and violent behaviour, providing further empirical support for the role of low ANS functioning (Portnoy & Farrington, 2015).

Summary

1. Neuropsychology is the study of the brain, its functions, and its part in behaviours and psychological processes. Tragic high-profile cases, such as the Chris Benoit murder-suicide, raise questions about how brain injuries may contribute to observed differences in personality, behaviour, and mood. Forensic neuropsychologists contribute to our understanding of criminal behaviour and aggression by studying the role of particular brain structures and neurochemicals in the production of behaviour and emotion.

2. Organic brain syndrome (OBS) refers to diseases, usually not psychiatric disorders, that result in decreases in mental functioning. Numerous studies reviewed in this chapter show that, following a severe head injury, people evidence changes in personality and behaviour, including aggressiveness. Further support for the link between

skin conductance
A measure of changes in the skin's resistance to electrical currents, which is closely connected to perspiration levels; it corresponds directly to autonomic nervous system functioning and indirectly to one's emotional state.

serious brain injury and aggressive behaviour comes from research employing neuropsychological tests of brain functioning.

3. Advances in neuropsychological techniques, including brain imaging technology, have allowed us to more accurately pinpoint the role of particular brain regions in the genesis of criminal and aggressive behaviour. Several trends have emerged from brain imaging studies employing CT, MRI, fMRI, PET, and SPECT scanning technologies. The frontal lobes and the prefrontal cortex have been singled out as playing an important part in aggressive behaviour. Temporal lobe dysfunction in the subcortical area, including the limbic system, may also influence aggressive behaviour.

4. Emotional and personality problems and deficits of behavioural production and management related to frontal lobe dysfunction may contribute to criminal behaviour. Individuals with serious frontal lobe damage may not fully appreciate the impact of their actions and may also evidence problems anticipating consequences. Additionally, an individual with frontal lobe damage may demonstrate sudden mood changes and have difficulties inhibiting behavioural responses.

5. The prefrontal cortex, which governs personality and executive control functions, has extensive neural connections with other areas of the brain, including the limbic system. The limbic system is part of the "emotional brain" and integrates sensory information, generating critical emotional drives associated with the fight-or-flight response. Research suggests that aggressive individuals may demonstrate an overactivation in the subcortical structures of the limbic system, generating negative emotions, and simultaneously exhibit underactivation in the prefrontal cortex. The reduced functioning in this part of the brain may mean that aggressive individuals are unable to inhibit their negative emotions and are more likely to act impulsively.

6. Theories of hemispheric dysfunction suggest that criminal and aggressive behaviour reflect problems with language lateralization. Some studies show that particular groups of violent offenders have difficulties recognizing or understanding "emotional" information. Ample research also indicates that juvenile delinquents evidence poorer performance on verbal subscales of intelligence tests. The relationship between reduced lateralization and criminal behaviour or violence may best be understood in the context of poor verbal comprehension in social situations.

7. Neurotransmitters are electrochemical messengers that transmit information or impulses throughout our nervous system. Several neurotransmitters—dopamine, norepinephrine, and serotonin—have been implicated in criminal and violent behaviour. A meta-analysis of the existing research literature identified low levels of serotonin as a particularly important neurotransmitter underlying impulsive aggression. Low levels of serotonin may reduce our ability to inhibit behavioural impulses, resulting in a high-risk, impulsive behavioural style.

8. Hormones, such as sex hormones and stress hormones, are chemical messengers that play a role in the regulation of several vital bodily functions. The most frequently studied sex hormone in forensic psychology, testosterone, has a positive but somewhat small impact on aggression. Methodological differences across studies may account for the weak nature of this connection. Alternatively, testosterone may be more pertinent for different forms of aggression, such as social dominance, or aggression in traditionally competitive social domains. Both low and high levels of cortisol, a stress hormone, have also been cited in the research literature on criminal and violent behaviour. Low levels may result in an "underappreciation" of the consequences of

aggression, while high levels may increase behavioural responses to relatively minor provocations.

9. The autonomic nervous system (ANS) is responsible for the regulation of automatic internal functions such as heart rate and blood pressure. According to some researchers, the acquisition of prosocial behaviours (and similarly the extinction of antisocial behaviours) occurs through a fear conditioning process whereby aversive stimuli (i.e. punishment) trigger an ANS response. Psychophysiological theories of crime suggest that low levels of ANS functioning are associated with stimulation-seeking and risk-taking behaviours, as well as lower levels of empathy and/or guilt. That is, individuals with poor autonomic functioning are less likely to experience fear or guilt. Empirical studies measuring indicators of autonomic functioning (skin conductance, heart rate) provide support for the argument that some criminal and violent offenders are psychophysiologically underaroused.

Review Questions

1. Identify and explain the various ways in which frontal lobe damage may facilitate aggressive or violent behaviour.
2. Discuss how deficits in the functioning of the prefrontal cortex and the subcortical structures of the limbic system might contribute to criminal and violent behaviour.
3. Explain how hemispheric asymmetry or dysfunction, particularly deficits in the lateralization of language, are related to criminal and violent behaviour.
4. Explain how the BAS and BIS contribute to criminal and violent behaviour. Identify and describe the specific roles played by various neurotransmitters in these two systems.
5. Explain how testosterone levels might be linked to social dominance.
6. Why might both high and low levels of cortisol be associated with criminal and violent behaviour?
7. Explain how ANS functioning may be connected to higher stimulation-seeking or lower levels of empathy. Use two indicators of ANS functioning to support your answer.

Additional Readings

Fabian, J. M. (2010). Neuropsychological and neurological correlates in violent and homicidal offenders: A legal and neuroscience perspective. *Aggression and Violent Behavior, 15*, 209–223.

Fishbein, D. (2002). *Biobehavioral perspectives in criminology*. Belmont, CA: Thomson-Wadsworth.

Hawkins, K. A., & Trobst, K. K. (2000). Frontal lobe dysfunction and aggression: Conceptual issues and research findings. *Aggression and Violent Behavior, 5*, 147–157.

Raine, A. (2013). *The anatomy of violence: The biological roots of crime*. New York, NY: Pantheon Books.

4

Developmental Pathways

Learning Objectives

At the end of this chapter, you should be able to:

- identify the three patterns or trends in delinquent and criminal behaviour that have emerged from longitudinal research;

- explain how coercive or negative parent–child interactions can contribute to the early onset of criminal and violent behaviour;

- compare and contrast the major differences between adolescence-limited and life-course persistent offenders;

- explore how age-graded informal social control mechanisms may influence commitment to or desistance from a criminal lifestyle;

- discuss the role of early behavioural and dispositional difficulties in the development of chronic antisocial behaviour over the life-course;

- examine the role of familial factors, such as parenting styles, parental monitoring, and parental discipline on the development of criminal and violent behaviour; and

- explain the role of peer factors, such as peer rejection and peer selection, on the development of criminal and violent behaviour.

CASE STUDY

Ethan Couch

Keller, Texas—Ethan Couch and eight of his friends spent much of 15 June 2013 drinking shots and playing beer pong in a vacant house owned by his parents. Late that evening, he rounded the group into his mother's pickup truck. On the street, he began driving 110 kilometres per hour on the wrong side of the road. When his passengers started yelling at him, he attempted to return to the correct lane, but he oversteered and plowed into a group of people. Four people died in the crash and many others were seriously injured, including one of Couch's friends, who was left paralyzed. Couch, whose blood alcohol level was triple the legal limit that night, pled guilty to four counts of intoxication manslaughter and two counts of intoxication assault. At the sentencing hearing, a defence psychologist testified that Couch was brought up in a wealthy family that never disciplined him for misbehaving and, as a result, he did not understand the consequences of his actions—something the psychologist characterized as "affluenza."

Certainly, Couch had a dysfunctional home life. His parents, Fred and Tonya, had a stormy marriage punctuated by frequent arguments and yelling matches that sometimes became physical. The police were often called to the house, although no one was ever arrested. The couple divorced in 2006, when Couch was nine years old. He lived mostly with his mother, who is described as a generous person who loves her son very much but has difficulty saying no to him. A court-ordered report completed during the divorce expressed concern over their codependent relationship. Her ex-husband claims that she referred to the boy as her protector.

Couch stayed with his dad occasionally, but the same court report identified Fred's "lack of regular and consistent relationship with Ethan" as a problem (para. 21). Tonya claimed that he did not properly supervise their son; Fred's defence was "I am not a mom" (para. 18). Discipline was left entirely up to Fred, who sometimes punished his son by taking away his privileges, but Tonya often undermined these efforts. For example, when Fred banned Couch from driving his truck, Tonya provided her vehicle. When Couch was 15, he was ticketed for possessing and consuming alcohol after police discovered him in the

Photo 4.1 Ethan Couch, known as the "affluenza teen," attends his hearing in Fort Worth, Texas, in April 2016, months after being apprehended in Mexico.

cab of his mother's truck with a naked 14-year-old girl and various containers of alcohol. Tonya lied about the incident to Fred, paid the fines, and even covered for her son when he failed to finish the court-ordered alcohol awareness class and community service hours, explaining that it was her fault for not reading everything properly. By the time Tonya and Fred reconciled in 2011, Couch was largely living on his own and frequently staying in the old family home vacated by his mother. Fred claims he visited the house once in a while to check up on Couch but acknowledged that he did not go by in the week prior to the crash.

This case did not end when the juvenile court sentenced Couch to 10 years probation and mandatory rehabilitation. In December 2015, a short video appearing to show Couch at a party with alcohol—and therefore in breach of his probation—appeared on social media (Kasperkevic, 2016). Shortly afterwards, he and his mother fled to Mexico. Sheriffs in Texas allege the two planned their disappearance and even held a going-away party (Kasperkevic, 2015). They were later apprehended by Mexican authorities and returned to the United States, after one of them used his or her phone to order pizza. Couch was sentenced to two years in jail for violating his probation; his mother is currently facing one charge of hindering the apprehension of a felon (Kasperkevic, 2016).

Source (except where otherwise noted): Mooney, M. J. (2015, May). The worst parents ever: Inside story of Ethan Couch and the "affluenza" phenomenon. *D Magazine*. Retrieved from http://www.dmagazine.com/publications/d-magazine/2015/may/affluenza-the-worst-parents-ever-ethan-couch?single=1

Introduction

Developmental theories of criminal behaviour focus on the dynamic (i.e. changeable) nature of criminality, particularly on the role of different factors at different stages of life. From a developmental perspective, early childhood behavioural problems, adolescent delinquency, and adult criminal behaviour are causally linked to one another (Sampson & Laub, 1993). Early predispositions or experiences are believed to interact with other situational factors to set individuals along certain life paths. For example, think about the interactions Ethan Couch had with his parents and the consequences on his subsequent behaviour. Likewise, events or new factors that arise in adolescence or adulthood can direct someone off a criminal trajectory and onto a more prosocial life-course. Often, the problems children encounter do not occur in isolation. Psychologist Rolf Loeber (1990) discussed the impact of what he referred to as a stacking of problems over the developmental life-course. According to Loeber, behavioural or psychological problems that are evident in early childhood can adversely impact the socialization process, leaving children ill-prepared for the future.

The Stability of Criminal Behaviour

Developmental or life-course perspectives on criminality are based on several important working premises drawn from numerous longitudinal examinations of delinquency. In a landmark study, Sheldon and Eleanor Glueck (1950) examined the relationship between early life experience and the development of chronic antisocial and criminal behaviour. They employed a matched cohort design, comparing several variables from a sample of 500 delinquent males between the ages of 10 and 17 with those from a sample of 500 non-delinquent boys. The researchers collected a vast array of information—demographic, psychological, and criminal history—on the participants and followed up on them until they were 32 years of age. The results showed that those boys who exhibited earlier antisocial behaviour were more likely to engage in chronic and more serious criminal behaviour across the life-course. In most cases, criminal behaviour appeared to tail off as the boys entered early adulthood.

Glueck and Glueck's findings (1950) have been observed in several subsequent studies. Wolfgang and colleagues' (1972/1987) Philadelphia Birth Cohort study, discussed in Chapter 1, is one example. Of the approximately 10,000 participants in this study, over one-third (3,475) had at least one officially recorded police contact. The rate of these contacts increased between the ages of 11 and 16 and began to decline after 17.

Another important contribution to our understanding of the developmental trajectories of criminal careers is David Farrington's (1995, 1997) *Cambridge Study in Delinquent Development*, a prospective longitudinal panel study of 411 boys born in London between 1952 and 1953. At the outset of the study, Farrington collected a wide range of information to determine potential correlates of delinquency. He gathered data through reports from the boys, their parents, and their teachers and through official file reviews. Several follow-ups were conducted between the ages of 8 to 46. Overall, approximately 40 per cent of the sample had at least one official criminal conviction by age 40. Two interesting findings emerged from this study. First, a small proportion of boys (6 per cent) included in the sample committed six or more crimes over the course of the study, accounting for half of the total number of convictions for the entire group. Second, criminal activity, on average, increased until the age of 17, when it began to decline. Approximately 3 per cent of the boys had an official criminal justice contact as adolescents (10 to 16 years), and those boys convicted at earlier ages tended to be the most persistent and chronic offenders over time.

Similar results have been obtained in other longitudinal studies (e.g. Dunford & Elliot, 1984; Guttridge, Gabrielli, Mednick, & Van Dusen, 1983; McCord & McCord, 1959; White, Moffitt, Earls, Robins, & Silva, 1990). Across these studies, three note-worthy trends or patterns are discernible (see DeLisi, 2005). First, longitudinal studies of delinquency indicate that a small proportion of high-rate, or chronic, offenders account for a relatively large proportion of criminal activity. Second, the existing research points to an age–crime curve with overall criminal activity increasing during adolescence, peaking in late adolescence (around 17 or 18), and declining in early adulthood (Agnew & Brezina, 2001; Caspi & Moffit, 1995; see Figures 1.1 and 1.2). Third, the age of onset of antisocial behaviour is strongly related to both the duration and the seriousness of later criminal activity (Loeber, Farrington, & Petechuck, 2003).

One of the major limitations of these studies is that their samples are composed entirely of boys. Historically, criminological research and forensic psychology have neglected girls and women in their study of delinquency and adult criminal behaviour. More recent research has begun focusing on the nature, stability, and developmental trajectories of female criminal behaviour. Cauffman, Monahan, and Thomas (2015) recently found that the developmental trajectories of female offending are very similar to patterns observed among males. For example, a small subset of female delinquents exhibited chronic criminal offending into middle age, and they can be distinguished from the majority of female delinquents on several childhood risk factors.

Major Developmental Theories

Patterson's Coercion Theory

Key elements of the theories discussed throughout this chapter were formulated in Gerald Patterson and colleagues' (Patterson, 1986, 1995; Patterson & Southamer-Loeber, 1984) **coercion theory**. One of Patterson's most important contributions to the developmental field is the idea that antisocial behaviour follows distinct developmental trajectories resulting in two groups of delinquents—early-onset and late-onset. According to coercion theory, the timing or developmental onset of delinquency is strongly related to the severity and stability of antisocial behaviour over the life-course. Consistent with the research identified in the previous section, this theory identifies early childhood as a critical period. Patterson argued that boys who evidence antisocial behaviours at a young age are distinct from late-onset delinquents and are at the greatest risk for chronic antisocial behaviour (Loeber, 1982; Patterson, DeBaryshe, & Ramsey, 1989). An important aspect of this theoretical perspective is that it casts early-onset delinquency as the start of a trend that characterizes an individual's entire life-course (Cullen & Agnew, 2006).

Coercion theory attributes importance to the family environment. Specifically, Patterson (1982, 1986) and colleagues (1989) suggested that parent–child interactions play a significant role in the genesis of chronic antisocial behaviour. This theoretical perspective views the family as a prominent learning environment where socialization begins. It acknowledges the difficult task faced by all parents—that is, teaching children communication skills, manners, and cooperative behaviours. Effective parenting, which includes supervision, discipline, and healthy family

coercion theory The idea that early-onset criminal and violent behaviour develops out of a family environment characterized by coercive and ineffective parent–child interactions.

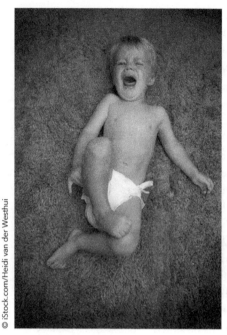

© iStock.com/Heidi van der Westhui

Photo 4.2 According to coercion theory, parents' reaction to their child's temper tantrums and other aversive tactics affects the child's social development.

coercive interactions
A pattern of dynamic parent–child interactions wherein the aversive behaviours of one individual elicit an equally aversive response from others, resulting in an escalation of dysfunctional behaviours toward one another.

cumulative disadvantage
An early difficulty that creates subsequent developmental problems for individuals over the life-course.

interactions, should result in children developing prosocial skills, thus enabling them to be successful as they transition into social interactions in school and the neighbourhood (Patterson, 1982, 1986, 1995; Patterson & Southamer-Loeber, 1984). Not all parents, however, are equally prepared for the challenges associated with raising a child. Some parents are young, inexperienced, and unable, or perhaps unwilling, to commit to the duties of effective parenting. One can easily imagine tired parents dismissing their child's requests for attention or relenting to his or her whining for a pre-dinner snack. Patterson and colleagues consider these types of parenting behaviour problematic.

Patterson envisioned the family as a dynamic environment characterized by a series of interactions between parents and children. Coercion theory argues that early-onset delinquents are raised in families characterized by inept or poor parenting strategies and a generally negative environment, where parental supervision and discipline are inconsistent, unduly harsh, or both (Patterson, 1982, 1986; Patterson & Dishion, 1998). At the centre of this negative family environment is a process that Patterson referred to as **coercive interactions**. This term refers to dynamic parent–child interactions wherein the aversive behaviours of one individual elicit an equally aversive response from the other, which develop into an escalating pattern of dysfunctional behaviours toward one another.

Coercive interactions begin with relatively innocuous aversive tactics, such as a child throwing a temper tantrum (Patterson, 1995). Coercion theory argues that a parent's response to these tactics is important for the child's development of prosocial behaviour. The diligent parent who maintains a disciplinary stance is likely to reduce the future use of such aversive actions. On the other hand, the parent who acquiesces to the child or withdraws punishment or a request reinforces the child's misbehaviour. The child's aversive tactics may prompt other types of negative responses from parents as well. They might respond to a child's whining or pouting by name-calling, shaming, yelling, or threatening excessive punishment. The child, in turn, becomes increasingly irritating and difficult, prompting even stronger and harsher responses from the parents.

Over time, these aversive tactics become functional for the child, meaning that he or she begins to adopt them as a method for daily problem-solving and interactions. Developmental perspectives of delinquency do not treat this type of problem as an isolated contributor or risk factor for future delinquency but define it as part of a continuous process that creates subsequent difficulties for children as they grow older and transition into new stages of life. In other words, coercion and other developmental theories characterize the failure to internalize prosocial interpersonal skills as a **cumulative disadvantage**—an early difficulty that creates subsequent developmental problems for individuals over the life-course.

Early-onset delinquency is thus characterized by a set of negativistic parenting traits that result in early child socialization failure; that is, children are not inoculated with the social skills that they will require as they get older and transition into new settings, such as school (Patterson, 1986, 1995). These children usually encounter difficulties early in life, including poor school performance, negative interactions with teachers, and peer relation problems such as rejection and delinquent peer association. Each childhood difficulty is further exacerbated by subsequent problems, making it increasingly difficult for the child to achieve what most people would consider a normal prosocial lifestyle. Research conducted by Patterson (1995) and his colleagues (Patterson & Southamer-Loeber, 1984) note that early-onset delinquents are significantly more likely to be either arrested or have some police contact by the age of 14.

Moffitt's Developmental Taxonomy

Another developmental theory of antisocial behaviour, developed by psychologist Terrie Moffitt, builds on Patterson's idea that early-onset delinquency is distinct from late-onset delinquency. Moffitt (1993a, 1993b, 2003) fleshes out Patterson's discussion of the late-onset delinquent and offers additional insight into why an adolescent becomes involved in delinquency and might desist in early adulthood. Specifically, she proposes that delinquency proceeds along at least two distinct developmental pathways. The **life-course persistent (LCP) pathway** consists of a small group of offenders who display a persistent, life-long pattern of serious antisocial behaviour. The **adolescence-limited (AL) pathway** consists of a much larger group of individuals who demonstrate delinquent or antisocial behaviour during only their teen years (see Figure 4.1). Moffitt's model posits that the two groups are qualitatively different from one another, distinguished by risk factors that arise early in development. The following section explores these pathways.

Life-Course Persistent (LCP) Offenders
LCP offenders represent the minority of delinquent activity. They begin to demonstrate behavioural problems in early childhood, which increase in severity through the life-course and persist into adulthood. Over the span of development, the LCP offender manifests a wide range of behavioural, antisocial, and criminal behaviours. Although the specific nature of these behaviours is believed to change with age, the key is that problem

life-course persistent (LCP) pathway The pathway consisting of delinquent offenders who display a persistent, life-long pattern of serious criminal and/or violent behaviour.

adolescence-limited (AL) pathway The pathway consisting of individuals who engage in less serious or normative patterns of criminal behaviour during the teen years and desist from offending upon entering adulthood.

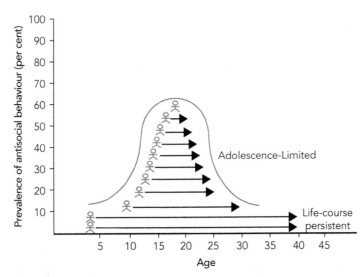

Figure 4.1 Hypothetical illustration of the changing prevalence of participation in antisocial behaviour across the life-course.

Source: Copyright © 1993 by the American Psychological Association. Reproduced with permission. T.E. Moffitt (1993). "Adolescence-limited and life-course persistent antisocial behavior: A developmental taxonomy." *Psychological Review*, 100(4), 674–701. The use of APA information does not imply endorsement by APA.

behaviours are always present. As an example, the LCP individual might start with biting and hitting in early childhood; progress into truancy, swearing, and lying in middle childhood; and finally develop into more serious forms of delinquency, such as robbery or drug dealing, in adolescence (Moffitt, 1993a). Moffitt believes that these behaviours are evidenced in all areas of a child's life, including home, school, and the community and so forth.

While Patterson (1986) focused on the family and parent–child interactions, Moffitt (1993a) adopted a broader approach to the root problems underlying chronic antisocial behaviour. She argues that the etiological roots of the LCP delinquent pathway can be traced to a range of neurological problems that are manifested early in childhood (Moffitt, 1993a; Moffitt & Silva, 1988). Difficulties emerging in early childhood are related to long-term negative outcomes through their more immediate impact on the acquisition of interpersonal skills during middle and late childhood. In other words, LCP offenders miss out on opportunities to develop and practise the social skills that they need to navigate socialization opportunities as they grow older (Moffitt, 1993a).

Imagine how difficult it would be to pass a post-secondary chemistry course if you had not taken a science class in high school. An academic prerequisite structure is somewhat analogous to a developmental perspective on socialization and the development of prosocial interpersonal skills. Hyperactive children who have difficult **temperaments** and have not learned or been reinforced for cooperative behaviour will have trouble making friends in school. They may also have problems with self-regulation and attention during school, prompting negative responses from teachers. These difficulties may result in further lost opportunities to develop interpersonal and academic skills (Coie, Dodge, & Kupersmidt, 1990; Moffitt, 1993a). Loeber (1990) argued that such problems would begin to accumulate, leaving these children less prepared for each developmental stage over the life-course.

temperament A person's natural mood state as evidenced by basic emotional and behavioural dispositions.

Adolescence-Limited (AL) Offenders

Although LCP offenders commit more serious and pervasive criminal acts, adolescence-limited (AL) offenders account for the majority of delinquent behaviour (Moffitt, 1993a). These offenders seem to experience a willingness to engage in antisocial behaviour during their teenage years, but the lustre of bad behaviour does not seem to last long. Moffitt's theory suggests that this form of delinquency represents a distinct developmental pathway, which accounts for the relative ease with which these young people can shift into more prosocial adult roles.

Unlike LCP offenders, AL offenders do not exhibit the same behavioural and mental health problems in early childhood. For instance, they are generally not characterized by difficult temperaments in infancy; you do not observe the same attentional problems or hyperactivity that marks the early developmental history of the LCP offender. The AL offender also tends to have a more stable family life. During the formative years of early childhood development, he or she is cared for, supported, and socialized by his or her parents and therefore inoculated with effective social skills. This appropriate early socialization leaves the AL offender better prepared for transitions into school and the fostering of relationships outside the family, allowing the child to get the most out of each successive developmental stage. This is a critical point for understanding why the AL offender is able to desist from antisocial behaviour in early adulthood.

Antisocial behaviour does not commence until early adolescence among the AL offenders and, while their delinquent behaviour may be similar to the LCP offender group, the delinquency is less serious and pervasive (Moffitt, Caspi, Dickson, Silva, & Stanton, 1996). Generally, the AL offender engages in what can be referred to as **normative offences**, delinquent acts that represent an attempt to gain some symbolic rank associated with maturity and adult privilege. Hence, the delinquency of the AL offender is more akin to rebellion than chronic criminality. AL offenders may engage in underage drinking, minor drug use, vandalism, truancy, or petty theft.

The driving force behind the AL offender's delinquency is social status or perhaps what has anecdotally been referred to as teen angst. Moffitt (1993a) described adolescence as an ambiguous period for many teens. For instance, a 15-year-old may have reached biological maturity but is probably still socially immature. Most important, our society has been organized to perceive and respond to adolescents as socially immature beings who require guidance and control. We place restrictions on driving, alcohol consumption, and voting, and we require adolescents to attend school until they reach a certain age. This treatment creates a maturity gap between biological age and social age.

During this period, adolescents also observe their LCP delinquent peers. This previously rejected group achieves a new-found popularity because it has access to a resource desired by all adolescents—social status. The "bad behaviour" of the LCP delinquents gains them autonomy and more adult status, which is witnessed and copied by other adolescents. Moffitt (1993a) referred to this process as **social mimicry**. In this process, two species share the same environment and compete for the same resources. When one species is more successful, the other will mimic or adopt the same behaviours to become more competitive and to ensure the acquisition of necessary resources. Empirical research shows that an increase in delinquent peer associations in adolescence is a consistent predictor of delinquent behaviour (Patterson et al., 1989; Patterson & Yoerger, 1995; Weerman, 2011).

But how or why does the AL delinquent desist from delinquency? According to Moffitt's (1993a) theory, there are two important factors to consider: a shift in reinforcement contingences and the availability of prosocial adult roles. As adolescents graduate from high school and enter the workforce or post-secondary studies, a variety of adult roles—marriage and family, a full-time job, higher education—become available. These roles reward prosocial attitudes and behaviours. In other words, how you acquire social status changes as you get older. This is a shifting **reinforcement contingency**, or a change in the types of behaviours that prompt rewards or reinforcement. (We will discuss reinforcement in more detail in Chapter 7.) Fighting and truancy are generally not rewarded with promotions and company cars in the business world. There is opportunity and incentive for AL delinquents to desist from criminal behaviour and take on more prosocial roles. They also have the ability to take advantage of these opportunities because they were properly socialized in early childhood and acquired the necessary social skills and appropriate behavioural repertoire. Conversely, the LCP delinquent has a limited behavioural repertoire and, as a result, adult prosocial roles are less accessible. Numerous studies indicate that the increased availability of prosocial opportunities is connected to a reduction in antisocial behaviour (Graham & Bowling, 1995; Mischkowitz, 1994; Uggen, 2000).

Moffitt's developmental taxonomy has faced some criticism from other prominent researchers. Criminologists Robert Sampson and John Laub (1993) were influenced by

normative offences Delinquent acts that represent an attempt to gain some symbolic status associated with maturity and adult privilege. These types of offences are less serious in nature than other crimes and might include petty theft, underage drinking, or truancy from school.

social mimicry A process in which two species share the same environment and compete for the same resources. When one species is more successful at obtaining resources, the other will mimic or adopt these behaviours to become more competitive and to ensure resource acquisition.

reinforcement contingency Consequences that increase or decrease the future possibility of a behaviour being repeated in the presence of an antecedent condition.

Researching Criminal and Violent Behaviour

A Follow-Up of AL and LCP Delinquents

Moffitt, Caspi, Harrington, and Milne (2002) conducted a follow-up study to test the hypothesis that the LCP developmental pathway is associated with chronic adult antisocial behaviour. The study involved 1,037 male children from New Zealand, who were identified at 3 years of age and measured at 26. The researchers used 79 measures of adult outcomes in 5 categories: criminal offending, personality, psychopathology, personal life, and economic life. They discovered that many AL delinquents were still in trouble. Although the AL men fared better overall than LCP delinquents, they fared poorly relative to the unclassified men, who had no remarkable delinquency history. Although the AL delinquents evidenced less antisocial behaviour as adults than the LCP offenders did, the researchers found that AL men accounted for twice their share of the property and drug convictions during adulthood, compared with non-offending men. Moffitt and colleagues speculated that adulthood in contemporary society may begin after 25 years of age. This new developmental stage—known as emerging adulthood—prolongs the crime-promoting conditions of adolescence.

Moffitt's life-course perspective on criminal behaviour, but they were critical of the LCP pathway. Specifically, they believed that Moffitt overstated the persistency of LCP delinquents' criminal behaviour. Based on a follow-up of Glueck and Glueck's (1950) famous study, Laub and Sampson (2003) concluded that all offenders eventually desist from crime, thereby suggesting that a reliance on childhood factors to predict long-term criminal behaviour is problematic. In response to these observations, Sampson and Laub (1993) introduced the concept of structural turning points.

Age-Graded Theory of Informal Social Control

Psychological theories of criminal behaviour often neglect the proposition that people can change. In their influential *Crime in the Making: Pathways and Turning Points through Life*, Sampson and Laub (1993) advanced similar, albeit more complex, ideas to explain the development of criminal careers. Consistent with Patterson's coercion theory and Moffitt's developmental taxonomy, they believed that people differed from one another in their individual propensities for criminal and antisocial behaviour. For instance, Sampson and Laub recognized that some individuals are more impulsive or perhaps have a more difficult temperament and are more likely to place themselves in troublesome situations or environments. Their **age-graded theory of informal social control** offers a developmental account of criminality over the life-course that considers both continuity and change in antisocial lifestyles (Cullen & Agnew, 2006).

Building on Travis Hirschi's (1969) social control theory, Sampson and Laub (1993) discussed the role of informal social controls on antisocial and prosocial behaviour. Formal social control refers to external controls, such as surveillance cameras and legal sanctions, which exert a pressure on us to adapt our behaviour. Informal social controls, including attachments to prosocial family members and friends, a legitimate career or job, or even a commitment to school, mediate our behaviour indirectly. According to Sampson and

age-graded theory of informal social control
A developmental theory of criminal behaviour, developed by Robert Sampson and John Laub, which argues that individuals desist from crime when they are subject to informal social controls. These controls are age graded such that the value or effect increases or decreases at different points of the lifespan.

Laub, informal social controls are like an investment in society that differentially increases or decreases the risk of antisocial behaviour. Children who struggle early in school—with poor academic performance, peer rejection, poor relations with teachers—have little investment in prosocial society. As these children develop, they will not be as heavily influenced by informal social control mechanisms. Because delinquents have less at stake and less to lose in conventional society as they get older, there is little to deter them from engaging in further crime. This lack of equity, or social capital, accounts for the continuity of antisocial behaviour that we observe among some individuals.

The criminal life-course trajectory, however, may also be characterized by change. Sampson and Laub's (1993) theory is a dynamic account of the development of antisocial behaviour. The researchers argued that many criminal offenders "go straight" and that the key to this change is establishing some stake in conventional society. They argued that people experience very significant life events, or **structural turning points**, that reintroduce the importance of informal social control networks into their lives. A parolee might fall in love with someone who has never committed an offence and subsequently desist from a criminal lifestyle. This new relationship would provide the offender with some form of social capital; he or she would have something to lose by continuing to commit crimes.

structural turning points Significant life events, such as marriage or the birth of a child, that introduce informal social controls to an individual's life.

Structural turning points can include new employment opportunities, marriage, religious experiences, or becoming a parent. They must be viewed as important and positive in nature. For example, a marriage that is not valued by the offender is unlikely to result in desistance from a criminal lifestyle. In addition, this type of social capital is age graded. That is, the value inherent in informal social controls will increase and/or decrease with age. A middle-aged adult would most likely place greater value on a career than would an adolescent. This proposition has been supported by research showing that employment training programs are more beneficial for adult offenders than for offenders under the age of 26 (Uggen, 2000).

Finally, Sampson and Laub (1993) posited that, following a structural turning point, desistance from crime generally occurs in one of two ways. In some cases, desistance from a criminal lifestyle occurs by default, or with little conscious effort on the behalf of the offender. You may notice that your time is currently monopolized by your course work; therefore, you probably have less time to get into trouble. Certain structural points, such as the birth of a child, will naturally introduce additional responsibilities that will result in significant investments of time and thereby pull individuals away from criminal lifestyles. However, Sampson and Laub also argued that an individual's desistance from crime can also involve a conscious decision to change his or her lifestyle, something they referred to as **human agency**.

human agency A term that refers to subjective free will and the conscious decision-making activities of an individual.

Early Childhood Factors and Delinquency

Numerous studies provide empirical support for life-course models of delinquency and criminal behaviour. Taking advantage of improved statistical techniques, Sampson and Laub (1990) re-examined Sheldon and Eleanor Glueck's (1950) famous archival database. In these updated analyses, Sampson and Laub looked at the links among job stability, occupational commitment, and attachment to a spouse with criminal behaviour. They reported that individuals with strong ties to work and family were significantly less likely to be involved in crime. Simons, Johnson, Conger, and Elder (1998) investigated the impact of a variety of risk factors connected to delinquency among Iowa families, including deviant peer associations, socio-economic status, parenting techniques, and the presence of externalizing disorders. They concluded that antisocial traits, such as oppositional child behaviour, had significantly less predictive power than did variables pertaining to parenting, school, and peers.

Neuropsychological Deficits

Although developmental theories focus on the impact of life experiences on the etiology of antisocial trajectories, the theories we have discussed acknowledge that early individual differences may interact with childhood situational factors and precipitate chronic antisocial behaviour. Numerous studies report a relationship between various prenatal and perinatal complications and the later onset of delinquency (Kandel & Mednick, 1991; Raine, Brennan, & Mednick, 1997). **Prenatal birth complications** refer to developmental difficulties experienced prior to birth, difficulties that may be caused by factors such as exposure to toxins during gestation; **perinatal birth complications** describe problems experienced immediately before or after birth. For instance, Kandel and Mednick's (1991) comparison of violent offenders and non-offenders found that the former were significantly more likely to have experienced problems during birth than the latter. These problems, as well as exposure to toxins in utero, may influence later delinquency by negatively affecting normal, healthy development during infancy and early childhood (McCord, Widom, & Crowell, 2001).

One aspect of early development that may be adversely impacted by prenatal and perinatal complications is infant temperament. As mentioned earlier, temperament describes a person's basic emotional and behavioural dispositions, as well as his or her innate and stable pattern of responding to and interacting with the environment (Stoff, Breiling, & Maser, 1997). Although all babies cry, some do so more frequently and may be inconsolable at times. Some babies are more fussy and irritable. One baby may be perfectly content while being held by a stranger; another will offer more protest. These situations reflect temperamental differences between people early in life. Thomas, Chess, and Birch (1968) studied infant temperament in a longitudinal study and identified nine qualities: activity, regularity, adaptability, intensity, mood, distractibility, attention span, initial reaction, and sensitivity.

A large body of research has observed that a difficult temperament in early infancy is related to the development of antisocial behaviours, such as externalizing problems, in middle childhood and later aggressive and delinquent behaviour (Bates, Petit, Dodge, & Ridge, 1998; Eley, Lichtenstein, & Stevenson, 1999; Loeber, 1990; Rubin, Burgess, Dwyer, & Hastings, 2003). The influence of difficult temperament on behaviour may manifest itself in a number of ways. Gottman and Katz (1989) outlined three major effects. Temperamental difficulties might impact a child's ability to focus on tasks, organize behaviour in a goal-directed fashion, or inhibit behaviour in response to positive or negative external events. According to Patterson (1982, 1986), a difficult temperament in infancy will influence later antisocial behaviour by affecting the quality of the child's interactions with parents, peers, and teachers. Fussy, irritable, and ill-tempered infants can have a reciprocal effect on parents by eliciting negative behaviours from them. The parent may become less responsive to the child, being less affectionate, showing less patience, and perhaps becoming short-tempered. These parental responses will exacerbate the child's negative temperament, prompting further maladaptive responses from him or her. This dynamic

prenatal birth complications Developmental difficulties experienced prior to birth, caused by such factors as exposure to toxins during gestation.

perinatal birth complications Developmental problems experienced immediately before or after birth.

reflects the coercive interactions identified by Patterson and discussed earlier in the chapter. One study, for example, found that parents of low-birth-weight (LBW) babies reported that their children were less pleasant to hold, less satisfying to feed, and more demanding to care for (Tinsley & Parke, 1983).

Childhood Externalizing Disorders

Many children evidence some behavioural and emotional problems—lying, stealing, temper tantrums, and/or hitting—over the course of their development. While these difficulties may be isolated and relatively minor incidents, ignoring more serious behavioural problems may have negative consequences for later stages of life. Several behavioural and emotional problems have been identified as potential risk factors for adolescent and adult antisocial behaviour (Huesmann & Eron, 1992; Moffitt et al., 2002; Sullivan, 2008). It is important to emphasize that there is always an inherent challenge in distinguishing between normal developmental changes and the emergence of a disorder. By its nature, children's behaviour fluctuates over time. Young children, for example, may tell small lies or spin fantastical tales for a short period growing up. Such behaviour is not necessarily indicative of any serious problem. **Externalizing behaviour disorders**, however, have an identified empirical relationship with antisocial behaviour.

Our discussion centres on three of these disorders, beginning with one of the most common mental health diagnoses among children (Popper, Gammon, West, & Bailey, 2003; Staller, 2006). According to the criteria outlined in *DSM-5*, **attention-deficit/hyperactivity disorder (ADHD)** is characterized by two categories of symptoms: (1) inattention and (2) hyperactivity and impulsivity (APA, 2013). Children evidencing attention problems may have difficulties organizing activities, remembering, paying attention to close details, or listening to directions. Hyperactivity and impulsivity may include problems with sitting still, fidgeting, or talking excessively. For a person to be diagnosed with ADHD, he or she must have six or more symptoms in each of these categories. Furthermore, the symptoms must have been present and causing impairment before age seven, existed for six months or more, caused clinically significant impairment in terms of interpersonal or academic functioning in two or more settings, and differed from normal developmental expectations.

Estimates of ADHD's prevalence vary but, using *DSM-IV-TR* (APA, 2000) diagnostic criteria, North American rates generally range from 3 per cent to 6 per cent of the general population (e.g. Popper et al., 2003). Determining the actual occurrence, however, is complicated by the overdiagnosis of symptoms among children (e.g. LeFever, Dawson, & Morrow, 1999). Research on externalizing disorders in general, and on ADHD specifically, notes that boys are significantly more likely than girls to exhibit these behavioural difficulties. Moreover, previous *DSM* diagnostic criteria for ADHD appear to be cross-culturally valid (Beiser, Dion, & Gotowiec, 2000). While there is some debate in the literature concerning the onset of ADHD, most children are typically diagnosed either between the ages of three and four or after their entry into the school system.

The inattention, hyperactivity, and impulsivity associated with ADHD create numerous difficulties for children. To date, a large body of research has documented several negative outcomes connected to a diagnosis, ranging from an increased risk for minor injuries (Byrne, Bawden, Beattie, & DeWolfe, 2003) to lower academic performance and higher rates of unpopularity and peer rejection (Erhardt & Hinshaw, 1994; Frick, 1994; Henker & Whalen, 1989; Ohan & Johnston, 2007). Most important,

externalizing behaviour disorders A category of mental disorders, that are characterized by behavioural indicators such as fighting, impulsivity, lying, or stealing.

attention-deficit/ hyperactivity disorder (ADHD) An externalizing behaviour disorder characterized by two broad categories of symptoms: (1) inattention and (2) hyperactivity and impulsivity.

the disorder has been identified as an early risk factor for antisocial and delinquent behaviour. Several empirical studies have reported that children with ADHD are at an increased risk for serious and pervasive antisocial behaviour in adolescence and adulthood (Moffitt, 1990, 1993b; Moffitt & Silva, 1988; Pfiffner, McBurnett, Rathouz, & Judice, 2005; Satterfield, Swanson, Schell, & Lee, 1994). Studies of adult ADHD symptoms also indicate that the prevalence among incarcerated adult offenders is quite high (Usher, Stewart, & Wilton, 2013).

Considerable debate has centred on the nature of the relationship between ADHD and antisocial behaviour. Some theorists have posited that the disorder indirectly increases the likelihood for antisocial and delinquent behaviour and have focused on its impact on interpersonal relationships and academic performance. Symptoms may increase the possibility of school failure and social isolation, thus pushing ADHD children further along a career criminal trajectory. While the nature of the relationship may not be perfectly understood, a meta-analysis of the existing literature suggests that the disorder is an important risk factor for antisocial behaviour and delinquency (Pratt, Cullen, Blevins, Daigle, & Unnever, 2002).

There is also evidence that ADHD is comorbid; that is, it frequently occurs in conjunction with other externalizing behaviour disorders, including oppositional defiant disorder and conduct disorder (Waschbusch, 2002; Offord, Boyle, & Racine, 1991). **Oppositional defiant disorder (ODD)** is characterized by three broad categories of symptoms: angry/irritable mood, argumentative/defiant behaviour, and vindictiveness (APA, 2013). Some research indicates that ODD boys are more likely to engage in antisocial behaviour and aggression in adolescence (Verhulst, Eussen, Berden, Sanders-Woudstra, & Van Der Ende, 1993). **Conduct disorder (CD)** is often considered a developmental precursor to antisocial personality disorder. CD is defined as a repetitive and persistent pattern of behaviour that violates the basic rights of others (APA, 2013). The symptoms fall into four broad categories: aggression toward people and animals, deliberate property destruction, deceitfulness or theft, and serious rule violations. Examples of symptoms include bullying or threatening, physical cruelty to people and/or animals, fighting, and truancy.

CD, which is more common among males than females, may develop at different points in the life-course, with the age of onset playing an important role in the severity of symptoms. The *DSM-5* identifies two subtypes of conduct disorder based on the age at which symptoms are initially manifested—childhood-onset and adolescent-onset. Childhood-onset conduct disorder is defined as the onset of CD symptoms prior to age 10, whereas adolescent-onset conduct disorder is characterized by an absence of symptoms before age 10. An early onset of CD is associated with more severe symptoms, as well as an increased risk for later antisocial and delinquent behaviour and the onset of antisocial personality disorder in adulthood (Loeber, Burke, Lahey, Winters, & Zera, 2000). In general, research has found that CD is related to adolescent substance use (Loeber, Stouthamer-Loeber, van Kammen, & Farrington, 1991) and delinquency (Eppright, Kashani, Robison, & Reid, 1993). A study of young girls found connections between patterns of CD and problems in later life, including criminal behaviour, early pregnancy, and unstable employment (Bardone, Moffitt, & Caspi, 1996). A study of lust killers found that over 75 per cent had a history of CD symptoms in childhood and adolescence (Ressler, Burgess, & Douglas, 1988).

The co-occurrence of ADHD and CD during childhood is linked to an increased risk of antisocial and delinquent behaviour. Loeber (1988), for example, conducted a follow-up

oppositional defiant disorder (ODD) A childhood externalizing behaviour disorder characterized by angry/irritable mood, argumentative/defiant behaviour, and vindictiveness.

conduct disorder (CD) A childhood externalizing disorder characterized by aggression toward people and/or animals, deliberate property destruction, deceitfulness or theft, and serious rule violations. This disorder is often viewed as a precursor to antisocial personality disorder.

study of boys who were 10, 13, or 16 during the original study. The boys were divided into four groups on the basis of parent and teacher ratings: high ratings on CD only, high ratings on ADHD only, high ratings on both disorders, and high ratings on neither disorder. Over five years, boys with high ratings on both CD and ADHD exhibited significantly higher rates of criminal offending than did boys in the other groups.

Parental Practices and Delinquency

None of the theories we have discussed in this chapter view early dispositional differences in temperament or activity as directly causing later criminal and violent behaviour. Recall that developmental theories are specifically interested in how various early risk factors interact with other environmental factors as the child grows older. An important set of environmental variables that must be considered is the family setting. For example, the coercion developmental theory contends that several family factors, such as parental monitoring and discipline, play a crucial role in the developmental onset of delinquent behaviour (Patterson, 1982).

Over the last three decades, a large body of research has demonstrated the importance of **parental practices** on the development of antisocial and delinquent behaviour (Loeber & Stouthamer-Loeber, 1998; Hoeve et al., 2009). Parental practices include the range of responsibilities that parents have in rearing their children. Not surprisingly, numerous conceptual definitions of the term exist in the literature. The working definition adopted in this chapter is "the diverse range of parental behaviours occurring in the family context, including disciplinary approaches, monitoring and supervision strategies, and interactional styles."

parental practices The diverse range of parental behaviours occurring in the family context, including disciplinary approaches, monitoring and supervision strategies, and interactional styles.

Parental Discipline

Developmental psychologist Diana Baumrind (1966, 1971, 1991) conducted a landmark study that resulted in one of the most commonly cited classification schemes of parenting styles. Baumrind made several detailed observations of preschool children in nursery school settings and within their own homes and identified two aspects of parenting that she believed were critical to healthy child development—parental responsiveness and parental demandingness. Parental responsiveness refers to how parents react to their child's needs and demands, such as providing warmth or comfort when the child is crying. Parental demandingness describes the expectations that parents place on their children. Based on these two dimensions, Baumrind described three distinct parenting styles: authoritarian, authoritative, and permissive.

Authoritarian parenting is a particularly rigid and restrictive approach to child-rearing. Authoritarian parents impose numerous rules—typically with little explanation of the reasons—and expect absolute obedience to and respect for their authority. This style can be thought of as the "my way or the highway" approach to rules and discipline. Although authoritarian parenting is not necessarily associated with **corporal punishment**, these parents commonly use punitive and forceful disciplinary tactics with their children.

The **authoritative parenting** style can perhaps best be described as a "firm but fair" method. Authoritative parents adopt a flexible approach to parenting, wherein rules are openly discussed and children contribute to decision-making. This type of parent engenders independence in his or her children, providing them with some freedom while

authoritarian parenting A rigid and restrictive approach to parenting characterized by punitive disciplinary methods and non-consultative limit-setting.

corporal punishment A form of discipline that employs physical force to correct or control a child's behaviour. The force is intended to cause the child pain, not injury.

authoritative parenting A "firm but fair" approach to parenting characterized by warmth, support, and consultative limit-setting.

offering warmth, support, and careful parental supervision. Punishment is consistent and fair but not excessive.

Lastly, **permissive parenting** is a warm, tolerant, but lax parental style. These parents act as less of an authority figure and more of a resource for their children. Permissive parents make few demands on their children, offer little monitoring of or control over behaviour, and permit considerable freedom. For a summary of Baumrind's parenting styles, see Table 4.1.

To date, a large body of research has examined the relationship between parenting styles and child development. Adolescents with neglectful or unresponsive parents generally tend to have higher rates of criminal offending than adolescents with authoritative parents (Hoeve, Dubas, Gerris, van der Laan, & Smeenk, 2011; Steinberg, Lamborn, Darling, Mounts, & Dornbusch, 1994; Steinberg, Blatt-Eisengart, & Cauffman, 2006). Authoritative parenting is associated with high levels of self-control among adolescents and may play an important role in the prevention of antisocial behaviour (Hay, 2001; Hollister-Wagner, Foshee, & Jackson, 2001). The overcontrolling and punitive features of the authoritarian style are related to an increased risk for CD (Loeber & Stouthamer-Loeber, 1986; Thompson, Hollis, & Richards, 2003) and aggression (Blitstein, Murray, Lytle, Birnbaum, & Perry, 2005; Ruchkin, 2002). A meta-analysis of 161 studies on the association between parenting and delinquency found that several negative aspects of parenting styles, such as rejection, hostility, and neglect, exhibited the strongest ties to delinquency (Hoeve et al., 2009).

Much of the research in this area simplifies the complex nature of parenting and parent–child interactions by assuming that parenting styles are stable. However, Schroeder and Mowen's (2014) longitudinal study on the impact of parenting style on delinquency suggests that approaches are often dynamic. The researchers found that transitions in parenting style can actually increase or decrease the risk for criminal and violent behaviour among youth. Specifically, shifts from authoritative parenting to permissive were connected to an increase in criminal behaviour. Other sociodemographic factors may also impact the relationship between parenting style and delinquency. For example, one recent study found that the effects of parenting style on adult criminal behaviour differed significantly by race (Schroeder, Bulanda, Giordano, & Cernkovich, 2010).

permissive parenting
A "hands-off" approach to parenting characterized by warmth, tolerance, and little parental limit-setting on the child's behaviour.

Table 4.1 Summary of Baumrind's parenting styles

	Characteristics	Outcomes in Children
Authoritarian	Rigid, restrictive Expect absolute obedience "My way or the highway" Punitive disciplinary tactics, which may include corporal punishment	Increased risk for aggression, conduct disorder, and delinquency Lower levels of happiness, self-esteem
Authoritative	Flexible, democratic "Firm but fair" Encourages independence Consistent and fair punishment	High levels of self-control Happy and capable Lower levels of delinquency
Permissive	Warm, tolerant Lax parental style Few demands Low parental monitoring and control	Lower levels of self-regulation Poor school performance

Researching Criminal and Violent Behaviour

Corporal Punishment and Spanking

Discipline can be defined as "parental actions that are part of a socialization process for children and adolescents" (Socolar, 1997, p. 355). Socolar (1997) identified a range of approaches to punishment that include withdrawing reward or privilege, changing a child's environment, and increasing parental monitoring of a child's activities. Corporal punishment is characterized by "the use of physical force with the intention of causing a child to experience pain but not injury for the purposes of correction or control of the child's behavior" (Straus, 1994, p. 4). This type of punishment, particularly spanking, has drawn the ire of numerous child welfare agencies in recent years. Debates on its merits have even found their way into courtrooms.

In spite of continued general support for corporal punishment, research has implicated its use in the development of aggressive behaviour among children (Patterson, 1982). Based on a meta-analysis of existing research, Elizabeth Gershoff (2002) concluded that spanking is associated with numerous long-term harms. She reported that while spanking produces compliance in the short term, it is also linked with 10 negative behaviours in the long term, including aggression, antisocial behaviour, and mental health problems. Gershoff's findings have drawn criticisms,

Peter Dazeley/Getty Images

Photo 4.3 What do you think about the use of spanking to discipline and/or correct a child's behaviour? Are there ages or types of behaviour that might warrant spanking or does spanking have no place in the disciplining of a child?

even among other psychologists. Robert Larzelere (2000; Baumrind, Larzelere, & Cowan, 2002) contends that mild forms of spanking can actually be an effective tool for controlling the behaviour of young children.

Parental Monitoring

Another aspect of parenting that has received a great deal of attention in the delinquency literature is **parental monitoring** (Patterson & Stouthamer-Loeber, 1984; Hoeve et al., 2009). Hayes, Hudson, and Matthews (2003) describe this process as involving several interrelated behaviours that occur in distinct stages. One aspect of parental monitoring is parents' awareness and knowledge of their children's activities, including who their friends are, how they spend their free time, and where they go outside the home (Dishion & McMahon, 1998; Patterson et al., 1992; Snyder & Patterson, 1987). Parental monitoring also includes setting limits on their child's time and activities (Dishion & McMahon, 1998). According to Hayes and colleagues (2003), parental monitoring unfolds in a predictable temporal sequence, wherein parents first establish rules and expectations for their children. When children return from school or social activities, parents interact with them, gathering information about their activities, learning about how they spent their time and evaluating whether the rules and expectations were followed.

parental monitoring
A process involving several interrelated behaviours, including parents' awareness and knowledge of their children's activities and limit-setting on their behaviour.

The quality of parental monitoring is related to several important outcomes in adolescence. Chilcoat and Anthony (1996), for instance, reported that higher levels of parental monitoring were associated with two-year delays in the onset of general drug use among adolescents. Other research found that adolescents from households with low parental monitoring reported consuming alcohol at an earlier age and drinking more frequently (Hayes, Smart, Toumbourou, & Sanson, 2004). Poor parental monitoring is also linked to an increased likelihood of delinquent peer associations and formal police arrests (Dishion, Patterson, Stoolmiller, & Skinner, 1991; Kilgore, Snyder, & Lentz, 2000; Laird, Pettit, Dodge, & Bates, 2005; Patterson & Stouthamer-Loeber, 1984). Findings from longitudinal studies offer further support of the important role that low parental monitoring, particularly parental permissiveness, plays in the development of delinquency (Coley, Morris, & Hernandez, 2004; Lahey, Van Hulle, D'Onoforio, Rogers, & Waldman, 2008; Roche, Ensminger, & Cherlin, 2007). These findings suggest that limit-setting may be critical for reducing the risk of delinquent behaviour. Interestingly, Roche and colleagues (2007) found that the rates of delinquency increased for youths who had permissive parents and lived in high-crime neighbourhoods. These results indicate that parental monitoring may act as a protective factor for children in high-risk neighbourhoods.

Peer and School Factors

Peer Rejection

As children grow older and transition into school, they spend increasingly less time at home with their parents and have a greater need to fit in with peers and make friends (Rubin, Bukowski, & Parker, 1998). In Patterson's (1982) coercion theory, an inability to form successful peer relations in middle childhood represents another link in the developmental chain of delinquency, resulting in further cumulative disadvantage for children. The absence of healthy friendships in elementary school may deprive children of the opportunity to develop and practise important social skills.

Additionally, the absence of prosocial peers in middle childhood may result in difficult children drifting into friendships with other antisocial peers. Teasing and ostracism lead some youths to seek approval from the "wrong crowd." To some extent, rejection played a role in the Columbine High School massacre in 1999, when Eric Harris and Dylan Klebold shot and killed 12 students and a teacher before committing suicide. Harris and Klebold were unpopular among their peers, and they were picked on by the athletic students. The boys were believed to be loosely tied to a group of other outcast students, known as The Trenchcoat Mafia, but they were largely isolated from their peers in the weeks leading up to the killings. Regardless of the exact nature of peer rejection in this case, longitudinal research suggests that childhood peer status is correlated with antisocial behaviour in adolescence (Coie, 2004).

In the psychological literature, peer rejection generally refers to a child's sociometric status in his or her peer group. **Sociometric status** is a measurement technique used in developmental psychology to gauge the extent that individuals are liked or disliked by their peers. A great deal of psychological research shows that peer rejection is associated with antisocial and aggressive behaviour (Dodge, 2003; Parker & Asher, 1987). The specific role of peer rejection in this relationship has yet to be determined, but two explanations have been proposed (Parker & Asher, 1987). One is that no direct causal relationship

sociometric status
A measurement technique in developmental psychology used to gauge the extent that an individual is liked or disliked by his or her peer group.

exists between peer rejection and later antisocial behaviour. According to this view, they are both consequences of maladaptive and bothersome traits displayed by some children; however, peer rejection is usually the first of these negative outcomes to emerge and therefore appears to cause delinquency. The other proposal is that peer rejection early in school maintains and perhaps even compounds earlier developmental difficulties, resulting in additional failures to acquire necessary social skills and further pushing the child toward a delinquent lifestyle. In Patterson's (1982) coercion theory, early difficulties with peer relationships and subsequent ties with antisocial peers represent successive stages of progression toward delinquency and antisocial behaviour. Thus, peer rejection is thought to make a unique contribution to antisocial behaviour.

Peer relationships are complex and dynamic and, as such, there are numerous explanations for why particular children are rejected by their peer groups. Evidence demonstrates that, in early and middle childhood, aggressive and difficult children are generally disliked by their peers. Some researchers argue that these antisocial behaviours, acquired and reinforced in early childhood, serve to socially distance the antisocial child from his or her peers. Coie and Kupersmidt (1983) examined the impact of aggressive behaviour on social status among fourth-grade boys. The boys first rated their peers using a sociometric measure of social status. The researchers then divided the boys into after-school playgroups of four boys each. The groups were either familiar (i.e. boys from the same classroom) or unfamiliar (i.e. from different schools). The boys who had been named "least liked" by their peers engaged in more antisocial verbal behaviour (e.g. threats, insults) and antisocial physical behaviour (e.g. hitting, kicking) during the playgroup sessions than did other boys. Moreover, unpopular boys' status and behaviour were consistent from the classroom to the after-school playground regardless of whether they were playing with familiar or unfamiliar peers. This result suggests that the boys' aggressive behaviour may have preceded their unpopular peer status.

Other research indicates that aggressiveness alone does not lead to peer rejection. Not all aggressive children are unpopular with their peers. According to some studies using sociometric ratings, some popular children are also described as dominant, arrogant, and aggressive (Cillessen & Mayeux, 2004; Rose, Swenson, & Waller, 2004). In these instances, physical aggression does not seem to prompt negative peer responses. Based on his research on peer rejection, psychologist John D. Coie (2004) argues that peer-rejected boys differ from their more popular peers in three ways. First, peer-rejected boys are impulsive, are disruptive, and have difficulty integrating in group play. Second, they are easily frustrated and provoked. The aggression exhibited by these boys is more likely to emerge due to their lower levels of tolerance and may often be unjustified given the circumstances (Coie et al., 1990). Third, peer-rejected boys are frequently characterized as lacking effective prosocial interpersonal skills. For instance, other researchers have observed low levels of cooperativeness among peer-rejected children (Deptula & Cohen, 2004). In other words, the aggressive behaviour of peer-rejected children may have a different form and function than the aggression demonstrated by some popular children.

Indeed, aggression is manifested in different ways and the social utility of certain forms may change over the life-course. According to Vitaro, Brendgen, and Barker (2006), physical aggression is more common in early childhood, but social or relational aggression becomes more prominent as children age and acquire more sophisticated verbal and social cognitive skills. Social or relational aggression refers to "the social manipulation of peer relations in order to harm another individual" (Vitaro et al., 2006, p. 14). A study of over 900 adolescent boys and girls reported that, while social or relational aggression was associated with high social prominence among peers, physical aggression was predictive of low social prominence (Cillessen & Mayeux, 2004). Some boys may be physically aggressive in childhood and maintain social prominence among their peers because they also possess and exhibit some interpersonal skills. As these boys age, they may rely less on physical aggression because they possess the social cognitive skills to use other forms of aggression more effectively. Comparatively, the aggression exhibited by peer-rejected boys may reflect their poor interpersonal skills, representing frustration or a lack of self-restraint. These boys may be rejected by their peers and thus miss out on further opportunities to develop social skills. Consequently, they continue to rely on physical aggression and maintain their peer-rejected status.

Peer rejection in middle childhood has also been empirically linked to subsequent involvement with other antisocial peers during adolescence (Coie, Terry, Lenox, Lochman, & Hyman, 1995; Dishion et al., 1991) and adolescent delinquency (Dodge & Petit, 2003). Interestingly, these findings have been obtained while taking into account earlier levels of rejection experienced by peer-rejected children. A study by Miller-Johnson, Coie, Maumary-Gremaud, Lochman, and Terry (1999) reported that peer rejection in the third grade predicted crime in early adulthood among males, even after controlling for aggressive behaviour observed in early childhood. Bierman and Wargo (1995) found that antisocial outcomes were more severe for children who were both socially rejected and aggressive than for children who were only aggressive. Using peer sociometric status and independent teacher ratings of behaviour problems in a sample of 613 elementary school children, Kupersmidt and Patterson (1991) found that rejected children were more likely to self-report negative outcomes. These findings indicate that peer rejection plays some role in the subsequent development of antisocial behaviour and that aggression manifested in early childhood does not merely prompt both peer rejection and antisocial outcomes.

Peer rejection may take on diverse forms as children become adolescents. Leary, Kowalski, Smith, and Phillips (2003) identified the following forms of rejection experienced in adolescence: active interpersonal, passive interpersonal, and romantic. Active forms of interpersonal rejection include name-calling, ridiculing, and bullying. Passive forms are characterized by social ostracism, wherein rejected children are excluded from peer events. In adolescence, romantic rejection represents another form of peer rejection, one that refers to intimate interpersonal relationships (i.e. dating) wherein rejection could involve a non-reciprocation of attraction or intimate feelings or the undesired termination of a dating relationship. In addition to general antisocial behaviour, these types of rejection have been linked to school violence and shootings, such as Columbine. Analyses of the characteristics of school shooters have identified social isolation and peer rejection as potential warning signs (Leary et al., 2003; Verlinden, Hersen, & Thomas, 2000). The extent of social rejection's impact on this specific type of youth violence, however, is not precisely understood.

Peer Selection

We previously mentioned that, as children enter school, they spend less time at home and become less reliant on their parents' opinions and guidance. Simultaneously, the influence of peer opinions on children's behaviours and decisions becomes more prominent

(DeRosier, Cillessen, Coie, & Dodge, 1994). Difficult, unpopular, and rejected children are not isolated from these peer influences. Although these children may be rejected by most of their peers, they are not without friends. Parker and Asher (1989) reported that 54 per cent of the low-accepted children in their study had reciprocating best friends within their classroom, and these friends were of similar sociometric status. As children with behavioural problems or low academic performance withdraw or are rejected from mainstream peer circles, they drift and gravitate toward other, similar children. Finding such peers becomes easier as children enter high school, where the student population increases and struggling or misbehaving students are streamlined into special courses or herded together in detention.

The idea that "birds of a feather flock together" is a consistent finding in the developmental literature on criminal and violent behaviour. This concept is formally referred to as **homophily**, which describes the tendency of individuals to socialize with similar others. For example, research suggests that antisocial children tend to mix with like-minded antisocial peers. A large body of general research on peer selection and child friendships illustrates the importance of similarity on a variety of factors, including behaviours, attitudes, interests, and personality on friendship formation (Epstein, 1989). In her research on adolescent friendship formation, Kandel (1978) showed that similarity between friends was due to two processes: selection and socialization. She found that children actively seek out, or select, similar children. The stability of friendship is influenced by socialization, wherein peers with similar attitudes, behaviours, and interests mutually influence and reinforce these shared characteristics.

Consistent with Kandel's (1978) proposed process of selection, empirical research has generally indicated that peer-rejected children frequently interact with one another or gravitate toward other antisocial peers (Laird et al., 2005). Developmental psychologist Thomas Dishion and colleagues (1991) found that aggressive pre-adolescent boys who were rejected by peers in early childhood eventually report associating primarily with other aggressive boys. Numerous studies show that antisocial peer groups in childhood and adolescence are similar on demographic characteristics (Cairns & Cairns, 1994), academic achievement (Ryan, 2001), aggression (Cairns & Cairns, 1994; Hektner, August, & Realmuto, 2000; Newcomb, Bukowski, & Bagwell, 1999), and delinquency (Urberg, Degirmencioglu, & Tolson, 1998). In a study using data from the Seattle Youth Study, Brownfield and Thompson (1991) examined the relationship between attachment to peers and self-reported delinquency in a sample of over 800 male adolescents. Those boys who self-reported involvement in delinquent acts were significantly more likely to have friends who had also committed delinquent acts.

A considerable body of research addresses Kandel's (1978) second process by demonstrating the impact of socializing with deviant peers. Delinquent peer association is a robust predictor of a variety of negative outcomes, including aggressive behaviour (Brendgen, Bowen, Rondeau, & Vitaro, 1999; Newcomb et al., 1999; Snyder, Horsch, & Childs, 1997), disruptive classroom behaviour (Berndt & Keefe, 1995), substance abuse (Cairns, Cairns, Neckerman, Ferguson, & Gariepy, 1989; Laird et al., 2005), and delinquent and criminal behaviour (Cairns et al., 1989; Patterson et al., 1989, 1992; Simons, Wu, Conger, & Lorenz, 2006). Delinquent peers play a particularly important role in reinforcing antisocial attitudes, beliefs, and behaviours (Cairns, Cairns, Neckerman, Gest, & Gariepy, 1988). Bagwell (2004) has coined the term **temptation talk** to refer to peer-group discussions of potential rule violations and antisocial behaviour. She observed that many youths openly

homophily The tendency of individuals to associate and socialize with similar others (i.e. "birds of a feather flock together").

temptation talk Peer-group discussions that reinforce rule violations and antisocial behaviour.

discuss and reinforce deviant ideas during middle childhood and adolescence. Some researchers have found that children who self-report having delinquent peers are more likely to produce aggressive solutions to hypothetical provocation situations (Brendgen et al., 1999).

Summary

1. Longitudinal research has identified three patterns or trends in delinquent and criminal behaviour. First, a small proportion of high-rate, or chronic, offenders account for a relatively large proportion of criminal activity. Second, the age–crime curve shows that criminal activity increases during adolescence, peaks in late adolescence, and declines in early adulthood. Third, the age of onset of antisocial behaviour is strongly related to both the duration and the seriousness of later criminal activity.

2. Coercion theory, developed by Gerald Patterson and colleagues, argues that criminal and violent behaviour develops along distinct developmental trajectories, resulting in two groups of delinquents: early-onset and late-onset. The chronic developmental pathway, early-onset delinquency, emerges in families characterized by coercive interactions among family members and a set of negativistic parenting traits that result in a failure in early child socialization. Patterson believes that the presence of these coercive family interactions distinguishes early-onset and late-onset delinquency.

3. Terrie Moffitt has also posited the existence of two qualitatively distinct developmental pathways to delinquency—the life-course persistent (LCP) offender and the adolescence-limited (AL) offender. According to Moffitt, the LCP offender exhibits behavioural problems early in childhood and progressively engages in more pervasive, serious criminal behaviour as he or she grows older. In contrast, the AL offender does not begin engaging in delinquent acts until early adolescence. His or her delinquent behaviour is less serious and usually desists in early adulthood due to the availability of prosocial opportunities and the ability to adopt these normative roles effectively.

4. Sampson and Laub's age-graded theory of informal social control argues that the developmental pathway to delinquency and adult criminality is characterized by both continuity and change. Their theory suggests that informal social controls, such as investment in school or family relations, regulate our behaviour. Continuity in criminal behaviour stems from a lack of informal social controls or equity in conventional society. Sampson and Laub argued that, at various points in life, people experience very significant life events, or structural turning points, that may reintroduce informal social control networks into their lives and provide opportunities to desist from crime.

5. Moffitt believed that early predispositional vulnerabilities distinguished early, chronic delinquents and that these vulnerabilities could be traced to neuropsychological functioning. Some early neuropsychological problems may stem from prenatal and perinatal complications. Early neuropsychological problems may impact behaviour by adversely affecting a child's temperament, the innate and stable pattern of responding to and interacting with the environment. Such temperamental difficulties in early childhood may influence the later development of externalizing behavioural deficits, such as conduct disorder.

6. Several aspects of parenting, including parental discipline and monitoring, play a role in the development of antisocial and delinquent behaviour. Diana Baumrind identified three major approaches to parenting based on responsiveness to the child's needs

and the demands placed on the child. While an authoritative parenting style has been associated with several healthy outcomes, authoritarian and permissive parenting have been linked to numerous negative consequences, including antisocial behaviour. Parental monitoring, which involves both parental awareness and limit-setting, has also been identified as a meaningful predictor of delinquency.

7. Several peer factors, including rejection and selection, are connected to delinquent behaviour. Peer-rejected youth are more likely to engage in antisocial and aggressive behaviour. Some streams of research indicate that peer rejection and subsequent antisocial behaviour are both outcomes of failed socialization earlier in the child's development. Other researchers argue that peer rejection plays a unique contributory role in the development of antisocial behaviour. One potential consequence of peer rejection is the absence of prosocial influences. Difficult, unpopular, and rejected children are not isolated from peer influences. Peer-rejected children tend to socialize with other like-minded antisocial peers. A large body of research has identified delinquent peer association as a robust predictor of aggressive and antisocial behaviour.

Review Questions

1. Identify and describe the three patterns or trends in delinquent and criminal behaviour that have emerged from longitudinal research.
2. What are coercive family interactions and, according to Patterson, how do they contribute to persistent criminal behaviour across the life-course?
3. Compare and contrast the major differences between the adolescence-limited and the life-course persistent offender. Why do adolescence-limited delinquents begin delinquency? Why do they desist from delinquency in early adulthood?
4. Describe three childhood externalizing behaviour disorders that may serve as early risk factors for delinquency and adult offending.
5. Review the case study of Ethan Couch. Describe the three parental disciplinary styles discussed in this chapter and identify which one(s) apply to his parents.
6. Identify different aspects of parental practices examined in the chapter. Review the case of Ethan Couch and discuss how shortcomings in his parents' approach to child-rearing likely contributed to his criminal offence.
7. What two peer factors may play a role in the development of criminal and violent behaviour? Explain how they may negatively influence children and adolescents.

Additional Readings

Moffitt, T. E. (1993). Adolescence-limited and life-course persistent antisocial behavior: A developmental taxonomy. *Psychological Review, 100,* 674–701.

Patterson, G. R. (1995). Coercion as a basis for early age of onset for arrest. In J. McCord (Ed.), *Coercion and punishment in long-term perspectives* (pp. 81–105). New York, NY: Cambridge University Press.

Sampson, R. J., & Laub, J. H. (1993). *Crime in the making: Pathways and turning points through life.* Cambridge, MA: Harvard University Press.

Savage, J. (2009). *The development of persistent criminality.* New York, NY: Oxford University Press.

5

Personality

Learning Objectives

At the end of this chapter, you should be able to:

- explain how anxiety or tensions from the dynamic interaction of the id, superego, and ego may trigger maladaptive defence mechanisms and result in criminal and violent behaviour;

- compare and contrast four major offender categories based on psychodynamic theory;

- explain how different patterns of adult attachment might influence criminal and violent behaviour;

- describe Eysenck's three major personality traits and discuss how they might relate to criminal and violent behaviour;

- define impulsivity and explain its relation to criminal and violent behaviour; and

- define the construct of personality disorder and explain the possible roles of different personality disorders in criminal and violent behaviour.

CASE STUDY

Dr Amy Bishop

Huntsville, Alabama—On 12 February 2010 University of Alabama professor Amy Bishop began shooting co-workers during a routine biology department meeting, killing three faculty members and wounding three others. According to Joseph Ng, a department member and co-worker, Bishop "got up suddenly, took out a gun and started shooting at each one of us. She started with the one closest to her, and went down the row shooting her targets in the head" (Bluestein, 2010, para. 3). After the gun ran out of ammunition, the other department members were able to force Bishop out of the room and keep her from re-entering. Arrested shortly after the shootings, she subsequently pled guilty to charges of capital murder and attempted murder and was sentenced to life in prison without parole.

Bishop's actions seemed to be at odds with her stable family life and her credentials as a Harvard-educated university professor, but stories portraying her as aggressive, hostile, and often belligerent soon began to emerge. Discussions with past associates suggested she was a frustrated and insecure individual. One colleague, Hugo Gonzales-Serratos, claimed that Bishop had become infuriated when co-authors in a research group failed to list her as first author on a published manuscript (Dewan & Zezima, 2010). She was also known to frequently dismiss graduate students from her laboratory for fear they would taint her research or potentially steal a first-author spot on publications.

Outside her academic career, Bishop was trying to carve out a future as a writer. She was part of a writing group, whose members described her as a difficult and entitled individual prone to citing her academic credentials and ties to novelist John Irving (her cousin) to boost her credibility (Irons, 2010). Bishop had apparently written and attempted to publish three novels. One depicted a female scientist struggling to

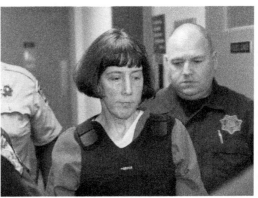

Photo 5.1 Amy Bishop apologized for her actions for the first time in 2015, five years after the killings. However, she has also filed numerous court documents stating that she was mentally ill at the time she pled guilty and that her lawyers were inadequate.

defeat a pandemic virus while coping with her own suicidal thoughts and fears of not earning tenure (Irons, 2010). This character was eerily similar to Bishop, who had her own tenure application rejected by the university several months prior to the shooting.

Further details of Bishop's past reveal a history of violent and aggressive behaviour. She was charged with assault in 2002, after punching a woman in the head for taking the last booster seat at a restaurant. Bishop demanded the booster seat for one of her children, screaming, "I am Dr Amy Bishop!" (Dewan & Zezima, 2010). She and her husband were also suspected of sending a mail bomb to a former mentor. In 1986, Bishop killed her brother in a shooting that was deemed an accident by investigating police officers; however, suspicious details surrounding the incident later surfaced. After the killing, Bishop left her parents' house and went to a local car dealership, where she threatened two employees with the gun in an attempt to steal a car (Slack & Rezendes, 2010).

Introduction

In both her personal and professional life, Amy Bishop exhibited a pattern in her response to obstacles—she lost her temper and behaved aggressively. The study of personality has long been an endeavour of psychology and has been approached from a variety of perspectives. Personality theory also has clear connections to our study of antisocial and criminal behaviour. The main issue of interest in this chapter is whether an offender's personality development differs from that of a prosocial individual in any remarkable way.

The Nature of Personality

personality The stable and distinct ways in which individuals think, feel, and behave in social interactions.

The concept of **personality** is often taken for granted. Most people think of it as simply "who we are." Like the images on a television screen, we see the full, completed picture but fail to comprehend or process the millions of pixels that comprise that finished image. The idea of a personality is, in fact, a complex hypothetical construct. You might describe one friend as "really outgoing" and consider another "shy and withdrawn." You might refer to a colleague as "abrasive and difficult" and another as "easygoing and dependable." These adjectives label observable indicators of what we believe to be the essence of personality. Each involves ways of thinking, feeling, and behaving that distinguish us from one another.

Distinctness has been identified as a core aspect of personality. We can then define personality as that aspect of an individual that makes him or her identifiable and offers some explanation for his or her behaviour. Another aspect of personality is stability. Individuals tend to behave in a consistent or predictable manner across time and context. For the purposes of this chapter, we can combine these ideas into the following definition: the stable and distinct ways in which individuals, think, feel, and behave in social interactions.

Psychology includes many theoretical traditions regarding personality. For example, the **psychodynamic perspective**, which has its roots in the work and ideas of Sigmund Freud, claims that personality is the result of a dynamic interaction between conscious and unconscious mental structures. Our navigation and resolution of several developmental conflicts over the course of childhood are integral to a psychodynamic understanding of abnormal personality. While Freud's theories came under criticism from students and colleagues such as Carl Jung and Alfred Adler, his belief that adult personality is contingent on childhood experiences remains an important cornerstone of this perspective (Engler, 2009; Schultz & Schultz, 2009).

psychodynamic perspective A theoretical approach that views personality as the product of a dynamic interaction between conscious and unconscious mental structures and argues that an abnormal or maladaptive personality results from early developmental conflicts.

The **trait perspective** views personality as the combination of various stable dispositional qualities that a person exhibits. This approach emphasizes developing systems for classifying personality in meaningful ways that distinguish us from one another. Test development and measurement play a large role within the trait perspective (Engler, 2009; Schultz & Schultz, 2009). Although other theoretical perspectives of personality exist, such as the behavioural and humanistic, this chapter examines criminal and violent behaviour using only psychodynamic and trait-related theories.

trait perspective A theoretical approach that views personality as the combination of various stable dispositional qualities that a person exhibits.

Psychodynamic Theories of Personality

Psychodynamic theories of criminal behaviour focus on the development of the personality or psyche across infancy and childhood. From this perspective, motivation for criminal behaviour is rooted in an individual's psychodynamic structure and development. Specifically, the approach believes that criminality stems from pathological development of the personality during the process of socialization in childhood. Contemporary psychodynamic theories of criminal behaviour are rooted in Freud's theory of the unconscious mind and personality structures.

Freud and Personality Development

Freud advanced the study of the unconscious mind during the early days of psychology, when behaviourism was the predominant paradigm in the field. He believed that the human mind was divided, a conceptualization many compare to an iceberg. The tip of the iceberg, the part visible to us, includes the conscious mind (our working thoughts, attitudes, perceptions, and feelings). The preconscious mind includes our available memory—those memories that we can recall with relative ease. Information that you transfer into memory while studying and then recall on exams comes from the preconscious mind. However, below the surface lies a vast array of fantasies, instincts, and motivations that form the unconscious mind, which Freud maintained is not readily accessible yet drives much of our behaviour. In *The Interpretation of Dreams* (1913), for instance, he argued that dreams contain hidden messages and symbols that can be analyzed to understand the hidden aspects of our psyche.

Human personality, according to Freud, is composed of three psychic structures that develop over the course of childhood (see Figure 5.1). Human personality is not fully developed at birth; the only aspect that is present is what Freud referred to as the **id**, which represents the basic human drive for food, shelter, and pleasure. The id is a reservoir of primal instincts that operates according to the **pleasure principle**, the demand to satisfy basic needs immediately. Imagine an infant crying because he or she is thirsty. The infant's personality is composed solely of the id, which drives the child to seek gratification of the

id A mental or psychic structure that represents the basic unconscious human drive for food, shelter, and pleasure.

pleasure principle The unconscious instinct to satisfy the id's needs and wants with no consideration of environmental demands or limitations.

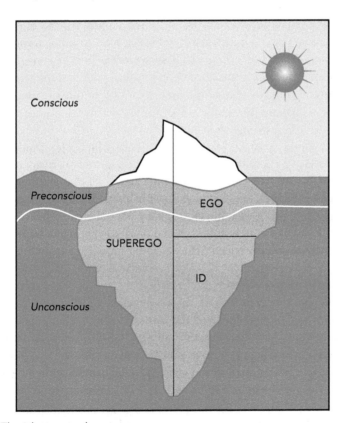

Figure 5.1 The id, ego, and superego.

ego A mental or psychic structure that regulates the id's demands according to the external environment and the limitations of the social context.

reality principle The way the conscious mind operates by recognizing the external world (i.e. reality) and regulating behaviour in accordance to the constraints of this realm.

superego A mental or psychic structure that represents an individual's conscience, or internalized standards of right and wrong.

socialization The teaching of values and morals and the setting of limits on behaviour within the family context.

defence mechanisms Unconscious processes employed by the ego to protect the psyche against unacceptable levels of anxiety.

displacement A psychodynamic defence mechanism that involves transferring a feeling about an object that causes discomfort onto another, usually less threatening, object or person.

reaction formation A psychodynamic defence mechanism that involves substituting unacceptable behaviour, thoughts, or feelings with the direct opposite.

desire for drink immediately without regard for the context. In addition, the personality remains uninfluenced by any sense of societal limits or morals, which have yet to be internalized.

As the child grows older and acquires more experiences, the conscious mind and the **ego** aspect of his or her personality develop. The ego functions like an office manager, regulating the id's demands in accordance with the external environment. Your ego is aware of the limitations your social context places on you and operates according to the **reality principle**, adjusting your drive to any external constraints. Socialization processes in the family eventually lead to the development of the **superego**, which represents your conscience, or internalized standards of right and wrong. **Socialization** refers to the teaching of values and morals and the setting of limits on behaviour that occurs in the family context (Andrews & Bonta, 2010; Blackburn, 1993).

Freud postulated that personality is the product of the dynamic interaction between these three psychic structures. The id seeks pure pleasure; the superego strives for morality and acceptable ethics; and the ego, the arbitrator of the personality triad, constantly seeks to mediate between these two forces and generally provides a compromise (Gallagher, 1987). On occasion, however, the battle between the id and superego produces a great deal of anxiety and overwhelms the ego.

In an effort to keep anxiety levels in check, the ego may employ **defence mechanisms**. These are unconscious coping strategies that protect the psyche from unacceptable degrees of anxiety (Barlow, Durand, & Stewart, 2009). Many defence mechanisms are normal or healthy approaches to reducing internal conflict. For example, have you ever received a grade you believed was unfair or inaccurate? Instead of expressing your anger and frustration with your instructor, you might have gone home and yelled at your parents or a sibling. This is an example of **displacement**. Your ego adaptively "decides" that expressing anger at your instructor might not be in your best interest. Because your parents or siblings do not have the authority to harm you in this situation, your anger is displaced to one of them.

Displacement and other defence mechanisms can also be maladaptive. A possible example is Edmund Kemper, known as the Co-ed Killer, who murdered six young women between May 1972 and February 1973. Kemper was raised by his abusive and domineering mother. In interviews following his arrest, he claimed that he went hunting for some of his victims after arguments with his mother. From a psychodynamic perspective, his relationship with his mother may have elicited a great deal of internal anxiety, which he displaced away from her and onto other women. Ultimately, Kemper murdered his mother and her friend before turning himself in to authorities (Douglas, Burgess, Burgess, & Ressler, 1992).

Reaction formation—a defence mechanism that involves substituting unacceptable behaviour, thoughts, or feelings with the direct opposite—can also be a factor in criminal and violent behaviour. John Wayne Gacy, the "Killer Clown," sexually assaulted, tortured, and murdered 33 young men between 1972 and 1978. Prior to his killing spree, he was accused of sexually assaulting young men who worked for him and was convicted of sodomy in 1968. In spite of his homosexual tendencies, he denied being a homosexual. He was married twice and was known to be quite virulent in his derision for homosexuals. Meadows and Kuehnel (2005) suggest that, from a psychodynamic perspective, Gacy's externalized aggression against young men may have been a maladaptive reaction to internal conflicts over his homosexual orientation. A summary of different psychodynamic defence mechanisms is provided in Table 5.1.

Bettman/Getty Images

Photo 5.2 Edmund Kemper, shown here during his preliminary hearing, was found guilty of eight counts of first-degree murder in November 1973 and sentenced to concurrent life sentences. He remains in prison at the California Medical Facility in Vacaville, California.

Bettman/Getty Images

Photo 5.3 Found guilty of multiple murders, John Wayne Gacy was executed by lethal injection at the Stateville Correctional Center in Crest Hill, Illinois, on 10 May 1994. Authorities have since stated that Gacy may have been responsible for other killings.

Table 5.1 Summary of Psychodynamic Defence Mechanisms

Mechanism	Definition	Example
Displacement	Redirecting an unacceptable urge away from the original object toward another one that is usually less threatening.	A student angry at the mark received on an assignment comes home and yells at his or her family.
Projection	Attributing one's own unacceptable urges, feelings, or thoughts to someone else.	Someone with a strong dislike for another person claims that the other hates him or her.
Reaction formation	Guarding against unacceptable urges, feelings, or thoughts by substituting them with the opposite.	Someone cheating on his or her spouse expresses strong views about the sanctity of marriage.
Repression	Pushing threatening thoughts, feelings, and memories into the unconscious.	A victim of childhood abuse has no recollection of these events.
Sublimation	Transforming an unacceptable urge into positive and socially acceptable behaviour.	Someone with aggressive urges plays hockey or football.

Sources: Adapted from Bernstein, D., Cramer, K. M., Fenwick, K. D., & Fraser, I. (2008). *Psychology* (1st Canadian ed.). Boston, MA: Houghton Mifflin, p. 522; Flett, G. L. (2007). *Personality theory and research: An international perspective. Mississauga*, ON: Wiley, p. 168.

Freud and the Psychosexual Stages of Development

Freud claimed that personality development involves five stages (outlined in Table 5.2). An unusual aspect of this theory is the amount of attention Freud devoted to sex. At each

Table 5.2 Freud's psychosexual stages of development

Stage	Description
Oral	The oral stage of psychosexual development spans from birth until two years. The primary erogenous zone is the mouth; as such, infants gain gratification from placing things in their mouths.
Anal	From the age of 15 months to 3 years, children occupy the anal stage of development, where the primary erogenous zone is the anus. Children gain gratification by eliminating bodily wastes and must master toilet training.
Phallic	The phallic stage spans from age three to six. The primary erogenous zone at this stage is the child's genitalia. Children discover their bodies, begin to make gender distinctions, and direct libidinal energies toward their opposite-sex parent. For instance, the Oedipal complex is characterized by the young boy's desire to possess his mother and his fear of his father. Comparatively, the Electra complex (identified by Jung) is characterized by mother–daughter competition for possession of the father.
Latency	From the age of six to puberty, the libidinal and instinctual drives that characterized the previous stages are repressed or become latent.
Genital	As the child grows into an adult and achieves independence from his or her parents, the primary erogenous zone is once again the genitalia, but libidinal energies are now directed at age-appropriate, consensual targets.

Source: Barlow, D. H., Durand, V. M., & Stewart, S. H. (2009). *Abnormal psychology: An integrative approach* (2nd Canadian ed.). Toronto, ON: Nelson.

stage of development, instinctual sexual energy associated with the id, or libidinal energy, is directed at particular areas of the body, or erogenous zones. Advancing through the stages requires children to develop control over this libidinal energy and to channel these drives in appropriate manners.

Freud believed that personality develops through these psychosexual stages and that the resolution of each libidinal conflict is a prerequisite for developing a healthy adult personality. The development of a maladaptive personality, then, occurs in the early years of infancy and childhood. However, Freud claimed that it was possible to become stalled or stuck in a stage, which can have important and long-lasting effects on personality (Andrews & Bonta, 2010; Blackburn, 1993). The concept of **fixation** refers to a failure to resolve particular conflicts at the appropriate stage. When this occurs, an individual's personality and behaviour become stuck, or fixated, at that stage. The anxiety that emerges from these conflicts manifests in what Freud called neuroses.

Fixation at different stages results in different problems. For example, an adult fixated in the oral stage might exhibit a sarcastic or manipulative personality and might engage in excessive smoking, nail-biting, or eating—behaviours symbolic of deriving pleasure from oral sensations. Fixation at the anal stage might lead to excessive neatness or messiness. American serial killer Ted Bundy, who is believed to have raped and murdered at least 30 young women, was linked to one of his victims by bite marks on her buttocks (McClellan, 2006). From a psychoanalytic perspective, Bundy's sexually sadistic personality and behaviour might reflect an oral fixation.

Much of Freud's theory of personality development, particularly his psychosexual stages, has been discarded in favour of other views. His emphasis on sexuality and the resolution of libidinal conflicts has been the subject of great criticism. Yet, notwithstanding his focus on all things related to sex, his belief that early childhood socialization processes are significant contributors to development remains an important and recognized factor in the study of criminality. A study by Nunberg (1955), for example, revealed that various forms of sexual assault on a child, including parental abuse, exposure to sexual activities,

fixation A psychodynamic process wherein an individual fails to resolve a conflict at the appropriate stage of development, resulting in later maladaptive personality development.

and acts of incest by older siblings, contributed to early childhood traumatization. Other research shows that a variety of similar early childhood difficulties can significantly influence the development of aggressive and antisocial tendencies.

Psychodynamic Theory and Criminal Behaviour

While Freud never directly addressed criminal behaviour, his concepts and ideas have been applied extensively to this subject. In fact, Freudian theory suggests many different routes to crime. Andrews and Bonta (2010) outlined the following four major offender types based on psychodynamic theory: weak superego type, weak ego type, the "normal" antisocial offender, and the neurotic offender.

The **weak superego offender** suffers from a weak, defective, or incomplete superego that is unable to control the instincts of the id. Because these offenders lack any internalized representation of morality and ethics, their behaviour is subject to the need for immediate gratification and the demands of the immediate external situation (Andrews & Bonta, 2010). Schoenfeld (1971), who offered a psychodynamic theory of juvenile delinquency, believed that parental deprivation and lack of affection, particularly during the first few years of a child's life, is the cause of a weak superego. This psychoanalytic conceptualization of criminality closely resembles the modern concept of the criminal psychopath (Milton, Simonsen, & Birket-Smith, 1998; see Chapter 6).

The **weak ego offender** is characterized by an underdeveloped ego. Recall that the ego acts like the office manager or executive of the personality and is responsible for conforming our behaviour to the external constraints of our environment. The consequence of an underdeveloped ego is a reduced ability to adapt one's behaviour to the particular demands of the situation. You may not be happy with your employer's criticism, but you probably recognize that pouting or being sarcastic or passive-aggressive are juvenile responses. According to Andrews and Bonta (2010), the weak ego offender is immature, gullible, and dependent and has poorly developed social skills. This offender often gets into trouble by misreading his or her environment.

The **"normal" antisocial offender** does not exhibit any features of a maladaptive personality and has passed through the normal stages of development to become a fully functioning adult (Andrews & Bonta, 2010). However, this offender has been primarily socialized by and has identified with a criminal parent. As a result, he or she has internalized procriminal attitudes and sentiments in the formation of the superego.

The **neurotic offender** is characterized by an overactive or strong superego (Andrews & Bonta, 2010; see also Meloy & Gacono, 1992). Recall that the superego is the conscience of personality, or the internalized representations of morality and ethics that individuals have learned through socialization. In some instances, an individual may be oversocialized and hence may perceive and judge moral transgressions more harshly. Another aspect of the superego is the ego ideal, which refers to our self-developed, inner, ideal image of the type of person we most aspire to be. In a sense, the ego ideal can be thought of as self-imposed personal standards of conduct, ethics, and appearance. From a psychoanalytic perspective, an individual with an overactive superego who commits a moral transgression will be judged harshly by his or her superego, thereby creating a great deal of anxiety and guilt. If these feelings are left unresolved, they may manifest later in antisocial or criminal behaviour. The criminal behaviour of the neurotic offender may reflect an unconscious desire to be punished for these past transgressions.

weak superego offender An offender who possesses a weak or incomplete superego that is unable to control the instincts of the id, resulting in a lack of internalized representations of morality and ethics.

weak ego offender An offender who possesses an underdeveloped ego, resulting in an inability to adapt his or her behaviour to the particular demands of the situation.

"normal" antisocial offender An offender who is a fully functioning adult with no maladaptive features but whose superego formation includes internalized procriminal attitudes and sentiments as a result of being primarily socialized by, and identifying with, a criminal parent.

neurotic offender An offender who possesses an overactive or strong superego, resulting in oversocialization and a potential tendency to perceive and judge moral transgressions more harshly.

Freud and the Hydraulic Model of Aggression

We previously referred to Freud's belief that much of human behaviour stems from innate instincts. In *Beyond the Pleasure Principle*, Freud (1920) described two opposing innate drives that he thought influenced much of our behaviour. Our instinct to survive—composed of the drive to satisfy hunger, thirst, love, and sex—was referred to as eros, or the life drive. This instinct conflicts with our death drive, or thanatos, our tendency toward self-destruction or an unconscious desire to die. For some individuals, this death instinct might express itself in an innate preference for being the "bottom" or "submissive" in bondage, discipline, sadism, and masochism (BDSM) relationships or involvement in extreme sports such as skydiving or cliff-diving.

Freud also theorized that we sometimes direct this death instinct away from ourselves in the form of aggression. Aggressiveness, or some forms of violence, could be natural expressions of an innate drive; however, society necessarily frowns upon most expressions of aggression. Much childhood socialization focuses on teaching children to refrain from engaging in hostile responses. Over time, children learn to repress expressions of anger and frustration. But what happens to our innate need to express aggression if that drive is denied?

The **hydraulic model of aggression** posits that our innate aggressive tendencies will build up like water in a dam if they are not channelled or expressed outward. The pressure eventually results in an explosion of aggressive behaviour (Berkowitz, 1965). Psychologists John Dollard and Neil Miller (1950) further developed this Freudian concept as an innate drive repressed by socialization practices: "We assume . . . that anger responses are produced by the innumerable and unavoidable frustration situations of child life . . . Society takes a special stand toward such anger responses, generally inhibiting them and allowing them reign only in a few circumstances" (p. 148). Ethnologist Konrad Lorenz (1966/2002) also developed and refined this model of aggression as an instinctual drive, focusing on the role of environment.

This Freudian view of aggression led other psychodynamic theorists to advance the idea of **catharsis**, a Greek word meaning "to cleanse" or "to purge." The term refers to the release of blocked anger, frustration, or aggression in mild, non-destructive ways (i.e. "blowing off steam"). Playing recreational contact sports or hitting a punching bag for exercise could be acts of catharsis that channel a person's innate aggressive tendencies in safe ways and prevent this energy from building to unhealthy levels. Some researchers have argued that watching acts of aggression and violence on television or in movies may serve as a form of catharsis, allowing viewers to vicariously channel their innate drives through another person. To date, research findings have largely failed to support this theory (e.g. Bushman, 2002). Media violence and real-world aggression is discussed in more detail in Chapter 7.

Attachment and Personality

Attachment theory, which originated with the work of British developmental psychologist John Bowlby (1969), offers us a more contemporary means to understand the development of a pathological personality. According to this theory, the early relationships and bonds that we form with primary caretakers in infancy significantly influence our capacity to form meaningful relationships with others as adults. Bowlby's work on the effects of maternal deprivation on infants was influenced by the findings of psychologist Harry Harlow, who conducted studies on maternal separation and social isolation with rhesus

---

hydraulic model of aggression The idea that unexpressed innate aggressive tendencies will accumulate over time until the pressure results in an explosion of aggressive behaviour.

catharsis A Greek word meaning "to cleanse" or "to purge" and referring to the release of blocked anger, frustration, or aggression in mild, non-destructive ways.

attachment theory The idea that early relationships and bonds formed with primary caretakers in infancy significantly influence our capacity to form meaningful relationships with others as adults.

monkeys. In a classic experiment, Harlow (1958) separated two groups of baby monkeys from their mothers. One group was placed in a cage with a terry-cloth substitute mother that provided no food and a wire-framed mother substitute that provided a bottle of milk. For the second group, the terry-cloth mother provided food, but the wire mother did not. Harlow observed that the isolated baby monkeys clung to the terry-cloth substitute regardless of whether it provided any food and clung to the wire-framed substitute only when it provided food. Based on these observations, he concluded that nourishment was not the only thing the babies craved; warmth and physical comfort were necessities as well.

In his attachment theory, Bowlby (1969) similarly surmised that bonding between infants and caretakers is a universal or innate need, like shelter and physical nourishment, and that the formation of these bonds is necessary for normal development to occur. From this perspective, attachment can be thought of as a series of behaviours designed to maintain a close interpersonal bond between an infant and a caretaker. Newborn babies cry for a variety of reasons, not only because they are hungry or uncomfortable but also because they simply want to be held. Toddlers may extend their arms when they want to be hugged, and young children will call out to their parents for comfort when they have awakened from a nightmare. All these behaviours are part of the attachment behaviour system; that is, they are goal-oriented behaviours designed to reassure the child that he or she is loved, safe, and protected.

Photo 5.4 A rhesus monkey in Harlow's experiment clings to its terry-cloth "mother."

A key aspect of attachment theory is that early attachments in infancy create internal working models of interpersonal relationships that we use in adulthood. Our early attachments create expectancies about the amount of safety and trust we can anticipate from other relationships. We may also develop insight into other people's thoughts and feelings (i.e. empathy) from these models. When primary caregivers are inaccessible, inconsistent, or fail to nurture or if there is disruption in the bonding process, infants will not attach and may even detach permanently, adversely impacting personality development.

Patterns of Attachment

Much of our current understanding of the effects of poor attachment is based on the work of Canadian psychologist Mary Ainsworth. To study parent–child interactions and patterns of attachment, Ainsworth (1979) developed the **strange situation**, an experimental research procedure that observes toddlers' responses to separation from, and reunion with, their mothers. In the strange situation, a mother and child arrive at an experimental, toy-filled room. Using a one-way mirror, researchers observe and record the child behaving with his or her mother present. Eventually, the mother leaves the room without the toddler's knowledge and a research confederate enters to observe the child exploring the room and playing with the toys. After a brief separation, the mother returns; the researchers observe and record the toddler's behaviour in response to the initial separation and eventual reunion.

strange situation An experimental research procedure in which researchers observe childrens' responses to separation from, and reunion with, their mothers or primary caretakers.

Ainsworth and colleagues (1979) observed different attachment patterns in their experiment. Some toddlers displayed secure attachment. When placed in a strange and unfamiliar environment, they played comfortably in their mothers' presence and demonstrated curiosity about their new setting. Following the mother's departure, the toddler was initially

JHU Sheridan Libraries/Gado/Getty Images

Photo 5.5 Mary Ainsworth's research on attachment was instrumental to the study of parent–child interactions.

distressed by her absence but eventually explored the room and toys. They used their mothers as a secure base and were able to separate effectively. When their mothers returned, the children were happy and warmly greeted them. Ainsworth observed that securely attached children had affectionate and consistently responsive caretakers. According to her, the securely attached infant is instilled with a basic trust of people.

In some cases, children stayed very close to their mothers rather than actively exploring the toys. These toddlers were suspicious of the stranger in the room and exhibited extreme emotional distress when their mothers left. Following the reunion, they were often indifferent and even hostile toward their mothers, occasionally pushing them away rather than seeking comfort. Caretakers of these children were inconsistent with providing affection and attention. Ainsworth surmised that the children developed feelings of uncertainty and insecurity, and she labelled this attachment style the anxious/ambivalent attachment pattern.

In avoidant attachment, toddlers basically ignored their mothers upon entering the experimental room and exhibited little or no sign of emotional distress when they left. These children either showed no regard for their mothers upon their return or casually acknowledged their presence with little emotion. Mothers of toddlers with avoidant attachment style were emotionally distant in their interactions, offering little or no response to their child's distress.

Subsequent research by Main and Solomon (1986, 1990) identified a fourth attachment pattern, which they called disorganized attachment. These infants exhibited a lack of clear attachment behaviours in the strange situation, often freezing or showing levels of fear.

internal working models
Mental templates of expectations about other people's trustworthiness and potential helpfulness. These models are developed in childhood as a result of attachment patterns with primary caretakers.

Early patterns of attachment with primary caretakers are believed to result in the development of **internal working models**, or templates of expectations about the trustworthiness and helpfulness of other people (Bretherton, 1992). These models guide our behaviour as we grow older by allowing us to anticipate and plan for how others will respond to us in social interactions and relationships. Another aspect of internal working models is children's perception of themselves and their worthiness of love and interpersonal closeness. For instance, children with a secure attachment style will view themselves as deserving of love and relationships.

Bartholomew and Horowitz (1991) have suggested that the internal working model developed through our attachment experiences consists of two dimensions. The first dimension concerns a model of self that ranges from positive to negative views (i.e. lovable or unlovable, respectively). The second dimension involves a model of others in relation to the self, wherein other people are viewed as either positive or negative (i.e. capable or incapable of giving love, respectively). According to attachment theory, these internal working models are stable and persist into adulthood. Four adult attachment styles have been identified and are shown in Figure 5.2. These styles are believed to develop from the childhood patterns we described and are assumed to influence interpersonal functioning (see Ward, Hudson, & Marshall, 1996, for a more detailed discussion).

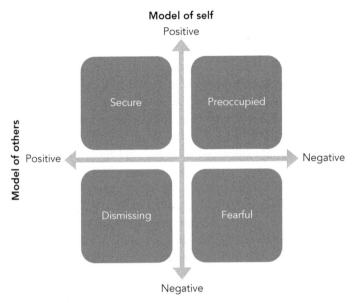

Figure 5.2 Adult attachment patterns.

The **secure adult attachment style** emerges from a secure attachment in childhood. The securely attached adult has high self-esteem and views others as warm and accepting. Not surprisingly, research findings show that adults exhibiting this pattern enjoy happier and healthier relationships (Ward et al., 1996). The **dismissing adult attachment style** emerges from avoidant attachment in childhood. An individual with this style harbours a strong positive self-image that is contrasted by a poor, mistrusting regard of others (Brennan & Shaver, 1995; Sawle & Kear-Colwell, 2001; Ward et al., 1996). Someone with **preoccupied attachment style**—a product of ambivalent/anxious attachment in childhood—has a negative view of himself or herself and a positive view of others (Ward et al., 1996). As the term suggests, these individuals are preoccupied with seeking relationships because they often evaluate their own self-worth based on others' responses. Given their poor self-image, they are prone to feeling insecure, jealous, and fearful that friends or intimate partners will leave them. Lastly, the **disorganized/fearful adult attachment style** emerges from disorganized attachment in childhood. The individual with this style exhibits a desire to be around others but at the same time avoids getting too emotionally close to people out of a fear of rejection (Ward et al., 1996).

Attachment and Criminal Behaviour

Attachment theorists and researchers have postulated that patterns of early parent–child relationships serve as templates for enduring adult attachment styles that influence several life outcomes, including the quality of romantic relationships and levels of empathy and self-esteem (Bartholomew & Horowitz, 1991; Feeney & Noller, 1990; Roberts, Gotlib, & Kassel, 1996; Young, Klosko, & Weishaar, 2003). Patterns of insecure attachment have also been linked to mental health problems among adolescents (Allen, Hauser, & Borman-Spurrell, 1996) and adults (McLaughlin et al., 2010; Ponizovsky,

secure attachment An adult attachment style that emerges from secure attachment in childhood and is characterized by a positive self-image and positive view of others.

dismissing attachment An adult attachment style that emerges from avoidant attachment in childhood and is characterized by a strong, positive self-image and a poor, mistrusting regard of other people.

preoccupied attachment An adult attachment style that emerges from ambivalent/anxious attachment in childhood and is characterized by a negative view of the self and a strong positive view of others.

disorganized/fearful attachment An adult attachment style that emerges from disorganized attachment in childhood and is characterized by a contradictory desire to be around others while also keeping them at an emotional distance out of a fear of rejection.

Nechamkin, & Rosca, 2007). A Dutch study of male forensic patients found associations between measured patterns of insecure attachment and diagnoses of personality disorders (van Ijzendoorn et al., 1997). Theoretically, the difficulties associated with insecure attachment—intimacy deficits, poor self-esteem, insecurity, hostile views of others, and lack of empathy—could facilitate criminal behaviour in a variety of contexts. For instance, Dutch psychologist Marinus van Ijzendoorn (1997) hypothesized that children with insecure attachment patterns are less likely to feel empathetic for their actions or to internalize moral standards of right and wrong.

To date, researchers have examined relationships between attachment patterns and several categories of predatory crime. Not surprisingly, early childhood attachment patterns have been examined as a potential developmental precursor to psychopathy, a personality disorder broadly characterized by a lack of affect, interpersonal manipulativeness, and an impulsive behavioural style (see Chapter 6). Some psychologists suggest that the lack of emotional depth and the interpersonal orientation of psychopaths may stem from patterns of attachment developed in early childhood (Fowles & Dindo, 2006; Saltaris, 2002). Associations have been observed between childhood attachment patterns and measures of psychopathy in adolescents (Kosson, Cyterski, Steuerwald, Neumann, & Walker-Matthews, 2002) and adults (Mack, Hackney, & Pyle, 2011). However, no universal consensus exists regarding the role of attachment in the development of psychopathic traits over the life-course, with some studies producing mixed results (e.g. Holmqvist, 2008).

Given the observed relationship between adult attachment patterns and adult intimacy, it is not surprising that research has identified attachment as a precursor to forms of interpersonal violence, including sexual offending and stalking. In addition to general intimacy deficits, some research has found links between insecure patterns of childhood and adult attachment and the employment of coercive sexual behaviours in relationships (Smallbone & Dadds, 2001). Canadian psychologist William L. Marshall used extensive research on sexual offending to suggest that insecure attachment may be a precursor to general criminality as opposed to a specific risk factor for violent sexual offending (Marshall, Serran, & Cortoni, 2000). Other studies suggest that sexual offenders are more likely to exhibit a disorganized pattern of attachment than are violent offenders and non-offenders (Baker & Beech, 2004; Burk & Burkhart, 2003; Van Ijzendoorn, Schuengel, & Bakermans-Kranenburg, 1999).

American forensic psychologist J. Reid Meloy (1988, 1992) was among the first researchers to postulate that insecure attachment may also serve as precursor to stalking, which he described as "an extreme disorder of attachment" (1992, pp. 37–38). Other researchers have observed that individuals with an insecure style of attachment may be more prone to jealousy and insecurity in intimate relationships, which may fuel extremely maladaptive responses to rejection or the dissolution of a relationship (Dennison & Stewart, 2006; Kienlen, 1998; Kienlen, Birmingham, Solberg, O'Regan, & Meloy, 1997; Patton, Nobles, & Fox, 2010). Research has indeed found that insecure attachment patterns are more frequently observed among stalkers than among other offenders and non-offenders (MacKenzie, Mullen, Ogloff, McEwan, & James, 2008; Tonin, 2004). Insecure attachment patterns have also been identified as precursors to interpersonal violence and stalking in intimate relationships (Dutton, Saunders, Starzomski, & Bartholomew, 1994; Dutton & Winstead, 2006; Dye & Davis, 2003).

CASE STUDY

Aileen Wuornos

Bruce Arrigo, an American forensic psychologist, applied attachment theory principles to the case of Aileen Wuornos—a serial killer convicted of murdering six men along Florida's highways between 1989 and 1990—to explain her behaviour (Arrigo & Griffin, 2004; Shipley & Arrigo, 2004). Wuornos's modus operandi was to wait by the roadside until somebody picked her up (Arrigo & Griffin, 2004). During the ride, Wuornos would disclose that she was a prostitute in need of money and persuade her victims to drive to secluded locations to have sex with her (Arrigo & Griffin, 2004; Myers, Gooch, & Meloy, 2005). It is assumed that she shot them with a small calibre handgun shortly after they parked their vehicle. In half the cases, the bodies were found naked; money and small personal effects were taken from a number of the victims as well (Myers et al., 2005).

Based on a review of available information, Arrigo and colleagues postulated that Wuornos exhibited a dismissing style of attachment as evidenced by "detachment, hostility, social withdrawal, impulsive behavior, and poor sensitivity and awareness" (Arrigo & Griffin, 2004, p. 386). In support of this assessment, Arrigo points to the history of fragmented relationships in Wuornos's past. She had no relationship with either of her parents. She had never met her father, Leo Pittman, a convicted child molester who committed suicide in prison, and her mother, Diane, abandoned her when she was four years old. Wuornos and her brother, Keith, were raised by their maternal grandparents, Lauri and Britta Wuornos. Accounts generally depict Lauri as a cold, stern disciplinarian who beat Wuornos on occasion and Britta as an alcoholic who did not intervene or protect her from the abuse. As a

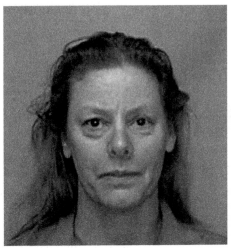

Photo 5.4 Convicted of murdering six men, Aileen Wuornos received a death sentence for each case; she was executed by lethal injection at Florida State Prison on 9 October 2002.

young girl and adolescent, Wuornos had few friends and was used by neighbourhood boys for sex.

These childhood experiences, especially the neglect and abuse she suffered at the hands of her primary caregivers, may have led Wuornos to form an internal working model of herself as worthless and hated and of others as hostile, untrustworthy, and uncompassionate (Arrigo & Griffin, 2004). As a result of these perceptions, she lived in constant fear of being abandoned, abused, and betrayed. The coping strategy that she adopted was to detach herself from her own emotions and those of the people around her. Arrigo and Griffin (2004) contend that this inability to form attachments and emotionally relate to other people made it relatively easy for Wuornos to devalue her victims and murder them in such a cold and calculated manner.

The Trait Perspective

The trait approach is one of the major theoretical areas in the study of personality. According to the trait perspective, individuals can be distinguished from one another based on qualities, or traits, that combine in unique ways. A personality **trait** is a durable

trait A durable disposition to behave in a particular way across a variety of situations.

disposition to behave in a particular way across a variety of situations. Adjectives such as *honest, dependable, moody, impulsive, suspicious, anxious, excitable, domineering*, and *friendly* describe dispositions that represent personality traits. Central to this perspective, trait theorists assume that these dispositions are relatively stable over time, differ among individuals, and influence behaviour (Engler, 2009; Schultz & Schultz, 2009).

The combination and interaction of traits contributes to the development of a distinct personality. Qualitative and quantitative differences exist in the combination of personality traits. Individuals may exhibit qualitative differences in the presence or absence of particular traits; for instance, some may be anxious and others may show no signs of anxiety. The amount of a trait, or the extent that it is quantitatively present, may also differ between people. One individual may be quantitatively more anxious than other people who exhibit some levels of anxiety.

American psychologist Gordon W. Allport (1961) argued that traits are hierarchically organized. In other words, some traits play a stronger role than others in determining how people behave and respond in their environment. According to Allport, traits are internally organized into three categories. **Cardinal traits** are dominant personality traits that are externally characteristic of an individual. If you were asked to describe yourself in one word, that single adjective would be a cardinal trait. **Central traits** refer to general characteristics that form the basic foundation of personality but are not necessarily dominant. **Secondary traits** are related to specific attitudes or preferences and typically appear only in certain situations or under particular circumstances. Examples include getting nervous when speaking to a group or becoming impatient while waiting in line.

Perhaps you have completed an online personality test to determine which television character or celebrity you most exemplify. These tests provide a straightforward, non-academic illustration of personality measurement and testing, which are prominent features of personality psychology. Personality psychologists focus much of their research efforts on measuring the presence and combination of personality traits in individuals (Engler, 2009; Schultz & Schultz, 2009). **Factor analysis**, a statistical technique in which correlations among variables are analyzed to identify closely related clusters, is frequently used to identify personality traits. Robert McCrae and Paul Costa Jr (1997, 1999, 2004) used factor analysis to identify a **five-factor model of personality**. According to this model, our personalities can be adequately described with five higher-order trait categories: extraversion, neuroticism, openness to experience, agreeableness, and conscientiousness. For example, conscientious people tend to be diligent, disciplined, well organized, punctual, and dependable. See Table 5.3 for more examples.

cardinal traits Dominant personality traits that are externally characteristic of an individual.

central traits General characteristics that form the basic foundation of personality but are not necessarily dominant aspects of an individual's dispositional style.

secondary traits Personality traits that are related to specific attitudes or preferences and typically appear only in certain situations or under specific circumstances.

factor analysis A statistical technique in which correlations among variables, such as personality traits, are analyzed to identify closely related clusters of those variables.

five-factor model of personality A trait perspective proposing that personalities can be described with five higher-order trait categories: extraversion, neuroticism, openness to experience, agreeableness, and conscientiousness.

Table 5.3 The five-factor model of personality

Trait	Examples
Extraversion	Talkative, sociable, fun-loving, assertive
Neuroticism	Anxious, self-conscious, insecure, irritable
Openness	Creative, non-conforming, broad interests
Agreeableness	Sympathetic, kind, trusting, cooperative
Conscientiousness	Ethical, dependable, efficient, organized

Source: McCrae, R. R., & Costa Jr, P. T. (1999). A five-factor theory of personality. In O. P. John, R. W. Robins, & L. A. Pervin (Eds.), *Handbook of personality: Theory and research* (pp.139–153). New York, NY: Guilford Press.

Eysenck's Theory of Personality and Crime

Perhaps the best-known theory of criminal personality was articulated by Hans Eysenck (1967, 1977, 1996; Eysenck, Eysenck, & Barrett, 1985). As discussed in Chapter 3, Eysenck believed that the development of a criminal personality is contingent on the interaction between biology and environment. Specifically, he argued that we are born with differences in autonomic nervous system (ANS) functioning, which impacts our ability to learn from the environment. Individuals with low ANS functioning do not experience the full impact of their environments. For example, a school-aged child with low ANS functioning who is singled out for misbehaving in class may experience very low levels of anxiety. In the absence of any genuine anxiety, this student may not learn from punishment and, as a result, may continue misbehaving.

Eysenck's outlook is a multidimensional theory of personality. Based on factor analyses, Eysenck identified and defined three basic personality dimensions: extraversion, neuroticism, and psychoticism (Eysenck & Eysenck, 1968). Each dimension can be understood as existing on a continuum; therefore, people vary in the degree to which they exhibit each trait. The dimensions are measured using the **Eysenck Personality Questionnaire–Revised (EPQ–R)**, developed by Eysenck (1996). It is a self-report questionnaire consisting of a series of yes or no questions organized across four scales: extraversion (E), neuroticism (N), psychoticism (P), and lie (L). The lie scale is designed to measure truthfulness in responding.

The first dimension Eysenck identified was the extraversion-introversion continuum (see Figure 5.3). People who have high levels of **extraversion** are characterized by thrill-seeking, sociability, and impulsivity, whereas introverts are unsociable, cautious, and emotionally controlled. According to Eysenck (1967, 1977, 1990, 1994), high levels of extraversion are caused by a lower functioning ANS, which creates a desire for added stimulation. Introverts are the opposite. They are believed to have a higher functioning ANS, which is easily overwhelmed by excessive stimulation. As a result, these individuals tend to be quiet and withdrawn and to avoid excitement. Eysenck expected individuals who scored high on the E-scale to engage more frequently in antisocial behaviour. In theory,

Eysenck Personality Questionnaire–Revised (EPQ–R) A self-report questionnaire or scale designed by Hans Eysenck to measure the presence or absence of specific personality traits. The scale consists of a series of yes or no questions organized across three personality categories—extraversion, neuroticism, and psychoticism—and a lie scale designed to measure truthfulness in responding.

extraversion A personality trait, identified by Hans Eysenck, that is generally characterized by thrill-seeking, sociability, and impulsivity.

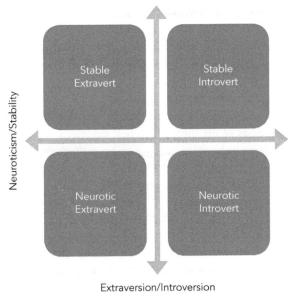

Figure 5.3 Eysenck's theory of personality.

the extravert's higher need for excitement and stimulation increases his or her likelihood of engaging in impulsive, risk-taking behaviour, including crime (impulsivity is discussed later in this chapter).

The second personality dimension, neuroticism-stability, is also shown in Figure 5.3 and refers to emotionality or emotional reactivity. Individuals high on the **neuroticism** scale exhibit elevated levels of emotional reactivity, or poor control of emotions. Neurotic individuals might be described as "emotionally unstable" or "melodramatic" and be more likely than the average person to experience anxiety, anger, guilt, and depressed moods. They respond poorly to environmental stress and are prone to interpreting ordinary situations as threatening, frustrating, and generally negative experiences. Typical neurotics also have an extremely hard time returning to normal levels of emotional functioning following exposure to a stressful or anxiety-provoking event. Individuals low on neuroticism are emotionally stable, calm, and more likely to manifest even-tempered behaviour. Eysenck expected individuals who scored high on the N-scale of the EPQ–R to engage in criminal behaviour more frequently. This prediction is not surprising given that highly neurotic people exhibit intense emotional responses to provocation and stress in their environment.

Eysenck added the psychoticism dimension to his theory years after its initial development, which accounts for its absence from Figure 5.3. The label *psychoticism* is unfortunate because it implies the presence of a serious mental disturbance that has no part of this dimension. A person who ranks high on **psychoticism** is typically aggressive, tough-minded, egocentric, non-conforming, and cold (Eysenck, 1996). At the other end of the continuum, individuals are described as empathetic, cooperative, tender-minded, and conforming. The psychoticism dimension is not clearly articulated and appears to overlap significantly with psychopathy. Higher scores on the P-scale are expected to correlate with antisocial and criminal behaviour.

A large body of research has been conducted to test the validity of Eysenck's personality dimensions and to determine the nature of their relationship with crime. Extensive reviews of this research may be found in a variety of sources (see, for example, Bartol & Bartol, 2012; Cale, 2006). In general, the P-scale exhibits the strongest relationship. Specifically, the emotionally cold and tough-minded nature of psychoticism has a moderate correlation with antisocial and criminal behaviour (Cale, 2006; Heaven, Newbury, & Wilson, 2004). Similarly, a high score on the N-scale has a significant, albeit weaker, relationship with these behaviours (Cale, 2006; Kemp & Center, 2003; van Dam, Janssens, & De Bruyn, 2005).

Contrary to expectation, high E-scale scores have not shown a consistent relationship to offending behaviour (Cale, 2006; Cochrane, 1974; Kemp & Center, 2003; Passingham, 1972). In reformulations of his theory, Eysenck suggested the subtraits that necessarily comprise extraversion may be more strongly active or displayed in adolescence and young adulthood, which might account for the E-scale's relative inability to predict offending. Some research indicates that extraversion may play a more significant role in antisocial and criminal behaviour at younger ages (e.g. Eysenck & Gudjonsson, 1989).

Extraversion, neuroticism, and psychoticism are independent from one another, but as shown in Figure 5.3, the specific combination of, or interaction between, these traits may also differentially contribute to risks for antisocial and criminal behaviour. For example, the stable extravert is outgoing and assertive but also emotionally stable and capable of navigating socially challenging environments. For our purposes, we are most

neuroticism A personality trait, identified by Hans Eysenck, that is generally characterized by high levels of emotional reactivity, anxiety, anger, guilt, and depressed mood.

psychoticism A personality trait, identified by Hans Eysenck, that is generally characterized by aggression, tough-mindedness, egotism, non-conforming, and coldness.

interested in individuals with high levels of extraversion and neuroticism or of neuroticism and psychoticism. Eysenck believed that the **neurotic extravert** would be overrepresented among offender populations. These individuals seek excitement and thrills while being very emotionally reactive (i.e. easily angered and upset and exhibiting problems calming down). Existing research also suggests that different combinations of Eysenck's personality dimensions explain different types of criminal behaviour (Carrasco, Barker, Tremblay, & Vitaro, 2006).

neurotic extravert A category of individuals who score high on both the extraversion and neuroticism scales of the EPQ–R. These individuals seek excitement and thrills and are very emotionally reactive (i.e. easily angered and upset).

Impulsivity, Personality, and Criminal Behaviour

Earlier in the chapter, we identified **impulsivity** as an important psychological concept in the discussion of criminal and violent behaviour, a sentiment shared by other psychologists and criminologists (e.g. Lynam & Miller, 2004). Nonetheless, impulsivity has proven difficult to define. For the purposes of this chapter, the term is used to describe a broad personality trait that encompasses stimulation-seeking behaviours and an inclination to initiate behaviours without adequate forethought.

impulsivity A broad personality trait characterized by stimulation-seeking behaviours and an inclination to initiate behaviours without adequate forethought.

Eysenck revised his personality theory several times in order to address the structure of impulsivity (Eysenck & Eysenck, 1968, 1977; Eysenck et al., 1985). You may recall from our earlier discussion that trait theorists propose that our personalities are composed of a series of hierarchically organized traits. At different points in the theory's history and development, Eysenck argued that impulsivity was composed of various subtraits differentially correlated with the higher-order traits of extraversion, neuroticism, and psychoticism. Eysenck and colleages (1985) proposed that impulsivity consisted of both adventurousness and sensation-seeking. They eventually included impulsiveness (e.g. "I usually think carefully before doing anything") as a component of psychoticism and designated adventurousness ("I would enjoy waterskiing") and sensation-seeking ("I sometimes like doing things that are a bit frightening") as facets of extraversion.

Other personality theorists have argued that the impulsivity trait comprises several lower-order traits, including sensation-seeking, susceptibility to boredom, risk-taking, and lack of premeditation (Depue & Collins, 1999). Psychologist Donald Lynam and colleagues proposed that four personality subtraits or pathways lead to impulsive behaviour: urgency, lack of premeditation, lack of perseverance, and sensation-seeking (Whiteside & Lynam, 2001). This model was supported in subsequent research, with lack of premeditation and sensation-seeking being most relevant to the manifestation of antisocial and criminal behaviour (Lynam & Miller, 2004).

Sociologists Michael Gottfredson and Travis Hirschi (1990) attempted to explore the role of individual propensities in criminal behaviour. Their **general theory of crime** argues that offending is a consequence of an inability to exercise self-control. According to them, low self-control is manifested through three personality pathways. Individuals who lack self-control are more likely to be impulsive, unable to delay gratification, or unable to consider future consequences for present behaviours. Low self-control individuals also have low levels of emotional tolerance, or an inability to tolerate frustration or stress. Finally, they engage in stimulation-seeking behaviours more frequently than other individuals. Some research has observed that, to some extent, low levels of self-control do contribute to the risk for engaging in offending behaviour (Keane, Maxim, & Teevan, 1993; LaGrange & Silverman, 1999; Sorenson & Brownfield, 1995). However, contrary to the title of the theory, these empirical studies do not suggest that low self-control is a general causal factor.

general theory of crime A theory of crime proposing that criminal behaviour is the result of an inability to exercise self-control.

Longitudinal studies examining the developmental course of delinquency in relation to numerous relevant variables have singled out impulsivity as an important psychological concept. Farrington (1992) reported a relationship between future delinquent behaviour among over 400 young boys and measures of impulsivity from three sources (teacher nominations, peer nominations, and self-report measures). In the Pittsburgh Youth Study, White and colleagues (1994) reported that several impulsivity measures are strongly correlated with self-reported rates of delinquency. Other research has shown that impulsivity may even act as a moderator between social context and criminal behaviour. Lynam and colleagues (2000) found that the risk for criminal behaviour among inner-city adolescent males was significantly higher for the impulsive boys than for the non-impulsive.

Personality Disorders

Our definition of personality focuses on how people think, feel, and behave in social interactions. Let's look at a few examples from real life and television. Amy Bishop, the subject of our opening case study, had a history of violent outbursts stemming from competitive behaviour and an entitled view of herself. Dexter Morgan, the titular character in the Showtime series *Dexter*, is a serial killer who admits to feeling emotionally disconnected from the people around him. Despite this lack of emotions, he maintains a relationship with his girlfriend, Rita, and superficial friendships with co-workers to blend in with society. Dale Gribble, a character in the animated *King of the Hill*, similarly evidences consistently odd behaviour in his social interactions. Paranoid, untrusting, and generally hostile toward most other characters, Dale is a conspiracy theorist who is so suspicious of the US government that he refuses to vote or be seen in public without his sunglasses. Across these examples, we can see problematic patterns. In this section, we will discuss the concept of a personality disorder and review specific disorders that are relevant to an examination of criminal behaviour.

personality disorder An enduring pattern of thinking and feeling about oneself and others that significantly and adversely affects how one functions in many aspects of life.

According to the *DSM-5*, a **personality disorder** is an enduring pattern of thinking and feeling about oneself and others that significantly and adversely affects how one functions in many aspects of life (APA, 2013; see Chapter 9). This dysfunctional pattern is associated with disturbances in two or more of the following areas: cognitions and perceptions of self and others, emotions, interpersonal functioning, and impulse control. Personality disorders usually emerge in adolescence or early adulthood and, once manifested, tend to persist regardless of age or situational context.

Antisocial Personality Disorder

antisocial personality disorder (ASPD) A personality disorder generally characterized by a consistent disregard for and violation of the rights of others. Symptoms may include a failure to conform to social norms or the criminal law, irritability, aggressiveness, consistent irresponsibility, and impulsivity.

The most commonly discussed personality disorder in reference to offending behaviour is **antisocial personality disorder (ASPD)**. According to the *DSM-5* (APA, 2013), individuals with ASPD must be at least 18 years old and, since the age of 15, must have shown a consistent disregard for and violation of the rights of others by demonstrating three or more of the symptoms listed in Table 5.4. Note that there is some conceptual overlap between ASPD and psychopathy, a topic discussed further in Chapter 6.

Given this diagnostic criteria, it should not be surprising that ASPD occurs much more frequently among offender populations than among non-offenders. Studies of correctional and jail intake populations place the occurrence of ASPD at anywhere from 50 per cent to 70 per cent among offenders (Corrado, Cohen, Hart, & Roesch, 2000; Hodgins & Côté, 1990; Motiuk & Porporino, 1992; Powell, Holt, & Fondacuro, 1997). For example, a study of inmates in a Canadian correctional facility found that mentally disordered offenders

CASE STUDY

Rorschach

"Because there is good and there is evil, and evil must be punished. Even in the face of Armageddon I shall not compromise in this." (Rorschach, Journal Entry, 13 Oct. 1985, as cited in Moore & Gibbons, 1986)

Walter Kovacs (aka Rorschach), the costumed vigilante in Alan Moore's critically acclaimed graphic novel, *Watchmen*, is clearly personality disordered. The unwanted child of an abusive prostitute, Kovacs adopted the persona of Rorschach after reading about the apathy displayed by neighbours during the rape and murder of Kitty Genovese. Extremely right-wing in his views, he is a moral absolutist who sees the world in stark black-and-white terms and believes that evil must be punished. Anti-communist and anti-liberal, Rorschach derides the societal permissiveness that condones overt sexuality and homosexuality, which he considers human weaknesses and the source of crime and disorder.

Rorschach imposes his idea of good on the world through an uncompromising use of violence, thus alienating himself from other heroes. In one particular scene, Rorschach captures child killer Gerald Grice, handcuffs him to a stove, and allows him to burn alive in his house. When the US government passes the Keene Act, outlawing masked vigilantes, he responds by killing a serial rapist and leaving his body outside a police station with a note bearing one word: "NEVER!" Rigid, uncompromising, aggressive, antisocial—what personality disorder does Rorschach exhibit?

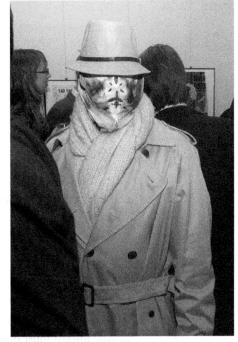

Joe Corrigan/Getty Images

Photo 5.7 An actor portraying Rorschach appears at the *Watchmen* movie premiere in New York City.

with ASPD began their criminal careers earlier and had significantly more prior convictions than inmates without ASPD (Hodgins & Côté, 1993).

Studies show that the disorder is correlated with numerous negative outcomes. A longitudinal follow-up study of males diagnosed with ASPD determined that it is chronic and associated with ongoing medical, mental health, and social problems (Black, Baumgard, & Bell, 1995). High rates of comorbidity between ASPD and substance use disorder among non-offenders are also frequently observed (Alterman & Cacciola, 1991; Kessler et al., 1997; Rutherford, Alterman, Cacciola, & McKay, 1997). Other studies report that people with ASPD exhibit higher rates of violent behaviour compared to those without it (Crocker et al., 2005; Robins & Regier, 1991). ASPD has also been connected to specific patterns of violence. Investigations of intimate partner violence have found that the disorder is generally correlated with proactive violence in domestic relationships (Ross & Babcock, 2009) and may moderate the relationship between intoxication and intimate partner violence (Fals-Stewart, Leonard, & Birchler, 2005). An examination of serial murderers' crime scene behaviours identified a number of patterns that are consistent with the characteristics of ASPD, including the use of domination, physical control, and humiliation (Geberth & Turco, 1997).

Table 5.4 ASPD diagnostic criteria

A. A pervasive pattern of disregard for and violation of the rights of others, occurring since age 15 years, as indicated by three (or more) of the following:

1. Failure to conform to social norms with respect to lawful behaviours, as indicated by repeatedly performing acts that are grounds for arrest.

2. Deceitfulness, as indicated by repeated lying, use of aliases, or conning others for personal profit or pleasure.

3. Impulsivity or failure to plan ahead.

4. Irritability and aggressiveness, as indicated by repeated physical fights or assaults.

5. Reckless disregard for safety of self or others.

6. Consistent irresponsibility, as indicated by repeated failure to sustain consistent work behaviour or honour financial obligations.

7. Lack of remorse, as indicated by being indifferent to or rationalizing having hurt, mistreated, or stolen from another.

B. The individual is at least age 18 years.

C. There is evidence of conduct disorder with onset before age 15 years.

D. The occurrence of antisocial behaviour is not exclusively during the course of schizophrenia or bipolar disorder.

Source: Reprinted with permission from the *Diagnostic and Statistical Manual of Mental Disorders*, Fifth Edition, (Copyright 2013). American Psychiatric Association.

Narcissistic Personality Disorder

narcissistic personality disorder A personality disorder characterized by a pervasive pattern of grandiosity (in fantasy or behaviour), need for admiration, and lack of empathy.

Narcissistic personality disorder has some relationship with aggressive behaviour, although the connection is less clear than the one between ASPD and aggression. The term *narcissism* refers to an excessive admiration or love of oneself and is derived from the Greek myth of Narcissus. A young hunter renowned for his physical beauty, Narcissus became so entranced by his reflection in a pool of water that he was unable to leave and eventually died by the water. The *DSM-5* (APA, 2013) describes narcissistic personality disorder as a pervasive pattern of grandiosity (in fantasy or behaviour), need for admiration, and lack of empathy that begins by early adulthood and presents in a variety of contexts, as indicated by five or more of the criteria listed in Table 5.5.

In contrast to the behavioural indicators of ASPD, the characteristics of narcissistic personality disorder do not immediately call to mind images of violent or aggressive offenders. However, the essential features of the narcissistic personality—the exaggerated self-esteem and accompanying sense of entitlement—may serve to moderate an individual's propensity for aggressive behaviour. There is a fundamental difference between confidence or high self-esteem and narcissism. People with high levels of self-esteem usually have accompanying social feedback (such as life accomplishments) that confirms or justifies their confidence. Comparatively, the narcissist's self-image is unrealistic. This individual does not have social feedback confirming his or her beliefs; they are self-perpetuated distortions. The inflated nature of this self-image leaves the narcissistic personality extremely vulnerable to any challenging feedback. Accepting the negative evaluation means lowering one's self-appraisal. Alternatively, highly narcissistic individuals may maintain their over-inflated sense of self by rejecting the negative feedback about themselves

Table 5.5 Narcissistic personality disorder diagnostic criteria

A pervasive pattern of grandiosity (in fantasy or behaviour), need for admiration, and lack of empathy, beginning by early adulthood and present in a variety of contexts, as indicated by five (or more) of the following:

1. Has a grandiose sense of self-importance (e.g., exaggerates achievements and talents, expects to be recognized as superior without commensurate achievements).

2. Is preoccupied with fantasies of unlimited success, power, brilliance, beauty, or ideal love.

3. Believes that he or she is "special" and unique and can only be understood by, or should associate with, other special or high-status people (or institutions).

4. Requires excessive admiration.

5. Has a sense of entitlement (i.e., unreasonable expectations of especially favourable treatment or automatic compliance with his or her expectations).

6. Is interpersonally exploitative (i.e., takes advantage of others to achieve his or her own ends).

7. Lacks empathy: is unwilling to recognize or identify with the feelings and needs of others.

8. Is often envious of others or believes that others are envious of him or her.

9. Shows arrogant, haughty behaviours or attitudes.

Source: Reprinted with permission from the *Diagnostic and Statistical Manual of Mental Disorders*, Fifth Edition, (Copyright 2013). American Psychiatric Association.

(Baumeister, Smart, & Boden, 1996). These narcissists are likely to see the criticism as unjustified, unfair, and provocative, and they may retaliate with anger and aggression against the source of the unwanted negative feedback (see Figure 5.4; Baumeister et al., 1996; Bettencourt, Tally, Benjamin, & Valentine, 2006).

Several studies have examined the relationship between high levels of narcissism and aggressive behaviour. Criticism, negative evaluations, and social rejection have all been observed to trigger the narcissist's anger and efforts to protect his or her self-image (Rhodewalt & Morf, 1998; Twenge & Campbell, 2003). For example, Kernis and Sun (1994) found

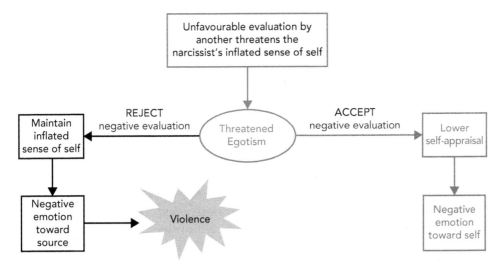

Figure 5.4 Threatened Egotism.
Source: Copyright © 1996 by the American Psychological Association. Adapted with permission. B.F. Baumeister, L. Smart, & J.M. Boden, (1996). "Relation of threatened egotism to violence and aggression: The dark side of high self-esteem." *Psychological Review*, 103(1), 5–33. The use of APA information does not imply endorsement by APA.

Researching Criminal and Violent Behaviour

Threatened Egotism, Narcissism, and Aggression

Social psychologist Roy Baumeister has studied and published extensively on self-esteem for over twenty years. Challenging traditional views linking low self-esteem with aggressive and violent behaviour, Baumeister, Smart, and Boden (1996) have proposed that threats to an inflated self-image may elicit anger and, in some instances, aggression. To examine this relationship, Bushman and Baumeister (1998) conducted a series of studies using the narcissistic personality inventory (Raskin & Terry, 1988) with undergraduate psychology students. On this measure, participants provide responses to statements such as "If I ruled the world it would be a much better place" and "I am more capable than other people."

Bushman and Baumeister (1998) told participants that they were studying how people react to positive and negative feedback. The experimental procedure consisted of two main components. In the first component, participants wrote a brief essay on abortion that was evaluated. Those in the ego threat condition received negative comments about their essay, while other participants received favourable evaluations. In the second component, the participants engaged in a competitive reaction time task with a fictional opponent. Slow participants were punished with a blast of noise. The winner of the task determined both the level and duration of noise blast administered to the loser; hence, it served as the dependent variable or measure of aggression. Ego threats in the form of insulting and negative evaluations from the first part of the study were found to increase aggression among all participants. More important, the strongest aggressive responses were displayed by those participants with the highest narcissism scores.

that narcissists respond to negative evaluations by attacking the credibility of their evaluator, thereby shifting the blame for failure and maintaining their positive self-image. Other studies have found links between forms of provocation and aggressive behaviours (see the "Researching" box). In these studies, connections have been established between ego threats and various forms of physical aggression (Girgis, 2006; Stucke & Sporer, 2002). However, the research does not suggest a direct causal link between narcissism and aggressive behaviour. Baumeister, Bushman, and Campbell (2000) have cautioned against adopting this conclusion, pointing out that research has found only that narcissists use aggression as a social response to protect against perceived threats to their ego.

Summary

1. Personality refers to the stable and distinct ways in which individuals, think, feel, and behave in their social interactions. We identified two cornerstones to this definition. First, our personality is distinct—it is that aspect of each individual that makes him or her identifiable. Second, our personality is relatively stable—most people behave in a fairly consistent and predictable manner across time and context.

2. Psychodynamic theories of criminal behaviour focus on personality development across infancy and childhood. From this perspective, criminality is rooted in an individual's psychodynamic structure and development. Specifically, the approach believes that criminality stems from the pathological development of the personality over the course of socialization in childhood. According to Freud, personality is the product of the interaction between psychic structures and dynamic unconscious

processes. Development of maladaptive personality styles is the outcome of a failure to successfully navigate specific developmental milestones and resolve unconscious levels of anxiety.

3. According to the hydraulic model of aggression, some levels of aggression reflect natural expressions of an innate drive. Freud argued that much of our childhood socialization processes focus on teaching children to refrain from engaging in aggressive responses, bottling up these innate drives like a dam blocking off flowing streams of water. Failure to find safe, non-destructive outlets to express our aggressive tendencies results in an unhealthy build-up of emotions, followed by a dangerous outburst of aggression. Catharsis refers to a safe release of blocked feelings of anger, frustration, and aggression in mild, non-destructive ways, such as involvement in recreational contact sports. While some researchers have suggested that various modes of violent media may serve cathartic purposes, little empirical research supports this claim.

4. According to attachment theory, early relationships formed with primary caretakers during infancy significantly influence our capacity to form meaningful relationships with others as adults. These early bonds result in the development of internal working models of interpersonal relationships that we use in adulthood. Our early attachments create expectancies about the amount of safety and trust we can anticipate from other relationships. Disruptions in early attachment relationships can result in the development of an insecure pattern of attachment. Research in forensic psychology suggests that patterns of insecure attachment may serve as a developmental precursor to psychopathy. Other studies indicate that sexual offenders and stalkers are more likely to exhibit insecure patterns of attachment than violent offenders and non-offenders.

5. Trait perspectives of personality focus on durable dispositions, or traits, that shape our consistent and predictable patterns of behaviour in a variety of situations. In his trait theory of personality and crime, Hans Eysenck argued that a criminal personality is contingent on the interaction between biology and environment. Specifically, people who commit crimes have not developed a strong conscience due to poor conditionability related to the autonomic nervous system. Eysenck identified three basic dimensions of personality: extraversion, neuroticism, and psychoticism. Across the existing research literature, the strongest relationship between Eysenck's personality dimensions and criminal behaviour has been observed with high levels of psychoticism. High levels of neuroticism may also be significantly correlated with antisocial and criminal behaviour. By comparison, high levels of extraversion have not shown a consistent relationship to antisocial and criminal behaviour.

6. Impulsivity refers to a broad personality trait composed of several subtraits that reflect stimulation-seeking behaviours and an inclination to initiate behaviours without adequate forethought. Donald Lynam and colleagues proposed four distinct personality pathways that lead to impulsive behaviour: urgency, lack of premeditation, lack of perseverance, and sensation-seeking. Based on existing research, impulsivity appears to play an important role in antisocial and criminal behaviour and may even act as a moderator between social context and offending.

7. A personality disorder is an enduring pattern of inner experience and behaviour that differs markedly from the expectations of the individual's culture. Antisocial personality disorder (ASPD), which is characterized by a consistent disregard for and violation of the rights of others, is a commonly diagnosed personality disorder among offender populations. Research suggests that ASPD is a chronic disturbance associated

with numerous negative outcomes, including substance use disorders, general criminality, and violent behaviour. Narcissistic personality disorder is characterized by a pervasive pattern of grandiosity, need for admiration, and lack of empathy. While there is no direct causal link between narcissism and aggressive behaviour, narcissistic individuals may respond to threats to their inflated egos with aggressive behaviour.

Review Questions

1. What are defence mechanisms? Explain how anxiety arising from the dynamic interaction among the id, superego, and ego may trigger defence mechanisms. In your answer, identify two examples of defence mechanisms and briefly describe how they might contribute to criminal or aggressive behaviour.
2. Identify and describe the four major offender types outlined by psychodynamic theory.
3. What is attachment? Define one of the following adult attachment patterns and explain how it might be related to criminal behaviour:
   a. dismissing attachment
   b. preoccupied attachment
   c. disorganized/fearful attachment
4. Identify and describe the three major traits outlined in Eysenck's theory of personality and crime. To what extent does research show that each trait is related to criminal and/or aggressive behaviour?
5. Provide a definition of impulsivity. According to Gottfredson and Hirschi's general theory of crime, how is impulsivity related to criminal behaviour?
6. What is a personality disorder? Define and explain how each personality disorder discussed in this chapter may contribute to criminal or aggressive behaviour.

Additional Readings

Andrews, D. A., & Bonta, J. (2010). *The psychology of criminal conduct* (5th ed.). Newark, NJ: LexisNexis/Anderson Publishing.

Arrigo, B. A., & Griffin, A. (2004). Serial murder and the case of Aileen Wuornos: Attachment theory, psychopathy, and predatory aggression. *Behavioural Sciences and the Law, 23,* 375–393.

Baumeister, R. F., Bushman, B. J., & Campbell, W. K. (2000). Self-esteem, narcissism, and aggression: Does violence result from low self-esteem or from threatened egoism? *Current Directions in Psychological Science, 9,* 26–29.

Eysenck, H. J. (1996). Personality and crime: Where do we stand? *Psychology, Crime, and Law, 2,* 143–152.

Lynam, D. R., & Miller, J. D. (2004). Personality pathways to impulsive behavior and their relations to deviance: Results from three samples. *Journal of Quantitative Criminology, 20,* 319–341.

Yu, R., Geddes, J. R., & Fazel, S. (2012). Personality disorders, violence, and antisocial behavior: A systematic review and meta-regression analysis. *Journal of Personality Disorders, 26,* 775–792.

6

Psychopathy

Learning Objectives

At the end of this chapter, you should be able to:

- describe the main symptoms of psychopathy;

- identify and describe some of the instruments commonly used to assess psychopathy;

- distinguish among other diagnostic labels and categories sometimes used interchangeably with psychopathy;

- explain the relationship of psychopathy to criminal and violent behaviour;

- discuss how the expression of psychopathy varies according to gender, age, and culture; and

- describe different theoretical explanations for psychopathy's links to crime and violence.

CASE STUDY

Clifford Robert Olson

Vancouver, British Columbia—Clifford Robert Olson—a confessed rapist and murderer of 11 youth in British Columbia during the early 1980s—has been described as a braggart, a silver-tongued charmer, a master manipulator, a habitual criminal, and a monster ("Braggart," 1982; Johnson, 1997; Worthington, 1993). His modus operandi was to approach potential victims on the pretense of looking for the employment office because he wanted to hire window washers for $10 an hour, a tempting wage at the time (Worthington, 1993). His appearance and manner were disarming: he was well dressed, polite, and had business cards to lend him legitimacy. His ploy successfully lured several young people into his car, where they were plied with a potent combination of alcohol and chloral hydrate. Once the victims were severely intoxicated, he drove them to a secluded location, where they were sexually assaulted, tortured, and killed. In some cases, Olson engaged in necrophilia with the bodies before burying them. Despite the victims' obvious lack of consent and the force involved in the attacks, he denied that anyone was sexually assaulted because "they never said no" (Worthington, 1993, p. 54).

When Olson became a suspect in one of the murders, he indicated that he would reveal the location of his victims for a price. In a deal that shocked and outraged the public, the police eventually placed $100,000 in a trust for Olson's ex-wife in exchange for information on the murders (Worthington, 1993). Olson pled guilty at trial and received 11 consecutive life sentences, with no parole eligibility for 25 years. He died in prison in 2011, at the age of 71, after spending 30 years behind bars (Mulgrew, 2011).

Photo 6.1   Clifford Olson leaves court on 8 August 1981, after being remanded for a 30-day psychiatric test in conjunction with one of his murder charges. Photo: The Canadian Press/Nick Didlick

Olson's murders were part of a larger pattern of antisocial behaviour that began in his youth. He recounted that, as a young boy, he often joined his father on milk deliveries, only to steal money from the collection tin. Later on, he started getting up earlier than his father and taking the money that customers left out for their milk (Worthington, 1993). School records show that Olson was frequently absent, uncooperative, and disruptive. He failed grade 7 twice and dropped out before finishing grade 8 (MacQueen & Hall, 1997). As a teenager, he began to steal "almost anything that wasn't nailed down" and received his first conviction at age 17 (MacQueen & Hall, 1997, p. A5; Worthington, 1993). Over the next 23 years, he amassed nearly 90 charges for offences ranging from breaking and entering, fraud, and drunk driving to armed robbery and escaping lawful custody (Johnson, 1997). He was paroled seven times but violated the conditions of his release or committed a further offence on all but one occasion.

Though Olson subsequently said that he felt remorse for the murders, a forensic psychiatrist who interviewed him described this declaration as "completely hollow" (Johnson, 1997, p. A41). By most accounts, Olson relished his notoriety and, despite his incarceration, managed to thrust himself into the limelight continually (Worthington, 1993). He launched a litany of legal challenges and complaints over his perceived mistreatment by prison officials, including a claim that being denied a sex doll was a violation of his human rights (Worthington, 1993). He even offered to assist various university criminology departments with developing a new course dedicated to studying him (Hare, 1993).

Introduction

The notion of psychopathy has found its way into the public's imagination through books, movies, and other forms of popular media, but its portrayal is as much fiction as fact. Some of the confusion undoubtedly stems from the root word *psycho*, which means "of the mind" but unfortunately is often used colloquially to connote a "crazed" criminal (*New Shorter Oxford English Dictionary*, 1993). To complicate matters further, the linguistic roots of *psychopathy* and *psychosis* are the same; this may explain why the two terms are sometimes mistaken for one another despite describing very different conditions. As we shall see in Chapter 9, psychosis is a condition marked by severely disturbed thinking processes typified by the presence of hallucinations and/or delusions. Psychopathy, on the other hand, is a personality disorder characterized by a profound lack of concern and emotional feelings for other people. Robert Hare (1996), a leading researcher in this area, colourfully describes psychopaths as "intraspecies predators who use charm, manipulation, intimidation, and violence to control others and to satisfy their own selfish needs. Lacking in conscience and in feelings for others, they cold-bloodedly take what they want and do as they please, violating social norms and expectations without the slightest sense of guilt and regret" (p. 26).

The past three decades have seen tremendous growth in the body of research linking psychopathy to criminal and violent behaviour. The connection is so well established that psychopathy has been called "the unified theory of crime" that draws together previously unconnected threads of research and theory (Delisi, 2009, p. 256).

The Clinical Description of Psychopathy

The contemporary clinical description of **psychopathy** is widely credited to Hervey Cleckley (1941/1976), who identified many of the disorder's key symptoms. Psychopathy is a higher-order construct comprising several underlying domains, just as wellness embodies physical, mental, and emotional health (Hare, 1996). The domains of psychopathy relate to interpersonal, affective, and behavioural symptoms. The case studies in this chapter are included to illustrate specific symptoms, but keep in mind that a diagnosis cannot be made on the basis of the limited information presented here. Furthermore, the presence of one or even a few symptoms does not mean that a person is a psychopath. For a more complete picture of psychopathy and its symptomology, consult the descriptions in Cleckley's (1941/1976) original work or Robert Hare's (1993) *Without Conscience: The Disturbing World of the Psychopaths among Us*.

psychopathy A personality disorder characterized by an absence of emotional attachment to others and a lack of concern for their rights and welfare, as well as a sense of entitlement and impulsivity.

Interpersonal Symptoms

Interpersonal symptoms correspond to a person's characteristic style of interacting with others. One key interpersonal symptom of psychopathy is superficial charm (Cleckley, 1941/1976; Hare, 1993). Psychopaths are masters of impression management. They are charismatic and engaging storytellers, but the more one listens to them, the more it becomes apparent that much of what they say cannot be true. They also appear grandiose and egocentric. For example, Olson's desire to be the subject of a university course and to get public attention illustrates the type of narcissism and blatant self-promotion that is prototypical of psychopathy. Given their self-centredness, psychopaths predictably attribute the

interpersonal symptoms Indicators of a person's characteristic style of interacting with other people.

source of their problems to the mistakes of others, misfortune, or mistreatment—anywhere but themselves (Hare, 1993). Psychopaths are also deceitful; they show a remarkable facility for lying and cheating. Cleckley's (1941/1976) case files describe a psychopath who managed to rent a room in his neighbour's house to a stranger and collect the rent in advance while the owner was out running errands. Even when psychopaths are caught in a lie, they tend to carry on unfazed and adjust the "facts" to suit their purpose (Hare, 1993).

Affective Symptoms

affective symptoms
Indicators of a person's emotional responses and feelings.

Affective symptoms relate to a person's emotional responses and feelings. Psychopaths lack the range of emotions that colour the normal human experience—for example, they seem incapable of feeling love, anger, sadness, or fear the way the rest of us do (Cleckley, 1941/1976; Hare, 1993). Psychopaths do not form strong emotional bonds with other people and, as a consequence, their lives are devoid of meaningful intimate relationships, close friendships, and strong family ties. In addition, psychopaths lack remorse for the harm they cause. This symptom is exemplified by Adremy Dennis, who accepted little responsibility for killing a man during a robbery and instead blamed the victim for moving at the wrong moment (see the case study). Although psychopaths sometimes express regret for their past deeds, Cleckley (1941/1976) explains that these statements often lack sincerity and appear "hollow and casual" (p. 343). It is interesting to note that similar language was used to describe Olson's claims of remorse. Psychopaths also exhibit a noticeable lack of empathy. That is, they are unable to appreciate the feelings of others. This may explain their apparent capacity to inflict immeasurable harm and misery on others without hesitation or discomfort.

CASE STUDY

Adremy Dennis

Akron, Ohio—In 1994, 18-year-old Adremy Dennis and an accomplice robbed Martin Eberhart and Kurt Kyle. Eberhart gave the robbers $15, but when Kyle began to search his pockets for money, Dennis shot and killed him. He was executed for the crime 10 years later. Rather than accept responsibility for the murder, Dennis shifted the blame to Kyle. He felt that Kyle should have cooperated and noticed that he was high. Dennis stated: "I ain't saying it's all his fault, but why did he move? Every day I think about that. It ain't 'Why did you kill that man?' It's 'Why did he move?'" He also told the parole board that, if "his mind had been right at the time," he would not have left any eyewitnesses (Nolan, 2004).

Photo 6.2 Adremy Dennis was 28 years old when he was executed for murdering Kurt Kyle, making him the youngest man to be executed in Ohio in 42 years.

Ohio Department of Corrections

Behavioural Symptoms

Psychopathy has several notable **behavioural symptoms**. One of the hallmarks is impulsivity (discussed in Chapter 5). Many of the things psychopaths do, including the crimes they commit, are spontaneous. Psychopaths seldom persevere in anything for very long (Cleckley, 1941/1976). As a result, their lives are characterized by constantly shifting goals and plans, as evidenced by frequent changes in their relationships, living arrangements, occupations, and activities (Hare, 1993). Another behavioural symptom is irresponsibility and unreliability (Cleckley, 1941/1976; Hare, 1993). Psychopaths fail to live up to their social obligations, and their actions frequently put the physical, emotional, and financial well-being of others at risk. It is not unusual for them to leave loans unpaid, violate conditions of parole or probation, or fail to care properly for dependants. Psychopaths also show a need for excitement (Hare, 1993). They are easily bored and often exhibit thrill-seeking behaviour. They may engage in risky activities that have no obvious purpose except for the apparent thrill derived from it. Some candidly report the "rush" they feel when committing crimes.

Disagreement has arisen in recent years over whether antisocial behaviour is a symptom of psychopathy or merely a common outcome of the disorder. One side of this debate argues that antisocial behaviour is a defining feature of psychopathy that distinguishes it from other disorders (Hare & Neumann, 2006). The implication of this view is that instruments and schemes intended to diagnose or measure psychopathy need to assess the onset, nature, severity, and scope of antisocial and criminal behaviours. Those who take the contrary position subscribe to the "consequence hypothesis" (Cooke, Michie, & Hart, 2006). It suggests that antisocial behaviour is a likely consequence or effect of the personality symptoms associated with the disorder but not a defining feature. In other words, antisocial and criminal behaviour are natural end-products of symptoms such as selfishness, deceit, lack of empathy, and impulsivity. Proponents of the consequence hypothesis favour excluding items addressing antisocial behaviours, on the grounds that they do not tap central features of the disorder (Cooke et al., 2006).

Assessing Psychopathy

One of the main difficulties previously associated with psychopathy was the absence of any means to reliably and validly assess it. To remedy this situation and to facilitate his own research, Hare (1980) developed a 22-item rating scale, which was subsequently shortened to a 20-item version (see Table 6.1) and published as a formal psychological instrument known as the **Hare Psychopathy Checklist–Revised** (PCL–R; Hare, 1991, 2003). Each item describes a different characteristic of psychopathy that is grounded in the clinical descriptions of the construct advanced by Cleckley (1941/1976) and others (Hare, 1996). Ratings are usually based on a clinical interview and a review of collateral information from other sources such as family, friends, school files, victim and witness statements, and police and correctional records. Each checklist item is rated on a scale from 0 to 2 according to how closely the person being assessed matches the symptom. A score of 0 indicates no match; 1 indicates a partial match; and 2 indicates a good match (Hare, 1991, 2003). The ratings are then totalled—the higher the score, the more strongly a person displays the characteristic symptoms of psychopathy. A score of 30 is the conventional diagnostic cut-off, but other scores have occasionally been used (Hare, 1996).

behavioural symptoms Indicators of a person's observable and characteristic manner of behaving.

Hare Psychopathy Checklist–Revised (PCL–R) A clinical assessment instrument developed by Robert Hare to evaluate the relative presence of psychopathic symptoms.

Table 6.1 PCL–R symptoms	
Interpersonal/Affective Symptoms	**Behavioural Symptoms**
Interpersonal	**Lifestyle**
Glibness/superficial charm	Need for stimulation
Grandiose self-worth	Parasitic lifestyle
Pathological lying	Lack of goals
Conning/manipulative	Impulsivity
	Irresponsibility
Affective	**Antisocial**
Lack of remorse	Poor behavioural controls
Shallow affect	Early behavioural problems
Lack of empathy	Juvenile delinquency
Will not accept responsibility	Revocation of conditional release
	Criminal versatility[2]
Other Symptoms[1]	
Promiscuous sexual behaviour	
Many short-term marital relationships	

Notes
1. "Other Symptoms" reflects PCL–R items that, according to early statistical analyses, did not fall clearly into any of the other groups.
2. Early analyses of PCL–R items suggest that criminal versatility does not fall clearly into the interpersonal/affective or behavioural groups of symptoms; however, more recent research based on a four-factor model indicates that this item should be grouped with the other antisocial items.

Source: Copyright © 2009 by the American Psychological Association. Reproduced with permission. R.D. Hare & C.S. Neumann, "Psychopathy and its measurement." *The Cambridge handbook of personality psychology.* P. J. Corr, & G. Matthews (eds.) (2009). New York: Cambridge University Press. The use of APA information does not imply endorsement by APA.

Early statistical analyses of the PCL–R suggested that the measure has two distinct components, or symptom groups, identified as Factor 1 and Factor 2 (e.g. Harpur, Hare, & Hakstian, 1989). Factor 1 consists mostly of items reflecting the interpersonal and affective symptoms of psychopathy, while Factor 2 primarily reflects the behavioural symptoms relating to the antisocial and deviant lifestyle characteristics (Harpur et al., 1989). Researchers and practitioners have sometimes found it useful to generate subscores for these factors, and this chapter occasionally refers to them. For simplicity, we will consider Factor 1 and Factor 2 as the interpersonal/affective symptoms and behavioural symptoms, respectively. More recent analyses indicate that the PCL–R may measure three (Cooke & Michie, 2001; Cooke, Michie, Hart, & Clark, 2004) or possibly four factors (Vitacco, Neumann, & Jackson, 2005), but there is no consensus on this issue.

Since its development, the PCL–R has been used in hundreds of studies, establishing it as a very reliable and valid measure of psychopathy (Hare, 1996; Hare, Clark, Grann, & Thornton, 2000; Hart & Hare, 1997). Its success with adult offenders prompted Hare and colleagues to develop modified versions suitable for other populations. This work resulted in the publication of the Hare Psychopathy Checklist: Screening Version (PCL:SV; Hart, Cox, & Hare, 1995), intended as a brief assessment tool primarily for psychiatric and civil settings, and the Hare Psychopathy Checklist: Youth Version (PCL:YV; Forth, Kosson, & Hare, 2003), used to assess psychopathic traits in offenders ages 12 to 18. Although the vast majority of the research on psychopathy conducted over the past 25 years utilizes the PCL-R or one of its derivative instruments, these measures do not constitute the only approach to the assessment of psychopathy. Over the years, an array of alternative assessment tools have been developed by other authorities in the field.

Related diagnostic categories and assessment schemes also exist. As noted in Chapter 5, antisocial personality disorder (ASPD) is a similar condition that is recognized in the *DSM-5*. According to the manual, ASPD relates to the same pattern of behaviour that is sometimes referred to as psychopathy. Nonetheless, notable differences exist between ASPD and the construct of psychopathy assessed by the PCL-R. ASPD is a diagnostic category—it is either present or absent—whereas the PCL-R provides a dimensional measure of how closely a person matches the prototypical psychopath. More important, ASPD is diagnosed primarily on the basis of observable behaviours involving social norm violations, such as stealing, fighting, lying, endangering others, and failing to pay bills. Reliance on observable behaviours stems from the assumption that interpersonal or affective characteristics are more difficult to assess reliably and should be avoided (Hart & Hare, 1997). Hare and colleagues argue that the emphasis on behavioural symptoms at the expense of affective and interpersonal symptoms has resulted in a diagnosis that diverges from the traditional clinical view of psychopathy, which is reflected in the PCL-R (Hare, 1996; Hart & Hare, 1997; Hare & Neumann, 2006).

The difference between ASPD and psychopathy is dramatically illustrated by comparing prevalence rates among offenders and forensic patients. You may recall from Chapter 5 that the diagnostic rate of ASPD in these groups ranges from 50 to 70 per cent, yet only 15 to 30 per cent are classified as psychopaths using the PCL-R (Hart & Hare, 1997). This diagnostic gap should not be surprising. People are imprisoned because of their behaviour, so it is to be expected that a large proportion of prisoners have engaged in the antisocial behaviours used to diagnose ASPD. Only a small proportion of these individuals also display the interpersonal and affective symptoms associated with psychopathy. The result is an **asymmetrical relationship between ASPD and psychopathy** (Hart & Hare, 1997). Nearly all the criminal offenders who are psychopaths according to the PCL-R also meet the diagnostic criteria for ASPD, but many of the offenders diagnosed with ASPD are not considered psychopaths based on the PCL-R (Hart & Hare, 1997). Hare (1996) has gone to great lengths to explain the difference between these two diagnostic labels, but the disorders continue to be mistakenly treated as equivalent.

Two related terms require brief explanation. **Dissocial personality disorder** is a diagnostic category contained in the tenth edition of the International Classification of Diseases (ICD-10), published by the World Health Organization (1990). This disorder most closely resembles the construct of psychopathy we have been discussing. Use of the category and the ICD-10 is prominent in Europe and some other parts of the world but is less common in North America. **Sociopathy** is also sometimes used interchangeably with psychopathy. It first emerged in the early twentieth century as a response to the prevailing view that the environment is the primary influence governing the development of psychopathic individuals (Hervé, 2007). The important role of social forces is even reflected in the name. The term was still in vogue in the 1950s and found its way into early editions of the *DSM* (Arrigo & Shipley, 2001; Hervé, 2007). The third edition, published in 1980, dispensed with this label in favour of ASPD (Arrigo & Shipley, 2001). Sociopathy has not existed as a diagnostic category in any formal classification scheme since, although the terminology still lingers.

asymmetrical relationship between ASPD and psychopathy The empirical finding that many people diagnosed with ASPD are not considered psychopathic but most people assessed by the PCL-R as psychopathic are also diagnosed with ASPD.

dissocial personality disorder A mental disorder that corresponds to the construct of psychopathy and is recognized in the World Health Organization's International Classification of Diseases.

sociopathy A label previously used to describe the construct of psychopathy. Early editions of the *DSM* included this term, but it no longer exists as a diagnostic category.

Empirical Links between Psychopathy and Criminal Behaviour

Psychopathy and criminality are empirically related yet distinct concepts. Some psychopaths—referred to as **subcriminal psychopaths**—engage in unethical and immoral conduct without attracting the attention of the criminal justice system and therefore are not criminals (Hare, 1996). For example, Babiak (1995, 2000) observed corporate employees who manifest all the affective and interpersonal symptoms of psychopaths without any accompanying criminal behaviours. Even in the absence of illegal behaviour, these "industrial psychopaths" are counterproductive and destructive to their workplaces (see the case study on "Dave").

Just as not all psychopaths are criminals, not all criminals are psychopaths (Hart & Hare, 1997). Only a relatively small proportion of criminals are psychopaths; however, the amount of crime and violence they commit far exceeds what is expected based on their representation in the population (e.g. Hare, 1996). This propensity to engage in crime is what makes psychopaths relevant to our understanding of criminal behaviour.

CASE STUDY

"Dave"

Paul Babiak (1995; Babiak & Hare, 2006), an industrial/organizational psychologist and leading authority on psychopaths in the workplace, described the case of "Dave." Dave was in his mid-thirties when he interviewed for a job at a rapidly growing electronics firm in the United States. He immediately impressed company officials: he was good-looking, articulate, and his resumé was exceptional for someone his age. After a routine reference check, he was hired. In the beginning, Dave came across favourably to his colleagues. He frequently arrived to the office early in the morning and appeared to stay late into the evening. He seemed creative, intelligent, and ambitious. He was also skillful at ingratiating himself to others and soon had a small circle of allies in various parts of the company, whom he could count on for support and assistance.

Those who worked closely with Dave were not impressed for long. He proved to be unreliable, and his work often failed to meet expectations. On one occasion, he submitted a major report containing plagiarized text and falsified business figures. He frequently

turned up to meetings late and tended to disrupt the discussion. Team members noted that he was domineering, aggressive, and rude. Other co-workers thought he was conceited because of his constant boasting, but he seemed indifferent to their opinion. He had also attempted to bring company equipment home without permission, purchased supplies without authorization, and padded his resumé. When Dave was confronted about his behaviour, he either dismissed the concerns as unimportant or became irate with those who spoke to him. He quickly developed a reputation as a phony who used lies to gain his colleagues' trust and then take advantage of them.

Those who worked less frequently with Dave saw him in a much more positive light. A number of senior executives identified him as someone with management potential, although none of them could provide specific examples of his accomplishments. When employees reported that Dave was misappropriating company time and materials to further a private business venture, management told them to leave him alone, making it plain to all that they continued to hold him in high regard. It became apparent that Dave had established relationships with some of the executives to secure his reputation and to bad-mouth his immediate supervisor, whose job Dave wanted.

Babiak (1995) conducted an organizational study of the company and, using the PCL:SV, concluded that Dave was psychopathic. He scored extremely high on the interpersonal and affective symptoms (11 out of a possible score of 12) and moderately high on the deviant lifestyle symptoms (8 out of 12), a common trend among corporate psychopaths. As an interesting epilogue to the case, Dave was promoted after his supervisor moved into a new position. According to Babiak (1995), fellow employees reported that Dave was even more overbearing than ever.

For the complete case history of Dave and more information on corporate psychopaths, see Babiak and Hare's (2006) *Snakes in Suits: When Psychopaths Go to Work.*

Frequency and Versatility of Offending

Criminal psychopaths are prolific offenders. They tend to commit a large number of offences, especially in relation to the time they spend free in society. Research consistently finds that psychopaths commit an average of 1.5 to 2 times more criminal offences than do non-psychopaths, a difference that extends to both non-violent and violent crimes (Haapasalo, 1994; Hare & McPherson, 1984b; Simourd & Hoge, 2000; Wong, 1984). Porter, Birt, and Boer (2001) examined the offence histories of more than 300 federal prisoners and found that, even without accounting for the time spent incarcerated, the psychopaths committed a significantly greater number of non-violent (27.9 versus 13.4) and violent (7.3 versus 4.5) offences on average than the non-psychopaths.

Psychopaths do not change their behaviour simply because they are incarcerated. Studies show that psychopaths continue to be disruptive and disregard the rules even when they are imprisoned (Guy, Edens, Anthony, & Douglas, 2005). Wong (1984) reported that the mean number of institutional infractions incurred per year by psychopaths (6.3) significantly outpaced the corresponding rate for non-psychopaths (0.7). Other studies do not directly compare the frequency of infractions but nevertheless confirm a relationship between psychopathy and various indexes of institutional misconduct, ranging from non-compliant behaviour and property damage to verbal aggression and physical assaults on inmates and staff (Edens, Buffington-Vollum, Colwell, Johnson, & Johnson, 2002; Hare & McPherson, 1984b; Hare et al., 2000).

Psychopaths also exhibit considerable criminal diversity. Studies report that psychopaths commit a significantly greater range of offences than non-psychopaths do (Kosson, Smith, & Newman, 1990; Simourd & Hoge, 2000; Porter et al., 2001). It appears that psychopaths are more likely to avail themselves of whatever criminal opportunities they come across than to pursue a single type of crime. This probably explains why some studies find that psychopathy exhibits a relatively weak relationship to sexual offending (Brown & Forth, 1997; Douglas & Webster, 1999; Porter et al., 2001). Psychopaths might engage in sexual offending, but they are just as likely to commit a different type of offence (Hare, 2003).

The Nature of Violence

Psychopaths are remarkable for not only the quantity of their offences but also the nature of those offences. Research shows that they are much more likely than non-psychopaths to incur convictions for violent offences. A study by Hare and McPherson (1984b) divided a sample of incarcerated offenders into three groups: psychopaths, mixed, and non-psychopaths. The percentage of each group with at least one violent conviction was 85, 64, and 54, respectively. Other researchers confirm these general results (Serin, 1991; Simourd & Hoge, 2000).

The violence of psychopaths is distinguishable from that of other offenders in several notable ways relating to their motivation, arousal level, victims, and degree of planning. Williamson, Hare, and Wong (1987) reviewed police reports to determine the surrounding characteristics of the most serious offence committed by a sample of incarcerated male offenders. They found that the violence of psychopaths was significantly more likely to target male strangers and involve motivations characterized by material gain or revenge, whereas non-psychopaths were more likely to commit violence against females known to them, usually during times of extreme emotional arousal (see Table 6.2). The researchers concluded that psychopathic violence lacked the "affective colouring and understandable motives" that characterize other offenders' violence (Williamson et al., 1987, p. 460). Similarly, Serin (1991) observed more weapons use, threats, and instrumental aggression in the criminal histories of psychopathic prisoners. In short, the violence of psychopaths tends to be characteristically instrumental in nature.

In an effort to measure instrumental and reactive violence more directly, Cornell and colleagues (1996) examined the criminal histories of incarcerated male offenders. The results revealed two groups: one committed reactive violence only and the other engaged in

Table 6.2 Characteristics of violence perpetrated by psychopaths and non-psychopaths

Characteristic	Psychopaths[1] %	Non-Psychopaths %
Offence		
Murder	14	46
Serious violent assaults	17	0
Robbery	45	12
Kidnapping	0	10
Criminal negligence, death, or serious injury	2	7
Sexual assault	21	24
Motive		
Material gain	45	15
High emotional arousal (e.g. jealousy, rage)	2	32
Revenge or retribution	10	0
Sexual gratification	21	24
Self-defence	0	2
None/no information	21	27
Perpetrator–victim relationships		
Family, friend, or acquaintance	36	66
Stranger	64	34

Note
1. Psychopaths n = 42; non-psychopaths n = 41.

Source: Copyright © 1987 by the American Psychological Association. Reproduced with permission. S. Williamson, R.D. Hare, & S. Wong. (1987). "Violence: Criminal psychopaths and their victims." *Canadian Journal of Behavioural Science*, 19, 454–462. The use of APA information does not imply endorsement by APA.

both types of violence. Virtually no one had a history consisting solely of instrumental violence. Comparisons of the two groups revealed that instrumentally violent offenders were much more psychopathic than the offenders who engaged in reactive violence alone. The findings support the view that most violent offenders engage in reactive violence but instrumental, predatory violence is more peculiar to individuals who manifest psychopathic traits.

Building on this research, Dempster et al. (1996) rated the most recent violent offence committed by a group of offenders, using Cornell and colleagues' (1996) coding scheme. Among other things, the results showed that the interpersonal/affective symptoms of psychopathy relate to features of instrumental violence and the behavioural symptoms relate to aspects of reactive violence. This result matches our earlier statement that many offenders exhibit the behavioural characteristics of psychopathy (Hart & Dempster, 1997). On the other hand, most non-psychopathic offenders lack the affective and interpersonal characteristics of psychopathy linked to instrumental violence, which probably explains why it is less common. Psychopaths manifest the full constellation of symptoms, which accounts for their tendency to commit both types of violence.

Hart and Dempster (1997) suggest that psychopathic violence is often imbued with characteristics of both forms of violence simultaneously because psychopaths tend to engage in goal-directed violence that is opportunistic and spontaneous. They fittingly refer to this violence as "impulsively instrumental" (p. 227). Hare (1993) describes an illustrative case involving a highly psychopathic individual who set out to buy beer but realized part way to the store that he had left his wallet at home. Instead of walking back the few blocks to retrieve it, he found a large piece of wood, which he used to rob a nearby gas station, seriously wounding the employee in the process.

Murder and Serial Murder

You may have noticed a curious finding in Table 6.2—psychopaths are less likely than other violent offenders to murder their victims. Other investigations have turned up similar results (e.g. Hare & McPherson, 1984b; Porter et al., 2001; Rasmussen, Storsaeter, & Levander, 1999). This finding seems counter-intuitive, but it makes sense if one is mindful of the fact that most homicides involve reactive violence occurring in emotionally charged, interpersonal conflicts between intimate partners or other close relationships. Psychopaths generally lack meaningful relationships and do not seem to experience the strong emotions, such as jealousy and rage, that often precede this type of violence. Thus, they are missing two of the key ingredients that ordinarily fuel murder. Two studies lend some, albeit limited, support to this view. Both investigations reviewed the files of incarcerated murderers and found that incidents of reactive homicide were exceedingly uncommon among the psychopaths in the samples (Porter & Woodworth, 2007, Woodworth & Porter, 2002).

Serial murder, which involves the same person killing two or more victims at different times (see Chapter 11), is very different. Unlike solitary acts of murder, serial murder does not tend to be the result of emotional interpersonal conflict. It is more often instrumental in nature and perpetrated against strangers for sexual purposes (Kraemer, Lord, & Heilbrun, 2004). Although it is generally assumed that serial killers must be psychopaths, studies show that this is not always the case (Beasley, 2004; Stone, 1998). Nevertheless, the traits of psychopathy are especially well-suited for someone who repeatedly engages in murder. It is easy to see how traits such as superficial charm, deceitfulness, egocentricity, and lack of empathy and remorse might be useful for luring strangers and getting them to drop their guard, committing the extreme acts of cruelty that often accompany serial murder, and ending victims' lives without psychological repercussions. Not surprisingly, assessments carried out on known serial killers reveal that many, perhaps even most, are also psychopaths (Beasley, 2004; Stone, 1998).

Sexual Violence

The unique nature of violence perpetrated by psychopaths also extends to sexual offences. Brown and Forth (1997) noted sharp differences in the emotional affect of psychopaths and non-psychopaths in the hours preceding the commission of a sexual offence: the former tended to experience a positive mood, whereas the latter were more likely to report feeling anxious and alienated. Their motivations for sexual offending also differ. Unlike many sexual offenders, psychopaths often have non-sexual motivations (Barbaree, Seto, Serin, Amos, & Preston, 1994; Brown & Forth, 1997). Research has established a relationship between psychopathy and rapes that are opportunistic acts of instrumental aggression, a finding that is consistent with Hart and Dempster's (1997) general observation that psychopathic violence tends to be impulsively instrumental. There is also evidence connecting psychopathy to sexual crimes that have angry and sadistic overtones (Barbaree et al., 1994; Brown & Forth, 1997; Porter, Woodworth, Earle, Drugge, & Boer, 2003).

Criminal Recidivism

One of the criminal justice system's overriding concerns is identifying offenders who are at risk of recidivating if they are released back into the community. Hart, Kropp, and Hare (1988) conducted the first study examining psychopathy's ability to predict recidivism using Hare's original PCL. They assessed a sample of incarcerated offenders and found that highly psychopathic individuals released into the community on conditions failed faster and more often than other offenders (see the "Researching" box). Subsequent studies replicated the findings for general recidivism and extended them by showing that psychopaths are also more likely to recidivate violently (Serin, 1996; Serin, Peters, & Barbaree, 1990; Serin & Amos, 1995). Despite the relatively poor success rate of released psychopaths in these studies, Wong (1984) found that psychopaths were just as likely as non-psychopaths to be granted parole. He speculated that their charming and manipulative interpersonal skills made psychopaths particularly adept at convincing parole boards that they had changed and were determined to lead law-abiding lives. Nowadays, many prison systems and parole boards are routinely provided with information concerning offender psychopathy assessments when they make case decisions.

Various meta-analytic reviews of the overall body of research confirm that psychopathy is a robust predictor of future criminal and violent behaviour (Gendreau, Goggin, & Smith, 2002; Hemphill, Hare, & Wong, 1998; Salekin, Rogers, & Sewell, 1996; Walters, 2003). Evidence specific to sexual recidivism is more ambivalent. Some studies find that psychopathy is related to the commission of future sexual offences (e.g. Firestone, Bradford, Greenberg, & Serran, 2000; Hanson & Harris, 2000; Quinsey, Rice, & Harris, 1995), while other studies do not (e.g. Barbaree, Seto, Langton, & Peacock, 2001; Hildebrand, de Ruiter, & de Vogel, 2004; Långström & Grann, 2000). The mixed nature of these results probably relates to the observation made previously: psychopaths are typically criminal generalists who show no particular tendency toward sexual offending.

Researching Criminal and Violent Behaviour

Psychopaths on Parole

Hart, Kropp, and Hare (1988) conducted an investigation of criminal recidivism in a sample of over 200 Canadian male federal offenders. Based on the men's PCL scores, the researchers divided the sample into three groups: non-psychopaths (n = 68), intermediate (n = 94), and psychopaths (n = 69). All the offenders had been released into the community on parole or mandatory supervision (another form of conditional release, available to offenders after serving at least two-thirds of their sentence). To evaluate offender performance, Hart and colleagues searched the parole service's official records. They considered a release to be a failure if the offender incurred a new conviction or his release was revoked (which could be due to breaching a condition) during the release period. It is clear from the results, shown in Figure 6.1, that the higher the psychopathy rating, the more likely the offender was to fail.

One difficulty with analyzing this type of data is that the length of the release period varies for each offender. Offenders released the earliest were studied for the longest amount of time and therefore had a greater chance (or more opportunity) to fail than offenders released later. To account for these differences, the researchers made use of survival analysis, which estimates the likelihood of an offender surviving (i.e. remaining free on release) over time. The results revealed that the psychopaths failed much more quickly than the other offenders. Hart and colleagues estimated that there was an 80 per cent chance of the non-psychopaths remaining free after one year, compared to 53 per cent of the intermediate group and only 38 per cent of the psychopaths. Extending the survival period to three years dropped these percentages to 71, 38, and 18, respectively.

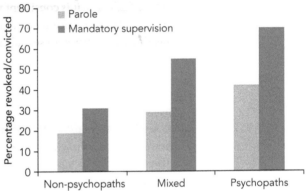

Figure 6.1 Performance on conditional release by level of psychopathy.

Source: Copyright © 1988 by the American Psychological Association. Reproduced with permission. S. D. Hart et al. (1988). Performance of male psychopaths following conditional release from prison. *Journal of Consulting and Clinical Psychology*, 56, 227–232. The use of APA information does not imply endorsement by APA.

That said, some evidence suggests that the combination of psychopathy and sexual deviance may be a powerful predictor of future sexual offences (Hildebrand et al., 2004; Rice & Harris, 1997). This possibility first emerged in a study conducted by Rice and Harris (1997), which followed up on sex offenders who had been released into the community for as many as 10 years. The researchers found that psychopathy was no better at predicting future sex crimes than sexual deviance; however, the combination of the two variables produced a strong interaction effect whereby sexually deviant psychopaths were significantly more likely to commit sexual reoffences than were non-deviant or non-psychopathic offenders. Thus, the presence of sexual deviance seems to provide a proclivity for sexual offences that does not otherwise exist among psychopaths.

Psychopathy and Gender

Psychopathy is not exclusive to males. In fact, Cleckley's (1941/1976) description of the disorder contains two case studies involving females. These women lied, stole, cheated, and generally failed to meet their social obligations and abide by the rules, much like the men Cleckley described. Aileen Wuornos, the subject of a case study in Chapter 5, was assessed for psychopathy by a three-person team that included the forensic psychiatrist who interviewed her before she was executed (Myers et al., 2005). She was rated 32 on the PCL-R, which exceeds the conventional cut-off used to diagnose psychopathy. Joanna Dennehy was also diagnosed as a psychopath (Chivers, 2014; Gover, 2014; see the case study). In 2013 she murdered three people in England over a two-week period, largely out of curiosity about how it would feel to kill someone. Like Wuornos, her case is unusual not only in terms of the extreme and predatory nature of the violence involved but also because of the sexual overtones associated with the killings.

A possible reason for the scant attention paid to female psychopaths may be that the disorder is more pronounced among males. Research using the PCL-R and its related measures generally reports that females receive lower mean scores than their male counterparts (Forth, Brown, Hart, & Hare, 1996; Grann, 2000; Rutherford, Cacciola, Alterman, & McKay, 1996). These lower scores correspond to lower base rates of psychopathy among females, which in correctional samples typically ranges from 11 to 16 per cent for females compared to 15 to 30 per cent for males (Jackson & Richards, 2007). More research is needed to uncover the reasons for this difference, but two possibilities include biased study samples and/or assessment criteria that favour characteristics more frequently exhibited by males (Jackson & Richards, 2007; Verona & Vitale, 2006). Of course, it could also be the case that psychopathy is genuinely more prevalent among males than females.

Researchers speculate that psychopathy does not present the same way in females as it does in males due to gender differences in socialization experiences (Cale & Lilienfeld, 2002; Jackson & Richards, 2007). Bolt, Hare, Vitale, and Newman's (2004) analyses of the individual items on the PCL-R reveal that interpersonal and affective items function much the same in both genders but that greater discrepancies exist for the behavioural symptoms. To illustrate, Verona and Vitale (2006) point out that the behavioural expression of aggression tends to be quite different. Males are much more likely to be physically aggressive—punching, kicking, or hitting an adversary—whereas females are more likely to rely on covert or relational aggression such as spreading malicious gossip or ostracizing someone they dislike from their social group. Other researchers also report that gender differences are most apparent on behavioural-related symptoms (Rutherford et al., 1996; Salekin, Rogers, & Sewell, 1997). To address this concern, there are calls to include items specifically tailored for assessing psychopathy in women, such as sexual promiscuity, child abuse and neglect, and covert forms of aggression (Vitale & Newman, 2001; Verona & Vitale, 2006).

With respect to criminal behaviour, the small pool of available research generally confirms that the relationship of psychopathic symptoms to criminal histories for violent and non-violent offences is the same for men and women (Cooke, 1995; Vitale, Smith, Brinkley, & Newman, 2002; Rutherford et al., 1996; Weiler & Widom, 1996). Few studies have investigated the ability of psychopathy to predict recidivism among female offenders

CASE STUDY

Joanna Dennehy

Peterborough, England—In March 2013 Joanna Dennehy stabbed three men to death and critically injured two more over a two-week period (Peachey, 2014). She lured her first victim, Lukasz Slaboszewski, to a house by sending him sexually suggestive texts and stabbed him in the heart when he arrived (Dodd, 2014). A week and a half later, she murdered her roommate, John Chapman, by stabbing him multiple times, including twice in the heart. She also murdered her landlord, Kevin Lee, later that same day (Peachey, 2014). In a final act of humiliation, she put his body in a black dress

Photo 6.3 Joanna Dennehy poses for a photo while on the run for murder. She is only the third woman in England's criminal history to be considered too dangerous to ever be released from prison. Photo: © Rex Features 2005. All rights reserved/The Canadian Press.

and dumped him in a ditch, purposely exposing his buttocks (Dodd, 2014). After the killings, Dennehy reportedly phoned a friend and sang Britney Spears's song "Oops . . . I Did It Again" (Peachey, 2014).

A few days later, Dennehy persuaded a male companion to travel with her to Hereford in search of more victims. There, in separate incidents occurring minutes apart, she spotted and attacked two men who were out walking (Duel & Hall, 2014). As she stabbed the second victim, John Rogers, she said, "Oh, look, you're bleeding. I'd better do some more" (Peachey, 2014, para. 1). Despite the gravity of their injuries, both victims managed to survive. When Dennehy and her accomplice were picked up by police a short time later, she jokingly told them that it had been a "hectic week" (Duell & Hall, 2014, para. 31).

One of the most striking things about Dennehy is that she enjoyed a relatively stable upbringing and was a well-adjusted, bright, and active child (Morris, 2014). Family members report that this all changed in

her mid-teens, when she began hanging out with older boys and skipping classes. At 15, she ran away with 20-year-old John Treanor and began drinking and using drugs. Her relationship with Treanor was a volatile one, plagued by constant arguments and violence, especially when she was drunk (Peachey, 2014). The pair had two children, but Dennehy, who complained she had not wanted kids, frequently walked out on the family for long stretches of time (Morris, 2014). Her violent outbursts eventually became too much for Treanor, who left with the children. Dennehy's behaviour continued to deteriorate and, in the years leading up to the murders, she drifted from one place to another, often resorting to theft and prostitution to support herself.

Criminologist Samantha Lundrigan noted that Dennehy is a "classic psychopath" ("Joanna Dennehy" 2014; Morris, 2014). The judge who sentenced her to life in prison described her as "cruel, calculating, selfish and manipulative" (Dodd, 2014, para. 1). The court also disclosed that she told a psychiatrist, "I killed to see how I would feel, to see if I was as cold as I thought I was" (Duell & Hall, 2014, para. 36). It seems that Dennehy revelled in the notoriety associated with the killings. She reportedly showed the corpse of one victim to a teenaged girl and celebrated when the first accounts of the murders were broadcast by the media (Dodd, 2014; Peachey, 2014). Dr Lundrigan speculated that "If she is a psychopath, she will like to have attention on her. Once the limelight is gone, she may feel compelled to offer some kind of explanation in order to keep the focus on her" (Peachey, 2014, para. 16).

thus far, and those that exist have produced mixed results (Douglas, Vincent, & Edens, 2006). Although more research is sorely needed, these findings suggest that psychopathy may not be as important for understanding and explaining the reoffence behaviour of women as it is for men.

Psychopathy and Crime across the Lifespan

Psychopathic Symptoms and Aging

There continues to be considerable debate around the onset of psychopathy. Some researchers suggest that tell-tale signs of the disorder can be found as young as preadolescence and even childhood. Supporters of this perspective point out it is unlikely that psychopathic personalities suddenly emerge the moment a person reaches adulthood without manifesting prior indications of the disorder (Salekin, 2006). Lynam (1996) has implicated hyperactivity, impulsivity, and attention deficits as a foreboding cluster of symptoms that elevate a child's risk of becoming a "fledgling" psychopath. Among the children with these difficulties, those with callous, unemotional traits—such as the absence of empathy, lack of remorse, and poverty of emotions—seem to exhibit the most serious antisocial behaviour (Barry et al., 2000; Christian, Frick, Hill, Tyler, & Frazer, 1997; Frick, Kimonis, Dandreaux, & Farell, 2003; Frick, Stickle, Dandreaux, Farell, & Kimonis, 2005). These and other findings have led to the suggestion that this interpersonal style may constitute an important formative step toward developing a fully blown psychopathic disorder as an adult (Frick, 2007).

Opponents of this view question whether personality disorders can exist at a point in the lifespan when, as is widely accepted, personality is still developing (Hart, Watt, & Vincent, 2002; Vincent & Hart, 2002). Some symptoms of psychopathy are common, temporary, and perhaps even normative features of human development (Edens, Skeem, Cruise, & Cauffman, 2001; Seagrave & Grisso, 2002; Vincent & Hart, 2002). For example, many children appear self-centred, impulsive, irresponsible, and even antisocial to one degree or another, but in most cases these tendencies diminish or disappear as they mature into adults (Edens et al., 2001; Seagrave & Grisso, 2002). Applying the construct of psychopathy to youth risks misidentification (Vincent & Hart, 2002). It is perhaps equivalent to saying someone is short before his or her adolescent growth spurt—while it might be true at that moment, the person's final height may be quite different in adulthood.

In an effort to address some of these questions, researchers are beginning to examine the extent to which psychopathic traits remain stable over time. Studies using a variety of measures report that overall ratings of psychopathy do not show large fluctuations during the formative years of development (Frick et al., 2003; Lee, Klaver, Hart, Moretti, & Douglas, 2009; Loney, Taylor, Butler, Iacono, 2007; Lynam et al., 2009). Moreover, there is evidence that the stability of psychopathic traits increases throughout adolescence (Lee et al., 2009). In other words, psychopathic traits displayed by older adolescents are less likely to change over time compared to those shown by younger adolescents. This pattern is consistent with our general understanding that personality becomes more inflexible with age.

The more critical question, however, is whether children with psychopathic traits grow up to become adult psychopaths (Seagrave & Grisso, 2002). One study addressing this issue found that many individuals who would be diagnosed as psychopaths on the basis of their symptoms as teenagers would not be in adulthood (Lynam, Caspi, Moffitt, Loeber, & Stouthamer-Loeber, 2007). This finding is encouraging because it suggests that the outcome of youths who show early signs of psychopathy can change with the right intervention. Unfortunately, the factors responsible for influencing the developmental pathway of those youths who did not become psychopaths are not yet entirely clear, but early indications point to the importance of parenting and peer relationships (Salekin, Rosenbaum, Lee, & Lester, 2009).

Research examining the stability of psychopathic traits in adulthood is confined to a single published study. Harpur and Hare (1994) employed a cross-sectional study design comparing different participants to see if younger and older individuals varied in terms of their psychopathy ratings. The weakness of this design is that it attributes any differences detected between younger and older study participants to age-related changes. The comparisons of mean scores revealed that the interpersonal/affective symptoms showed no change with age but that behavioural symptom ratings declined steadily with advancing age. These results may indicate that the antisocial and deviant lifestyle components of psychopathy undergo age-related changes but core personality characteristics remain intact and unaltered.

The Criminal Careers of Psychopaths

The criminal careers of psychopaths begin early and endure for many years. Wong (1984) examined a random sample of more than 300 federal offenders and observed that the age at first arrest was 18 years for the psychopaths versus 24 years for the non-psychopaths. Other investigations have yielded similar results (Devita, Forth, & Hare, 1990; Hare, McPherson, & Forth, 1988; Moltó, Poy, & Torrubia, 2000; Porter et al., 2001; Rasmussen et al., 1999). Moreover, adolescents displaying psychopathic traits are remarkably similar to adult psychopaths in terms of their antisocial and criminal behaviour. They exhibit greater criminal diversity, have more extensive criminal involvement, and commit more serious criminal offences than adolescents without psychopathic traits (Brandt, Kennedy, Patrick, & Curtin, 1997; Kosson et al., 2002; Murrie, Cornell, Kaplan, McConville, & Levy-Eklon, 2004; Vincent, Vitacco, Grisso, & Corrado, 2003). Adolescent psychopathy is also related to general and violent recidivism, although some studies indicate that the relationship to the former is more attenuated in adolescents relative to adults (Brandt et al., 1997; Catchpole & Gretton, 2003; Corrado, Vincent, Hart, & Cohen, 2004; Forth, Hart, & Hare, 1990; Gretton, Hare, & Catchpole, 2004; Vincent et al., 2003).

A handful of studies have looked at whether the criminal activity of adult psychopaths changes as they age (Hare, Williamson, & Harpur, 1988; Harris, Rice, & Cormier, 1991; Porter et al., 2001). Investigations by Hare et al. (1988) and Porter et al. (2001) calculated the number of crimes committed by incarcerated psychopaths and non-psychopaths for different five-year periods during adulthood (e.g. ages 21–25, 26–30, 31–35, etc.). Several findings common to both investigations emerged. Generally speaking, the psychopaths proved to be significantly more criminally active than the non-psychopaths at every interval, from early adulthood until approximately 40 years of age. This finding was consistent for both violent and non-violent offences. By the time the psychopaths entered their forties, however, their criminal offending declined steeply to the point that it was no longer different (Hare et al., 1988) and, in some cases, was below the non-psychopaths' activity level (Porter et al., 2001). With respect to this latter finding, a major difference appeared between the two studies. Porter et al. (2001) noticed major reductions in both non-violent and violent offending after age 40, but Hare et al. (1988) observed a decline in only non-violent offences while the level of violent offences appeared largely unchanged.

Whether these discrepant results represent genuine differences or methodological artifacts is unclear. Hare et al.'s (1988) finding is the product of a methodologically stronger study. Unlike the cross-sectional study by Porter et al. (2001), it employed longitudinal analyses, albeit with a relatively small number of offenders. The only other study to use this approach found that the rate of violent recidivism for psychopaths showed little fluctuation as a function of age and remained significantly higher than the rate for non-psychopaths across all periods (Harris et al., 1991). These findings support the results reported by Hare and colleagues. Keep in mind that all three studies are hampered by very small samples of psychopaths in the most senior age brackets and, as a consequence, the results would change dramatically if the outcomes of even a few participants were different.

The pattern of age-related decline in criminal activity observed among psychopaths in these studies corresponds roughly to the downward slope of the age–crime curve. This raises the possibility that psychopaths experience the same age-related changes that appear to occur in many other criminals as they pass through middle age. Hare (1996) argues that these outward signs of change are deceptive and that psychopaths continue to be self-absorbed, deceitful, and remorseless throughout their lives, as evidenced by the aforementioned finding that interpersonal/affective symptom ratings remain relatively constant. Hare (1996) believes that, rather than undergoing any meaningful change, older psychopaths become weary of, or perhaps more adept at, avoiding the most overtly criminal acts and transition to antisocial behaviours that are less likely to bring them into contact with the criminal justice system.

Psychopathy across Culture

The construct of psychopathy appears to cut across historical, political, and cultural lines. Documentary evidence of individuals we might identify as psychopaths can be traced throughout the ages and as far back as biblical times (Berrios, 1996; Cleckley, 1941/1976; Rotenberg & Diamond, 1971). Anthropological investigation has revealed the presence of psychopathic-like individuals in non-industrial societies. According to Murphy (1976), the Yorubas people of Nigeria speak of *aranakan*, individuals who resemble the Western construct of psychopathy. Similarly, the Inuit of northwest Alaska refer to the *kunlangeta*— members of their community who show no regard for the accepted rules. They lie, cheat, steal, avoid their responsibility to hunt and provide for the community, and sexually exploit the partners of other community members while they are away. The Inuit solution for dealing with the *kunlangeta* is to take them hunting and push them off the ice when no one is looking (Murphy, 1976).

The emergence of the PCL–R and its derivatives has provided a common instrument for measuring and comparing psychopathy across cultures. Numerous studies have investigated the international presence of psychopathy, although most of this research is concentrated within European countries (Sullivan & Kosson, 2006). Using the traditional cut-off score of 30, these studies confirm the presence of psychopaths outside North America (e.g. Cooke, 1998; Folino, Marengo, Marchiano, & Ascazibar, 2004). While psychopaths appear to exist in every society, there is evidence that the prevalence or level of the disorder fluctuates from culture to culture. Reviews of international studies using the PCL-R report that mean scores for prisoners are higher in North America than in other countries, but the pattern is just the opposite for psychiatric settings (Cooke, 1998; Sullivan & Kosson, 2006). Sullivan and Kosson (2006) suggest that this pattern could reflect different practices in criminal justice and mental health systems rather than cultural differences in psychopathy. It may be that psychopaths are more likely to end up in prison in North America and in the mental health system in Europe.

The empirical relationships found between psychopathy and criminal behaviour in North American studies have largely been replicated in international research. Studies outside North America also find that the offending behaviour of psychopaths is more extensive, diverse, and extreme in nature and frequency compared to that of non-psychopaths (e.g. Hare et al., 2000; Moltó et al., 2000; Rasmussen et al., 1999). As in North America, psychopathy has proven to be a powerful predictor of general and violent recidivism in studies with European samples (Hare et al., 2000; Grann, Långström, Tengström, & Kullgren, 1999). Sullivan and Kosson (2006) claim that the most potentially persuasive evidence of psychopathy's universality would be experimental studies demonstrating that the same cognitive and psychophysiological deficits can be found in psychopaths everywhere, regardless of cultural context. Unfortunately, research in these areas is almost exclusively confined to North American samples. Nevertheless, the body of available evidence suggests that psychopathy is a meaningful construct for understanding criminal behaviour across cultures.

Theoretical Explanations of the Psychopathy–Crime Link

As we have seen, a considerable body of research demonstrates a link between psychopathy and various dimensions of crime, including its frequency, nature, and severity. There is also limited evidence supporting the generalizability of this connection across age, gender, and cultures. Although the ties between psychopathy and crime are well established, the underlying mechanism(s) responsible remains uncertain. Researchers have developed various theories on the subject, five of which are outlined in this section: Lykken's fearlessness model, Hare's hypoemotionality model, Newman's response modulation model, hostile attribution bias, and Baumeister's threatened egoism hypothesis.

Lykken's Fearlessness Model

Introduced more than half a century ago, David Lykken's (1957, 1995) **fearlessness model** is grounded in two lines of research discussed in Chapter 3. One shows that psychopaths exhibit weak physiological responses in anticipation of aversive stimuli. You may recall that people normally show heightened responses (e.g. increased heart rate and skin conductance) when they expect an impending electrical shock or some other unpleasant stimulus, which is believed to reflect their level of fear. The comparatively low physiological reaction of psychopaths in these situations is generally viewed as an indication that they feel little anxiety or fear.

The other line of research reveals impaired passive avoidance learning among psychopaths. Passive avoidance learning tasks require participants to inhibit a response; for example, most people would not knowingly make an incorrect choice while navigating a

fearlessness model A theory postulating that the failure to experience fear increases a person's likelihood of committing criminal behaviour because he or she is unafraid of the consequences, such as being caught and punished.

mental maze if that mistake resulted in an electric shock (Lykken, 1957). Psychopaths are able to learn the correct path through the maze just as well as non-psychopaths, but they perform relatively poorly at avoiding the incorrect choices. Lykken (1957, 1995) believes this is because they are not afraid of the shock. The same fearlessness also explains psychopaths' tendency to engage in criminal behaviour—they are not afraid of getting caught and punished for the things they do (Lykken, 1995).

Hare's Hypoemotionality Model

hypoemotionality model
A theory postulating that psychopaths' emotional deficits increase their likelihood of committing criminal behaviour because they have no feelings for other people and do not experience any distress over causing harm.

Hare's (1993, 1996) **hypoemotionality model** is broader than Lykken's. It proposes a more generalized emotional deficit that includes the failure to experience fear but extends to the full range of emotions that are all thought to be impaired (Hart & Dempster, 1997). Evidence from a variety of studies supports the hypoemotionality model. One such investigation examined the psychopath's ability to grasp the emotional meaning of different statements (Hare et al., 1988). Participants were presented with a series of target phrases (e.g. "a man thrown overboard from a sinking ship") and asked to match their emotional tones with one of four other phrases. Although the task is relatively straightforward for most people, psychopaths often made mistakes. They were much more likely than non-psychopaths to choose "a man surfing on a large wave" as a match than "a man running from a monster." Both situations are highly arousing, but they convey very different emotional tones. The former depicts the excitement of surfing; the latter involves the fear of being chased, which correctly matches the fear of being thrown overboard. Hare (1998) interprets the inability of psychopaths to discriminate between positive and negative emotions as evidence that they show a "confusion of emotional polarity" (p. 119). It seems that they do not appreciate the emotional quality or significance of the events around them.

In a similar vein, Blair and colleagues (1995) observed that, when psychopaths are presented with a story in which the protagonist intentionally harms someone else, they are much more likely than non-psychopaths to believe that he or she will feel happy. Non-psychopaths appropriately attribute feelings of guilt. These impairments in emotion recognition extend to the detection of voice tone and facial expression. Several studies show that psychopaths perform very poorly when it comes to detecting sad and fearful facial expressions and sad vocal tones (Blair, et al., 2002; Blair et al., 2004; Stevens, Charman, & Blair, 2001). The implication of these affective deficits for criminal behaviour is not difficult to grasp. Anyone who fails to recognize or appreciate the pain and suffering of others is missing an important restraint that might otherwise dissuade them from victimizing another person.

Newman's Response Modulation Model

response modulation model
A theory postulating that psychopaths display an impaired ability to monitor and adjust their behaviour, leading them to overlook or disregard factors that would stop most people in the same situation from initiating or continuing a criminal course of conduct.

Over the past 20 years, Newman and colleagues (MaCoon, Wallace, & Newman, 2004; Newman, Patterson, & Kosson, 1987; Patterson & Newman, 1993) developed and elaborated the **response modulation model**, which accounts for the failure of psychopaths to regulate their behaviour. *Response* refers to behaviour and *modulation* to adjusting or changing. The focus of the response modulation model, then, is on the process of adjusting or changing behaviour. It hypothesizes that psychopaths have an impaired ability to inhibit an established behavioural response and shift their attention briefly to evaluate the consequences. The failure of psychopaths to do the latter means that they generally do not adjust their behaviour even when the circumstances warrant it.

Patterson and Newman (1993) believe that psychopaths tend to intensify their original response rather than evaluate and adjust it. Newman and colleagues (1987) demonstrated this pattern using a card-playing task. Participants in the study were instructed to draw one card at a time from the top of the deck. They won money if they drew a face card and lost money for a number card. They could quit the task at any time and keep whatever money they still possessed. Unbeknownst to the participants, the deck was rigged so that the odds of drawing a winning face card diminished throughout the task: 9 of the first set of 10 cards were face cards (90 per cent), then 8 of the second set (80 per cent), 7 of the third set (70 per cent), and so on until there was no chance of winning.

Psychopaths performed much more poorly on the task than non-psychopaths, choosing to play the task longer and losing more money as a consequence. The results suggest that, once the card-drawing behaviour was initiated, psychopaths did not notice the diminishing odds of finding a winner; instead of inhibiting this response, they continued to repeat it long after it stopped being profitable. Administering a modified version of the task with a mandatory five-second delay between each draw eliminated the performance difference between the psychopaths and non-psychopaths. Presumably, the delay forced the psychopaths to evaluate the effect of their responses and, when doing so, they were just as capable of monitoring and making appropriate adjustments to their behaviour as the non-psychopaths.

This same process may explain the criminal and violent behaviour displayed by psychopaths (Vitale & Newman, 2009). Once launched upon a particular course of action, they do not evaluate the effect of their behaviour or notice when it is failing. As a consequence, they "blindly" continue performing the same behaviour and do not make the adjustments needed to realize their goal. It is like following GPS directions to a desired destination without watching the road. Somewhere along the way, you are bound to encounter a red light, a detour, or a pedestrian. If you are not paying attention, you will not alter the course or speed of your vehicle, with potentially disastrous results. Vitale and Newman (2009) postulate that, once psychopaths decide to commit a crime, they become similarly blind to factors that might cause another person to reconsider their actions. Once they have a crime in mind, it is virtually inevitable that they will attempt to carry it out. This theory is attractive because it explains the impulsive and unconsidered qualities that often characterize psychopathic criminal behaviour, especially offences that are almost certain to result in detection and arrest.

Hostile Attribution Bias

Hostile attribution bias, discussed in more detail in Chapter 8, has been advanced to explain violent behaviour. Hostile attributions are cognitions or thinking processes that interpret ambiguous behaviours as antagonistic or malicious. Research has shown that this type of antisocial cognition is associated with an elevated risk of engaging in aggressive and violent behaviour (see Dodge, Price, Bachorowski, & Newman, 1990).

The current view of psychopathy is generally consistent with the presence of an attribution bias. Many clinicians observe that psychopaths see society as a hostile and inhospitable place where the laws of the jungle prevail and everyone must look after himself or herself to survive. Emerging evidence supports these clinical impressions. In one study, Serin (1991) showed psychopaths and non-psychopaths a series of vignettes that described different hypothetical situations with frustrating outcomes. The psychopaths were more likely to view the behaviour depicted as deliberately disrespectful or self-righteous. Compared to

> **hostile attribution bias** The tendency to interpret others' neutral or ambiguous conduct as indications of aggressive intent or behaviour.

the non-psychopaths, they also reported that the behaviour would make them more angry. A subsequent investigation confirmed the presence of hostile attributions among psychopaths; however, the researchers were unable to show that this bias was related to the frequency of past criminal charges for violence (Vitale, Serin, Bolt, & Newman, 2005). While this failure may be due, as the researchers suggest, to the rather crude measure of violence used in the study, it is clear that more research is needed to determine if and how hostile attributions influence psychopathy-related violence.

Baumeister's Threatened Egotism Model

threatened egotism model
A model stating that individuals with an inflated sense of themselves may defend against unfavourable feedback that threatens this unrealistic self-appraisal by reacting aggressively against the information source.

The **threatened egotism** hypothesis was previously covered in Chapter 5 and will be discussed here only as it relates to psychopathy. You will recall that, according to the hypothesis, people who hold the most favourable and distorted opinions of themselves are the individuals most likely to react aggressively against anyone who hurts their pride (Baumeister, 2001; Baumeister et al., 1996). Because psychopaths are extremely narcissistic and grandiose, they should be particularly sensitive to acting violently whenever they feel insulted, negatively evaluated, or treated disrespectfully (Cale & Lilienfeld, 2006; Baumeister et al., 1996). This may explain Williamson and colleagues' (1987) finding that psychopaths appear to be more prone than non-psychopaths to committing violence for revenge (see Table 6.2).

Cale and Lilienfeld (2006) investigated the hypothesis by examining the relationship of self-report measures of psychopathy to collateral reports and documents of aggressive incidents in a sample of approximately one hundred prisoners. They found that psychopathy was significantly related to self-reported anger and documented verbal aggression in situations involving threats to one's self-concept. In short, the more psychopathic an individual, the greater the likelihood that he or she will respond aggressively to insults.

Putting It All Together: A "Perfect Storm" for Crime

All five of the theories discussed above explain how a different subset of psychopathy symptoms can lead to crime and violence. While each theory is independent, it is possible that some combination of the theories, or even all five together, might explain psychopathy's relationship to crime. Accordingly, each theory and its related symptomology may account for some aspects of psychopathic criminal behaviour. The theories could also explain why psychopathy is potentially so devastating; the disorder consists of many symptoms that are each capable of contributing to criminal behaviour in different ways. Hare (1993), in fact, describes psychopathy as a "formula for crime" (p. 86).

Regardless of which theory or theories apply, the symptoms of psychopathy constitute a particularly potent and toxic mix (see Figure 6.2). Many promote crime by making it rewarding or, at the very least, desirable (Hart, 1998a). These crime-promoting symptoms are primarily interpersonal and behavioural in nature. For instance, the need for excitement may lead individuals to go joyriding, steal things for the "rush" it brings, use drugs, and commit other antisocial acts. The enjoyment that psychopaths derive from deceiving others means that acts of forgery, fraud, and personation are likely to be particularly gratifying to them, and their grandiosity increases the chances that they will find the actions of others insulting or unreasonable and feel provoked into violence. This does not mean that

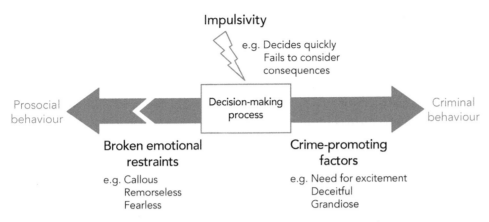

Figure 6.2 The influence of psychopathic symptoms on decision-making.

crime is an automatic or inevitable outcome—the need for excitement, for instance, can lead people to participate in risky or exhilarating sports rather than antisocial behaviour—but the presence of these symptoms can make crime more appealing and thus increase the likelihood of deciding to engage in illegal conduct. In this sense, crime-promoting symptoms serve to "push" psychopaths toward offending.

Other symptoms of psychopathy represent loosened or absent behavioural restraints. These symptoms effectively dampen or remove the inhibitions that stop most people from acting criminally even when it may be attractive or rewarding to do so. Although there are many reasons why most of us do not cheat, steal, or murder, one very powerful set of restraints is the emotional connections we feel toward other people. We understand how people feel when they are victimized and we feel badly when we hurt them. These emotional restraints are missing in psychopaths. They lack remorse and empathy, and they do not feel an attachment or bond to other people. As a consequence, the emotional restraints that normally hold behaviour in check are broken (Hare, 1993; Hart, 1998a; Porter, 1996).

Compounding matters further is the psychopath's characteristic impulsiveness—the tendency to act first and think later. Hart (1998a) identifies two ways in which impulsiveness may increase psychopaths' chances of engaging in crime. First, psychopaths often decide to commit a crime before they have adequately assessed their situation and weighed the different factors that, with more time and consideration, might dissuade them from such acts. Second, psychopaths may impulsively say (e.g. "You're a #$&!! jerk") or do things (e.g. buying things they cannot possibly pay for) that indirectly raise the likelihood of subsequent criminal and violent acts.

Collectively, these symptoms may interact with one another in a synergistic manner. Crime-promoting symptoms that push psychopaths toward behaviours and situations in which crime is a likely outcome go unchecked because of weak or absent emotional restraints. Moreover, their impulsivity means decisions are made quickly and without considering the consequences. That these ill-considered choices frequently involve illegal behaviour is hardly surprising given that psychopathy symptoms create the "perfect storm" for criminal behaviour.

Summary

1. Psychopathy is a disorder defined by a distinct pattern of interpersonal, affective, and behavioural symptoms. The interpersonal style of psychopaths is superficially charming, grandiose, and deceitful. Affectively, psychopaths fail to experience the normal range of human emotions and seem to lack remorse and empathy. Psychopaths' behaviour is characterized by impulsivity, irresponsibility, and a need for excitement. Although antisocial behaviour is commonly associated with psychopathy, there is debate over whether it is a core symptom of the disorder or merely a frequent consequence of the other symptoms.

2. Research of psychopathy over the past several decades has been facilitated by the development of the Hare Psychopathy Checklist. The revised version of this instrument (PCL–R) uses ratings on 20 items to generate scores, ranging from 0 to 40, that reflect how closely an individual resembles clinical descriptions of the prototypical psychopath. A score of 30 or higher is conventionally used as the cut-off for diagnosing someone as psychopathic. The success of the PCL–R has spawned the development of several modified versions intended for different contexts and populations.

3. Antisocial personality disorder (ASPD) is a diagnostic category used by the American Psychiatric Association in the current version of the DSM. ASPD is conceptually similar to psychopathy but, due to differences in assessment criteria, it is not equivalent to a diagnosis made using the PCL–R. Dissocial personality disorder is recognized by the World Health Organization as the diagnostic category most similar to psychopathy. Sociopathy is a historical term that was once used in the DSM instead of psychopathy. It no longer exists as a formal diagnostic category in any major contemporary scheme of mental disorder.

4. Psychopathy and criminality are distinct concepts, yet research shows that there is a strong relationship between the two. Compared to non-psychopaths, the offending behaviour of psychopaths tends to be more frequent, diverse, and serious. Psychopaths are also much more likely than non-psychopaths to engage in instrumental violence.

5. Psychopathy exists in all segments of the population, although the specific expression of the disorder may vary somewhat with gender, age, and culture. Studies show that some women manifest psychopathy, but the disorder does not appear to be as important for understanding women's criminal behaviour as it is for men. Psychopathic traits appear in individuals of all ages and are related to problematic conduct throughout the lifespan. Some data suggest that the overt criminal behaviours of psychopaths may decline in later life, but there is no evidence of any fundamental change in their core personality traits. Instead, psychopaths may simply transition to other forms of antisocial behaviour as they age. Research and anthropological evidence have also extended the construct of psychopathy outside North America; however, the prevalence and expression of the disorder may vary somewhat as a function of culture.

6. Several existing theories may explain psychopathy and its connection to crime. Lykken's fearlessness model and Hare's hypoemotionality model implicate emotional deficits as the mechanism responsible for the psychopath's offending behaviour. In contrast, Newman's response modulation model focuses on impairments in the psychopath's ability to evaluate the consequences of their behaviour. Two other theories

just relate to violence. Hostile attribution bias suggests that the decisions of psychopaths to act violently are influenced by faulty thinking processes that tend to interpret the ambiguous behaviours of others in a hostile and aggressive manner. Baumeister's threatened egoism hypothesis proposes that grandiose and narcissistic people, such as psychopaths, are more prone to committing violence against anyone they perceive is insulting them or treating them disrespectfully.

Review Questions

1. Describe the three main symptom domains of psychopathy and identify a key symptom within each.
2. Explain the "consequence hypothesis" as it relates to possible symptoms of psychopathy involving antisocial behaviour.
3. Explain how differences in the assessment criteria of the PCL–R and ASPD impact the resulting diagnostic rates of these two conditions among offenders.
4. Describe some of the ways that violence perpetrated by psychopaths typically differs from violence perpetrated by non-psychopaths.
5. Discuss whether there is any evidence to indicate that psychopaths experience age-related changes.

Additional Readings

Babiak, P., & Hare, R. D. (2006). *Snakes in suits: When psychopaths go to work*. New York, NY: HarperCollins.

Hare, R. D. (1993). *Without conscience: The disturbing world of the psychopaths among us*. New York, NY: Pocket Books.

Hare, R. D. (1996). Psychopathy: A clinical construct whose time has come. *Criminal Justice and Behavior, 23*, 25–54.

Hart, S. D., & Hare, R. D. (1997). Psychopathy: Assessment and association with criminal conduct. In D. M. Stoff, J. Breiling, & J. D. Maser (Eds.), *Handbook of antisocial behaviour* (pp. 22–35). New York, NY: Wiley.

Hervé, H., & Yuille, J. C. (2007). *The psychopath: Theory, research, and practice*. Mahwah, NJ: Lawrence Erlbaum Associates.

Patrick, C. J. (2006). *Handbook of psychopathy*. New York, NY: Guildford Press.

7

Learning

Learning Objectives

At the end of this chapter, you should be able to:

- define learning and identify its principle processes;

- describe the process of classical conditioning and explain how it may facilitate offending;

- explain Hans Eysenck's theory about the development of the human conscience as a classically conditioned response;

- describe the principles of operant conditioning and explain how people learn to offend as a result of differential reinforcement;

- use the principles of operant conditioning to explain why punishment imposed by contemporary criminal justice systems is ineffective;

- explain the process of observational learning and identify factors that increase the likelihood of children mimicking the violence they see in the media; and

- discuss Ronald Akers's differential association-reinforcement theory of deviant and criminal behaviour.

CASE STUDY

Devalon Armstrong

New Orleans, Louisiana—On 16 June 2013, 13-year-old Devalon Armstrong was babysitting his younger half-sister, Viloude Louis. During the evening, she began to complain of a stomach ache. When Louis did not return from brushing her teeth, Armstrong went to check on her. He found her lying on the bathroom floor, still in pain. He led her downstairs and helped her lie on the couch. A short time later, her breathing stopped. Armstrong called 911 and, following the operator's instructions, administered CPR until the paramedics arrived (Hunter, 2013). Despite these efforts, Louis was pronounced dead at the hospital.

The coroner's office initially deemed Louis's death "unclassified"; however, an autopsy showed that the five-year-old had suffered broken ribs, a lacerated liver, and internal bleeding from blunt force trauma. In a police interview, Armstrong revealed that he had performed wrestling moves he had seen on TV on his half-sister, who was little more than one-third of his size (Purpura, 2013). He had punched her in the stomach, done elbow drops on her, and body slammed her onto her bed (Hunter, 2013; Thornhill, 2013). He also said that he continued with the wrestling

Photo 7.1 Devlon Armstrong's killing of his half-sister, Viloude Louis (shown here), brought attention to the possible connection between watching violence and committing violence.

after Louis began to complain of being hurt and that he stopped only because the phone rang (Hunter, 2013). Armstrong pled guilty to negligent homicide and was sentenced to three years in juvenile detention (Thornhill & Farberov, 2013).

Introduction

The wrestling moves that killed Viloude Louis were learned by her half-brother. **Learning**—which can be defined as a change in our behavioural repertoire due to experience—is our principal means of acquiring behaviour (see Domjan, 2005; Lieberman, 2000). Central to all learning theories is the assumption that no one is inherently good or evil; everyone begins life as a blank slate, free of pre-existing behavioural tendencies. Our behaviour is simply a function of what we learn as we go through life. In this respect, learning theories of crime depart markedly from the biologically oriented concepts covered in previous chapters. The latter posit that biological differences predispose some individuals to behave criminally, whereas the former contend that differences in learning experiences lead some to develop criminal behaviours.

> **learning** A process in which experience causes a change in a person's behavioural repertoire.

Learning occurs in a variety of ways. Observational learning results from watching what others do, just as Armstrong learned wrestling moves from seeing them on television. Learning can also occur through association, which happens when we realize that two events are reliably connected (Lieberman, 2000). In psychology, this process is known as conditioning and is divided into two types. Classical conditioning involves associations between two events that precede a certain behaviour. For example, when the taillights of the car ahead go on, we apply the brakes because we associate these lights with the vehicle decelerating. Operant conditioning involves associations between a behaviour and its consequence; we press the remote's power button because we know it will turn on the TV. This chapter reviews all three types of learning and explains how they may contribute to offending behaviour.

Classical Conditioning

Overview

classical conditioning A learning process whereby two stimuli are repeatedly paired and result in a neutral (conditioned) stimulus being able to evoke the response originally evoked by the other (unconditioned) stimulus.

unconditioned stimulus (UCS) A stimulus in classical conditioning that evokes a response naturally and without learning.

Learning through **classical conditioning** was first confirmed in a series of experiments conducted by Ivan Pavlov at the turn of the twentieth century (Lieberman, 2000). Pavlov discovered the process accidentally while studying the digestive system. His research involved placing meat powder in a dog's mouth to observe the animal salivate. When this task was done repeatedly, an unexpected behaviour occurred: the dog began to salivate before receiving the food. Pavlov realized that the dog was salivating when stimuli associated with the food, such as the sight and sound of the person responsible for feeding it, were present (Lieberman, 2000).

To Pavlov's credit, he recognized the significance of his discovery and began to investigate it more methodically. One of his early attempts involved sounding a tone and then presenting food to the dog. Initially, the tone produced no effect; however, when Pavlov paired the tone with the food many times, the dog eventually associated the two stimuli and began to salivate at the sound of the tone, even when the food was absent. Various labels are used to describe these events (see Lieberman, 2000; Mazur, 2013). The food is identified as the ***unconditioned stimulus*** (UCS) because the salivation it stimulates is automatic and *un*learned. Salivation is the *un*learned response elicited by the presence of the food and is labelled the ***unconditioned response*** (UCR). The tone is a **conditioned stimulus** (CS) because its ability to stimulate salivation depends on the dog learning to associate the tone and food. The salivation produced as a learned response to the tone is a **conditioned response** (CR). Note that the salivation is both the UCR and the CR; the label switches depending on whether it is elicited by the unconditioned or conditioned stimulus. Figure 7.1 presents a diagram of classical conditioning.

In classical conditioning, the learned association forms between events that occur prior to the response (e.g. the sounding of the tone and the presentation of the food). Note too, that the person or organism plays a passive role. The environment acts on the person and elicits an automatic reflexive response over which he or she has little control.

A.

FOOD
UCS ————————→ SALIVATION
UCR

B.

Repeated pairings

FOOD
UCS ————————→ SALIVATION
UCR

TONE
CS

C.

Repeated pairings

FOOD
UCS ————————→ SALIVATION
UCR

TONE
CS

D.

SALIVATION
CR

TONE
CS

Figure 7.1 Summary of classical conditioning processes.

Classical Conditioning and Criminal Behaviour

Classical conditioning can facilitate deviant and criminal acts in some situations. If past deviant behaviour repeatedly occurred in the presence of particular stimuli or environmental cues, the future presence of these prompts could evoke the same feelings and motivate new offences. Evidence that these classical conditioning mechanisms contribute to offending is limited, but it is well established that drug addicts often feel a renewed desire to relapse in settings associated with their past drug use (Siegel, 2005; Siegal & Ramos, 2002). Deviant sexual preferences for things such as animals or inanimate objects could also develop in some cases because early experiences of sexual arousal occurred in the presence of these items (McGuire, Carlisle, & Young, 1965). Laboratory studies have successfully conditioned male participants to become sexually aroused to previously neutral objects, including women's boots and coloured shapes, by repeatedly pairing them with erotic pictures (Rachman, 1966; Rachman & Hodgson, 1968; McConaghy, 1970). Richard Ramirez, "The Night Stalker," is thought to have become sexually aroused by his cousin's stories and graphic photographs of the young women he raped and murdered. Ramirez's later crimes might have been partly fuelled by this association between sex and violence (Meadows & Kuehnel, 2005; see the case study).

unconditioned response (UCR) A response in classical conditioning that is evoked by a stimulus naturally and without learning.

conditioned stimulus (CS) A stimulus in classical conditioning that was originally neutral but, as a result of repeated pairings with an unconditioned stimulus, triggers the response evoked by the unconditioned stimulus.

conditioned response (CR) A response in classical conditioning that was originally evoked by the unconditioned stimulus but, as a result of repeated pairings between the unconditioned and the conditioned stimuli, is evoked by the conditioned stimulus.

CASE STUDY

Richard Ramirez

Los Angeles, California—During the spring and summer of 1985, the residents of southern California were terrorized by Richard Ramirez, who became known as "The Night Stalker" because he used the cover of darkness to enter his victims' homes through unlocked doors or windows. Ramirez immediately killed any adult males present, usually with a single gunshot to the head. He bound the women with pieces of clothing, electrical cords, or other items he found in the home. Once they were completely under his control, he viciously beat and raped them, sometimes repeatedly. The pain and terror he caused seemed to excite and arouse him further. When he was finished, he would ransack the home and take any valuables he could find. In some cases, he made victims swear to Satan or drew a pentagram as a sign of his allegiance to the devil.

Ramirez's reign of terror ended when local citizens recognized him from a mug shot in the newspaper and held him until police arrived. He was eventually convicted of 13 murders, 5 attempted murders, 11 sexual assaults, and 14 burglaries (Botelho, 2013). On being

Photo 7.2 During his trial, Richard Ramirez shows the pentagram symbol on his hand.

sentenced to death, he is quoted as saying "Big deal, death always went with the territory" (Martin, 2013, p. D8). He died at the age of 53, awaiting execution.

How might this criminal behaviour be tied to classical conditioning? Born in El Paso, Texas, in

continued

1960, Ramirez grew up with his three older brothers, Ruben, Joseph, and Robert, and his older sister, Ruth. His father laid railway track for a living, which kept him away from the family for long periods. When he was home, he took his explosive temper out on his children, especially Ruben and Robert, who had constant run-ins with the law during their teens. Although Ramirez had a kindly mother, she worked full-time, so he was raised mostly by his sister. He was described as a relatively happy boy who achieved satisfactory grades throughout most of elementary school.

Things seemed to change around the seventh grade, when Ramirez's cousin Miguel returned from the Vietnam War. Ramirez revered Miguel and spent more and more time with him. He began to smoke marijuana with him and listen to stories of his war exploits, which included binding, raping, and murdering Vietnamese women. On numerous occasions, Miguel showed Ramirez a shoebox full of photos depicting these sadistic acts. Ramirez found the photos sexually arousing and masturbated with these images in his mind. Miguel also taught him the ways of war and how to move with stealth and kill. Miguel remained an influential figure in his cousin's life until he was apprehended and confined to a psychiatric institution for murdering his wife. Ramirez, just 13 at the time, witnessed the killing.

Shortly before Miguel's arrest, Ramirez began breaking into homes. It excited him and gave him a sense of power to look through other people's belongings, ponder what he would steal, and fantasize about scenarios of sexual bondage. Most of the stolen items were handed over to Miguel to be sold and the profits split between them. After Miguel was arrested, Ramirez went to Los Angeles to spend the summer with his brother Ruben. Ruben was addicted to heroin and supported himself by stealing cars and burglarizing homes. Ramirez accompanied him several times and learned how to avoid detection when entering people's houses. When Ramirez returned to El Paso, he was no longer interested in school and, by grade nine, he was failing every subject except physical education. At the age of 15, he landed a job at a hotel. He was entrusted with a master key, which he used to slip into the rooms of guests while they slept and steal their belongings. He was arrested when he hid in the room of a female guest and tried to sexually assault her as she came out of the bathroom.

A couple of years later, Ramirez returned to the LA area and came to believe that Satan was his protector. He committed burglaries and, within a few years, escalated to the brutal string of crimes for which he is notorious.

Source (except where otherwise noted): Carlo, P. (1996). *The Night Stalker: The life and crimes of Richard Ramirez*. New York: Pinnacle.

Classical Conditioning and the Human Conscience

Hans Eysenck (1977) used classical conditioning processes to explain why people obey the law rather than why they violate it. He claimed that our conscience is, in essence, a classically conditioned emotional reflex that normally develops through socialization during childhood. When this conditioned response is weakly developed or fails to develop, people behave as they please without regard for the law. How does this classically conditioned "conscience" develop? According to Eysenck (1977, 1983), the punishments children receive for misbehaving cause them to experience pain, fear, or other uncomfortable feelings. In the language of classical conditioning, the punishment is the UCS and the unpleasant feeling it produces automatically and without learning is the UCR (Eysenck, 1983).

Suppose one young child hits another. The behaviour is equivalent to the CS. So long as the child is caught and punished, the unpleasant feelings will follow. If hitting other people (CS) is consistently and repeatedly punished (UCS), the child will learn to associate these two events so that the act of hitting alone (i.e. in the absence of any punishment) will cause him or her to experience the same feelings of discomfort (CR; see Figure 7.2).

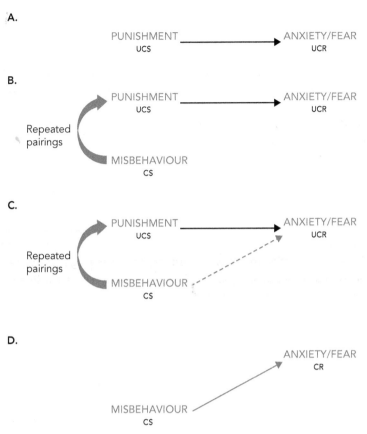

Figure 7.2 Summary of Eysenck's classically conditioned conscience.

Eysenck (1977, 1983) believed that, once this conditioned anxiety and fear response is established, the mere thought of misbehaving will sufficiently evoke the associated unpleasant consequences to deter most people from offending. Furthermore, anyone who does offend experiences the feelings of distress that are now associated with doing something wrong. We call this feeling guilt.

Of course, it is impossible to develop a conditioned fear response in people for every illegal or antisocial behaviour, but doing so is unnecessary. Eysenck (1977) reasoned that, once the conditioned reflex is established in relation to some prohibited activities, it would extend to others through **stimulus generalization**. In this context, stimuli similar to the original CS will elicit the same CR (Mazur, 2013). Pavlov demonstrated stimulus generalization when he found that presenting different tones to the dogs he was studying yielded the same salivary reflex as the original tone. A conditioned anxiety and fear response to one antisocial behaviour presumably generalizes to all antisocial behaviours the same way. In fact, Eysenck (1977) believed that the tendency of parents and other authority figures to label a diverse range of conduct as "bad" or "naughty" enhances this process by lumping all these behaviours into a single group deserving of punishment (p. 116).

While this classically conditioned conscience may be strong enough to keep most people's behaviour in line, it appears to be missing in some people. This absence could come about in at least two ways. First, antisocial behaviour must be repeatedly paired with punishment for classical conditioning to occur. When punishment is inconsistent

stimulus generalization
In classical conditioning, the capacity of stimuli that are similar to the conditioned stimulus to evoke the same conditioned response.

or absent, it produces a weak or non-existent classical conditioning response. Good adult supervision and disciplinary practices during a child's formative years are needed to avoid this outcome. Eysenck (1983) believed that society's growing permissiveness and failure to consistently punish misbehaviour has severely limited opportunities for conditioning to take place. The consequence is a more weakly developed conscience and greater crime.

conditionability The degree to which classical conditioning responses can be easily and strongly formed in a person.

The second factor is **conditionability**, or how easily and strongly people form associations between a CS and a CR and develop classical conditioning responses. Eysenck (1977, 1983) hypothesized that some people are inherently more conditionable than others due to biological differences in our nervous systems. Highly conditionable individuals who experience appropriate and consistent discipline growing up are expected to be relatively law-abiding because of the strong association they make between offending and unpleasant consequences. Unfortunately, as we saw in Chapter 3, some people exhibit poor classical conditioning responses. Eysenck (1977, 1983) predicted that these individuals are more likely to behave badly even if they experience good parenting because they fail to associate offending with its aversive consequences; therefore, the conscience necessary for ongoing prosocial behaviour can never develop. Study findings discussed in Chapter 3 are consistent with this theory (e.g. Gao et al., 2010).

Operant Conditioning

Overview

operant conditioning A learning process whereby anticipated consequences influence voluntary behavioural choices.

The term *operant conditioning* was coined by B.F. Skinner, who did much of the pioneering work in this area, to reflect his view that this type of learning involves the organism operating on the environment (Mazur, 2013). During operant conditioning, people learn to associate behaviour with its consequences. The essence of this type of learning is that people tend to repeat behaviours that bring about desirable outcomes and avoid behaviours that have undesirable results.

Operant conditioning can be distinguished from classical conditioning by the timing of the associations and the degree to which the behaviour involved is voluntary. Remember, operant conditioning concerns an association between a behaviour and what happens after it, whereas classical conditioning involves an association between a response (i.e. behaviour) and what happened before it. Another major distinction is that the action performed in operant conditioning is usually viewed as voluntary. People initiate the behaviour because they learned that it produces a desired result.

Discriminative stimulus In operant conditioning, a stimulus that signals whether a certain response is likely to be reinforced or punished.

Operant conditioning consists of three basic elements: a discriminative stimulus, a response, and the consequence of the response (Mazur, 2013). A **discriminative stimulus** is a specific context or environmental cue that indicates whether a particular response is likely to be reinforced. In a football game, tackling the person carrying the ball stops the opposition's advance down the field. The context (football game) tells players that a specific behaviour (tackling the ball carrier) will yield a desired consequence (stopping the play). Discriminative stimuli are important because they exert a strong influence over how people choose to behave at any given time. Take the previous example and change the context to a basketball game. Now tackling the player with the ball has a very different consequence. Thus, the discriminative stimuli in these examples give us important clues about the anticipated consequences of a behaviour.

Reinforcement

The fundamental principle of operant conditioning is that people behave in ways intended to bring about specific outcomes. Consequences that increase the likelihood of a response are labelled **reinforcement**. **Positive reinforcement** increases a behavioural response by presenting something that is pleasant or rewarding, such as getting a scholarship for maintaining high grades or a job promotion for doing good work. **Negative reinforcement** strengthens a behavioural response by removing something that is unpleasant or painful, such as allowing a child out of his or her room once it is clean or turning off a morning alarm to stop its annoying sound. The key to all reinforcement is that it encourages a particular response.

Research with animals reveals that reinforcement is most effective when it follows immediately or shortly after the target behaviour and learning is reduced the longer it is delayed (Lieberman, 2000). This makes sense because operant conditioning depends on the animal or person connecting the applicable behaviour to the reinforcer. Lengthy delays increase the likelihood of intervening events taking place, which makes it more difficult for the necessary connection to form (Schwartz, Wasserman, & Robbins, 2001). When the delay becomes too long, no connection is established and the association will not be learned.

Extinction and Schedules of Reinforcement

A behaviour will be repeated as long as it continues to be reinforced. If reinforcement stops, responding tends to taper off until it disappears, a process known as **extinction**. Behavioural responses vary in terms of their resistance to extinction. Some responses are highly resistant to extinction and continue long after reinforcement has ended; others are less resistant and disappear very quickly. Resistance to extinction has real-world implications because it governs how enduring desirable behavioural responses will be if reinforcement stops and how easy it will be to extinguish undesirable behaviours by eliminating all reinforcement.

One of the chief factors influencing resistance to extinction is the reinforcement schedule that established the behavioural response. **Reinforcement schedules** are the rules governing the delivery of reinforcement, which may be broadly classified as either continuous or intermittent (Lieberman, 2000; Mazur, 2013). **Continuous reinforcement** schedules deliver the reinforcer every time the appropriate response is made. These schedules generally yield higher rates of responding and faster learning than intermittent ones, but they rarely exist outside a laboratory (Schwartz et al., 2001). **Intermittent reinforcement** schedules deliver the reinforcer after only some appropriate responses (Lieberman, 2000; Sundel & Sundel, 1993). Under intermittent reinforcement schedules, learning occurs more slowly, but a learned behaviour is more enduring and disappears more gradually when reinforcement stops (Schwartz et al., 2001).

The reason extinction is impacted by the type of reinforcement schedule is not difficult to grasp. With continuous reinforcement schedules, it is immediately obvious when reinforcement is no longer delivered and further responding has become futile. The unpredictability of intermittent reinforcement creates a lingering hope that the next behaviour is the one that will be reinforced; hence, responding continues much longer in the absence of reinforcement (Schwartz et al., 2001). This is precisely what casino operators count on and why people find it so hard to stop gambling.

reinforcement In operant conditioning, an event following a response that increases the likelihood of the response being made again.

positive reinforcement A type of reinforcement that increases the likelihood of a certain response by administering something pleasant or rewarding when that response occurs.

negative reinforcement A type of reinforcement that increases the likelihood of a certain response by removing something unpleasant or aversive when that response occurs.

extinction In operant conditioning, a process that occurs when reinforcement is discontinued and responding subsequently diminishes until it stops.

reinforcement schedules The rules under which appropriate responses are reinforced.

continuous reinforcement Rules specifying that reinforcement should be delivered after every appropriate response.

intermittent reinforcement Rules specifying that reinforcement should be delivered after some but not every appropriate response.

Punishment

Behaviour can also bring about punishment, which has the opposite effect of reinforcement. Within the context of operant conditioning, **punishment** is anything that decreases the likelihood of a response. As with reinforcement, it can be classified as either positive or negative. **Positive punishment** involves the application of an unpleasant or aversive stimulus, such as requiring a student to write an essay about the impact of their disruptive behaviour on their classmates or giving a child extra chores for misbehaving. **Negative punishment** involves the removal of a rewarding or pleasant stimulus, for example, removing a child's privilege to watch TV or play computer games. Table 7.1 summarizes the different types of reinforcement and punishment.

When carried out properly, punishment can reduce problem behaviours. Years of animal research has shed light on three factors that make it effective: intensity, timing, and consistency (see Azrin & Holz, 1966; Church, 1967; Johnston, 1972; Van Houten, 1983). These studies show that higher-intensity punishments are generally more effective than lower-intensity punishments (Azrin, 1960; Camp, Raymond, & Church, 1967). Mild punishments can reduce problem behaviours as well, but if the punished behaviour occasionally pays off or leads to reinforcement, any reduction tends to be short-lived and the behaviour soon rebounds to its original level (Azrin, 1960). In terms of timing, punishment should follow the unwanted behaviour as closely as possible. The longer punishment is delayed, the lower its suppressive effect and the more likely the behaviour will reappear (Camp et al., 1967; Solomon, Turner, & Lessac, 1968). Ideally, punishment should be administered every time the unwanted behaviour appears. Infrequent or inconsistent delivery weakens the punishment's inhibitory effect (Azrin, Holz, & Hake, 1963).

Unfortunately, punishment only suppresses the targeted behaviour as opposed to substituting it with something more acceptable (Johnston, 1972). One way to enhance punishment's effectiveness is to combine it with reinforcement for some alternative and desirable behaviour (Azrin & Holz, 1966; Sundel & Sundel, 1993). This point is clearly demonstrated in a study of four individuals who lived in residential care and were prone to inappropriate and self-injurious behaviour (Thompson, Iwata, Conners, & Roscoe, 1999). The researchers examined the impact of delivering punishment alone, which consisted of verbal reprimands and mild physical restraint (e.g. holding the patient's arms for 15 seconds), and punishment plus positive reinforcement in the form of access to pleasurable and socially appropriate activities and objects. As Figure 7.3 shows, punishment alone reduced the levels of self-injurious behaviours across all four patients, but the reductions were much larger when punishment was accompanied by reinforcement. Schwartz and colleagues (2001) suggest that even relatively mild punishments can be completely effective so long as acceptable behaviours that yield the same reinforcement as the unwanted behaviour are found.

punishment In operant conditioning, an event following a response that decreases the likelihood of the response being made again.

positive punishment A type of punishment that decreases the likelihood of a certain response by administering something unpleasant or aversive when that response occurs.

negative punishment A type of punishment that reduces the likelihood of a certain response by removing something pleasant or rewarding when that response occurs.

Table 7.1 Summary of the different types of reinforcement and punishment

	Positive (administering)	Negative (removing)
Reinforcement (increases responding)	Administering something pleasant	Removing something unpleasant
Punishment (decreases responding)	Administering something unpleasant	Removing something pleasant

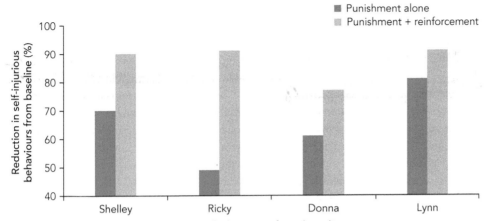

Figure 7.3 Reduction in self-injurious behaviours from baseline.

Sources: Data from Thompson et al. (1999). Effects of reinforcement for alternative behavior during punishment of self-injury. *Journal of Applied Behavior Analysis*, 32, 317–328.

Operant Conditioning and Crime

Although Skinner did not research operant conditioning to explain crime, the principles he delineated have been applied to it. Jeffery (1965) outlined one of the earliest accounts of criminal behaviour based on operant conditioning more than half a century ago. No doubt he would soundly reject the adage "crime never pays." Jeffrey believed that criminal behaviour is the product of reinforcement and that people commit crime precisely because it is rewarding. He emphasized the role of **nonsocial reinforcement**, such as material goods and physiological and emotional states, on criminal behaviour. Theft is a prime example (Jeffery, 1965). The stolen item—a pair of sneakers, a wallet, or a restaurant meal—serves as positive reinforcement for the act of shoplifting, pickpocketing, dining and dashing, or whatever illegal behaviour was used to acquire it.

Violent crime can also be positively reinforced (Jeffery, 1965). Think back to Richard Ramirez. The items he looted, together with the feelings of power and pleasure he derived from dominating and abusing his victims, served as positive reinforcement for his sexually violent behaviour (Meadows & Kuehnel, 2005). There is also evidence of negative reinforcement in the Ramirez case. Violent behaviour is negatively reinforced when it removes an aversive stimulus, such as threats or assaults that scare off a rival drug dealer (Jeffery, 1965). Negative reinforcement may account for Ramirez's tactic of immediately murdering adult males in the homes he burglarized. This action eliminated a major obstacle to his goal of ransacking the home and sexually attacking the female occupants.

Crime can be reinforcing, but would-be offenders sometimes fail and, on other occasions, they are caught and punished. This raises the question: Why do people continue to commit crime when the consequences are so mixed and unpredictable? The key, according to Jeffery (1965), is **differential reinforcement**, the difference between the reinforcing and punishing consequences brought about by the behaviour. People repeat criminal acts when the net effect of past reinforcement exceeds the suppressing effect of any punishments. Put simply, offending will continue if it produces more reinforcement than punishment. Criminal conduct that pays off only occasionally and is therefore on an intermittent

nonsocial reinforcement Any event that does not depend on social interaction but follows a response and increases the likelihood of it reoccurring. The event may include attaining certain material items or internal physiological and emotional states.

differential reinforcement The net effect of all reinforcement and punishment received for a certain response.

reinforcement schedule can be explained the same way. So long as the overall effect of the periodic reinforcement is greater than the effect of any associated punishment, the offending behaviour will persist.

Jeffery (1965) acknowledged that other people can strongly influence someone's decision to break the law but argued that they function primarily as discriminative stimuli and not as sources of reinforcement. In other words, the people around us are indicators of whether offending behaviour is likely to be reinforced or punished. For instance, many drivers immediately slow down when they spot a police car ahead, only to resume speeding as soon as they see it turn off the road. Parents, teachers, police officers, and other authority figures are all examples of discriminative stimuli that tell us disobeying the rules is likely to result in punishment (Williams & McShane, 2010). On the other hand, someone who is alone on a dark street or in the midst of a riot is operating under a very different set of expectations about what is likely to happen if they break the rules.

In addition to the principles of operant conditioning already discussed, Jeffery (1965) added the concepts of satiation and deprivation. Though not explicitly defined, they reflect the notion that current access to a reinforcer determines its strength (Williams & McShane, 2010). The reinforcing effect of food, for example, is much greater for someone who is hungry than someone who just ate (Azrin et al., 1963). Satiation and deprivation are useful for explaining the concentration of crime in impoverished communities. Illegal activities such as theft and drug trafficking are highly rewarding for people living in poverty-stricken conditions characterized by inadequate food, clothing, and shelter. Those living in more affluent areas seldom lack these important reinforcers and therefore they gain less reinforcement from committing crime and, presumably, are less likely to break the law.

While satiation and deprivation help to account for the distribution of crime in society, it does not follow that people living in the same environment are inevitably bound to behave the same way. Every individual has a unique conditioning history of past reinforcement and punishment, and every situation he or she encounters differs in terms of both the discriminative stimuli present and the available reinforcement. Jeffery (1965) believed that variations in these and other learning-related factors explain the widely different behavioural responses exhibited by people sharing the same living conditions.

Why Criminal Justice System Punishments Fail

The ongoing problem of crime is a clear sign that the current system of punishment does not adequately offset the reinforcing properties of illegal behaviour. Critics claim that Western society's manner of imposing punishment flouts virtually everything known about the conditions necessary for it to be effective. Much of this criticism is based on animal studies, but there is little evidence to suggest that the processes and principles elucidated so far do not apply to humans as well. This section offers a summary of the most prominent shortcomings associated with current criminal justice system practices. For more information, see Andrews & Bonta, 2006; Huesmann & Podolski, 2003; McGuire, 2004; Moffitt, 1983.

Punishment Severity Is Gradually Increased

The criminal justice system tends to impose relatively mild punishments on first-time offenders, which are gradually made more severe for subsequent offences, rather than imposing strong punishments at the outset. Yet laboratory research suggests that the same punishment that completely inhibited a behaviour when it was delivered from the beginning has much less impact if it is administered at the end of a long sequence of gradually increasing punishments (Azrin et al., 1963; Miller, 1960). To be sure, the appropriate manner of imposing punishments is an issue that must be resolved on the basis of ethical, humanitarian, and legal considerations and not just the science of operant conditioning (Schwartz et al., 2001). The point here is that the current practice of gradually increasing sentence severity may not be an effective approach for reducing future reoffending (Lieberman, 2000; Schwartz et al., 2001).

Punishment Is Delayed

Punishment is most effective when it is delivered immediately after the behaviour. Unfortunately, the wheels of justice turn at a notoriously slow pace. Overburdened criminal justice systems and delays in due process result in offenders being held accountable and punished long after they commit a crime. Analyses of criminal case processing in North America reveal that, even under relatively favourable circumstances, the time between an offender being arrested and being sentenced is typically three to eight months (Boyce, 2013; Ostrom & Kauder, 1998). Not only does the delay weaken the association between the behaviour and the punishment, but it also creates an opportunity for offenders to commit further crimes and gain more reinforcement. For example, an offender apprehended in the midst of one car theft may successfully steal several other cars while out on bail. This reinforcement has the potential to outweigh the effect of any subsequent punishment (Andrews & Bonta, 2006).

Punishment Is Inconsistent

Criminal justice systems deliver punishment erratically, which is unfortunate in light of evidence showing that consistent punishment leads to lower rates of recidivism. Brennan and Mednick (1994) examined the impact of criminal sanctions in a cohort of more than 28,000 Danish men. They looked at participants with a history of arrests and found that the recidivism rate fell as the proportion of arrests resulting in punishment rose. For example, someone arrested on four occasions and punished three times (i.e. 75 per cent of the time) was less likely to reoffend than someone arrested on four occasions but punished only once (i.e. 25 per cent of the time).

The failure to deliver punishment consistently is a function of at least two shortcomings within the criminal justice system: the perpetrator of a crime is often not caught and many of those who are caught are not punished (McGuire, 2004). North American clearance rates highlight the scope of the first problem. Statistics show that at least three-quarters of all property crimes are never solved (Hotton Mahony & Turner, 2012; Federal Bureau of Investigation, 2011). Higher clearance rates are reported for violent crimes, but even for serious offences such as homicide and sexual assault, one-quarter or more of cases remain unsolved. In reality, the situation is more dismal than official figures indicate because victimization surveys reveal that the majority of criminal incidents are never reported to police (see Perreault & Brennan, 2010; Truman & Langton, 2014). If unreported incidents are considered, the proportion of crimes for which the perpetrator is caught is very small. Even when perpetrators are apprehended, they go unpunished more than half the time because the charges are subsequently withdrawn by the prosecutor, plea bargained away, or dismissed by the court (Boyce, 2013). In the UK it has been estimated that as little as 2 per cent of reported and unreported offences end in a conviction (Home Office, 1993).

Offending Behaviours Are Not Replaced with Acceptable Alternatives

The design and operation of the criminal justice system centres on punishing unwanted behaviour rather than promoting prosocial behaviour. Ideally, punishment should be augmented with reinforcement for acceptable alternative behaviours; however, there is little opportunity to do so within most legal systems. One of the few times that authorities have sufficient control over the environment to make reinforcing alternative and socially acceptable behaviour feasible is when offenders are institutionalized. Over the past five decades, a number of so-called token economies founded on the principles of operant conditioning have been implemented in various institutions across North America and Europe. A **token economy** typically awards an offender points each time he or she performs a desired behaviour and deducts points whenever he or she violates institutional rules or behavioural expectations. The offender can exchange the points earned for privileges, snacks, or other desired items.

Numerous studies report that a token economy can measurably improve offenders' behaviour while they are participating in it (see Kirigin, Braukmann, Atwater, & Wolf, 1982). The challenge is to maintain behavioural changes after the offender leaves the program and reinforcement ends (Kazdin & Bootzin, 1972). Unfortunately, many offenders return to their old environment, where they are once again reinforced for performing the same antisocial behaviours that led to their previous incarceration.

token economy A structured behaviour modification system that awards tokens or another symbolic reward whenever certain desirable behaviours are exhibited; the accumulated tokens can be exchanged for privileges or prizes.

Observational Learning

Anyone who has taken a commercial flight is familiar with the preflight safety demonstration. It is expected that, after seeing this demonstration, passengers can operate the oxygen mask and inflatable life vest even if none of them have done so before. The airlines, in this instance, are relying on **observational learning**, the process of learning by watching and imitating the actions of others. The person performing the observed behaviour is the **model**. Models are everywhere—they are the people we see and encounter daily, and they provide us with a constant supply of behavioural examples that we learn from and sometimes replicate. Albert Bandura (1973), who is widely credited with conducting some of the early ground-breaking research in this area, believes that much of our behaviour is socially transmitted in this manner.

observational learning A learning process whereby a person acquires a new behaviour after seeing it performed by someone else.

model The person performing a behaviour observed and learned by someone else.

Observational Learning Processes

Observational learning can be broken into two basic components: acquisition and imitation. **Acquisition**, the first step, is a cognitively demanding process that involves the observer paying attention to what the model is doing and retaining it in his or her memory, where it can be drawn on later when the model can no longer be observed (Bandura, 1973; see Chapter 8). The second step is the performance, or **imitation**, of the acquired behaviour. Just because a behaviour has been acquired does not necessarily mean that it will be imitated. The observer must be both capable of reproducing the behaviour and sufficiently motivated to carry it out.

Bandura (1973) believed that the desire to perform a behaviour is greatly influenced by the consequences it brings. Based on our knowledge of operant conditioning, we know that people will be motivated to act in ways that lead to reinforcement and avoid punishment. So far, our discussion of reinforcement has been confined to **direct reinforcement**,

acquisition In observational learning, the process of paying attention to and memorizing an observed behaviour.

imitation In observational learning, the process of replicating an observed behaviour.

direct reinforcement Reinforcement that is personally experienced.

which is personally experienced, such as a child receiving an allowance for performing chores. Bandura (1973) explained that people are also influenced by the reinforcements and punishments they witness other people experiencing. This is known as **vicarious reinforcement**. The sight of one child receiving an allowance for doing chores serves as vicarious reinforcement that encourages his or her siblings to do their chores as well. Think back to Devalon Armstrong. What vicarious reinforcement did he observe? When it comes to imitation, it is not just seeing a model's behaviour that counts but also the consequences that are seen to follow that behaviour.

It should be apparent that observational learning differs from other forms of learning in several ways. Unlike classical and operant conditioning, which view people (and other organisms) as simply responding to their environment, observational learning is highly dependent on mental processes, or cognition. This distinction is evident by the infusion of attention, memory, and motivation into the learning process. Further, classical and operant conditioning depend on repeated personal experience, whereas observational learning occurs by watching others in the absence of personal experience (Mazur, 2013). The role played by reinforcement in operant conditioning and observational learning is also very different. In operant conditioning, learning is a product of reinforcement; we learn to behave in certain ways to obtain reinforcers and avoid punishers. Attention and retention are the keys to acquiring new behaviours through observational learning, while reinforcement and punishment govern which of these behaviours are performed and maintained.

Observing and Imitating Offending Behaviour

Observational learning contributes to everyone's behavioural repertoire. Precisely what behaviours are learned depends critically on the models a person is exposed to and how those models conduct themselves. Models can be a rich source of cooperative and prosocial behaviour, but the opposite is also true. People just as readily pick up the antisocial and aggressive behaviours they see. While the effects of modelling can be felt at any age, a great deal of attention has been paid to the impact of parents on their children. Parents sometimes deliberately model and actively involve their children in antisocial or criminal behaviour. For example, a few years ago, police in one North American city solicited the public's help to identify a couple who entered a large electronics store accompanied by their two young children (Sinoski, 2010). As they walked down the store aisles, the children picked out DVDs they wanted while the parents hid the items in a baby stroller they were pushing. Authorities estimate that the family stole nearly $3,000 worth of merchandise.

Fortunately, most parents have no intention of modelling blatantly illegal behaviour in front for their children, but they may do so inadvertently by littering, engaging in internet piracy, violating traffic regulations, and so forth. When children see these behaviours, they are more likely to engage in them too. A recent study revealed that teenagers of parents who drive aggressively or under the influence of intoxicating substances are more likely than others to report the presence of these habits in their own driving (Schmidt, Morrongiello, & Colwell, 2014). Moreover, evidence indicates that as the number of models increases from one to both parents, so does the risk of the child taking up the behaviour (Jackson & Henriksen, 1996). Telling children how to act can reduce the impact of negative behavioural models, but it does not eliminate the effects (Jackson & Henriksen, 1996).

vicarious reinforcement
Reinforcement that other people are observed experiencing or are known to have experienced.

It appears there is some truth to the proverb that actions speak louder than words because children often continue to imitate behaviour modelled by their parents despite verbal directions from them to behave differently.

Children will also imitate the aggressive and violent behaviours they observe non-parental models perform. One of the best-known demonstrations of modelling behaviour is a series of studies by Bandura, Ross, and Ross (1961, 1963), which showed that young children who observed models acting aggressively toward a Bobo doll tended to mimic these behaviours when they played with the doll. Consistent with the principle of vicarious reinforcement, the children were more likely to display aggressive behaviours when they saw the model rewarded with treats rather than punished (see the "Researching" box). Research outside the laboratory supports the generalizability of these findings. For example, numerous studies report that childhood exposure to physical and sexual violence is linked to violent offending later in life (Ehrensaft et al., 2003; Felson & Lane, 2009; Widom, 1989).

Researching Criminal and Violent Behaviour

The Bobo Doll Experiments

In one of the first Bobo doll experiments—a series of now classic studies conducted by Bandura and colleagues (1961) at Stanford University during the 1960s—children attending the campus nursery school were separately escorted to a room where they were seated at a table and given an activity to do. An adult who "happened" to be nearby was also invited to join the fun. He or she went to the other end of the room, where a Tinkertoy set, mallet, and Bobo doll were situated. The five-foot inflatable Bobo doll, a popular toy at the time, had a weighted bottom that caused it to pop upright whenever it was struck or knocked over. Depending on the study condition, the child saw the adult model engage in a variety of aggressive or non-aggressive play activities. Aggressive activities included repeatedly punching the doll, hitting it with the mallet, and kicking it. These physical acts were accompanied by the model speaking aggressively (e.g. "Sock him in the nose.") or non-aggressively ("He sure is a tough fella."). In the non-aggressive condition, the adult quietly played with the Tinkertoys and ignored the doll. After a short time, the experimenter returned and escorted the child into another room

Photo 7.3 Bandura's famous Bobo doll experiments supported his theory that children learn behaviour, such as aggression, through observation and imitation.

containing all the previous toys plus some others. The child was left to play while a researcher, blind to the study condition, watched through a one-way mirror and recorded the number of aggressive behaviours displayed. Children exposed to the aggressive model exhibited significantly more verbally and physically aggressive behaviours than those exposed to the non-aggressive model or no model.

In a follow-up study, the researchers examined how the consequences of the model's behaviour influenced the children's tendency to mimic these actions. They modified the original procedure so that the children viewed a short film before entering the playroom (Bandura, Ross, & Ross, 1963). In the aggressive model–rewarded version of the film, Rocky acts aggressively, first toward a Bobo doll and then toward Johnny, who was another boy playing with some attractive-looking toys. At the end of the film, an announcer states that Rocky is the victor and he is shown playing with the toys and helping himself to soft drinks and cookies. The aggressive model–punished version of the film is the same except that, when Rocky acts aggressively, Johnny overpowers and spanks him. When the film ends, Rocky is shown cowering in the corner and the narrator comments on his punishment.

Two further conditions served as control groups. One watched a film depicting two models playing vigorously but non-aggressively with the toys, while the other group had no exposure to any of the models. As seen in Figure 7.4, the children displayed the most aggressive behaviour when they saw the aggressive model being rewarded and the least aggression when the model was punished. Children who were not exposed to the aggressive models exhibited intermediate levels of aggression. These findings suggest that decisions to imitate the behaviour of those around us is greatly influenced by the consequences witnessed.

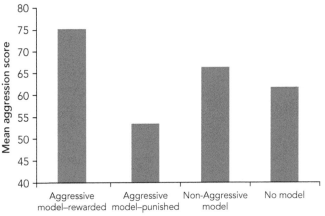

Figure 7.4 Level of aggression exhibited by children exposed to different models.
Source: Copyright © 1963 by the American Psychological Association. Adapted with permission. A. Bandura, D. Ross, & S.A. Ross. (1963). "Vicarious reinforcement and imitative learning." *Journal of Abnormal and Social Psychology*, 67, 601-607. The use of APA information does not imply endorsement by APA.

The Effects of Violent Media

Needless to say, Bandura and colleagues' findings raise important questions about the possible effects of television and other electronic media on aggressive and violent behaviour. The presence of media violence may affect behaviour through any one of the forms of learning reviewed in this chapter. As noted earlier, people sometimes appear to simply imitate violent acts they see performed in the media, something we now know is more likely to occur when those acts are rewarded. Observational learning may also affect behaviour in less obvious ways. Rowell Huesmann (2007) argues that exposure, especially repeated exposure, to violent media can have a long-lasting impact on our thoughts and normative beliefs about the world and what constitutes appropriate conduct, which in turn influences how people choose to behave (see also Bandura, 1979). The nature of these thinking patterns and beliefs and the role they may play in criminal and violent behaviour is discussed in Chapter 8. Finally, Savage (2008) has raised the possibility that classical conditioning responses may develop from repeatedly viewing exciting scenes of violence. If such viewing produces a rewarding sensation and the scenes are constantly paired with violence, the violence alone may eventually produce a rewarding sensation.

Television Violence

The bulk of media violence research addresses the effects of television because this technology has existed much longer than other forms of electronic media. Investigations employ two basic study methodologies: experimental (or quasi-experimental) and correlational. Much like Bandura's original research, most experimental or quasi-experimental studies compare participants who watch violent television programming to a control group that does not. Another example of this type of investigation is Josephson's (1987) study, which showed boys in grades 2 and 3 short videos of violent or non-violent scenes and then had them play floor hockey. Observers recorded all incidents of inappropriate aggression and violence during the game, including giving verbal insults, elbowing, and pushing. They found a connection between viewing the violent scenes and exhibiting higher levels of aggression during the game but only among boys previously rated as aggressive by their teachers, a point we will return to later. The main concern with this type of investigation is that the relatively short-term behavioural effects produced in such contrived situations may or may not generalize to longer-term behavioural changes in the real world (Savage, 2004). Williams's (1986) field study of a small Canadian town receiving TV for the first time—discussed in the "Researching" box—overcomes this limitation and is an interesting variation on the quasi-experimental design.

The second group of studies employs correlational designs. These investigations better reflect real-world conditions because they examine the relationship between the usual viewing habits and general behaviour of study participants. As noted in Chapter 1, the main difficulty with correlational studies is isolating cause and effect. Assuming a relationship is found, it could be that watching violent programs causes aggression. Alternatively, the relationship might run in the other direction, such that people who are aggressive prefer to watch violent programs. The best correlational studies for addressing this issue use longitudinal designs, which allow researchers to measure aggressive behaviour and viewing habits at one time and then see if the amount of violent television watched relates to aggressive behaviour at a later time. A study by Huesmann, Moise-Titus, Podolski, and Eron (2003) is representative of this approach. These investigators interviewed more than 500 elementary school children about the amount of violent television they watched and followed up with as many participants as they could locate 15 years later ($n = 329$). They found that viewing violent television as a child was associated with having higher aggression scores as an adult, even after the childhood aggression level was taken into account.

Several reviews of the scientific literature have concluded that watching violent media is significantly related to aggressive behaviour (e.g. Hogben, 1998; Paik & Comstock, 1994; Wood, Wong, & Chachere, 1991; cf. Ferguson, 2009; Savage & Yancey, 2008). The relationship tends to be larger in experimental investigations than in correlational studies, a finding that might be expected given that researchers are better able to eliminate or control extraneous variables that could otherwise obscure any media-related effect

Researching Criminal and Violent Behaviour

The Town without Television

In 1973 television was about to be introduced into a small Canadian community for the first time. Tannis Williams and her colleagues seized the opportunity to conduct a natural experiment looking at the impact of TV on the residents (Williams, 1986). The town, which the researchers called Notel, was similar to its neighbours in most major respects, except that it was situated in a geographic blind spot that prevented it from getting TV reception. Shortly before a new transmitter was installed to eliminate this problem, the researchers collected data on a wide range of variables, including the level of aggression displayed by the town's elementary school children. They observed the children playing on multiple occasions over a two-week period, noting both verbal and physical acts of aggression (Joy, Kimball, & Zabrack, 1986). Two years later, they returned to conduct follow-up observations of the same children to see if aggression levels had changed following the introduction of TV.

Williams and colleagues found that the average level of verbal and physical aggression rose between the two study periods (Joy et al., 1986; see Figure 7.5). To rule out the possibility that the changes were caused by age-related developmental processes rather than the effects of television,

they simultaneously studied two control groups of children from nearby towns that already had TV reception. As no differences were found in the control groups, the researchers concluded that maturation processes could not explain the elevated level of aggression observed in the experimental group (Joy et al., 1986).

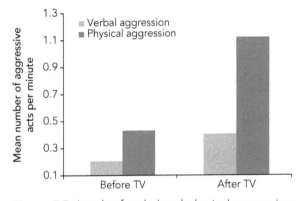

Figure 7.5 Levels of verbal and physical aggression exhibited by children before and after the introduction of television to their town.

Source: Based on data from Joy et al. (1986). Television and children's aggressive behavior. In T. M Williams (Ed.), *The impact of television: A natural experiment in three communities*. Orlando, FL: Academic Press.

(Anderson et al., 2010). Although the impact of violent television programming is statistically significant, the effect is relatively small and many other factors probably have a stronger and more direct bearing on individual decisions to act criminally or violently (Savage, 2008).

The research also indicates that media effects likely vary depending on the depiction of violence and the characteristics of the viewer. Huesmann (2007) points out that people who identify more closely with the character perpetrating the violence have a greater chance of exhibiting aggression. Several studies, including the one by Josephson (1987), found the strongest media effects among participants with the highest levels of past aggression (see also Friedrich & Stein, 1973; Robinson & Bachman, 1972). Although this finding is inconsistent in the literature, it raises the possibility that viewing media violence has a more pronounced effect on some people than others, depending on their individual personality. With respect to media content, the most problematic depictions involve violent actions that are seen as justified or that fail to show any unpleasant consequences (Hogben, 1998). Finally, depictions of violence that are perceived to reflect real life may have a greater negative impact on viewers than those believed to be implausible and far-fetched (Hogben, 1998).

Video Game Violence

Not only has there been a radical transformation in the forms and availability of electronic media, but the violent content of that media has also arguably become much more graphic. As a result, it is unclear what decades-old studies of television might tell us about the influence of the violence portrayed in contemporary media. A newer medium that has been the subject of empirical investigation is video gaming. Video game violence is qualitatively different from TV violence in at least two important respects. First, television viewing is passive, whereas video games are interactive and may involve the participant "performing" acts of violence, as occurs in first-person shooter games (Huesmann, 2007). Second, violent video games often provide direct reinforcement in the form of points or some other virtual reward (Smith, Lachlan, & Tamborini, 2003). Based on the principles of learning already reviewed, it is easy to see why some people suspect that video game violence may have a greater negative impact on human behaviour than television violence (Huesmann, 2007).

A recent meta-analytic review of more than 130 studies found a significant relationship between playing violent video games and acting aggressively; however, the magnitude of this relationship fell within the range generally reported for television violence (e.g. Hogben, 1998; Paik & Comstock, 1994). One of the only studies to examine the impact of playing violent video games versus watching them being played was conducted by Polman, Orobio de Castro, and van Aken (2008), who randomly assigned children in grades 5 and 6 to one of the following three conditions: playing a non-violent video game, playing a violent video game, or passively watching someone play a violent video game. The key to the study is that the first and third groups viewed the same content but had different interactions with it. The researchers found that the average level of aggressive behaviour during a post-video game session was significantly higher among boys in the interactive–violent condition than those in the passive–violent condition. This finding did not extend to the girls in the study. Furthermore, the level of aggressive behaviour did not differ significantly between the interactive–violent and interactive–non-violent conditions. The study provides some support for the view that playing violent video games raises the risk of aggressive behaviour, but it does not appear from these results that the risk is any higher than that associated with viewing violent TV shows.

Differential Association-Reinforcement Theory

Ronald Akers (2009) has woven the various learning theories and principles we have described into a comprehensive theory of criminal and deviant behaviour known as differential association-reinforcement theory. Within criminology, Akers's theory is often called the social learning theory of crime (Akers & Sellers, 2013). Outside criminology, **social learning** is used in connection with any behaviour acquired through interaction with other people and the environment and therefore encompasses a wide array of related

social learning A theory that behaviour is acquired through interaction with other people and the environment.

learning theories and processes, including differential association-reinforcement theory (Bandura, 1977). To avoid any confusion, Akers's theory will be referred to in this text as differential association-reinforcement theory (DA-reinforcement theory) only.

Differential Association

The origins of DA-reinforcement theory lie in the pioneering ideas and work of Edwin Sutherland (Akers, 2009). Sutherland (1947) argued that criminal behaviour is the result of learning and set out nine principles that he thought governed this process (see Table 7.2). He believed that all behaviour, be it good, bad, or indifferent, is learned primarily from interacting and communicating with other people. According to this perspective, everyone is capable of becoming a gangster or a respectable citizen; the outcome depends on the people in our lives and whether they endorse procriminal or prosocial attitudes and behaviour. Thus, human behaviour varies as a result of differences in our social interactions, or what Sutherland called **differential association**.

Knowing other people who engage in criminal behaviour does not necessarily doom a person to a life of crime (Akers, 2009). Not everyone we contact and communicate with has the same social significance to us. Some people matter a great deal and have a profound impact on our lives, whereas others matter very little and have no impact at all. Sutherland believed that four **modalities of association** govern the relative influence of our social interactions (Akers, 2009). Think of the people who have been especially influential on your beliefs and social perspectives. Chances are they all played a prominent role in your life at one time or another and were people you liked and admired. This reflects the modality of **intensity**—associations that are personally meaningful, respected, and enjoyed are much more important than trivial or insignificant ones. A measure of intensity

differential association
A theory, proposed by Edwin Sutherland, that the behaviour people learn and exhibit varies as a function of their social interactions and relationships.

modalities of association
In differential association theory, qualities that impact the degree of social influence a person has over another.

intensity In differential association theory, a modality of association that reflects how personally meaningful and respected an individual is to a specific person.

Table 7.2 Sutherland's principles of differential association

1. Criminal behaviour is learned.

2. Criminal behaviour is learned in interaction with other persons in a process of communications.

3. The principal part of the learning of criminal behaviour occurs within intimate personal groups.

4. When criminal behaviour is learned, the learning includes (a) techniques of committing the crime, which are sometimes very complicated, sometimes very simple; (b) the specific motives, drives, rationalizations, and attitudes.

5. The specific direction of motives and drives is learned from definitions of the legal codes as favourable and unfavourable.

6. A person becomes delinquent because of an excess of definitions favourable to violation of law over definitions unfavourable to violation of law.

7. Differential associations may vary in frequency, duration, priority, and intensity.

8. The process of learning criminal behaviour by association with criminal and anti-criminal patterns involves all of the mechanisms that are involved in any other learning.

9. While criminal behaviour is an expression of general needs and values, it is not explained by those general needs and values since non-criminal behaviour is an expression of the same needs and values.

Source: Sutherland, E. H. (1947). *Principles of criminology* (4th ed.). Chicago, IL: Lippincourt Company, pp. 6–7.

is the closeness of the relationship; family, good friends, and romantic partners tend to have a greater influence on us than do more distant relationships, such as those that typically exist with casual acquaintances, neighbours, and other people in the community and media (Akers, 2009).

The three other modalities are priority, frequency, and duration (see Akers, 2009; Akers & Sellers, 2013). **Priority**—the timing or onset of the association—reflects the relative importance of interactions formed earlier in life over later ones. **Frequency** refers to the rate of contact; hence, associations with a high rate of contact are more important than ones characterized by only rare contact. Finally, **duration** encompasses both the length and proportion of time spent with an association. Connections that have endured across many years and/or account for a large proportion of a person's time are more important than those of a more fleeting nature. To summarize, criminal behaviour is most likely to be learned when someone spends much of their youth immersed in a social circle dominated by criminal associates. A wealth of research supports this general proposition and shows that a person's peer group is one of the strongest predictors of antisocial behaviour (see Akers & Jensen, 2006).

The Learning Processes

Sutherland (1947) focused almost exclusively on the learning that occurs from exposure to different "definitions" in our social environment, a topic we will address shortly. Burgess and Akers (1966), swayed by Skinner's research on operant conditioning, expanded the theory by integrating the principles of reinforcement and punishment. Akers (2009) later refined the theory further with the addition of imitation behaviour based on Bandura's work in observational learning. He even acknowledged the potential contribution of classical conditioning. We can see, then, that DA-reinforcement theory brings all the major learning processes discussed in this chapter into a single learning-based theory of criminal behaviour. The following sections explore the specific role of each process, with the exception of classical conditioning, which Akers (2009) believes is the least important.

Definitions

Sutherland (1947) believed the primary importance of one's social associations is that they expose us to different **definitions**, which are generally understood to be a person's values, attitudes, norms, and beliefs (Akers, 2009; Jensen, 2007). The process of learning socially appropriate definitions by interacting with others is often called socialization (Jensen, 2007). Thus, people are socialized in either a prosocial or criminal manner depending on the definitions they are exposed to and adopt. Akers distinguished definitions based on whether they support criminal behaviour (see Akers, 2009; Akers & Sellers, 2013). He termed attitudes and beliefs that disapprove of law-breaking as **negative definitions**. Conversely, **positive definitions** are the attitudes and beliefs that view offending behaviour as appropriate or even desirable. **Neutralizing definitions** recognize that criminal conduct is not normally acceptable but rationalize it as justified in the particular circumstances.

Definitions are important for two reasons (Akers, 2009). First, they act as discriminative stimuli that tell people whether a behaviour is likely to be welcomed and reinforced

---

priority In differential association theory, a modality of association that reflects the timing of a person's social relationship with a specific individual.

frequency In differential association theory, a modality of association that reflects how often a person is in contact with a specific individual.

duration In differential association theory, a modality of association that reflects both the length and proportion of time that a person has had a social relationship with a specific individual.

definitions In Edwin Sutherland's differential association theory, the values, attitudes, norms, and beliefs held by people.

negative definitions In differential association-reinforcement theory, the values, attitudes, norms, and beliefs that disapprove of law-breaking behaviour.

positive definitions In differential association-reinforcement theory, the values, attitudes, norms, and beliefs that approve of law-breaking behaviour.

neutralizing definitions In differential association-reinforcement theory, the values, attitudes, norms, and beliefs that recognize law-breaking behaviour as normally unacceptable but rationalize or excuse it in the applicable circumstances.

or frowned upon and punished. We will expand on this role later in the text. Second, they serve as guideposts for what behaviour is socially and morally appropriate. People holding neutral or positive definitions are apt to offend because they tend to see this type of behaviour as moral or at least justified (Akers & Sellers, 2013). The more pervasive and engrained these definitions become, the more likely a person is to commit crime. Negative definitions have the opposite effect and therefore lower the likelihood of crime.

It may be helpful to imagine a set of scales with negative definitions on one side and neutral and positive definitions on the other. When negative definitions are more strongly held, the scales tip heavily toward law-abiding behaviour. When neutral and positive definitions are stronger, the scales tip heavily in the opposite direction. The overall balance is influenced as much by the absence of definitions as by their presence. As a result, it is possible for the scale to be heavily weighted in favour of crime simply because definitions favouring law-abiding behaviour are missing (Akers, 2009). Such was the case of mobster Henry Hill, discussed in the next case study. What about when the definitions favouring prosocial and antisocial behaviour are fairly even? In this case, behaviour is the most uncertain and highly dependent on situational factors such as the person's immediate desire or need and the opportunities available to him or her (Akers, 2009).

Akers (2009) stresses that definitions establish a frame of mind or mental outlook that makes crime more or less likely as opposed to directly causing it. The exception may be when antisocial definitions are so deeply and strongly held that people feel obligated to act on them, as illustrated by the horrific acts of violence committed by members of some groups espousing extremist and violent political or religious ideologies.

CASE STUDY

Henry Hill

Brooklyn, New York—Henry Hill grew up on the east side of Brooklyn in the 1950s, the son of hard-working immigrants who believed that work taught children the value of money. They were thrilled when 11-year-old Hill announced that he had found a job at the cabstand across the street from their house. For years, he had dreamed of being like the finely dressed, cash-flashing men he saw pull up to the stand in Cadillacs and Lincolns. As it turned out, the business was actually the centre of operations for Paul Vario, an emerging figure in the Lucchese crime family. As an errand boy, Hill saw men move stolen merchandise in and out of the cabstand and listened to their illegal money-making schemes. Before long, he was helping with Vario's gambling operations, cashing counterfeit money, using stolen credit cards, and collecting loan-shark payments.

The benefits of being associated with the Mob were not lost on Hill. He no longer had to wait in line at the bakery, no one dared park in his family's driveway, and he had more money than he could spend. When his parents received a truancy letter from his school, the Varios threatened to kill the mail carrier if another school letter was ever delivered to the Hill home. After his first arrest—at the age of 16 and for using a stolen credit card—Hill followed the instructions he had been given long before and refused to cooperate with the police. Less than an hour after being apprehended, the Varios had arranged for a lawyer and paid his bail. As Hill left the courtroom, he was met by various members of the Varios family, who all smiled and hugged him and took him out to celebrate. Perhaps

continued

more important than the money and assistance, Hill felt a sense of belonging with people he admired, and he did his best to emulate everything they did. When he bought the same suit he saw them wearing, his mother was horrified and screamed that he looked like a gangster. She could not have paid him a greater compliment.

Like all the mobsters he knew, Hill wanted the luxuries in life that everyone desires, but he refused to follow society's rules to obtain them and viewed law-abiding people as fools to be preyed upon. He graduated to bigger schemes, including smuggling cigarettes, stealing cars, committing arson and insurance scams, and hijacking truckloads of merchandise—all under the protection of Paul Vario. The rules of being part of the family were simple and everyone knew them: get out of line or cross the wrong person and you were dead. Run-ins with law enforcement were accepted as a cost of doing business and usually managed without much difficulty through Vario's connections and bribes to the right people. In return, Hill and his associates gave a portion of their proceeds to Vario as "tribute."

Photo 7.4 Henry Hill's life in the Mob formed the basis of the book *Wiseguy*, which was adapted into the Martin Scorsese film *Goodfellas*.

Photo: AP Photo/Nati Harnik

Hill was involved in some of the largest heists of the day. He and his acquaintances stole nearly half a million dollars from an Air France cargo warehouse at Kennedy airport. He also helped facilitate the theft of nearly $6 million in cash and jewellery from Lufthansa's cargo vaults. Over the years, Hill accumulated numerous charges and convictions and served 10 years in federal prison. He was arrested for drug trafficking in 1980 and found himself under investigation by five different law enforcement agencies. Moreover, he was convinced that his associates were going to kill him to tie up "loose ends." He did the only thing he thought he could in the circumstances: he became an FBI informant and, with his wife and children, entered the Witness Protection Program. He was eventually expelled from the program in the early 1990s for committing several crimes while in protection. Hill died of heart failure in Los Angeles in 2012 (Adams, 2012).

Source (except where otherwise noted): Pileggi, N. (1985). *Wiseguy*. New York: Simon & Schuster.

Observational Learning and Imitation

Social interactions not only expose us to what others think, but also what they do; therefore, the people we associate with are an important source of observational learning and imitation (Akers, 2009). Because the four modalities of association tell us that models residing within the family are typically the most influential, there are good theoretical reasons to identify children raised in families with one or more criminal relatives as being the most likely to learn and display offending behaviour (Akers, 2009). These same modalities suggest that models seen in media, such as television and video games, will have considerably less influence on the observer's behaviour.

Reinforcement

In keeping with the principles of operant conditioning, DA-reinforcement theory assumes that people who repeatedly break the law do so because it is reinforcing and seldom punished. In a marked departure from Jeffery's (1965) exclusive focus on nonsocial reinforcers, the theory also recognizes the powerful impact of **social reinforcement**, the verbal and non-verbal behaviour of the people around us (Lieberman, 2000). This behaviour encompasses what people say, the facial expressions and gestures they make, the amount of attention they give us, and other signs of approval. It is not difficult to find examples of social reinforcers of antisocial and criminal behaviour: a coach gives a player a "thumbs up" and more playing time for making a dirty play, a street racer receives a huge number of social media hits to the video of a race, a street gang accepts a prospective member after he or she shoots a rival gang member. Think about the celebratory reaction Henry Hill received from his Mob associates after he refused to cooperate with police and was released from jail.

In any given situation, people usually have access to a range of behavioural options that offer the possibility of reinforcement. They will choose the most reinforcing one based on the intrinsic value of the reinforcer and the frequency and likelihood of reinforcement (Akers, 2009). This is why the associations a person keeps are so important—they act as both discriminative stimuli and sources of social reinforcement (or punishment). Their presence signals which acts are likely to be reinforced, and their subsequent reactions to a person's behaviour affect the likelihood of that individual repeating the behaviour. For people with strongly procriminal social networks, such as Henry Hill, the implications are clear: the available discriminative stimuli are overwhelmingly positive and neutralizing in nature and there is a great deal of social reinforcement for criminal and antisocial acts.

social reinforcement The verbal and non-verbal behaviour and gestures made by others following a response, which increase the likelihood of that response being repeated.

Putting It All Together: DA-Reinforcement Theory in Action

DA-reinforcement emphasizes the role of early family and childhood experiences in the development of criminal behaviour because they represent the child's first social associations. When these associations are procriminal, they are a source of definitions and models that are the basic ingredients of delinquency. Akers (2009) contends that, with few exceptions, a person commits delinquent and criminal acts only after exposure to procriminal associates in their family or among their peers. Procriminal associates also supply reinforcement that may lead a person to repeat and maintain this behaviour. Moreover, a person's associations impact their behaviour and vice versa. As we learned in Chapter 4, criminally involved individuals are more likely to maintain social interactions with people who approved and reinforced this type of behaviour in the past. They also tend to form new social associations and friendships with like-minded people who share their involvement in crime.

The formation and maintenance of these procriminal relationships further enhances the availability of definitions, models, and reinforcement that support continued offending, which in turn impacts future social choices. In this way, associations and behaviours influence one another in an ongoing and reciprocal fashion. Over time and with reinforcement, especially intermittent reinforcement, criminal behaviour gains "habit strength" and becomes an engrained way of responding (Akers, 2009, p. 159). At this point, an entrenched pattern of criminal behaviour has developed and will continue until the reinforcement or punishment contingencies surrounding it are altered, something that typically cannot be accomplished without a wholesale change in one's social associations, such as the one that occurred when Hill entered witness protection (Akers, 2009).

Summary

1. Learning represents a change in our behavioural repertoire due to experience and is responsible for most of the behaviours we acquire during our lives. All learning theories share the same general belief that people are born "neutral" and any subsequent behaviour they display, be it prosocial or antisocial, is a product of learning. This chapter overviewed three principal forms of learning—classical conditioning, operant conditioning, and observational learning—and explained how each one may contribute to crime.

2. Classical conditioning involves learning an association between two events that precede a behaviour. It was first recognized during Pavlov's research with dogs that were presented with food (unconditioned stimulus), which elicited a salivary response (unconditioned response). The dogs learned to associate the food with the approaching sights and sounds of the assistant who fed them. Once the association was formed, these sights and sounds alone (conditioned stimulus) caused the dogs to salivate (conditioned response). Criminal offending may be classically conditioned in the same manner. If past criminal acts repeatedly occur in the presence of the same environmental stimuli, the future presence of these stimuli could evoke the same feelings and desires that previously led them to offend.

3. Hans Eysenck theorized that most people have a classically conditioned conscience that stops them from committing crime. This conscience will develop if children are consistently punished when they misbehave so that they learn to associate "bad" behaviour with the unpleasant feeling of being punished. As a result of this association, children who behave badly automatically experience feelings of anxiety and discomfort even in the absence of punishment. Eysenck believed that, once this classical conditioning response is established, the mere thought of doing something wrong will elicit the same unpleasant feelings, which will be sufficiently strong to deter most people from misbehaving. This classically conditioned "conscience" will not develop in children who exhibit poor conditionability or whose bad behaviour is not consistently punished.

4. Operant conditioning is founded on the premise that people behave to bring about particular consequences. Reinforcement is anything that increases the likelihood of a response: positive reinforcement strengthens responding by presenting something pleasant; negative reinforcement strengthens responding by removing something aversive. In contrast, punishment is anything that decreases the likelihood of a response. Like reinforcement, there are two types of punishment—positive punishment decreases responding by administering something aversive, while negative

punishment decreases responding by removing something pleasant. C.R. Jeffery hypothesized that offending reflects differential reinforcement. That is, people tend to repeat criminal behaviour because it results in more reinforcement than punishment. Jeffery focused on the importance of nonsocial reinforcement, such as material goods, and argued that people will continue to offend if their behaviour produces more nonsocial reinforcement than punishment.

5. The criminal justice system puts a great deal of emphasis on the use of punishment to deter offending. Unfortunately, this approach is not likely to meet with much success because contemporary systems violate the principles of effective punishment. Punishment is imposed in an incremental fashion, the delay between the act and the punishment is too long, and punishment is imposed inconsistently. Legal systems also do a poor job of providing offenders with reinforcement for engaging in alternative, prosocial behaviour.

6. Observational learning occurs when people acquire new behaviours they see performed by another person, known as a model. An observer is more likely to imitate behaviour that results in vicarious reinforcement (i.e. the model was seen being reinforced for performing the same behaviour). Recognition that learning can occur by observation has raised concerns over the potential impact of television and other forms of electronic media. Research on the effects of viewing violence in the media has produced mixed results, but there appears to be a small yet statistically significant relationship between watching violent images and aggressive behaviour in young people. Studies suggest that the negative effects of watching violent media are greater when viewers identify with the character perpetrating the violence and the violence is depicted in a manner that is realistic and justified but lacks any of the unpleasant consequences that accompany it in real life.

7. Ronald Akers's differential association-reinforcement theory integrates all three forms of learning into a comprehensive explanation of deviant and criminal behaviour. DA-reinforcement is founded on the ideas of Edwin Sutherland, who believed behaviour is learned through social interactions that expose people to different definitions. These definitions consist of the values, attitudes, norms, and beliefs that people hold and are classified as negative, positive, or neutralizing depending on whether law-breaking is construed as unacceptable, acceptable, or excusable in the circumstances, respectively. According to Sutherland's principle of differential association, people are likely to act criminally when their social networks expose them to definitions that are predominantly positive and neutralizing rather than negative.

8. DA-reinforcement marries Sutherland's ideas with the principles of operant conditioning and reinforcement. According to the theory, the behavioural choice a person makes in a situation is the one associated with the greatest reinforcement, taking into account the value, frequency, and likelihood of the reinforcer. Both nonsocial as well as social reinforcement, such as verbal and non-verbal expressions of approval, influence these behavioural choices, although Akers believes the latter are more important. This is why the personal associations we maintain are so influential. First, the people around us act as discriminative stimuli that give us clues about which behaviours are likely to be reinforced. Second, their reactions to our behaviour may be socially reinforcing and therefore increase the likelihood that we will choose to repeat the behaviour.

Review Questions

1. Using classical conditioning theory, diagram how repeated exposure to his cousin's sexually violent stories and photographs caused Richard Ramirez to become sexually aroused to violence. Be sure to identify the unconditioned stimulus, unconditioned response, conditioned stimulus, and conditioned response.
2. Explain Eysenck's theory about the development of a classically conditioned "conscience."
3. Indicate whether each of the following situations involves positive reinforcement, negative reinforcement, positive punishment, or negative punishment:
   a. An offender is sentenced to perform 100 hours of community service.
   b. An incarcerated inmate is released from prison early.
   c. A shoplifter steals a cellphone and leaves the store undetected.
   d. A qualified driver has his or her licence suspended.
4. Identify the two main processes involved in observational learning. What factors appear to increase the likelihood that children who observe media violence will behave the same way?
5. Explain the distinction between social and nonsocial reinforcement. Review the case study of Henry Hill and identify examples of both types of reinforcement.
6. Using DA-reinforcement as the framework, identify different ways that social networks influence the likelihood of a person offending.

Additional Readings

Akers, R. L. (2009). *Social learning and social structure: A general theory of crime and deviance*. New Brunswick, NJ: Transaction.

Bandura, A. (1977). *Social learning theory*. Englewood Cliffs, NJ: Prentice-Hall.

Jeffery, C. R. (1965). Criminal behavior and learning theory. *The Journal of Criminal Law, Criminology and Police Science, 56*, 294–300.

Moffitt, T. E. (1983). The learning theory model of punishment: Implications for delinquency deterrence. *Criminal Justice and Behavior, 10*, 131–158.

Paik, H., & Comstock, G. (1994). The effects of television violence on antisocial behavior: A meta-analysis. *Communication Research, 21*, 516–546.

Savage, J. (2008). The role of exposure to media violence in the etiology of violent behavior: A criminologist weighs in. *American Behavioral Scientist, 51*, 1123–1136.

8

Social Cognition

Learning Objectives

At the end of this chapter, you should be able to:

- describe the field of cognitive psychology and explain social cognition;

- explain how low moral reasoning contributes to criminal behaviour;

- explain the various mechanisms of moral disengagement employed by people to avoid the negative feelings associated with violating their moral standards;

- identify and describe different thinking patterns that contribute to criminal behaviour;

- explain how affect and cognition can interact in ways that lead to violent behaviour;

- explain how groups and authority figures influence individual decisions to engage in criminal and violent behaviour;

- identify different social information processing errors and explain how they contribute to criminal and violent behaviour; and

- describe the general aggression model (GAM).

CASE STUDY

Umar Farouk Abdulmutallab

Detroit, Michigan—"Hey dude, your pants are on fire," exclaimed the passenger sitting beside 25-year-old Umar Farouk Abdulmutallab, who became known as the Underwear Bomber (Harris, 2011, para. 15). Noticing the smoke and flames, fellow passengers aboard Northwest Airlines Flight 253, flying to Detroit on Christmas Day 2009, rushed to Abdulmutallab's aid and set about extinguishing the flames (Lewis, 2012). Once the fire was doused and Abdulmutallab's pants were stripped away, it became apparent that there was something odd about his underwear. As one person explained, "All I know is they

Photo 8.1 This photo of Umar Farouk Abdulmutallab was released by the US Marshals Service in December 2009, after Abdulmutallab's arrest.
AP Photo/US Marshals Service

were bulky and they were burning" (Gardham, 2011, p. B5). The bulkiness was from a bomb that, when it failed to denotate, caught fire. The FBI later learned Abdulmutallab believed that, if he blew up the plane, he would become a martyr and go to heaven (Rosenfield, 2011). According to one agent who interviewed him, "He did not bat an eye in saying if that plane was going to go down, it was going to go down. That was God's call. . . . His responsibility was just to detonate the bomb, and whatever happened, happened" (Lewis, 2012, para. 10).

The FBI's subsequent investigation of Abdulmuttalab's background revealed that he came from a wealthy family who cared deeply about him (Lewis, 2012). Although he was raised in the Islamic faith, his family did not share his fanatical beliefs and were shocked to hear of his bombing attempt. His mother reported that he was exposed to radical Islam at a young age through the Internet and became convinced that he should join the jihad, or holy war, against the West. While completing his masters' degree in engineering, he broke off communication with his family and made his way to Yemen, where he tried to contact Al-Qaeda operatives. The group was initially skeptical of him, but his persistence convinced them to train him. He was eventually instructed to blow himself up in a plane flying over a densely populated area of the United States so as to maximize the loss of life.

The agents who interviewed Abdulmutallab described him as "different because of his absolute devotion to Jihad. The degree of conviction that he had to the cause is unparalleled" (Lewis, 2012, para. 49). He reported wearing the underwear bomb for the three weeks leading up to the incident to ensure that he was comfortable with the device and could get it through airport security, something authorities think may have contributed to the bomb's failure to detonate (Ferran, 2012). During his various court proceedings, Abdulmutallab called the United States "a cancer" (Harris, 2011, para. 10) and described the bomb he was carrying as a "blessed weapon to save the lives of innocent Muslims" (White, 2012, para. 21). He claimed to have acted out of a religious duty and that attacks like the one he launched were "the most virtuous of deeds" (Rosenfield, 2011, para. 14). Even at the end of his sentencing hearing, he was unrepentant, declaring that he was "proud to kill in the name of God" (Ferran, 2012, para. 5).

Introduction

Many of Abdulmutallab's statements reveal the deeply held beliefs and engrained thinking patterns that supported and justified his attempt to blow up Flight 253. The study of how we perceive, think, remember, and make decisions is called **cognitive psychology**. Within this field, a distinction is sometimes drawn between nonsocial and social cognition. **Nonsocial cognition** focuses on how information about the physical world, such as time, space, and action, is perceived, processed, stored, and utilized in decision-making (Ross & Fabiano, 1981). **Social cognition** is concerned with how we understand ourselves and other people (Fiske & Taylor, 1991). It involves our abilities to perceive what others are thinking and feeling, understand their perspectives, appreciate their perceptions of us, and solve interpersonal problems (Ross & Fabiano, 1981). This chapter examines social cognition and how it contributes to offending.

Moral Reasoning

Morality is the ability to discern right and wrong. The dominant model of moral development continues to be the one put forward by Lawrence Kohlberg half a century ago. Kohlberg (1976) was interested in **moral reasoning**, the analytical or logical process that people use to make judgments about what is right and wrong. To investigate moral reasoning, he created a series of hypothetical moral dilemmas, the best-known of which involves Heinz, who stole the drug his wife desperately needed to survive (Kohlberg, 1969). Participants presented with this dilemma were asked if they agreed with Heinz's actions. Kohlberg was not really interested in what participants decided; he wanted to know why they approved or disapproved of stealing the drug and the logic they used to arrive at their judgment.

Based on this research, Kohlberg (1976) developed his theory of moral development. The resulting model identifies three major levels of moral reasoning, each with two stages (see Table 8.1). The first is the **preconventional** level, which encompasses the earliest forms of moral reasoning that are typical of young children, who assess right and wrong with reference to external circumstances such as avoiding punishment or gaining rewards from people with authority over them. You may recognize this type of reasoning if you have ever heard a child tell a friend that they should not do something because they might get in trouble. Individuals operating at the second, or **conventional**, level have internalized society's rules, which they see as important for maintaining order. They determine what is right and wrong according to the expectations of people who are important to them (e.g. family, close friends) or out of a sense of obligation toward society as a whole. The average adolescent and most adults exhibit this type of moral reasoning. The third and highest level is the **postconventional**. Individuals at this level do not accept society's rules uncritically and instead develop their own set of moral principles based on equality, dignity, and a respect for human rights. They recognize that their principles will occasionally clash with society's rules and laws but believe they should stand by their own beliefs. According to Kohlberg, only a small minority of adults ever attain this level.

As a stage-based theory, Kohlberg's model makes several assumptions. First, it presupposes that individual moral reasoning operates only one stage at a time. Second, changes in moral development always occur in an upwards direction. Once you achieve a higher stage, you never regress to a lower one. Third, each stage is a prerequisite for the next one and

cognitive psychology The study of the mental processes involved in human perception, thought, memory, and decision-making.

nonsocial cognition The study of how we understand the physical world and other matters unrelated to people and their social interactions.

social cognition The study of how we understand ourselves and other people.

morality The ability to distinguish between right and wrong.

moral reasoning The analytical process used to arrive at decisions about what is right and wrong.

preconventional moral reasoning The lowest of Lawrence Kohlberg's levels of moral development, whereby right and wrong are determined by the anticipated rewards or punishments.

conventional moral reasoning The middle of Lawrence Kohlberg's levels of moral development, whereby right and wrong are determined by the expectations of other significant people, such as family members, close friends, or society at large.

postconventional moral reasoning The highest of Lawrence Kohlberg's levels of moral development, whereby right and wrong are determined by an individual's own principles of equality, justice, and respect for human rights.

Table 8.1 Kohlberg's six hierarchical stages of moral development

Level	Stage	
3. Postconventional	**Stage 6: Universal ethical principle orientation** Right is determined by one's conscience, according to principles such as justice, equality, and respect for human dignity.	A minority of adults
	Stage 5: Social contract, legalistic orientation Right is determined by society's rules, which should be upheld with some exceptions.	
2. Conventional	**Stage 4: "Law and order" orientation** Right is determined by society's rules, which must be upheld for the system to work.	The average adolescent and adult
	Stage 3: "Good boy–nice girl" orientation Right is determined by the expectations of those who are close or important to you.	
1. Preconventional	**Stage 2: Instrumental relativist orientation** Right is determined by what will be rewarded.	
	Stage 1: Punishment and obedience orientation Right is determined by what will be punished.	Children less than 9–11

Source: Adapted from Kohlberg, L. (1978). The cognitive developmental approach to behavior disorders: A study of the development of moral reasoning in delinquents. In G. Serban (Ed.), *Cognitive defects in the development of mental illness* (pp. 207–219). New York, NY: Brunner/Mazel.

therefore movement through the stages always follows the same sequence and no stage is ever skipped. Although the sequence of development is the same for everyone, the rate of progress and the highest stage attained show individual variation. Jennings, Kilkenny, and Kohlberg (1983) speculate that interacting with others operating at higher levels of moral reasoning reveals shortcomings in our own judgments, which in turn spurs further moral growth. Thus, the speed of moral development and the stage at which development peaks are both highly dependent on a person's individual circumstances. People with extensive social interactions dominated by high moral reasoners are expected to develop more quickly and attain higher levels of moral reasoning than individuals with smaller and morally immature social circles.

Moral Development and Offending

Investigations of delinquent youths typically find that they are dominated by preconventional moral reasoning, whereas nondelinquent groups exhibit a much higher proportion of conventional moral reasoning (see Table 8.2 for a summary of selected studies). A recent meta-analysis confirms that delinquents exhibit significantly lower moral reasoning than their nondelinquent counterparts (Stams et al., 2006). Moreover, this difference persists after controlling for other variables such as socio-economic status, cultural heritage, age, intelligence, and gender. Studies also show that morally immature offenders are much more likely to recidivate than morally mature ones (Van Vugt et al., 2011) and that treatment programs designed to boost moral maturity can significantly reduce run-ins with the law (e.g. Wilson, Bouffard, & MacKenzie, 2005).

While Kohlberg's model of moral development was not originally expounded as a theory of crime, it has subsequently been elaborated on and used to explain offending behaviour.

Table 8.2 Percentage of preconventional and conventional moral reasoning usage among delinquent and nondelinquent samples in selected studies

Study	Preconventional (%)	Conventional (%)
Kohlberg (1958a)		
Delinquents	80	20
Controls	25	75
Hickey (1972)		
Delinquents	53	47
Controls	7	93
Kohlberg (1958b)		
Delinquents	92	8
Controls	58	42
Critchley (1961)		
Delinquents	87	13
Controls	15	85
Hudgins & Prentice (1973)[1]		
Delinquents	80	20
Controls	30	70
Jurkovic & Prentice (1977)		
Delinquents	71	29
Controls	42	58
Lee & Prentice (1988)[2]		
Delinquents	71	29
Controls	49	51
Basinger et al. (1995)[3]		
Delinquents	71	29
Controls	33	67
Palmer & Hollin (1998)[1,4]		
Delinquents	50	50
Controls	17	83
Trevethan & Walker (1989)[1]		
Delinquents	93	7
Controls	47	53

Notes
1. Figures reflect the percentage of youth operating at each level rather than the percentage of usage.
2. Figures reflect a subgroup of "psychopathic" delinquents.
3. Transitions between levels were grouped according to the lowest level.
4. Percentage is based on conversion of scores on the Sociomoral Reflection Measure–Short Form (Gibbs, Basinger & Fuller, 1992).

Source: Republished with permission of Simon and Schuster, from Jennings, W. S., Kilkenny, R., & Kohlberg, L. (1983). Moral-development theory and practice for youthful and adult offenders. In W. S. Laufer & J. M. Day (Eds.), *Personality theory, moral development, and criminal behavior* (pp. 281–355). Lexington, MA: Lexington Books.

Kohlberg and colleagues do not propose that low moral reasoning is a causal factor in offending, but they do believe that it can promote self-serving behaviour (Jennings et al., 1983). Remember, preconventional moral reasoners determine how they should act based primarily on the probable consequences of the behaviour. This sensitivity to their immediate surroundings means that they are likely to offend when the chances of being caught are slim or the expected payoffs are high. This does not pose much of a problem with young children because their parents or other responsible adults are usually close at hand to punish or reward their behaviour as appropriate. It presents more of a problem among morally immature adolescents (Palmer, 2003). Parental supervision and control are loosened for adolescents, which means that they increasingly encounter opportunities where the perceived costs of offending are low (i.e. likelihood of getting caught) and the anticipated benefits are high (e.g. material rewards). Adolescents who are still operating at the preconventional level will be strongly influenced by these situational factors and thus likely to offend (Jennings et al., 1983).

High moral reasoners are better equipped to withstand opportunities to commit crime because they determine what is right and wrong based on their internal sense of social obligation and moral principles. This is why Kohlberg theorizes that high moral reasoning is essential for consistent and stable prosocial behaviour (Jennings et al., 1983). In this sense, preconventional moral reasoning does not cause offending, but conventional and postconventional moral reasoning help to prevent it. While it may be true that high moral reasoning increases our resistance to situational factors, it does not immunize us from committing crime. Table 8.2 shows that anywhere from 10 to 50 per cent of the moral reasoning in the delinquent groups was at the conventional level or higher. One explanation for this apparent contradiction is that offending behaviour does not always involve moral judgments. Some offences flow from disturbed thinking processes associated with mental disorders (see Chapter 9) or from impulsive acts committed without time to engage in moral reasoning (Jennings et al., 1983).

Moral development theory also highlights a major pitfall of criminal justice system policies that promote incarceration. Because institutions are dominated by low moral reasoners, prison offers few opportunities for moral growth through exposure to higher levels of moral reasoning (Jennings et al., 1983). While imprisonment does not preclude offenders from attaining conventional moral reasoning, their progress will probably be much slower than if they remained in the community and were surrounded by peers operating at higher levels. The situation for conventional moral reasoners is even worse. Because they will encounter few, if any, inmates who are morally more mature, their moral development will stagnate. Incarcerating offenders, then, impedes moral development and leaves them vulnerable to situational factors that promote criminal behaviour when they are released back into the community.

Moral Disengagement

At one time or another, most of us have done something we knew was wrong. Perhaps you stayed silent when a cashier undercharged you for an item or gave you too much change. Maybe you accidently damaged someone's parked vehicle but did not leave a note for the owner or you ran a red light despite knowing you could stop safely. Put bluntly, we sometimes do things we know are wrong. One of the criticisms levelled against Kohlberg's theory is that it does not consider how the cognitive processes surrounding morality relate to actual behaviour (Lytton, Maunula, & Watts, 1987). As we saw in Chapter 7, human behaviour is, at least initially, governed by the presence of external rewards and punishments. Albert Bandura (1999) suggested that, over time, internal moral standards develop, a shift that resembles the change from preconventional to conventional moral reasoning. He argues that people apply consequences to themselves depending on the degree to which they live up to their internal moral standards. People feel good about themselves when they adhere to their morals, and this serves as motivation for behaving morally in the future. When they fall short of their moral expectations, they feel badly, which deters them from engaging in amoral conduct again. In this sense, our morals serve as an internal compass guiding our behaviour.

Bandura (1999) speculated that people can turn off this self-regulatory mechanism through **moral disengagement**, which refers to a variety of processes that people employ to avoid the negative psychological consequences of violating their moral standards. Although this theory can be applied to minor incidents such as those described at the beginning of this section, Bandura's main purpose was to explain the senseless, cruel, and inhumane acts that are universally regarded as wrong yet occur with shocking regularity around the world. Disengagement processes operate in four ways: to minimize the reprehensible nature of the behaviour, to minimize responsibility for the behaviour, to minimize the consequences of the behaviour, or to minimize the worth of the victims or shift blame on to them. As we shall see shortly, Umar Farouq Abdulmutallab employed many of these mechanisms.

> **moral disengagement**
> A process, described by Albert Bandura, in which people employ a variety of psychological mechanisms to avoid the negative feelings they might otherwise experience as a result of violating their moral standards.

Mechanisms of Moral Disengagement

Minimize the Reprehensible Nature of the Behaviour

One group of moral disengagement processes work by recasting the perpetrator's behaviour in a more favourable moral light. This shift can be accomplished by **euphemistic labelling**, which makes the behaviour sound less offensive (Bandura, 1999). For example, Abdulmutallab called himself a martyr instead of a suicide bomber and described his acts a jihad rather than terrorism. Euphemistic labelling is not restricted to terrorists. Government and military officials routinely do the same thing. They refer to civilians who are wounded or killed during military operations as collateral damage and waterboarding has been called an enhanced coercive interrogation technique (Henley, 2007). A second cognitive strategy is **moral justification**, whereby otherwise objectionable behaviour is construed as acceptable because of the important goal it is designed to achieve—something Abdulmutallab did when he justified blowing up the plane as a way to save Muslim lives (Bandura, 1999). Finally, people sometimes engage in **advantageous comparisons** to make their conduct appear less offensive and to demonstrate their moral superiority by pointing out that what they have done is, at least in their eyes, less egregious than other people's acts.

> **euphemistic labelling**
> A moral disengagement mechanism whereby people apply a positive description to their immoral behaviour to make it sound less offensive.
>
> **moral justification** A moral disengagement mechanism whereby people rationalize their immoral behaviour on the grounds that it was necessary to achieve an important goal or avoid a more serious, harmful consequence.
>
> **advantageous comparisons** A moral disengagement mechanism whereby people construe their immoral behaviour as less offensive by judging it against another's more egregious acts.

Minimize Responsibility for the Behaviour

Another group of disengagement mechanisms operate by diminishing the perpetrator's perceived responsibility for the objectionable conduct. This is achieved by displacing or diffusing responsibility (see Figure 8.1). **Displacement of responsibility** occurs when people attribute responsibility for their immoral acts to people in positions of control and authority. In Abdulmutallab's case, this authority was God. Abdulmutallab thought that his task was merely to detonate the bomb and that it was up to God to determine if the plane would actually blow up. Psychologically, displacement relieves offenders of personal responsibility by attributing their immoral acts to a higher authority. Stanley Milgram's research on obedience, discussed later in this chapter, attests to the powerful effect of displacement on human aggression. **Diffusion of responsibility** is similar, except that the person spreads the responsibility across a group of people who are jointly culpable for the harm. As Bandura (1999) explains, "When everyone is responsible, no one really feels responsible" (p. 198).

> **displacement of responsibility** A moral disengagement mechanism whereby people avoid responsibility for their immoral acts by attributing them to people in positions of control and authority.
>
> **diffusion of responsibility** A moral disengagement mechanism whereby people minimize their responsibility for immoral acts on the grounds that they are merely one among many involved.

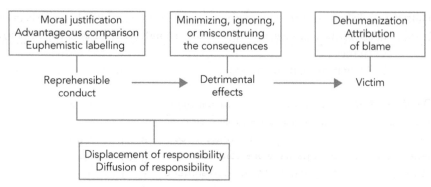

Figure 8.1 Mechanisms of Moral Disengagement.

Source: A. Bandura, Moral disengagement in the perpetration of inhumanities (*Personality and Social Psychology Review* 3(3)) pp. 193–209, copyright © 1999 by SAGE. Reprinted by Permission of SAGE Publications , Inc.

Minimize the Consequences of the Behaviour

Disengagement mechanisms also minimize the harmful effects of the offender's behaviour (Bandura, 1999). For example, an offender might lessen the perceived harm of stealing by explaining that the homeowners can buy new products with the insurance money while he or she is stuck with their old junk. Research shows that, the more removed perpetrators are from their victims and the consequences, the easier it is for them to ignore or minimize the harm they cause (Milgram, 1965).

Minimize the Worth of the Victim and Blame the Victim

The remaining disengagement processes loosen any connection the offender feels toward the victim by characterizing him or her as different or deserving of mistreatment. One such process is **dehumanization**, which equates victims to monsters, subhuman creatures, or even inanimate objects (Bandura, 1999). Recall that Abdulmutallab referred to the United States as cancer, as though it were a disease to be eradicated. In a similar vein, serial killer Gary Ridgway referred to his victims as "garbage" (Doughton, 2003, para. 4). Psychologically, it is easier to hurt something inhuman rather than human. The **attribution of blame** focuses on the victim's conduct, which is seen as an extreme provocation that left the offender no choice but to respond as he or she did.

dehumanization A moral disengagement mechanism that loosens the perpetrators' connection to their victims by viewing them as devoid of human qualities or as objects deserving mistreatment.

attribution of blame A moral disengagement mechanism whereby the victims are blamed for provoking the perpetrators and leaving them with no alternative but to respond as they did.

Individual Development and Operation of Moral Disengagement

Most people endorse similar moral standards. Where they tend to vary is in how badly they feel about violating their moral standards and their reliance on disengagement processes. Even the same person can employ different disengagement mechanisms from one situation to the next. Bandura (1999) believes that this is why people who exhibit the same level of moral reasoning do not always exhibit the same behaviour. Furthermore, there is evidence that the combined effect of several disengagement processes is greater than any individual mechanism (e.g. Bandura, Underwood, & Fromson, 1975). A series of studies conducted by Bandura and colleagues (1975) found that participants exposed to both diffusion of responsibility and dehumanization of the victim applied higher-intensity shocks to the victim than did participants exposed to only one of these conditions (see the "Researching" box). Given the enormity of the violence attempted by Abdulmutallab, it is not surprising to see numerous disengagement processes.

Researching Criminal and Violent Behaviour

Moral Disengagement in Action

Bandura and colleagues (1975) investigated the impact of dehumanization and diffusion of responsibility on aggression in a sample of college students. Participants were told that the study was examining the effect of punishment on decision-making and that they would be supervising a three-member team situated in another room. The team had to complete a series of tasks. If any of the proposed solutions were unsatisfactory, the supervisor was to select and administer a mild to painful shock to the team. In reality, there was no team and therefore no one was shocked; however, the researchers used the shock level selected to measure the participants' aggression.

The study included several conditions. The researchers told participants in the personal responsibility condition that they each supervised a single team member and that any shock they administered applied to that person alone. Participants in the diffusion of responsibility condition were told that they were one of three supervisors and their shocks would be averaged before being administered to the whole team. The researchers also varied the humanization and dehumanization of the team members by making comments about them in front of the participants. In the humanization condition, they were described as understanding, perceptive, and having other human qualities; in the dehumanization condition, they were characterized as rotten and animalistic. No comments were made in the neutral condition.

Figures 8.2 and 8.3 show the results of the study. Participants in the diffuse responsibility condition applied significantly greater shocks than those in the personal responsibility condition. They also applied much stronger shocks when the team members were dehumanized than when they were humanized or not described.

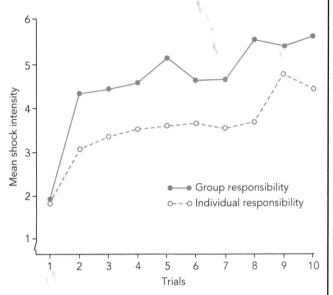

Figure 8.2 Average shock intensity applied when operating under conditions of diffused responsibility or individual responsibility.

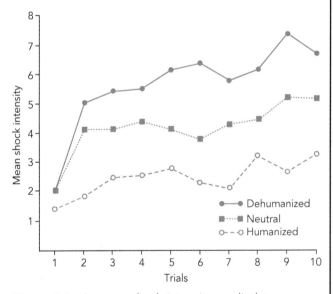

Figure 8.3 Average shock intensity applied to persons represented as humanized, neutral, or dehumanized.

Source: Reprinted from *Journal of Research in Personality, 9*(4), Albert Bandura, Bill Underwood, and Michael E Fromson, "Disinhibition of aggression through diffusion of responsibility and dehumanization of victims," 253–269, Copyright (1975), with permission from Elsevier.

Criminal Thinking

criminal thinking Cognitive processes and content that facilitate the initiation and continuation of offending behaviour.

Several theories focusing on **criminal thinking** have emerged over the past several decades. Criminal thinking refers to cognitive processes and content that facilitate the initiation and maintenance of offending behaviour (Walters, 2006). The underlying premise of these theories is that our thinking determines our behaviour. By logical extension, the only way to understand criminal behaviour is to gain an appreciation of how offenders think (Walters, 1990).

Yochelson and Samenow's Criminal Personality

Samuel Yochelson and Stanton Samenow's *The Criminal Personality* (1976) summarized nearly 15 years of their clinical work at a secure psychiatric hospital in Washington, DC. During this time, they conducted countless interviews with 240 offenders—most of whom were male—found not guilty by reason of insanity. Based on these interviews, Yochelson and Samenow concluded that offenders think differently than other people. They described 52 common criminal thinking errors and behavioural patterns that permeated all aspects of the offenders' cognitions, including what they thought before, during, and after committing a crime. The researchers claimed that a criminal act, like anything else a person might do, is simply the result of the offender's thought processes.

Yochelson and Samenow's work represented an important step forward because it highlighted cognition's role in criminal behaviour; however, their research has not escaped criticism. One difficulty is that they studied a fairly unusual group of offenders, raising questions over whether the thinking errors identified might be unique to that sample (Ross & Fabiano, 1981). In addition, the absence of a control group makes it impossible to assess the extent to which these same thought processes might exist among the general public. Critics also argued that many of the thinking errors were poorly operationalized and therefore difficult to validate scientifically (Walters, 2006). These weaknesses aside, Yochelson and Samenow's clinical descriptions formed the foundation for subsequent work in this area.

Criminal Thinking Styles

Combining Yochelson and Samenow's research with their own clinical experience at the federal penitentiary in Leavenworth, Kansas, Glenn Walters and Thomas White (1989) distilled eight cognitive errors that they believed were associated with criminality. They labelled these cognitive errors, or criminal thinking styles, mollification, cutoff, entitlement, power orientation, sentimentality, superoptimism, cognitive indolence, and discontinuity (see Table 8.3). Walters (1990) argues that the presence of these thinking styles perpetuates the criminal lifestyle. To be clear, he is not trying to explain isolated law-breaking but the persistent and serious offending of people firmly entrenched in a criminal lifestyle.

The central tenet of Walters's (1990) theory is that the choices and early life experiences of people who engage in lifestyle criminality produce a belief system that consists of the eight criminal thinking styles. Once established, this belief system promotes, justifies, and rationalizes continued criminal conduct. Walters (1990) acknowledges that surrounding social conditions such as family upbringing and neighbourhood environment impact

Table 8.3 Criminal thinking styles

1.	**Mollification**	The process of rationalizing criminal behaviour and avoiding responsibility by blaming it on other external factors or perceived injustices.
2.	**Cutoff**	A psychological mechanism for ignoring the fear and anxiety associated with offending that might otherwise serve as a deterrent. A cutoff can be internal, such as a stated phrase (e.g. "Nothing risked, nothing gained"), or external, such as the use of an intoxicating substance prior to committing an offence.
3.	**Entitlement**	The belief that the usual rules do not apply and that one has the right to do or take anything.
4.	**Power orientation**	The view that the world can be divided into people who exert power and control over others and those who are powerless and submissive.
5.	**Sentimentality**	An emphasis on one's positive attributes and actions as a means of overshadowing and justifying the negative and harmful things one has done.
6.	**Superoptimism**	An overly confident and optimistic view of one's abilities, especially the ability to avoid the undesirable consequences of one's law-breaking.
7.	**Cognitive indolence**	Lazy and uncritical thought processes and the tendency to be easily bored.
8.	**Discontinuity**	A lack of commitment and general failure to follow through on things one starts.

Sources: Adapted from Walters, G. D., & White, T. W. (1989). The thinking criminal: A cognitive model of lifestyle criminality. *Criminal Justice Research Bulletin*, 4, 1–10; Walters, G. D. (1990). *The criminal lifestyle: Patterns of serious criminal conduct*. Newbury Park, CA: Sage Publications.

people's opportunities and likelihood of criminal behaviour, but he strongly rejects the general sociological perspective that some people are essentially compelled into a life of crime by their social situation. According to Walters, the choices people make ultimately set them on a path toward or away from a criminal lifestyle.

To facilitate criminal lifestyle theory research, Walters (1995) created the Psychological Inventory of Criminal Thinking Styles (PICTS), a self-report instrument that measures all eight styles. Studies show that the presence of criminal thinking, as measured by the PICTS, is associated with criminal reoffending among men and women (Walters, 2002, 2012; Walters & Elliot, 1999). In one study, women prisoners scored significantly higher on the PICTS than their male counterparts (Walters, Elliot, & Miscoll, 1998). Walters and colleagues (1998) speculate that women may be more open and candid in their responding and, as a result, receive higher scores. Alternatively, criminal behaviour is generally seen as less socially acceptable for women than for men; therefore, the women who engage in this lifestyle and end up incarcerated may have more severe procriminal thinking patterns. On a more positive note, there is some evidence that cognitive-based treatments can reduce criminal thinking styles, but more research is needed to show that these changes can lower reoffending (Walters, 2002; Walters, 2012).

Hostile Thoughts and Affect

The discussion so far has focused on the role of cognition in offending behaviour, largely to the exclusion of affect or emotion. Yet it would be naïve to think that cognition and affect do not influence one another. We know that our feelings shape our thinking. For example, we tend to express more negative and pessimistic views when we are sad or dejected than when we are happy. Likewise, what people think impacts how they feel. Receiving a compliment on our looks evokes quite different feelings depending on whether we think the person is flirting with us or about to ask us for money. The excitation transfer theory and the frustration-aggression hypothesis highlight different ways that cognition and affect may interact to produce aggressive and violent behaviour.

Excitation Transfer Theory

Dolf Zillman's excitation transfer theory is based on the idea that emotional arousal can carry over from one situation to another (Zillman, Katcher, & Milavsky, 1972). The theory assumes that the physiological arousal of people who are excited dissipates gradually. Eventually, the excitement subsides to a level where people are no longer aware of their arousal despite its lingering presence. In this state, they tend to mistakenly attribute any remaining physiological arousal to their current environment. This remaining arousal could also drive their behaviour. Imagine that someone walking across a narrow cable bridge suspended high above a canyon encounters a good-looking stranger. In this context, the arousal generated by the thrill (or fear) of walking on the bridge might be mislabelled as an intense attraction to the stranger and could even fuel efforts to contact him or her later on (Dutton & Aron, 1974).

In a carefully controlled investigation of this effect, Zillman and colleagues (1972) showed that participants who were angered and then physiologically aroused by riding an exercise bike administered significantly more intense electric shocks to an antagonist than did participants who were not angered or physiologically aroused by exercise. Presumably, the arousal was misidentified as anger and energized their aggressive behaviour. To borrow Donald Hebb's (1955) analogy, physiological arousal is like the engine that propels us, but it is cognition and our ability to recognize and process information from our surroundings that serves as the steering wheel that guides the way we label our emotions and behave. Although the excitation transfer effect has not been consistently demonstrated in research (e.g. Bornewasser & Mummendey, 1982), it may help us understand incidents such as the one involving French international soccer star Zinedine Zidane, who headbutted Marco Materazzi in the chest after the Italian defender allegedly insulted him during the 2006 World Cup final ("I'm sorry but no regrets," 2006). The theory suggests that insults or provocations are more likely to evoke intensely angry and even violent responses during highly arousing events such as close sports matches.

Berkowitz's Cognitive Neoassociation Model

Frustration-Aggression Hypothesis

The frustration-aggression hypothesis is the foundation for Berkowitz's (1989, 1990) cognitive neoassociation model of aggression. Originally articulated by John Dollard and colleagues at Yale University in 1939, the hypothesis consists of two basic propositions: every aggressive act is proceeded by a frustration and every frustration produces aggression (Dollard, Doob, Miller, Mowrer, & Sears, 1939). Their definition of **frustration** is steeped in the language of behaviourism that prevailed at the time, but Berkowitz (1989), using more contemporary language, describes it as being unexpectedly blocked from attaining an anticipated goal. The Dollard group noted that frustration does not always result in overt acts of physical violence but can lead to verbal threats or no visible signs of aggression. Nevertheless, they were firm in the belief that every aggressive act can be traced to an underlying frustration.

frustration In the context of the frustration-aggression hypothesis, the state produced when a person is blocked from attaining an expected goal.

The frustration-aggression hypothesis has been attacked on a number of grounds over the years, but its greatest weakness is this claim of universality (Berkowitz, 1978). For instance, contract killers commit violence to fulfill a goal, not as a response to a blocked goal. As this example illustrates, the hypothesis has little application to instrumental violence.

The Role of Negative Affect

Berkowitz (1989) recognized that a body of research demonstrates that people are more likely to exhibit aggression when faced with a host of unpleasant experiences—such as personal insults, pain, foul odours—that do not constitute frustrations according to the theory (Berkowitz, Cochran, & Embree, 1981; Geen, 1968; Rotton, Frey, Barry, Milligan, & Fitzpatrick, 1979). To accommodate these findings, he suggested that all **aversive events**, not just those that are frustrating, are capable of sparking aggression. According to Berkowitz (1989, 1978), an aversive event generates **negative affect**, or feelings of unpleasantness and discomfort. Not every aversive event is equally unpleasant, but in some cases the negative affect generated is sufficiently intense that it evokes an aggressive response. For example, a goal that is deliberately and unfairly thwarted by someone has an added unpleasantness, which explains why this sort of frustration is more likely to result in violence than goals frustrated accidently or for legitimate reasons (Berkowitz, 1978).

aversive events Incidents that produce pain, frustration, and unpleasant feelings.

negative affect A feeling of discomfort or unpleasantness.

The Role of Cognition

The cognitive neoassociation model of aggression—Berkowitz's (1989, 1990, 1993, 2003) most recent theoretical work—expands on what happens after negative affect is generated, including the influence of cognition. The central role played by negative affect means the model is best suited to explaining reactive violence and, like the frustration-aggression hypothesis, it offers little insight into instrumental acts of violence.

The cognitive neoassociation model incorporates two distinct phases, each governed by different processes. The initial phase is dominated by associative processes that occur in a largely automatic fashion and with little cognitive processing. The negative affect automatically and simultaneously activates the flight-or-flight response, discussed in Chapter 3 (Berkowitz, 1989). The theory assumes that this response involves networks of associated feelings, thoughts, physiological responses, and expressive motor reactions such as facial expressions and other body language. Activating one part of a network leads to a **spreading activation** of other parts. When the fight response tendency is activated, an array of interconnected ideas (e.g. hostile thoughts), feelings (arousal), physical expressions (clenched teeth, fists) associated with aggression are stimulated and are collectively experienced as a rudimentary form of anger. In the flight response tendency, the activation of this associative network is experienced as fear. The response tendency that dominates on any given occasion primarily hinges on the person (e.g. biological influences, previous learning) and situational factors (Berkowitz, 1989).

spreading activation A process that occurs when activation of one part of an interconnected neural network leads to the activation of the other parts.

As we are interested in antisocial and violent behaviour, we will assume that the aggressive response prevails. The fight associative network includes links to the motor actions or behaviours relating to violence as well as the inclination to attack and injure. When it is strongly stimulated by unpleasant events, people feel a powerful urge to lash out violently and hurt someone (Berkowitz, 1993, 2003). This phase unfolds automatically and without cognitive input, which explains the impulsive acts that characterize reactive violence.

The mere fact that the fight associative network is activated more strongly than the one for flight does not mean that physical acts of violence are inevitable. Situational factors are very influential—the threat of certain punishment usually stops people from acting violently unless the instigation to attack is extremely powerful (Berkowitz, 1993). On the other hand, the presence of an obvious target for the violence, especially one that is the source of the aversive event, facilitates aggression. Berkowitz (1969) believes that aggressive cues in the environment (e.g. weapons, violent media images) also increase the chance of violence occurring (see the "Researching" box).

Researching Criminal and Violent Behaviour

The Influence of Aggressive Cues on Behaviour

Berkowitz and LePage (1967) conducted a now classic study on how aggressive cues in the environment influence behaviour. The participants were male university students who believed that they were partaking in a study on physiological responses to stress. The students were paired up and put in separate rooms. They were told that they would take turns working on an assignment and giving feedback to their partner. Depending on the quality of their work, they would receive from 1 (good) to 10 (poor) mild electric shocks. Unbeknownst to the participants, their partner was a confederate of the researchers. The naïve participants always completed the assignment first and, when it was done, they received either one or seven shocks. The number administered was predetermined and independent of the quality of their work. The researchers expected that the participants given seven shocks would be angry at their poor evaluation.

At this point, the participant was brought to the control room to judge his or her partner's work and observed the device for administering the shocks. Some of the participants also saw either two guns or some badminton racquets situated on a nearby table. The researchers found that the angry students visually exposed to the firearms administered significantly more shocks than the other participants (see Figure 8.4). They interpreted this finding as an indication that aggressive cues can stimulate aggressive behaviour, which Berkowitz (1968) later summarized by stating, "The

finger pulls the trigger, but the trigger may also be pulling the finger" (p. 22).

Critics of the study argue that the results simply reflect demand characteristics, which inadvertently encourage participants to respond in the predicted manner (Page & Scheidt, 1971). A follow-up study by Turner and Simons (1974) casts doubt on this assertion. They found that, the more participants believed the study was about aggressive responses, the fewer shocks they delivered. Comprehensive reviews conducted since this time confirm that the presence of weapons tends to increase aggression (Bettencourt & Kernahan, 1997; Carlson, Marcus-Newhall, & Miller, 1990).

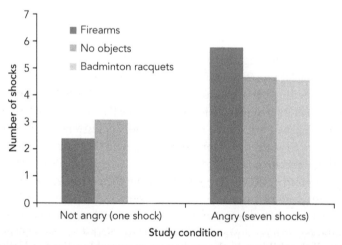

Figure 8.4 Mean number of shocks delivered with and without firearms present.

Source: Based on a figure in Berkowitz, L. (1993). *Aggression: Its causes, consequences, and control.* Philadelphia, PA: Temple University Press.

The second phase, during which deeper cognitive processing occurs, begins immediately after the initial phase is underway. Now people start to think about and evaluate the causes of the event, the motives of the other people involved, and their emotions (Berkowitz, 2003). They will likely form conclusions about whether their goals were accidently or intentionally thwarted, which will diminish or intensify their anger. Their rudimentary anger will become more clearly differentiated into such feelings as irritation or rage. Berkowitz (1990) notes that, if they have not acted already, people are apt to become aware of their feelings and weigh their actions more carefully during this phase. Although this stage does not eliminate the possibility of violence, it increases the likelihood of pro-social responses, especially among people with appropriate prior learning experiences.

Social Interactions

Decisions to act criminally or violently do not occur in a vacuum. As the preceding discussion highlights, what happens to and around people, such as experiencing aversive events, affect their behaviour. The features and events in someone's immediate surroundings are known as **situational** (or **contextual**) **factors**. One of the most powerful situational factors is human social interaction. Deindividuation and obedience, which are discussed next, exemplify this type of situational factor.

> **situational (or contextual) factors** Features, events, or social interactions that characterize a person's surrounding circumstances.

Deindividuation

Deindividuation, a term coined by Festinger, Pepitone, and Newcomb (1952), is a psychological state marked by a decreased sense of personal identity, self-awareness, and self-evaluation, which can result from being submerged in a group (Diener, 1977). Evidence indicates that, the larger the group, the greater the deindividuated effect (Postmes & Spears, 1998). The worry is that people in this state are more prone to violating social norms and offending (Festinger et al., 1952; Zimbardo, 1970). A study by Diener, Fraser, Beaman, and Kelem (1976) illustrates the possible consequences of deindividuation on trick-or-treaters. The study was conducted in more than two dozen homes around Seattle, Washington. When the door was answered at the pre-selected locations, trick-or-treaters saw two bowls on a table: a large one containing candy and a smaller one containing coins. Children in the anonymous condition were not asked anything by the adult occupant who answered the door, but those in the non-anonymous condition were asked their name and where they lived. After directing the children to take one candy from the bowl, the adult left them alone and went to another room while a hidden observer recorded the size of the group and the children's behaviour. The researchers reported that children in conditions conducive to deindividuation (i.e. trick-or-treating in a group) were more likely than the other children to violate social expectations by taking multiple candies or money (see Figure 8.5).

> **deindividuation** A psychological state characterized by a loss of individual identity, self-awareness, and self-evaluation, which is often associated with being immersed in large groups.

The study's results point to another factor—anonymity—that also contributes to deindividuation. It is no coincidence that the children who did not disclose their names or addresses were more likely to violate the situation's social expectations. Keep in mind that all the children in the study were presumably attired in Halloween costumes, which added to their feeling of anonymity. In fact, anything that makes us less identifiable, such as masks, dark glasses, similar uniforms, or even darkness, is thought to promote deindividuation (Zimbardo, 1970). For instance, fifth graders randomly assigned to teams and issued the same colour t-shirts engaged in significantly more aggressive play than

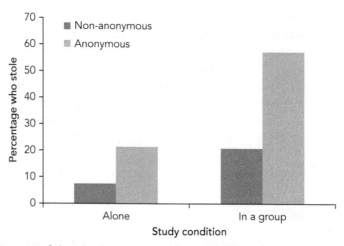

Figure 8.5 Impact of deindividuation on stealing by Halloween trick-or-treaters.

Source: Copyright © 1976 by the American Psychological Association. Reproduced with permission. E. Diener et al. (1976). Effects of deindividuation variables on stealing among Halloween trick-or-treaters. *Journal of Personality and Social Psychology, 33,* 178–183. The use of APA information does not imply endorsement by APA.

the members of the opposing team, who were playing in their regular clothes (Rehm, Steinleitner, & Lilli, 1987). The role anonymity plays in deindividuation may explain the finding of an ethnographic study that observed people of cultures who adorn themselves in masks or face paint prior to going into battle tend to inflict more extreme violence than people whose faces are not obscured (Watson, 1973).

The effect of deindividuation is frequently implicated in the results of the well-known Stanford prison experiment (Haney, Banks, & Zimbardo, 1973; Zimbardo, Maslach, & Haney, 2000). Despite the absence of some basic methodological elements required for a true scientific experiment, the study is still relevant because of its realism. In this study, two dozen volunteers were assigned the role of guard or prisoner in a simulated prison constructed in the basement of Stanford University's psychology department. Before the study formally began, the guards drafted rules governing prisoner behaviour and were supplied with military-style uniforms and mirrored sunglasses, items thought to foster the sense of anonymity (Zimbardo et al., 2000; Haney et al., 1973). The prisoners wore ankle chains and were dressed in smocks that had a number sewn on the front and back. The prisoners were confined to the simulated prison around the clock, with teams of guards working in shifts and maintaining a constant watch over them. As the study went on, the researchers witnessed the guards becoming increasingly aggressive, punitive, and degrading toward the prisoners. In fact, the guards' behaviour and the detrimental effects it had on the prisoners eventually forced the researchers to terminate the study after six days instead of the two weeks originally scheduled (Zimbardo et al., 2000). The outcome of this study hints at the possible deindividuating effect of prison settings and may explain events such as those at Abu Ghraib (see the following case study).

Different ideas exist about why deindividuation leads to social transgressions. The classic view is that it reduces the anxiety and fear of being singled out and subjected to social disapproval and, as a consequence, people engage in behaviours they would otherwise inhibit (Festinger et al., 1952; Zimbardo, 1970). In short, deindividuation promotes antisocial behaviour by diminishing social controls. The social identity model of deindividuation effects (SIDE; Reicher, Spears, & Postmes, 1995; Spears, Postmes, Lea, & Watt, 2001)

CASE STUDY

Lynndie England and US Military Personnel at Abu Ghraib

Bagdad, Iraq—During the Iraq War, Abu Ghraib prison served as a detention facility for the US military. In 2004 disturbing photos of various army personnel abusing Iraqi prisoners came to light. Some of the photos show Private Lynndie England smoking a cigarette while pointing at the genitals of a hooded naked prisoner being forced to masturbate, holding a leash attached to a crawling naked prisoner wearing a dog collar, and standing behind a pyramid of naked prisoners, giving a thumbs-up. England and 10 other members of the 372nd Military Police Company were eventually convicted of offences stemming from the abusive conduct ("Lynndie England still haunted," 2009).

England and many of the other convicted personnel admitted that prisoners were stripped naked, forced to wear women's clothing and crawl across the floor, denied access to toilets, deprived of sleep, and subjected to other abuses; however, they maintained that these practices were established prior to their arrival. England claimed: "When we first got there, we were like, what's going on? Then you see staff sergeants walking around not saying anything [about the abuse]. You think, OK, obviously it's normal" (Brockes, 2009, para. 29). Many of the accused

Photo 8.2 This image, showing Private Lynndie England holding a naked Iraqi detainee by a leash, was just one of the many photos revealing prisoner abuse at Abu Ghraib.

argued at trial that they were simply following orders and that the abusive treatment was actively encouraged to break the will of the prisoners before being interrogated (Brockes, 2009; Hersh, 2004). The prosecutor at England's trial soundly rejected this assertion, pointing out that none of the prisoners in the photos with England was ever questioned ("Lynndie England still haunted," 2009).

takes a very different stance. SIDE postulates that people in groups shift from identifying themselves as individuals to identifying as a member of the group and, as a result, begin to adopt the behavioural norm of those around them (Reicher et al., 1995; Spears et al., 2001). According to SIDE, deindividuation facilitates both antisocial and prosocial behaviour—it just depends on the norm of the particular group (Reicher et al., 1995). It also suggests that the behaviour of people in groups becomes increasingly "socially regulated" rather than "deregulated," as the traditional view suggests (Spears et al., 2001, p. 337). How do anonymity and crowds contribute to this process? With greater anonymity and larger crowds, an individual has less and less sense of his or her own identity; at the same time, the identity of the group grows in prominence (Spears et al., 2001).

SIDE aligns deindividuation theory with the well-established body of social psychological research on conformity, which shows that individuals usually adapt their

Doug Pensinger/Getty Images

Photo 8.3 A lone American fan stands in a crowd of Canadians celebrating at the 2010 Winter Olympics.

The Canadian Press/Geoff Howe

Photo 8.4 A crowd watches a car burn during the Vancouver riots of 2011, which began after the Canucks lost game 7 of the Stanley Cup finals to the Boston Bruins.

behaviour to be consistent with those around them. Deindividuation studies also appear to support SIDE. A meta-analysis of deindividuation research found that participant behaviour tends to follow the situational norm of the group, be it good or bad, as opposed to always acting contrary to the norms of society (Postmes & Spears, 1998). Finally, the theory appears better able to account for the wide range of behaviour displayed by different crowds, a point aptly illustrated by two events occurring a short time apart in Vancouver, British Columbia. In 2010 the city hosted the Winter Olympics, during which thousands of people thronged through the streets in a jovial and festive atmosphere (Sin, Cooper, & Mercer, 2010). Sixteen months later, a crowd in the same area of the city and probably involving some of the same individuals rioted, causing injuries to 150 people and millions of dollars in property damage, after the home team Canucks lost the Stanley Cup to the Boston Bruins (Chan, 2011). Many of the people eventually identified as participants in the riot claimed that they were "swept up" in the moment (e.g. Coleburn, 2011; Dhillon, 2012). While the traditional view of deindividuation accounts for the rioters' actions, it does not fit the positive behaviour seen throughout the Winter Olympics. SIDE theory, on the other hand, can explain both events. It suggests that people adopted the emerging normative behaviour of the crowd, which happened to be good-natured and prosocial during the Olympics but decidedly antisocial and destructive following the Canucks' defeat.

Obedience

As mentioned in the Abu Ghraib case study, many of the convicted military personnel claimed that they were simply following orders. Similar defences were advanced by people tried for their role in the Holocaust, a matter of deep interest to Stanley Milgram, an American psychologist with a strong Jewish identity who had grown up during World War II (Milgram, 2000). In a well-known series of studies, he investigated the degree to which ordinary Americans complied with commands to inflict pain on another person.

obedience The action of complying with the directions of a higher authority.

All Milgram's (1963, 1965) studies of **obedience** employed the same basic design. Community members were recruited through newspaper ads to participate in a study they believed was exploring the effect of punishment on learning. Pairs of participants drew to determine whether they would be the teacher or the learner. In reality, the draw was rigged so that a confederate of the researcher was always the learner and the naïve participant was always the teacher. The teacher administered a task to the learner, who was in a separate room and hooked up to a shock generator. Whenever the learner made a mistake, the teacher was to deliver a shock, the strength of which increased with each incorrect answer to a maximum of 450 volts. Participants who expressed an unwillingness to continue at any point were given up to four verbal prompts by the experimenter, beginning with the relatively mild "Please continue" and escalating to the strong command of "You have no choice, you must go on."

When Milgram (1965) asked a group of psychiatrists how far participants would go, they predicted that less than 1 per cent would remain obedient to the very end. The actual results were dramatically different. Despite obvious signs that many participants felt uneasy at what they were doing, 65 per cent of them delivered the maximum shock, even though the learner pounded on the wall and stopped answering after the twentieth shock (300 volts).

Milgram (1965) conducted a series of follow-up studies using the same basic design and involving close to a thousand participants. He discovered that various situational factors, including the learner's proximity, affected people's obedience. In the most remote study condition, the teacher could not see or hear the learner except for the protest occurring after the 300-volt shock. Proximity was increased in the second condition by adding a series of audible protests, beginning with grunts (75 V), followed by statements such as "I can't stand the pain" (180 V) and ending with agonizing screams of pain. The third condition included the verbal protests but situated the learner only 1.5 feet away from the teacher. Finally, in the fourth condition, the teacher had to physically hold the learner's hand against a shockplate. Milgram observed an inverse relationship between obedience and victim proximity. Participants were most obedient when the victim was farthest removed and least obedient when the victim was closest (see Figure 8.6).

Milgram (1965) also examined the effect of changing the proximity of the authority figure. Putting the experimenter only a few feet away from the teacher was associated with the greatest obedience, whereas removing the experimenter from the room and issuing instructions to the teacher via a phone or recording was associated with the least obedience.

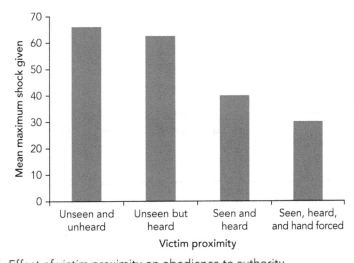

Figure 8.6 Effect of victim proximity on obedience to authority.

Source: Adapted from Stanley Milgram, *Human Relations 18*(57), pp. 57–76, copyright © 1965 by SAGE. Reprinted by Permission of SAGE Publications, Ltd.

In short, proximity to the victim and authority work in opposite ways. Obedience increases the closer the individual is to the source of authority and decreases the closer the individual is to the victim.

One reason so many participants continued giving the shocks may be the task's incremental nature. The intensity of the shocks increased in relatively small steps. Once participants decided to apply the shock at one level, it became difficult to justify not going just a little bit further and applying the next shock. While it is impossible to know with certainty what happened in Abu Ghraib, similar processes were probably at work. There is evidence that the low-ranking military personnel convicted of perpetrating the abuses were acting under orders, although who gave them is not clear (Hersh, 2004). As we learned in our discussion of moral disengagement, acting on the authority of someone else serves to minimize personal responsibility. Moreover, the abuse may have started as relatively minor and isolated incidents that gradually progressed into more egregious abuses and human rights violations.

Social Information Processing Theories

Social information processing (SIP) theories liken the human mind to a computer that generates output based on the data going in and how they are processed (Huesmann, 1998). The "data" consist of the stimuli or **social cues** people perceive, such as the words and actions of others, which give them clues about their social situation; the "output" is the behaviour generated in response to the information processed (Dodge, 1986; Huesmann, 1998). Human behaviour, then, is the product of the underlying sequence of mental operations used to process social cues (Dodge & Schwartz, 1997). Do not let the computer analogy mislead you into thinking that these theories assume everyone is destined to behave exactly the same way. Human behaviour is highly complex and variable because every situation presents a unique set of social cues and everyone possesses different "hardware" and "software," which they use to process this information (Huesmann, 1998).

Since the 1980s, several models based on SIP theory have been proposed to explain the occurrence of antisocial and, more particularly, aggressive behaviour (Anderson & Bushman, 2002; Crick & Dodge, 1994; Huesmann, 1988). While these models diverge from one another in a number of ways, they share four key processing stages: encoding social cues, interpreting social cues, searching for behavioural responses, and evaluating and selecting a response (Anderson & Huesmann, 2003; Huesmann, 1998). Theorists speculate that information deficiencies and errors in the cognitive processes at one or more of these stages lead to poor decision-making and inappropriate behaviour. The following section summarizes the basic information processing stages of the models proposed by Kenneth Dodge (Crick & Dodge, 1994; Dodge, 1986) and Rowell Huesmann (1988, 1998).

Encoding Process

To respond effectively in any social situation, we must first understand it. Situational awareness begins when people perceive and organize incoming social cues, a process known as **encoding**. This process depends on our perceptual abilities (e.g. seeing and hearing) as well as where we direct our attention and what we remember (Dodge & Schwartz, 1997). Encoding is akin to the acquisition stage of observational learning discussed in Chapter 7. Central to SIP theories is the notion that everyone differs in their perception, attention,

social cues The words, gestures, and actions of other people that provide clues about their feelings, thoughts, and motives.

encoding The process of perceiving and organizing incoming stimuli such as social cues.

and memory; therefore, even people experiencing the same event do not acquire or retain exactly the same version of it. This appears to be particularly true for antisocial and aggressive individuals. Studies show that youngsters who engage in aggressive behaviour are more likely than other children to seek out, focus on, and remember aggressive social cues in their environment (Dodge & Frame, 1982; Gouze, 1987). Not surprisingly, distorted or deficient information of this sort creates difficulties when it comes to accurately interpreting the social situation (Dodge & Schwartz, 1997).

Interpretation Process

Interpretation involves integrating the available encoded social cues and other information to form a mental picture or understanding of the situation (Dodge, 1986). The interpretation generated is affected by the available social cues as well as the person's mood, arousal, memories of similar past experiences, and attributions (Crick & Dodge, 1994; Huesmann, 1998). **Attribution** is the process of making causal judgments about behaviour and events (Fiske & Taylor, 1991). For example, imagine that a child is hit with a ball thrown by someone playing with other children. In most cases, without more information, the child will assume it was simply an accident and not attribute any intention on the part of the ball thrower. We all use attributions on a daily basis because they help us make sense of others' actions and inform our decisions about how we should respond (Fiske & Taylor, 1991).

Unfortunately, the attributions we make are prone to errors such as hostile attribution bias, which is the tendency to interpret the ambiguous actions of others as signs of aggressive intent or behaviour and is one of the major information processing errors identified by Dodge's model (Crick & Dodge, 1994; Dodge, 1986). Returning to our example, someone exhibiting hostile attribution bias would assume that he or she was hit with the ball on purpose, despite the equivocal nature of the surrounding circumstances. This error in information processing can lead to problems because people tend to retaliate when they believe others are acting aggressively against them (Dodge, 1980).

Dodge (1980) demonstrated the presence of hostile attribution bias among aggressive children who discovered the puzzle they were assembling was destroyed by a peer on purpose (i.e. hostile intent), by accident (i.e. benign intent), or in unclear circumstances (i.e. ambiguous intent). When participants were given an opportunity to act against the puzzle-wrecker, differences only emerged in the ambiguous intent condition. Boys known to be aggressive who were in the ambiguous condition displayed the same level of aggression as they did in the hostile intent condition. The non-aggressive boys' level of aggression in the ambiguous intent condition matched the level they displayed in the benign intent condition. These results suggest that the aggressive boys faced with ambiguous social cues were biased toward making hostile attributions, whereas the non-aggressive boys made non-hostile attributions. Other studies support this general finding (Nasby, Hayden, & DePaulo, 1980; Steinberg & Dodge, 1983).

Response Search Process

Once they interpret a social situation, people search their long-term memory for suitable behavioural responses (Crick & Dodge, 1994; Huesmann, 1998). Central to Huesmann's model is the idea that the behavioural responses retrieved from memory take the form of scripts. A **script** is an organized unit of knowledge or mental template that lays out

attribution The process of making causal judgments about people's behaviour and events.

script An organized unit of knowledge or mental template that lays out the expected sequence of behaviour for a particular social situation as well as the likely outcome of that behaviour.

the expected sequence of behaviour for a particular social situation as well as the likely outcome of that behaviour (Crick & Dodge, 1994; Huesmann, 1988). For instance, most children have a well-defined script for Halloween: ring the bell, yell "Trick or Treat" when the door is opened, and hold out the treat bag. The expected outcome of this script is that the person answering the door will put candy in the child's bag. Thus, scripts serve as guidelines for behaviour that help people navigate their daily social interactions and social problems (Huesmann, 1998).

People maintain countless scripts in their memory, which are based on their experiences and observations of others (Huesmann, 1998). The particular scripts retrieved on any given occasion depend heavily on the interpretation assigned to the situation and past information processing patterns. Scripts that are frequently accessed, rehearsed, and utilized are more likely to be retrieved over ones that are not (Huesmann, 1988, 1998). Script retrieval is also influenced by **priming**, which occurs when recent exposure to stimuli increases the accessibility of associated mental structures such as scripts and, as a result, increases the chance of subsequent activation (Huesmann, 1998). In other words, recent experiences involving particular objects, media, or emotions may "ready" certain scripts so they are more accessible and likely to be retrieved in the near future. In Berkowitz and LePage's (1967) study, discussed in the "Researching" box on aggressive cues, visual exposure to guns was accompanied by higher levels of aggression. Presumably, the sight of the weapons primed aggressive scripts in the study participants, which they subsequently retrieved and enacted (Carlson et al., 1990).

Less socially competent people manifest a number of difficulties during the response search process. Research indicates that they tend to retrieve fewer scripts, especially as young children, and those they do retrieve are often less effective or inappropriate for the situation (Gouze, 1987; Richard & Dodge, 1982). Furthermore, scripts become increasingly rigid and automatic with more use. This practice does not pose a problem if scripts are prosocially oriented, but it means that frequently repeated maladaptive processing patterns and behaviours eventually become habitual and resistant to change (Crick & Dodge, 1994). This is one reason why recurrent fantasies involving acts of violence are so troubling.

Response Evaluation Process

A script will be activated only if it is perceived to be the most appropriate choice among those retrieved (Crick & Dodge, 1994; Huesmann, 1998). The process of evaluating scripts and selecting one for enactment is theorized to encompass three main considerations. One is what Dodge calls **response evaluation** and involves assessing the script's content against the individual's values and moral beliefs (Fontaine & Dodge, 2006; Crick & Dodge, 1994; Huesmann, 1998). Scripts that fit, or at least do not conflict with, a person's values are preferred for enactment. Keep in mind that individual beliefs do not always reflect those held by society at large and, consequently, people with antisocial attitudes may view a violent or otherwise procriminal script as perfectly acceptable (Huesmann, 1998). A second consideration concerns **outcome expectations** (Crick & Dodge, 1994). Here, the script's anticipated positive outcomes are weighed against the possible negative outcomes (Fontaine & Dodge, 2006). The last consideration, **self-efficacy**, focuses on the likelihood that the person can successfully perform the response in the current situation. Research indicates that maladaptive scripts may be selected when people feel they lack the requisite

priming The process that occurs when recent exposure to stimuli increases the accessibility of associated mental structures such as scripts, raising the possibility of their subsequent activation.

response evaluation One of the considerations used to evaluate whether to enact a particular script based on how closely it fits one's values and moral beliefs.

outcome expectations One of the considerations used to evaluate whether to enact a particular script based on a cost–benefit analysis of the possible positive and negative outcomes.

self-efficacy One of the considerations used to evaluate whether to enact a particular script based on the likelihood that it can be successfully performed.

social skills to execute more prosocial ones. In one study, aggressive children expressed significantly greater confidence in their ability to enact aggressive behaviours and significantly less in their ability to perform more conciliatory responses than non-aggressive children (Crick & Dodge, 1989).

The evaluation process ends with the selection of a script, which is immediately enacted (Crick & Dodge, 1994). Fontaine and Dodge (2006) acknowledge that people do not always engage in a careful evaluation process before they act. They suggest that impulsive behaviour is an indication that the evaluation process has been skipped altogether. This may occur when something in the situation brings forth an especially salient script that is performed at once and "preempts" further processing (p. 617).

Enactment of Antisocial and Violent Behaviours

The decision to enact antisocial or violent behaviour does not appear to hinge on any particular error in SIP. In cognitive terms, it is the scope and depth of the processing deficiencies that seem to separate people who regularly resort to antisocial and violent behaviour from the rest of us. It appears that chronically aggressive people habitually make multiple errors affecting more than one processing stage (Yoon, Hughes, Cavell, & Thompson, 2000). Studies also demonstrate that, as the deficiencies in information processing become more serious, the associated behavioural problems increase in severity (Lochman & Dodge, 1994).

Nonetheless, certain patterns of deficient information processing are thought to promote specific types of aggression (Dodge, 1991). Studies find that errors in the initial stages of processing, such as hypervigilance to aggressive social cues and hostile attribution bias, correlate most strongly to reactive violence (Dodge & Coie, 1987; Dodge, Lochman, Harnish, Bates, & Pettit, 1997). These types of processing errors explain the emotional responses to (mis)perceived insults and provocations that are characteristic of reactive violence. The roots of these problems may lie in early childhood abuse, which fosters the development of hypervigilance to signs of aggression as well as instilling fear and rage reactions (Dodge et al., 1997). In contrast, people who perceive and interpret social cues accurately but possess scripts dominated by aggressive responses and believe this type of behaviour will be rewarded tend to engage in instrumental violence (Dodge et al., 1997; Schwartz et al., 1998). The origin of the processing deficiencies associated with instrumental violence is thought to be quite different. Dodge (1991) hypothesizes that exposure to violent role models at home or in the media is responsible for expanding a person's inventory of aggressive scripts. Moreover, when people learn through observation or personal experience that these violent responses are rewarding, it increases the probability that they will retrieve these scripts from memory and enact them (Dodge, 1991).

While SIP theories were developed in an effort to explain chronically aggressive behaviour, the theories can also be applied to explain isolated incidents of violence, such as the case of George Zimmerman, a neighbourhood watch coordinator whose misplaced suspicions led to a lethal confrontation with unarmed teen Trayvon Martin (see the case study). It is not difficult to see how misattributions and other social information processing errors might have contributed to the tragic sequence of events in this case. Theorists are also beginning to extend the maladaptive patterns of information processing identified in SIP theories—especially those surrounding response evaluation—to other antisocial behaviours unrelated to aggression, such as cheating, theft, and drug use (e.g. Fontaine, 2006).

CASE STUDY

George Zimmerman and Trayvon Martin

Sanford, Florida—On 26 February 2012 George Zimmerman shot and killed Trayvon Martin in the gated community where both men were staying. Zimmerman was the coordinator of the neighbourhood watch, which he had helped organize after a number of homes in the complex were burglarized. He took up the role with evident vigour, contacting police dozens of times to report disturbances, open windows, break-ins, and suspicious people (Robles, 2012). Zimmerman had ambitions of becoming a law enforcement officer and, several years before the shooting, he had even pursued and helped apprehend a shoplifter ("In Trayvon Martin shooting," 2012).

The evening of the shooting was dark and rainy. Zimmerman was running errands in his truck when he spotted Martin. The 17-year-old was walking back to a home in the complex owned by his father's fiancée. He was wearing a gray hoodie, with the hood pulled over his head. Zimmerman called 911 and told the dispatcher, "We've had some break-ins in my neighbourhood. And there's a real suspicious guy" (para. 58). He described Martin as being in his late teens and black. After asking when the police would arrive, Zimmerman remarked, "These assholes, they always get away" (para. 62).

Meanwhile, Martin was talking to his girlfriend on his cellphone and told her that someone was watching him. When she told him to run, he replied that he would walk quickly. Zimmerman noticed the change in pace and informed the dispatcher that Martin was now

Photo 8.5   George Zimmerman testifies at his bond hearing on 20 April 2012.

running. Despite police recommendations that neighbourhood watch volunteers be unarmed, Zimmerman took his gun from his truck and began trailing the teenager on foot. When the dispatcher became aware he had left his vehicle, Zimmerman was advised that they did not need him to follow Martin and arrangements were made for him to meet police. What happened next is unclear, but the two men encountered each other and a violent confrontation ensued. Witnesses reported seeing the two men wrestle and someone was heard screaming for help numerous times, followed by the sound of a single gunshot which killed Martin.

At the trial, the jury accepted Zimmerman's claim that he shot Martin in self-defence and found him not guilty of both second-degree murder and the lesser charge of manslaughter (Alvarez & Buckley, 2013).

Source (except where otherwise noted): Barry, D., Kovaleski, S. F., Robertson, C., & Alvarez, L. (2012, April 1). Race, tragedy and outrage collide after a shot in Florida. *The New York Times*. Retrieved at http://www.nytimes.com/2012/04/02/us/trayvon-martin-shooting-prompts-a-review-of-ideals.html.

Putting It All Together: The General Aggression Model

distal factors Factors that indirectly increase the risk of future violent behaviour by enhancing proximate factors that encourage violence or diminishing proximate factors that disinhibit violence.

Craig Anderson and Brad Bushman's (2002) general aggression model (GAM) combines many of the theories discussed in this chapter, including social information processing, cognitive neoassociation, and excitation transfer, as well as elements of the learning theories covered in Chapter 7. The GAM is intended to help us understand individual episodes of violence that, according to the model, are products of both distal and proximate factors (Anderson & Carnagey, 2004). **Distal factors** are typically biological (e.g. executive functioning problems, ADHD) or environmental (e.g. high-risk neighbourhood, antisocial peers) in nature. These factors operate in the background and either increase proximate factors that encourage violence or reduce proximate factors that inhibit it.

Proximate factors relate to the characteristics of the immediate episode and exert a direct influence on behaviour. Person-based proximate factors pertain to the characteristics of the individual. For example, we saw in Chapter 5 that people vary in the degree to which they exhibit self-control, narcissism, sensation-seeking, and other personality traits conducive to violence. Individual characteristics are important because they influence how people perceive and interpret their situation and this affects how they will react (DeWall & Anderson, 2011). GAM views cognition as critically important, especially those aspects that are the subject of frequent exposure and practice. As outlined in our discussion of SIP theories, when cognitive structures such as scripts are repeatedly accessed and rehearsed, decision-making becomes more automatic, which leads people to act with little or no active processing of their situation or their response to it (DeWall & Anderson, 2011). Situation-based factors, mentioned earlier in the chapter, relate to features of the surrounding circumstances. Many of the situational factors identified in GAM incorporate aspects of other theories, such as frustrations, provocations, aggressive stimuli, and physiological arousal. Alcohol, which is discussed in Chapter 10, is also identified as a situational factor because of its disinhibiting role.

The GAM proposes that person and situation factors affect arousal, affect, and cognition. Like some of the theories already discussed, these three are thought to be highly interconnected and therefore impact one another through the process of spreading activation. Collectively, they represent a person's present internal state, which in turn impacts his or her behaviour. In this sense, they serve as routes through which person and situation factors influence behaviour.

The arousal, affect, and cognitions generated by person and situation factors are constantly appraised. Much of this evaluation occurs automatically without our awareness, something that is dubbed **immediate appraisal**. Immediate appraisal can lead to impulsive and unconsidered acts, including violence, but this is highly dependent on the characteristics of the individual involved. Where the immediate appraisal is associated with an undesirable outcome and people have sufficient time and cognitive abilities, they will enter into a reappraisal. During the **reappraisal**, people look for further social cues about the event, comb their minds for relevant memories, and consider alternative explanations of what happened. The cycle of forming a possible explanation of the situation, evaluating it, and then discarding it may be repeated numerous times. Once the person settles on a satisfactory explanation, he or she will act. The more extensive cognitive processing undertaken during reappraisal means the behavioural responses that follow are more purposeful and considered than acts flowing out of immediate appraisals. An overview of the GAM is presented in Figure 8.7.

The GAM model can be applied to the Abdulmutallab case. Few distal factors seem to be present because Abdulmutallab is a bright person raised in a warm, loving, and stable family. Although his family did not support violence, he became preoccupied with radical Islamic views that appear to have promulgated ideas of hatred and violence directed against the West. Essentially, he immersed himself in a social network that supported violence, a distal factor that likely fostered the development of person-based proximate factors such as normative beliefs about aggression and retaliation, attitudes about violence, and cultural stereotypes. It is evident from Abdulmutallab's statements that other

proximate factors Factors that relate to the characteristics of the person or situation and directly impact the risk of violence.

immediate appraisal A largely automatic, subconscious process in which arousal, affect, and cognition are constantly evaluated to make inferences about a situation. Immediate appraisals may lead to impulsive behavioural responses or a reappraisal.

reappraisal The process of re-evaluating arousal, affect, and cognition to make inferences about a situation when the initial or immediate appraisal was unsatisfactory and time and cognitive resources permit a further evaluation.

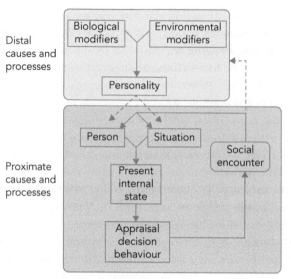

Figure 8.7 The general aggression model

Source: Republished with permission of Guilford Publications, from *The social psychology of good and evil*, A. G. Miller (ed), 2004; permission conveyed through Copyright Clearance Center, Inc.

person-based proximate factors existed, including moral justification for violence, displacement of responsibility, and dehumanization. His training with Al-Qaeda made numerous aggressive scripts cognitively available and, by wearing the bomb for three weeks prior to boarding the plane, he was repeatedly rehearsing mentally and, to some extent physically, the violent act he was going to perform. The bomb represents a situation-based proximate factor. Ultimately, his extreme and violent ideology, the presence of the bomb, and the situational opportunity he was afforded aboard the plane, came together in his decision to carry out his plan.

Summary

1. Cognitive psychology is the study of the mental processes involved in perceiving, thinking, remembering, and decision-making. The subfield of social cognition is concerned with how people understand themselves and others. This chapter focused on theories of criminal and violent behaviour relating to social cognition.

2. Moral reasoning is the analytic process people use to make decisions about what is right and wrong. Lawrence Kohlberg proposed that moral reasoning passes through three levels of development: preconventional, conventional, and postconventional. Research and theory indicate that people operating at the lowest, or preconventional level, are the most likely to offend. Low moral reasoners decide what is right or wrong based on what will be punished or rewarded by those in authority. This environmental sensitivity explains the high rate of offending of preconventional reasoners because situations where crime is highly rewarding or the risk of punishment is very low arise frequently in modern society.

3. Albert Bandura proposed the process of moral disengagement to account for occasions when people do not abide by their own morals. Moral disengagement involves

the use of psychological mechanisms to avoid self-censure or feeling bad about acting immorally. These mechanisms centre on reinterpreting objectionable behaviour to make it less grievous, avoiding responsibility by shifting the blame elsewhere, minimizing the harm caused to victims, or dehumanizing victims so they appear less human or even deserving of harm.

4. Samuel Yochelson and Stanton Samenow identified more than 50 different thinking errors and behavioural patterns that facilitated criminal behaviour based on their clinical work with offenders. Glenn Walters and Thomas White extended this work by distilling it into eight cognitive errors or criminal thinking styles labelled mollification, cutoff, entitlement, power orientation, sentimentality, superoptimism, cognitive indolence, and discontinuity. Importantly, Walters overcame one of the major shortcomings of Yochelson and Samenow's work by showing that the presence of these criminal thinking styles relates to reoffending.

5. Some theories covered in the chapter explicitly recognize that cognition and affect interact with one another in ways that can produce aggression. Dolf Zillman's excitation transfer theory assumes that arousal dissipates slowly, which may lead people to mistakenly attribute the residual arousal to their current environment. Studies show that, in the wrong circumstances, pre-existing arousal can be mislabelled as anger and fuel aggressive behaviour. Affect also lies at the heart of the cognitive neoassociation model. It theorizes that aversive events, such as having one's expected goals blocked, create unpleasant feelings. This negative affect automatically activates two different networks of associated thoughts, feelings, physiological responses, and motor reactions. One network centres on the tendency to attack the aversive source and the other one on avoiding it. The dominating behavioural tendency varies with the person and situation. This initial phase unfolds automatically; however, Berkowitz believes that people begin to cognitively process their feelings and consider their actions within moments, which increases the chances that they will restrain any urge to lash out violently.

6. Research shows that the presence of other people can exert a strong influence on what we think and how we act. Being immersed in large crowds can produce deindividuation, a state characterized by a decreased sense of personal identity. Anonymity also promotes deindividuation. The traditional view of deindividuation is that it encourages social transgressions; however, a more recent theory suggests that it may simply influence people to adopt the behavioural norm of the crowd, which could be either prosocial or antisocial. In addition, Stanley Milgram showed that the presence of an authority figure can profoundly influence people's behaviour. He observed that the closer people are to authority, the more likely they are to obey commands, even if it means hurting other people.

7. Social information processing theories suggest that inappropriate behaviour is due to deficiencies in one or more of the following stages of cognitive processing: encoding social cues, interpreting social cues, searching for behavioural responses, and evaluating and selecting a response. One type of processing error identified by Kenneth Dodge is hostile attribution bias, the tendency to interpret others' ambiguous actions as aggressive, which in turn can lead to unjustified acts of retaliation. Rowell Huesmann emphasizes the role played by cognitive scripts or mental blueprints that set out the sequence of expected behaviours in a situation. He believes that aggressive people are more likely to maintain, access, and enact scripts involving aggressive behaviour.

8. The general model of aggression (GAM) integrates many of the theories and research findings discussed in this chapter into a comprehensive model that explains aggressive episodes. According to the model, distal factors relating to a person's biology and environment enhance or diminish the presence of proximate factors. Proximate factors relate to the characteristics of the immediate situation, such as the presence of provocation or weapons, as well as the characteristics of the person, such as his or her personality. Collectively, these proximate factors directly impact the person's arousal, affect, and cognition, which are appraised and, if necessary and time permits, reappraised until the person settles on what seems to be an appropriate behavioural response.

Review Questions

1. Explain why Kohlberg's theory of moral development suggests that incarcerating young offenders is counterproductive.
2. Define moral disengagement and describe two different mechanisms that people may employ.
3. Define the term *priming* and use this concept to explain what Berkowitz (1968) meant when he stated, "The finger pulls the trigger, but the trigger may also be pulling the finger" (p. 22).
4. Define deindividuation and provide two different theories for how it may contribute to offending.
5. Using SIP theory, identify possible processing errors and biases that might have contributed to George Zimmerman's killing of Trayvon Martin.

Additional Readings

Anderson, C. A., & Carnagey, N. L. (2004). Violent evil and the general aggression model. In A. G. Miller (Ed.), *The social psychology of good and evil* (pp. 168–192). New York, NY: Guildford Press.

Bandura, A. (1999). Moral disengagement in the perpetration of inhumanities. *Personality and Social Psychology Review, 3,* 193–209.

Berkowitz, L. (1989). Frustration-aggression hypothesis: Examination and reformulation. *Psychological Bulletin, 106,* 59–72.

Blass, T. (2000). *Obedience to authority: Current perspectives on the Milgram paradigm.* Mahwah, NJ: Erlbaum.

Dodge, K. A., & Schwartz, D. (1997). Social information processing mechanisms in aggressive behavior. In D. M. Stoff, J. Breiling, & J. D. Maser (Eds.), *Handbook of antisocial behaviour* (pp. 171–180). New York, NY: Wiley.

Huesmann, L. R. (1998). The role of social information processing and cognitive schema in the acquisition and maintenance of habitual aggressive behavior. In R. G. Geen & E. Donnerstein (Eds.), *Human aggression: Theories, research, and implications for social policy* (pp. 73–109). New York, NY: Academic Press.

Palmer, E. J. (2003). An overview of the relationship between moral reasoning and offending. *Australian Psychologist, 38,* 165–174.

Walters, G. D. (1990). *The criminal lifestyle: Patterns of serious criminal conduct.* Newbury Park, CA: Sage.

9

Mental Disorder

Learning Objectives

At the end of this chapter, you should be able to:

- identify and describe the major mental disorders;

- identify the three main lines of research investigating the relationship of mental disorder to criminal and violent behaviour;

- discuss the extent to which criminalization may account for empirical evidence linking mental disorder to criminal and violent behaviour;

- identify and explain how specific symptoms of mental disorder may lead to criminal and violent behaviour; and

- discuss the potential for substance use, social disadvantage, victimization, treatment, and other factors to impact the criminal and violent behaviour of people with mental disorders.

CASE STUDY

Rene Poole

Richmond, British Columbia—It was a clear summer evening in 1989 when motorist Carol Ireland heard the roar of a car engine behind her. In the rear-view mirror, she observed a vehicle hurtling toward her. Ireland let the car pass and, as it did so, the vehicle veered sharply into the slow lane, where it nearly collided with another car, before swerving abruptly back into the passing lane and speeding off down the road.

Moments later, the same car came up behind two other vehicles driving in adjacent lanes. Without any visible attempt to slow down, the car plowed into the vehicles ahead. The one in the slow lane careened off the road and slammed into a street lamp, causing fatal injuries to the only occupant. The car responsible for the collision swerved back and forth several times, as though the driver was attempting to regain control, before eventually stopping more than 150 metres beyond the initial impact site. Traffic accident reconstruction experts later determined that the vehicle's brakes had been applied only in the last metre.

Witnesses who stopped to provide assistance noticed that the driver, Rene Poole, emerged from the vehicle unscathed but exhibiting odd behaviour. She asked bystanders repeatedly if they had seen her ex-husband, removed her clothes, and defecated at the side of the road. She then lay down at the edge of the highway and began to laugh. Witnesses sensed that she did not grasp that she was responsible for causing a very serious accident. Indeed, Poole told police that it was "the second best day of her life" (para. 37). She later explained that God had broadcast driving directions to her through the car's radio and, in the final seconds before the collision, she had let go of the steering wheel, shut her eyes, and let God steer the car.

After the accident, it emerged that Poole suffers from bipolar disorder, a serious mood disturbance. She had been hospitalized several times and treated with lithium carbonate, a medication that helps control but cannot cure the disorder. During the time leading up to the crash, she was not receiving psychiatric care and had stopped taking her medication.

Source: Based on *R. v. Poole*, [1991] B.C.J. No. 199 (S.C.) (Q.L.).

mental disorder An abnormal pattern of thoughts, emotions, or behaviours caused by a personal dysfunction and associated with significant personal distress or disability.

major mental disorders A group of mental disorders characterized by severe and potentially debilitating disturbances of thought and/or emotion. Schizophrenia, major depression, bipolar disorder, and other conditions featuring psychosis are commonly identified as major mental disorders.

psychosis A group of symptoms that involve impaired reality testing, whereby a person has difficulty perceiving what is real and what is fantasy. The hallmarks of psychosis are delusions and hallucinations.

Introduction

Mental disorder is generally defined as an abnormal pattern of thoughts, emotions, or behaviours caused by a personal dysfunction and associated with significant personal distress or disability (APA, 2013; Wakefield, 1992). This broad definition encompasses a great number and variety of conditions, including the personality and substance abuse disorders covered elsewhere in this text. Within this large group is a smaller subset of conditions sometimes identified as **major mental disorders** or serious mental illness. Major mental disorders are characterized by severe and potentially debilitating disturbances of thought and/or emotion. Schizophrenia, major depression, and bipolar disorder are all considered major mental disorders; however, other conditions in which psychosis is a prominent feature may also be included (e.g. Hodgins & Janson, 2002).

Psychosis describes a cluster of symptoms involving impaired reality testing (Sadock, 2005). Someone who is psychotic (i.e. a person experiencing psychosis) has difficulty perceiving what is real and distinguishing it from fantasy. In the narrowest sense, psychosis consists only of delusions and/or hallucinations but, under more expansive definitions, it encompasses other signs of serious mental disturbance, such as disorganized speech and behaviour. Psychosis may be present alone or in combination with other symptoms or disorders, including depression and mania. This chapter focuses on the major mental disorders including psychosis and their relationship to criminal and violent behaviour.

Systems for Classifying Mental Disorders

The two main classification and diagnostic schemes for mental disorders are the *DSM* (APA, 2013) and the *International Classification of Diseases and Health Related Problems* (*ICD*; WHO, 1992). Historically, substantial differences in diagnostic criteria, nomenclature, and even the mental conditions each system recognized made it difficult to equate diagnoses between the two systems. The situation has improved considerably because of steps taken to better harmonize the *DSM* and *ICD*; however, differences still exist and a diagnosis made using one system does not necessarily correspond closely to a diagnosis in the other (Barlow et al., 2009).

The *DSM* has been the subject of considerable criticism over the years. One prominent complaint is that, by establishing diagnostic categories of mental disorder, it has created an artificial distinction between what is "normal" and "abnormal" when psychological phenomena actually exist on a continuum and people differ only in the degree to which they exhibit any particular condition (Maddux, 2004). Another argument levelled against the *DSM* is that many of the disorders cannot be consistently or reliably diagnosed by mental health experts (Kirk & Kutchins, 1994). Critics also charge that the diagnostic categories are social, not scientific, constructions that inappropriately medicalize normal aspects of the human condition (Brown, 1990; Maddux, 2004). Notwithstanding these criticisms, the existence and debilitating nature of the major mental disorders is not seriously in doubt and, as the *DSM* remains the dominant classification system in North America, we will base our discussion on its diagnostic criteria and categories.

Major Mental Disorders

Schizophrenia

Schizophrenia does not have a single defining feature but is identified by the presence of psychosis. Diagnoses are made on the basis of various possible psychotic symptoms that must persist for an extended period of time (APA, 2013). The symptoms are often organized into positive, negative, and disorganized domains, based on their clinical presentation (Buchanan & Carpenter, 2005). **Positive symptoms** represent excesses or distortions of psychological functioning—that is, thoughts, feelings, or behaviours that should not exist are present. Delusions and hallucinations are the chief examples of positive symptoms (Sadock, 2005). A **delusion** is a false belief that is rigidly maintained despite evidence to the contrary and is not shared by other members of the same culture. We would probably all agree that someone who believes a neighbour is radiating electricity that is making him or her ill is delusional. A **hallucination** is a false sensory perception that occurs in the absence of an appropriate external stimulus (Sadock, 2005). Hallucinations may affect any one of our five senses (APA, 2013). For example, Rene Poole experienced an auditory hallucination when she heard God speaking through the car radio.

Negative symptoms—the opposite of positive symptoms—are characterized by deficits in psychological functioning. Thoughts, feelings, or behaviours that should exist are missing or attenuated. The main negative symptoms of schizophrenia include affective flattening, alogia, and avolition (APA, 2013). Affect refers to the way observable behaviours such as facial expressions, gestures, and other forms of body language display our feelings. As such, someone with **flattened affect** shows little or no sign of emotion in his or her physical

schizophrenia A mental disorder characterized by a mixture of psychotic symptoms that are present for a prolonged period.

positive symptoms A group of symptoms characterized by an excess or distortion of psychological functioning.

delusion A strongly held but false belief.

hallucination A false sensory perception that occurs in the absence of an appropriate external stimulus.

negative symptoms A group of symptoms characterized by a deficit of psychological functioning.

flattened affect A lack of appropriate emotion in a person's observable expressions and behaviours (e.g. facial expressions).

alogia Speech that is impoverished in terms of the quantity of spoken words or the content of the ideas communicated.

avolition A lack of energy and/or disinterest in one's usual activities.

disorganized symptoms A group of symptoms involving bizarre behaviour or confusing speech that reflect a severe underlying disturbance of thought.

formal thought disorder A serious disturbance in the organization, process, or flow of a person's thoughts.

word salad Nonsensical speech characterized by a series of unconnected words and phrases.

loosening of associations A train of thought that seems to shift from one unrelated idea to another.

major depression A mental disorder characterized by an extended period of profound sadness and/or anhedonia.

anhedonia A loss of enjoyment from social and recreational activities that are usually a source of pleasure.

expressions (Kirkpatrick & Tek, 2005). **Alogia** is an impoverishment of speech that may be characterized by a brevity or absence of speech, lack of content, or abrupt interruptions, as though the person's mind went blank. **Avolition** describes a lack of energy and apparent disinterest in, or inability to carry out, one's usual activities and therefore it tends to negatively impact personal hygiene, work, and routine chores (APA, 2013).

    Disorganized symptoms generally reflect **formal thought disorder** as evidenced by disturbances in the organization, process, and flow of a person's thoughts (Sadock, 2005). It is usually most apparent in a person's speech, which tends to be difficult to follow and understand. In the extreme, disorganized speech consists of nothing more than **word salad**, an incomprehensible mixture of words and phrases. Less severe forms may involve **loosening of associations**, whereby the person seems to drift from one unrelated idea to another with no apparent direction in his or her train of thought. Disorganized symptoms can also encompass bizarre, purposeless, or socially inappropriate behaviours, such as a person walking endlessly in circles while repeating the same peculiar hand motions.

    The worldwide prevalence of schizophrenia is probably not more than 1 per cent (APA, 2013; Buchanan & Carpenter, 2005). The disorder afflicts both genders; however, it is more commonly found among men. The onset typically occurs between the ages of 18 and 25 for men and somewhat later for women (Buchanan & Carpenter, 2005). The symptoms are usually most severe during the first 5 to 10 years, after which the disorder stabilizes. During this period, symptoms may appear more or less continuously or fluctuate between phases of activity and inactivity. Symptom intensity tends to diminish with the person's age, although the disorder rarely disappears altogether.

Major Depression

Major depression is a serious mood disturbance marked by the presence of one or both of the following two core features: deep sadness and **anhedonia** (Barlow et al., 2009). The latter symptom refers to a loss of enjoyment and interest in one's usual social and recreational activities. For example, a person might withdraw socially, perhaps refusing to attend family gatherings, go out with close friends, or even answer the phone. Other physical symptoms associated with depression reflect markedly lower levels of activity, such as insomnia, loss of appetite, and fatigue (APA, 2013). Thinking can also be affected and is often characterized by pessimism, guilt, and difficulty concentrating. Thoughts of self-harm are relatively commonplace and, in more serious cases, the person may have made plans or preparations to commit suicide. We have all probably experienced some of these symptoms on occasion, but that does not mean that we are clinically depressed. What distinguishes a major depression from the feeling of being down that everyone experiences from time to time is the severity and duration of the symptoms. A person is considered to be suffering from a major depression only if he or she is depressed for several weeks or more and the depression is a source of significant personal distress or impairment.

    Major depression is the most common mood disorder, affecting approximately 5 to 7 per cent of people at any one time (Rihmer & Angst, 2005). The rate of occurrence is at least twice as high among women as men, although the reason for this difference is not yet clear. The average age of onset is in the mid-twenties and initial episodes are frequently triggered by stressful events (APA, 2013; Rihmer & Angst, 2005). Depression may be experienced in a single episode, but recurring bouts are more common (Akiskal, 2005a).

The duration of each episode varies considerably; most last several months, while more prolonged ones can persist for two years or more.

Bipolar Disorder

Bipolar disorder, which is characterized by fluctuating manic and depressive episodes, is another mood disorder. A **manic episode** is a period of unusually elevated mood, thinking, and activity (Akiskal, 2005b; APA, 2013). Although a person with this disorder may experience manic episodes alone, a mix of manic and depressive episodes is much more common (Barlow et al., 2009). During a manic episode, people typically feel euphoric and far happier than the circumstances warrant. Their activity levels are accelerated and it often seems that their mind is racing so fast that their body cannot keep up. For example, they may exhibit **pressured speech**. Their behaviour is frequently impulsive and shows poor social judgment, such as investing large sums of money into dubious business ventures, giving away treasured possessions, or making dramatic life changes (Akiskal, 2005b). Thinking also tends to be distorted. They may appear grandiose, overly confident, and believe that they are capable of virtually anything. Irritability is another common feature of bipolar disorder and a frequent source of interpersonal conflict.

Conventional estimates suggest that the prevalence rate of bipolar disorder is around 1 per cent, but this figure may be low (Akiskal, 2005a; Rihmer & Angst, 2005). Regardless of the precise rate, the proportion of men and women manifesting the disorder appears to be nearly equal (Akiskal, 2005b; APA, 2013). Onset typically occurs in late adolescence or early adulthood, but occasionally cases emerge much later in life (APA, 2013). There are indications that manic episodes are frequently precipitated by psychosocial stressors. Most episodes last from several weeks to a few months; however, there may be a rapid shift between manic and depressive episodes without an intervening period that is symptom free (APA, 2013).

Other Psychotic Disorders

The *DSM-5* identifies several psychotic disorders in addition to schizophrenia. **Delusional disorder** is defined by the presence of one or more persistent, non-bizarre delusions (APA, 2013). A delusion is considered non-bizarre if it is plausible and based on ordinary life experiences (Fennig, Fochtmann, & Bromet, 2005). For example, a person with **erotomania** is delusionally convinced that someone, often a celebrity, is in love with him or her. Although this scenario is unlikely, people fall in love all the time. The belief that a family member has been abducted by aliens and replaced by an identical-looking imposter is implausible and therefore a bizarre delusion. The initial presentation of this disorder usually occurs during the mid- to late thirties and tends to remain fixed. The primary distinction between delusional disorder and schizophrenia is that the former lacks the hallucinations and other disorganized thoughts and behaviours that typify the latter. Moreover, people with delusional disorder do not exhibit the same degree of impairment or deterioration typically observed among those with schizophrenia. Several other psychotic disorders are very closely related to schizophrenia. **Schizophreniform disorder** and **brief psychotic disorder** present much the same as schizophrenia, except that the symptoms do not last as long (APA, 2013). **Schizoaffective disorder**, as its name suggests, combines symptoms of schizophrenia and mood disorders. Table 9.1 summarizes the major mental disorders and their symptoms.

bipolar disorder A mental disorder characterized by episodes of mania alone or varying episodes of mania and depression.

manic episode A period featuring unusually elevated mood, thinking, and/or motor activity that is inappropriate for the circumstances.

pressured speech Extremely rapid speech, delivered as though the speaker cannot express his or her ideas fast enough.

delusional disorder A mental disorder marked by the presence of one or more persistent, non-bizarre delusions, without any other accompanying psychotic symptoms.

erotomania A subtype of delusional disorder characterized by a person's false belief that another person is in love with him or her.

schizophreniform disorder A mental disorder similar to schizophrenia, except that the symptoms are not present for as long.

brief psychotic disorder A mental disorder like schizophrenia and schizophreniform disorder, except that the symptoms are present for only a very short time.

schizoaffective disorder A mental disorder characterized by symptoms of both schizophrenia and a mood disorder.

Table 9.1 Major mental disorders and related symptoms

	Schizophrenia	Major Depression	Bipolar Disorder	Delusional Disorder
Defining features	Persistent psychosis and impaired functioning	Persistent feeling of deep sadness and/or loss of interest in usual activities	Persistent elevated mood and behavioural activity	Persistent non-bizarre delusions
Associated symptoms	Positive symptoms • Delusions • Hallucinations Negative symptoms • Flat affect • Alogia • Avolition • Asociality Disorganized symptoms • Disorganized speech • Disorganized behaviour	• Loss of appetite • Insomnia • Fatigue • Feelings of guilt or worthlessness • Difficulty thinking or concentrating • Suicidal thoughts or actions	• Grandiosity • Pressured speech/talkative • Flight of ideas • Distractibility • Increased activity level	• No other symptoms apart from the delusion • Non-bizarre behaviour apart from the delusion • Delusion not caused by drugs or medications

Source: Adapted from American Psychiatric Association (APA). (2013). *Diagnostic and statistical manual of mental disorders* (5th ed.). Washington, DC: Author.

Mental Disorder and Crime

Does mental disorder cause crime? This question, like so many others in the behavioural sciences, is easy to ask but difficult to answer. As we will see next, researchers looking for evidence of such a link have usually adopted one of three broad approaches: studying the prevalence of mental disorder among known criminals, studying the criminal behaviour of people with known histories of mental disorder, and studying the mental health and criminal behaviour of a community sample (see Eronen, Angermeyer, & Schulze, 1998; Hodgins, 1995, 2001; Monahan, 1992; Walsh, Buchanan, & Fahy, 2002).

Mental Disorder among Criminal Offenders

Numerous studies conducted in various Western countries have evaluated the mental health of inmates. At first glance, the level of mental disorder reported in representative samples—from 50 to 80 per cent or more—appears startlingly high, but closer examination reveals that these figures often include personality and substance use disorders, which are particularly prominent among offenders (Andersen, 2004; Brink, 2005; Fazel & Danesh, 2002). Excluding these disorders so that the spectrum of possible diagnoses more closely resembles the major mental disorders reveals prevalence rates that range between 15 and 25 per cent (Andersen, 2004; Brink, 2005; Diamond, Wang, Holzer, Thomas, & des Anges, 2001; Lamb & Weinberger, 1998). Depression is the most widespread major mental disorder, present in approximately 10 to 12 per cent of all inmates (Andersen, 2004; Fazel & Seewald, 2012). Probably none of the psychotic disorders, including schizophrenia and bipolar disorder, has a prevalence rate that exceeds 5 per cent in offenders (Fazel & Seewald, 2012; Andersen, 2004; Brink, 2005).

While these figures indicate that the level of mental disorder among criminal offenders is relatively high, it is far more important to know how it compares to the level in the general public. Keep in mind that, if mental disorder contributes to criminal behaviour, the rate of mental disorder among offenders should be higher than the rate for non-offenders. Making such comparisons is complicated because reported levels of mental disorder vary greatly depending on the diagnostic scheme (*ICD* versus *DSM*), assessment procedure employed (clinical interview versus review of patient records), the period of interest (current versus lifetime diagnosis), the setting (jail versus prison), and the specific disorders diagnosed (Andersen, 2004). One way to address this issue is to compare investigations that incorporate the same major design features, that is, to compare so-called apples to apples. Table 9.2 presents the results of some selected studies conducted in North America. None is especially recent, but they all employed clinical interviews using the same set of structured questions to arrive at a diagnosis based on a similar scheme and all reported a breakdown of prevalence rates for essentially the same group of disorders. These results show that the rates of major mental disorders for inmate samples are generally two or three times higher than those for members of the community.

Other research has focused on offenders accused of homicide (e.g. Côté & Hodgins, 1992). The primary advantage of these studies is that, because homicide is such a grave offence, it is relatively immune to biases that may arise with less serious crimes due to non-reporting or discretionary law enforcement. Hodgins and Janson (2002) point out that Scandinavian studies are particularly valuable because extensive mental health evaluations are routinely conducted on nearly everyone accused of homicide, meaning that these investigations include the entire population of all known homicide perpetrators. Regardless of the country of origin, the results are very consistent. The rates of the major mental disorders far exceed what would be expected for the general population (Eronen, Tiihonen, & Hakola, 1996; Lindqvist, 1986; Pétursson & Gudjónsson, 1981; Taylor & Gunn, 1984; Yarvis, 1990).

Although research consistently finds that offenders suffer from mental disorder at much higher rates than community members, it does not necessarily follow that mental disorder causes criminal behaviour. Perhaps people with mental disorder are simply more likely to be arrested or imprisoned (Monahan, 1992), a possibility explored later in the chapter. Alternatively, some of the mental health problems identified in these studies could have developed after the offence took place, perhaps in reaction to the experience

Table 9.2 Prevalence rates of major mental disorders in North American jails and prisons

Study	Country	Setting	Diagnosis			
			Depression	Mania[1]	Bipolar Disorder	Schizophrenia
Bland et al. (1990)	Canada	Jail	16.7[2]	4.4	—	2.2
Hodgins & Côté (1990)	Canada	Prison	16.9	—	4.8	7.5
Motiuk & Porporino (1992)	Canada	Prison	13.6[2]	2.8	1.6	4.4
Powell, Holt, & Fondacaro (1997)	USA	Jail/Prison	15.5	7.5	5.2	3.8
Teplin (1990)	USA	Jail	5.8	2.5	—	3.7
General male population[3]			**3.2–5.9**	**0.3–0.7**	**—**	**0.5–1.7**

Notes
1. Manic episode.
2. Major depressive episode.
3. Based on representative community samples from Edmonton, Alberta (Bland, Orn, & Newman, 1988), and the Epidemiological Catchment Area of the United States, as presented in Teplin (1990).

of being arrested or incarcerated (Hodgins, 2001). Prison studies can be especially problematic in this regard because there is a relatively long intervening period between the commission of the offence and the admission to prison, during which the offender's mental condition may have changed considerably. Due to these methodological shortcomings, it is important to look at other lines of inquiry.

Criminal Behaviour among Psychiatric Patients

If mental disorder elevates the likelihood of a person violating the law, the rate of illegal behaviour among psychiatric patients should be higher than the rate among people without mental disorder. The criminality of former patients with mental disorder has been the subject of research for much of the past hundred years (Monahan, 1992). During the 1960s and 1970s, numerous investigations studied samples of patients released from American psychiatric hospitals to determine the extent to which they committed criminal or violent acts in the community. Much of this research challenged the prevailing view that psychiatric patients were less likely than the general public to commit crime. Instead, it showed that they often had higher rates of arrest and conviction (e.g. Durbin, Pasewark, & Albers, 1977; Giovannoni & Gurel, 1967; Rappeport & Lassen, 1966; Sosowsky, 1978; Steadman, Cocozza, & Melick, 1978; Zitrin, Hardesty, Burdock, & Drossman, 1976). Although findings for property offences were more ambiguous, the rates of violent offences, especially assault and homicide, were consistently higher for the psychiatric patients. Unfortunately, it is not clear whether the elevated rates were due to the presence of major mental disorders or the high concentration of other mental conditions such as substance abuse and personality disorders. Reviews of the research also point to numerous other methodological weaknesses, including overlapping diagnoses, possible confounding variables such as prior arrest history, non-equivalent comparison groups, small group sizes for some of the statistical comparisons, or the absence of statistical comparisons (Hodgins, 1995; Rabkin, 1979).

Many of these methodological concerns were addressed in later investigations. These studies reproduced earlier results showing that the rate of offending among psychiatric patients exceeded that of the general public (Belfrage, 1998; Lindqvist & Allebeck, 1990; Link, Andrews, & Cullen, 1992; Modestin, Hug, & Ammann, 1997; Modestin & Wuermle, 2005; Mullen, Burgess, Wallace, Palmer, & Ruschena, 2000; Tiihonen, Hakola, Eronen, Vartiainen, & Ryynänen, 1996; Wallace et al., 1998; Wessely, Castle, Douglas, & Taylor, 1994). Once again, there is evidence that rates of violent offences are elevated among psychiatric patients but not rates of non-violent or property offences.

It would be remiss to leave this topic without mentioning the landmark McArthur study of mental disorder and violence (Monahan et al., 2001; Steadman et al., 1998). More than 1,100 psychiatric patients and 500 non-patient controls recruited from the community took part in this study. It employed a prospective, or forward-oriented, design that evaluated participants for mental disorder at the beginning of the investigation and then collected follow-up data in the community. Instead of relying exclusively on self-reported behaviour, the researchers also consulted with a close family member or friend of the participant and reviewed official records for any indication of violent behaviour. A comparison of violence rates after 10 weeks revealed that patients without symptoms of substance abuse were no more likely to engage in violence than community controls without substance abuse symptoms (Steadman et al., 1998). Only when individuals with symptoms of substance abuse were included in the analyses did the patient group appear more violent. In other words, any difference in the level of violence between the two groups could be attributed to a larger proportion of violent substance abusers among the patients than the community controls.

These findings run counter to much of the existing research supporting a connection between mental disorder and violent behaviour. Several reasons have been put forward to explain the results, including the low participation rate associated with some diagnostic groups (e.g. schizophrenia) and the short follow-up period (Joyal, Dubreucq, Gendron, & Millaud, 2007). Nevertheless, the scale and methodological rigour of the MacArthur study are cause for reflection, and the results have renewed questions about the relationship of mental disorder to violence and the possible role of other underlying factors.

Mental Disorder and Crime in Community Samples

A major problem with studying former patients is that samples tend to be highly selective and therefore potentially biased (Hodgins, 1995; Monahan, 1992). For example, patients in some of these investigations were originally hospitalized due to previous violent behaviour, so it may not be all that surprising to find that these same individuals were more likely to be arrested or convicted later on. A better tactic is to select unbiased samples of people from the community and compare the behaviour of those individuals with mental disorder (who may or may not have ever received psychiatric treatment) to those without. One way to assemble unbiased samples is through random selection. The seminal study employing this strategy was carried out by Swanson, Holzer, Ganju, and Jono (1990), who capitalized on the largest set of survey data ever collected on psychiatric disorders in the United States at the time (see the "Researching" box). Their analyses yielded a positive relationship between mental disorder and violent behaviour, a finding replicated in subsequent studies using the same basic design (Corrigan & Watson, 2005; Stueve & Link, 1997).

An alternative way to study unbiased community samples without employing random sampling strategies is to examine total birth cohorts. A **total birth cohort** consists of everyone born within a specified time period in a particular jurisdiction. It is largely immune to sampling bias because no one in the selected birth years is excluded. An added advantage of this approach is that the samples are usually quite large. For example, one such study by Brennan, Mednick, and Hodgins (2000) included more than 350,000 individuals born in Denmark between 1944 and 1947. The trade-off in this type of investigation is that the measures of mental disorder and crime are usually rudimentary. Most rely on searches of official registries, using conviction records to indicate the presence of criminal and violent behaviour and psychiatric hospitalization records for information concerning mental disorder (cf. Arseneault, Moffitt, Caspi, Taylor, & Silva, 2000). In general, these studies find that community members with a documented history of mental disorder are more likely to have records for criminal and violent convictions than community members without a known history of mental disorder (Arseneault et al., 2000; Brennan et al., 2000; Hodgins, 1992; Hodgins & Janson, 2002; Hodgins, Mednick, Brennan, Schulsinger, & Engberg, 1996; Tiihonen, Isohanni, Räsänen, Koiranen, & Moring, 1997). Several of these investigations report that the difference between the two

total birth cohort A group of people born in the same jurisdiction during a specific time period.

Researching Criminal and Violent Behaviour

The Epidemiological Catchment Area Study

Swanson and colleagues (1990) avoided a major pitfall of earlier investigations that relied on potentially biased samples by drawing on data collected for the National Institute of Mental Health's Epidemiological Catchment Area (ECA) study. As part of this project, thousands of randomly selected household residents were surveyed at five different sites across the United States. Swanson and colleagues (1990) analyzed the data from three of these sites, involving more than 10,000 participants. Each participant was surveyed using a structured interview schedule that allowed the diagnosis of mental disorders according to the *DSM-III*. Embedded in the interview schedule were five questions about different violent behaviours. For the purposes of the study, anyone who acknowledged engaging in one or more of these behaviours was considered to have been violent. Using the data, the researchers calculated the violence rate associated with the presence and absence of different mental disorders for the 12-month period preceding the survey interview.

Two notable findings emerged, as depicted in Figure 9.1. First, survey participants with a major mental disorder were over five times more likely to report violent behaviour than those with no disorder. Second, the rates of reported violence for participants diagnosed with alcohol or substance abuse or dependence were dramatically higher than those for participants with a major mental disorder or no disorder. On the basis of their data, the researchers concluded that a modest relationship between mental disorder and violence exists that cannot be explained away by the presence of other clinical or demographic variables.

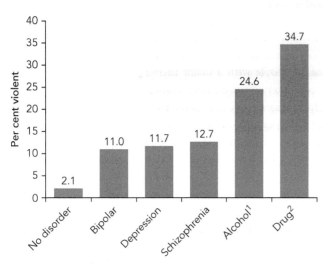

Figure 9.1 Twelve-month violence rates by *DSM-III* diagnosis

Notes
1. Alcohol abuse/dependence.
2. Drug abuse/dependence, excluding cannabis.

Source: Copyright © 1990 by the American Psychological Association. Reproduced with permission. J.W. Swanson, C.E. Holzer, V.K. Ganju, & R.T. Jono, (1990). Violence and psychiatric disorder in the community: Evidence from the Epidemiological Catchment Area survey. *Hospital and Community Psychiatry, 41,* 761–770. The use of APA information does not imply endorsement by APA.

groups is more pronounced for violent as opposed to criminal offences (Hodgins, 1992; Hodgins & Janson, 2002; Tiihoneen et al., 1997).

Putting It All Together: The Relationship of Mental Disorder and Crime in Context

Evidence of a connection between mental disorder and crime has emerged along three lines of research: mental disorder among criminal offenders; criminal behaviour among psychiatric patients; and the relationship of mental disorder and crime in community samples.

Each of these approaches has methodological weaknesses, but there is widespread agreement that, when the body of research is considered as a whole, it establishes the presence of a relationship between mental disorder and crime (Angermeyer, 2000; Hodgins, 1995, 2001; Joyal et al., 2007; Monahan, 1992; Mulvey, 1994; Walsh et al., 2002). The relationship appears stronger for violent rather than general criminal behaviour, but even the link to violence is, at best, small in magnitude (Angermeyer, 2000; Monahan, 1992; Mulvey, 1994). Moreover, the correlational nature of the research and other associated limitations mean that any conclusion regarding causality is premature. Although mental disorder might lead to criminal behaviour, the possibility that repeated criminal behaviour and its consequences contribute to mental disorder cannot be ruled out (Mulvey, 1994). Even if mental disorder proves to be a causal factor, there is probably a wide range of intermediate variables capable of strengthening or diminishing the connection.

To better appreciate the association of mental disorder and crime, it needs to be put in context. The fact is that the vast majority of people with major mental disorders do not engage in criminal or violent behaviour (Mulvey, 1994; Wallace et al., 1998). Figures vary, but studies typically report that 90 per cent or more of all people with a major mental disorder do not act violently (Corrigan & Watson, 2005; Swanson & Holzer, 1991; Wallace et al., 1998). Thus, most of the crime and violence perpetrated in society is committed by people without a mental disorder. Walsh and colleagues (2002) estimate that individuals with mental disorder are probably responsible for 10 per cent or less of all violent crime, a conclusion supported elsewhere in the literature (Taylor, 2008; Wallace et al., 1998). Finally, many other factors show stronger relationships to crime and violence and are therefore more important and influential (Angermeyer, 2000; Corrigan & Watson, 2005; Monahan et al., 2001). As is evident from a brief glance back to Figure 9.1, there is a much greater risk of being assaulted by someone with an alcohol or drug abuse problem than by a person with a major mental disorder (Swanson & Holzer, 1991).

The Criminalization of Mental Disorder

One theory put forward to explain the association of mental disorder and offending is the criminalization hypothesis. The **criminalization of mental disorder** refers to the idea that people with mental disorder who engage in nuisance or disruptive behaviour are processed as offenders through the criminal justice system instead of treated as patients in the mental health system (Abramson, 1972; Lamb & Weinberger, 1998; Teplin, 1983, 1984). According to this hypothesis, differences in the way the criminal justice system handles people with and without mental disorder have created the appearance of a relationship that does not actually exist. In other words, people with mental disorders are not more likely to offend, but they are more likely to be arrested, convicted, and imprisoned than others who engage in the same behaviour.

criminalization of mental disorder The processing of individuals with mental disorder through the criminal justice system for committing nuisance or disruptive behaviours instead of treating these individuals as patients in the mental health system.

Deinstitutionalization

The idea that the criminal justice system is used to control individuals with mental disorder is not new. British researcher Lionel Penrose (1939) made a connection between the size of the mental health and prison populations after reviewing European statistical data more than 75 years ago. He noticed that the population of European asylums and prisons appeared inversely related such that any change in the size of one system was matched by an equal and opposite change in the size of the other. Penrose concluded that expanding the mental health system would help to prevent crime whereas contracting mental health services would lead to more people with mental disorder being imprisoned. A more recent analysis of US mental health and prison systems from 1934 to 1985 found a relationship similar to the one Penrose observed in Europe (Palermo, Smith, & Liska, 1991).

Beginning in the 1960s, many jurisdictions in North America and elsewhere implemented policies of **deinstitutionalization**, the large-scale transfer of psychiatric patients out of dedicated hospital facilities and into community-based settings (Lamb, 2001). The hope was that this policy shift would lead to greater personal liberty and better life quality for the patients. Unfortunately, the dramatic cuts made to the number of beds at large psychiatric hospitals were not always offset with corresponding increases in community-based resources (Sealy & Whitehead, 2004; Lamb, 2001; Lamb & Weinberger, 2005). Critics complained that many of the patients simply ended up in the criminal justice system (Hoffman, 1990; Lamb, 2001; Lamb & Weinberger, 2005; Teplin, 1983).

It is difficult to assess the effects of deinstitutionalization because good estimates concerning the prevalence of mental disorder among inmates prior to this time do not exist. Without this information, it is hard to know whether the level of mental disorder currently observed in prisons is different than it was before deindustrialization began (Lamb, 2001). In the United States, initial efforts to get around this problem focused on reviewing prison records for changes in the proportion of prisoners with documented histories of psychiatric hospitalization before and after deinstitutionalization. If the proportion grew during this period, it would indicate more mental health patients were ending up in prison; however, study results proved inconsistent and conflicting (e.g. Steadman & Ribner, 1980; Steadman, Monahan, Duffee, Hartstone, & Robbins, 1984). Investigations commenced after deinstitutionalization—some of which were discussed earlier in the chapter—provide better prevalence estimates of mental disorder among prisoners. Although these data are available only for the period of time following deinstitutionalization, they still shed light on the potential impact of this process. A meta-analytic review of studies from Western countries between 1966 and 2010 showed no change in the levels of depression or psychosis in prisons, with one exception (Fazel & Seewald, 2012). A separate analysis of studies conducted in the United States revealed that the prevalence of depression, but not psychosis, rose significantly, yet it is unclear whether this increase is due to deinstitutionalization, escalating rates of depression among the American public, or some other factor (Fazel & Seewald, 2012).

Research of psychiatric patients and their contact with the criminal justice system is another valuable source of information. If deinstitutionalization has led to criminalization, there should be signs of increasing psychiatric patient involvement in the criminal justice system. An early review by Rabkin (1979) reported that studies of psychiatric patients completed before deinstitutionalization (i.e. prior to 1965) generally reported lower arrest rates than studies conducted after. Critics claim that this difference reflects nothing more than shifting mental health practices that began to hospitalize substance abusers and people with antisocial personality disorder, two groups known to have high arrest rates, when the later studies were conducted (Hiday & Burns, 2010). More recent investigations in Denmark and Australia avoided this difficulty by looking at psychiatric patients diagnosed with schizophrenia only (Kramp, 2004; Wallace, Mullen, & Burgess, 2004). Both studies noted that the prevalence of psychiatric patients passing through the criminal justice system grew following deinstitutionalization but reached opposite

deinstitutionalization
A policy implemented in many Western jurisdictions that involves transferring psychiatric patients out of large-scale institutions and into community-based care.

conclusions over whether this shift was the result of deinstitutionalization policies or broader societal changes that increased the criminal justice system involvement of the entire population.

Police Discretion

Studies of policing in North America reveal that law enforcement officers frequently encounter people with mental disorder during the course of their duties (Arboleda-Florez & Holley, 1988; Bonovitz & Bonovitz, 1981; Wilson-Bates, 2008). How these situations are handled and whether arrests are made is largely a matter of police discretion. There is a concern that, when police exercise their discretion, they are more likely to arrest someone with mental disorder causing a disturbance or committing a relatively minor crime than someone else engaging in the same conduct (Abramson, 1972; Davis, 1992; Lamb & Weinberger, 1998).

This issue is at the centre of Linda Teplin's (1984) classic field study of policing practices. In this investigation, graduate students in clinical psychology observed police–citizen interactions over a 14-month period. The field researchers used a standardized checklist to note any evident symptoms of mental disorder displayed by the citizens and document the police officers' responses. Teplin (1984) analyzed 884 of these interactions, involving nearly 1,800 citizens. Of the 506 suspects identified by the police, 29 per cent were arrested and approximately 6 per cent were considered to have mental disorder by the field researchers. A comparison of the arrest rates for suspects with and without mental disorder was particularly illuminating. Forty-seven per cent of those with mental disorder were arrested compared to only 28 per cent of those without (see Table 9.3). When the arrest rate was broken down by offence, Teplin (1984) noticed that the discrepancy was greatest for minor offences and largely disappeared for more serious ones.

Teplin (1984) attributed these results, in part, to the failure of police to recognize the symptoms of mental disorder. Most of the time (97 per cent), the field researchers and police agreed on the suspect's mental status, but whenever they disagreed, the field researchers felt the suspect was mentally disordered and the police did not. Teplin (1984) suggested that annoying symptoms of mental disorder reflected in behaviours such as verbal abuse, belligerence, and disrespect may not be recognized as such by police and, consequently, they may respond in a more punitive fashion with suspects they perceive are being difficult. Deficiencies with the mental health system also seemed to influence police decisions to arrest. The field researchers noted that the police frequently took the steps necessary to make an arrest as a precautionary measure in case they could not get the suspect hospitalized. In these situations, arrests were consciously being used to manage the suspect and overcome shortcomings in the mental health system.

Table 9.3 Comparison of arrest rates for suspects with and without mental disorder

	Number of participants	Suspects arrested (%)
With mental disorder	30	46.7
Without mental disorder	476	27.9
Total sample	506	29.1

Source: Copyright © 1984 by the American Psychological Association. Reproduced with permission. L.A. Teplin (1984). "Criminalizing mental disorder: The comparative arrest rate of the mentally ill." *American Psychologist, 39*, 794–803. The use of APA information does not imply endorsement by APA.

This issue was re-examined by two large-scale studies carried out in the United States (Engel & Silver, 2001; Novak & Engel, 2005). Unlike Teplin's (1984) original investigation, these later studies relied on the lay opinions of either the investigating police officer (Engel & Silver, 2001) or the investigating officer in conjunction with a non-clinically trained field observer (Novak & Engel, 2005). Both studies found that suspects judged by police to have a mental disorder were either no more likely or significantly less likely to be arrested than suspects without a mental disorder. These results suggest that police do not intentionally criminalize people with mental disorders; however, it does not preclude the possibility advanced by Teplin (1984) that criminalization occurs unintentionally when the symptoms of mental disorder go unrecognized. Interestingly, suspect disrespect and noncompliance significantly increased the likelihood of arrest in the studies by Engel and Silver (2001) and Novak and Engel (2005). Teplin (1984) pointed out that these same annoyances can be subtle signs of mental disorder and are easily overlooked by police.

Offenders with Mental Disorder Are More Likely to Be Apprehended

A variation on the criminalization hypothesis is that offenders and their crimes are more readily detected and identified when a mental disorder is involved (Hodgins & Janson, 2002). The relative ease of "catching" these offenders—not discriminatory criminal justice system practices—could account for the high arrest rates found among people with mental disorder. Why might these offenders be more prone to getting caught? It could be that they are less likely to conceal the offence, flee the scene, deny their involvement, and so forth. To explore this possibility, Robertson (1988) examined the arrest circumstances of detainees at a remand centre in England. Robertson reported that individuals with mental disorder made little effort to avoid identification or apprehension and, as a consequence, the vast majority (86 per cent) were arrested the same day the offence was committed. In particular, they showed a greater tendency to commit crimes when witnesses were present and were significantly more likely to remain at the scene of the crime. They also turned themselves over to police at rates approximately 1.5 to 3 times higher than other offenders. Perhaps the most telling finding, however, is the amount of investigative effort required by police to solve the case. Further detective work was needed before an arrest could be made for 55 per cent of the cases involving offenders without mental disorder but only 10 per cent of the cases of offenders with mental disorder.

Putting It All Together: Making Sense of Criminalization

The number of people with mental disorder living in the community rose dramatically after deinstitutionalization. Evidence shows that police contact and criminal justice system involvement in the post-deinstitutionalization era is relatively high for at least some of these individuals. Research showing the criminalization of people with mental disorder is more ambivalent and probably depends greatly on various factors, including the severity of the offence committed, the perpetrator's tendency to stay at the scene of the crime, police training and familiarity with mental disorder, and the availability of psychiatric care and support (Hiday & Burns, 2010; Hodgins & Janson, 2002). Where mental health services and psychiatric care are inadequate or difficult to access, police may turn to the criminal justice system as a way to manage those with mental disorders (Davis, 1992; Hoffman, 1990; Teplin, 1984). Conversely, the presence of extensive mental health systems and specialized police–mental health teams diminishes police reliance on the criminal justice system in these situations (Lamb, Shaner, Elliot, DeCuir, & Foltz, 1995).

Based on the available evidence, criminalization alone cannot adequately account for the relationship detected between mental disorder and crime. To the extent that criminalization occurs, it is largely confined to minor offences and nuisance behaviour, where police exercise the widest discretion (Robertson, Pearson, & Gibb, 1996; Teplin, 1984). Serious offences, such as those involving violence, are most appropriately processed through the criminal justice system regardless of the suspect's mental status (Lamb & Weinberger, 1998; Teplin, 1984). Thus, criminalization is not especially well-suited to explain the connection between mental disorder and violent behaviour (e.g. Corrigan & Watson, 2005; Swanson et al., 1990). It should also be kept in mind that the relationship of mental disorder and crime has been demonstrated in studies using self-reported behaviours that did not necessarily come to the attention of police and could not be the result of criminalization (e.g. Corrigan & Watson, 2005; Link et al., 1992; Steadman & Felson, 1984; Swanson et al., 1990).

Symptom-Based Theories of Crime

We know that mental disorders are characterized by different clusters of symptoms. Perhaps the unusual thoughts and feelings that people with mental disorder experience interfere with their decision-making and ability to abide by the law. Certainly, there are anecdotal accounts of criminal behaviour that, by all appearances, were propelled by mental disorder. Recall the case study from the beginning of this chapter—it seems very unlikely that Poole would have released the steering wheel if not for the auditory hallucination directing her to do so. Explanations of criminal behaviour that centre on particular symptoms of mental disorder and their role in influencing decisions to act criminally may be referred to as **symptom-based theories**. These explanations stand in sharp contrast to the criminalization hypothesis, which suggests that the link between mental disorder and crime is simply an artifact of how society and the criminal justice system respond to people with mental disorder.

symptom-based theories of crime Theories that attribute the criminal behaviour of a person with a mental disorder to the altered perceptions, thoughts, and emotions experienced as a result of his or her mental condition.

Among the major mental disorders, psychosis appears to be the cluster of symptoms most likely to lead to crime. There is even speculation that affective disorders such as major depression and bipolar disorder do not show a relationship to crime and violence once the psychotic forms of these disorders are taken into account (Eronen et al., 1998). One way to evaluate the role of psychosis and other symptoms in criminal behaviour is to review offences for signs of **symptom-consistent behaviour.** Taylor (1985) adopted this approach, interviewing men detained on charges to see if there was a connection between their mental state and self-reported motivation for offending. Almost everyone with psychosis appeared to have been actively psychotic at the time he offended. In 46 per cent of these cases, offenders described their acts in a manner that implicated their psychotic symptoms, although they did not always grasp the connection. The balance of the psychotic offenders identified more conventional motives, such as material gain or self-defence. The results of this study and other investigations show that there are occasions when symptoms of mental disorder drive crime (Junginger, Claypoole, Laygo, & Crisanti, 2006; Junginger, Parks-Levy, & McGuire, 1998; Taylor et al., 1998); it also appears that

symptom-consistent behaviour Conduct that appears to reflect the symptoms of a person's mental disorder and therefore makes it reasonable to infer that the disorder contributed to his or her behaviour.

many of the offences committed by people with mental disorder have very little or nothing to do with their mental condition.

A large body of research has investigated whether a statistical relationship exists between psychosis and violence in groups of offenders, psychiatric patients, and community members. A very comprehensive review of this literature by Douglas, Guy, and Hart (2009) analyzed more than 200 studies and revealed that, despite contradictory findings between individual studies, psychosis is positively related to violence. Even more persuasive is evidence showing that the strength of the relationship varies according to the type of symptom. If symptomology is influential, different symptoms should exhibit different relationships to violence. This is precisely what the researchers found. The relationship to violence is strongest for positive symptoms, intermediate for disorganized symptoms, and weakest for negative symptoms. These findings make conceptual sense. Positive symptoms tend to fuel the sort of ideas and behaviours that could conceivably lead to crime. On the other hand, individuals manifesting negative symptoms generally lack the energy, interest, and social interaction necessary for criminal and violent behaviour (Modestin et al., 1997; Swanson et al., 2006). Douglas and colleagues (2009) suggest that disorganized symptoms probably have a destabilizing effect that interferes with normal decision-making processes and behaviour, leading to a greater chance of impulsive criminal behaviour. In extreme cases, however, thinking and behaviour may be so disorganized that the likelihood of criminal action is actually reduced (Estroff & Zimmer, 1994).

Delusions and Hallucinations

Much of what is understood about psychotic symptoms and the circumstances under which they contribute to crime is based on clinical observations and research of delusions and hallucinations. Of these two symptoms, delusions are both more common and more important in terms of motivating criminal behaviour (Taylor, 1998). It is worth pointing out that behaviours initiated in response to delusional beliefs are not always illegal; however, delusionally driven behaviour can sometimes bring a person into conflict with the law. For example, research shows that a small proportion of stalkers suffer from the delusional belief that another person, often a celebrity, is in love with him or her (see Chapter 12). Even when the relationship is denied and the would-be suitor is flatly rejected, these individuals often continue contacting and communicating with the target in a misguided effort to carry on the delusional romance. As illustrated by the case study of Margaret Mary Ray, who stalked David Lettermen for several years, these efforts can persist long after the police and courts become involved.

persecutory delusions A strongly held, false belief that others are conspiring against you or wish to cause you harm.

delusional distress A sense of fear, anxiety, or sadness experienced as a result of delusions.

belief maintenance The effort by a delusional person to corroborate or discredit his or her delusions.

Delusions are not all the same. If present, some phenomenological qualities greatly increase the risk of violence (Bjørkly, 2002a). **Persecutory delusions**, which involve the false belief that others are conspiring against you or wish to cause you harm, are especially troubling. Individuals with persecutory belief systems often feel fearful, which may prompt them to make a violent pre-emptive strike against their perceived enemy. **Delusional distress**, which includes feelings of fear, anxiety, and sadness, is also a cause for concern. Distress can result from the content of a delusion—for instance, if a person believes a contract has been put out on his or her life—but it can also arise when the delusional person becomes anxious over his or her inability to control delusional thoughts. Regardless of the source, the presence of delusional distress increases the chance of violence. A third phenomenological quality, **belief maintenance**, involves the delusional

CASE STUDY

Margaret Mary Ray

New Canaan, Connecticut—Margaret Mary Ray's unwanted contact with late night television host David Letterman became the subject of wide attention in the 1980s (Bruni, 1998). Ray suffered from schizophrenia, a condition shared by several members of her family, and believed that she was romantically involved with the celebrity. Her fixation came to light in 1988, after she stole his Porsche from his driveway and, unable to pay the Lincoln Tunnel toll, informed the collector that she was Letterman's wife ("Letterman stalker," 1997). No charges were laid as a result of this incident, but Ray was arrested a few days later when she reappeared at Letterman's house—police found her in the living room, where she was reportedly writing scripts for him ("Bogus wife of Letterman," 1988).

Ray made repeated visits to Letterman's home, breaking in on several occasions. Most of these incidents were fairly innocuous. Once, she entered through an unsecured garage door and left behind some letters, cookies, and a bottle of whisky ("Letterman gets stalker's visit," 1993). On another occasion, she was discovered camping out in his yard (Bruni, 1998). Letterman reported feeling threatened by her behaviour only once, when he and a girlfriend were in bed and saw Ray watching them from the hallway. She fled as soon as they spotted her.

Legal intervention provided only temporary relief. Ray was arrested seven times and repeatedly cycled in and out of prison and psychiatric hospitals ("Plea deal in case of Letterman plot," 2005). Institutionalized and on medication, her condition would improve

AP Photo/Peter Cosgrove

Photo 9.1 On 26 September 1997, Margaret Mary Ray made her first court appearance for stalking Story Musgrave. She had previously stalked David Letterman for several years.

until she was well enough to be released (Bruni, 1998). Unfortunately, she denied having a mental disorder and frequently discontinued her medications due to the unpleasant side effects. Without medication, her behaviour changed dramatically. As Letterman explained, "When she was on [her medication] it was like hearing from your aunt. When she was off them it was like hearing from your aunt on Neptune" (para. 24). Ray's fixation on Letterman persisted for many years and subsided only after she became obsessed with retired astronaut Story Musgrave ("Letterman stalker," 1997). In 1998 she committed suicide by running in front of a train in Colorado (Bruni, 1998).

---

person expending time and effort to confirm or refute his or her delusional belief. Buchanan and colleagues observed that people were more likely to act on their delusions if they had actively searched for, or identified, evidence to corroborate them (Buchanan, 1997; Buchanan et al., 1993).

The presence of hallucinations giving commands is another potential concern. Poole experienced a **command hallucination** when she heard the voice on the radio directing her where to drive. Command hallucinations are relatively common among patients with psychosis but are seldom disclosed (Hellerstein, Frosch, & Koenigsberg, 1987; McNiel,

command hallucination
A false auditory perception of being ordered to do something.

Eisner, & Binder, 2000; Rogers, Gillis, Turner, & Frise-Smith, 1990). Sometimes, the command orders the person to perform a criminal or violent act. One study of psychiatric inpatients found that, during the previous year, 30 per cent reported hearing a voice instructing them to hurt someone (McNiel et al., 2000). But command hallucinations are not always obeyed. Reviews of the literature reveal wide variations in reported compliance rates, ranging from less than 10 per cent to 80 per cent or more (Bjørkly, 2002b; Hersh & Borum, 1998; Kasper, Rogers, & Adams, 1996; Rudnick, 1999). In part, this discrepancy may be a function of the study context, with lower rates associated with very structured and secure hospital settings (where compliance is more difficult) and higher rates associated with unstructured community settings (Hersh & Borum, 1998).

Compliance is also influenced by the phenomenological qualities of the hallucination. Familiar, trusted, or benevolent voices are more likely to be obeyed than voices lacking these qualities (Beck-Sander, Birchwood, & Chadwick, 1997; Chadwick & Birchwood, 1994; Junginger, 1990, 1995). Hersh and Borum (1998) posit that people are more likely to carry out the orders of trusted and recognizable sources because they feel that these commands must be in their best interests. The fact that Poole was told to let go of the steering wheel by God, a source in which she presumably had great faith, probably affected her decision to obey the order. There are also indications that the seriousness of the command impacts compliance; therefore, orders to commit acts of violence are more likely to be resisted than ones related to non-violent acts (Beck-Sander et al., 1997; Chadwick & Birchwood, 1994; Junginger, 1995). Still, violent command hallucinations are occasionally carried out, and research confirms that there is a greater risk of violence when hallucinations are present (Douglas et al., 2009; McNiel et al., 2000; Monahan et al., 2001). Two other phenomenological qualities—the pressure and persistence of the voice issuing the command—seem to influence compliance as well (Bjørkly, 2002b).

Behavioural responses to command hallucinations are also impacted by the presence of delusions (Junginger, 1990; Taylor et al., 1998). In particular, delusional beliefs about the consequences of obeying or disobeying a command exert a tremendous influence on compliance (Taylor, 1998). Speculation also exists that people are more inclined to act on hallucinations that match their belief system as opposed to those that do not (Beck-Sander et al., 1997; Hersh & Borum, 1998). Taylor and colleagues (1998) have gone so far as to suggest that hallucinations alone are seldom sufficient to trigger violence. They reached this conclusion after detecting a relationship between hallucinations and criminal behaviour among patients in high-security hospitals only when the hallucination was accompanied by a delusion.

Threat/Control-Override Symptoms

Many of the findings described in the previous section are integrated into a symptom-based explanation of mentally disordered violence proposed by Link and colleagues (Link, Monahan, Stueve, & Cullen, 1999; Link & Stueve, 1994). The foundation of their model is the **principle of rationality-within-irrationality**, which posits that the violent behaviour of individuals with mental disorder is often a reasonable response to their illogical and bizarre symptoms. The behaviour of a man who smashes his household furniture, uses a meat cleaver to inflict a superficial laceration to his wife's chest, and swings his infant child over his head by the ankle is befuddling to outside observers but makes more sense once it is understood that he is operating under the delusion that his family is being attacked by the devil and that performing these actions will save them (*R. v. Swain*, 1992).

principle of rationality-within-irrationality The theory that violence committed by individuals with psychosis is often a rational response to irrational symptoms that they experience and perceive as real.

As we can see from this example, the symptoms provide the context necessary for making sense of otherwise seemingly random and senseless acts.

Applying the principle of rationality-within-irrationality, Link and colleagues identified two types of psychotic symptoms that they believed were likely to culminate in violence, which they collectively called threat/control-override (T/CO) symptoms (Link et al., 1999; Link & Stueve, 1994). **Threat symptoms** are equivalent to the persecutory delusions discussed earlier in this section, and their conceptual link to violence is the same. **Control-override symptoms** interfere with a person's sense of free will and ability to control his or her own body and actions. These symptoms might involve an external force that intrudes on the person's perception of independence and bodily autonomy such as **thought insertion**, command hallucinations, or the feeling that one's mind is dominated by an external force.

At the conceptual level, control-override symptoms leave a person with a diminished feeling of self-control and free will and, as a result, violent behaviour that ordinarily would be inhibited is more likely to be expressed. Both threat and control-override symptoms were exhibited by Vincent Li, who stabbed and beheaded a fellow bus passenger near Portage La Prairie, Manitoba, in 2008 (see the following case study). The extreme nature of the violence in this case is exceptionally rare, but it serves as a poignant reminder of the tragic consequences that can follow when society fails to recognize and adequately assist those in distress.

threat symptoms A term used by Bruce Link and colleagues to describe psychotic symptoms that cause an individual to feel that he or she is likely to be harmed. These symptoms are equivalent to persecutory delusions.

control-override symptoms A term used by Bruce Link and colleagues to describe psychotic symptoms that may lead to a diminished sense of control and autonomy over one's body and actions.

thought insertion The perception that ideas or thoughts that do not belong to a person are being put inside his or her mind.

CASE STUDY

Vincent Li

Portage La Prairie, Manitoba—The first obvious signs of Vincent Li's mental disorder appeared in the summer of 2004 (Lett, 2009). Li began to cry uncontrollably and his wife, Ana, noticed that he would not eat or sleep for days at a time. He told her that he saw God and heard voices that provided him with "direction and guidance" (para. 10). Less than a year later, the couple separated and Li began living a somewhat transient existence. His first contact with the mental health system occurred when he attempted to follow "God's instructions" to leave Toronto and return to Winnipeg. Police spotted him north of Toronto, looking disoriented and exhausted after trying to walk the 1,500-kilometre journey. They took him to a psychiatric facility for assessment, but he was later released without being formally diagnosed. Psychiatrists now believe he was suffering from schizophrenia (McIntyre, 2009).

Over the next few years, Li's overall mental health continued to decline. Near the end of July 2008, Li left Edmonton pursuant to God's instructions and boarded a passenger bus (McIntyre, 2009). During a

Photo 9.2 Found not criminally responsible for killing Tim McLean, Vincent Li spent five years in the Selkirk Mental Health Centre. In February 2016 he won the right to live independently; the conditions of his release include daily monitoring, regular appointments with mental health professionals, and random drug tests.

stop in Erickson, Manitoba, God told him that a man circling the bus station in a vehicle was going to kill him (Lett, 2009). Li had a knife and was prepared to

continued

use it, but the man drove away without incident. Li resumed his bus journey despite God's orders that he remain in Erickson. He heard God warn him that the passenger next to him, Tim McLean, was an evil force who was going to kill him (McIntyre, 2009). Believing he had to act quickly or be killed, Li began stabbing McLean repeatedly in the chest and back. Even after McLean was obviously dead, Li continued the attack and then dismembered the body out of fear that it might come back to life and cause him harm. Li later stated, "It's not my kill, God kill him. God angry at me because God asked me to stay in Erickson forever. God choose my hand to kill, I truly believe that." (Lett, 2009, para. 32).

While all psychotic symptoms are potentially disturbing and upsetting to those who experience them, Link and colleagues (1999) speculate that only T/CO symptoms are likely to lead to violence. Their analysis of data from preliminary investigations bears this out (Link & Stueve, 1994; Link et al., 1999). These studies show that violence is related to T/CO symptoms but not other psychotic symptoms (see the "Researching" box). Two studies report similar findings but observe that the relationship varies, and may disappear, when factors such as treatment and substance use are taken into account (Swanson, Borum, Swartz, & Monahan, 1996; Swanson et al., 1997). Other studies are less supportive. One reported no difference in the prevalence of T/CO symptoms when violent offenders with mental disorder in a high-security institution were compared to non-violent civil psychiatric patients; however, T/CO symptoms were associated with more severe forms of violence in the former group (Stompe, Ortwein-Swoboda, & Schanda, 2004). Another study failed to find any evidence of a relationship (Appelbaum, Robbins, & Monahan, 2000).

T/CO symptoms provide a useful framework for thinking about the type of symptoms that are likely to lead to violence and the reason that the risk of violence is elevated when these symptoms are present. On the other hand, the theory does not attempt to explain non-violent criminal behaviour nor does it account for the offending behaviour of individuals who manifest different symptoms. In addition, the research reviewed provides hints that other factors, such as substance abuse and treatment, may strongly affect the relationship of mental disorder and crime.

Factors Influencing the Relationship between Mental Disorder and Crime

Alcohol and Substance Use

Over the years, researchers have identified a host of factors that appear to affect the relationship observed between mental disorder and crime. Substance use is arguably the most noteworthy of these factors, but the research paints a confusing picture of its role. There is evidence that substance use has an additive effect (Walsh et al., 2002). Several investigations report that the risk of criminal behaviour associated with mental disorder is elevated even higher by the presence of substance use (Brennan et al., 2000; Kushel, Hahn, Evans, Bangsberg, & Moss, 2005; Modestin & Wuermle, 2005; Swanson, 1994; Swanson et al., 1997; Swartz & Lurigio, 2007; Tiihonen et al., 1997). For example, an Australian study that reviewed the psychiatric and criminal records of all adults in the state of Victoria between 1993 and 1995 found that men with schizophrenia were 1.9 times more likely to have a criminal record

Researching Criminal and Violent Behaviour

Threat/Control-Override Symptoms

Link and colleagues (1999) investigated the value of T/CO symptoms for explaining violence among a group of young adults in Israel. Clinical interviews were used to diagnose mental disorders and to rate the degree to which each participant exhibited either T/CO or other psychotic symptoms. When the researchers examined self-reported fighting (engaging in a physical fight) and weapon use (holding, for example, a knife, stick, or gun during a fight) over the previous five years, they found that rates among participants manifesting psychotic and bipolar disorders were more than double those observed for participants without these disorders. Further analyses revealed that T/CO, but not other psychotic symptoms, were significantly related to fighting and weapon use. Moreover, the relationship between T/CO symptoms and violence was positive and linear such that, as the level of the former rose, so did the likelihood of the latter (see Figure 9.2).

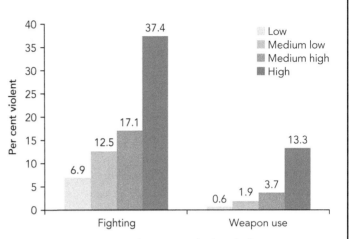

Figure 9.2 Five-year violence rates by level of T/CO symptoms

Source: Link, B. G., Monahan, J., Stueve, A., & Cullen, F. T. (1984). Real in their consequences: A sociological approach to understanding the association between psychotic symptoms and violence. *American Sociological Review, 64*, 316–332.

than those without a disorder (Wallace et al., 1998). This figure jumped to 12.4 times for men with schizophrenia and substance abuse. The reason that mental disorder and substance use form such a potent combination is not known. Intoxicating substances might further cloud perceptions and judgment already impaired by mental disorder or perhaps substance use exacerbates existing symptoms such as hallucinations and delusions (Pristach & Smith, 1996).

These results must be considered in light of different studies that find substance use explains away the relationship of mental disorder to crime (Fazel, Gultai, Linsell, Geddes, & Grann, 2009; Modestin & Ammann, 1995; Monahan et al., 2001). Generally speaking, these studies find that substance use is strongly related to criminal behaviour and that the apparent association of mental disorder and crime merely reflects greater drug and alcohol use among people with mental disorder than those without. This argument is reminiscent of the third variable problem discussed in Chapter 1 and is illustrated in a study by Elbogen and Johnson (2009). These researchers examined predictors of self-reported violence in a national sample of nearly 35,000 community residents in the United States. They found that the presence of a major mental disorder was not significantly related to future violence, except when it was coupled with substance abuse and/or dependence. Although individuals with major mental disorders reported more violence, Elbogen and Johnson (2009) concluded it was because they were more likely to manifest other risk factors, such as substance abuse.

In a more direct assessment, Junginger and colleagues (2006) reviewed the files of a group of offenders with mental disorder and found that substance abuse was responsible for their criminal behaviour twice as often as their mental disorder. Though more research is clearly needed to disentangle the effect of substance abuse and mental disorder, there already exists a great deal of confidence in one conclusion: people with substance use problems and a major mental disorder are more likely to commit crime and violence. Less certain is whether this behaviour is due to the presence of the mental disorder alone, the substance abuse alone, or the combination of both conditions.

Social Situation

Social situation is another potentially influential factor. The link between mental disorder and low socio-economic status is well documented. Dohrenwend (1980) reported that 15 of 21 investigations conducted between 1950 and 1980 found that the highest rates of mental disorder were located in the lowest socio-economic classes. Subsequent research has extended the relationship of mental disorder to other indicators of social disadvantage, including low educational achievement, unemployment status, and homelessness (Hudson, 1988, 2005). The poor social conditions that surround many individuals with mental disorder may constitute an important pathway to criminal behaviour (Draine, Salzer, Culhane, & Hadley, 2002; Junginger et al., 2006). One clue is that offenders with mental disorder are unemployed or homeless prior to their arrest at significantly higher levels than other offenders (Ditton, 1999; Lamb & Grant, 1982; Martel, 1991; Martell, Rosner, & Harmon, 1995; McCarthy & Hagan, 1991; Robertson, 1988). Research has also found that psychiatric patients discharged into extremely poor neighbourhoods are significantly more likely to be violent than their counterparts discharged into more affluent areas (Silver, 2000; Silver, Mulvey, & Monahan, 1999). Draine and colleagues (2002) argue that the conditions of impoverishment and not the mental disorder per se are the most salient factor in criminal behaviour. They contend that poverty and other aspects of social disadvantage raise the risk of criminal behaviour and that the concentration of these factors among people with mental disorder largely explains their criminality.

Efforts to understand the criminal behaviour of people with mental disorder extend to other situational factors. Silver and Teasdale's (2005) analyses of survey data from more than 3,400 household residents in the United States show that individuals with major mental disorders report the highest levels of violence, stressful life events, and poor social support. The researchers found that the strength of the relationship between mental disorder and recent acts of violence diminishes once life stresses and poor social support are considered. The results suggest that much of the violence perpetrated by people with mental disorder may in part be a function of the stressful situations they experience and the lack of adequate social support available to them. But simply having a large social network is not the answer. The probability of violence is greatest when social networks are large and characterized by relationships perceived as hostile and coercive (Estroff & Zimmer, 1994). These relationships are typically reported by the people who are most dysfunctional and severely mentally disordered, probably because they are the least able to appraise their social situation accurately, relate to others, and resolve conflict (Swanson et al., 1998). Finally, social networks that include antisocial peers who condone and promote illegal or violent behaviour have the same negative impact on individuals with mental disorders as they do on individuals without these conditions (Silver, 2006). Hence, it is probably the quality rather than the sheer size of the social network that is most important.

Victimization

The relationship of mental disorder and crime is also affected by victimization. Reported rates of criminal and violent victimization among people with mental disorder are uniformly high (Hiday, Swartz, Swanson, Borum, & Wagner, 1999; Hodgins, Alderton, Cree, Aboud, & Mak, 2007; Maniglio, 2009; Walsh et al., 2003) and often exceed those for community residents with no mental disorder several times over (Pandiani, Banks, Carroll, & Schlueter, 2007; Silver, 2002; Silver, Arseneault, Langley, Caspi, & Moffitt, 2005; Teplin, McClelland, Abram, & Weiner, 2005). The vulnerability of mentally disordered populations is a consequence of both their mental and social conditions—including a general lack of adequate, safe housing and the tendency to inhabit poorer, riskier neighbourhoods—and makes them attractive targets (Hiday, Swanson, Swartz, Borum, & Wagner, 2001; Silver, 2002; Maniglio, 2009; White, Chafetz, Collins-Bride, & Nickens, 2006). Victimization experiences in turn increase the risk of criminal and violent behaviour among those suffering from mental disorder (Elbogen & Johnson, 2009; Estroff & Zimmer, 1994; Hiday et al., 2001; Swanson et al., 2002; Swartz et al., 1998). Although more work is needed to uncover how victimization leads to criminal behaviour, a couple of possibilities have been identified (Hiday, 1997). One is behavioural modelling, which was described in Chapter 7. There is evidence that psychiatric patients who witness violent behaviour in the community are more likely to use violence themselves (Swanson et al., 2002). Another possibility is that recent criminalization experiences may leave victims feeling fearful, suspicious, and threatened and therefore more likely to react violently in the future (Hiday, 1997). This latter mechanism is bolstered by research showing that recent victimization experiences are more predictive of violence than victimization experiences occurring in early life (Hiday et al., 2001).

Treatment

If mental disorder is causally related to offending, effective treatment should help to reduce this behaviour. Indeed, research has found that, when individuals with mental disorder follow their prescribed medication regimes, they are significantly less likely to commit acts of violence in the community (Bartels, Drake, Wallach, & Freeman, 1991; Elbogen, van Dorn, Swanson, Swartz, & Monahan, 2006; Swanson, Swartz, & Elbogen, 2004). Unfortunately, compliance with medication is a challenge for a myriad of reasons, including inconvenient dosing schedules, forgetfulness, and unpleasant side effects. An American study found that only one-quarter of federal inmates treated with psychiatric medication at some point in their lives reported being on medication at the time of their arrest (Wilper, et al., 2009). **Insight**, which reflects an individual's appreciation of his or her mental disorder and need for treatment, is another factor thought to affect compliance (Buchanan & David, 1994). Having regular contact with mental health professionals and instilling positive perceptions of treatment are both effective ways to increase treatment compliance and reduce the risk of violence (Elbogen et al., 2006; Elbogen, Mustillo, Van Dorn, Swanson, & Swartz, 2007).

insight The appreciation a person has of his or her mental disorder and the need for treatment.

The combination of nonadherence to treatment regimens and substance abuse appears to be particularly dangerous and greatly elevates the risk of violence (Swartz et al., 1998).

The reason for this finding is poorly understood, but it may be that these factors negatively impact one another. Substance abuse interferes with the ability or willingness to follow a treatment regime, yet the failure to comply with treatment probably increases the chances of using drugs and alcohol as a form of self-medication.

Mental Disorder Creates "Tense Situations" that Lead to Violence

Much of what we have discussed so far is incorporated into the model of violence developed by Virginia Hiday (1995, 1997). The model acknowledges that mental disorder can cause violence in the manner put forth by Link and colleagues (Link & Stueve, 1994; Link et al., 1999) when T/CO symptoms are produced, but it also implicates other forms of psychosis (Mojtabai, 2006). According to Hiday, T/CO and disorganized symptoms involving bizarre or disturbing behaviour can create **tense situations** when people who come into contact with individuals suffering from mental disorder become frustrated or attempt to manage or stop their behaviour. These situations can erupt into angry confrontations and physical violence. The notion of tense situations and their consequences fits well with the aforementioned finding that violence is more prevalent among people with mental disorder who describe their social networks as unfriendly and coercive (Estroff & Zimmer, 1994). Hiday (1995, 1997) emphasizes that violence is likely to occur only if one or more of the parties see it as an acceptable solution to conflict, something that is facilitated by behavioural modelling in social environments characterized by repeated violent victimization. The pathways linking these symptoms and tense situations to violence are diagrammed in Figure 9.3.

Hiday's (1995, 1997) model is more complex than it appears in Figure 9.3 and identifies many other factors that contribute to violence. Substance use and antisocial personality are each identified as direct causes of violence. It also hypothesizes that both factors can lead indirectly to violence by causing stressful events (e.g. relationship break-up or job loss) and tense situations (e.g. someone tries to prevent an alcoholic from drinking) that boil over into physical confrontations. Regardless of the precise chain of events, the critical point is that the substance abuse or antisocial personality is responsible for the

tense situations A term used by Virginia Hiday to describe incidents of interpersonal distress and/or conflict that result when other people get frustrated or attempt to confront or control a person manifesting psychosis.

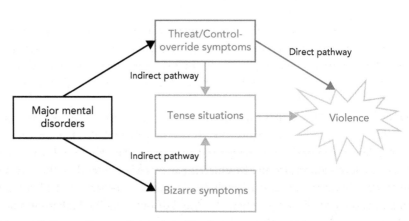

Figure 9.3 Pathways between mental disorder and violence

Source: Reprinted from *International Journal of Law and Psychiatry*, *20*(4), Virginia Aldigé Hiday, "Understanding the connection between mental illness and violence", 399–417, Copyright (1997), with permission from Elsevier.

violence along these pathways. Mental disorder is associated with violence in these situations only because it is **co-morbid**, or co-occurs with the substance abuse or antisocial personality. Put differently, substance abusers with mental disorder are likely to become violent as a result of their substance abuse and not their mental disorder (Hiday, 1997). A variety of other factors leading down different pathways are also hypothesized to result in violence, and readers are encouraged to consult Hiday's (1995, 1997) original articles for a more complete description. One further point deserves mention here. While neurobiological factors are identified as the cause of serious mental disorder, the surrounding social environment determines the extent to which mental disorder is likely to lead to violence in the model. Hiday (1995, 1997) believes that social conditions such as poverty and dysfunctional communities produce substance use problems and antisocial personalities as well as environments plagued by violence, victimization, and other stressful life events. It is only when mental disorder is combined with one or more of these adverse conditions that it is likely to lead to violence.

One attraction of Hiday's (1995, 1997) model is its ability to account for the spectrum of findings reported by studies investigating mental disorder and violence. It proposes that the relationship of mental disorder and violence is partly attributable to certain symptoms of mental disorder that lead to violent interactions. But symptoms alone do not provide the full explanation, and the model takes into account the multitude of other forces, including social disorganization, victimization, and life stresses that can also lead to violence. It recognizes that violence is rarely the result of unilateral action by a single person and is instead much more commonly the result of a dynamic process between people in the context of heated or tense social interactions.

co-morbid A mental disorder or condition that presents with another mental disorder or condition.

Summary

1. Mental disorder is an abnormal pattern of thoughts, emotions, or behaviours caused by some personal dysfunction and associated with significant distress or disability. Within the broad spectrum of mental disorder, a subgroup sometimes referred to as major mental disorder is characterized by serious disturbances of emotion or thought. The three major mental disorders reviewed in this chapter were schizophrenia, major depression, and bipolar disorder. Schizophrenia is a persistent condition marked by seriously impaired functioning and the presence of delusions and/or hallucinations. Major depression embodies two core symptoms, at least one of which must be present: a persistent feeling of profound sadness and anhedonia (a loss of interest in a person's usual activities). Finally, bipolar disorder is a persistent condition characterized by periods of elevated mood and activity levels that may be mixed with episodes of depression.

2. The search for evidence of a link between mental disorder and crime has followed three lines of research. One observed higher rates of mental disorder among convicted offenders in comparison to the general population. Another found that arrest and conviction levels among former psychiatric patients are greater than the corresponding levels among the general population. The third approach studied community samples and reported that people with mental disorder exhibit higher rates of criminal and violent behaviour than those without. The general conclusion based on this collective body of research is that a small relationship exists between mental disorder and crime. It must be kept in mind that the vast majority of people with a mental

disorder do not commit serious criminal or violent acts—most of society's crime and violence is committed by people who do not have a mental disorder.

3. A possible explanation for the link between mental disorder and crime is the criminalization hypothesis. According to this theory, individuals with mental disorder are no more likely to commit crime than those without, but their behaviour is more likely to result in arrest and conviction. Although there is some evidence to suggest that police may intentionally or unintentionally employ the criminal justice system as a way to manage people with mental disorder, criminalization alone cannot adequately account for all the evidence establishing a link between mental disorder and crime.

4. Anecdotal case reports and research indicate that some of the criminal behaviour committed by people with mental disorder is driven by psychotic symptoms. Theory and research suggest that psychosis-driven violence is more likely to occur in the context of threat/control-override symptoms that involve perceived threats of harm and/or the sense that outside forces are interfering with one's autonomy and internal controls. It is also theorized that symptoms of a bizarre nature sometimes create tense interpersonal situations with other people that can become confrontational and violent. While symptomology occasionally propels illegal behaviour, the majority of offences committed by people with mental disorder are characterized by conventional motives (e.g. material gain) that are unrelated to their disorder.

5. Numerous factors influence the relationship between mental disorder and criminal behaviour. Chief among them is substance use. Research consistently finds that the combination of mental disorder and substance use is strongly related to criminal and violent behaviour. It remains unclear whether the strength of this relationship is due primarily to the effect of substance use alone, the effect of mental disorder alone, or the effect of the two conditions together. Other factors that also appear to be important include social environment, support, stress, victimization experiences, and treatment.

Review Questions

1. Identify and describe the main characteristics of each major mental disorder.
2. Describe the three main areas of research that support the existence of a relationship between mental disorder and crime and identify methodological weaknesses associated with each approach.
3. Describe the criminalization hypothesis and discuss research that supports it.
4. Review the case of Vincent Li and identify examples of threat and control-override symptoms. Explain why the presence of these two types of symptoms is believed to elevate the likelihood of violence.
5. Identify and explain two or more factors that may strengthen or weaken the relationship between mental disorder and crime.
6. Describe Hiday's (1995, 1997) model concerning the possible relationship between major mental disorder, tense situations, and violent behaviour.

Additional Readings

American Psychiatric Association (APA). (2013). *Diagnostic and statistical manual of mental disorders* (5th ed.). Washington, DC: Author.

Hiday, V. A., & Burns, P. J. (2010). Mental illness and the criminal justice system. In T. L. Scheid & T. L. Brown (Eds.), *A handbook for the study of mental health: Social contexts, theories, and systems* (2nd ed.) (pp. 478–498). New York, NY: Cambridge University Press.

Hodgins, S. (2008). Criminality among persons with severe mental illness. In K. Soothill, P. Rodgers, & M. Dolan (Eds.), *Handbook of Forensic Mental Health* (pp. 400–423). Cullompton, UK: Willan Publishing.

Monahan, J., & Steadman, H. J. (1994). *Violence and mental disorder: Developments in risk assessment*. Chicago, IL: University of Chicago Press.

Taylor, P. J. (2008). Psychosis and violence: Stories, fears, and reality. *The Canadian Journal of Psychiatry, 53,* 647–659.

10

Substance Use

Learning Objectives

At the end of this chapter, you should be able to:

- explain the nature of psychoactive substances and identify common factors that influence their effects on human behaviour;

- explain and distinguish substance use, intoxication, misuse, and substance use disorders;

- identify and describe the three major classes of psychoactive substances;

- use Goldstein's framework to describe three types of drug-related crime;

- explain how the intoxication and withdrawal effects of different psychoactive substances may contribute to criminal and violent behaviour; and

- identify and explain three major theories of alcohol-related violence.

CASE STUDY

Robert Osborne

Langley, British Columbia—"Oncoming! Oncoming!" Robert Osborne screamed at the vehicles heading toward him. High on crystal methamphetamine, he was driving on the wrong side of the road in a frantic effort to escape police. Moments earlier, he had stolen a bait car containing a hidden camera and electronic tracking device that allowed police to monitor his whereabouts. The recovered video shows him repeatedly trying to fire a jammed handgun inside the vehicle and making several stops to break into parked cars and steal the valuables inside. On the last stop, he spotted police, triggering his desperate getaway. During the ensuing chase, Osborne drove through residential streets at over 140 kilometres per hour, struck three motorists, and then switched into another stolen vehicle. Although police called off the pursuit, Osborne was identified using the bait car video and was eventually apprehended and convicted on nearly two dozen charges (O'Connor, 2006a).

From the beginning, drugs were a constant part of Osborne's life. He lived with his single mother, an alcoholic, until he quit school and ran away at age 13 (O'Connor, 2006a). He found solace with other homeless kids, who quickly taught him how to survive on the streets and support himself through crime (O'Connor, 2006b). It was not long before he was using drugs and, within a few years, he had developed a serious addiction to crack cocaine and meth. He spent most of the next decade abusing drugs and committing crime. It is estimated that, over the course of his criminal career, he stole as many as a thousand

Photo 10.1 In this still from bait car video taken on 6 June 2004, Robert Osborne is seen holding a gun and driving a stolen car.

vehicles. He was such a prolific offender that police had him on their most-wanted list for two years running (O'Connor, 2006a).

While Osborne was in custody for the bait car incident, he learned that his mother—missing for over a year—had been found dead. This news proved to be a seminal point in his life, prompting him to immediately stop using meth. He later recounted that "Something just changed inside of me because I had seen how her addiction had led her to that" (O'Connor, 2006b, p. A4). He admits that quitting his habit was difficult, especially during the first two weeks, when his withdrawal symptoms were most pronounced. Nevertheless, he was determined: "[My mother's] life ended the way it did because of her addiction to alcohol. It's a promise I made to her to honour her memory. I've been absolutely true to it" (O'Connor, 2006a, p. A3). At last report, Osborne was out of prison, employed, and still drug-free (O'Connor, 2008).

Introduction

It is difficult not to be struck by the profound impact that drugs had on Osborne's life. He confronted drug use at every major juncture as a child being raised by an alcoholic parent, a runaway teen on the streets, a young adult with a serious drug habit, and an inmate surrounded by drug users. The branch of psychology that studies the effects of drugs on our cognition, emotion, and behaviour is referred to as **psychopharmacology** or **behavioural pharmacology** (McKim & Hancock, 2013).

psychopharmacology (or behavioural pharmacology) The branch of psychology that studies the effects of drugs on human cognition, emotion, and behaviour.

psychoactive drug A substance that acts on the central nervous system and produces changes in a person's cognition, emotion, or behaviour.

Psychopharmacology examines **psychoactive drugs**, substances that act on the central nervous system and produce changes in our mental state (Advokat, Comaty, Julien, 2014). In this chapter, the term *drug(s)* refers to these substances. Several examples of psychoactive substances can be found in the Osborne case study, including alcohol, meth, and crack cocaine. Drugs are not necessarily harmful, despite the negative connotations associated with their use (Tupper, 2012). The problem is not usually the drug but how people use it and the moral judgments made about them. For instance, oxycodone is often prescribed for its powerful pain-relieving abilities; however, some people take advantage of this analgesic effect and use it solely to get high. Psychologists and other health professionals call the practice of taking drugs or products at levels or for purposes other than those prescribed or intended as **substance misuse** (Ksir, Hart, & Ray, 2006).

substance misuse The intake of a psychoactive substance in doses or for purposes other than those prescribed or intended.

Governments have used the powerful effects of psychoactive substances and their potential for misuse as justification for legislating drug use. The degree of legislative control varies considerably depending on the substance and jurisdiction. Some drugs, such as caffeine, tobacco, alcohol, and codeine, are subject to relatively little regulation in most jurisdictions and are therefore known as **licit drugs**. Others, including heroin, crack, and lysergic acid diethylamide (LSD), are subject to extensive regulatory regimes that severely restrict or even ban their use. Substances that are illegal to possess or use are called **illicit drugs**. This chapter focuses on the relationship between both types of drugs and offending.

licit drug A psychoactive substance that is legal to possess or use.

illicit drug A psychoactive substance that is illegal to possess or use.

Drug Use and Its Effects

Intoxication, Tolerance, and Withdrawal

Many people use a variety of psychoactive substances on a regular, even daily, basis. Consuming drugs at moderate levels that do not cause any significant impairment in functioning is called **substance use**. Substance use can cause **intoxication**—a temporary and reversible state of disturbed cognition, emotion, and/or behaviour—if a sufficiently large dose is consumed at any one time (APA, 2013; Brands, Sproule, & Marshman, 1998). As we will see shortly, the specific nature of the intoxicated state depends on the particular substance, but common effects include elated or depressed moods, impaired thinking and judgment, altered perceptual experiences, and decreased motor coordination and interpersonal behaviour (APA, 2013).

substance use The consumption of psychoactive drugs in amounts that do not cause significant impairment in a person's functioning.

intoxication A temporary and reversible state induced by the intake of a psychoactive substance and characterized by disturbed cognition, emotion, or behaviour.

When a drug is used regularly, the body begins to adjust to its constant presence and eventually develops a **tolerance** to it. As a result, increasing drug amounts are required to produce the same level of effect; alternatively, the same drug amount produces diminishing effects (McKim & Hancock, 2013). The obvious downside of tolerance is that psychoactive drug users must continually up their usage to achieve the same level of intoxication they once obtained with a much smaller dose. The development of tolerance is closely connected to the phenomenon of **withdrawal**, which occurs when prolonged drug use is abruptly stopped and unpleasant symptoms appear (Brands et al., 1998). These symptoms are typically the opposite of the effects produced by the drug and reflect the body's continued attempt to compensate for a substance that is now absent (Brands et al., 1998; McKim & Hancock, 2013). Symptoms subside as the body readjusts, but this process can take several days or weeks. For example, Osborne acknowledged suffering severe withdrawal symptoms for 10 days after he stopped using meth. Of course, withdrawal can be quickly alleviated by taking the drug again, and some people will maintain their drug habit, at least in part, to avoid this experience.

tolerance A condition caused by regular drug intake, whereby a higher dose is required to produce the same effects previously obtained with a lower dose.

withdrawal A condition characterized by symptoms that emerge when a person who has developed tolerance to a drug abruptly stops taking it. These symptoms are usually the opposite of the effects produced when the drug is taken.

Substance Use Disorders

For some people, casual substance use progresses into a more problematic pattern of consumption. In the past, maladaptive substance use was categorized as either substance abuse or substance dependence. The *DSM-5* moved away from this approach in favour of placing **substance use disorder** on a continuum with 11 diagnostic criteria (APA, 2013). Under this system, the disorder's severity is determined by the number of presenting symptoms. A diagnosis requires a minimum of two symptoms that appear within a 12-month period and cause the person significant personal distress or functional impairment. The disorder is considered mild when two or three symptoms are present, moderate with four or five, and severe when there are six or more. A severe substance use disorder corresponds loosely to what many people call addiction, although this term is no longer officially recognized or defined in the *DSM*. Table 10.1 presents the 11 diagnostic criteria for alcohol use disorder, but the same symptoms are used to diagnose substance use disorders in relation to other classes of drugs such as cocaine, cannabis, and the opioids (e.g. heroin, morphine). Review the Osborne case and see how many of these criteria apply to his meth use.

substance use disorders
A pattern of problematic psychoactive drug use that causes significant distress or impairment and is typically associated with impaired control over drug taking and harm to the user.

Table 10.1 *DSM-5* alcohol use disorder criteria

A problematic pattern of alcohol use leading to clinically significant impairment or distress, as manifested by at least two of the following, occurring within a 12-month period:

Impaired control

1. Alcohol is often taken in larger amounts or over a longer period than was intended.
2. There is a persistent desire or unsuccessful efforts to cut down or control alcohol use.
3. A great deal of time is spent in activities necessary to obtain alcohol, use alcohol, or recover from its effects.
4. Craving, or a strong desire or urge to use alcohol.

Social impairment

5. Recurrent alcohol use resulting in a failure to fulfill major role obligations at work, school, or home.
6. Continued alcohol use despite having persistent or recurrent social or interpersonal problems caused or exacerbated by the effects of alcohol.
7. Important social, occupational, or recreational activities are given up or reduced because of alcohol use.

Risky use

8. Recurrent alcohol use in situations in which it is physically hazardous.
9. Alcohol use is continued despite knowledge of having a persistent or recurrent physical or psychological problem that is likely to have been caused or exacerbated by alcohol.

Pharmacological

10. Tolerance, as defined by either of the following:
    a. A need for markedly increased amounts of the substance to achieve intoxication or desired effect.
    b. A markedly diminished effect with continued use of the same amount of the substance.

11. Withdrawal, as manifested by either of the following:
    a. The characteristic withdrawal syndrome for alcohol (refer to Criteria A and B of the criteria set for alcohol withdrawal).
    b. Alcohol (or a closely related substance, such as a benzodiazepine) is taken to relieve or avoid withdrawal symptoms.

Source: Reprinted with permission from the *Diagnostic and Statistical Manual of Mental Disorders*, Fifth Edition, (Copyright 2013). American Psychiatric Association.

While none of the listed symptoms is necessary or sufficient for a diagnosis, two elements are typically considered indicative of maladaptive substance use: impaired control over drug taking and harm to the user. As West (2001) notes, these two elements in combination can be extremely damaging because individuals persist in their drug use even when they realize it is harming them or those around them. The first four symptoms in Table 10.1 reflect impaired control. Perhaps the most notable symptom within this group is **craving**, which refers to an intense longing or urge for the drug (APA, 2013). The harm element is formally integrated into the definition of substance use disorder, which requires significant impairment or distress. It is also reflected in the social impairment and risky use symptoms. Tolerance and withdrawal are important because they indicate chronic substance use and are thought to elevate the risk of future problematic drug use.

craving An intense longing or urge for something, such as a drug.

Factors Impacting Drug Effects

The drugs responsible for most substance use disorders appear to activate the brain reward systems, especially those involving the neurotransmitter dopamine (Advokat et al., 2014). This has naturally led to speculation that drug use behaviour arises, at least initially, because it is pleasurable and rewarding but becomes problematic as the brain reward system adjusts to the drug's chronic presence (e.g. Kenny, 2007; Koob & Le Moal, 2008; Robinson & Berridge, 2001). Presumably, more intensely pleasurable and rewarding drug use experiences pose a greater risk of problematic drug use behaviour developing. The nature of the experience is governed primarily by factors associated with the drug, the person, or the setting.

Drug-Related Factors

At least three drug-related factors affect the drug use experience (Brands et al., 1998). The most important is the drug selected. As shall be discussed shortly, different drugs produce different effects according to their specific neurochemical action, some of which are much more pleasurable than others. Another factor is the route of administration. Intravenous injection and inhalation facilitate faster and more efficient uptake, which produces more intense effects than if the same drug is taken orally or absorbed through the skin. The third drug-related factor is the size of the dose. Generally speaking, larger doses produce more intense effects. Table 10.2 ranks various drugs with respect to their associated risk of problematic use. Consistent with our discussion, the risk varies with the type of drug and the method of administration.

Person-Related Factors

Characteristics of the individual user also influence drug effects. Consider the impact of drinking beer on a petite person who took valium a short time earlier and is drinking to "loosen up" before a party versus a 250-pound linebacker who drinks regularly and is having a couple of beers after practice. The alcohol effects will not be the same for these two people. Individual differences in their physical attributes, substance use history, and psychological expectations will result in distinct drinking experiences (Advokat et al., 2014; DeWall, Bushman, Giancola, & Webster, 2009; Vogel-Sprott, 1992).

Setting

A study by Siegel, Hinson, Krank, and McCully (1982) demonstrated the potential power of the drug-use setting on the pharmacological effects experienced. The researchers gave a

Table 10.2 The proneness of different drugs to problematic use

Proneness	Substance
Very high	Heroin (injected)
	Crack cocaine (smoked)
High	Morphine (injected)
	Opium (smoked)
Moderate/high	Cocaine powder (snorted)
	Nicotine (tobacco; smoked)
	Phencyclidine (PCP; smoked)
	Barbiturates (secobarbital; oral)
Moderate	Benzodiazepine (Valium; oral)
	Alcohol (oral)
	Amphetamine (oral)
Moderate/low	Caffeine (coffee; oral)
	Marijuana (smoked)
Very low	LSD (oral)

Source: Data from Gable, R. S. (1993). Toward a comparative overview of dependence potential and acute toxicity of psychoactive substances used nonmedically. *American Journal of Drug and Alcohol Abuse, 19,* 263–281, reprinted by permission of the publisher (Taylor & Francis Ltd, http://www.tandfonline.com).

sample of rats a dose of heroin in a certain setting one day and a placebo dose in another setting the next day. A group of control rats was administered injections of only the placebo in the same two settings. After 30 days, the researchers administered the same potentially lethal dose of heroin to every rat. Rats in the control group had the highest mortality rate (96 per cent) because they received only the placebo and had no tolerance to the drug. The others exhibited significantly different mortality rates depending on the setting of the final dose: 64 per cent in an unfamiliar setting and 32 per cent in a familiar setting.

Why the difference? The familiar setting signalled the impending heroin injection, leading the rats to unconsciously compensate for the effect of the drug before it was administered. Rats injected in an unfamiliar setting unassociated with the heroin essentially had no advance warning. Consequently, their bodies were completely unprepared for the heroin and many did not survive the injection.

Major Classes of Drugs

Psychoactive substances may be classified a variety of ways, including their origin, chemical structure, mechanism of action, and therapeutic use (Brands et al., 1998). The drug classifications used in this chapter (see Figure 10.1) are based largely on the drug's action within the brain and its effects on the user but be aware that, even when drugs are organized in this manner, they can still be grouped in more than one way.

Stimulants

The **stimulant** class of drugs typically produce effects involving increased attention, mood, and activity levels. The usual action of these drugs is to stimulate the central

stimulant A class of drugs that elevate aspects of central nervous system function.

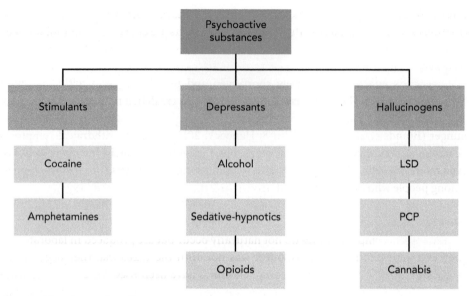

Figure 10.1 Drug classifications

nervous system by enhancing the activity of dopamine, norepinephrine, and epinephrine (Advokat et al., 2014). As we learned in Chapter 3, these neurotransmitters (especially dopamine) play an important role in the reward system or pleasure pathway of the brain, which is probably why people find stimulants so pleasant to use and, in some cases, so difficult to resist (Advokat et al., 2014; Grilly, 2006). Among the drugs in this class are cocaine, amphetamines, nicotine, and caffeine. The last two are by far the most popular stimulants, but they do not exhibit the links to criminal behaviour associated with cocaine and amphetamines and are not reviewed here.

Cocaine

Cocaine has a long history of use that can be traced back to the people of modern-day Bolivia and Peru who chewed the leaves of the coca plant to ward off fatigue and improve their mood (Ksir et al., 2006). The drug eventually made its way to Europe and North America, where it became increasingly popular during the late nineteenth and early twentieth centuries (Advokat et al., 2014). Cocaine powder can be either snorted or dissolved in water and injected. It cannot be smoked in this form because the high temperature necessary to vapourize the drug destroys its psychoactive property (Daamen, Penning, Brunt, & Verster, 2012; Grilly, 2006). The answer to this problem is crack, which is produced by dissolving cocaine powder in water, mixing it with baking soda, and then heating the solution to evaporate the liquid (Daamen et al., 2012). The residue of this process consists of rocklike crystals that can be smoked (Daamen et al., 2012).

rush The sudden and intensely pleasurable feeling users may experience immediately following the administration of a psychoactive drug.

binge To consume a large amount of something, such as a drug, in a continuous fashion for an extended time.

Cocaine consistently produces alertness, euphoria, and enhanced energy (Bezchlibnyk-Butler, Jeffries, Procyshyn, & Virani, 2014). Large doses taken intravenously or smoked can lead to an intense euphoria, or **rush**, that has been equated to being lifted into the air or having an orgasm (McKim & Hancock, 2013). Some users find the experience so pleasurable that they go on a **binge**, during which they take cocaine nonstop for hours or even days at a time (Brands et al., 1998). Using cocaine chronically or in high doses, however, can produce agitation, anxiety, and paranoia. In extreme cases, users may have a psychotic break, during which they experience delusions and/or hallucinations such as "coke bugs"—the sensation that insects are crawling over or under one's skin (Bezchlibnyk-Butler et el., 2014; Grilly, 2006). Overdoses can result in convulsions, respiratory and cardiac arrest, and death (McKim & Hancock, 2012).

Cocaine's effects are relatively short-lived and usually dissipate within an hour (Brands et al., 1998). The euphoria is often followed by a **crash** that normally occurs within 30 minutes of taking the drug and is characterized by a period of depression, lethargy, and hunger (Brands et al., 1998; McKim & Hancock, 2013). Physical withdrawal symptoms peak one or two days after drug use stops, but a craving may persist for many weeks or even months (Grilly, 2006). The risk of developing cocaine problems appears to be highest among people who experience a rush from using the drug (Brands et al., 1998).

crash The period following a binge on stimulant drugs, when the intoxication effects rapidly diminish and the user experiences feelings of depression, lethargy, and/or hunger.

Amphetamines

Unlike cocaine, amphetamines do not naturally occur but are produced in laboratories. They first appeared in the 1800s, but it was not until the 1920s that they began to be used medicinally. Since this time, amphetamines have been used for everything from asthma and narcolepsy to depression and weight control. In recent years, their medical use has been substantially curbed and is now largely confined to treating narcolepsy and ADHD (Ksir et al., 2006; McKim & Hancock, 2013). The decline in the pharmaceutical manufacture of amphetamines has been largely replaced by the illicit production of these and other related designer drugs, such as meth (Brands et al., 1998; McKim & Hancock, 2013).

Amphetamines are most commonly smoked, injected, or ingested orally, although it is also possible to snort them (Brands et al., 1998). The short-term intoxication effects are very similar to those of cocaine. As with cocaine, amphetamine can produce a rush and users are prone to binge. Paranoia, delusions, and hallucinations are known to appear with high or repeated doses, and discontinuing regular use is likely to be followed by a psychological desire or craving (Brands et al., 1998; Grilly, 2006). In fact, the effects of amphetamines and cocaine are so analogous that the two drugs cannot be reliably distinguished from one another when administered intravenously, except that the effects of the former last much longer (Fischman et al., 1976). These prolonged effects probably account for the less pronounced crash and more gradual appearance of withdrawal symptoms associated with amphetamines (Grilly, 2006).

Depressants

Depressants are labelled as such because their major effect is to depress, or slow down, central nervous system function. The precise action of these drugs varies from compound to compound, but it generally involves reducing neuron excitability, which in turn lowers overall neural activity in the central nervous system (Grilly, 2006). The main types of depressants are alcohol, sedative-hypnotics, and opioids.

depressants A class of drugs that dampen certain aspects of central nervous system function.

Alcohol

Ethanol—the proper name for the alcohol we drink—has a history of use that stretches back thousands of years and to many different regions of the world because it is so easy to make. Its wide availability, pleasurable effects, and general social acceptability have combined to make it one of the most misused of all drugs (Brands et al., 1998).

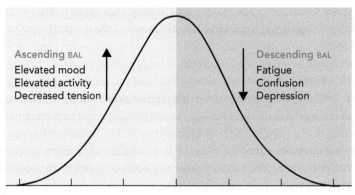

Figure 10.2 The biphasic effects of alcohol intoxication

biphasic Something that has
two phases.

The effects of alcohol are **biphasic**, meaning that there are two phases (see Figure 10.2). During the first phase, blood alcohol levels (BAL) increase and there is a corresponding rise in mood and activity, similar to that seen with the stimulants (McKim & Hancock, 2013). You may have observed this effect if you have witnessed someone become more talkative and animated after consuming a couple of drinks. Despite this elevated state, alcohol is not considered a stimulant because its effects are thought to be caused by depressing certain areas of the brain (Brands et al., 1998; Grilly, 2006). For example, rising BALs slow motor performance, coordination, and reaction time (LeBlanc, Kalant, & Gibbins, 1975; Martin & Earleywine, 1990; Vogel-Sprott & Fillmore, 1993). The second phase occurs as BALs drop, producing more depressant-like effects such as lethargy, drowsiness, and confusion (McKim & Hancock, 2013). People in this phase often appear more depressed and they may show signs of anger and irritability (Brands et al., 1998). At extreme levels of intoxication, alcohol may result in a loss of consciousness, coma, and death, usually due to respiratory failure (McKim & Hancock, 2013).

The biphasic effects of alcohol have prompted speculation that people display more aggression when BALs are ascending and less when they are descending. Giancola and Zeichner's (1997) findings on alcohol's effect on aggression are consistent with this hypothesis (see the "Researching" box).

Tolerance to alcohol develops quickly and plateaus within a matter of weeks (McKim & Hancock, 2013). Abstaining may cause withdrawal but usually only after years of prolonged use (Adokat et al., 2014; Grilly, 2006). Withdrawal symptoms can appear within a few of hours of the last drink and, in mild cases, may consist of irritability, headache, and insomnia (Bezchlibnyk-Butler et al., 2014). More serious reactions progress through several stages, typically starting with less serious symptoms such as tremors, nausea, and vomiting before escalating to visual and auditory hallucinations, delusions, and convulsions. **Delirium tremens (DTs)** is a potentially life-threatening condition characterized by these later withdrawal symptoms and cardiovascular stress (Brands et al., 1998). Withdrawal symptoms usually disappear within 7 to 10 days of onset but may persist for many weeks in severe cases (Ksir et al., 2006).

delirium tremens (DTs)
A pattern of severe symptoms
caused by withdrawal from
alcohol and characterized by
tremors, delusions, hallucinations, and convulsions.

Sedative-Hypnotics

Sedative-hypnotics are primarily used to treat anxiety and insomnia (Ksir et al., 2006). Barbiturates were the first drugs of this class to be developed, but they have been largely supplanted by benzodiazepines, which are just as effective and much safer.

Researching Criminal and Violent Behaviour

The Biphasic Effects of Alcohol on Aggression

Giancola and Zeichner (1997) used an aggression paradigm to study the biphasic effects of alcohol on aggression. Participants were told that they were competing against an opponent in a task designed to study alcohol's effects on reaction time. On each of several trials, the participant with the quickest reaction was the "winner" and delivered an "electric shock" to the loser. The winner chose the level of shock by pressing one of numerous buttons arranged in a line and labelled from low to high. Unbeknownst to the participants, their opponent was really a confederate of the researchers and the outcome of each task was determined by a computer program designed to have the participants win half the trials. The participants controlled only the level and duration of the shock applied to their fictional opponent. The shock's duration and intensity were totalled and used as the measure of participant aggression.

The researchers recruited 60 male participants for the study by using ads in community newspapers. Half the participants served as sober controls and the other half were randomly assigned to an alcohol ascending condition (AAC) or an alcohol descending condition (ADC). Participants in the two experimental conditions drank a glass of orange juice containing a quantity of alcohol calibrated to their body weight. Their BAL was tested every few minutes until it reached 0.08 per cent, the designated level for commencing the reaction task. Participants in the AAC did the task when their BAL ascended to the designated level, whereas those in the ADC did it after their BAL had peaked and descended to the designated level. Individual participants in both conditions reached the designated BAL level at different times. To account for this variation, each participant was paired with a control participant who remained sober. The controls drank a glass of orange juice with no alcohol and, after waiting the same amount of time as it took their partner to reach the required BAL, completed the reaction task.

Giancola and Zeichner (1997) found that participants in the AAC delivered shocks of significantly greater average intensity than did participants in the ADC or the sober control groups. The shock intensities of the ADC and the control groups did not differ significantly from one another (see Figure 10.3). The investigators speculated that alcohol-related aggression was greatest when the BAL was ascending because this phase tends to produce stimulating and arousing effects similar to those linked to aggression with substances such as amphetamines.

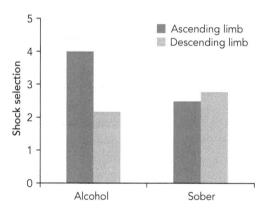

Figure 10.3 Mean shock intensity selections for each limb and beverage group

Source: Copyright ©1997 by the American Psychological Association. Reproduced with permission. P.R. Giancola & A. Zeichner (1997). "The biphasic effects of alcohol on human physical aggression." *Journal of Abnormal Psychology, 106*, 598–607. The use of APA information does not imply endorsement by APA.

Sedative-hypnotics are taken recreationally by people who enjoy the intoxicated state these drugs produce, which resembles that caused by alcohol consumption in many respects (Brands et al., 1998). Common effects include impaired mental performance, memory, and judgment, as well as slurred speech, decreased coordination, slowed reaction times, fatigue, and drowsiness (Bezchlibnyk-Butler et al., 2014). A particularly potent benzodiazepine, capable of producing all these effects as well as amnesia, is ro-hypnol (Grilly, 2006). These properties have been exploited by some individuals, who slip the drug into the drinks of unsuspecting victims and then sexually assault them once the drug has taken effect—hence rohypnol's reputation as the "date rape drug" (Grilly, 2006; Ksir et al., 2006).

The onset of effects range widely among the sedative-hypnotics. As might be expect-ed, the most popular ones on the street usually have a rapid onset and produce effects for short to moderate periods (Grilly, 2006). Discontinuing these drugs can lead to a variety of withdrawal symptoms, including tremors, agitation, insomnia, nausea, and, in severe cases, seizures and even coma (Bezchlibnyk-Butler et el., 2014).

Opioids

Opioids are a large family of drugs related to the main psychoactive ingredients found in the opium poppy native to various parts of Asia and the Middle East (Grilly, 2006; Ksir et al., 2006). People have capitalized on opium's psychoactive properties for thou-sands of years, although its main active ingredients—morphine and codeine—were not chemically isolated and identified until the early 1800s (Brands et al., 1998). Near the end of that century, Bayer Laboratories made some minor chemical refinements to morphine, which dramatically increased its potency, and then marketed the resulting product to the public under the name heroin (Ksir et al., 2006). Chemists have since synthesized a number of drugs, such as Demerol and methadone, which produce sim-ilar analgesic effects, as well as opioid antagonists, such as naloxone and naltrexone, which block the action of these drugs and counteract their effects (Brands et al., 1998; Ksir et al., 2006).

Opioids are taken for both medicinal and recreational purposes. Medically, the opioids continue to be prescribed because they remain among the most effective drugs available for pain control (Brands et al., 1998). People also take them recreationally for the pleasant feeling they induce. Early users simply chewed or smoked opium; nowadays, substances such as morphine and heroin are usually injected because this route of admin-istration generates the most intense effects (Brands et al., 1998; Grilly, 2006). The intoxi-cated state produced by this group of drugs involves feelings of relaxation, pleasant mood, and in some cases an intense rush (Grilly, 2006). Because opioids are depressants, they generally lower the user's level of consciousness, which may result in a dreamy, cloudy, or drowsy mental state that some people report enhances their creative processes. Psychomo-tor performance may also decrease (McKim & Hancock, 2013).

The acute effects of opioid use are not always pleasant. Many first-time users experi-ence nausea and vomiting, and it may take repeated applications of the drug before these symptoms disappear (McKim & Hancock, 2013). Large doses carry the risk of coma and depressed breathing, which in some cases leads to respiratory arrest and death (Bezch-libnyk-Butler et al., 2014). That said, the most common negative health impacts associat-ed with the opioids are not due to the drugs per se but to the lifestyle that accompanies their use, which commonly features non-sterile needles, impure drugs, and poor nutrition (Brands et al., 1998; McKim & Hancock, 2013).

Tolerance to most opioid drug effects develops quickly, and regular users are con-tinually forced to increase the dose to achieve the same pleasurable effects. Users even-tually reach a point where further increases are no longer effective and continued use merely staves off withdrawal (Brands et al., 1998). The signs of withdrawal—restlessness, agitation, tremors, cramps, chills, nausea, vomiting, and body aches—usually emerge 6 to 12 hours after the last dose (Bezchlibnyk-Butler et al., 2014; Grilly, 2006). Opioid withdrawal is often compared to a bad case of the flu and, although very unpleasant, is rarely life-threatening (McKim & Hancock, 2013). It is widely recognized that, once a pattern of problematic opioid use has developed, it is very difficult to break. Cravings for the drug can last for months after drug taking stops and withdrawal symptoms have disappeared (Brands et al., 1998; Grilly, 2006). Moreover, a large proportion of users who manage to abstain from drug taking eventually relapse (Grilly, 2006).

Hallucinogens

Hallucinogens are the most heterogeneous of the three drug classes. This group encompasses an array of chemically unrelated substances that, when taken in sufficiently large doses, are all capable of producing one common effect: hallucinations (Grilly, 2006; Ksir et al., 2006). This ability to create altered states of consciousness and perception—and not the effects on the brain reward systems—appears to be reinforcing and the reason that these drugs are used recreationally (Grilly, 2006).

hallucinogens A class of drugs that are chemically unrelated but are all capable of producing hallucinations.

Lysergic Acid Diethylamide (LSD)

LSD first appeared in the 1930s, when it was accidently ingested during experimental efforts to find a new medicine (McKim & Hancock, 2013). It can be smoked, injected, or swallowed. The latter route is the most common means of administration and, once in the digestive system, LSD is absorbed quite quickly (Advokat et al., 2014). Intoxication is associated with positive mood states and euphoria, as well as distortions of time, space, and self (Brands et al., 1998; Ksir et al., 2006). One of the most notable effects is the ability to induce a kaleidoscopic array of visual hallucinations composed of different patterns and vivid colours or distorted images such as faces or objects that exist in real life. In the extreme, LSD may precipitate psychotic episodes, during which the person cannot distinguish between what is real and what is not (Brands et al., 1998). Adverse reactions are relatively common and may include feelings of anxiety or panic (Ksir et al., 2006). Some users experience **flashbacks**, spontaneous reoccurrences of the drug-induced perceptual experience in a drug-free state (Brands et al., 1998; Ksir et al., 2006). Apart from the possibility of these unpleasant symptoms, there are no known long-term negative health effects.

flashback A spontaneous re-occurrence of a drug-induced perceptual experience that happens during a drug-free state.

Tolerance develops very quickly and, after taking LSD on several successive days, the drug will no longer produce effects (Brands et al., 1998). The only way to re-establish drug effects is to abstain from it for a number of days. LSD does not produce symptoms of withdrawal when drug taking ceases, nor does it appear to be especially prone to problematic usage patterns given the infrequent case reports of people who crave it or show an inability to control their use (Brands et al., 1998).

Phencyclidine (PCP)

Phencyclidine (PCP) was originally developed as a surgical anaesthetic but was abandoned due to complications with post-operative delirium and hallucinations (Brands et al., 1998). This drug may be swallowed, snorted, injected, or sprinkled on another substance, such as marijuana or tobacco, and smoked (Brands et al., 1998). Like the other hallucinogens, PCP intoxication causes distortions to self, time, and space (Ksir et al., 2006).

It also produces euphoria, but this effect is not universal and positive past experiences are no guarantee against future adverse reactions involving anxiety, alienation, depression, and panic (Brands et al., 1998; Ksir et al., 2006). The literature suggests that the distortions in sensory input caused by PCP can lead to exaggerated, and perhaps even violent, responses to environmental stimuli (Advokat et al., 2014). Thinking can become suspicious and confused, and in severe cases there may be a full psychotic break (Advokat et al., 2014; Grilly, 2006). Flashbacks are also a possibility, and very large doses may result in stupor or coma (Advokat et al., 2014; Brands et al., 1998). Some evidence suggests that PCP tolerance can develop so that regular users must increase their dose over the course of several weeks to maintain the same effects. Paradoxically, users do not appear to suffer withdrawal symptoms when drug use is discontinued, although cravings for the drug are common (Advokat et al., 2014).

Cannabis

The cannabis sativa plant's ability to survive in a wide range of climates has allowed people to cultivate it in many regions of the world (Ksir et al., 2006). The plant's main psychoactive ingredient, delta-9-tetrahydrocannabinol (THC), is present at higher levels in the flowering tops and at lower levels in the leaves and stalks (Ksir et al., 2006). Three drug-related products are derived from the cannabis plant (Brands et al., 1998). The most common is marijuana, which consists of the dried flowers and leaves of the plant and it has the lowest concentration of THC (Ksir et al., 2006). Hashish is the plant resin that has been scraped off and dried. The THC level of hashish is between that of marijuana and hash oil, which is made by boiling the cannabis plant in alcohol and then evaporating the liquid off to produce a thick, oily concentrate (Brands et al., 1998; Ksir et al., 2006). Cannabis products are generally smoked, but they are sometimes included in baked items, such as cookies (Brands et al., 1998; McKim & Hancock, 2013).

Cannabis is used medically to treat glaucoma, conditions involving involuntary muscle contractions (e.g. Tourette's syndrome), and chemotherapy-induced nausea (McKim & Hancock, 2013). It is used recreationally for its intoxicating effects, which induce feelings of well-being, relaxation, mild euphoria, amusement, and laughter (Advokat et al., 2014). Impairments in judgment, cognition, memory, balance, and motor coordination may be noticeable (Brands et al., 1998; Ksir et al., 2006). As with the other drugs of this class, cannabis can produce distortions of self, time, and space, but hallucinations are relatively uncommon (Advokat et al., 2014; McKim & Hancock, 2013). Higher doses have an increased risk of adverse reactions involving paranoia, panic, and disorientation, but there appears to be little, if any, risk of a lethal overdose (Brands et al., 1998; Ksir et al., 2006). Over the longer term, smoking cannabis may negatively impact health in ways similar to smoking tobacco products (Brands et al., 1998).

The occasional use of cannabis does not result in tolerance, but it may occur with heavy and prolonged use (Grilly, 2006). Individuals who abruptly discontinue taking the drug are likely to show signs of withdrawal, which may include changes in appetite, sleep disturbances, anxiety, irritability, and restlessness (Advokat et al., 2014). Some users experience persistent cravings for the drug and have difficulty controlling or eliminating their use (Brands et al., 1998). Nevertheless, it is widely believed that the craving and compulsive need people exhibit for cannabis is not as strong as that for alcohol, stimulants, or opioids (Grilly, 2006).

Goldstein's Tripartite Model

Paul Goldstein (1985) provided one of the first conceptual frameworks describing the major interconnections of drugs and violence. It outlines three possible links, labelled as follows: systemic violence, economic compulsive violence, and psychopharmacological violence. Although the original focus was the drug–violence nexus, Goldstein's ideas have been adapted in this chapter and broadly applied to all drug-related criminal behaviour.

Systemic Crime

Systemic crime involves illegal behaviour that occurs as a consequence of the drug trade's illicit nature. Because the drug trade operates outside the law, those involved in it are unable, or at least unwilling, to seek recourse from the usual legal authorities when disagreements arise. In short, participants must be prepared to safeguard themselves and their business interests and to resolve their own disputes (Johnson, Williams, Dei, & Sanabria, 1990).

systemic crime A form of drug-related crime identified in Paul Goldstein's tripartite model that occurs because the drug trade is illegal and its participants cannot turn to authorities for assistance.

Reiss and Roth (1993) identified three dimensions of systemic crime: organizational, transaction, and third party. Organizational crime concerns the overall operation of the gang or cartel involved in the drug trade and presumably encompasses actions to establish, maintain, or expand the organization's position within it. This requires internal accountability and discipline so that individual members live up to the organization's expectations of them. Violence in this context is often a response to individuals who are "messing up" the money; that is, they fail to return the expected amount of money to their supplier considering the quantity of drugs they were given to sell (Johnson et al., 1985, p. 174).

Externally, an organization must contend with rival groups that may try to encroach on its territory. Sometimes informal agreements are reached, whereby one organization pays tribute, or hands over a portion of its profits, to a more powerful rival. At other times, disputes between competing drug organizations erupt into open warfare, as illustrated by the extreme episodes of violence observed in northern Mexico in recent years. The organization must also avoid being investigated and prosecuted by the authorities. Organizations typically employ a variety of strategies for this purpose, which commonly include concealing their operations, bribing and threatening local officials, and laundering the proceeds. There is perhaps no better example of the organizational dimension of systemic crime than the Medellin Cartel, led by Pablo Escobar. For a time, this group controlled much of the illegal cocaine flowing into the United States through a ruthless strategy of eliminating competitors and bribing or threatening state officials (see the case study).

Transaction-related systemic crime typically revolves around a single business deal or the business relationship of a seller and buyer. Reiss and Roth (1993) note that violence may be used to resolve disputes over the quality and quantity of the drugs or the payment. In addition, dealers are sometimes robbed by those wishing to capitalize on the large quantities of drugs and money they usually carry with them.

Third-party systemic crime involves those at the periphery of the drug trade. Illicit drugs are frequently a visible part of many other illegal markets, including protection rackets, prostitution, and stolen property. Criminal and violent behaviour from the drug trade can spill over into these other areas. For example, drug violence has created an illegal market for stolen and illegal firearms and body armour. More alarming for the general public are cases of innocent bystanders being injured or killed in drug-related conflicts.

CASE STUDY

Pablo Escobar

Medellin, Colombia—Pablo Escobar emerged from relatively humble beginnings to become one of the most powerful drug lords the world has ever known. Born near Rio Negro, Colombia, in 1949, he grew up poor, living in a one-bedroom house in the country before his family moved him to the city of Medellin. There are rumours that Escobar engaged in some petty crime as a teenager, but it wasn't until his twenties that he ventured into smuggling, first contraband cigarettes and then cocaine. He started in the cocaine trade by purchasing cocaine paste in Peru and transporting it back to Colombia, where it was processed into powder and then smuggled into the United States. Initially,

Photo 10.2 Drug lord Pablo Escobar, seen here at a soccer game with an unidentified bodyguard, served only one year in prison before escaping. He was killed by the Columbian police when they found him hiding out in a house in Medellin. AP Photo

Escobar was actively involved in the operation and drove cars with cocaine stashed in the fenders over the border into Colombia. As his operation grew, he formed the Medellin Cartel with several other cocaine producers in the area and together they directed vast drug-trafficking empires from the relative safety of their country estates.

Escobar was the cartel's natural leader. At the height of his dominance, it is estimated that he controlled 80 per cent of the global cocaine trade, and *Forbes* listed him as the seventh wealthiest person in the world in 1989 (Pressly, 2014). His brother claims that they spent $2,500 per month just on elastics to hold all the money they were collecting. Escobar funnelled some of his profits into real estate and other business investments to create the appearance of legitimacy. He also funded many housing and community projects, such as hospitals and soccer fields, where he lived and developed a well-cultivated reputation as Robin Hood among the locals. He became so popular that he even managed to briefly hold a seat in parliament.

Much of Escobar's success is attributed to his personal charisma, criminal business savvy, and ruthlessness. He had a reputation for following a policy of *"plata o plomo"* ("silver or bullets"), whereby officials either accepted his bribes or faced his bullets (Bowden, 2001). During his time in power, intimidation, kidnappings, torture, and assassinations were regular features of life around Medellin and elsewhere in Colombia. In the end, his wealth and prominence proved his undoing. He caught the eyes of American officials, who pressed Colombia's government to turn him over to them. Escobar responded by unleashing a campaign of terror and violence on state officials in an effort to coerce them into blocking a Colombian law that would permit drug traffickers to be extradited to the United States (Pressly, 2014). He is thought to be responsible for ordering the deaths of a minister of justice, an attorney general, legislators, judges, and hundreds of police officers (Bowden, 2001; Escobar, 2009). The violence wrought by Escobar, which included bringing down an airliner with more than a hundred people aboard, backfired and turned public opinion against him (Pressly, 2014). Escobar died amid a barrage of gunfire as he tried to escape from Colombian security forces in 1993.

Source: (except where otherwise noted): Escobar, R. (2009). *Escobar. Drugs. Guns. Money. Power. The inside story of Pablo Escobar, the world's most powerful criminal.* London, UK: Hodder & Stoughton.

Goldstein and colleagues applied the tripartite classification system to two samples of drug-related homicide cases occurring in New York State in 1984 and 1988 (Goldstein, Brownstein, Ryan, & Bellucci, 1989; Goldstein, Brownstein, & Ryan, 1992). The first sample consisted of 129 homicides committed outside New York City in 1984 and the second of 218 homicides in the city in 1988. The percentage of cases involving systemic violence was 21 and 74 per cent, respectively. The researchers believe one reason for the large discrepancy was the widespread growth in the marketing and distribution of crack after 1984. Analyses of data from a multi-year national survey in the United States supports the general proposition that participating in the illicit drug trade raises the risk of becoming both a perpetrator and a victim of violent crime (Menard & Mihalic, 2001).

Economic Compulsive Crime

Economic compulsive crime is committed for the purpose of supporting an existing drug habit (Goldstein, 1985). It can occur in several different ways: crimes may be committed to get money for purchasing drugs, illegal commodities such as stolen property may be bartered for drugs, or the drugs may be stolen from other users or drug dealers. Robert Osborne, featured in this chapter's opening case study, committed economic compulsive crime when he stole motor vehicles to pay for drugs.

In Goldstein and colleagues' (1992) research, economic compulsive crime was the least common of the three types of illegal behaviour identified in the model, constituting less than 5 per cent of the incidents examined. Keep in mind that this figure relates to drug-related homicides only and the results might have been quite different had all drug-involved crime been examined. Other research suggests that economic compulsive crime accounts for a much larger proportion of drug-related crime. For example, studies in the United States and Britain reveal that 20 to 30 per cent of arrestees and inmates committed their offence to purchase drugs (Bennett, 2000; Mumola & Karberg, 2006).

There are two major factors that contribute to the financial cost of using psychoactive drugs. One is the level of drug use. In the past, this factor was attributed primarily to the desire to alleviate withdrawal symptoms, but there is growing recognition that the psychological craving and compulsive need to use a drug may be just as important for driving consumption (Bean, 2004). The second factor is the cost of the drug. Illicit substances cannot be purchased on the open market and therefore come at grossly inflated costs. The most expensive drug habits are associated with psychoactive substances that are both strongly addictive and expensive. This is why cocaine and heroin users typically need much more money to pay for their drugs than users of less addictive and cheaper substances such as cannabis and other hallucinogens (Goldstein, 1985). Data collected by the Office of National Drug Control Policy (ONDCP, 2014a) estimate the average expenditures incurred by chronic users of several illicit drugs. As shown in Table 10.3, the average monthly cost of heroin and cocaine, which takes into account the typical patterns of consumption associated with these drugs, lies in the neighbourhood of US$1,000. In view of these high costs, it is not surprising that these two drugs show the strongest relationships to crime (Bennett, Holloway, & Farrington, 2008).

economic compulsive crime A form of drug-related crime identified in Paul Goldstein's tripartite model that occurs as a result of drug users engaging in illegal behaviour as a means to support their drug habit.

Table 10.3 Estimated average monthly drug expenditures among American drug users, 2010 (US dollars)

Substance	Average cost per month		
	21+ days/month	4–10 days/month	Weighted average
Cocaine	1,737	382	883
Heroin	1,834	530	1,457
Methamphetamine	1,256	165	655

Source: Adapted from Office of National Drug Control Policy. (2014). *What America's users spend on illegal drugs: 2000–2010*. Washington, DC: p. 32–33.

Many illicit drug users have no need to resort to crime to pay for drug purchases because they use drugs only occasionally and are gainfully employed (Slaymaker, 2014). A national survey of American adolescents and young adults found that only 2–4 per cent of the respondents acknowledged committing an offence to fund drug purchases (Menard & Mihalic, 2001). People with more serious habits, however, find paying for drugs poses a more significant challenge (Faupel & Klockars, 1987). Not only do they spend more money on drugs, but they are also less likely to have full employment (Slaymaker, 2014). Whether this situation is the result of people losing their jobs as a consequence of their drug use or the persistently unemployed becoming drug users is difficult to disentangle. Regardless, many persistent drug users find themselves supporting expensive drug habits without an adequate source of legitimate income (Stewart, Gossop, Marsden, & Rolfe, 2000).

Numerous studies support the connection between economic compulsive crime and the amount of money users spend on drugs. Several investigations report that criminal activity levels are higher or lower depending on the amount of drugs being consumed and the user's need for money (e.g. Anglin & Speckart, 1988; Ball, Shaffer, & Nurco, 1983; Nurco, Hanlon, Kinlock, & Duszynski, 1988). Likewise, drug users who enter treatment programs and reduce their drug consumption exhibit lower levels of criminal activity (Farabee, Shen, Hser, Grella, & Anglin, 2001; Gossop, Marsden, Stewart, & Kidd, 2003; Ross et al., 2006). One of the only studies to directly examine the relationship of drug-related spending and crime found that drug-using offenders who committed crimes to get money were spending significantly more on drugs than users who did not commit these crimes (Hayhurst et al., 2013). Relatedly, employment programs appear to reduce economic compulsive crime because users gain a legal source of income to pay for their drugs, not because their drug intake has decreased as a result of working (Uggen & Shannon, 2014).

With respect to the nature of economic compulsive crime, drug users demonstrate a preference for non-violent over violent offending (Anglin & Speckart, 1988; Ball et al., 1983; Nurco, Kinlock, & Hanlon, 1990). Property offences and drug dealing are the most common crimes committed for this purpose (Ball et al., 1983). Users who resort to violence to obtain drug money typically do so during periods of intense drug use, when they may feel there is no alternative (Anglin & Speckart, 1988; Johnson et al., 1985; Hunt, Lipton, & Spunt, 1984; Nurco, et al., 1990). Nevertheless, Goldstein (1985) believes that, when economic compulsive crime involves violence, it is usually a function of situational factors. In other words, the perpetrators do not intend to inflict physical harm on victims but do so as a result of their own nervousness, the victim's actions, the presence of weapons, or the intervention of bystanders.

Psychopharmacological Crime

Psychopharmacological crime encompasses offending behaviour that stems from the acute and chronic effects of using psychoactive substances (Goldstein, 1985). In Goldstein and colleagues' (1992) original studies, 14 and 59 per cent of the homicide cases reviewed from the years 1984 and 1988, respectively, were classified as psychopharmacological violence. Although these figures cover a broad range, they correspond loosely to the 25 to 50 per cent of incarcerated offenders in North America who report being under the influence of a drug at the time of their offence (Brochu et al., 2001; National Center on Addiction and Substance Abuse at Columbia University, 2010; ONDCP, 2014b). Of course, the fact that someone is intoxicated while offending does not prove that a psychoactive substance caused him or her to commit a crime, but it is consistent with this possibility. Pharmacologically, the effects of intoxication, withdrawal, or long-term neurological changes caused by prolonged use could all increase the likelihood of crime and violence (Hoaken et al., 2014). As most research focuses on the possible psychopharmacological connections that exist between the major drugs and violent as opposed to criminal behaviour, the following review adopts the same approach.

> psychopharmacological crime A form of drug-related crime identified in Paul Goldstein's tripartite model that occurs as a result of the acute and chronic effects produced by a psychoactive substance.

Stimulants

Stimulants, especially amphetamine, are the drugs most frequently implicated in violent offending (Goldstein, 1985). A sizeable body of research substantiates the presence of a relationship between amphetamines and violence, but most of it is correlational in nature (Hoaken et al., 2014). Moreover, Hoaken and colleagues (2014) note some inconsistent findings, which they suggest point to the role of other factors. In contrast to the research on amphetamines, evidence that cocaine use leads to violence is more equivocal. Reviews of the literature note that, while some studies report positive relationships between cocaine and aggressive or violent behaviour, others ascribe these findings to the underlying characteristics of the cocaine users (Hoaken et al., 2014; Kretschmar & Flannery, 2007; Kruesi, 2007; Moore et al., 2008). In particular, two studies found that cocaine users with a history of aggression or antisocial traits were at risk of behaving aggressively, but users without these traits were not (Moeller et al., 1997; Moeller et al., 2002).

The reason stimulant intoxication may facilitate aggression is not well understood, but all these substances enhance arousal, mood, and activity, which may increase social interactions and the potential for interpersonal conflict. Reduced impulse control as a result of prolonged amphetamine use is another factor that may contribute to aggressive behaviour (Semple, Zians, Grant, & Patterson, 2005; Simons, Oliver, Gaher, Ebel, & Brummels, 2005). In extreme cases, these substances can produce psychosis, which elevates the risk of violence, especially if it involves paranoid and persecutory themes. After examining 13 individuals who committed homicide under the influence of amphetamines, Ellinwood (1971) concluded that the violence in most cases was directly attributable to the symptoms of amphetamine intoxication, including the presence of paranoid delusions either alone or in combination with emotional instability and impulsivity. Interestingly, Ellinwood identified a number of additional factors that contributed to violence, such as the presence of another drug and the personality of the perpetrator.

Depressants

Studies of the relationship between the sedative-hypnotics and violence concentrate on the benzodiazepines. Reviews note the research paints a confusing picture because individual studies often present divergent results; nevertheless, the general conclusion is that the use of benzodiazepines is associated with violent behaviour (Kruesi, 2007; Boles & Miotto, 2003; Hoaken et al., 2014). Hoaken and colleagues (2014) suggest that the mixed pattern of results indicates that individual factors such as impulsivity and a pre-existing tendency to behave aggressively likely influence the relationship.

The benzodiazepine–aggression relationship is somewhat counter-intuitive considering that these drugs are typically used for their sedative and calming effects. This paradox could be due to dose-dependent psychopharmacological effects, whereby low doses increase aggression and high doses capable of producing stronger sedative effects decrease it (Hoaken & Stewart, 2003). The precise mechanism(s) responsible for producing aggressive behaviour remains uncertain. Boles and Miotto (2003) point out that, like alcohol, these drugs can lead to a state of disinhibition and poor judgment that contributes to unconsidered and, in some instances, violent behaviour.

Alcohol is by far the psychoactive drug most strongly associated with criminal and violent behaviour. Although many of the studies reporting this relationship are correlational, the drug's violence-related pharmacological effects have been reproduced in experimental studies involving animals and humans and confirmed by meta-analytic reviews of the literature (Hoaken & Stewart, 2003; Bushman, 1993, 1997; Bushman & Cooper, 1990; Ito, Miller, & Pollock, 1996). Numerous theories have attempted to explain the role of alcohol in crime and violence, some of which will be canvassed near the end of the chapter.

Often overlooked is the fact that the sedative effects of benzodiazepines and alcohol have been exploited to perpetrate offences. Some offenders intentionally administer these substances to prospective victims, who may or may not know what they are consuming, to render them vulnerable to attack. As mentioned earlier, rohypnol is notorious for being used in this manner. Karla Homolka surreptitiously gave her sister the powerful sedative Haldol so that she would be incapacitated while being raped by Homolka's husband, Paul Bernardo (see the opening case study in Chapter 13). Serial killers such as Jeffery Dahmer, John Wayne Gacy, and Clifford Robert Olson plied their victims with alcohol and other psychoactive depressants prior to assaulting them. Under the effects of intoxication, the victims not only became relaxed and less guarded, but they were also more physically vulnerable and easier to overpower.

With respect to opioids, there is widespread agreement that the intoxication effects do not increase the risk of aggression and violence (Boles & Miotto, 2003; Hoaken & Stewart, 2003; Roth, 1994). Although reports of a positive relationship between opioid use and violence do exist, these findings are generally believed to reflect pre-existing tendencies among some individuals who harbour and display feelings of aggression (Hoaken et al., 2014). Indeed, opioid intoxication is associated with what Goldstein (1995) calls a "**reverse psychopharmacological effect**" that lowers the risk of crime and violence (p. 256). This reverse effect is probably caused by the lowered activity levels and mood brought about by opioid use, together with the general disabling effect of intoxication that makes it difficult to carry out offences (Bean, 2004).

Although opioid intoxication does not appear to facilitate aggression, there are numerous suggestions that withdrawal, especially from heroin, may have this effect (Boles & Miotto, 2003; Kretschmar & Flannery, 2007; Reiss & Roth, 1993). In fact, Bean (2004) argues that increased aggression from heroin withdrawal probably outweighs any reversal or reduction brought about by the acute effects of intoxication. The usual explanation

reverse psychopharmacological effect The reduced, rather than enhanced, likelihood of criminal behaviour, brought about by the acute and chronic effects of a psychoactive substance.

provided for aggressive behaviour in this context is that the symptoms become unbearable for some users and, in their desperation to get more drugs, they become violent (Boles & Miotto, 2003). An alternative explanation is the **self-medication hypothesis**. Khantzian (1985) proposes that some people specifically use heroin because of its suppressing effect on their irritable, angry, and aggressive feelings. As they withdraw from the drug and this suppressing effect is lifted, the risk of expressing these feelings increases.

Hallucinogens

Of the three classes of psychoactive substances reviewed here, hallucinogens exhibit the weakest relationship to crime and violence (Boles & Miotto, 2003; Reiss & Roth, 1993; Roth, 1994). Indeed, one recent study found that hallucinogen use was associated with reductions in criminal recidivism in a large sample of offenders under community supervision (Hendricks, Clark, Johnson, Fontaine, Cropsey, 2014). With respect to LSD specifically, there is virtually no evidence of any association with offending behaviour (Boles & Miotto, 2003; Roth, 1994).

More questions surround the possible effects of PCP. Some commentators suggest that it increases aggressive and violent behaviour, while others reject this claim (Boles & Miotto, 2003; Roth, 1994). Resolving this issue is hampered by the fact that only a small number of studies on this relationship have been conducted. According to Reiss and Roth (1993), some laboratory studies with animals show that the administration of PCP increases aggression, but the treated animal is typically the target, not the perpetrator of the violence. Research with humans is mixed. One early study found no differences in documented aggressive behaviour between patients in PCP and heroin detoxification and rehabilitation units (Khajawall, Erickson, & Simpson, 1982). On the other hand, a more recent study reported that chronic PCP users were significantly more likely than other drug users to have a history of general and partner violence (Crane, Easton, & Devine, 2013). Neither study examined whether the participants involved in these incidents were under the influence of PCP at the time they were aggressive. As with many of the other substances discussed, it appears that any relationship between PCP and violence is probably influenced by personality characteristics such as a pre-existing tendency to act aggressively (Fauman & Fauman, 1982; McCardle & Fishbein, 1989).

Reiss and Roth (1993) speculate that PCP led to violent victimization in animal studies because the intoxicated animals were hyperactive and displayed inappropriate or provocative social signals. A further way PCP intoxication may contribute to violence is by reducing impulse control (Fauman & Fauman, 1982). It has also been pointed out that PCP can produce psychosis that, depending on the nature of the presenting symptomology, could lead to violence (Fauman & Fauman, 1982; Kruesi, 2007). Police report that arresting people intoxicated with PCP can be challenging because the drug's analgesic properties often render conventional techniques relying on pain ineffective (Ksir et al., 2006).

A sizeable body of research has examined the relationship of cannabis and offending behaviour. Plenty of studies report a positive relationship between cannabis use and aggression (see Moore & Stuart, 2005); however, Hoaken and colleagues (2014) claim that this link generally disappears when common risk factors are taken into account. They identify two studies that continued to find a relationship between cannabis and violence despite controlling for common risk factors but point out that the researchers attributed their findings to systemic violence associated with drug trafficking, not to the pharmacological effects of the drug (see Friedman, Glassman, & Terras, 2001; Kinlock, O'Grady, & Hanlon, 2003).

self-medication hypothesis A theory proposing that some individuals take psychoactive drugs to suppress pre-existing feelings of anger and aggression; it is thought that, without this suppressing effect, such individuals are prone to act on these feelings.

The general view seems to be that cannabis intoxication has a predominantly calming effect that does not raise the risk of violence and, at higher doses, may even lower it (Boles & Miotto, 2003; Hoaken et al., 2014; Kruesi, 2007; Reiss & Roth, 1993; Moore & Stuart, 2005).

In contrast to cannabis intoxication, there is evidence that cannabis withdrawal can induce aggressive and violent behaviour (Arendt, Rosenberg, Foldager, Sher, & Munk-Jogensen, 2007; Budney, Moore, Vandrey, & Hughes, 2003; Budney, Vandrey, Hughes, Moore, & Bahrenburg, 2007; Kouri, Pope, & Lukas, 1999; Moore et al., 2008). Two explanations for this relationship have been advanced, both of which implicate negative feelings such as irritability and anger but in different ways. One suggestion is that withdrawal produces feelings of irritability and anger that are not normally present but lead some people to behave aggressively (Moore et al., 2008). The other is the aforementioned self-medication hypothesis, which assumes that the feelings of irritability and anger are pre-existing. The latter possibility was empirically tested by Arendt and colleagues (2007), who found that individuals with a history of violence were more likely than individuals with no such history to report using cannabis as a way to control their aggression (Arendt, Rosenberg, Fjordback et al., 2007). Yet paradoxically, these same people were also more likely to act aggressively when they used cannabis. This finding may be another indication that personality variables influence the relationship between cannabis and violent behaviour (Hoaken et al., 2014).

Putting It All Together: Making Sense of Psychopharmacological Violence

It is abundantly clear that a relationship between psychopharmacological effects and aggressive and violent behaviour exists, but its nature is exceedingly complex and varies with the particular drug. There is little evidence that any psychoactive substance directly causes violence as one of its pharmacological effects. It does appear that the intoxicating effects of several psychoactive substances commonly produce symptoms that increase the likelihood of interpersonal violence, but these effects are indirect. In addition, studies report fairly consistently that the relationship of drugs to violence depends on the characteristics of the individual user. One of the more common findings in this regard is that drug users with antisocial or aggressive personality traits are more likely to behave violently while intoxicated than are people without these traits. This fits many anecdotal observations of alcohol intoxication and the notion that some people are "happy" drunks while others are "mean" drunks. In short, the relationship of substance use to violent behaviour seems to vary not only from drug to drug but probably from person to person as well.

Theories of the Alcohol–Violence Relationship

Alcohol stands apart from the other psychoactive substances in terms of both the scope and depth of the theories developed to explain its relationship to offending. Most focus on explaining alcohol-related violence, but many of them can be easily adapted to explain general criminal behaviour. These theories can be loosely organized into the following three groups: disinhibition theories, cognitive-disruption theories, and expectancy theories.

Disinhibition Theories

Probably the most widely held explanation of alcohol-intoxicated behaviour is disinhibition (Collins, 1988; Graham, 1980). The essence of **disinhibition theories** is that alcohol intoxication depresses functioning in those areas of the brain responsible for behavioural control and, as a consequence, behaviours normally suppressed are exhibited (Graham, 1980). Taylor and Leonard (1983) assert that, as it relates to aggressive and violent behaviour, disinhibition theory is founded on the following two propositions: alcohol exerts a direct and universal effect on our inhibitory controls, and people possess an inherent tendency or predisposition to act aggressively that is normally restrained by such controls. Together, these propositions suggest that people act on their underlying aggressive tendencies when alcohol has sufficiently weakened the usual inhibitory controls (Giancola et al., 2012). Taylor and Leonard (1983) criticize this theory on the grounds that alcohol intoxication does not inevitably lead to aggressive behaviour but varies widely depending on the individual circumstances.

To address this weakness, Parker and colleagues refined the theory and relabelled it **selective disinhibition** (Parker & Auerhahn, 1998; Parker & Rebhun, 1995). They argue that alcohol disinhibits violence in a very selective manner according to its perceived effectiveness. The perception of violence as a useful course of action depends on the nature of the person, interpersonal dynamics, and the surrounding context (Parker & Rebhun, 1995). When violence is seen as an effective solution, it takes a conscious effort and willingness to adhere to society's behavioural expectations and resist the temptation to act violently (Parker & Auerhahn, 1998). This deliberate and proactive decision-making process is referred to as **active constraint**. A physically imposing individual outside a bar where fights regularly occur might be engaged in active constraint if he turns away from a lone stranger hurling insults at him. **Passive constraint** reflects situations where little or no conscious and deliberate effort is required to refrain from violence because it is perceived to be ineffective or at least less effective than non-violent courses of action. It might apply to a slightly built employee who does not react to being publicly berated by the boss at an office party.

Parker and Rebhun (1995) argue that alcohol intoxication disinhibits the usual constraints in a situation. This effect is most pronounced in active-constraint situations, when the use of violence is seen as advantageous. For example, our muscular friend might wish to teach his antagonist a lesson. Even with the disinhibiting effects of alcohol, violence is unlikely in passive-constraint situations such as the one experienced by the slight employee because the outcome of acting in this manner is expected to be physically and/or economically harmful. Parker and Rebhun (1995) stress that the level of intoxication required to override active constraint is a function of both the person and situation. This is the reason that intoxication effects appear so inconsistent and why alcohol consumption in the same situation, or even by the same person, does not always end in violence.

Cognitive-Interference Theories

Cognitive-interference theories are premised on the idea that alcohol intoxication impairs cognition in ways that interfere with our abilities to encode and process information from the social environment. In other words, alcohol intoxication causes people to misinterpret the thoughts and actions of others during the course of social interactions. When social misunderstandings occur, the chance of interpersonal conflict and inappropriate or even violent behaviour increases. These theories are reminiscent of the social

---

disinhibition theories of alcohol intoxication Theories based on the common premise that alcohol impairs areas of the brain responsible for inhibiting responses and, as a result of intoxication, behaviours normally suppressed are exhibited.

selective disinhibition A theory that the effect of alcohol in disinhibiting violence depends on the perceived effectiveness of acting violently in the particular circumstances.

active constraint The relatively large conscious and deliberate effort needed to act in a socially acceptable manner in situations where acting violently is perceived to be an effective and desirable course of action.

passive constraint The relatively small conscious and deliberate effort needed to act in a socially acceptable manner in situations where acting violently is perceived to be an ineffective or undesirable course of action.

cognitive-interference theories Theories based on the common premise that alcohol intoxication impairs human social cognition in ways that increase the chance of aggressive and violent behaviour.

information processing theories reviewed in Chapter 8. The main difference is that cognitive-interference theories attribute information processing errors to the temporary psychopharmacological effects of alcohol rather than the individual's characteristic way of perceiving and thinking.

Cognitive-interference theories vary with respect to the hypothesized source of the information processing errors. The **self-awareness model** centres on the cognitive awareness a person has of his or her behaviour. According to Hull (1981), appropriate behaviour can be maintained only if people are constantly aware of what they are doing and able to judge their actions against their internal standards of behaviour as well as the external standards set by the people around them and society at large. Hull argues that alcohol impairs the cognitive processes necessary for maintaining self-awareness and, in the absence of this information, people are likely to act inappropriately and perhaps even violently. Research by Bailey, Leonard, Cranston, and Taylor (1983) provides support for this theory. They reported that intoxicated individuals who were made self-aware administered less severe shocks to an adversary compared to those who were not self-aware (see the "Researching" box).

In contrast to the self-awareness model, the **appraisal-disruption model** focuses on stimuli in the external environment. It proposes that alcohol impairs an individual's ability to accurately appraise stressful information. Sayette (1993) claims that, after alcohol

self-awareness model The theory that people must be actively conscious of what they are doing in order to evaluate their conduct against relevant standards of behaviour; people with an impaired sense of self-awareness are likely to act inappropriately.

appraisal-disruption model The theory that alcohol interferes with the cognitive abilities people need to appraise social cues in the environment properly; as a consequence of alcohol intoxication, they may behave inappropriately for the situation.

Researching Criminal and Violent Behaviour

Intoxication, Self-Awareness, and Aggression

Bailey and colleagues (1983) examined the relationship of alcohol intoxication and self-awareness to aggression using an aggression paradigm similar to the one employed by Giancola and Zeichner (1997) discussed earlier in the chapter. Participants were informed that the study was testing the effect of alcohol on perceptual skills and that they would be performing a series of reaction-time tasks against an opponent situated in another room. At the beginning of each trial, participants chose 1 of 10 different shock levels. As long as their performance on the reaction task was faster, the level of shock selected would be administered to their opponent. If their performance was slower, they would receive whatever level of shock their opponent had selected. As in the other studies, there was no opponent and the outcome of each trial was fixed ahead of time. The researchers' only interest was the severity of the shock participants chose for their fictional opponent.

The study employed a 2 x 2 design that randomly assigned participants to an alcohol/placebo condition as well as a self-aware/self-unaware condition. All participants consumed two drinks that contained either a lot of or very little alcohol, depending on the study condition. Those in the self-aware condition were positioned so that they could see their reflection in a large mirror during the reaction task and were told that the reaction task was being filmed. Those in the self-unaware condition could not see their reflection and were not told the reaction task was being recorded.

The researchers reported that aggressive behaviour, as indicated by the intensity of the shock selected by the participants, varied according to the amount of alcohol consumed and self-awareness. Participants who received a large quantity of alcohol administered greater shock intensities than participants in the placebo condition. Furthermore, and in line with predictions, participants with a heightened self-awareness due to the mirror and filming administered lower intensity shocks than did participants who were less self-aware.

is consumed, social cues that should be a cause for concern are not properly evaluated. Consequently, the intoxicated person does not appreciate the seriousness of the situation or the behaviourally appropriate response for it. More particularly, the absence of fear and inhibition in situations where it is warranted is thought to increase the chance of interpersonal conflicts and physical altercations (Giancola, 2000). Imagine that two men are talking and one begins to speak about the other's girlfriend in unflattering terms. The boyfriend becomes increasingly angry—perhaps he stares intently, responds in a hostile tone, or bangs his fist on the table for emphasis. The appraisal-disruption model suggests that, if the person speaking is intoxicated, he is less likely to appraise these warning signs or appreciate the perilousness of his situation. He will carry on fearlessly with the conversation until the boyfriend lashes out violently. The theory may have a similar application to a real-life situation involving Shia LaBeouf (see the case study).

The **attention allocation model (AAM)** also centres on alcohol's impact on our cognitive ability to process external stimuli (Giancola, Josephs, Dewall, & Gunn, 2009). It proposes that alcohol intoxication makes it hard for us to shift our attention among multiple

> **attention allocation model (AAM)** The theory that alcohol interferes with the cognitive capacity needed to pay attention to multiple sources of information and, as a consequence of intoxication, people's attention focuses on only the most salient social cues in a situation, which are often aggressive in nature.

CASE STUDY

Shia LaBeouf

London, England—On 16 January 2014, actor Shia LaBeouf—noted for roles in *Indiana Jones and the Crystal Skull*, *Transformers*, and *Holes*—was filmed screaming at a fellow pub patron and then headbutting him, apparently after becoming upset at remarks the man made about his girlfriend's mother ("What are you saying," 2014). Immediately after striking the man, LaBeouf exclaimed, "What are you saying about my girl's mom? Are you f****** kidding me, bro?" One bystander stated, "I think also everyone's drunk and things are said . . . things got misconstrued." (para. 5). Sometime later, LaBeouf appeared to apologize for his actions:

> I'm not trying to have any more problems. You know what I'm saying . . . I'm really just trying to make peace . . . I mean, I'm a normal human being . . . I accept what I gotta get into to do what I love . . . And I'm not trying to s**t on nobody. I am a human being. I'm super normal, I am super normal. More normal than most . . . When people get hostile. They s**t on my girl's mom. They say things that are out of turn . . . And I'm sorry

about that. I had no control over that. I just want peace you know what I mean . . . I got nothing wrong with him. ("Shia Labeouf gives rambling apology," 2014, para. 4).

Photo 10.3 Shia LaBeouf has had several encounters with police, including being arrested for disorderly conduct and criminal trespassing in New York in June 2014, after he chased a homeless man and disturbed a live Broadway performance of *Cabaret*.

sources of information and to remain aware of everything that is going on (Taylor & Leonard, 1983). As a result, intoxicated people are much more limited in terms of what they can pay attention to and focus on only the most salient features in the environment. More subtle features receive little or no attention and are not adequately processed so the intoxicated person is left with an incomplete picture of the situation (Giancola et al., 2009). This effect has been dubbed alcohol myopia because, like short-sightedness, people fail to grasp everything that is happening (Steele & Josephs, 1990).

The theory does not see alcohol as the cause of violence per se but as directing behaviour by focusing attention on only the most salient cues in the environment (Giancola, Duke, & Ritz, 2011, p. 1021). If the most salient cues in a situation are hostile and provocative, such as insults or verbal threats, people are more likely to react violently; conversely, if those cues are peaceful, people are more likely to engage in non-violent behaviour. This is where the appraisal-disruption model and AAM diverge. In the former, people fail to appreciate anxiety-eliciting stimuli, whereas in the latter, these are the only stimuli that people appreciate. The problem, according to the AAM, is that hostile cues invariably have the greatest salience because of their alarming and threatening nature. These cues will dominate the intoxicated person's perception of the situation because, in an impaired state, he or she has no "spare" attention to process the more subtle, violence-inhibiting cues that may be present (Giancola et al., 2009). In these circumstances, violent action becomes more probable. This outcome is less likely for sober people, who acquire a better appreciation of the whole situation because they possess sufficient attentional resources to process both salient and subtle cues.

Expectancy Theories

Expectancy theories represent a marked shift away from the theories just discussed which emphasize the psychopharmacological effects of psychoactive substances. Instead, expectancy theories are based on the notion that the behaviour of intoxicated people is strongly influenced by their pre-existing expectations or beliefs about how the drug they took is going to affect them (Hoaken et al., 2014; Quigley & Leonard, 2006). One of the two general versions of this theoretical approach addresses **outcome expectancies**, a mental image, or cognitive template, about the behavioural consequence of drug taking. McMurran (2012) describes it as an "if-then" relationship such as, "If I take drug X, it will loosen me up and make it easier for me to socialize" (p. 215). The outcome expectancies a person holds are probably acquired through a combination of observational learning and personal experience (Jones, Corbin, & Fromme, 2001). Most important, outcome expectancies are thought to influence how people behave. To oversimplify, drug expectancies act as self-fulfilling prophesies, whereby a drug produces whatever behavioural effect the user believes it will. In the context of aggressive and violent behaviour, the theory assumes that some individuals believe drinking alcohol leads to aggressive behaviour and, consequently, they tend to act aggressively when they drink.

The other version of expectancy theory is **deviance-disavowal**. Rather than focus on specific behavioural outcomes, this theory centres on the learned expectation that behaviour displayed in a state of intoxication will be attributed to the effects of the drug rather than the individual (Zhang, Welte, & Wieczorek, 2002). Accordingly, the usual social standards of behaviour are temporarily suspended while people are intoxicated and they are seen as less responsible, or even excused, for the way they act in this state (Quigley & Leonard, 2006). The expectation that antisocial behaviours committed while intoxicated

expectancy theories
Theories based on the common premise that the behaviour of people who are intoxicated is strongly influenced by their pre-existing beliefs about how the drug they took is going to affect them.

outcome expectancy
A mental template of the behavioural result anticipated to follow an action such as drug taking; it is theorized that people will behave in a manner consistent with the results they anticipate.

deviance-disavowal theory
The theory that, when people are intoxicated, the usual social standards of behaviour are temporarily suspended so that they are viewed as less responsible for their actions.

will be tolerated presumably encourages people under the influence to exhibit behaviours they would normally restrain. Moreover, these expectations create the opportunity for some individuals to purposefully use drugs prior to offending so that they have an excuse for their behaviour (Collins, 1988; Zhang et al., 2002).

Consistent with expectancy theory, research confirms that people believe alcohol intoxication leads to aggression, but evidence linking these expectancies to aggression is more tenuous (Quigley & Leonard, 2006). Some research does support the existence of such a link. For example, one recent study demonstrated these expectancy effects in a group of alcohol-consuming participants given the opportunity to retaliate aggressively against someone who had previously provoked them (Bègue et al., 2009). Only the participants' belief about the quantity of alcohol consumed, and not the actual amount, seemed to affect their behaviour. Specifically, the larger the amount of alcohol participants thought they drank, the more retaliatory aggression they displayed. On the other hand, a meta-analysis by Quigley and Leonard (2006) revealed that people tend to believe alcohol consumption causes others to behave aggressively, but not themselves. This latter finding runs contrary to expectancy theory. Furthermore, several other meta-analytic reviews of this topic report that outcome expectancies are relatively unimportant as explanatory factors of alcohol-related violence (Bushman, 1997; Bushman & Cooper, 1990; Hull & Bond, 1986).

Research regarding the deviance-disavowal version of the theory is mixed (Quigley & Leonard, 2006). Some studies find that people who engage in offending behaviour are considered less blameworthy when they are intoxicated, but other studies find people tend to blame them even more. In conclusion, empirical support for expectancy theories of alcohol aggression is currently limited.

Putting It All Together: Integrating Theories of Alcohol-Related Aggression

Giancola (2000) presented an overarching model of alcohol-related aggression that ties the various cognitive-interference theories together, arguing that the different cognitive abilities are simply components of executive functioning (see Chapter 3). Previous research shows that alcohol intoxication affects the prefrontal cortex and therefore is likely to disrupt executive functioning and all its component processes, such as paying attention, appraising social information, maintaining self-awareness, taking the perspective of others, and formulating appropriate non-violent behavioural responses. When these cognitive processes are impaired, aggression becomes more likely—though not inevitable—especially in response to provocation.

Giancola (2000) maintains that people with a high capacity for executive functioning will be less likely to act aggressively because, even under the impairing effects of alcohol, they still possess sufficient cognitive resources to inhibit this type of reaction. People with less executive functioning capacity have few cognitive resources left to inhibit aggression once the effects of alcohol have taken their toll. Both Giancola's model and the AAM see alcohol intoxication as taxing a finite cognitive capacity. The difference is that the former involves the global or overall cognitive capacity of a person, whereas the latter is concerned with only the cognitive capacity to pay attention. In addition, Giancola's model integrates an element of disinhibition theory; it suggests that diminished cognitive resources interfere with a person's ability to inhibit themselves from reacting violently to a provocation. A study by Giancola (2004) provides some empirical support for the model. It revealed the expected relationship between executive functioning and alcohol-related aggression such that high executive functioning was associated with less aggression and lower executive functioning with more aggression, but this pattern appeared for the male participants only.

Summary

1. This chapter discussed how psychoactive drugs influence criminal and violent behaviour. Psychoactive drugs are substances that act on the central nervous system and produce changes in our mental state. Due to concerns over the psychopharmacological effects of these substances, governments typically regulate their use, even prohibiting the use of some altogether. Drugs that cannot be used legally are known as illicit drugs.

2. Many people engage in substance use for medical or recreational purposes in ways that do not negatively impact their lives. When people take psychoactive substances in doses or for purposes other than those prescribed or intended, it is referred to as substance misuse. In some cases, people develop substance use disorders, characterized by a pattern of problematic usage that causes the person significant impairment or distress for an extended period of time. The hallmarks of problematic substance use include drug tolerance, withdrawal symptoms, drug craving, and difficulty regulating drug use.

3. Several factors impact the effect drugs have on people, including the characteristics of the user, the setting where the drug is taken, and the properties of the drug consumed. Psychoactive drugs can be broadly classified as stimulants, depressants, or hallucinogens, depending on the nature of their effects. Stimulants (e.g. caffeine, nicotine, amphetamine, and cocaine) typically produce effects that increase arousal, activity, and mood. Depressants, at least at higher doses, generally have the opposite effect of stimulants. Examples include benzodiazepines, alcohol, and opioids. Hallucinogens, such as LSD, PCP, and cannabis, are an eclectic class of drugs that produce distorted perceptual experiences that may include hallucinations.

4. Goldstein (1985) developed a framework to describe three major dimensions of the drug–violence relationship, which we extended to include criminal behaviour. Systemic crime consists of drug-related offending that occurs because of the illegal nature of the drug use. It includes acts such as illegally selling drugs or using violence to enforce payment of drug debts. Economic compulsive crime involves offences committed as a way to obtain drugs and support a habit. Finally, psychopharmacological crime encompasses criminal and violent behaviours precipitated by the acute or chronic effects of drug taking.

5. The chapter examined the extent to which the major classes of drugs exhibit a relationship to psychopharmacological violence. Stimulants are widely acknowledged as the class with the strongest relationship to violence, although the empirical evidence is not uniform. This connection may be due to the increased activity and arousal associated with stimulant intoxication. Impulsivity and paranoid thinking may also play a contributory role. The relationship of depressants to violence is highly dependent on the drug. Benzodiazepine and alcohol intoxication are linked to violence, but opioid intoxication is not. On the other hand, opioid withdrawal may lead to violence in some cases. Hallucinogens show the weakest relationship to violence.

6. Numerous theories have been developed to explain alcohol-related violence. One group of theories, based on the notion of disinhibition, proposes that alcohol acts on areas of the brain responsible for controlling behaviour; consequently, actions that would be inhibited in a sober state find expression in an intoxicated one. Cognitive-interference theories constitute a second group. According to these theories, alcohol disrupts aspects of cognition important for perceiving and interpreting social situations. As a result of possessing biased or incomplete information about a situation, people may misinterpret others' actions and respond inappropriately or even violently. Finally, expectancy theories represent a departure from the psychopharmacological emphasis of disinhibition and cognitive-interference theories. Expectancy theories suggest that people's behaviour while intoxicated is influenced by their pre-existing expectations about the effect the drug will have on them.

Review Questions

1. Identify and describe the dimensions of the drug–crime relationship set out in Goldstein's tripartite framework.
2. Explain what Goldstein meant by a reverse psychopharmacological effect. Identify some drugs covered in the chapter that are thought to exhibit this effect.
3. Explain the self-medication hypothesis. What two drugs covered in this chapter exhibit a relationship to violence consistent with this theory?
4. Identify and explain the three broad groups of alcohol-related aggression theories.
5. Review the case study of Shia LaBeouf. Suppose the actor could see his reflection in a large mirror situated behind the bar where he was sitting. Why might the presence of the mirror have changed his behaviour? Identify and explain the theory pertaining to alcohol-related violence that accounts for the mirror's effect.
6. Explain which of the three broad theories of alcohol-related aggression best accounts for the following statement, made by a witness to LaBeouf's behaviour: "I think also everyone's drunk and things are said . . . things got misconstrued."

Additional Readings

Advokat, C. D., Comaty, J. E., & Julien, R. M. (2014). *Julien's primer of drug action: A comprehensive guide to the actions, uses, and side effects of psychoactive drugs* (13th edition). New York, NY: Worth Publishers.

Boles, S. M., & Miotto, K. (2003). Substance abuse and violence: A review of the literature. *Aggression and Violent Behavior, 8*, 155–172.

Giancola, P. R. (2012). Alcohol and aggression: Theories and mechanisms. In M. McMurran (Ed.), *Alcohol-related violence: Prevention and treatment* (pp. 37–59). Chichester, UK: Wiley-Blackwell.

Goldstein, P. J. (1985). The drugs/violence nexus: A tripartite conceptual framework. *Journal of Drug Issues, 14*, 493–506.

Hoaken, P. N. S., Hamill, V. L., Ross, E. H., Hancock, M., Lau, M. J., & Tapscott, J. L. (2014). Drug use and abuse and human aggressive behavior. In J. C. Verster, K. Brady, M. Galanter, & P. Conrod (Eds.), *Drug abuse and addiction in medical illness: Causes, consequences, and treatment* (pp. 467–477). New York, NY: Springer.

11

Homicide

Learning Objectives

At the end of this chapter, you should be able to:

- explain how the statistical pattern of homicide more closely resembles reactive violence than instrumental violence;

- discuss how affect, cognition, and self-regulatory abilities influence the reactive forms of aggression that commonly characterize acts of homicide;

- describe filicide and parricide and explain how different mental health problems and psychosocial factors may explain their patterns;

- identify and describe the major characteristics of serial killers;

- discuss two etiological models of serial murder;

- explain how cult leaders use psychological theories of influence and attitudinal change to recruit and indoctrinate members; and

- identify and describe the major risk factors for school shootings.

CASE STUDY

The Manson Family Murders

Los Angeles, California—Charles Manson was born on 12 November 1934 in Cincinnati, Ohio, to unwed 16-year-old prostitute Kathleen Maddox. He had a turbulent childhood—nearly half his formative years were spent in reform schools and juvenile homes. By 1967 he had been arrested for numerous offences, including petty theft, auto theft, armed robbery, and pimping. That same year, he made his way to the Haight-Ashbury district of San Francisco, the nexus of hippie culture. Taking advantage of the movement's openness and "free love," Manson presented himself as a self-styled guru and gained a following that he called the Family.

Manson and his group travelled around California. During one of these trips, he happened to meet Beach Boys member Dennis Wilson, who introduced Manson—an aspiring musician—to some of his music contacts, including producer Terry Melcher. These encounters did not lead to a recording contract as Manson hoped they would, a slight he never forgot. The Manson Family eventually settled at the Spahn Ranch in Los Angeles in August 1968. Here Manson took increasing control of his followers and frequently spoke about his vision of the apocalypse. He considered The Beatles' *White Album* as a directive to initiate a race war between black and white Americans, which he named after the album's song "Helter Skelter." He thought that he and his followers would survive by hiding in the Death Valley desert and they would take control when the war ended.

Manson set his plans for Helter Skelter in motion on 9 August 1969. He instructed four of his followers—Charles "Tex" Watson, Susan Atkins, Linda Kasabian, and Patricia Krenwinkel—to go to 10050 Cielo Drive and kill everyone inside. This house belonged to Melcher

Photo 11.1 Charles Manson has spent over four decades in prison. He was denied parole for the twelfth time in 2012, when it was also decided that his case would not be reconsidered for another 15 years. AP Photo/Eric Risberg, File

but, unbeknownst to Manson, it was being leased by film director Roman Polanski, who was out of the country at the time. The group broke into the house and brutally murdered Sharon Tate (Polanski's pregnant wife), Jay Sebring, Abigail Folger, Wojciech Frykowski, and Steven Parent. Tate was stabbed 16 times, and Atkins used her blood to write the word *pig* on the front door. The next night, Manson accompanied the group, which also included Leslie Van Houtten, to the residence of Leno and Rosemary LaBianca. They stabbed Mrs LaBianca 41 times and left her husband with a carving fork in his chest. Again, the group adhered to Manson's instructions to scrawl messages such as "Rise," "Death to Pigs," and "Helter Skelter" on the walls and doors. Manson and the killers were eventually apprehended and brought to trial. Kasabian, who did not participate in the murders, agreed to testify against Manson.

The celebrity status of some of the victims and Manson's bizarre behaviour during the trial garnered national media attention. Manson carved an *x* into his forehead, as did the three women charged. Attempting to get a mistrial, he flashed the jury an edition of the *Los Angeles Times* with the headline "Manson Guilty, Nixon Declares." He once lunged across the defence table and tried to attack the judge. Outside the courtroom, his followers gathered daily, adding to the proceedings' circus-like atmosphere. Despite these efforts, the defendants were convicted. Manson was sentenced to death, but this decision was later commuted to life in prison. No member of the group has been released from prison, but Leslie Van Houten was recommended for parole in April 2016 (Hamilton, 2016).

Sources: (except where otherwise noted): Bugliosi, V., & Gentry, C. (1974). *Helter Skelter: The true story of the Manson murders.* New York: Norton; Goldberg, A. (Writer), & Zeff, L. (Producer). (2002). *Charles Manson: Journey into evil* [Television series episode]. In A. Nixon (Creator), *A&E Home Video.* New York: New Video.

Introduction

Over 40 years have passed since Charles Manson gained infamy as the catalyst behind the Helter Skelter murders. The subject of numerous books and documentaries, he illustrates the often intense public fascination with violent crimes and offenders (Schmid, 2005). Mainstream news focuses on statistically rare occurrences of violence, and TV shows such as *True Detective*, *Criminal Minds*, and *Hannibal* provide audiences with familiar narratives of violent, homicidal individuals (Cavender & Deutsch, 2007; Eschholz, Mallard, & Flynn, 2004). Although the occurrence of such crimes in Western countries has generally decreased over the last 15 years, the associated societal costs remain high (Dauvergne & Brennan, 2011; Boyce, Cotter, & Perreault, 2014). In this chapter, we will focus on one specific form of violent crime—homicide. We will discuss theoretical frameworks for making sense of its patterns and outline specific types of this crime, including family homicide, serial murder, and mass murder.

Theoretical Models of Homicide

homicide The intentional killing of another person.

For the purposes of this chapter, we define **homicide** as the intentional killing of another person. Although the media's narrative usually portrays homicide as an instrumental act (see Chapter 1), North American statistics are more consistent with reactive violence. Canadian and American data show that both offenders and victims are typically males under the age of 25 (Cooper & Smith, 2011; Cotter, 2014). Most of the victims were murdered by someone they knew, usually an acquaintance or family member, with less than one-quarter of all homicides involving strangers. Given that the perpetrator and victim are often familiar with one another, it is not surprising that most homicides unfold in private residences (Miladinovic & Mulligan, 2015). Quarrels appear to be the most common precipitating factor for murder in Canada and the United States, at least in cases where motivation could be determined (Cooper & Smith, 2011; Cotter, 2014).

Another prominent feature of North American homicides is substance use. Figures for the United States indicate that nearly half the cases of homicide reported by offenders in state prisons involved perpetrators and/or victims who were drinking alcohol at the time of the incident (Greenfeld, 1998). Canadian data echo these general results. More than 40 per cent of accused perpetrators were believed to be under the influence of alcohol at the time of the murder (Cotter, 2014). If other intoxicating substances are taken into account, the proportion expands considerably. Analysis of Canadian homicide cases for 2013 indicates that nearly 60 per cent of the victims and more than 70 per cent of the alleged perpetrators were under the influence of one or more intoxicating substances. In their meta-analysis of data across nine countries, Kuhns, Exum, Clodfelter, and Bottia (2013) noted a similar relationship between alcohol and homicide.

Collectively, these statistics tell us that homicides arise in the context of alcohol-fuelled interpersonal conflicts among young people who know one another. With this in mind, the initial part of our discussion covers theories of personality, affect, cognition, and self-regulation, which are broadly applicable to reactive forms of aggression. As we move on to examine serial murder, we address theories more relevant to instrumental violence.

Personality Types and Reactive Aggression

In Chapter 5 we briefly discussed the concept of traits—the basic, stable qualities of an individual that influence how he or she behaves and reacts in social environments. One of the basic assumptions of trait psychology is that personality characteristics exist on a continuum (e.g. introversion–extraversion) and people vary in the amount they have of each one. Both the amount and the particular combination of these attributes (e.g. high extraversion, high openness) contribute to our individuality. Some trait psychologists have pursued the identification of specific **personality types**, the psychological classifications of people into discrete categories based on a particular combination of specific attributes. The concepts of traits and types are easily confused and, in some cases, the two terms have been used interchangeably. We suggest that a trait reflects a quantitative difference between individuals on a particular attribute, whereas a type involves a qualitative difference. According to trait theory, extraversion and introversion are polar ends of a continuous personality dimension where the difference is a matter of degree. Type theories posit that an introvert and an extravert are fundamentally different categories of people. Several personality types have been identified and discussed in the aggression literature, including Type A (e.g. Adorno, Frenkel-Brunswick, Levison, & Sanford, 1950; Altemeyer, 1988) and Machiavellian (e.g. Paulhus & Williams, 2002).

Psychologist Edwin Megargee (1966) conducted numerous investigations of aggressive behaviour and worked extensively on the development of offender classification systems. Based on his research, he believed that individuals with a history of extremely aggressive behaviour could be divided into two distinct personality types—under- and overcontrolled offenders. The first type constitutes a familiar figure in the criminal justice literature. The **undercontrolled offender** has failed to internalize inhibitions or behavioural restraints against the use of aggression. He or she is described as having a quick temper and being easily pushed over the edge. Megargee claimed that the undercontrolled offender would typically have a long documented history of violent, assaultive behaviour. In contrast, the **overcontrolled offender** has developed an extremely rigid behavioural inhibition system against expressing aggressive impulses. These individuals restrain or suppress their emotions in response to provocations until the strain causes them to inevitably explode in a burst of excessive emotional rage. This type of personality might apply to the 17-year-old suspect implicated in the shooting deaths of four people in La Loche, Saskatchewan, in 2016. Prior to the shooting, he had endured years of bullying about his appearance without any sign of violence (see the case study).

In the 1960s Megargee, Cook, and Mendelsohn (1967) developed the overcontrolled hostility (O-H) scale for the Minnesota Multiphasic Personality Inventory (MMPI; Hathaway & McKinley, 1943) to identity individuals who exhibit signs of overcontrolling emotional responses to provocations. Several studies show that this scale has some ability to distinguish between extremely assaultive offenders and non-violent offenders. Blackburn (1968) found that extremely assaultive psychiatric patients were significantly less hostile, more introverted, and more self-controlled than moderately assaultive patients. Salekin, Ogloff, Ley, and Salekin (2002) examined the scale's ability to distinguish among adolescent offenders. Specifically, they compared scores of adolescent murderers, violent but non-murdering adolescent offenders, and non-violent adolescent offenders. The first group was subdivided into those with a history of aggression and those without. Findings

personality type The psychological classification of people into discrete categories based on the statistical combination of specific attributes. Personality types reflect qualitative differences between individuals on these characteristics.

undercontrolled offender A personality type identified by Edwin Megargee and characterized by an individual's quick temper, low tolerance to frustration or provocation, and failure to internalize inhibitions or restraints against behaving aggressively.

overcontrolled offender A personality type identified by Edwin Megargee and characterized by an individual's extremely rigid behavioural inhibition system against the expression of aggressive impulses. The acts of violence committed by these individuals are typically explosive, occurring after long periods of building anger and frustration.

CASE STUDY

The La Loche Shooter

La Loche, Saskatchewan—At approximately 1:00 p.m. on 22 January 2016, a string of messages started appearing in a group chat: "done with life," "just killed 2 ppl," "bout to shoot ip [sic] the school," "Dayne and lul . . . are dead" (Stueck, Tait, & Blaze, 2016, para. 19). Minutes later, a 17-year-old student at La Loche Community School allegedly blasted his way into the building and began shooting the people he encountered. Seven people were shot, two fatally, before he was apprehended by police. Sometime later, the bodies of brothers Dayne and Drayden "Lul" Fontaine were discovered in their home a short distance away.

Those who knew the accused describe him as a quiet loner. For years prior to the shooting, he had been mocked mercilessly about his big ears. Despite the insults, he never got upset or acted violently toward his antagonists or anyone else. His childhood friend, Emilio Montgrand, explained that any anger he felt over the taunting must have been kept "bottled up" (p. A 6).

Source: Spurr, B., & Smith, J. (2016, January 26). Shooting suspect was bullied, source claims: 17-year-old who allegedly killed four, injured seven kept to himself, friend says. *Toronto Star*, p. A6.

indicated that adolescent murderers had higher O-H scores than the non-murdering groups; however, previously aggressive homicide offenders were not distinct from homicide offenders with no history of aggression.

Affect, Cognition, and Reactive Aggression

In Chapter 8 we introduced several social cognition theories that apply to reactive aggression and homicide. As noted elsewhere, our emotional responses to events and subsequent cognitive processing are integral to understanding criminal and aggressive behaviour (e.g. Berkowitz, 1990). In the following section, we will briefly review key ideas from the frustration-aggression hypothesis, the cognitive neoassociation model of aggression, the excitation transfer theory, and the general aggression model.

Recall from Chapter 8 that the frustration-aggression hypothesis proposed that frustration produces aggression when an individual is unexpectedly blocked from attaining a specific anticipated goal. Berkowitz (1989) argued that aversive events produce a sufficient degree of discomfort or pain (or negative affect), which subsequently leads to aggressive behaviour. From this theoretical perspective, the insults and provocations involved in a rapidly escalating argument between acquaintances could reasonably be expected to produce negative affect, thereby accounting for the reactive violence that characterizes many homicides. However, the hypothesis does not explain how cognition—our thoughts, ideas, and decision-making—plays (or fails to play) a role in acts of reactive violence.

Berkowitz (1989, 1990) addressed the role of cognition in his revised cognitive neoassociation model of aggression. As you will recall, negative affect in this two-stage model initially activates a fight-or-flight response. A fight response is triggered by a network of associated feelings, thoughts, and physiological responses—things that we have learned to associate with aggression over time. Imagine you are carrying a drink in a crowded bar, accidentally bump into a stranger, and spill some of your drink on his shirt. He calls you a derogatory term and clenches his fist as he leans in to you. Both the derogatory term and the clenched fist will trigger particular feelings and thoughts you have associated with aggressive responses, simultaneously activating other ideas, physical expressions, and motor respons-es connected with aggression. Strong aversive events can automatically activate this "fight" associative network, thereby producing the kind of impulsive and violent behaviour that characterizes reactive violence observed in many homicide cases (Berkowitz, 2003).

In the second phase of this model, which quickly follows the initial step, cognitive processes are activated as individuals begin to think about and evaluate the causes of the event, the motives of the other people involved, and their emotions. The inclusion of cog-nitive processes in this phase provides some explanation for why most individuals do not engage in reactive violence when experiencing negative affect. Despite being angered and frustrated, they become aware of their feelings, weigh their actions carefully, and select a prosocial response (Berkowitz, 1990).

The excitation transfer theory may also provide a theoretical account for the impul-sive nature of reactive violence in many homicides. As we discussed in Chapter 8, Zillman and colleagues (1972) proposed that the emotional arousal from a situation may be carried over to a new one. Physiological arousal from one context does not immediately disappear when an individual moves to another but instead it gradually reduces over time. An indi-vidual who has experienced an extremely stressful, provoking incident at work does not immediately feel at ease upon leaving the workplace. He or she will carry a residual level of arousal—anger, hostility, emotional upset—into another physical situation. People in this state tend to mistakenly attribute any remaining physiological arousal to their current environment. The individual who has been disciplined or perhaps dismissed at work may more readily lash out in a relatively minor incident when he or she gets home (e.g. child whining or nagging, a dish dropped at the dinner table).

Craig Anderson and Brad Bushman (2002) present a more integrated model of ag-gressive or violent behaviour. Their general aggression model (GAM) proposes that in-dividual and situational characteristics (inputs) influence a person's arousal, affect, and cognition (routes), which in turn are subject to appraisal and decision processes that end in a behavioural response (outcomes). High levels of anger and of alcohol are examples of inputs that would influence an individual's routes. According to the GAM, affect and cog-nitions are highly interconnected and therefore impact one another through the process of spreading activation. An individual who has higher levels of psychopathic traits, has consumed a large amount of alcohol, and is then provoked may experience higher levels of physiological arousal, anger, and cognitions supportive of aggression than other people do. Collectively, this internal state is more likely to influence the reactive violence that often characterizes homicide.

Self-Regulation and Pathway Models of Homicide

A potential key to understanding the reactive violence that characterizes many homicides is **self-regulation**, which we define as the ability to control our emotional responses and evaluate and select appropriate behavioural responses. In their extensive work on relapse prevention and sex offenders, Tony Ward, Thomas Keenan, and Stephen Hudson (2000) developed a model of violent offending based on self-regulation. While the model was initially created to account for sex offending, it offers a good framework for understanding how the ability to self-regulate might contribute to reactive forms of violence such as ho-micide. Ward and colleagues identified different patterns of dysfunctional self-regulation, including **underregulation**—the disinhibited or impulsive behaviour that results from a

self-regulation The ability to control our emotional re-sponses and evaluate and se-lect appropriate behavioural responses.

underregulation Disinhib-ited or impulsive behaviour that results from a failure to exert control over one's feelings and subsequent behaviours.

failure to exert control over one's feelings and subsequent behaviours. The reactive violence of many homicides stems from underregulation.

Other research on aggression and violent behaviour suggests that there may be distinct causal pathways linking dysfunctional self-regulation with homicide. For example, Canadian researchers Grant Harris, Marnie Rice, and Martin Lalumière (2001) proposed a two-pathway model for general criminal violence. In the pathological pathway, criminal violence results from the types of neuropsychological problems outlined in Chapter 3, causing poor inhibitory control and impulsive violence. The second pathway involves a strong tie between psychopathic personality traits and impulsive violence. (Psychopathy and its relationship with criminal and violent behaviour were discussed in Chapter 7.) Recent research has validated this model in samples of homicide offenders found not guilty by reason of insanity (NGRI; Gilligan & Lennings, 2013). More complex explanatory pathway models for homicide have also been identified. Cassar, Ward, and Thakker (2003) recognized four different routes to violent behaviour based on self-regulation. One of these pathways is characterized by poor self-regulation abilities, with offenders being further distinguished from one another based on their goals and strategies to achieve them in relation to homicide.

Homicide in the Family

The dynamics of family violence and specifically spousal homicide, are discussed in Chapter 12. Here we will focus on two types of family homicide—filicide and parricide. **Filicide** is a broad term that refers to the killing of a child by his or her parent (Porter & Gavin, 2010). Researchers have typically distinguished between **neonaticide**, the killing of an infant within the first 24 hours of his or her birth, and **infanticide**, the killing of a child older than 24 hours (Resnick, 1970). A large body of research has compared the characteristics of neonaticidal and infanticidal women and identified several important differences (see Porter & Gavin, 2010).

In the first thorough comparison, Resnick (1970) examined the existing literature, dating back to the eighteenth century, and concluded that evidence of psychopathology at the time of the homicide often distinguished neonaticidal and infanticidal women. This oft-cited study reports that women who commit infanticide are more likely to be mentally ill at the time of the murder. Several later studies have similarly reported that mental illness is more commonly observed in cases of infanticide (e.g. Hatters-Friedman, Heneghan, & Rosenthal, 2007; Meyer & Oberman, 2001; Putokonen, Collander, Weizmann-Henelius, & Eronen, 2007).

That said, not all infanticidal perpetrators have a serious mental health problem (Porter & Gavin, 2010). Numerous psychosocial factors, such as poverty, unemployment, or lack of education, may play important roles (McKee & Shea, 1998). Studies of neonaticidal women usually highlight the impact of such elements rather than the presence of mental health problems. For example, poverty and social isolation have been reported as underlying contributors (e.g. Hatters-Friedman & Resnick, 2009; Dobson & Sales, 2000). Women who commit neonaticide often are poor and single and hid their pregnancy. The murder of the newborn is thus a means to continue the concealment and perhaps avoid potential stigmatization (Beyer, Mack, & Shelton, 2008; Hatters-Friedman & Resnick, 2009).

Dobson and Sales (2000) identified three categories of mental health problems that women may experience following childbirth and that may play a role in infanticide.

filicide A general term that refers to the killing of a child by his or her parent.

neonaticide A form of filicide, specifically, the killing of an infant within the first 24 hours of his or her birth.

infanticide A form of filicide, specifically, the killing of a child older than 24 hours.

Postpartum blues refers to relatively minor and common symptoms of depression (e.g. anxiety, crying, irritability, and mood changes) that last for a short time. No real link between these symptoms and infanticide has been identified. Postpartum depression involves relatively more serious and somewhat prolonged symptoms of depression—loss of appetite, sleep disturbances, and suicidal ideation—and may persist for several weeks. According to Dobson and Sales (2000), this experience is often indicative of ongoing problems with depression and is not necessarily connected to childbirth. Moreover, little empirical relationship between postpartum depression and infanticide exists. **Postpartum psychosis** is a rare form of depression that can directly follow childbirth (Dobson & Sales, 2000; Friedman, Cavney, & Resnick, 2012). Women with postpartum psychosis often experience breaks with reality. For example, they may believe that their child has been taken from them and switched with another newborn. Symptoms may include delusional and/or disorganized thinking, rapid mood shifts, and bizarre behaviour (Friedman & Resnick, 2009). While an empirical link between postpartum psychosis and infanticide has been established, the risk among women diagnosed is still low, suggesting that a number of factors contribute to the risk.

postpartum psychosis
A rare form of depression experienced by some women after childbirth that can cause delusional and/or disorganized thinking, rapid mood shifts, and bizarre behaviour.

Most existing filicide research centres on the maternal type (Putkonen et al., 2011). While paternal neonaticide is rare, men are not less likely than women to commit filicide (West, Hatters-Friedman, & Resnick, 2009). However, the research suggests that several important differences exist (Bourget, Grace, & Whitehurst, 2007). Based on their analysis of filicide cases, Putkonen and colleagues (2011) suggest that paternal filicide offenders can be separated into two distinct categories: men with a history of violent behaviour and the "emotionally overloaded" offender. For the former type, the murder of a child is part of a pattern of violent or aggressive behaviour rather than an anomalous or unique act of violence. Emotionally overloaded offenders murder a child in response to the accumulation of various stressors. Across these two categories, several factors seem to distinguish male and female filicide offenders. For instance, male filicide offenders are more likely to murder their spouse as well as their child and to murder their child as an act of revenge against their spouse. Male filicide is more apt to occur within the context of ongoing family abuse. Alcohol is also more likely to be involved in acts of filicide committed by men. Although male filicide offenders are less likely to have serious mental health problems at the time of the homicide, they are probably unemployed or in low-paying jobs or experiencing other types of stress, such as marital separation.

Parricide refers to the murder of a parent by his or her child, with matricide being the murder of the mother and patricide of the father (Walsh, Krienert, & Crowder, 2008; Meyers & Vo, 2012). Because little research exists on parricide, our understanding of its causal factors is poor. Much of the investigation has focused on identifying a common set of characteristics associated with the offence (Heide & Petee, 2007). In general, adult males are more likely to kill their parent than either adult females or juveniles, and fathers are more likely to be murdered than mothers (Bourget, Gagne, & Labelle, 2007; Heide & Petee, 2007; Meyers & Vo, 2012; Walsh et al., 2008). Based on their examination of FBI data spanning 24 years, Heide and Petee (2007) reported that parricide offences do not typically emerge from other ongoing criminal enterprises but seem to be triggered by distinct familial events.

parricide The murder of a parent by his or her child. Matricide refers to killing one's mother and patricide to killing one's father.

An interesting finding is that key differences exist in the characteristics of adult and juvenile parricide offenders, prompting some researchers to propose that a different set of explanatory factors may exist for each group (Walsh et al., 2008). For instance, adult parricide offenders may be more likely to have a serious mental illness, and the killing is often connected to ongoing financial problems or an argument. Juvenile parricide offenders may murder a parent to end ongoing abuse or to protect the other parent from further abuse (Dantas et al., 2014; Marleau, Auclair, & Millaud, 2006; Meyers & Vo, 2012; Walsh et al., 2008). A Canadian study examining coroners' files in parricide cases identified delusional thinking as the most common underlying factor (Bourget, Gagne, & Labelle, 2007).

Multiple Murder

Defining Multiple Murder

mass murder A form of multiple murder that involves killing four or more victims as part of one event at a single geographic location.

spree murder A form of multiple murder that involves killing the victims during one continuous event at two or more geographic locations.

serial murder A form of multiple murder that involves killing two or more victims at different times.

The phenomenon of multiple murder has traditionally been organized into three distinct categories (Holmes & DeBurger, 1988; Ressler, Burgess, & Goulas, 1988). **Mass murder** is defined by the FBI as an incident of multiple murder involving four or more victims in a single geographic location during the same event (Douglas, Burgess, Burgess, & Ressler, 2013). The Columbine school shootings is an example of mass murder. Historically, **spree murder** involved killing multiple victims during one event but at more than one geographic location. (This term is no longer used by the FBI.) An example is the murder spree of Charles Starkweather and Caril Anne Fugate, the inspiration for Oliver Stone's *Natural Born Killers*. The couple murdered 11 people on an 8-day road trip across Nebraska and Wyoming (Fox & Levin, 2005). **Serial murder** is the killing of at least two victims at different times (Douglas et al., 2013). As these definitions reveal, the existence of a cooling-off period distinguishes the mass or spree murderer from the serial murderer. While the number of his victims and the time span between his murders have been debated, serial killer Ted Bundy is believed to have killed over a five-year period.

Serial Murder

Photo 11.2 Ed Gein, shown here in a Wisconsin court, was found guilty of murder but legally insane in 1968. Confined to various criminal psychiatric institutions, he died at the Mendota Mental Health Institute in 1984. Photo: Bettman/Getty Images

Criminologist Ray Surette (2011) identified the psychotic super-male criminal—typically represented by the serial killer—as the most common narrative of criminality in the media. A keyword search on the Internet Movie Database turns up over 2,000 film titles with some link to the topic of serial killers. Ed Gein, an American serial killer who gained notoriety for keeping human skulls and lampshades made from flesh, has reportedly served as the basis for popular fictional serial killers, including Norman Bates, Hannibal Lecter, and Leatherface (Oleson, 2005, 2006). In spite of its ubiquity in the media, serial murder is statistically rare.

Most researchers agree that estimating the number of serial killers is a difficult and perhaps unrealistic task (Holmes & DeBurger, 1988; Quinet, 2007). The methods for detecting and policing serial homicide have changed remarkably over the years, casting doubt on the accuracy of older data (Egger, 2002). US estimates suggest that approximately 30 serial killers operated between 1970 and 1984 (Rowlands, 1990) and between 3,500 and 5,000 victims were murdered by serial killers (Holmes & DeBurger, 1988). Comparable British assessments indicate that approximately 1.7 per cent of murders committed in England and Wales between 1940 and 1985 could be attributed to serial killers. Hickey (2006), a forensic psychologist who specializes in research on serial homicide, more recently estimated that 340 serial killers operated between 1800 and 2004, with the largest proportion of active serial killers operating between 1975 and 2000.

The amount of empirical research on serial murder is relatively small, and much of what is currently known is based on case studies. As such, the information is composed primarily of patterns and characteristics associated with serial killers. Hickey (2006) conducted a detailed review of 399 serial murderers who killed between 1800 and 1995, identifying several patterns in their victim selection, motives and methods, and criminal backgrounds. He found that the male serial killer tends to target strangers and most are young women who are vulnerable in some way. Prostitutes are the most common victims in Hickey's dataset; other stranger-victims include hitchhikers, runaways, students walking alone, or women living alone. An acquaintance is the next most prevalent perpetrator–victim relationship, and women are once again the most frequently identified victims.

Sex, power, and control are common underlying motivations of the male serial killer (Hickey, 2006). Researchers have also highlighted the role played by vivid fantasies fraught with sexual domination and control over a human (Fox & Levin, 1998; Skrapec, 1996). Based on a study of 25 serial killers, Prentky and colleagues (1989) found that 86 per cent of serial killers reported that they had violent fantasies on a regular basis, in comparison to only 23 per cent of single-victim murderers. Other studies similarly suggest that male serial killers frequently experience intrusive, violent fantasies (Silva, Leong, & Ferrari, 2004).

A number of serial killers exhibit bizarre patterns of sexual arousal, referred to as paraphilia. A **paraphilic disorder** is a paraphilia that causes the person distress or impairment or involves inflicting psychological distress or physical harm on another person (APA, 2013). Several paraphilic disorders are found frequently among both clinical and criminal populations, including exhibitionism, pedophilia, and sexual sadism (Holmes & Holmes, 2002; Palmero, 2004; see Chapter 12 for more on these disorders). Jeffrey Dahmer, who murdered 17 young men, exhibited several paraphilias, including necrophilia, cannibalism, and vampirism (Purcell & Arrigo, 2006).

Erotophonophilia, or **lust murder**, is a paraphilia that involves the murder of an unsuspecting sexual partner (Hazelwood & Douglas, 1980; Purcell & Ariggo, 2006; Simon, 1996). The power/domination and sexual motivations of male serial killers are also evident in their methods. According to Hickey (2006), they often use a combination of non-lethal and lethal force. They may shoot, stab, or strangle a victim to death, but they might also employ elements of non-lethal torture, which is consistent with the portrait of an individual seeking to exercise ultimate control over another human being (Fox & Levin, 1998).

paraphilic disorder A paraphilia that causes the person distress or impairment or involves inflicting psychological distress or physical harm on another person.

erotophonophilia (or *lust murder*) A paraphilia involving the murder of an unsuspecting sexual partner.

Female Serial Killers

In Chapter 5 we reviewed the case of Aileen Wuornos, a high-profile female serial killer. To what extent does she represent the prototypical female serial killer? While the research is limited, it suggests that female serial killers differ from their male counterparts in a few important ways (Farrell, Keppel, & Titterington, 2011; Hickey, 2006). Female serial killers may be "active," on average, for longer periods, which might be partially explained by their use of more subtle methods. Hickey (2006) has described the female serial killer as the "quiet killer" who prefers poison as her weapon of choice. A popular conception of female serial killers stems from the stereotype that women's violence is typically connected to their maternal roles; thus, they are more likely to target a lover or acquaintance. The "black widow" killer (the wife who kills her husband) and the "angel of death"

The Green River Killer

On 30 November 2001, 52-year-old factory employee Gary Ridgway was arrested in Renton, Washington, for the murders of four women. Two years later, he pled guilty to 48 counts of aggravated murder, placing him among the most infamous serial killers in American history. His victims were all women, primarily prostitutes and teenage runaways whom he picked up along the highway. To make his victims feel more at ease, he would often show them a photograph of his son. In many instances, he would have sex with the women prior to strangling them to death. He would then dump their bodies along the Green River (which earned him the moniker "the Green River Killer"), sometimes posing them in the nude. On some occasions, he returned to

Photo 11.3 During the 1980s and 1990s, Gary Ridgway killed at least 48 women; he has claimed that the total is a high as 80. Photo: King County Sheriff's Office

have sex with the bodies. Eventually, he began burying them to resist his sexual urges.

Ridgway's killings reflected an intense hatred toward women and the power/domination motivations characteristic of many male serial killers. According to Ridgway, his mother was a domineering woman who verbally abused his father. Despite being married, Ridgway routinely solicited prostitutes. His first two marriages were characterized by infidelity and ultimately failed. His second wife testified at his trial that Ridgway had once placed her in a chokehold. Ridgway committed most of his murders during his third marriage. He was sentenced to life in prison without parole.

Sources: Guillen, T. (2007). *Serial killers: Issues explored through the Green River murders.* Upper Saddle River, NJ: Pearson/Prentice Hall; Hickey, E. W. (2013). *Serial murderers and their victims* (6th ed.). Belmont, CA: Wadsworth.

(the female caretaker who murders her patients) are consistent with this theory. To some extent, research supports this view—female serial killers are more likely than male serial killers to kill people they know, including family members or dependants (Farrel et al., 2011; Miller, 2014a). In contrast to male serial killers, however, female serial killers are more likely to be motivated by financial gain (Hickey, 2006; Miller, 2014a). Based on these patterns, Wuornos appears to represent a departure from the typical female serial killer.

Typology of Serial Killers

Numerous efforts have been made to develop a useful serial killer typology from observable patterns in the murders (see Miller, 2014a). To gain a better understanding of serial murder and sexual homicide specifically, the Behavioral Science Unit (BSU), a former division of the FBI, interviewed incarcerated sexual murderers in the 1980s, collected information pertaining to their behavioural and personality traits, and thoroughly examined a number of crime scene variables. Based on this research, the BSU proposed two major categories of sexual homicide offenders: the organized and the disorganized killer (Ressler, Burgess, & Douglas, 1988; Ressler, Burgess, Hartman, Douglas, & McCormick, 1986).

The **organized killer** is generally intelligent, socially and sexually adept, emotionally controlled, and able to maintain some façade of normalcy, such as holding a job or

organized killer The type of serial killer who is generally intelligent, socially and sexually adept, emotionally controlled, and able to maintain some façade of normalcy. The organized killer's crime scenes reflect elements of planning and premeditation.

having a family. His or her crime scenes reflect this intelligence and emotional control. For instance, they will typically show signs of premeditation and control over the victim. The organized killer may bring tools to the crime scene to restrain the victim, such as handcuffs or rope, and will often move the victim's body and remove evidence to conceal the crime and avoid apprehension. It is not unusual for the organized killer to also take a trophy from the scene, such as articles of clothing, jewellery, or photographs, which help him or her to relive the murder later. In addition, organized killers usually carefully select their victims, watching or stalking them for some time before murdering them (Ressler, Burgess, Douglas, 1988; Ressler, Burgess, Hartman, et al., 1986).

The **disorganized killer** is usually socially and sexually inept, possesses below-average levels of intelligence, and often lives alone. His or her murders tend to be spontaneous attacks that reflect a sudden outburst of anger at the victims. The crime scenes reflect this frenzied style of attack: the disorganized killer is much more apt to use something readily available at the scene (e.g. a kitchen knife) as a weapon than to bring one and is unlikely to make any effort to conceal the crime or alter the evidence. Victim-targeting reflects opportunity and accessibility rather than planning. The disorganized killer seldom has any prior contact with his or her victims (Ressler, Burgess, Douglas, 1988; Ressler, Burgess, Hartman, et al., 1986). Some other major differences between the two types are outlined in Tables 11.1 and 11.2.

disorganized killer The type of serial killer who is typically socially and sexually inept and has below-average intelligence. The disorganized killer's crime scenes reflect spontaneous attacks, suggesting sudden outbursts of anger.

Table 11.1 Crime scene differences between organized and disorganized killers

Organized Killers	Disorganized Killers
Plan the offence	Leave weapon at scene
Use restraints	Position dead body
Commit sexual acts with live victims	Perform sexual acts on dead body
Display control of victim (e.g. threatening)	Keep dead body
Use a vehicle	Do not use a vehicle

Source: Ressler, R. K., Burgess, A. W., Douglas, J. E., Hartman, C. R., & D'Agostino, R. B. (1986). Sexual killers and their victims: Identifying patterns through crime scene analysis. *Journal of Interpersonal Violence, 1*, 288–308.

Table 11.2 Characteristic differences between organized and disorganized killers

Organized killers are more likely to . . .	Disorganized killers are more likely to . . .
be intelligent	be low birth-order children
be skilled in occupation	come from a home with unstable work for the father
think and plan the crime	have been treated with hostility as a child
be angry and depressed at the time of the murder	be sexually inhibited and have sexual aversions
have a precipitating stress (e.g. financial, marital, employment)	know the victim
follow crime events in media	live alone and have committed the crime closer to home and work

Source: Ressler, R. K., Burgess, A. W., Douglas, J. E., Hartman, C. R., & D'Agostino, R. B. (1986). Sexual killers and their victims: Identifying patterns through crime scene analysis. *Journal of Interpersonal Violence, 1*, 288–308.

Perhaps the most familiar and widely cited classification system is the one developed by criminologist Ronald M. Holmes (Holmes & DeBurger, 1988; Holmes & Holmes, 1998). This typology distinguishes serial killers on the basis of their motivations and the absence of psychopathology. Holmes identified four major types of serial killers: visionary, mission-oriented, hedonistic, and power/control (see also Miller, 2014a).

Visionary serial killers are driven to murder primarily by a serious psychotic disorder. These individuals suffer from delusions or hallucinations and often report hearing voices instructing them to target and kill certain individuals. They may have bizarre beliefs that killing is necessary to prevent certain tragedies. For example, Herbert Mullin, who murdered 13 people in California in the early 1970s, believed that a tragic earthquake was inevitable unless blood sacrifices were made to nature. He thought the Vietnam War had produced enough deaths, but as the conflict began to wane in 1972, he claimed that a voice instructed him to continue the sacrifices (Jenkins, 1989; Ressler & Schactman, 1992). The visionary serial killer is generally not geographically mobile, preferring to target his or her victims within a comfort zone. Perhaps due to the severity of their mental health problems, visionary serial killers commit chaotic murders that would most often fit into the disorganized category (Holmes & Holmes, 1998; Miller 2014a).

As the name implies, **mission-oriented serial killers** target victims based on an agenda or mission—they select victims who they feel are unworthy and should be systematically eliminated from society. Common victim groups include prostitutes, runaways, or elderly or homeless people. Unlike the visionary serial killer, the mission-oriented serial killer does not suffer from a serious psychotic disorder and is typically able to fit into society, maintain a job, and perhaps even has a spouse and family (Holmes & Holmes, 1998; Miller 2014a).

The third category, the **hedonistic serial killer**, is motivated by the thrill or enjoyment that he or she takes from the act of killing others (Holmes & Holmes, 1998; Miller 2014a). They derive some form of satisfaction from selecting, stalking, and eventually murdering their victims. Researchers have identified different subtypes of this serial killer. The lust killer, for example, is sexually aroused by sadistic violence and torture, and the murders are fuelled by an overactive and deviant sexual fantasy. The creature-of-comfort serial killer commits murder for financial profit or to maintain a lifestyle. Contract killer Richard Kuklinski, the "Iceman," claimed to have murdered over 200 people. His acts were driven by a cold-hearted, merciless pursuit of profit (Carlo, 2006).

Lastly, the **power-oriented serial killer** is motivated by the power and enjoyment derived from exercising an ultimate life-or-death form of control over another human being (Holmes & Holmes, 1998; Miller 2014a). The desire to use this control often stems from the killer's feelings of inadequacy and powerlessness. The Zodiac Killer, who has yet to be identified, is believed to be responsible for over 30 murders involving teen couples who were shot or stabbed to death in "lovers lane" settings during the late 1960s and 1970s. Exhibiting a desire for attention and demonstration of control, he sent several letters containing puzzles and codes to taunt law enforcement and the media (Haugen, 2010).

Etiology of Serial Murder

To date, we have surprisingly little understanding of the etiological mechanisms underlying serial homicide. In the 1960s J.M. MacDonald (1963) introduced what is now referred to as the **MacDonald triad**, a set of three behavioural problems—fire-setting,

visionary serial killer The type of serial killer who is motivated by a serious psychotic disorder. These individuals suffer from delusions or hallucinations and often report hearing voices instructing them to target and kill certain people.

mission-oriented serial killer The type of serial killer who targets victims based on an agenda or mission, selecting people who he or she feels are unworthy and should be systematically eliminated from society.

hedonistic serial killer The type of serial killer who is motivated by the thrill or enjoyment derived from killing.

power-oriented serial killer The type of serial killer who is motivated by the power and enjoyment derived from exercising an ultimate life-or-death form of control over another person.

MacDonald triad A set of three behavioural problems—fire-setting, cruelty toward animals, and enuresis (bedwetting)—that emerge early in childhood and may be precursors to serious forms of adult antisocial behaviour.

cruelty toward animals, and enuresis (bedwetting)—that emerge early in childhood and may act as precursors to serial homicide. Though these problems have not been identified as common risk factors for general adult violence, some researchers suggest that they are more often observed among serial killers and may, at the very least, serve as a warning sign that a child is troubled or experiencing early psychological difficulties (Hellman & Blackman, 1966; Hickey, 2006). Kellert and Felthous (1985) reported that a history of cruelty to animals was observed more frequently among violent offenders than either non-violent offenders or non-offenders. Hellman and Blackman (1966) found links between enuresis, violent fantasies, and aggression among a sample of inmates. Both fire-setting and cruelty toward animals are diagnostic criteria of conduct disorder in the DSM. As Hickey (2006) has pointed out, the link between enuresis and aggression is more tenuous given that it is both an involuntary and a non-violent act.

Regardless of the MacDonald triad's value as an early warning sign for the development of serial homicide, it does not offer much insight into why an individual commits multiple murders. In the 1980s, psychologist Joel Norris (1988) advanced his **addiction model of serial homicide**, which argued that the act of murder takes on a ritualistic aspect for serial killers and eventually develops into an addiction. Based on a series of interviews with convicted serial killers, Norris argued that this type of killer progresses through several incremental psychological phases, detailed in Table 11.3.

Hickey (2006) also formulated a theoretical model to account for the etiology and maintenance of serial homicide. His **trauma-control model** is particularly useful because, rather than outlining a single pathway, he argues that an interaction among several factors underlies the etiological development of a serial murderer (see Figure 11.1). He claims that certain predispositional factors (e.g. built-in traits such as an aggressive temperament, low empathy levels, or high anxiety) exist in some individuals, leaving them less able to cope effectively with traumatic events. Consistent with this notion, Alley and colleagues reviewed the existing literature and identified several possible early neuropsychological precursors among serial killers, including head injuries (Alley, Minnis, Thompson, Wilson, & Gillberg, 2014).

According to Hickey, **traumatic events** are severely negative incidents that occur during an individual's formative years; these could include repeated parental rejection, physical and/or sexual abuse, or the death of a parent. An examination of the child histories of serial killers reveals that many experienced childhood traumas. For instance, Henry Lee Lucas was physically abused by his mother, a prostitute (Egger, 2002). The Boston Strangler was reportedly sold as a slave by his own father (Kelly, 1995). These events create problems with self-image and interpersonal connectedness. Hickey argued that traumatic events experienced in childhood lead to low self-esteem. Traumatized individuals grow up with a poor self-image, feel helpless and hopeless, have difficulty negotiating social relationships with peers from an early point, and eventually become socially disconnected. The consequence of this lack of social investments is an overreliance on fantasies. We all have daydreams or fantasies, but the extent to which we rely on them is limited because we are constrained by the demands of our social relationships and obligations. The developing serial killer, who does not have these types of relationships, spends increasingly more time in a fantasy world. Furthermore, the feelings of hopelessness and powerlessness that stem from low self-esteem have a significant impact on the nature of fantasies.

Photo 11.4 The San Francisco Police Department released these sketches of the Zodiac Killer, which are based on eyewitness accounts, on 18 October 1969. Photo: Bettman/Getty Images

addiction model of serial homicide A theory of serial murder that states the act of murder has a ritualistic aspect for serial killers that leads them to become addicted to or compelled to kill.

trauma-control model of serial homicide A theory of serial murder that argues that the combination of certain predispositional factors and early traumatic events interact with several other factors (e.g. low self-esteem and abnormal fantasies) over the life-course to create a serial murderer.

traumatic events Severely negative events that occur during a person's formative years.

Table 11.3 The addiction model of serial homicide

Aura Phase	Serial killers begin at the aura phase, where they start to withdraw from social reality and spend increasing amounts of time fantasizing about power, control, and violence. These fantasies serve to disinhibit the serial killer, relaxing restraints on his or her murderous impulses.
Trolling Phase	During the trolling phase, the serial killer begins to live out aspects of his or her fantasy, seeking out suitable victims and watching and following them. Although nobody has been murdered, the prospective killer is becoming comfortable with the fantasy. This is akin to a "warming up" or "feeling-out" stage.
Wooing Phase	In the wooing phase, the serial killer interacts with potential victims, gaining their confidence and trust and eventually luring them into a trap.
Capture and Murder Phases	The serial killer catches and/or confines the victim and then engages in the actual act of murder. In particular, the murder phase represents an emotionally intense experience for the serial killer, who, in many cases, has long fantasized about the moment.
Totem Phase	The serial killer realizes his or her long-rehearsed fantasy of domination and murder over another human being. The emotional intensity of the murder phase quickly vanishes and, in an effort to maintain it, some serial killers take a symbolic trophy of their actions to relive the act and, specifically, to re-experience the sensation of power that he or she had at the time of the murder.
Depression Phase	In spite of the souvenirs taken during the totem phase, the serial killer's emotional high disappears and is often replaced by a period of depression and emptiness. This emotional let-down triggers a return to the aura phase, and the killer becomes increasingly addicted to the ritualistic aspects of identifying, pursuing, and capturing his or her prey.

Source: Hickey, E. W. (2013). *Serial murderers and their victims* (6th ed.). Belmont, CA: Wadsworth.

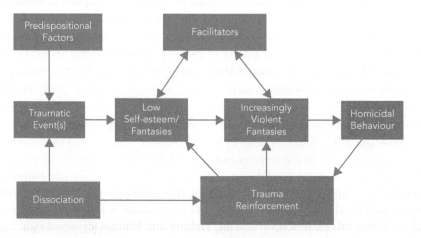

Figure 11.1 The trauma-control model of serial homicide

The powerless individual creates a fantasy world wherein he or she is omnipotent or exerts extreme domination over others.

Another important concept in the trauma-control model is dissociation. Stephen Porter (1996), a forensic psychologist, has discussed its role in the development of secondary psychopathy. Dissociation can be viewed as an adaptive response to serious traumatic events that provoke intense feelings of anxiety. In some cases, people will slowly "deactivate" or "numb" their emotional response to trauma as a self-protective measure. Porter argued that some individuals are predisposed with a reduced capacity to deal with traumatic events and are increasingly likely to dissociate.

Two final components of Hickey's (2006) model are trauma reinforcers and facilitators. **Trauma reinforcers** are events experienced in adulthood that reinforce or trigger responses experienced during similar or related traumatic events in childhood. For example, a child who has been rejected by cold, abusive parents may have problems dealing with rejection from a co-worker or a poor work evaluation. These types of events are benign for most adults, but the developing serial killer who has suffered earlier traumatic rejection will be reminded of their childhood experiences. These individuals lack the effective coping skills to deal with these events adequately and will instead rely on their fantasy worlds as a way to escape and cope. Furthermore, serial killers often increasingly rely on facilitators, such as alcohol, drugs, or pornography, which serve to disinhibit an individual and make them more comfortable exploring their fantasies of power and domination.

> trauma reinforcers Events experienced in adulthood that reinforce or trigger responses felt during similar or related traumatic events in childhood.

All the factors in Hickey's (2006) model interact and eventually culminate in murder. The act of killing reinforces the fantasies experienced by the serial murderer, which tends to perpetuate the cycle. While other models may offer further insights into the development of serial homicide (see Purcell & Arrigo, 2006), recent literature reviews support the notion that a complex interaction of neuropsychological, psychological, and psychosocial factors play a role in the etiology of serial homicide (Miller, 2014b).

Mass Murder

In their extensive work on mass murder, Ronald M. Holmes and Stephen T. Holmes (2001) identified several key differences between serial killers and mass murderers. As noted earlier, the latter is a single, continuous event and lacks the temporal breaks that occur with the former. For example, Jared Lee Loughner shot 18 people—including then-US congresswoman Gabrielle Giffords—killing 6 of them, in a Safeway parking lot in Tucson, Arizona, in 2011. His actions are considered mass murder because the shootings occurred within a single time frame and at one geographic place. Although Loughner was apprehended, mass murderers often kill themselves or commit "suicide by police." By comparison, serial killers often express no desire to stop killing and typically continue until they are apprehended.

Holmes and Holmes (2001) developed a typology for mass murder based on motivation, anticipated gain, victim selection, victim relationship, and spatial mobility. Some mass murderers appear to be motivated by extrinsic pressures, such as the influence of a group or individual, whereas others are motivated by intrinsic forces, such as delusional thinking. Using this classification scheme, Holmes and Holmes identified eight types of mass murderer: the disciple mass killer, the family annihilator, the disgruntled employee mass killer, the ideological mass killer, the set-and-run mass killer, the disgruntled citizen mass killer, the school shooter, and the psychotic mass killer. Some offenders may fit more than one category or may not fit any. Loughner, for instance, exhibited mental health problems but also expressed negative attitudes toward women and the US government (Barry, 2011). In the following sections, we outline two of these categories—the disciple mass killer and the school shooter.

Cults and the Disciple Mass Killer

The **disciple mass killer** is an individual(s) who kills "because of the relationship with someone who dictates the murder" (Holmes & Holmes, 2001, p. 35). The Manson Family murders, discussed at the outset of this chapter, illustrate the potential influence a charismatic group or cult leader may exert over the behaviour of followers. One of the first challenges in discussing cults is establishing a definition that adequately distinguishes these groups from legitimate subculture or religious organizations. What separates Manson's "family" from the hippie movement of the 1960s or Jim Jones's Peoples Temple (see the case study) from the Church of Scientology or the Roman Catholic Church?

CASE STUDY

The Jonestown Massacre

The Jonestown Massacre remains one of history's most shocking mass murders. The events of 18 November 1978 were set in motion by Jim Jones, a self-styled communist who was dissatisfied with McCarthy-era American politics in the 1950s and saw religion as a way of living communist values without state oppression. Borrowing the theatrics and showmanship he observed in Baptist faith-healing sermons, he opened what eventually became the Peoples Temple in a racially mixed neighbourhood in Indianapolis. Jones had a heavy influence over his church members from the start, instructing them to abstain from sex and encouraging them to spend holidays with fellow members rather than their own families. His sermons endorsed a communal lifestyle, urging members to give their belongings to the temple and assuring them that he would meet their needs. Over time, these sermons became more bizarre, referring to an imminent nuclear Armageddon in the United States, and more frequently focused worship onto Jones (Galanter, 1989; Holmes & Holmes, 2001).

In the mid-1970s Jones moved the Peoples Temple and its members to Guyana, forming what he referred to as Jonestown. He described it as a "socialist paradise" and explained to his members that it was the only place where they could escape oppression.

Photo 11.5 Jim Jones, leader of the Peoples Temple, promised his followers utopia.

However, many Jonestown members were unhappy. In response to allegations of abuse, US Congressman Leo Ryan visited the commune on 17 November 1978, and several residents asked to return to the United States with him. At the local airport, Ryan, three journalists, and a Jonestown member were shot and killed by Jones's security guards. The next day, Jones informed his followers of the incident and said that it was only a matter of time before more outsiders arrived to end their way of life. He ordered everyone to drink Flavor Aid laced with cyanide. Many drank the poison; those who refused were shot. Over 900 people died at Jonestown, including Jones, who allegedly shot himself in the head (Galanter, 1989; Holmes & Holmes, 2001).

The term *destructive cult* was coined by Frank MacHovec (1989), who defined it as "a rigidly structured group under a charismatic leader, which isolates itself from establishing societal traditions, values, and norms, recruits members deceptively without informed consent, and retains them by manipulative techniques which deny freedom of choice" (p. 10). Psychologist Margaret Thaler Singer (1996), a world-renowned expert, identified three factors that distinguish cults: the origin and role of the leader, the power structure between the leader and followers, and the use of a coordinated program of persuasion. According to Singer, cult leaders are self-appointed, charismatic, and dominating individuals who claim to either have a special mission in life or to possess some special knowledge that they can pass to their followers. The relationship structure of cults is authoritarian in nature; rules are rigidly set and pronounced by the leader, but a double standard exists in their implementation. For example, cult leaders may have multiple spouses but separate other married couples and forbid them from engaging in intimacy. Singer described cults as totalitarian organizations wherein leaders implement a program of coercive persuasion geared at influencing significant shifts in group members' behaviour, thoughts, and ideologies.

> **destructive cult** A strictly organized group that has a charismatic leader, uses deceptive means to recruit members, and retains them through manipulative strategies that negate freedom of choice.

Much of the existing research on cults focuses on the leader's explicit role and use of coercive persuasion to exercise control over others (Galanter, 1989; Ofshe & Watters, 1994; Zimbardo & Leippe, 1991). **Coercive persuasion** refers to forms of social influence that produce significant changes in an individual's behaviour and thought processes (Schein, 1961). Not unlike advertising campaigns, cults selectively target particular demographics, namely, ones that are more likely to be vulnerable. Several key factors—including depression, social isolation, and weak or absent affiliations—make individuals attractive for cult recruitment (Olson, Breckler, & Wiggins, 2008). Generally, cults focus their recruitment efforts on people who are between 18 and 30 years of age attending high school, college, or university and are at a vulnerable transition point in their lives. Many first-year university students are living away from home for the first time and, especially on larger campuses, may feel anonymous and alone, rendering them particularly susceptible to a group offering companionship (Tao, Dong, Pratt, Hunsberger, & Pancer, 2000; Wintre & Yaffe, 2000). Cults often try to make potential recruits feel unique or important by telling them that they were "specially" selected, a tactic identified as effective for luring young people (Ando et al., 1998).

> **coercive persuasion** Forms of social influence that produce significant changes in an individual's behaviour and thought processes.

Cults use numerous tactics to recruit members, including isolation and invitations to group meals, lecture sessions, or weekend retreats (Hassan, 1988). Another technique is what Singer (1996) calls **love bombing**:

> **love bombing** A recruitment technique often employed by cults that involves showering potential recruits with unconditional love, affection, flattery, and security.

> Love bombing is a coordinated effort, usually under the direction of leadership that involves long-term members' flooding recruits and newer members with flattery, verbal seduction, affectionate but usually nonsexual touching, and lots of attention to their every remark. Love bombing—or the offer of instant companionship—is a deceptive ploy accounting for many successful recruitment drives. (p. 114)

Manson effectively used many of these approaches to break down and eventually exert a great deal of control over his members, who were primarily young adults from middle-class backgrounds (Bugliosi & Gendry, 1974). As noted in the opening case study, he attracted many of his followers by adopting a hippie persona, preying on the recruit's disenfranchisement with parents and the older generation and isolating members from competing sources of information by moving them to the Spahn Ranch. He also used Paul Watkins, a younger and attractive male follower, to seek out young girls and bring them to group orgies, where Manson passed out drugs and instructed people to strip and engage in various sexual acts. According to Watkins, Manson used these orgies to "eradicate hang-ups" and to reduce people's inhibitions (p. 317). However, he always took smaller amounts of drugs, putting him in a position of control. Brooks Poston, a former Manson Family member, described how he gained power:

> He had various techniques. With a girl, it would usually start with sex. Charlie might convince a plain girl that she was beautiful. Or, if she had a father fixation, have her imagine that he was her father. Or, if he felt she was looking for a leader, he might imply that he was Christ. Manson had a talent for sensing and capitalizing on a person's hang-ups and/or desires. When a man first joined the group, Charlie would usually take him on an LSD trip, ostensibly "to open his mind." Then, while he was in a highly suggestible state, he would talk about love, how you had to surrender yourself to it, how only by ceasing to exist as an individual ego could you become one with all things. (Bugliosi & Gentry, 1974, p. 316)

Psychological theories of social influence can shed light on cult recruitment and indoctrination techniques. Initial recruitment approaches can be partially explained by the **foot-in-the-door technique**, a compliance tactic that convinces someone to fulfill a large or extreme request by first getting him or her to do small or benign tasks and gradually increasing them (Burger, 1999; Freedman & Fraser, 1966). This tactic relies on the need felt by many people to maintain a consistent self- and public image, which recruitment strategies frequently manipulate. A cult leader might first ask a recruit to attend a one-hour lecture and then to take home several pamphlets that will take a few hours to read. Eventually, he or she may be asked to give up a weekend to meet other cult members and learn more about the group. As the recruit consistently complies with increasingly more demanding requests, the leader may ask the person to quit working and donate all his or her savings to the cult.

The efforts and sacrifices that cults request of new recruits may trigger dissonance and consequently increase commitment to the cult. Psychologist Leon Festinger (1954) proposed a theory of attitudinal change called **cognitive dissonance theory**, which posits that, when we experience inconsistent thoughts (or dissonant cognitions), we will experience anxiety. For instance, "I have stolen from someone" and "Stealing is wrong" are inconsistent thoughts. An individual who steals from people but knows that doing so is wrong will experience dissonance. People are generally motivated to reduce this anxiety; however, behaviours can be difficult to change. It is hard to stop smoking or to change one's eating habits. Changing how we think about things and rationalizing our behaviour is often an easier way to reduce dissonance. You can rationalize stealing from someone by convincing yourself that the person you stole from deserved it or was stupid for not protecting their belongings more diligently. Manson's insistence that his members engage in personally distressing public sexual acts may have triggered dissonance ("I am embarrassed by this sexual act"; "I am engaging in this sexual act in front of strangers"). To reduce their anxiety, his followers may have rationalized their behaviour by increasing their affinity to the group (i.e. "I must like them") and attributing their actions to an acceptance of Manson's philosophies.

Other techniques used to engender feelings of confusion and uncertainty during the stages of indoctrination may also facilitate dissonance. According to research by social psychologist Ian McGregor (2003; McGregor & Marigold, 2003; McGregor, Zanna,

foot-in-the-door technique A compliance tactic that involves getting someone to fulfill a more extreme request by first gaining his or her agreement to perform smaller, benign tasks and gradually increasing them.

cognitive dissonance theory A social psychological theory that proposes the experience of inconsistent thoughts (i.e. dissonant cognitions) results in anxiety that people may reduce by changing their attitudes to minimize the inconsistency.

Holmes, & Spencer, 2001), people are much more likely to adopt extreme views when they experience feelings of personal uncertainty. These feelings may make people uncomfortable or lead to dissonance, which can be reduced by strongly adopting a set of ideas or beliefs. Manson was able to convince several members that Helter Skelter was inevitable and that it was their responsibility to set the events in motion. The personal uncertainty that some may have experienced—perhaps partly due to the social and political turbulence of the 1960s and psychedelic drug use—could have resulted in dissonance that was reduced by wholeheartedly accepting Manson's belief system.

School Shootings

School shootings are a statistically rare phenomenon. Public concerns about safety and school violence are in large part fuelled by mainstream media reporting practices, which selectively focus on rare, extreme events and thereby increase their perceived salience (see Chyi & McCombs, 2004; Surette, 2011). Nevertheless, the social costs of these incidents to families, schools, and communities are immeasurable and highlight the importance of gaining further insight into their nature and frequency.

A US report indicates that mass school shootings may have increased during the 1990s (Vossekuil, Fein, Reddy, Borum, & Modzeleski, 2004). The School Associated Violent Death Study (Modzeleski et al., 2008), conducted by the Centers for Disease Control and Prevention, found that the rate of multiple-victim homicides in American schools stabilized between 1999 and 2006. The same study found that the majority of homicides at schools involved single victims. Yet accurate estimates of the exact number of school shootings are difficult to obtain for a variety of reasons, including definitional issues (Muschert, 2007; Ferguson & Ivory, 2012). While the Columbine massacre perhaps represents the prototypical school shooting, a clear and consistent definition of the term *mass school shootings* remains elusive. Some researchers have suggested that it refers to an incident of "targeted" school violence, where the target includes specific individuals, groups of individuals, or the school community (Flannery, Modzeleski, & Kretschmar, 2013). According to Newman (2004), a mass school shooting involves a student or former student targeting random victims or victims who hold some symbolic value in a public area (e.g. classroom, cafeteria) on school property. Interestingly, Newman excludes shootings of specific individuals due to conflicts, such as rival gang shootings, thereby introducing sociocultural parameters to the definition.

Much of the research on school shootings focuses on the identification of a statistical profile based on potential risk factors, many of which are microfactors discussed in the chapters on neuropsychology, developmental theories, and psychopathology. Poor temperament, impulse control problems, anxiety, and depression have all been highlighted as possible contributors (see Flannery et al., 2013). Peer status, bullying victimization, and peer rejection have also been discussed in this context (Leary et al., 2003; Verlinden et al., 2000; Wike & Fraser, 2009). At present, the growing perspective in the literature is that, while peer rejection may have been a common feature observed across several prior incidents, it is probably a more distal risk factor that serves to influence others more directly related to the violent behaviour (Wike & Fraser, 2009). Dave Cullen (2009) argues that the Columbine shooters, Dylan Klebold and Eric Harris, not only had friends at their school but also frequently bullied other children. Kenneth Dodge and colleagues (2003) found that peer rejection was correlated with increases in anxiety, depression, and general antisocial behaviour—all of which are factors found to play a more direct role in school shootings.

CASE STUDY

Adam Lanza and the Sandy Hook Elementary School Shooting

On 14 December 2012, 20 school children and 6 adults were murdered at Sandy Hook Elementary School in Newton, Connecticut, making it the deadliest mass school shooting in US history (*The Economist*, 2012). The shootings began at approximately 9:35 a.m., when 20-year-old Adam Lanza, who had killed his mother earlier that morning, shot through the school's front entrance. Armed with a rifle and a pistol, he shot indiscriminately as he went from classroom to classroom. Principal Dawn Hochsprung and school psychologist Marey Sherlach were killed trying to stop him. Teachers such as Victoria Soto, who was also killed, blocked classroom doors and rushed children into closets in an attempt to shield them (Blackwell, 2012). Like many other mass murderers, Lanza committed suicide in the school following the shootings. At a memorial service, Connecticut Governor Dannel Malloy said, "Evil visited this community" (Blackwell, 2012).

Little is known about Lanza's motivation. Discussion has centred on mental health problems and abnormal patterns of behaviour (Curry, 2013). Lanza also exhibited a fascination with school shootings, particularly Columbine (Stoller, 2013). Lanza's actions at Sandy Hook sparked a renewed debate around gun control in the United States.

The role of some potential risk factors, such as peer rejection and bullying, may play a smaller direct role in school shootings because they interact with other factors within a larger sociocultural framework. For example, accessibility to firearms and a wider "gun culture" may contribute to school shootings in the United States (e.g. Sung Hong, Cho, Allen-Meares, & Espelage, 2011; Wike & Fraser, 2009). Other research has focused on broader ecological factors, including toxic social views around traditional masculinity (Sung Hong et al., 2011). From this perspective, social norms defining and governing masculinity around rigid notions of entitlement, dominance, and aggression may result in grossly exaggerated responses to perceived provocations, such as peer or romantic rejection, triggering the violence observed in mass school shootings (Sung Hong et al., 2011).

Other researchers have attempted to create categories of school shooters based on particular groupings of risk factors. Langman (2009) identified three distinct types. The traumatized school shooter demonstrates a distinct pattern of developmental risk factors; he or she comes from a "broken home" characterized by physical and/or sexual abuse, parental substance use, or parental criminal history. The psychotic school shooter is characterized by serious mental health problems. While a person in this category may have an intact family, he or she is more likely to exhibit symptoms of schizophrenia, including paranoid delusions and auditory hallucinations. Finally, the psychopathic shooter exhibits symptoms consistent with psychopathy, including a lack of empathy and high levels of narcissism.

Summary

1. Homicide refers to the intentional killing of another person. North American statistics indicate that homicides most often resemble forms of interpersonal conflict among young males familiar with each other and involve alcohol and/or drug use. This statistical pattern is consistent with reactive aggression.

2. Affective or emotional responses to events, cognitions, and the ability to regulate our emotional responses all play an integral role in reactive aggression. Stressors or provocations may trigger intense emotional responses that subsequently prompt cognitions that support or do not support aggressive behavioural responses. Our ability to think about potential behavioural responses and effectively regulate both our emotions and reactions serves to increase or decrease the likelihood of violent behaviour.

3. Filicide and parricide are both major types of family homicide. Filicide refers to the killing of a child by his or her parent. Much of the research on neonaticide and infanticide—forms of filicide—focuses on mothers who kill their children. While psychosocial factors such as poverty have been identified as playing a significant role in neonaticide, research has generally found that women who commit infanticide are more likely to exhibit mental health problems. Postpartum psychosis, a rare and serious form of depression, may play a role in some cases of infanticide. The little research that exists on men who kill their children has found that male filicide often occurs in the context of ongoing family violence. Parricide refers to the murder of a parent by his or her child. Differences have been observed between adult and juvenile parricide offenders. The former may be more likely to suffer from a serious mental illness, whereas the latter are more likely to kill to end ongoing abuse in the family.

4. Generally, serial murder is defined as the murder of at least two victims at different times. Statistically rare and difficult to research, much of what is known about serial killers is based on analyses of case studies. According to this research, the male serial killer typically targets strangers and, in many cases, his victims come from vulnerable and/or marginalized groups. Sex, power, and control are core aspects of the male serial killer's motivation, with many of these individuals exhibiting features of both paraphilic disorders and intrusive and violent fantasies. The addiction model of serial homicide focuses on the intrusive role of these violent fantasies and the ritualistic aspects of serial murder that gradually develop into compulsive behaviour. The trauma-control model suggests that serial murder is the result of an interaction between predispositional factors and early-life traumatic events, which are subsequently shaped and reinforced by later life events and personality factors.

5. Mass murder involves the killing of four or more people at one time and in one geographic location. Two types of mass murderers were described. The first is disciple mass killers, who murder because of their relationship with a charismatic and authoritarian leader who orders the murders. This cult leader targets vulnerable groups, typically young people at transitional points of life, and employs a series of coercive persuasive techniques to gain and maintain control. These methods may include isolation, love bombing, and compliance tactics (e.g. the foot-in-the-door technique). Cognitive dissonance theory may explain how the efforts and sacrifices cults require of members result in total commitment to the leader's mission.

6. The second type of mass murder described concerns school shooters. Although mass school shootings are statistically rare, some research suggests that the number of such incidents increased in the United States in the 1990s before stabilizing over the following decade. Emerging statistical profiles of school shooters have identified a number of micro-risk factors, including poor impulse control, anxiety, depression, and peer status and rejection. The small or indirect role of some of these factors, such as bullying and peer rejection, suggests that broader sociocultural factors, such as societal norms around masculinity and gun culture, most certainly play a role in these murders.

Review Questions

1. Explain how our affective responses, cognitions, and ability to self-regulate may play a role in the reactive aggression that characterizes many acts of homicide. In your answer, define reactive aggression and contrast it with instrumental aggression.
2. Identify and define the two major forms of family homicide discussed in this chapter. Compare and contrast the different mental health and psychosocial factors that account for the patterns observed in these forms of family homicide.
3. According to the trauma-control model, how does an individual develop the repetitive homicidal behaviour that characterizes serial murder?
4. Charles Manson was able to recruit young adults and convince them to commit murder. Identify and discuss two psychological theories that might explain how Manson was able to recruit them and gain their compliance.

Additional Readings

Hickey, E. W. (2006). *Serial murderers and their victims* (6th ed.). Belmont, CA: Wadsworth.

Miller, L. (2014a). Serial killers: I. Subtypes, patterns, and motives. *Aggression and Violent Behavior, 19*, 1–11.

Miller, L. (2014b). Serial killers: II. Development, dynamics, and forensics. *Aggression and Violent Behavior, 19*, 12–22.

Porter, T., & Gavin, H. (2010). Infanticide and neonaticide: A review of 40 years of research literature on incidence and causes. *Trauma, Violence, and Abuse, 11*, 99–122.

Purcell, C. E., & Arrigo, B. A. (2006). *The psychology of lust murder: Paraphilia, sexual killing, and serial homicide*. New York, NY: Academic Press.

12

Interpersonal Violence

Learning Objectives

At the end of this chapter, you should be able to:

- define stalking and describe the major patterns of this behaviour;
- identify and describe major typologies of stalkers;
- define intimate partner violence (IPV) and describe its major patterns;
- identify and describe major typologies of spousal assaulters;
- apply two psychological theories that explain stalking and IPV;
- identify and describe major patterns of sexual violence;
- discuss various theoretical explanations for sexual violence; and
- identify and describe major categories of risk factors for sexual violence.

CASE STUDY

Ray Rice

Atlantic City, New Jersey—On 15 February 2014, former Baltimore Ravens running back and his fiancée (now wife), Janay Palmer, were arrested for assault following an altercation at Atlantic City's Revel Casino. Four days later, TMZ released a video showing Rice dragging an unconscious Palmer out of a casino elevator. He was indicted on charges of third-degree aggravated assault, but the case was dropped; the National Football League (NFL) suspended him for two games and fined him $58,000. Public criticism of what was widely considered an insufficient punishment led the NFL to revise its position on domestic violence (Elliott, 2014; Kantor, 2014).

At the start of the 2014 football season, TMZ released a second video of the assault, which showed Rice punching Palmer in the face, knocking her unconscious. In response to public backlash over this video, the Ravens cut Rice from the team, and the NFL—which claimed that it hadn't seen the footage prior to its release—suspended him indefinitely. Palmer took to social media to defend her husband, prompting some criticism.

Photo 12.1   During an NFL news conference in May 2014, Ray Rice and Janay Palmer make statements about his assaulting her. Both apologized and stated that they were working things out together.

This second video sparked conversations about intimate partner violence and how organizations such as the NFL, along with society in general, respond to it. Victim advocates pointed out that the Rice incident and Palmer's comments follow common patterns in such cases.

Introduction

The term *interpersonal* simply means "between people"; hence, interpersonal violence encompasses any incident of threatened, attempted, or actual physical harm between two or more persons. Rice's assault of Palmer is interpersonal violence, as well as an example of intimate partner violence (IPV). As this case illustrates, interpersonal violence can take many forms, but this chapter focuses on just three: stalking, IPV, and sexual violence.

Stalking

The Extent and Nature of Stalking

Stalking has been referred to as harassment or obsessional following (Kropp, Hart, & Lyon, 2002; Meloy, 1996; Spitzberg & Cupach, 2007; Westrup & Fremouw, 1998). According to the *Oxford English Dictionary*, to harass is to "torment [someone] by subjecting them to constant interference or intimidation." The *DSM-5* defines obsession as "recurrent and persistent thoughts, urges, or impulses that are experienced, at some time during the disturbance, as intrusive and unwanted" (APA, 2013 , p. 826). References to stalking as obsessional harassment conceptualize it as an abnormal or long-term pattern of threat or persecution directed toward a specific individual (Meloy, 1996; Meloy & Gothard, 1995; Zona, Sharma,

& Lane, 1993). Tjaden and Thoennes (2000) define stalking as "a course of conduct direct-ed at a specific person that involves repeated visual or physical proximity; nonconsensual communication; verbal, written, or implied threats; or a combination thereof that would cause fear in a reasonable person (with *repeated* meaning on two or more occasions)" (p. 5).

Legal definitions of stalking vary from jurisdiction to jurisdiction, but most incor-porate three basic elements. First, the perpetrator must exhibit a pattern of behaviour typically involving repeated attempts to contact the victim. Second, the contact must be non-consensual and against the victim's wishes. Finally, the perpetrator's behaviour must cause the victim to reasonably fear for his or her safety or the safety of people known to him or her. Combining these elements gives us the following definition of **stalking**: a pat-tern of repeated contact with another person that is unwanted and causes that person to reasonably fear for his or her safety or the safety of people known to him or her (Kropp, et al., 2002).

The best prevalence estimates for stalking are found in several large-scale victim-ization surveys conducted with representative samples in North America, England, and Wales (Black et al., 2011; Budd & Mattinson, 2000; Sinha, 2013). Although these surveys are methodologically strong, each uses a different definition of stalking, which may have impacted the results. According to these surveys, the annual and lifetime prevalence rates for women probably range from 3 to 5 per cent and from 15 to 17 per cent, respectively. The corresponding rates for men are substantially lower, probably 1 to 2 per cent annually and 5 to 7 per cent lifetime.

Research such as these studies contradicts the media's image of stalkers as physically violent women pursing strangers. In fact, research consistently shows that between 80 and 90 per cent of stalkers are male and that most victims know the perpetrator (Black et al., 2011; Budd & Mattinson, 2000; Sinha, 2013). Stalking cases involving strangers represent only about one-quarter of all cases. Some research indicates that a majority of stalkers are former intimate partners, although these findings appear to be more consistent in police samples and may reflect a greater tendency of these victims to notify authorities (e.g. Garrod, Ewert, Field, & Warren, 1995; Sinha, 2013; Zona et al., 1993). Some vic-timization surveys, by comparison, report that former intimate partners comprise about 30 per cent or less of stalking perpetrators (Budd & Mattinson, 2000; Sinha, 2013; cf. Black et al., 2011). Nevertheless, stalking behaviours appear to be a common tactic employed by former partners. For example, a study of university students reported that nearly 40 per cent of respondents admitted to having engaged in at least one type of stalking behaviour following a break-up (Davis, Ace, & Andra, 2000).

The majority of perpetrators engage in different stalking behaviours, with perhaps 20 per cent or less confining themselves to a single type (Budd & Mattinson, 2000; Mullen, Pathé, Purcell, & Stuart, 1999). As Table 12.1 shows, the behavioural range of stalking is immensely diverse. Although the most commonly reported tactic in Canada and the United States is unwanted phone calls, a remote behaviour that generally occurs away from the victim, it is evident that a substantial proportion of respondents experienced other approach-oriented (e.g. following or besetting) and more intrusive behaviours.

Although crime is typically a "young man's game," stalkers are, on average, older in comparison to other offender groups, with their mean or median age ranging in the mid- to late thirties (Gill & Brockman, 1996; Harmon, Rosner, & Owens, 1995a, 1995b; Meloy & Gothard, 1995; Mullen et al., 1999; Zona et al., 1993). Stalkers are also relatively more edu-cated than other offenders. Generally, the average offender has not completed high school,

stalking A pattern of repeat-ed contact with a person that is unwanted and causes the person to reasonably fear for his or her safety or the safety of people known to him or her.

Table 12.1 The prevalence of various stalking behaviours reported in two victimization surveys

	Percentage of respondents	
Behaviour	Canada	United States[1]
Phone calls	47	79
E-mails or messages	6	13
Gifts	9[2]	26
Watched or followed	28	39
Approached or showed up	N/A	58
Waited outside home	15	N/A
Waited outside other place	19	N/A
Left strange items	N/A	12
Snuck into home or car	N/A	23
Persistently asked you on a date and refused to take no for an answer	12	n/a
Tried to communicate with you against your will in any other way	8	N/A
Tried to intimidate or threaten you by intimidating or threatening someone else	43	N/A
Tried to intimidate or threaten you by hurting your pets or damaging your property	20	N/A

Notes
1. Female respondents only.
2. Gifts, letters or cards.
Sources: AuCoin, K. (2005). *Family violence in Canada: A statistical profile 2005*. Ottawa, ON: Canadian Centre for Justice Statistics, Statistics Canada; Black, M. C., et al. (2011). *The national intimate partner and sexual violence survey (NISVS): 2010 summary report*. Atlanta, GA: National Center for Injury Prevention and Control, Centers for Disease Control and Prevention.

but stalkers are significantly more likely to have graduated and have some post-secondary education (Harmon et al., 1995a, 1995b; Meloy & Gothard, 1995). Finally, stalkers have problems maintaining regular employment—they are significantly more likely than other criminal offenders to be unemployed at the time of the offence (Meloy, 1996; Kienlen, Birmingham, Solberg, O'Regan, & Meloy, 1997).

Stalkers also appear to suffer from interpersonal and mental health difficulties. Several studies point out that stalkers have problems both establishing and maintaining healthy intimate relationships (Harmon et al., 1995a, 1995b; Meloy & Gotthard, 1995). Mullen and colleagues (1999) found that some stalkers had never had a long-term relationship. Lyon (1997) reported that stalkers were significantly more likely to have experienced serious marital problems, such as separation or divorce, as compared to other types of criminal offenders. Regarding mental health problems, schizophrenia, delusional disorders, and substance abuse problems are the most frequently diagnosed Axis I disorders among stalkers (Mullen et al., 1999). Although many stalkers are also personality disordered, psychopathy is usually not associated with this crime. A study of men convicted of stalking found that psychopathic traits were not commonly observed; in cases of elevated psychopathy levels, victims were usually casual acquaintances, not former intimate partners (Storey, Hart, Meloy, & Reavis, 2009).

Researching Criminal and Violent Behaviour

Cyberstalking

With the growth of the Internet and the expansion of social media, cyberstalking (and cyberbullying) is a growing area of concern for law enforcement and lawmakers. Like traditional stalking, cyberstalking involves a range or pattern of interrelated behaviours. Its three major categories are hyper-intimacy, threat, and real-life transfer (Spitzberg & Rhea, 1999; Spitzberg, Marshall, & Cupach, 2001). Aspects of hyper-intimacy may include repeated, unsolicited efforts at cybercommunication with the victim, such as sending tokens or exaggerated messages of affection or sending pornographic messages. Threat refers to online invasions of privacy and may include intimidating e-mails or text messages and various forms of electronic sabotage, such as spamming or sending viruses (Bocij, 2002; Burgess & Baker, 2002; Finn, 2004; Finn & Banach, 2000; McGrath & Casey, 2002; Spitzberg & Hoobler, 2002). Real-life transfer refers to physical intrusions into the victim's life that have emerged from online encounters, including the victim being followed or physically harmed by a person whom he or she met online.

Studies on the prevalence of cyberstalking suggest that the rates of victimization are low, with the more commonly experienced forms being relatively minor in nature (Alexy, Burgess, Baker, & Smoyak, 2005; Finkelhor, Mitchell, & Wolak, 2000; Fisher, Hartman, Cullen, & Turner, 2002). Another major area of inquiry is whether cyberstalking represents a distinct social problem (e.g. Bocij & McFarlane, 2002) or whether electronic media merely provides an extension of such behaviour (e.g. Burgess & Baker, 2002; Meloy, 1998; Ogilvie, 2000). The rationale for considering cyberstalkers as a distinct group rests on the assumption that the Internet and its expansive opportunities to monitor and contact individuals may prompt stalking behaviour from people who would not engage in such actions in face-to-face social settings (Finn, 2004; McGrath & Casey, 2002). While some studies have identified differences in stalking patterns between cyberstalkers and traditional stalkers (Lucks, 2004), others suggest that the Internet merely provides stalkers with an additional means to exert control over victims. Sheridan and Grant (2007) found that only 7 per cent of self-reported stalking victims indicated that they had been stalked online only; nearly half of these participants had received an e-mail from their stalker. The majority of respondents were harassed offline.

Stalking, Violence, and Risk Factors

While serious physical violence is rare, there are certainly stalking cases that end tragically. An important research area concerns identifying factors that might indicate the probability of violence to law enforcement. Rosenfeld and Harmon (2002) examined 204 stalking and harassment cases referred to the New York City Forensic Psychiatry Clinic between 1994 and 1998. They found several demographic and psychological factors that significantly predicted violence in stalking cases. Stalkers who were under 30, non-Caucasian, and had less than a grade 10 education were significantly more likely to use violence. Higher incidents of violence were also observed among perpetrators who were stalking former spouses or intimate partners. Stalkers who threatened to hurt their victims were more likely to do so. Consistent with the general violence risk assessment literature, stalkers with a history of substance abuse were more likely to be violent than those with no such history. Surprisingly, gender, prior criminal history, and past history of violence—all traditional predictors of general violence—were not associated with violence in stalking cases.

To further examine these risk factors, Rosenfeld (2004) subsequently performed a meta-analysis of 13 published studies involving over 1,000 stalkers. He found that violence was observed in nearly 40 per cent of cases. Consistent with his earlier results, he discovered that violence was associated with threats, substance abuse, the absence of a serious psychotic mental disorder, and a former intimate partner stalker. The only contradictory finding was that a history of violent behaviour predicted violence in stalking in the meta-analysis but not Rosenfeld's original study.

A recurring element in the studies we have discussed is the context of the stalking behaviour. Violent behaviour was most commonly observed when the victim and the stalker had a prior intimate relationship. Moreover, victimization surveys show that stalking frequently occurs in the context of a failed intimate relationship. These findings have led researchers to posit a connection between IPV and stalking (Davis et al., 2000; Burgess, Nelson, & Myers, 1998; Douglas & Dutton, 2001). Two complementary lines of research support such a link. One shows that former intimate partner stalkers are more likely than non-stalkers to be psychologically or physically abusive within their intimate relationships (e.g. Coleman, 1997; Logan, Leukefeld, & Walker, 2000). The other demonstrates that stalking behaviour is more prevalent among men who are physically abusive to their intimate partners than among men who are not (e.g. McFarlane, Campbell, & Watson, 2002; McFarlane et al., 1999). The overlap between stalking and IPV may relate to the stalker's need for control. Former intimate partner stalkers likely perceive the need to engage in stalking because more direct means of controlling and monitoring the victim no longer exist. In this context, stalking may simply represent the continuation of IPV beyond the end of the relationship.

Typology of Stalkers

As the research literature on stalking has expanded, several researchers have developed typologies of stalkers. Zona and colleagues (1993) distinguished between three major categories of stalkers: simple obsessional, love obsessional, and erotomanic. The **simple obsessional stalker** category represents the most common form of stalking and involves cases where the victim and stalker had a relationship (e.g. marriage, common law, or brief dating). In many instances, the stalker is a former intimate partner and the stalking is an extension of domestic violence. Most cases of simple obsessional stalking involve male perpetrators and female victims.

The simple obsessional stalker is usually socially immature, low in self-esteem, insecure, and prone to jealousy in relationships. These individuals have difficulty maintaining relationships; it is hypothesized that they use violence to maintain control over their partners and engage in stalking behaviours to continue this domination after the relationships end. Their motives often reflect two opposing desires—to force their ex-partner back into the relationship and to exact some measure of revenge. Zona et al. (1993) described the behaviour as a "sustainable rage in response to a perceived narcissistic injury" (p. 901). Simple obsessional stalkers frequently attempt to contact their victims by phone and are also significantly more likely than other types to attempt face-to-face contact with their victims, which represents a significant risk for violence (Meloy & Gothard, 1995).

In contrast to the simple obsessional, the **love obsessional stalker** has no prior intimate relationship with his or her victim; the two are strangers or, at most, casual acquaintances (neighbours, co-workers, or classmates). Cases in which the stalker becomes familiar with the victim through the media—as John Hinckley, Jr, did—often involve celebrity stalking. After

simple obsessional stalker
A stalker who has had a relationship with his or her victim (e.g. former intimate partner); the most common type of stalker.

love obsessional stalker
A stalker who has no prior relationship with his or her victim; the parties are strangers or, at most, casual acquaintances (e.g. neighbours, co-workers).

viewing *Taxi Driver* multiple times, Hinckley became obsessed with Jodie Foster, one of the film's stars. He made several attempts to make contact with her but failed. On 30 March 1981, he attempted to assassinate US President Ronald Reagan in a bid to gain Foster's attention and affection. Hinckley wounded Reagan and others, including Press Secretary James Brady, who was paralyzed by the shooting. In August 2016 Hinckley was released from the psychiatric facility where he had spent the last 34 years.

Love obsessional stalkers often suffer from a mental illness, such as depression, and struggle with their self-image. They pursue their victims in a misguided hope of establishing a relationship and, by associating with famous people, raising their own level of worth. Love obsessional stalkers will typically send written correspondence, such as fan letters or poems, and may also attempt phone contact with their victims. They may even attempt to visit the victim's home to satisfy the fantasy that a relationship is possible, but they rarely attempt face-to-face contact.

The **erotomanic stalker** suffers from erotomania—which, as explained in Chapter 9, causes a person to believe that someone is in love with him or her. The obsession is not always based on sexual attraction but may reflect an idealized love; erotomanic stalkers believe that their victim is a "perfect match" and that their relationship was meant to be. In most cases of this type, the perpetrator is a female and the victim is a male of higher social status. Margaret Mary Ray, who believed she was married to David Letterman, was an erotomanic stalker (see the case study on page 217). Despite the bizarre behaviour of erotomanic stalkers, they are less likely than other stalkers to seek direct face-to-face contact with their victims and thus present a lower risk for violence (Wahl, 2003).

AP Photo

Photo 12.2   John Hinckley Jr has reportedly claimed that his attempt to assassinate Ronald Reagan was an "unprecedented demonstrations of love" and compared himself and Jodie Foster to Romeo and Juliet.

Intimate Partner Violence

The Extent and Nature of Intimate Partner Violence

The term *domestic violence* refers broadly to violence and aggression in a family context and includes a wide spectrum of behaviour, such as child abuse and neglect, elder abuse, spousal abuse, and violence among non-married intimate partners and family cohabitants (Wallace, 2004). Our focus is **intimate partner violence** (IPV), which is defined by the World Health Organization (WHO, 2002, para. 2) as "acts of physical aggression, psychological abuse, forced intercourse and other forms of sexual coercion, and various controlling behaviours such as isolating a person from family and friends or restricting access to information and assistance." The Centers for Disease Control and Prevention (CDC; Breiding, Basile, Smith, Black, & Mahendra, 2015, p. 11) defines IPV as "physical violence, sexual violence, stalking, and psychological aggression by a current or former intimate partner." The organization considers an intimate partner "a person with whom one has a close personal relationship that may be characterized by partners' emotional connectedness, regular contact, ongoing physical contact and sexual behaviour, identity as a couple, and familiarity and knowledge about each other's lives" (Breiling et al., 2015, p. 11).

These definitions emphasize that IPV is characterized by a range of behaviours that extend beyond physical and sexual aggression, highlighting the role of psychological and emotional abuse noted by other researchers (e.g. Williams, Richardson, Hammock, & Janit, 2012). Further, the CDC conceptualization of intimate partner is broad and allows for a consideration of violence in homosexual and dating relationships.

erotomanic stalker A stalker who suffers from erotomania and therefore delusionally believes that a relationship with his or her victim already exists.

intimate partner violence (IPV) Acts of physical, psychological, and/or sexual violence and other forms of controlling behaviour against a current or former intimate partner.

Available information on IPV rates and patterns clearly illustrates that this behaviour is a pressing and ongoing health concern. Police-reported data for 2011 show that there were 97,500 victims of IPV in Canada, representing a rate of 341 victims per 100,000 in the population (Sinha, 2013). Young women were disproportionately represented as victims across both age groups and types of IPV. In the United States, over one-third of women and just over one-quarter of men reported experiencing at least one form of IPV in their lifetime (Black et al., 2011). Data from the Crime Survey for England and Wales (Office for National Statistics, 2014) indicate that 7 per cent of women and 4 per cent of men had experienced some form of IPV over a one-year period, with 30 per cent of surveyed women and 16 per cent of men reporting that they had experienced some form of IPV since the age of 16.

Each relationship, violent or non-violent, is unique, which makes identifying patterns difficult. Nonetheless, some common elements of IPV have emerged, giving us more insight into the nature of this type of violence. Based on an examination of violent relationships, Meuer, Seymour, and Wallace (2002) identified a common sequence of interactions that occur in several distinct stages. In the "honeymoon phase," the abusive partner is flattering and extremely attentive, with early hints of obsessiveness or controlling behaviour that may be misinterpreted for passion. Over the course of the relationship, this attentiveness transitions into overtly controlling behaviour, increasingly demanding expectations, psychological abuse, and then physical abuse. According to the researchers, physical abuse is often quickly followed by a period of contrition, where the perpetrator expresses remorse and promises that the abuse will cease. Eventually, the physical and psychological abuse begins again, thereby creating a cycle that leaves the victim feeling helpless and socially isolated.

The observation that IPV occurs in a cyclical pattern also underlies the theory of **battered woman syndrome**, a psychological condition that has gained recognition over the past several decades. According to Lenore Walker (1984), who coined the term, women manifest certain psychological sequelae in response to persistent and serious physical and mental abuse by their intimate partners. They become depressed, develop low self-esteem, and gradually begin to feel powerless to alter their situation. Walker explains that many women stay with abusive partners because of their perceived helplessness and may even accept the blame for their victimization.

Two important streams of psychological theory shaped Walker's concept of battered woman syndrome: learned helplessness and the cycle of abuse. Psychologist Martin Seligman (1975) developed his influential theory on **learned helplessness** while working at Cornell University in the 1960s. The term refers to a psychological condition in which an individual learns to accept his or her current situation as something that is unchangeable regardless of the course of conduct he or she adopts. In other words, the individual believes that nothing can be done to alter his or her situation. For example, a student struggling in his or her studies may begin to believe that no amount of effort will result in a good grade and eventually give up.

Seligman (1975) developed his theory while conducting research with dogs. In his study, some dogs were placed in cages that had a small barrier dividing it down the middle. When a tone sounded, electric shocks were administered through the floor. The dog could easily escape the shock by jumping over the barrier to the other side. In another condition, the dogs were unable to jump to a safe location and avoid the shock. Seligman noticed that these dogs eventually stopped trying to escape and simply lay on the floor of the cage, absorbing the shocks. In essence, the dogs "learned" that they were helpless (Seligman & Maier, 1967).

Seligman and other investigators claim that learned helplessness triggers other psychological problems, such as depression. This research is the basis of battered woman syndrome.

battered woman syndrome
The term for the collection of psychological responses commonly experienced by female victims of persistent and serious IPV, including depression, low-self-esteem, and powerlessness.

learned helplessness
A psychological condition in which an individual learns to accept his or her current conditions or situation as unchangeable regardless of his or her actions.

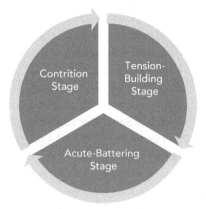

Figure 12.1 Lenore Walker's cycle of abuse

Victims of IPV are often subjected to unpredictable assaults, cut off from friends and family, and financially controlled by their abusive partners. Walker argued that these women undergo a psychological process similar to the one experienced by Seligman's dogs and "learn" helplessness. They come to believe that there is nothing they can do to escape or change their situation.

Walker (1984) based her **cycle of abuse theory** on a series of comprehensive interviews conducted with abused women. Similar to the observations made by Meuer and colleagues (2002), the theory depicts abusive relationships proceeding through a distinct and predictable pattern of interactions that unfold in three stages. During the **tension-building stage**, interactions between the partners become increasingly tense. The abusive partner is irritable, critical of the victim, and intermittently explodes over trivial things. For example, he or she may complain bitterly about the quality of dinner, criticize his or her partner's physical appearance, and scream in rage when a glass of milk is spilled. During the **acute-battering stage**, the victim experiences various forms of abuse—physical, psychological, or sexual—at the hands of his or her partner. This stage is followed by the **contrition stage**, when the abusive partner apologizes, promises to change, and (in many cases) lavishes gifts on the victim in an effort to persuade him or her to stay. According to Walker, this cycle repeats over and over again in the same fashion, except that the seriousness of violence steadily increases. The repetitive pattern creates an expectancy among victims and they begin to anticipate the violence, which they feel less and less capable of stopping.

Typology of Spousal Assaulters

Several researchers have attempted to create a typology of spousal assaulters based on their observable behavioural and personality characteristics (e.g. Dutton, 1995a, 1995b; Gottman, Jacobson, Rushe, & Shortt, 1995; Holtzworth-Munroe & Stuart, 1994; Saunders, 1992). Don Dutton (1998, 2007), a Canadian psychologist and expert on IPV, summarized much of the research on typologies in *The Abusive Personality*. Based on their review of the literature, Fowler and Westen (2011) suggest that at least two major subtypes of abusive men exist: psychopathic men who use instrumental violence in and out of intimate relationships (see Dutton, 1995a, 1995b) and men with borderline personality features and an insecure attachment history that manifest in patterns of jealousy and anger. The most frequently cited typology was developed by Holtzworth-Munroe and Stuart (1994), who identified three major categories of male spousal assaulters—family-only, dysphoric/

cycle of abuse theory The theory of intimate partner violence, proposed by Lenore Walker, that abusive relationships exhibit a predictable cycle of behaviour characterized by the following three stages: tension-building, acute-battering, and contrition.

tension-building stage The first stage in Lenore Walker's cycle of abuse theory; characterized by the abusive partner becoming increasingly tense, irritable, angry, and psychologically abusive.

acute-battering stage The second stage in Lenore Walker's cycle of abuse theory; characterized by the abusive partner subjecting the victim to various forms of physical, psychological, or sexual abuse.

contrition stage The final stage in Lenore Walker's cycle of abuse theory; characterized by the abusive partner trying to persuade the victim to remain in the relationship by apologizing, promising to change, and, in many cases, lavishing gifts on him or her.

borderline, and generally antisocial—that are distinguished by the seriousness and frequency of domestic violence, the generality of their violence or extent to which they are violent outside the domestic context, and the presence or absence of psychopathology.

According to Holtzworth-Munroe and Stuart (1994), the **family-only assaulter** is generally not violent outside the household and, compared to the other two types, engages in less frequent and less serious levels of violence against his spouse and family members. The violence is often a response to situational stressors or frustration. Psychologically, this assaulter does not exhibit any serious psychopathology or substance use problems. His violence usually reflects cognitive distortions and poor coping and communication skills. He is the least likely spousal assaulter in this typology to have a criminal record.

The **dysphoric/borderline assaulter** is emotionally dependent on the relationship and often exhibits mental health problems. These assaulters frequently engage in moderate to severe violence, including both psychological and sexual abuse. Although the violence is typically confined to a domestic context, it can extend outside the family. This type of assaulter often shows signs of psychopathology, such as **dysphoria**, or negative mood states, such as depression.

Dutton (1995a, 1995b) argues that borderline personality features frequently characterize spousal assaulters. According to the *DSM-5* (APA, 2013), **borderline personality disorder** is a persistent pattern of unstable interpersonal relationships, self-image, and affects and discernible impulsivity that exists in several contexts and begins by early adulthood. To be formally diagnosed with this disorder, an individual must exhibit five or more of the symptoms listed in Table 12.2. Dutton (1995a, 1995b) explains that these individuals tend to be excessively dependent on their intimate relationships, crave control, and fear abandonment and rejection by their partners. If they perceive their relationship as threatened, they experience intense jealousy and humiliation.

family-only assaulter One of three male spousal assaulter types identified by Holtzworth-Munroe and Stuart; an assaulter who engages in abusive behaviour in the household but generally not outside the domestic sphere and whose abusive behaviour reflects problems with coping skills and cognitions.

dysphoric/borderline assaulter One of three male spousal assaulter types identified by Holtzworth-Munroe and Stuart; an assaulter who engages in moderate to serious forms of abusive behaviour in the domestic sphere and exhibits serious mental health problems (e.g. borderline personality disorder).

dysphoria A mental state characterized by a negative mood, such as depression.

borderline personality disorder A persistent pattern of unstable interpersonal relationships, self-image, and affects and discernible impulsivity that begins by early adulthood and exists in several contexts. Symptoms include chronic feelings of emptiness, affective instability, identity disturbance, and frantic efforts to avoid real or imagined abandonment.

Table 12.2 *DSM-5* borderline personality disorder diagnostic criteria

A pervasive pattern of instability of interpersonal relationships, self-image, and affects, and marked impulsivity, beginning by early adulthood and present in a variety of contexts, as indicated by five (or more) of the following:

1. Frantic efforts to avoid real or imagined abandonment (*Note:* Do not include suicidal or self-mutilating behaviour covered in Criterion 5.)

2. A pattern of unstable and intense interpersonal relationships characterized by alternating between extremes of idealization and devaluation.

3. Identity disturbance: markedly and persistently unstable self-image or sense of self.

4. Impulsivity in at least two areas that are potentially self-damaging (e.g., spending, sex, substance abuse, reckless driving, binge eating). (*Note:* Do not include suicidal or self-mutilating behaviour covered in Criterion 5.)

5. Recurrent suicidal behaviour, gestures, or threats, or self-mutilating behaviour.

6. Affective instability due to a marked reactivity of mood (e.g., intense episodic dysphoria, irritability, or anxiety usually lasting a few hours and only rarely more than a few days).

7. Chronic feelings of emptiness.

8. Inappropriate, intense anger or difficulty controlling anger (e.g., frequent displays of temper, constant anger, recurrent physical fights).

9. Transient, stress-related paranoid ideation or severe dissociative symptoms.

Source: Reprinted with permission from the *Diagnostic and Statistical Manual of Mental Disorders*, Fifth Edition, (Copyright 2013). American Psychiatric Association.

The **generally violent/antisocial assaulter** frequently exhibits violence that can range from moderate to severe. The main distinguishing feature of these assaulters is that they engage in general violence. In other words, they are violent inside and outside the relationship, making extensive criminal histories that extend beyond spousal violence common. With respect to psychopathology, this type of assaulter often has serious substance abuse problems and may show psychopathic characteristics.

generally violent/antisocial assaulter One of three male spousal assaulter types identified by Holtzworth-Munroe and Stuart; an assaulter who is frequently violent in intimate relationships and other contexts.

Theories of Stalking and Intimate Partner Violence

As you may recall from Chapter 5, attachment theory proposes that our early childhood relationships and bonds exert a strong influence over our capacity to form meaningful relationships as adults. While individuals who form secure attachments in childhood are trusting and secure in their adult relationships, insecure attachment patterns result in long-term maladaptive interpersonal functioning. Meloy (1992) describes stalking as "an extreme disorder of attachment" (pp. 37–38). Indeed, stalking behaviour that emerges after a failed romantic relationship often represents a misguided attempt to maintain an attachment that the other party wishes to terminate. Support for Meloy's view is bolstered by a large body of empirical research establishing a relationship among insecure attachment styles, borderline personality traits, and IPV (Dutton, 1998; Dutton et al., 1994). Individuals with preoccupied or disorganized/fearful styles of attachment are more prone to jealousy and insecurity in their intimate relationships, which may in turn fuel extremely maladaptive responses to rejection or a break-up, including psychological and physical abuse (Dennison & Stewart, 2006; Kienlen, 1998; Kienlen et al., 1997; Patton et al., 2010). Further, studies show that insecure attachment patterns are more frequently observed among samples of stalkers than other offender and non-offender populations (MacKenzie et al., 2008; Tonin, 2004). These patterns have also been identified as precursors to interpersonal violence and stalking in intimate relationships (Dutton et al., 1994; Dutton & Winstead, 2006; Dye & Davis, 2003).

Several researchers—most notably, Dutton (1995a, 1995b)—have adapted and applied social learning theory (see Chapter 7) to IPV and stalking. According to this theory, we learn new behaviours by observing our families, neighbours, and the media. In relation to stalking and IPV, we detect specific behaviours (e.g. hitting, emotional abuse) and attitudes from these sources. For example, children may witness their fathers using physical and emotional aggression in their households and may conclude from media representations of dating and relationships that boys should be dominant and aggressive. We know from our discussion of learning earlier in the text that observed and reinforced behaviours are more likely to be used in the future.

Dutton (1995a, 1995b) argued that instigators and regulators of aggression also play a role in the development of IPV. **Instigators** are events or stimuli in the environment that trigger learned behaviours. **Aversive instigators** produce specific emotional responses (e.g. anger, jealousy) that may initiate IPV, and **incentive instigators** act as perceived rewards for abusive behaviour (e.g. withdrawal of unwanted behaviours, maintenance of control or power). **Regulators** of aggression refer to various forms of punishment that potentially inhibit IPV if present or enacted. Because abuse in the context of relationships typically occurs in private domestic settings, regulators that might otherwise help to inhibit it are largely absent. Moreover, many critics argue that society has broad cultural supports for negative attitudes and behaviours toward women that may impede the regulation of IPV.

instigators Events or stimuli in the environment that trigger learned behaviours.

aversive instigators Cues in the environment that produce specific negative emotional responses that may trigger intimate partner violence.

incentive instigators Cues in the environment that act as perceived rewards for abusive behaviour.

regulators Various forms of punishment that potentially inhibit intimate partner violence if present or enacted.

Sexual Violence

The Extent and Nature of Sexual Violence

sexual violence A threatened, attempted, or actual sexual act against another person without his or her consent.

Sexual violence is defined as a threatened, attempted, or actual sexual act with another person without his or her consent (Basile, Smith, Brieding, Black, & Mahendra, 2014; Boer, Hart, Kropp, & Webster, 1997). There are two main elements to this definition: the presence of a sexual act and the absence of consent (Boer et al., 1997). With respect to the first, sexual acts encompass both contact and non-contact behaviours (Basile et al., 2014). Sexual contact includes behaviours that involve penetration or the intentional touching of a person's genitalia, breasts, or buttocks regions, either directly or through clothing. Non-sexual contact refers to other acts, such as sexual communications (e.g. exhibitionism, obscene phone calls) and violations of sexual privacy (e.g. voyeurism, posting sexually explicit images of the person). The second element can arise in several ways. Some victims are unwilling to consent and are coerced, threatened, or physically forced to engage in unwanted sexual acts. Other victims may be unable to consent due to a mental disability (including being under age) or lack of awareness, as might occur if the person is unconscious or surreptitiously being watched or filmed.

Sexual violence affects a substantial number of people every year in North America and elsewhere in the world. For example, the sexual victimization rates per thousand people for men and women in Canada in 2014 were 5 and 37, respectively. Although these figures may not sound large, they correspond to approximately 80,000 men and 550,000 women annually (Perreault, 2015). Similar rates are reported for the United States and England and Wales (Black et al., 2011; UK Ministry of Justice, 2013). In the United States, where lifetime estimates are available, as many as 1.3 million men and 22 million women are believed to be the target of a serious assault involving attempted or actual sexual penetration during their life (Black et al., 2011).

The overwhelming majority of sexual violence victims are women. Data from official police records and victimization surveys in both Canada and the United States consistently find that 85 per cent or more of all sexual violence victims are women (Kong, Johnson, Beattie, & Cardillo, 2003; Planty, Langton, Krebs, Berzofsky, & Smiley-McDonald, 2013; Sinha, 2013). The risk of sexual victimization is generally highest during the early teens and then declines from this age on (Kong et al., 2003; UK Ministry of Justice, 2013; Perreault, 2015; Planty et al., 2013). In most cases, the victim knows the perpetrator, who is usually an acquaintance, relative, or intimate partner (Black et al., 2011; Kong et al., 2003; Planty et al., 2013). Canadian data suggest that young children, especially girls, are most likely to be sexually victimized by a family member, whereas teens and adults are most often victimized by an acquaintance (Kong et al., 2003). Depending on the report, strangers account for between 20 and 45 per cent of identified perpetrators, with higher figures found for adult victims and less serious forms of sexual violence (Black et al., 2011; Kong et al., 2003; Perreault, 2015; Planty et al., 2013).

While most victims are female, the opposite is true for sexual violence perpetrators. Data show that males comprise more than 90 per cent of all sex offenders in Canada (Cotter & Beaupré, 2014; Perreault, 2015). Alcohol or other intoxicating substances were reportedly used by the perpetrator in about 40 per cent of cases in Canada and the United States (Kong et al., 2003; Planty et al., 2013). Most officially reported incidents of sexual violence do not involve physical injuries (Sinha, 2013). For example, slightly more than

75 per cent of the offences reported to police in Canada involved unwanted sexual touching (Kong et al., 2003). Similarly, less than 1 per cent of surveyed women in England and Wales reported being a victim of the most serious sexual offences in the prior 12 months (Ministry of Justice, 2013). Weapons are reported present in less than 15 per cent of cases (Perreault, 2015; Planty et al., 2013). It is important to emphasize that an absence of serious physical injury does not suggest that other forms of sexual violence are minor.

Sex Offenders

Rapists

In this text, the term *rapist* refers to an adult who sexually assaults someone 16 years of age or older (e.g. Prentky & Knight, 1991). A recurring theme throughout our discussion is the incredibly diverse nature of offenders, even with respect to a specific group, such as rapists. Knight and Prentky (1990; Knight, Prentky, & Cerce, 1994) developed the **Massachusetts Treatment Center (MTC) typology**, which uses theoretical and exploratory ideas about men who commit rape, as well as observable behavioural and motivational indicators, to categorize this heterogeneous group. Their model was statistically tested over several years and its categories further refined. The revised scheme, known as MTC: R3, classifies adult male rapists into four major categories and nine subtypes (see Figure 12.2).

The first major category, the **opportunistic rapist type** (types 1 and 2), describes an adult male rapist who exhibits a general pattern of impulsive behaviour. Rapes committed by these men are opportunistic and may occur in the context of another crime. For example, an opportunistic rapist might break into a residence with the sole intent of stealing valuables but impulsively commit rape if he unexpectedly encounters an occupant. Usually, this type of rapist does not use any more violence than is necessary to force the victim to comply. This does not mean that no violence is present, as all acts of sexual assault are inherently violent. It simply means that there is a lower level of violence relative to some of the other types. The opportunistic rapist, as with all the categories, can be further classified based on his level of social competence (Knight et al., 1994; Knight & Prentky, 1990).

Massachusetts Treatment Center (MTC) typology
An offender typology that categorizes adult male rapists based on observable behavioural and motivational indicators into four broad groups: opportunistic, pervasively angry, sexually motivated, and vindictive.

opportunistic rapist type
The type of adult male rapist who exhibits a general pattern of impulsive behaviour and typically commits his sexual offences in the context of another crime using lower levels of violence. The category can be further distinguished based on levels of social competency.

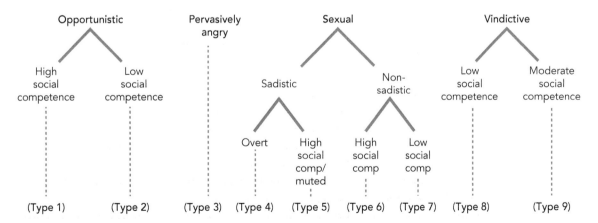

Figure 12.2 The MTC: R3 adult male rapist typology

Source: *Sexual deviance: issues and controversies* by Hudson, Stephen M. ; Laws, D. Richard ; Ward, Tony Reproduced with permission of Sage Publications, Inc in the format Republish in a book via Copyright Clearance Center.

pervasively angry rapist type The type of adult male rapist who has a high level of generalized anger and frequently engages in antisocial and violent behaviour that includes sexual violence against women.

sexually motivated rapist type The type of adult male rapist who is motivated by sexually deviant fantasies. This type can be further distinguished based on levels of social competency and the presence or absence of sadistic expressions of these fantasies.

vindictive rapist type The type of adult male rapist who is a misogynist and whose sexual offences are characterized by a high level of anger specifically intended to humiliate and degrade women. This category can be further distinguished by levels of social competency.

intra-familial child molester A person who sexually abuses a biologically related child or a child for whom he or she assumes a parental role.

extra-familial child molester A person who sexually abuses a child outside his or her family.

The **pervasively angry rapist** (type 3) describes an adult male rapist who exhibits a high level of anger and typically has a history of general antisocial and violent criminal behaviour. High levels of extra-violence—that is, excessive violence beyond what is required to force victim compliance—is evident in their rapes. As a consequence, pervasively angry rapists often inflict much more serious injuries on their victims than other types of rapists.

In the MTC: R3 typology, **sexually motivated rapists** are driven by deviant sexual fantasies. This group of rapists is further divided into four subtypes. Sadistic rapists are motivated by violent sexual fantasies that they explicitly act upon during the offence (overt) or merely serve as implicit motivators (muted). Non-sadistic rapists may be motivated by fantasies of omnipotence, for example, but are usually not sexually aroused by the physical suffering or humiliation of their victims. These rapists are categorized by their level of social competence.

The **vindictive rapist type** describes an adult male rapist who exhibits a high level of anger specifically directed at women. This rapist has a sense of entitlement in regards to intimate relationships and other areas of life and attributes his failures and shortcomings to women. He rapes women to humiliate and degrade them.

Child Molesters

A child molester is a significantly older adult who engages in sexual acts with someone who is below the legal age for providing consent (Lanning, 1992). As we shall see shortly, a child molester may or may not be a pedophile. The nature of sexual offences against children varies widely, and offender characteristics differ depending on victim characteristics and the nature of sexual interests. Child molesters can be distinguished from one another based on whether they are intra-familial or extra-familial. An **intra-familial child molester** sexually abuses his or her biologically related children or children for whom he or she assumes some parental role. **Extra-familial child molesters** sexually abuse children outside their family.

Child sex offenders may also be differentiated from one another based on the primary sexual interests they demonstrate (Camilleri & Quinsey, 2008). A fixated child molester is one whose primary sexual interest is prepubescent children (i.e. not reached puberty; Groth, Hobson, & Gary, 1982). In other words, they prefer sexual activity with sexually immature children. These offenders usually meet the DSM definition of pedophilia because they have recurrent urges, fantasies, or behaviours involving sexual activity with children. Regressed child molesters, by comparison, normally have a sexual interest in age-appropriate peers, but due to a psychosocial stressor such as marital problems, they exploit children who may be readily accessible.

Female Sex Offenders

Most research on sexual violence focuses on males as perpetrators, and only a comparatively small amount has examined female sex offenders. Existing research on the latter reveals that their victims are largely males and tend to be child relatives or acquaintances (Cortoni & Hanson, 2005; Vandiver & Kercher, 2004). Some research also suggests that female sex offenders are less likely to reoffend (Cortoni & Hanson, 2005; Freeman & Sandler, 2008) and more likely to report being sexually abused as a child than are male sex offenders (Vandiver & Kercher, 2004). Typologies of female sex offenders have been developed; for example, Vandiver and Kercher (2004) identified the teacher–lover/heterosexual nurturer—female sex offenders who exploit a position of trust to sexually abuse adolescent boys—as the most frequent female sex offender category (see also Matthews, Matthews, & Speltz, 1989).

Internet Sex Offenders

Somewhat surprisingly, research on Internet sex offenders is still rather limited. According to Robertiello and Terry (2007), the Internet often serves as a tool for child sex offenders, who use it to view and post child pornography and lure victims. A meta-analysis of studies comparing online and offline sex offenders identified youth and unemployment as significant risk factors for the former. The same study found that Internet offenders were disproportionately Caucasian and, despite evidencing higher levels of victim empathy than other sex offender categories, they exhibited greater sexual deviancy (Babchishin, Hanson, & Hermann, 2011).

Theories of Sexual Violence

Deviant Sexual Preference and Sexual Offending

According to the **deviant sexual preference hypothesis**, men who engage in sexually deviant and violent behaviour are motivated by a recurrent and intense pattern of deviant sexual preferences (Laws & Marshall, 1990; Ward, Polaschek, & Beech, 2006). Paraphilia, introduced in Chapter 11, is central to our discussion of deviant sexual preferences. The *DSM-5* describes **paraphilia** as recurrent and intense sexual urges, fantasies, or behaviours to anomalous or inappropriate stimuli (APA, 2013). Various paraphilic disorders are described in Table 12.3.

Sexual fantasies are a central component of the deviant sexual preference theory. Numerous researchers have argued that deviant sexual fantasies play a role in the acquisition and maintenance of deviant sexual preferences (Laws & Marshall, 1990; McGuire et al., 1965). There have also been several attempts to define both terms (Bartels & Gannon, 2011). According to Leitenberg and Henning (1995) a **sexual fantasy** is "any mental imagery that is sexually arousing or erotic to the individual" (p. 470). However, fantasy is an integral part of all sexual behaviour (Holmes & Holmes, 2002). Identifying what constitutes a deviant sexual fantasy has proven a difficult undertaking. Fantasies of domination and/or control, which might be viewed as deviant or unusual by some segments of society, do not necessarily constitute the types of deviant sexual fantasies that may increase a risk for sexual offending. They may be more illustrative of the consensual sadomasochism, bondage,

deviant sexual preference hypothesis A theory of sexual violence that posits that men who engage in sexually deviant and violent behaviour are motivated by a recurrent and intense pattern of deviant sexual preferences.

paraphilia Recurrent and intense sexual urges, fantasies, or behaviours to anomalous or inappropriate stimuli.

sexual fantasy Any mental imagery that an individual experiences as sexually arousing or erotic.

Table 12.3 Paraphilic disorders

A person experiences recurrent and intense sexual urges, fantasies, or behaviours that involve . . .

Voyeurism	Surreptitiously observing people who are naked, undressing, or engaging in sexual activity.
Exhibitionism	Exposing one's genitals to an non-consenting person.
Frotteurism	Touching or rubbing against a non-consenting person.
Fetishism	Using inanimate objects or normally non-sexual parts of the body.
Sexual masochism	Being the target of humiliation, pain, or other forms of suffering.
Sexual sadism	Inflicting humiliation, pain, or suffering on another person.
Pedophilia	Sexual activity with prepubescent children.
Zoophilia	Sexual activity with animals.
Necrophilia	Sexual activity with corpses.

Source: Adapted from American Psychiatric Association. (2013). *Diagnostic and statistical manual of mental disorders* (5th ed.). Washington, DC: Author.

or fetish play communities. Fantasies that involve non-consensual domination, feelings of omnipotence, violence, or the fear and/or humiliation of others are more characteristic of the deviant sexual fantasies that may play a role in sexual offending. Based on an extensive review of the relevant literature, Bartels and Gannon (2011) define a high-risk sexual fantasy as "any mental imagery involving an elaborate sexual scenario or script with distorted aims and/or means, whose repeated use can increase the risk of the fantasizer committing a sexual offense in the presence of certain context and/or dispositions" (p. 553).

Both classical conditioning and operant conditioning, discussed in Chapter 7, have been used to identify how deviant sexual fantasies and preferences are acquired and maintained, respectively (e.g. Laws & Marshall, 1990). Based on interviews with 45 sexually deviant men, McGuire and colleagues (1965) noted that their initial sexual experiences were often deviant in nature with a strong stimulus value. For example, this experience might involve a pre- or early adolescent boy masturbating after accidentally glimpsing a female neighbour undressing. In terms of classical conditioning, the non-consensual viewing of a woman undressing is a conditioned stimulus and masturbation is the unconditioned stimulus that leads to the unconditioned response of sexual arousal. Repeated pairing of the act of voyeurism with masturbation could result in the development of a conditioned response, namely, sexual arousal from the non-consensual sexual behaviour of voyeurism.

Conditioned behaviours eventually disappear through extinction. Deviant sexual preference theory proposes that deviant patterns of sexual arousal are maintained through operant learning processes. Once a deviant pattern of arousal is established, individuals often supplement it with sexual fantasies. Pairing the deviant sexual fantasy with masturbation, for example, will act as a form of positive reinforcement and ultimately maintain a deviant pattern of sexual arousal beyond initial acquisition (see Ward et al., 2006).

The empirical research examining the relationship among deviant sexual fantasies, deviant sexual preferences, and sexual offending is inconclusive. Nevertheless, some studies suggest that deviant sexual fantasies are part of a process that increases the risk of sexual offending, with some sex offenders progressing from general sexual fantasies prior to any offending to offence-based or deviant sexual fantasies leading up to their first sexual offence (Bartels & Gannon, 2011; Gee, Devilly, & Ward, 2004). Case studies and reviews of existing research indicate that deviant sexual fantasies may interact with other risk factors, such as early traumatic experiences, to produce sexual offending (Carabellese, Maniglio, Greco, & Catanesi, 2011; Maniglio, 2010). A study by Warren, Hazelwood, and Dietz (1996) found evidence of sadistic sexual offenders acting out their violent sexual fantasies in some of their offences. Yet other research reveals that some sex offenders report the same sexual fantasies commonly expressed by heterosexual adult males (Sheldon & Howitt, 2008).

The relationship between paraphilic disorders and sexual offending is also complex and poorly understood. Although research demonstrates a consistent link between pedophilia and child sex offences, there is little evidence of a clear association between other paraphilic disorders and specific categories of sex offenders (Hanson & Bussiere, 1998). In a recent study of 139 high-risk sexual offenders in Canada, Michael Woodworth and colleagues (2103) examined the influence of sexual fantasy and paraphilias on sexual offending. Offenders were divided into three categories: exclusive child molesters, exclusive rapist offenders, and mixed sexual offenders. The researchers found that a large portion of offenders reported deviant sexual fantasies, and those who reported violent sexual fantasies were more likely to have committed a violent sexual offence. Another interesting finding is that offender type was related to the number of paraphilia identified. Offenders in the exclusive rapist category were most likely to have no paraphilia, whereas child sex offenders were likely to have one and the mixed offenders to have two or more.

Cognitive Theories of Sexual Offending

In Chapter 8 we discussed the concept of the script, an organized unit of knowledge or mental template that lays out the expected sequence of behaviour for a particular social situation. Comparatively, a **schema** is a broader cognitive structure that helps us organize general information into meaningful categories, allowing us to process and interpret it in new settings and experiences more efficiently. According to Mann and Beech (2003), a schema contains "beliefs or attitudes that follow a similar theme or pattern that [has] developed as a result of trying to make sense of early life experiences" (p. 145). We have schemas to help us organize and understand sexual behaviour, sexuality, and gender. For example, young men develop schemas about consent and "masculinity" through their interactions with family, peers, and media.

Several cognitive theories of sexual violence have been developed. The **schema-based model of sexual assault** proposes that dysfunctional schemas about sexuality and sexual behaviour interact with environmental variables and lead to sexual offending (Mann & Beech, 2003). According to this model, schemas serve as a distal factor largely interacting with more proximate risk factors such as empathy or emotional regulation. As shown in Figure 12.3, early developmental experiences influence the development of dysfunctional

schema A cognitive structure that helps us organize and interpret general information.

schema-based model of sexual assault A theory of sexual assault that proposes sexual offending is precipitated by dysfunctional schemas about sexuality and sexual behaviour interacting with environmental variables.

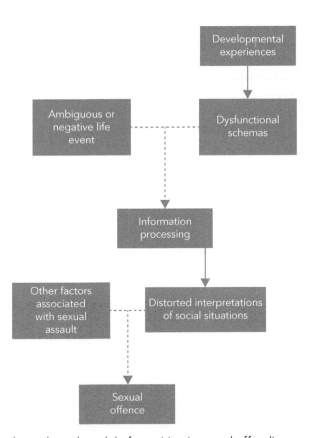

Figure 12.3 A schema-based model of cognition in sexual offending

Source: *Sexual deviance: issues and controversies* by Hudson, Stephen M. ; Laws, D. Richard ; Ward, Tony Reproduced with permission of Sage Publications, Inc in the format Republish in a book via Copyright Clearance Center.

or deviant schemas. A pre-adolescent boy who obtains most of his early knowledge about sex from pornography may make erroneous assumptions about normal or appropriate sexual behaviour. Images in film, television, and fashion magazines may lead to the development of dysfunctional schemas about body image (see the "Researching" box). Individuals with dysfunctional schemas may be more likely to process social information inaccurately and offer grossly distorted rationalizations for their behaviour that are consistent with their inaccurate beliefs. The figure shows that these cognitive distortions interact with a variety of other factors in ways that often result in sexual offending. In other words, dysfunctional schemas play a smaller role in sexual offending than do risk factors such as impulsivity or emotional regulation.

Researching Criminal and Violent Behaviour

Sex and Violence in Pornography and Slasher Horror Films

The development of dysfunctional schemas about gender, sex, and sexuality and links to media content is a well-studied subject. Concerns about ties between pornography consumption and sexual aggression have been debated for decades. Even Ted Bundy infamously suggested that pornography played a significant role in his homicidal behaviour (Marshall, 2000). Nevertheless, attempts to understand potential connections have been complicated by differences in the studies' operational definition of pornography (Bridges, Wosnitzer, Scharrer, Sun, & Liberman, 2010). For instance, Seto, Maric, and Barbaree (2001) distinguish between erotica and pornography. Like many other attempts to define pornography, this distinction focuses on the presence or absence of violence, degradation, and consent (see also Bridges et al., 2010). According to the researchers, erotica is sexually explicit material that "depicts adult men and women consensually involved in pleasurable, non-violent, non-degrading, sexual interactions" (Seto et al., 2001, p. 37). In contrast, pornography is sexually explicit material characterized by the inclusion of violence, degradation, and/or non-consensual sexual activity. Content analyses of popular pornographic movies have found high levels of physical and verbal aggression, with women being the primary target (Bridges et al., 2010).

To date, empirical research has found little evidence of a direct causal relationship between viewing pornography and sexual aggression (Seto et al., 2001). Most research suggests that pornography's impact on sexual aggression depends on several factors. Ed Donnerstein, a psychologist who has conducted extensive research on media–violence links, proposes that a relationship between pornography and sexual aggression depends on the level of arousal generated by the pornographic content, the level of aggressive content, and the reactions of victims depicted in the pornographic material (Donnerstein, 1980, 1984; Donnerstein & Berkowitz, 1981; Linz, Donnerstein, & Penrod, 1984; Malamuth & Donnerstein, 1982). More recent research suggests that pornography consumption may influence sexual aggression indirectly by increasing attitudes supporting violence against women (e.g. Malamuth, Hald, & Koss, 2012). In addition, the effects may be observed only among men who are already predisposed to sexual aggression (Hald & Malamuth, 2015; Malamuth et al., 2012; Vega & Malamuth, 2007). Hald and Malamuth (2015) found that viewing pornography in the past together with recent exposure in a research setting significantly predicted attitudes supporting violence against women but only among men who were low in agreeableness, one of the big five personality traits (McCrae & Costa, 1999; see Chapter 6).

The slasher subgenre of horror film, which includes the *Friday the 13th* and *Halloween* series, has similarly faced criticism for its depictions of violence against women. Early content analyses of such films suggest that female characters are less likely to be victimized than male characters and more likely to survive violence (Cowan & O'Brien, 1990; Molitor & Sapolsky, 1993; Sapolsky, Molitor, & Luque, 2003; Weaver, 1991). Yet more recent examinations report that female characters are the more frequent victims of violence (Welsh, 2009, 2010). Welsh (2009) studied a sample of 50 slasher films and found that scenes of violence involving female characters were longer in duration and tended to linger on their suffering, with more extensive use of close-ups. Scenes involving a juxtaposition of both violent and sexual imagery were also more likely to involve a female character. In a follow-up analysis of the same sample, Welsh (2010) found that female characters involved in sexual activity were significantly less likely to survive than were those not involved in any sexual activity. Death scenes were also longer on average for the first group. These differences were not observed for male characters.

These findings fit the research literature on the media portrayals of women, the role of schemas concerning traditional gender roles, and the impact of these portrayals on real-life victims. A large body of research suggests that media depictions of female victims overwhelmingly reinforce negative gender stereotypes (Anastasio & Costa, 2004; Dietz, 1998; Milkie, 1994). Researchers have observed that exposure to sexually violent media (films, music videos, television shows, song lyrics) can have a number of detrimental effects. It may lead to emotional desensitization (Linz, Donnerstein, & Adams, 1989; Linz et al., 1984, 1988); it appears to increase adversarial sexual beliefs, aggressive thoughts, and male stereotypic dominance behaviour (Barongan & Hall, 1995; Golde, Strassberg, & Turner, 2000; Johnson, Adams, Ashburn, & Reed, 1995; Mulac, Jansma, & Linz, 2002; Peterson & Pfost, 1989); and it tends to promote negative views of and decrease sympathy for female victims (Krafka, Linz, Donnerstein, & Penrod, 1997; Linz et al., 1984, 1988, 1989).

Paramount/The Kobal Collection

Photo 12.3 Shots such as this one from *Friday the 13th Part VII: The New Blood* are typical in slasher movies, which were most popular in the 1970s and 1980s.

Another cognitive theory of sexual violence, developed by Tony Ward and colleagues (Ward, 2000; Ward & Keenan, 1999), focuses on **implicit theory**, a set of beliefs or schemas used to "explain, predict, and interpret interpersonal phenomenon" (Ward, 2000, p. 49). An implicit theory can be thought of as a specific type of schema that serves as a causal hypothesis—it is an idea that we form about why people's behaviour unfolds in certain ways. Unlike hypotheses derived from research, implicit theories are not tested or analyzed by individuals but are reinforced through an anecdotal process of selectively attending to evidence consistent with existing beliefs (Ward, 2000; Ward et al., 2006). For example, Ward and Keenan (1999) proposed a set of five implicit theories developed and held by child sex offenders, listed in Table 12.4.

In summary, cognitive theories of sexual violence look at the role of inaccurate and deviant attitudes, beliefs, and thought processes that influence the likelihood of sexual violence. The concept of a **rape myth**, an inaccurate and/or stereotypical attitude about sexual violence, is similar in principle to the cognitive distortions proposed by the schema-based model (Burt, 1980; Suarez & Gadalla, 2010). The belief that drunkenness signals consent or that women routinely lie about sexual assault are common examples of rape myths.

implicit theory A set of beliefs or schemas used to explain, predict, and interpret interpersonal phenomenon.

rape myth An inaccurate and/or stereotypical attitude or belief regarding sexual violence and victims of sexual violence.

Table 12.4 Implicit theories of child sex offenders	
Children as sexual objects	The belief that children are sexual beings with adult sexual motivations and are capable of desiring and enjoying sex.
Nature of harm	The belief that sexual molestation is beneficial or not harmful.
Uncontrollability	The belief that sexual behaviour and sexual offending is outside the offender's control.
Entitlement	The belief that the offender's wants or needs are more significant or important than those of other people.
Dangerous world	The belief that the world is a hostile and dangerous place where no one or only children can be trusted.

Source: Adapted from Ward, T., & Keenan, T. (1999). Child molesters' implicit theories. *Journal of Interpersonal Violence, 14*, 821–838.

These dysfunctional schemas develop through an ongoing socialization process; in other words, they are learned and reinforced. Feminist scholars have long discussed the existence of a rape culture that perpetuates dysfunctional or deviant ideas about gender, sexuality, and sexual violence across social institutions (e.g. family, education systems, politics, and media).

The Confluence Model of Sexual Aggression

American psychologist Neil Malamuth (2003) has conducted extensive research on sexual violence for five decades. Based on this large body of work, he proposed the **confluence model of sexual aggression**, an integrated causal model for sexual violence that proposes there are two distinct pathways that increase the risk or motivation to engage in sexual violence: hostile masculinity and an impersonal sexual orientation. The **hostile masculinity** pathway features attitudes and beliefs that accept violence against women. This general cognitive framework develops into a narcissistic personality characterized by hostile attitudes toward women, aggressive attitudes about sexual relationships, and sexual dominance. For example, men high in hostile masculinity are often easily angered by women. **Impersonal sexual orientation pathways** stem from an abusive home environment that initially manifests in early delinquent behaviour and later develops into impersonal views about sex and sexuality. That is, men high in impersonal sexual orientation do not view sex as a form of emotional intimacy but prefer casual, promiscuous sexual encounters and view sex as a game defined by "winners" and "losers."

According to Malamuth, Addison, and Koss (2000), the pathways may work independently or collectively. It is anticipated that, as the number of risk factors in the latter case increases, the risk for sexual aggression increases in kind (see Figure 12.4). The confluence model is consistent with other researchers' views that a good theory of sexual aggression probably incorporates a variety of risk factors (Ward et al., 2006), and there is existing research supporting a relationship between its pathways and sexual aggression (e.g. Abbey, Jacques-Tiura, & LeBreton, 2011).

Sex Offender Recidivism and Risk Factors

A large body of empirical research has been dedicated to identifying risk factors for sexual aggression and recidivism. Canadian psychologist Karl Hanson and his colleagues (Hanson & Bussiere, 1998; Hanson & Morton-Bourgon, 2005; Mann, Hanson, & Thorton, 2010) have conducted several meta-analyses that identified and organized major risk factors into

confluence model of sexual aggression An integrated theoretical model of sexual violence that proposes the risk for sexually violent behaviour is influenced by two distinct pathways of factors: hostile masculinity and an impersonal sexual orientation. These pathways may work independently or collectively.

hostile masculinity One of the pathways of risk factors in the confluence model of sexual aggression; refers to a general cognitive framework characterized by hostile attitudes and beliefs that accept violence against women.

impersonal sexual orientation pathway One of the pathways of risk factors in the confluence model of sexual aggression. Men high in this pathway do not view sex as a form of emotional intimacy and tend to prefer casual, promiscuous sexual encounters.

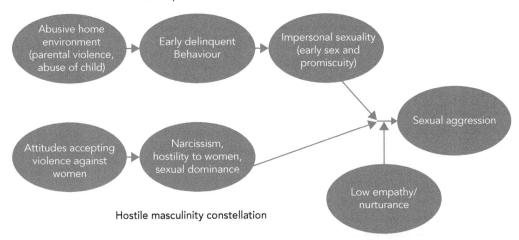

Figure 12.4 The confluence model of sexual aggression

Source: Malamuth, N. M. (2003). Criminal and non-criminal sexual aggressors: Integration psychopathy in a hierarchical-mediational confluence model. In R. A. Prentky, E. S. Janus, & M. C. Seto (Eds.), *Annals of the New York Academy of Sciences, Vol. 989, Sexually coercive behaviour: Understanding and management* (pp. 35–58). New York, NY: New York Academy of Sciences.

two categories: sexual deviancy and antisocial lifestyle factors. We discussed theories of sexual aggression based on deviant sexual preferences earlier in this chapter. According to Hanson and Morton-Bourgon (2005), **deviant sexual interests** refer to "enduring attractions to sexual acts that are illegal or highly unusual" (p. 1154). An orientation to deviant sexual arousal patterns has typically been assessed using **penile plethysmography (PPG)**, a psychophysiological measure of penile tumescence (i.e. an erection) as various stimuli—both sexually appropriate and inappropriate—are presented to an individual. Higher levels of penile tumescence in response to sexually inappropriate material indicate higher levels of deviant sexual interests (Lalumière, Harris, Quinsey, & Rice, 2005; Seto, 2008).

Several risk factors indicating deviant sexual preferences have been linked with sexual aggression and recidivism. For example, Mann, Hanson, and Thornton (2010) found that sexual pre-occupation, or intense and recurrent thoughts about sex in the absence of meaningful emotional connections, is a common risk factor. Other examples include sexual interest in prepubescent children, sexual sadism or sexualized violence, multiple sexual paraphilia, and the absence of emotionally intimate relationships with adults.

Antisocial lifestyle factors are more general patterns of antisocial behaviour and lifestyle problems, such as antisocial personality traits, impulsiveness, hostility and anger, employment difficulties, and a criminal history (Hanson & Bussiere, 1998; Hanson & Morton-Bourgon, 2005; Mann et al., 2010). According to Hanson and Morton-Bourgon (2005), this category represents a broader risk for not only sexual aggression but also general and violent (non-sexual) recidivism.

Risk assessment, discussed in greater detail in Chapter 13, refers to strategies for evaluating an offender's likelihood of reoffending and for developing strategies to manage and reduce this risk. The literature on risk assessment practices in the criminal justice system is large, and there are a number of approaches to risk assessment and specific tools. Furthermore, distinct risk assessment tools exist for general recidivism, violent recidivism, and specific offender categories (e.g. stalkers, sex offenders). Even within the specific practice

deviant sexual interests Persistent attractions to illegal or highly unusual sexual acts.

penile plethysmography (PPG) A psychophysiological measure of penile tumescence, or an erection, used to assess for deviant sexual preferences among sex offenders.

antisocial lifestyle factors A category of risk factors for sexual aggression and recidivism that includes general patterns of antisocial behaviour and lifestyle problems such as impulsivity, employment problems, and a criminal history.

of sex offender assessment, a number of risk assessment instruments have proliferated over the last 20 years. Over a hundred studies have been conducted with the express intent of better understanding the effectiveness of risk assessment measures with sex offenders. At this point, it is important to once again emphasize the diversity of sex offender populations. While some risk factors (e.g. general antisocial orientation) may have predictive validity across most subgroups, others may be unique or have greater predictive ability for specific offender types. Additionally, the predictive accuracy for the many approaches may vary (see Chapter 13). Existing evaluations of multiple studies have generally found that sex offender risk assessment measures exhibit moderate predictive accuracy for sexual recidivism (Hanson & Morton-Bourgon, 2009; Parent, Guay, & Knight, 2011).

Summary

1. Stalking may be defined as a pattern of repeated contact with another person that is unwanted and causes that person to reasonably fear for his or her safety or the safety of people known to him or her. Existing research shows that the majority of stalkers are male and the victims female. Stalking often occurs between former intimate partners and is an extension of domestic violence. Studies confirm that stalking encompasses a diverse range of behaviours, the most common being phone calls. While serious physical violence is infrequent, violence against victims is more likely to be observed in cases where offenders are stalking former intimate partners and/or struggling with substance abuse problems.

2. A typology developed by Zona, Sharma, and Lane (1993) identifies three major categories of stalkers that are distinguished according to the nature of the offender–victim relationship and the offender's psychological problems. The simple obsessional, the most common type of stalker, had prior relationship with the victim. This type of stalker is typically an insecure, jealous individual whose behaviour is an extension of the fear and control exercised in a previous intimate relationship. The love obsessional stalker has no prior relationship with the victim and may only know him or her from casual or infrequent encounters or through distant, indirect means such as the media (e.g. celebrity stalking). This stalker usually suffers from mental health problems, such as depression. Lastly, the erotomanic stalker suffers from the delusional belief that another individual (often of higher social status) is already in love with him or her.

3. Intimate partner violence (IPV) includes acts of physical, psychological, and/or sexual violence and other forms of controlling behaviour against a current or former intimate partner. Examinations of IPV patterns indicate that abusive relationships often feature a cycle of increasingly controlling and violent behaviour. Lenore Walker proposed a cycle of violence defined by three distinct stages that progress from periods of increasing tension and anger to acute stages of physically violent behaviour followed by a period of contrition and promises to change. According to Walker, these stages play out repeatedly and, as a result, the victim begins to feel helpless and uncertain about her ability to effect any change in or escape from the relationship, a psychological condition known as learned helplessness. The cycle of violence and learned helplessness underlie the concept of battered woman syndrome.

4. The most frequently cited typology of domestic abusers, developed by Holtzworth-Munroe and Stuart (1994), organizes offenders into three categories based on the generality of the exhibited violent behaviour, the severity and frequency of violence, and

the presence or absence of psychopathology. The violence of the family-only assaulter is generally confined to the household, less serious than the other two types, and stems from poor coping skills and distorted cognitive patterns. The dysphoric/borderline assaulter engages in more serious forms of IPV and exhibits mental health concerns, particularly personality problems and issues with depression and jealousy. Lastly, the generally violent/antisocial assaulter is frequently violent across a range of contexts and exhibits problems with substance abuse and antisocial/psychopathic traits.

5. Several psychological theories have been applied to IPV, such as attachment theory and Bandura's social learning theory. Meloy (1992) has described stalking as an attachment disorder, and research suggests that individuals with preoccupied or disorganized/fearful attachment styles may be more prone to jealousy and insecurity in intimate relationships. Social learning theory proposes that aggressive and abusive behaviours in intimate relationships are learned through an ongoing process of observation, reinforcement, and a lack of social regulation.

6. Sexual violence continues to be a pressing health and safety concern. Official police-reported crime statistics and self-report data from victimization surveys consistently find that younger women are disproportionately the victims of sexual violence and, in the majority of cases, the offender is a person known to the victim. The vast majority of perpetrators are male and many are intoxicated with alcohol or other substances at the time of the offence.

7. In the early 1990s Raymond A. Knight and Robert A. Prentky developed the Massachusetts Treatment (MTC) typology of adult male rapists. This model classifies adult male rapists into four broad categories—opportunistic, pervasively angry, sexually motivated, and vindictive—based on extensive research on behavioural and motivational indicators from past sex offences. For example, while the sexually motivated rapist is fuelled by deviant sexual fantasies often involving sadistic predilections, the vindictive rapist is a misogynistic offender who uses gendered and sexualized violence to degrade and humiliate women. Other typologies of male sex offenders (and other sex offender groups) offer insights into underlying causal factors and potential treatment paths.

8. In this chapter, we reviewed several different theories of sexual violence, including the deviant sexual preference hypothesis, cognitive theories, and the confluence model of sexual aggression. According to the deviant sexual preference hypothesis, male sex offenders are motivated by recurrent and intense patterns of deviant sexual preferences that are acquired and maintained through a complex interaction between classical and operant conditioning processes. Many sex offenders evidence distorted attitudes and beliefs about gender, sexuality, and sexual behaviour. One cognitive theory, the schema-based model of sexual assault, argues that sex offenders develop dysfunctional schemas about sexuality and sexual behaviour from various sources, such as the media, that result in distorted views of and rationalizations for deviant and aggressive sexual behaviour. Another cognitive theory focuses on implicit theories, which serve as dysfunctional causal hypotheses about the way people behave that some individuals subscribe to and that influence sexual aggression. The confluence model of sexual aggression proposes that there are two pathways of factors that influence the risk for sexual aggression—hostile masculinity and an impersonal sexual orientation.

9. Meta-analyses of existing research generally identify deviant sexual interests and antisocial lifestyle factors as the two broad categories of risk factors for sexual violence

and recidivism. Several indicators of deviant sexual preferences have been linked to sexual violence, including multiple sexual paraphilia, sexual sadism, sexual interest in prepubescent children, high levels of pre-occupation with sex, and lack of emotionally intimate relationships with adults. Several indicators generally associated with an antisocial lifestyle (e.g. impulsivity, hostility, and anger) have also been linked to sexual violence. Numerous risk assessment measures and approaches have been developed for the assessment and management of sex offenders, with research suggesting moderate predictive accuracy.

Review Questions

1. Compare and contrast the three major types of stalkers, providing examples in your answer.
2. Define intimate partner violence (IPV), describe its patterns, and explain how physical and emotional abuse occurs in a cyclical pattern that can result in victims feeling helpless and powerless.
3. Compare and contrast the three major types of spousal assaulters.
4. Use one of the following psychological theories to explain stalking and IPV: attachment theory or social learning theory.
5. Explain how deviant sexual preferences can develop and contribute to sexually violent behaviour.
6. Identify and describe (with examples) two major categories of risk factors for sexual violence and recidivism.

Additional Readings

Dutton, D. G. (2007). *The abusive personality: Violence and control in intimate relationships* (2nd ed.). New York, NY: Guilford.

Meloy, J. R. (1998). *The psychology of stalking: Clinical and forensic perspective.* San Diego, CA: Academic Press.

Spitzberg, B. H., & Cupach, W. R. (2004). *The dark side of relationship pursuit: From attraction to obsession and stalking.* Mahwah, NJ: Erlbaum & Associates.

Ward, T., Polaschek, D. L. L., & Beech, A. R. (2006). *Theories of sexual offending.* West Sussex, England: Wiley.

13

Assessment and Treatment

Learning Objectives

At the end of this chapter, you should be able to:

- explain the importance of coordinating risk assessment and risk management activities for reducing the risk of offending;

- describe the three basic steps in the risk assessment process;

- discuss different risk assessment methods, including their strengths and weaknesses;

- explain the risk-need-responsivity (RNR) model of offender treatment;

- explain the good lives model (GLM) as an alternative approach to offender treatment;

- identify and describe elements of effective offender treatment programs; and

- discuss strategies for ensuring that the design and delivery of treatment programs reflect best practices.

CASE STUDY

Karla Homolka

St Catharines, Ontario—Karla Homolka and her husband, Paul Bernardo—dubbed the "Ken and Barbie killers" by the media—were responsible for the sexual homicides of three young women in Ontario during the early 1990s. The couple's first victim was Homolka's younger sister, Tammy. As a gift to Bernardo, Homolka drugged Tammy unconscious so that he could rape her (Williams, 1999). Tammy died during the sexual assault, when she aspirated her own vomit. In two separate incidents committed nearly a year apart, Homolka and Bernardo abducted teenagers Leslie Mahaffy and Kristen French from the streets of St Catharines. They took each girl home, where they sexually assaulted and tortured her for several days before killing, dismembering, and disposing of her. When the couple was arrested in 1993, Homolka struck a plea bargain with prosecutors, agreeing to testify against her husband in exchange for being allowed to plead guilty to manslaughter and thus avoiding a possible first-degree murder conviction. She began serving her 12-year sentence in July 1993 (Shephard, 1999). Meanwhile, Bernardo was sentenced to life in prison with no chance of parole for 25 years. He was also declared a dangerous offender, which means he can be imprisoned indefinitely (Canadian Press, 2015).

After six years in prison, Homolka unsuccessfully applied for temporary releases under the escort of a correctional official, claiming that they would help her "develop a positive support network along with reducing [her] social isolation" (Shephard, 1999, p. 1). At the same time, her parole officer reported that Homolka needed to "focus on assuming responsibility and the role as an assailant that she played in committing these offences, before any real social reintegration can be

Photo 13.1 Although Karla Homolka told investigators that she was an unwilling accomplice to the rape and murder of young women, video tapes of the crimes—found after her plea bargain was arranged—revealed that she was an active participant. Photo: The Canadian Press/Frank Gunn

considered" (Shephard, 1999, p. 1). Normally, federal offenders are released on conditions after serving two-thirds of their sentence, but the Parole Board of Canada (PBC) continued to have Homolka detained because they considered her likely to commit another offence causing death or serious harm (Mofina & Audbry, 2001).

Despite the concern surrounding Homolka, finding suitable treatment to reduce her risk of re-offending proved complicated. At the time, Canadian correctional facilities contained so few female sex offenders—only 16 in the entire federal system—that no treatment program existed for them (Roman, 2001). Correctional officials first tried to deal with the situation by transferring Homolka to an institution for offenders with mental disorders, where they planned to adapt a program intended for male sex offenders ("Homolka moved," 2001). They soon concluded that none of the institution's treatment programs would be beneficial so moved her again. Eventually, she was treated at another correctional facility, with a program designed for juvenile sex offenders. She had completed most of this program when her parole application was rejected for a fourth time ("Twelve years," 2005). In fact, Homolka never received early release and remained in prison until her sentence expired in July 2005.

The restrictions on Homolka did not end with her release. In an unusual legal move, government officials convinced a court to impose conditions on her freedom beyond the end of her sentence, on the basis that she remained a danger to the public (Hamilton, 2005). However, the legal order was soon quashed and all the restrictions removed (Haines, 2005). Homolka is now remarried and, at last report, is living in Montreal with her husband and children (Wilton, 2016).

Introduction

After people are convicted of a criminal offence, they typically come under the authority of the correctional system, which is responsible for administering sentences and preparing offenders for eventual reintegration into society. Carrying out these responsibilities is complicated because, as we have seen throughout this book, offenders differ from one another in many aspects, including upbringing, social skills, education, personality, and cognitions (Van Voorhis & Salisbury, 2014). This diversity means an approach that is appropriate for one offender may be inappropriate or even counterproductive for someone else. Put succinctly, one size does not fit all when it comes to managing offenders. Corrections officials plainly recognized this point when they struggled to find suitable treatment for Homolka. The process of assessing an offender's personal characteristics and circumstances and matching them to appropriate treatment and other management strategies is known as **offender classification** (Andrews, Bonta, & Hoge, 1990; Clements, 1996; Van Voorhis & Salisbury, 2014). This chapter focuses on how offenders are assessed, differentiated, and managed in ways that promote public safety.

offender classification The process of assessing an offender's personal characteristics and circumstances and matching them to appropriate management strategies and services aimed at lowering his or her risk of reoffending.

Risk of Offending

A risk represents a possible adverse or undesirable outcome (Hart, 2001; Kraemer et al., 1997). While we might not think in these terms, considerations of risk govern many of our daily choices. Decisions to invest in a mutual fund or undergo a medical procedure are both influenced by our perceptions about the likelihood of an unwanted outcome, whether it be declining financial markets, poor health, or something else. Risk is no less a consideration in the criminal justice system, although the adverse outcome of concern in this context is offending behaviour. It is evident that Homolka's **risk of offending** explicitly or implicitly entered into the decisions to find appropriate treatment for her and to reject her applications for temporary escorted absences and early release. In fact, Homolka's risk was considered so great that efforts were made to have restrictions imposed on her even after her sentence was over.

risk of offending The likelihood that a particular person will engage in an act of criminal or violent behaviour, usually within a specified time frame.

Effectively reducing the risk of offending requires two complementary activities: risk assessment and risk management (Hart, 1998b). **Risk assessment** centres on developing an accurate picture of the risk posed by an offender. This activity has sometimes been referred to as risk prediction, but as Hart (2001) has pointed out, a good assessment goes beyond merely forecasting the likelihood that someone will commit a crime. It also involves determining what it is about an individual offender and his or her circumstances that may contribute to future offending behaviour. A parallel can be drawn to the field of medicine. Knowing that a patient is in critical condition and likely to die is not especially helpful unless the physician understands what is putting the patient's life in peril so that a suitable course of treatment can be initiated. Similarly, once it is understood why an offender poses a risk, it is possible to undertake **risk management**, which involves implementing strategies and delivering services designed to mitigate the risks identified during the assessment process (Hart, 1998b; Snowden, 1997). In short, the best way to prevent acts of criminal and violent behaviour is to assess and manage offender risk in a coordinated fashion (Guy, Douglas, & Hart, 2015).

risk assessment The process of evaluating the likelihood of someone's risk of offending and the reasons that the person poses a risk.

risk management The process of implementing strategies and services intended to mitigate identified risks.

Figure 13.1 The interconnected nature of risk assessment and risk management

Risk Assessments of Offenders

Steps in the Risk Assessment Process

As we shall see shortly, the risk of offending can be assessed in several ways; however, all methods have three basic steps in common. The first is information gathering. While the precise information collected is influenced somewhat by the method used and the risk of interest, assessments typically canvass the offender's past antisocial behaviour, social adjustment, psychological adjustment, and current or anticipated circumstances.

The value of any assessment depends on the accuracy and comprehensiveness of the data it is based on. To safeguard against incomplete or biased information, it is generally recommended that evaluators use multiple sources (Borum, Swartz, & Swanson, 1996). Information may be gathered by interviewing the offender, victims, and collateral informants (e.g. the offender's family and friends) as well as reviewing relevant documents such as the individual's criminal and mental health records and police reports. In some cases, evaluators may administer psychological tests or use other assessment tools.

The second step is to identify and evaluate the presence (or absence) of relevant risk and protective factors. A **risk factor** is something associated with an increased likelihood of future criminal behaviour (Kraemer et al., 1997). For example, we know from previous chapters that individuals who exhibit poor educational achievement or prior antisocial behaviour have a greater probability of committing crime, so these characteristics are risk factors. On the other hand, a **protective factor** is something associated with an increased likelihood of prosocial behaviour (Kraemer et al., 1997). Most protective factors represent the opposite condition characterized by a risk factor. Using the examples above, it is evident that high educational achievement and the absence of previous antisocial behaviour are protective factors. Because these types of factors are generally the reciprocal condition of one another, it is usually unnecessary to refer to both; therefore, we will frame our remaining discussion only in terms of risk factors.

risk factor A characteristic associated with an increased likelihood of future criminal behaviour.

protective factor A characteristic associated with a decreased likelihood of future criminal behaviour.

A distinction can be made between static and dynamic risk factors. A **static risk factor** is permanent or at least extremely resistant to change, whereas a **dynamic risk factor** is changeable. Returning to our examples once again, prior antisocial behaviour constitutes a static risk factor because it is impossible for an offender to undo these misdeeds. By comparison, offenders may choose to upgrade their education, making educational achievement a dynamic risk factor. This changeable quality has two important implications. Most notably, it means that the risk currently posed by an offender may differ from past or future risk. Risk is expected to fluctuate depending on the status of relevant dynamic risk factors, including whether the offender is currently abusing drugs or alcohol, experiencing psychosis, maintaining relationships with antisocial peers, or failing to comply with a prescribed treatment and medication regime (Douglas & Skeem, 2005). In addition, dynamic risk factors make ideal targets for treatment precisely because they can change and reduce an offender's risk.

The third basic step is to arrive at a judgment about risk. Every risk assessment involves some sort of decision-making process that considers, weighs, and synthesizes the various risk and protective factors (Hart, 2001). Decision-making in this context is either the product of professional judgment or actuarial methods (Grove & Meehl, 1996; Hart, 2001). Professional judgment is involved if the evaluator has input into the final decision; actuarial methods rely exclusively on a fixed and explicit set of predetermined rules (Grove & Meehl, 1996; Hart, 2001). The critical distinction between these processes is the presence or absence of human discretion. Professional judgment allows the evaluator to exercise discretion, whereas actuarial methods eliminate it.

Risk Assessment Methods

While every risk assessment involves the same basic steps, considerable variation exists in how these steps are performed. The literature published over the past two decades delineates at least half a dozen methods for conducting risk assessments (e.g. Hanson, 1998; Hart, 2001; Melton, Petrila, Poythress, & Slobogin, 2007; Otto, 2000). Four major methods are described here: unstructured professional judgment, anamnestic, structured professional judgment, and actuarial. The main distinction among them is the degree of specificity and structure surrounding information gathering, risk factor identification and operationalization, and decision-making.

Unstructured Professional Judgment Method

As its name suggests, the **unstructured professional judgment method** lacks structure at all three steps of the assessment process (Hart, 2001). Evaluators gather any information they believe is relevant, using the methods they feel are most suitable and/or convenient in the circumstances. They also decide which factors to emphasize and which ones to ignore and how this information will be integrated into an overall judgment of risk (Bonta, 1996; Melton et al., 2007; Monahan, 2008). In general, this approach is highly dependent on the evaluator's personal knowledge and experience (Hart, 2001; Melton et al., 2007).

The main advantage of this approach is flexibility; it can be readily adjusted to accommodate a wide range of contexts and unique, case-specific features (Hart, 2001; Melton et al., 2007). The downside is that the approach varies tremendously from evaluator to evaluator, which critics claim leads to low **interrater reliability**—that is, the level of agreement between different evaluators' assessments of the same person or thing (Grove & Meehl, 1996;

static risk factor A permanent, or at least very difficult to change, characteristic associated with an increased likelihood of future criminal behaviour.

dynamic risk factor A changeable characteristic associated with an increased likelihood of future criminal behaviour.

unstructured professional judgment method The risk assessment method that gives the evaluator complete discretion over all aspects of the process, including information gathering, risk factor identification and operationalization, information synthesis, and making the judgment about risk.

interrater reliability The extent to which different evaluators' independent assessments of the same person or thing match.

Hart, 2001; Melton et al., 2007). In other words, if one evaluator concludes that someone presents a high risk of offending, we expect other evaluators examining this person to arrive at the same conclusion. Accuracy appears to be another problem. Research generally shows that unstructured professional judgment is not particularly accurate relative to other types of decision-making processes (Grove & Meehl, 1996, Hart, 2001; Melton et al., 2007). The absence of structure also means a lack of transparency (Hart, 2001). Only the evaluator knows what considerations were used and how they were put together, which makes it very difficult for anyone else to scrutinize or test the conclusions (Bonta, 1996; Hart, 2001).

Anamnestic Method

anamnestic method The risk assessment method that involves inquiring into an offender's history to identify the sequence of personal and situational factors that the evaluator believes led to past offending.

The **anamnestic method** involves reviewing an individual's offence history to identify the circumstances surrounding his or her criminal behaviour (Hart, 2001; Melton et al., 2007). It is founded on the premise that, if the same factors and sequence of events that led to previous criminal behaviour should reappear, the offender is likely to repeat the same behaviour (Miller & Morris, 1988). Imagine that Offender X has an extensive criminal record for motor vehicle theft. A review of these offences reveals that some of his associates have substance abuse problems and he uses drugs whenever he is in their company. Once he starts using drugs, it quickly becomes habit-forming, and he requires a constant source of money to purchase drugs. Unfortunately, his work performance slips so dramatically when he is using that he is usually fired from whatever job he has at the time. In the absence of any legitimate source of income to support his habit, he resorts to the only means he knows for acquiring money fast: stealing cars. The behavioural sequence, or **offence cycle**, in this case is straightforward (see Figure 13.2) and shows that associating with drug users, personal drug use, and employment problems are all important risk factors for this offender.

offence cycle The particular sequence of personal and situational factors that led an offender to commit past criminal acts.

As this example illustrates, the anamnestic approach imposes some structure on the risk assessment process by requiring evaluators to gather information about the offence history (Hart, 2001). This method does not, however, prescribe the risk factors that must be considered or specify rules for judging risk. The approach's primary strength lies in its ability to guide risk management (Melton et al., 2007). Once the offence cycle is known, strategies can be developed to interrupt the behavioural sequence and avert future offences (Hart, 2001). For example, Offender X's case presents a number of opportunities to intervene and break his offence cycle by developing relationships with prosocial individuals, avoiding drug-using associates, attending drug counselling, securing short-term financial

Figure 13.2 Identifying the offence cycle through an anamnestic risk assessment

aid, and participating in employment skills training. Despite its practical appeal, the anamnestic approach is largely unproven in terms of reliability and accuracy for predicting and preventing reoffending (Hart, 2001; Melton et al., 2007). Moreover, anamnestic assessments ignore the fact that risk factors shift over time and that offenders may behave differently in the future (Hart, 2001).

Structured Professional Judgment Method

A third and more recent trend in the field of risk assessment is the **structured professional judgment (SPJ) method**. Central to this method are guidelines intended to reflect good risk assessment practices with respect to training, qualifications, and assessment considerations (Hart, 1998b, 2001). SPJ adds structure to the process in two fundamental ways: it specifies the information that should be gathered to carry out a risk assessment, and it identifies and operationalizes key factors that research, theory, and/or practice indicate are important for risk assessment purposes (Douglas & Reeves, 2010).

structured professional judgment (SPJ) method The risk assessment method that prescribes the minimum information that must be gathered and identifies and operationalizes the risk factors that must be considered but gives the evaluator discretion over how to synthesize this information and make the judgment about risk.

The HCR-20^{V3}, now in its third version, is a popular example of the SPJ method (Douglas, Hart, Webster, & Belfrage, 2013). This tool was designed for assessing violent, rather than general, offending among adults with mental health issues. Its guidelines direct evaluators to rate the relative presence or absence of 20 risk factors according to definitions contained in the HCR-20^{V3} manual and then use this information to form an opinion about the offender's risk (Douglas et al., 2013). Thus, the HCR-20^{V3} structures the initial steps of the assessment process, including the information to be gathered and the risk factors to be examined, but leaves evaluators free to determine the relative importance of each risk factor and how the factors should be integrated into a judgment of risk.

Researching Criminal and Violent Behaviour

The HCR-20^{V3}

Consistent with the SPJ approach, the HCR-20^{V3} guidelines outline some general principles of good risk assessment practices and articulate the evaluator's expected training and qualifications (Douglas et al., 2013). Its 20 risk factors were identified through reviews of the literature, using a rational selection process based on reason or logic (Douglas & Reeves, 2010). That is, a factor might be selected because it is empirically related to violence, implicated by contemporary theories of violence, widely recognized by professionals in the field as relevant, or some combination thereof (Douglas & Reeves, 2010; Hart, 2001). Ultimately, the goal is to capture a broad collection of key risk factors (Douglas & Reeves, 2010).

The risk factors of the HCR-20^{V3} are organized into three scales: historical, clinical, and risk management (see Table 13.1). The historical scale contains 10 items related to aspects of the person's past. Five items addressing the person's current or recent functioning make up the clinical scale. The remaining five items, in the risk management scale, concern the person's anticipated future circumstances (Douglas & Reeves, 2010). All the risk factors are defined, and evaluators assess and rate each one on a 3-point scale, where 0 indicates the factor is absent, 1 indicates it is partially or possibly present, and 2 indicates the item is definitely present (Douglas et al., 2013). Evaluators are instructed to determine whether an offender poses a low, moderate, or high risk after taking into account the number of presenting risk factors, the relevance of these risk factors, and other considerations, such as the nature and intensity of management needed in the case. Thus, decisions about risk remain the responsibility of the evaluator.

Table 13.1 HCR-20^V3 Scales and Items

Historical (Past)	Clinical (Present)	Risk Management (Future)
H1. Violence	C1. Insight	R1. Professional services and plans
H2. Other antisocial behaviour	C2. Violent ideation or intent	R2. Living situation
H3. Relationships	C3. Symptoms of major mental disorder	R3. Personal support
H4. Employment	C4. Instability	R4. Treatment or supervision response
H5. Substance use	C5. Treatment or supervision response	R5. Stress or coping
H6. Major mental disorder		
H7. Personality disorder		
H8. Traumatic experiences		
H9. Violent attitudes		
H10. Treatment or supervision response		

Source: Douglas, K. S., Hart, S. D., Webster, C. D., & Belfrage, H. (2013). *HCR-20 (Version 3): Assessing risk of violence—User guide*. Burnaby, BC: Mental Health, Law, and Policy Institute, Simon Fraser University, p. 115.

One benefit of the SPJ method is greater interrater reliability because every evaluator examines the same risk factors using a common set of definitions (Hart, 2001; Melton et al., 2007). The validity of the judgments is also expected to be better because evaluators consider well-established risk factors. This arrangement minimizes the problem of evaluators who might overlook important risk factors or attach great weight to extraneous details (Douglas & Reeves, 2010). Finally, transparency is increased because the information and risk factors going into the judgment are obvious (Hart, 2001). The approach's main drawbacks are the time and expense required to develop the guidelines (Hart, 2001). Suitable guidelines may not even exist for some cases, giving evaluators little choice but to rely on other approaches. Moreover, the evaluator's discretion over the judgment of risk is objectionable to those who prefer the purely mechanical process of actuarial methods (e.g. Quinsey, Harris, Rice, & Cormier, 2006).

Actuarial Method

The **actuarial method** is the most structured risk assessment method. It specifies the information to be gathered, identifies and operationalizes the risk factors, and uses a predetermined formula or set of rules to make judgments about risk (Hart, 2001; Otto, 2000). Actuarial risk assessment instruments are usually derived through research with a **construction sample**, which is the original group of research participants used to develop, or "construct," the instrument. Typically, the construction sample is composed of offenders studied for a specified time to see who engages in further criminal or violent acts. Statistical analyses identify the best combination of risk factors for predicting which offenders in the construction sample reoffended and which ones did not (Melton et al., 2007). These findings are then used to formulate the actuarial instrument.

actuarial method The risk assessment method that prescribes all aspects of the process, including information gathering, risk factor identification and operationalization, and the rules for combining this information and making the judgment about risk.

construction sample The original group of participants studied to develop a new psychological test or assessment tool.

This general approach was employed to develop the Violence Risk Appraisal Guide (VRAG), a 12-item actuarial instrument for assessing the risk of violence among offenders with mental disorders (Harris, Rice & Quinsey, 1993). All the items in the VRAG relate to factors that predicted subsequent violent reoffending in the construction sample. Like other actuarial instruments, the VRAG prescribes all steps of the assessment process. The information that must be collected is specified by the 12 items; each item or risk factor is operationalized so that evaluators know how to organize and score it; and judgments about risk are made using a fixed set of formal rules. Evaluators sum the 12 individual item scores to obtain a total VRAG score, which is converted into a precise estimate of the offender's probability of reoffending violently. Most important, the VRAG makes no provision for evaluators to modify this risk estimate, which is solely the product of a mathematical exercise (see the "Researching" box).

The high degree of structure associated with actuarial methods provides instruments such as the VRAG with many of the same advantages observed for SPJ, including good

Researching Criminal and Violent Behaviour

The Violence Risk Appraisal Guide

The Violence Risk Appraisal Guide (VRAG) was developed by a group of researchers working at a maximum security psychiatric institution located at Penetanguishene, Ontario (Harris et al. 1993; Quinsey et al., 2006). The construction sample involved more than 600 mentally disordered, male offenders assessed or treated at the institution. The researchers reviewed each offender's file and recorded information concerning approximately 50 potential "predictor" variables covering aspects of the offender's sociodemographic characteristics (e.g. age, marital status), childhood and adult adjustment (e.g. elementary school maladjustment, criminal history, alcohol use), index offence (e.g. relationship to the victim, victim injury), and psychological assessments (e.g. IQ, psychopathy).

After the participants were released back into society, the researchers followed up, searching the national database of arrests and convictions to see who had reoffended. By this time, the participants had been free for an average of nearly seven years. A participant was deemed to have reoffended if he had been charged with a new violent offence or returned to the institution in connection with an act that, in the researchers' opinion, could have resulted in such a charge. Violence was defined broadly to encompass offences ranging from simple assault to homicide and included sexual assaults, armed robbery, forcible confinement, threatening, and pointing a firearm (Harris et al., 1993; Quinsey et al., 2006). Based on these parameters, 31 per cent of the construction sample recidivated violently during the follow-up period (Harris et al., 1993).

The researchers performed a series of statistical analyses to determine which study variables proved to be the best predictors of violent reoffending in the construction sample. The 12 most predictive variables were selected for inclusion in the VRAG (see Figure 13.3). Harris and colleagues performed a further series of computations to develop a scoring scheme for each item that was designed to optimize the instrument's overall predictive ability. Scores for each item were added to yield a total VRAG score, which could range from –27 to +35. The researchers divided the total possible score into nine brackets spanning seven points each and calculated the recidivism rate for each bracket based on the construction sample. For example, 44 per cent of the offenders in the +7 to +13 bracket recidivated within 7 years. The percentage of offenders who recidivated grew to 58 per cent when the follow-up period was extended to 10 years (see Table 13.2). It is assumed that other offenders who were not in the construction sample but receive similar scores will reoffend at the same rate.

1.	**Lived with both biological parents to age 16** (except for death of parent) ☐ Yes = –2 ☐ No = +3	Score: _____
2.	**Elementary school maladjustment** (up to and including grade 8) ☐ No problems = –1 ☐ Slight or moderate discipline or attendance problems = +2 ☐ Severe (i.e. frequent or serious) behavior or attendance problems (e.g. truancy or disruptive behaviour that persisted over several years or resulted in expulsion) = +5	Score: _____
3.	**History of alcohol problems** ☐ 0 points = –1 ☐ 3 points = +1 ☐ 1 or 2 points = 0 ☐ 4 or 5 points = +2	Score: _____

> **Allot one point for each of the following:**
> Alcohol abuse in biological parent   Alcohol involved in a prior offence
> Teenage alcohol problem   Alcohol involved in index offence
> Adult alcohol problem

4.	**Marital status** (at time of index offence) ☐ Ever married (or lived common law in the same home for at least 6 months) = –2 ☐ Never married = +1	Score: _____
5.	**Criminal history score for convictions and charges for non-violent offences prior to the index offence** (Cormier–Lang Criminal History Score) ☐ Score of 0 = –2 ☐ Score of 3 or above = +3 ☐ Score of 1 or 2 = 0	Score: _____

> **Cormier–Lang Criminal History Scores**
>
> | | |
> |---|---|
> | Robbery (bank, store) = 7 | Break & enter (incl. intent to commit offence) = 1 |
> | Robbery (purse-snatching) = 3 | Fraud (extortion, embezzlement) = 5 |
> | Arson and fire-setting (church, house, barn) = 5 | Fraud (forged cheque, impersonation) = 1 |
> | Arson and fire-setting (garbage can) = 1 | Possession of a prohibited/restricted weapon = 1 |
> | Threatening with a weapon; pointing firearm = 3 | Living on avails prostitution or procuring = 1 |
> | Threatening (uttering threats) = 2 | Trafficking in narcotics = 1 |
> | Theft over (incl. possession stolen property) = 5 | Dangerous driving, impaired driving = 1 |
> | Mischief to public or private property over = 5 | Obstruct a peace officer (incl. resisting arrest) = 1 |
> | Break & enter and commit indictable offence = 2 | Causing a disturbance =1 |
> | Theft under (incl. possession stolen property) = 1 | Wearing a disguise with intent = 1 |
> | Mischief to public or private property under = 1 | Indecent exposure = 2 |

6.	**Failure on prior conditional release** (includes parole violation or revocation, breach of or failure to comply with recognizance or probation, bail violation, and any new charges, including the index offence, while on a conditional release)	Score: _____
7.	**Age at index offence** (at most recent birthday) ☐ ≥39 = –5 ☐ 27 = 0 ☐ 34–38 = –2 ☐ ≤26 = +2 ☐ 28–33 = –1	Score: _____
8.	**Victim injury** (index offence only; most serious injury is scored) ☐ Death = –2 ☐ Treated and released = +1 ☐ Hospitalized = 0 ☐ None of slight (incl. no victim) = +2	Score: _____
9.	**Any female victim** (for index offence) ☐ Yes = –1 ☐ No (incl. no victim) = +1	Score: _____
10.	**Meets *DSM-III* criteria for any personality disorder** ☐ Yes = +3 ☐ No = –2	Score: _____
11.	**Meets *DSM-III* criteria for schizophrenia** ☐ Yes = –3 ☐ No = +1	Score: _____
12.	**Hare Psychopathy Checklist-Revised score** (PCL–R; Hare, 1991) ☐ ≤4 = –5 ☐ 15–24 = 0 ☐ 5–9 = –3 ☐ 25–34 = +4 ☐ 10–14 = –1 ☐ ≥26 = +2	Score: _____
		TOTAL: _____

Figure 13.3 Violence Risk Appraisal Guide (VRAG)

Source: Copyright © 2006 by the American Psychological Association. Adapted with permission. V.L. Quinsey, et al. (2006). *Violent offenders: Appraising and managing risk* (2nd ed.). Washington, DC: American Psychological Association. The use of APA information does not imply endorsement by APA.

interrater reliability, validity, and transparency. In addition, the use of actuarial decision-making means that human discretion and the frailties associated with it are eliminated from the judgment part of the process. In this respect, these methods address past concerns

Table 13.2 Recidivism rates associated with different VRAG scores

VRAG Total Score			Rate of Recidivism	
			Over 7 Years	Over 10 Years
	≤	−22	0.00	0.08
−21	to	−15	0.08	0.10
−14	to	−8	0.12	0.24
−7	to	−1	0.17	0.31
0	to	+6	0.35	0.48
+7	to	+13	0.44	0.58
+14	to	+20	0.55	0.64
+21	to	+27	0.76	0.82
	≥	+28	1.00	1.00

Source: Copyright © 2006 by the American Psychological Association. Adapted with permission. V.L. Quinsey, et al. (2006). *Violent offenders: Appraising and managing risk* (2nd ed.). Washington, DC: American Psychological Association, p. 286. The use of APA information does not imply endorsement by APA.

Table 13.3 Characteristics of the four major risk assessment methods

	Risk assessment method	Prescribed information gathering	Prescribed and operationalized risk factors	Prescribed rules for decisions about risk
Less structure	Unstructured professional judgment	✗	✗	✗
	Anamnestic	✓	✗	✗
	Structured professional judgment	✓	✓	✗
More structure	Actuarial	✓	✓	✓

Source: Copyright © 2008 by the American Psychological Association. Adapted with permission. J. Monahan "Structured risk assessment of violence." *Violence assessment and management.* R. I. Simon & K. Tardiff (Eds.), 2008. Washington, DC: American Psychiatric Publishing. The use of APA information does not imply endorsement by APA.

over the evaluator's ability to effectively process and integrate large amounts of information into clinical opinions and avoid many of the biases that exert subtle yet influential effects on human decision-making (Grove & Meehl, 1996; Quinsey et al., 2006). Actuarial methods are also grounded in scientific research and rely on risk factors with an established relationship to criminal behaviour (or some other outcome of interest) in the construction sample.

On the other hand, creating an instrument designed to achieve maximum predictive accuracy in the construction sample has a cost. The more finely tuned an instrument is for one sample, the more poorly it tends to perform in different samples (Hart, 2001). Another concern is the inadvertent omission of risk factors. Useful risk factors may be excluded from actuarial instruments because the researchers did not think of them, it was impractical to include them in the original pool of test variables, or they appear unrelated to criminal behaviour due to the idiosyncratic characteristics of the construction sample (Douglas & Reeves, 2010). Two other limitations of actuarial methods mirror those mentioned for SPJ, namely, the time required for development and the absence of suitable instruments for some cases. Table 13.3 provides a summary of the four major methods of risk assessment and their associated characteristics.

The Clinical versus Actuarial Debate

For many years, there has been a great deal of controversy over whether professional judgment (also called clinical judgment) or actuarial methods produce better assessment decisions (e.g. Holt, 1970; Meehl, 1954). This dispute—sometimes referred to as the clinical versus actuarial debate—originated in other fields but has spilled over into the area of risk assessment during the past two decades (Dvoskin & Heilbrun, 2001; Webster, Hucker, & Bloom, 2002). Proponents of actuarial methods usually base their stance on the superior accuracy of this method relative to human judgment. They often point to the large body of research, in a wide array of fields ranging from health to employment, that shows actuarial methods typically exceed the accuracy of unstructured professional judgment (e.g. Ægisdóttir et al., 2006; Grove, Zald, Lebow, Snitz, & Nelson, 2000).

Meta-analytic reviews of research specific to risk assessment echo these general results and confirm that actuarial methods are also more accurate than unstructured professional judgment in this field (Bonta, Law, & Hanson, 1998; Hanson & Morton-Bourgon, 2009; Mossman, 1994). Individual studies conducting head-to-head comparisons using the same information, sample, and outcome measures also show that actuarial methods come out on top (e.g. Bengston & Långström, 2007). In view of the accumulated evidence, it is widely recognized that the disadvantages of unstructured professional judgment usually outweigh the advantages and, as a consequence, this method should be avoided whenever possible (Heilbrun, Yasuhara, & Shah, 2010).

The debate has now shifted to one between structured professional judgment and actuarial methods. But why would anyone continue to use decision-making processes that incorporate human judgment in the face of evidence supporting the greater relative accuracy of actuarial methods? Research reveals that, when risk assessments are appropriately structured, they generally fare as well as actuarial methods in terms of accuracy (see Guy et al., 2015). Bear in mind that actuarial instruments are often fine-tuned to the construction sample for maximum predictive accuracy and, as a result, there can be a noticeable decline in performance when they are applied to other samples (e.g. Blair, Marcus, & Boccaccini, 2008). By comparison, the SPJ method is expected to perform robustly across different samples because it selects risk factors on the basis of the literature as a whole and is not optimized for a construction sample (Douglas & Reeves, 2010; Hart, 2001).

Supporters see one further advantage of the SPJ method. With control over the judgment of risk, evaluators are able to consider the relevance of each risk factor based on the case's unique characteristics. Douglas and colleagues (2013) explain that evaluators might reasonably decide that an offender poses a high risk on the basis of only a few or even a single risk factor if that factor is highly relevant and concerning (e.g. the offender expresses a clear intent to carry out a terrorist attack). Of course, exercising this type of discretion is exactly what critics claim reduces the reliability and accuracy of non-actuarial approaches (Quinsey et al., 2006; Rice, Harris, & Hilton, 2010). At this juncture, there is insufficient evidence to conclude that either the SPJ or actuarial method clearly outperforms the other in terms of predictive accuracy. The only way to settle this debate, if it needs settling, is to conduct more studies employing head-to-head comparisons, as is often done in the medical field when there are questions about best practices involving different medical procedures.

Perhaps in an attempt to find an intermediary position, another approach that combines professional judgment and actuarial methods, known as the **adjusted-actuarial approach**, has emerged (Hanson, 1998; Melton et al., 2007). It is often construed as separate and distinct from the others discussed so far. The challenge that evaluators face is how to

adjusted-actuarial approach The risk assessment method that involves generating an initial judgment of risk using the actuarial method and then subjecting it to the evaluator's professional discretion.

blend these two methods to form a single overall judgment of risk. There are two possibilities. One approach is to use the actuarial instrument to form a risk estimate that the evaluator may increase or decrease to account for important case-specific factors that would otherwise be overlooked (Hanson, 1998). The other is to generate an actuarial estimate that the evaluator considers along with all the other gathered information (Litwack, 2001). The difference between the approaches is really a matter of emphasis (Melton et al., 2007). With the former, the actuarial estimate is the foremost consideration and it is modified only to the extent necessary. The latter places more emphasis on the evaluator's professional judgment, and the actuarial estimate merely represents one piece of information among many.

The prospect of combining professional judgment and actuarial approaches has evoked a number of criticisms. On some level, a combined approach is an oxymoron. Once professional discretion enters into the decision-making process, it is no longer actuarial. As others have noted, a decision is either rule-bound or without rules; it cannot be both (Douglas & Reeves, 2010). Of course, actuarial purists warn against the dangers of allowing professional judgment, arguing that it will inevitably result in diminished accuracy (Rice et al., 2010; Quinsey et al., 2006). Dvoskin and Heilbrun (2001) suggest that evaluators should not tamper with an actuarial estimate of risk once it is derived. They recommend contextualizing the information for consumers (e.g. courts, parole boards) by explaining the estimate's strengths and limitations. In other words, evaluators should freely identify and explain other considerations that might affect the actuarial estimate, but they should stop short of adjusting it based on these considerations. Unfortunately, there is virtually no published empirical research on the practice of modifying actuarial assessments. Descriptions of the few unpublished studies completed to date suggest that actuarial assessments of risk overridden by evaluators tend to be less accurate than the original estimate (see Hanson & Morton-Bourgon, 2009; Heilbrun et al., 2010).

Putting It All Together: Good Risk Assessment Practices

While the clinical versus actuarial debate is often cast in black and white terms, the actual division may not be so distinct. Actuarial methods frequently incorporate one or more risk factors that require clinical or professional judgment (Litwack, Zapf, Groscup, & Hart, 2006; Monahan, 2008). The VRAG is a useful case in point because it includes items based on the Hare Psychopathy Checklist–Revised (PCL–R) and DSM-III diagnoses of personality disorder and of schizophrenia. All these items require evaluators to make professional judgments about whether these conditions are present. Thus, the VRAG eliminates professional judgment only from the final step by dictating how the items are to be combined and interpreted. Furthermore, while the actuarial and SPJ approaches differ with respect to the involvement of professional judgment in decisions about risk, they are very similar in many other ways. Both use empirical evidence to inform the selection of risk factors, albeit through somewhat different methods (Heilbrun et al., 2010). Each approach prescribes what information needs to be gathered, what risk factors must be considered, and how those risk factors are operationalized. Litwack and colleagues (2006) have gone so far as to suggest that professional judgment and actuarial assessments share so much in common that the two are "blurring to the point where there is often no meaningful distinction" (p. 504).

The evident overlap in these approaches indicates some degree of agreement over how risk assessments should be conducted. Rather than emphasizing areas of discord, it may

Table 13.4 Essential elements for good risk assessment practices
1. Risk assessment practices need to be evidence-based (Douglas, Cox, & Webster, 1999; Melton et al., 2007; Webster et al., 2002). That is, the procedure should reflect current research and consider factors with established relationships to the hazard of interest.
2. When available, structured methods are preferable to unstructured methods (e.g. Bonta, 2002; Melton et al., 2007; Monahan, 2008).
3. Risk assessments should be comprehensive and balanced so that all major known risk and protective factors are reviewed and considered (Bonta, 2002; Hart, 2001; Lavoie, Guy, & Douglas, 2009; Rogers, 2000; Webster et al., 2002).
4. Risk assessment practices should be sensitive to changes over time and therefore should take static and dynamic risk factors into account (Douglas & Skeem, 2005; Hart, 2001; Reid, 2003; Rogers, 2000).
5. Risk reassessments should be carried out at appropriate intervals so that any changes in dynamic risk factors are noted and evaluated.
6. Risk assessment practices should provide helpful information that can be used to guide risk management strategies (Hart, 2001; Lavoie et al., 2009; Snowden, 1997; Webster et al., 2002).

be more constructive to identify those elements that are generally recognized as essential for good risk assessment practices. No definitive list currently exists, but the six elements identified in Table 13.4 are widely supported in the literature.

Treatment of Offenders

Treatment is one of the major strategies used to manage offenders and their risk of committing a future offence. The remainder of this chapter discusses the main assessment considerations surrounding offender treatment and the program features that enhance treatment efficacy.

The Decline and Revival of Offender Treatment

The idea that offenders should be treated to "correct" their behaviour (hence the term *corrections*) is not new. Offender rehabilitation was the dominant force behind correctional thinking and practices in North America throughout most of the twentieth century. Although several factors contributed to its waning influence during the latter part of the century, Robert Martinson's article on the effectiveness of prison treatment proved to be a pivotal event. Martinson (1974) began the piece by asking, "What works?" (p. 22) and then discussed a report that he and colleagues had completed on behalf of the New York State government, which reviewed, in painstaking detail, 231 studies on prison rehabilitation carried out between 1945 and 1967 (Lipton, Martinson, & Wilks, 1975). Martinson's (1974) conclusion was that "with few and isolated exceptions, the rehabilitative efforts that have been reported so far have had no appreciable effect on recidivism" (p. 25). Although Martinson outlined several caveats to this statement, it seems the message that most people took away from it was simply "Nothing works."

Others disagreed with Martinson's rather bleak assessment of the literature. In a rebuke published the following year, Palmer (1975) reported that nearly half the studies Martinson reviewed actually showed some sign of positive treatment effects. A few years later, Gendreau and Ross (1979) responded with an article pointedly entitled "Bibliotherapy for Cynics," which examined 95 methodologically stronger studies conducted after Martinson's report and noted the presence of beneficial treatment effects in many of these investigations. When the studies were quantified, it was found that treatment had a positive impact in 86 per cent of the investigations (see Andrews, Zinger, Hoge, Bonta, Gendreau, & Cullen, 1990). These and other assessments of the available research revealed that treatment worked at least some of the time or at least under the right conditions. Five years after the publication of his article, Martinson (1979) publicly conceded that his original conclusion was inaccurate. By this time, however, the nothing works doctrine was so firmly embedded into conventional thinking that not even his retraction could dislodge it (McGuire & Priestley, 1995).

Although a steady flow of studies continued to report encouraging results, two investigations published in the early 1990s were instrumental in restoring confidence in the potential value of correctional treatment (Andrews & Bonta, 2010). One was Mark Lipsey's (1992) quantitative review of results from studies examining the effectiveness of delinquency treatments using what was then the relatively new technique of meta-analysis. This review was not the first meta-analysis of the offender treatment literature, but it stood apart both in terms of its quality and sheer magnitude. Lipsey analyzed over 400 studies, nearly three times more than any other meta-analysis of offender treatment at the time, which made its results extremely convincing. In contrast to the view that nothing works, he reported that treating juvenile offenders was associated with an average 10 per cent drop in recidivism compared to untreated juvenile offenders. Lipsey (1992) acknowledged that the size of the reduction was very modest, but it was nonetheless statistically significant and non-trivial. Just as noteworthy, Lipsey (1992) found that treatment success varied with the type, integrity, and intensity of the intervention.

The second notable investigation was conducted by Andrews, Zinger, and colleagues (1990), who believed that offender assessment was the key to effective correctional treatment. They hypothesized that treatments appropriately matched to the offender would outperform mismatched or unmatched treatments. To explore this possibility, they reviewed 80 studies that examined the effects of treatment on recidivism. The type of treatment was categorized in one of four ways: criminal sanctions (the type or level of criminal disposition varied), inappropriate treatment (no or inappropriate matching of treatment type and offender), appropriate treatment (appropriate matching of treatment type and offender), or unspecified treatment. The study revealed that, compared to inappropriate treatments or unspecified treatments, appropriate treatments significantly lowered recidivism. Together, the results of these investigations went a long way to restoring faith in correctional treatment, as well as sparking interest in the use of assessments for matching offenders to treatments.

The Rise of the RNR Model of Offender Treatment

Over the past two decades, our understanding of what makes a treatment appropriate, or inappropriate, has grown tremendously thanks in large part to the pioneering work of Donald Andrews, James Bonta, and their colleagues (Andrews, Zinger, et al., 1990; Andrews, Bonta, & Hoge, 1990). These researchers combined theory and empirical evaluation to identify three core principles of effective correctional treatment they termed risk, needs, and responsivity (RNR). These principles describe the who, what, and how of correctional treatment and together form the RNR model that is now a mainstay of contemporary correctional systems in many parts of the world (Andrews & Bonta, 2010).

The Risk Principle

The **risk principle** identifies who should receive correctional treatment. It specifies that treatment should be matched to the offender's level of risk such that the most intense treatment efforts should be dedicated to the highest risk offenders. Conversely, very little or no treatment should be given to the lowest risk offenders. Research confirms the soundness of this principle, generally showing that allocating treatment in this manner has the greatest overall impact on lowering recidivism (Andrews & Dowden, 2006; Landenberger & Lipsey, 2005; Lipsey, 2009; Lowenkamp, Latessa, & Holsinger, 2006). The reason it is better to target high-risk offenders may be no different than the reason a C student will probably benefit more from tutoring than an A student: there is simply more room for improvement (Lipsey, 1995).

Other factors may also lie behind this principle. Andrews and Bonta (2006) note that subjecting low-risk offenders to high levels of treatment not only appears unhelpful, but it may also be counterproductive and increase recidivism. Although the reason for this finding is not entirely certain, two hypotheses have been put forward. The most frequently cited possibility is that placing low-risk offenders in intensive treatment programs typically means surrounding them with higher risk offenders who model and reinforce antisocial behaviour (Andrews & Bonta, 2010). The other explanation is that putting these offenders into treatment programs disrupts and weakens many of the protective factors that contribute to their low-risk level, such as employment and relationships (Lowenkamp et al., 2006).

The Need Principle

The **need principle** concerns what should be targeted for treatment, namely, an offender's dynamic, or changeable, risk factors. The logic behind this principle is straightforward. Treating and changing dynamic risk factors will lower the risk of reoffending, whereas treatment directed at static risk factors or at factors unrelated to criminal behaviour will not. Accordingly, Andrews and Bonta (2006) recommend targeting factors such as antisocial thoughts and attitudes, procriminal peers, substance abuse, and lack of employment skills, all of which have a known relationship to criminal behaviour. The RNR model does not dismiss the possibility of treating an offender's other needs, but these are seen as much less important because they do not directly impact the risk of offending.

The Responsivity Principle

The **responsivity principle** addresses how the treatment should be carried out. Generally speaking, treatment must be delivered in a manner that matches the offender's abilities and learning style. There are two aspects to responsivity. **General responsivity** refers to the broad approach to treatment, which should involve a structured program that is delivered in a positive therapeutic environment. Program structuring is discussed later in the chapter. To create a positive therapeutic environment, client–therapist relationhips must be established that are characterized by trust, respect, collaboration, support, empathy, and understanding (Andrews & Bonta, 2006; Marshall, Marshall, Serran, & O'Brien, 2013). **Specific responsivity** involves adjusting the broad treatment approach to suit the unique characteristics and abilities of the individual offender, including his or her maturity level, cognitive abilities, learning styles, and cultural background. For example, journal writing exercises might be useful for high-functioning, well-educated offenders but are

---

risk principle A guideline of the RNR model stipulating that, for treatment to be effective, the intensity level must be matched to the offender's risk of reoffending such that low-risk offenders receive little or no treatment and high-risk offenders receive the most treatment.

need principle A guideline of the RNR model stipulating that, for treatment to be effective, it should be directed at dynamic risk factors.

responsivity principle A guideline of the RNR model stipulating that, for treatment to be effective, it must be delivered in a manner that matches the offender's abilities and learning styles.

general responsivity An aspect of the RNR model's responsivity principle stipulating that, for treatment to be effective, it must be structured and delivered within the context of a positive therapeutic environment.

specific responsivity An aspect of the RNR model's responsivity principle stipulating that, for treatment to be effective, the therapeutic approach must be tailored to the offender's particular characteristics and abilities.

entirely unsuitable for illiterate offenders. Similarly, treatment sessions delivered to an offender with ADHD should be relatively short and involve active participation to maximize the likelihood of success.

One important aspect of responsivity is treatment motivation. As the cases of Darnell Pratt and Brenden Sarginson illustrate, offenders differ vastly in their motivation to seek out and participate in treatment programs. Pratt showed little interest in receiving treatment for his substance abuse after correctly anticipating that he was going to be released from prison even without it. In contrast, Sarginson turned himself into authorities when he breached a term of his probation and asked the judge for a longer sentence to facilitate his treatment (see the case study). Although it is not well studied, treatment motivation is thought to have a major impact on the extent to which treatment gains are realized.

CASE STUDY

Darnell Pratt and Brenden Sarginson

Maple Ridge, British Columbia— In March 2005, 16-year-old Darnell Pratt committed a gas-and-dash at a service station. When Grant De Patie, the station attendant, tried to prevent the crime, Pratt struck him with the vehicle and dragged him several kilometres, causing his death. Pratt was convicted of manslaughter and ordered to serve seven years in prison. He admitted drinking daily during the months prior to the offence and was given the opportunity to participate in a prison substance abuse program (Chan, 2010). Parole documents describe Pratt as exhibiting a negative attitude to the program and making minimal effort to complete treatment-related assignments. Correctional authorities suspended him from the program after only six weeks for failing to attend or arriving late for over one-third of the sessions. Pratt indicated that he was not interested in participating because his conditional

Photo 13.2 Since being released from prison, Darnell Pratt has reportedly committed several parole violations and pled guilty to car theft.

release date was coming up and he would be allowed to leave prison whether he finished the program or not.

The documents further indicate that Pratt was occasionally "uncooperative" with his case management team and was suspected of using drugs and alcohol while in prison (Chan, 2010). Two days following his release, he failed to return to his halfway house, putting him in breach of his release conditions (Campbell, 2010). He was arrested a short time later. At his revocation hearing, it came to light that he had been found drinking in a pub twice in two days, contrary to his release conditions that required him to abstain from all drugs and alcohol use (Campbell, 2010).

Regina, Saskatchewan—One day after finishing a two-year stint in prison for sexually assaulting a six-year old girl, Brenden Sarginson went to a park, in

continued

violation of probation conditions that prohibited him from, among other things, being anywhere children congregate (Pruden, 2010). Sarginson recognized that he had taken the first step in his offence cycle, which he described as "disturbing" (Pruden, 2010, p. A1). Of his own volition, he went to police and admitted to violating the terms of his probation. At court, the prosecutor requested that Sarginson receive 12–18 months for breaching his probation. Sarginson argued for a two-year sentence so that he would serve the time in a federal penitentiary rather than a provincial institution. He stated, "I need help, and I can't get it on the street . . . The only place for me to get it in Saskatchewan is the federal penitentiary" (Pruden, 2010, p. A1). The judge noted that the term of imprisonment was too harsh for a breach of probation but acquiesced to Sarginson's request. On hearing the news, Sarginson is reported to have smiled and said, "Now I can go up to the pen and I can start the treatment I need" (Pruden, 2010, p. A1).

Photo 13.3 At court for violating the terms of his probation, Brenden Sarginson, requested the judge impose a longer sentence to facilitate his treatment.

The RNR model illustrates why good offender assessment is so vital. To apply RNR principles, it is necessary to differentiate lower and higher risk offenders from one another, identify individual dynamic risk factors, and determine personal attributes that are likely to influence treatment response. All these tasks involve assessing offenders, but assessments alone are insufficient. The assessment information must be used to match offenders to suitable correctional programs. Think back to the Homolka case. The indecision over her treatment probably related to the difficulties correction officials encountered in finding a program that fit her particular risk, needs, and responsivity.

The Good Lives Model

Despite its success, the RNR model is not without critics. While acknowledging the approach's success and merits, Ward and colleagues criticize its single-minded focus on risk factors, which in many ways represent problems or deficits in the offender (Ward, 2002; Willis & Ward, 2013). They argue that this emphasis on deficits is unappealing to offenders and does not inspire or motivate them to become engaged in treatment (Willis & Ward, 2013). The good lives model (GLM) was developed as an alternative framework that provides a more positive, strengths-based approach to offender treatment (Ward, 2002; Ward & Maruna, 2007).

primary human goods Personal characteristics, states of mind, and experiences that are intrinsically valued by people and promote their psychological well-being.

The GLM is grounded in the belief that offenders, like everyone else, desire personal meaning and fulfillment in their lives, which is achieved through primary human goods. **Primary human goods** represent personal characteristics, states of mind, and experiences that are intrinsically valued and promote psychological well-being (Ward & Maruna, 2007). So far, Ward and colleagues have identified 10 classes of primary goods, which are listed

Table 13.5 Primary human goods identified by the good lives model

1.	**Life**	Physical needs required for healthy living and functioning.
2.	**Knowledge**	Desire to understand ourselves, others, and our environment.
3.	**Excellence in play and work**	Desire to engage in recreational activities for pleasure and develop competence in work and non-work activities.
4.	**Autonomy**	Desire to freely choose one's goals and the means of achieving those goals without interference from others.
5.	**Inner peace**	Desire to achieve and maintain a stable emotional state free of turmoil and stress.
6.	**Relatedness**	Desire for warm and caring attachments to others, including friends, family, and romantic partners.
7.	**Community**	Desire to belong to social groups of people who share the same beliefs and interests.
8.	**Spirituality**	Desire for a sense of meaning and purpose in life.
9.	**Happiness**	Desire for the feeling of gratification and general contentment with one's life.
10.	**Creativity**	Desire to come up with new ideas or ways of doing things or to produce artistic works.

Source: Day, A., Casey, S., Ward, T., Howells, K., & Vess, J. (2010). *Transitions to better lives: Offender readiness and rehabilitation.* Portland, OR: Willan, pp. 51–52.

in Table 13.5 (Day, Casey, Ward, Howells, & Vess, 2010). Although everyone pursues some measure of all 10, the significance and priority attached to each class varies from individual to individual (Willis & Ward, 2013). Most important, GLM assumes that people commit crime to attain, directly or indirectly, one or more of these primary human goods. For example, someone who lacks romantic companionship, which reflects the primary human good of relatedness, might stalk someone as part of an inappropriate effort to establish a relationship with a desired partner.

The GLM suggests that the key to treatment is to develop an offender's capacity to attain primary human goods in a prosocial manner (Ward & Marshall, 2004). This goal can be accomplished by strengthening the internal capabilities of offenders, such as furthering their knowledge, skills, and beliefs, as well as addressing their external conditions, such as providing them with assistance and opportunities (Ward & Gagnon, 2006). Treatment on stalking might work on enhancing the offender's interpersonal skills and confidence in social situations (i.e. internal capabilities) and on identifying social activities and other opportunities where meaningful and consensual relationships might develop (i.e. external conditions). It is expected that the risk of future criminal behaviour will diminish as a natural consequence of improving the capabilities of offenders and enriching their lives (Ward & Marshall, 2004).

As our discussion makes clear, RNR and GLM differ in terms of their principal objectives and the means used to attain them. For the RNR model, the primary goal is to decrease reoffending. Treatment, then, targets an offender's risk needs. The main objective of GLM is to improve the offender's well-being and life satisfaction—reduced offending, though expected, is a corollary of this goal. According to proponents, one major advantage of GLM is that it focuses on achieving the very things that matter most to offenders so that they are more likely to be motivated to engage in therapy (Ward, Mann, & Gagnon, 2007). Detractors worry that GLM may undo many of the gains made in correctional treatment over the last several decades by re-directing scarce resources away from an offender's risk-related needs to his or her general psychological well-being, a shift that has not been shown to reduce recidivism (e.g. Bonta & Andrews, 2003).

Elements of Effective Treatment

Structured Treatment

Since the three original principles of RNR were first articulated, research has continued to identify treatment features associated with improved outcomes for offenders. A key finding from this work is that structured treatments are typically more effective than unstructured ones (Lipsey, 1992). Treatment structure is a function of its goals and content. Treatment goals are usually derived from criminological theory and must be specific and clearly stated (McGuire, 2004). Treatment content, in turn, must be designed to achieve the identified therapeutic goals (McGuire, 2004). Thus, all the activities that make up the content need to be carefully defined and explained and their sequence set out. An intervention that incorporates these structural elements is usually referred to as a **treatment program**. The most effective treatment programs tend to work on developing identifiable skills and/or behaviours (Lipsey, 1992). Cognitive, behavioural, or cognitive-behavioural methods have all generally proven to be better at bringing about desired changes in offenders than alternatives such as punishment, psychodynamic approaches, or unspecified methods (Lipsey, 1992; Lösel, 1995).

treatment program
A highly structured treatment incorporating specific treatment goals and treatment content that is defined and sequenced.

Multimodal Program

Multimodal programs, which have two or more treatment components, are generally more effective than interventions that rely on a single therapeutic activity (e.g. Lipsey, 1992). Typically, each component has a specific object that may or may not be addressed by the other components using different methods or techniques. The obvious advantage of multimodal approaches is that numerous treatment needs can be targeted within the framework of a single program. One meta-analytic review found that multimodal treatments featuring cognitive-behavioural therapy (discussed on next page) coupled with other components, such as mental health counselling or employment upgrading, were associated with significantly larger decreases in recidivism than interventions restricted to CBT alone (Landenberger & Lipsey, 2005). Likewise, Andrews and Bonta (2006) note that targeting a greater number of dynamic risk factors (relative to the number of static risk factors) produces stronger treatment effects.

multimodal program An intervention that addresses more than one need.

Treatment Dosage

Research shows that the **treatment dosage**, or the amount of treatment delivered in a program, is another factor that impacts outcome. Reviews of the literature indicate that higher treatment dosages are associated with lower rates of recidivism (Lipsey, 1992; Landenberger & Lipsey, 2005). The dose required to achieve maximum treatment efficacy is not known with any degree of certainty, but it is recommended that offenders receive around a hundred hours of programming (Lipsey, 1992; Smith, Gendreau, & Swartz, 2009). The treatment dosage an offender receives is a function of several factors, including the number of sessions per week, the duration of each session, and the number of weeks in the program. In their quantitative review of CBT programs, Landenberger and Lipsey (2005) observed that the frequency and duration of weekly contact have a stronger bearing on outcome than does the length of the program. Thus, high frequency sessions that concentrate treatment into a small number of weeks appear to be more effective than delivering the same amount of treatment over a longer period of time.

treatment dosage The amount of treatment, usually measured in hours, delivered to participants during the course of a treatment program.

Treatment dosage is also affected by **attrition**, which refers to the number of intended program participants who do not complete treatment. Attrition may come about in a variety

attrition In terms of a treatment program, the number of intended participants who do not complete the program.

of ways. For instance, offenders may not commence programs that the courts or correctional officials directed them to take; they may leave the program before reaching the end; or they may be expelled for violating program rules or expectations. The case of Darnell Pratt, discussed earlier, is an example of attrition. Attrition is problematic because it often reflects an offender's lack of motivation to change. Furthermore, non-completers receive less than the full treatment dosage and therefore any therapeutic gains they derive are likely attenuated.

Treatment Setting

The treatment setting appears to be another important factor. Meta-analytic reviews of the research report differential treatment effects for programs implemented in the community versus institutions (e.g. Andrews & Bonta 2006; Lipsey, 1999; Lipsey & Wilson, 1998). McGuire (2002a) estimates that community-based programs may be nearly twice as effective than institutionally based programs, but only if the programs are structured. Unstructured programs tend to perform poorly regardless of where they are situated. Setting-related treatment differences could be the result of one or more of the negative impacts of institution-based programs previously mentioned, such as removing offenders from their social supports and/or immersing them in the procriminal environment of custodial institutions.

Cognitive-Behavioural Therapy

Cognitive-behavioural therapy (CBT) is widely hailed as one of the most promising forms of treatment for offenders. CBT is not unique to the correctional field; it is a prominent therapeutic approach used by clinical psychologists to treat a wide variety of problems, including mood, eating, and anxiety disorders. The generic term *cognitive-behavioural* describes a group of related clinical interventions that meld behaviourism and cognitive psychology (McGuire, 2000). The therapy's central tenet is that our thoughts and behaviours are inextricably linked and therefore, to change the latter, we must alter our cognitive content and processes—that is, we must change what and how we think (Dobson & Dozois, 2001). CBT assumes that people who exhibit maladaptive behaviour also have underlying cognitive problems. Treatment typically concentrates on getting individuals to recognize and change errors in their thinking and to develop skills that will help them avoid problem behaviours in the future (Dobson & Dozois, 2001).

> **cognitive-behavioural therapy (CBT)** An approach to psychological treatment that focuses on individuals recognizing and changing errors in their thinking as well as developing cognitive skills as a way to avoid problem behaviours.

Offender treatment programs based on CBT operate on the same principles. As we have seen, especially in Chapter 8, offenders' thought content and processes tend to differ from non-offenders' in several important respects. Offenders are more likely to display poor moral reasoning, distorted cognitions, and antisocial attitudes and to misinterpret the actions and intentions of others. Presumably, these maladaptive thinking patterns, together with poor interpersonal and coping skills, lead offenders to frequently make poor decisions and engage in criminal acts. When delivered appropriately, CBT is consistent with the principle of general responsivity and is one of the treatment approaches recommended by leading authorities in this area (Andrews & Bonta, 2006; Smith et al., 2009). Cognitive-behavioural methods may involve cognitive restructuring, cognitive skills development, or both approaches at the same time (Van Voorhis & Salisbury, 2014).

Cognitive restructuring is mostly concerned with distortions and other flaws in the way offenders think (MacKenzie, 2006). It works on getting offenders to monitor and change the attitudes, beliefs, and assumptions they hold that support and promote their criminal behaviour (Van Voorhis & Lester, 2009). For instance, cognitive restructuring

> **cognitive restructuring** A form of cognitive-behavioural therapy that focuses on changing behaviour by altering a person's thought content. It typically involves challenging the person's distorted beliefs and working to replace undesirable thoughts with more appropriate ones.

might seek to identify and challenge the distorted beliefs of a child molester who views his or her actions as harmless and educational for the victim. Specific cognitive restructuring techniques include challenging offenders with evidence that contradicts their distorted beliefs, getting them to actively monitor their thoughts in journals, and having them replace undesirable thoughts with more appropriate alternatives. In short, cognitive restructuring aims to alter cognitive content, or what the offender thinks (Van Voorhis & Lester, 2009).

cognitive skills development
A form of cognitive-behavioural therapy that focuses on changing behaviour by altering how a person processes information and decides how to act. It typically involves the use of modelling and role-playing exercises to develop the person's ability to analyze, consider, and respond effectively to different situations.

Cognitive skills are concerned with how an offender processes information and makes decisions to act in a particular way (Van Voorhis & Lester, 2009). The aim of **cognitive skills development** is to help the offender adapt his or her behaviour appropriately to different social situations (MacKenzie, 2006). Thus, cognitive skills address faulty decision-making processes as opposed to faulty thought content. Cognitive skills interventions work on improving the offender's ability to effectively analyze a situation, generate possible responses to it, and weigh the consequences of those responses, as a way to deal effectively to a wide variety of interpersonal problems and stressful events (Dobson & Dozois, 2001). Interventions of this sort typically utilize modelling, guided instruction, feedback and reinforcement, and role-playing to teach offenders such skills as effective communication, critical reasoning, perspective-taking, goal-setting and planning, negotiation, and conflict resolution. Once they master the individual skills, offenders practise putting them together to deal with the problems they encounter in their day-to-day lives (McGuire, 2006).

How Effective Are Offender Treatment Programs?

As our discussion shows, the "right" kinds of offender treatment can make a difference. The question that remains is, "How effective are treatment programs at reducing recidivism?" The body of accumulated research has grown to the point where it is feasible to calculate meta-analytic estimates of treatment effectiveness. In fact, so many meta-analyses exist on this issue that investigators have begun "reviewing the reviews" (e.g. McGuire, 2004). In one such review, Lipsey and Cullen (2007) reported that every meta-analysis they looked at found that correctional treatment had a positive impact on reoffending. The minimum average drop in recidivism associated with treatment across the more than three dozen meta-analyses they examined was 10 per cent.

This reduction is modest and may even seem trivial in the absence of some appropriate context. To gain a better appreciation of what this figure means, some researchers have compared the effect sizes of offender treatment programs with those achieved by interventions in other fields (e.g. Andrews & Bonta, 2010; McGuire, 2002b). Effect sizes provide a common metric for comparing the outcomes of different studies, with larger figures reflecting stronger treatment effects. The effect size associated with offender treatments overall lies in the neighbourhood of 0.10 (e.g. Lösel, 1995). As Table 13.6 shows, treating offenders is not out of line with other medical and psychological interventions.

The problem with looking at the average effectiveness across treatments is that it lumps everything together. Of course, treatments are not all equal; their effectiveness depends greatly on the appropriateness of the intervention. Programs that reflect good treatment practices may be expected to attain recidivism reductions beyond the average 10 per cent. Most illuminating in this regard are analyses carried out by Andrews and Bonta (2006), who examined how adherence (or nonadherence) to RNR principles impacted offender treatment outcome. They reviewed 374 studies of treatment and criminal justice sanctions and rated each one according to the number of core RNR principles followed, from 0 (none

Table 13.6 Effectiveness of selected interventions		
Type of intervention	**Target**	**Mean effect size (r)**
Medical		
Cyclosporine (Rosenthal, 1991)	Organ rejection	0.19
Bypass surgery (Lynn & Donovan, 1980)	Angina pain	0.37
Psychological		
Counselling (Erford et al., 2015)	Youth anxiety	0.29
Cognitive-behavioural treatment (Butler et al., 2006)	Depression	0.44
Correctional		
Offender treatments in general (Lösel,1995)	Recidivism	0.10
Offender treatments adhering to RNR (Andrews & Bonta, 2010)	Recidivism	0.26

Source: Adapted from McGuire, J. (2002b). Criminal sanctions versus psychologically-based interventions with offenders: A comparative empirical analysis. *Psychology, Crime and Law, 8*, 183–208. Reprinted by permission of the publisher (Taylor & Francis Ltd, http://www.tandfonline.com).

of the principles) to 3 (all three principles of risk, need, and responsivity). As the level of adherence rose, the likelihood of reoffending dropped lower and lower. Table 13.6 shows that the effect size associated with programs adhering to the principles of RNR is much larger than the overall average. Andrews and Bonta (2006) estimate that following all three principles could translate to a 35 per cent decrease in recidivism. By comparison, treatments that failed to apply any RNR principles were associated with increased recidivism.

Research has also shown that treatment programs based on CBT are very effective. A meta-analysis of European studies found, on average, a 23 per cent decrease in recidivism with CBT compared to a much more modest 12 per cent decline with other treatments (Redondo, Sánchez-Meca, & Garrido, 1999). Other reviews have produced similar results. Lipsey, Chapman, and Landenberger (2001) examined 14 high-quality studies of CBT with offenders and found that treatment was associated with an overall drop in recidivism of 30 per cent. A broader review by Landenberger and Lipsey (2005), encompassing a larger number of studies exhibiting a greater range of methodological quality, arrived at a slightly lower average reduction of 25 per cent. These researchers identified the treatment features associated with the greatest declines in reoffending (e.g. focusing on high-risk offenders, delivering a reasonable treatment dose, and including components that address anger control and interpersonal problem-solving) and then calculated that a CBT program incorporating these "best practices" might reduce recidivism by as much as 50 per cent.

Treatment Integrity

Unfortunately, standardized treatment programs incorporating many best practices frequently fall short of expectations when they are more widely implemented (e.g. Tong & Farrington, 2006; Wilson, Gallagher, & MacKenzie, 2000). For example, Lipsey's (1992) meta-analytic review of the juvenile delinquency treatment literature discussed earlier in this chapter reported that treatment effectiveness was enhanced by smaller study size and greater researcher involvement in the design and implementation of the program. The essence of this finding has been replicated by other researchers comparing so-called demonstration projects involving small-scale, tightly controlled treatments to real-world applications in which treatment is part of an established program broadly available within a correctional institution or system (e.g. Andrews & Bonta, 2006; Landenberger & Lipsey, 2005). One estimate indicates that correctional treatments operated on a large scale may be only half as effective as those that are part of small demonstration projects (Lipsey, 1999).

The difference in treatment effectiveness between demonstration projects and routine practice has two plausible explanations. One possibility is that the prominent role of researchers in demonstration projects sometimes leads to findings that are biased toward treatment success. The other is that demonstration projects tend to have better quality control, or **treatment integrity**, meaning that they are delivered in the manner intended (Hollin & Palmer, 2006, Lipsey & Cullen, 2007). Lipsey (1992) surmised that, when researchers are heavily involved in small-scale treatment studies, there is probably better quality control and therefore stronger treatment effects. By comparison, treatment programs implemented on a larger scale, in the real world, may not be delivered as carefully or consistently and, as a result, treatment outcomes suffer. Neither explanation has been definitively confirmed or ruled out, but general opinion seems to favour treatment integrity as the most likely reason.

Elements contributing to treatment integrity are numerous and varied. Andrews and Dowden (2005) identified 10 indicators they used to gauge the integrity of correctional programs (see Table 13.7). In a review of almost 300 treatment studies, they found a significant, positive relationship between the number of integrity indicators and treatment effectiveness. That is, better integrity was associated with better treatment results. Although treatment integrity can enhance the effectiveness of "good" treatments, Andrews and Dowden (2005) note that it cannot improve the performance of poor treatments that do not adhere to RNR principles. This makes perfect sense, as delivering an ineffective treatment exactly as it was intended does not change the fact that the treatment was ineffective in the first place. It is akin to building an airplane with serious design flaws that prevent it from flying. No matter how meticulously the design plans are followed or how much care is taken to assemble the plane, it will never get airborne.

treatment integrity The extent to which a treatment is delivered in the manner intended.

Table 13.7 Indicators of program integrity

1. Specific model of desired practice
2. Selection of appropriate staff
3. Staff are trained on program delivery
4. Supervision of staff by someone trained on program delivery
5. Training manuals are available on program delivery
6. Procedures for monitoring service and assessing treatment gains
7. Clients receive adequate treatment dosage
8. New or fresh program
9. Small participant treatment group
10. Program evaluator involved in the design, delivery or supervision of treatment

Source: Adapted from Andrews, D. A., & Dowden, C. (2005). Managing correctional treatment for reduced recidivism: A meta-analytic review of programme integrity. *Legal and Criminological Psychology, 10*, 173–187.

In practice, delivering and maintaining high-quality treatments is a tremendous challenge. Staff turnover, training costs, waning staff enthusiasm, scarce resources, and the time-consuming nature of continually monitoring and supervising treatment all threaten treatment integrity. While all correctional programs face these problems to some degree, larger ongoing programs are the most vulnerable, which may explain the relatively superior performance of small, one-off, demonstration projects. Despite the importance of treatment integrity to treatment success, it has yet to make its way firmly into mainstream correctional practice. Andrews and Dowden (2005) report that only two of their indicators were mentioned in even half the treatment studies they reviewed. References to most integrity indicators were present in only 20 to 40 per cent of treatment programs. The extent to which these results reflect a true lack of treatment integrity as opposed to the researchers' failure to include it in their published reports is less certain, but the figures suggest that much more could be done to improve efforts around treatment integrity.

Putting It All Together: Effective Programs in Practice

Great strides have been made in our understanding of effective correctional treatment programming over the last few decades. We now have a much clearer picture of the elements that make treatment effective. For instance, we know to target high-risk offenders, focus treatment on dynamic risk factors, accommodate the offender's learning style, and use cognitive-behavioural approaches that are multimodal and of sufficient dosage. We have also learned that treatment integrity is critical to maintaining maximum treatment effectiveness. Attention is now increasingly turning to how this knowledge can be effectively integrated into contemporary correctional practices. Program accreditation and program audit are two new developments in this area.

Program accreditation, which has been undertaken primarily in the UK, is a process of assessing and approving treatment programs that reflect best practices (Goggin & Gendreau, 2006). The first step in developing a program accreditation process is to identify the essential elements that make treatment effective and then integrate them into a set of minimum program standards. Correctional treatment programs undergoing accreditation are then evaluated against these standards. Programs that satisfy the criteria are accredited and receive what amounts to an "official" stamp of approval. Presumably, only accredited programs can be used to treat offenders within the correctional system administering the accreditation program. The main advantage is the assurance that accredited programs incorporate the basic features that the available evidence suggests make treatments effective. Accreditation does not guarantee that a particular program works or is better than another program. These are questions that can be answered only by careful research of the program and its impact on offender recidivism.

The primary focus of program accreditation is confirming that correctional programs are well designed at the outset, but it provides little insight into their day-to-day delivery. A **program audit** verifies treatment integrity by assessing whether treatment is being delivered the way it is supposed to be delivered (Hollin & Palmer, 2006). Hollin (1995) recommends that program audits tap three information sources. First, independent external observers should watch the program as it is being administered. Second, program participants should be solicited for their experiences in the program. Finally, program

program accreditation A process for assessing and approving offender treatment programs that incorporate best practices.

program audit An inspection of an offender treatment program that assesses whether treatment is being delivered in the intended manner.

staff should provide a self-reflective review of how they deliver treatment. Once this information has been gathered and collated, program supervisors and administrators can assess how closely the treatment being delivered comes to matching the original design. More important, shortcomings can be identified and strategies to correct them can be implemented. Regular program audits (e.g. once per year) help to ensure that problems are rectified and that program delivery does not drift over time.

Summary

1. The risk of offending represents the likelihood that a particular person will engage in an act of criminal or violent behaviour. Effectively reducing this risk requires the complementary activities of risk assessment and risk management. The risk assessment process focuses on evaluating the level of risk a person poses and the reasons that the person poses a risk. Information from the risk assessment is used to inform risk management, which involves implementing strategies to reduce the offender's identified risks as much as possible. Thus, both activities should be carried out in a coordinated fashion.

2. Every risk assessment has three basic steps: information must be gathered about the offender; the information gathered must be used to identify the presence of risk and protective factors; and some sort of decision-making process must be used to form a judgment about the offender's risk based on the relevant risk and protective factors. One of two types of decision-making processes may be used for this purpose. Decisions based on professional judgment allow the evaluator to exercise discretion, whereas actuarial methods rely on a fixed set of predetermined rules.

3. There are four main methods for conducting risk assessments, which vary in terms of the degree of structure imposed at each step of the process. The unstructured professional judgment method has no structure. The anamnestic method requires the evaluator to gather information about the offender's criminal history (i.e. the personal and situational circumstances that led to the crime) to identify his or her offence cycle, but it does not prescribe specific factors or how factors should be combined into a judgment about risk. The structured professional judgment method directs the evaluator to gather certain information and evaluate the presence (or absence) of particular factors that are operationalized; however, the evaluator has discretion over the final judgment about the offender's risk. Actuarial methods structure all steps of the risk assessment and, most important, it is the only method that eliminates human discretion from the judgments about risk.

4. Treatment is an important strategy for managing the risk of offending. The popular view of offender treatment during the 1970s and 1980s was that "nothing works," but more current research shows that it can reduce reoffending when carried out appropriately. Our present understanding of what constitutes appropriate treatment has been largely guided by the risk–need–responsivity (RNR) model. The risk principle specifies that treatments should be dedicated to high-risk rather than low-risk offenders. According to the needs principle, treatment must target dynamic, or changeable, risk factors, not static ones. The responsivity principle recommends using a structured treatment delivered in a positive therapeutic environment (general responsivity), which should be tailored to suit the offender's unique characteristics and abilities (specific responsivity).

5. In recent years, the good lives model (GLM) has emerged as an alternative to the RNR model. The GLM is a positive, strength-based approach to treatment grounded in the belief that everyone, including offenders, seeks fulfilling and meaningful lives, which are achieved through primary human goods. These goods represent personal characteristics, states of mind, and experiences that are intrinsically valued and promote psychological well-being. GLM assumes that people commit crime to attain primary human goods; therefore, treatment is geared toward developing an offender's capabilities to realize these things using prosocial behaviour. It is expected that the risk of criminal behaviour will diminish as a natural consequence of improving the capabilities of offenders and enriching their lives. Furthermore, the GLM's emphasis on achieving what matters to the offender should serve to motivate them to engage in therapy.

6. Research evidence indicates that a variety of other features, such as a clearly defined program structure, a multimodal intervention, sufficient treatment dose, and delivery in community settings, also enhance treatment effectiveness. One particularly promising therapeutic approach is cognitive-behavioural therapy (CBT), which typically involves changing offender behaviour by altering their thinking through the use of cognitive restructuring, cognitive skills development, or both at the same time. Cognitive restructuring emphasizes getting offenders to recognize and change the errors in their thinking that led to their past offending. Cognitive skills development focuses on teaching offenders how to analyze, consider, and respond appropriately in social situations.

7. The impact of appropriate offender treatment programs in reducing recidivism is relatively small but non-trivial. Moreover, the size of these treatment effects is equivalent to many other interventions in education and medicine. Current efforts are looking at ways to ensure that existing knowledge on best treatment practices are incorporated into the programs delivered to offenders. One strategy is to develop an accreditation process that sets out required criteria for treatment programs based on the available evidence and then approves treatment programs that meet these minimum standards. Another development is the program audit, which involves inspecting a treatment program to verify that it is being delivered consistently and in the manner intended.

Review Questions

1. Explain the difference between static and dynamic risk factors. Indicate whether each of the following is static or dynamic:
    a. exposure to criminal role models growing up
    b. symptoms of psychosis
    c. low educational achievement
    d. a history of past criminal behaviour
    e. a diagnosis of narcissistic personality disorder
    f. a social network dominated by antisocial peers
2. Identify the four risk assessment methods and explain one advantage and one disadvantage of each.
3. Describe the clinical versus actuarial debate and explain how it has shifted recently. Discuss your position on it.
4. Reread the case study of Darnell Pratt. Discuss whether the RNR or GLM model is a better treatment option, given his obvious reluctance to participate in treatment. Give reasons to support your choice.

5. Explain the concept of primary human goods as it relates to the GLM. For each example in the following list, indicate the primary human good(s) the offender was trying to obtain:
   a. a female offender who steals food to feed herself and her children
   b. a young offender who deals and uses drugs as a way to escape from his conflicted relationship with his parents
   c. a male offender who feels he has little control of his life outside his home but gets satisfaction from dominating and abusing his family

Additional Readings

Andrews, D. A., & Bonta, J. (2010). Rehabilitating criminal justice policy and practice. *Psychology, Public Policy, and Law, 16*, 39–55.

Craig, L. A., Dixon, L., & Gagnon, T. A. (2013). *What works in offender rehabilitation: An evidence-based approach to assessment and treatment.* New York, NY: Wiley.

Douglas, K. S., Hart, S. D., Groscup, J. L., Litwack, T. R. (2014). Assessing violence risk. In I. B. Weiner & R. K. Otto (Eds.), *The handbook of forensic psychology* (pp. 385–441). Hoboken, NJ: Wiley.

Otto, R. K., & Douglas, K. S. (2010). *Handbook of violence risk assessment.* New York, NY: Routledge.

Van Voorhis, P., & Salisbury, E. J. (2014). *Correctional counselling and rehabilitation* (8th ed.). Waltham, MA: Anderson Publishing.

Glossary

acquisition In observational learning, the process of paying attention to and memorizing an observed behaviour.

active constraint The relatively large conscious and deliberate effort needed to act in a socially acceptable manner in situations where acting violently is perceived to be an effective and desirable course of action.

actuarial method The risk assessment method that prescribes all aspects of the process, including information gathering, risk factor identification and operationalization, and the rules for combining this information and making the judgment about risk.

acute-battering stage The second stage in Lenore Walker's cycle of abuse theory; characterized by the abusive partner subjecting the victim to various forms of physical, psychological, or sexual abuse.

addiction model of serial homicide A theory of serial murder that states the act of murder has a ritualistic aspect for serial killers that leads them to become addicted to or compelled to kill.

adjusted-actuarial approach The risk assessment method that involves generating an initial judgment of risk using the actuarial method and then subjecting it to the evaluator's professional discretion.

adolescence-limited (AL) pathway The pathway consisting of individuals who engage in less serious or normative patterns of criminal behaviour during the teen years and desist from offending upon entering adulthood.

advantageous comparisons A moral disengagement mechanism whereby people construe their immoral behaviour as less offensive by judging it against another's more egregious acts.

affective symptoms Indicators of a person's emotional responses and feelings.

age–crime curve The distribution of criminal behaviour over the lifespan, which consistently shows that crime rates rise sharply throughout adolescence, peak in early adulthood, and taper off during middle and old age.

age-graded theory of informal social control A developmental theory of criminal behaviour, developed by Robert Sampson and John Laub, which argues that individuals desist from crime when they are subject to informal social controls. These controls are age-graded such that the value or effect increases or decreases at different points of the lifespan.

allele An alternative form of a gene that exists in more than one form.

alogia Speech that is impoverished in terms of the quantity of spoken words or the content of the ideas communicated.

amygdala An almond-shaped subcortical structure that is part of the limbic system, which processes emotional information in the environment, and plays a role in somatic or emotional memory.

anamnestic method The risk assessment method that involves inquiring into an offender's history to identify the sequence of personal and situational factors that the evaluator believes led to past offending.

anhedonia A loss of enjoyment from social and recreational activities that are usually a source of pleasure.

antisocial lifestyle factors A category of risk factors for sexual aggression and recidivism that includes general patterns of antisocial behaviour and lifestyle problems such as impulsivity, employment problems, and a criminal history.

antisocial personality disorder (ASPD) A personality disorder generally characterized by a consistent disregard for and violation of the rights of others. Symptoms may include a failure to conform to social norms or the criminal law, irritability, aggressiveness, consistent irresponsibility, and impulsivity.

appraisal-disruption model The theory that alcohol interferes with the cognitive abilities people need to appraise social cues in the environment properly; as a consequence of alcohol intoxication, they may behave inappropriately for the situation.

asymmetrical relationship between ASPD and psychopathy The empirical finding that many people diagnosed with ASPD are not considered psychopathic but most people assessed by the PCL–R as psychopathic are also diagnosed with ASPD.

attachment theory The idea that early relationships and bonds formed with primary caretakers in infancy significantly influence our capacity to form meaningful relationships with others as adults.

attention allocation model (AAM) The theory that alcohol interferes with the cognitive capacity needed to pay attention to multiple sources of information and, as a consequence of intoxication, people's attention focuses on only the most salient social cues in a situation, which are often aggressive in nature.

attention-deficit/hyperactivity disorder (ADHD) An externalizing behaviour disorder characterized by two broad categories of symptoms: (1) inattention and (2) hyperactivity and impulsivity.

attribution The process of making causal judgments about people's behaviour and events.

attribution of blame A moral disengagement mechanism whereby the victims are blamed for provoking the perpetrators and leaving them with no alternative but to respond as they did.

attrition In terms of a treatment program, the number of intended participants who do not complete the program.

authoritarian parenting A rigid and restrictive approach to parenting characterized by punitive disciplinary methods and non-consultative limit-setting.

authoritative parenting A "firm but fair" approach to parenting characterized by warmth, support, and consultative limit-setting.

autonomic nervous system (ANS) The part of the peripheral nervous system that is responsible for regulating automatic or involuntary functions, including the fight-or-flight response.

aversive events Incidents that produce pain, frustration, and unpleasant feelings.

aversive instigators Cues in the environment that produce specific negative emotional responses that may trigger intimate partner violence.

avoidance learning A process whereby individuals learn to initiate or inhibit certain behaviours in response to aversive stimuli.

avolition A lack of energy and/or disinterest in one's usual activities.

battered woman syndrome The term for the collection of psychological responses commonly experienced by female victims of persistent and serious IPV, including depression, low-self-esteem, and powerlessness.

behavioural activation system (BAS) A biological system that triggers emotional responses in the amygdala and activates behaviours in response to rewards and non-punishment.

behavioural genetics The field of study concerned with understanding the influence of genetics on the expression of characteristics and behaviours within a population.

behavioural inhibition system (BIS) A biological system that triggers emotional responses in the amygdala and activates behaviours in response to aversive stimuli, such as punishment.

behavioural symptoms Indicators of a person's observable and characteristic manner of behaving.

belief maintenance The effort by a delusional person to corroborate or discredit his or her delusions.

binge To consume a large amount of something, such as a drug, in a continuous fashion for an extended time.

biphasic Something that has two phases.

bipolar disorder A mental disorder characterized by episodes of mania alone or varying episodes of mania and depression.

borderline personality disorder A persistent pattern of unstable interpersonal relationships, self-image, and affects and discernible impulsivity that begins by early adulthood and exists in several contexts. Symptoms include chronic feelings of emptiness, affective instability, identity disturbance, and frantic efforts to avoid real or imagined abandonment.

brain plasticity The brain's ability to change structure and function and to develop new neural connections.

brief psychotic disorder A mental disorder like schizophrenia and schizophreniform disorder, except that the symptoms are present for only a very short time.

cardinal traits Dominant personality traits that are externally characteristic of an individual.

case study An in-depth examination or observation of a single individual.

catharsis A Greek word meaning "to cleanse" or "to purge" and referring to the release of blocked anger, frustration, or aggression in mild, non-destructive ways.

causal inference A logical conclusion made when experimental results show that one variable is responsible for changing another.

central traits General characteristics that form the basic foundation of personality but are not necessarily dominant aspects of an individual's dispositional style.

challenge hypothesis A theory that attempts to account for observed relationships between testosterone levels and aggression. The hypothesis proposes that males' testosterone levels will rise in situations that challenge reproductive success or mating.

cheating behaviour Accepting a benefit from another without reciprocating the favour.

chromosome A microscopic structure that contains DNA.

classical conditioning A learning process whereby two stimuli are repeatedly paired and result in a neutral (conditioned) stimulus being able to evoke the response originally evoked by the other (unconditioned) stimulus.

coercion theory The idea that early-onset criminal and violent behaviour develops out of a family environment characterized by coercive and ineffective parent–child interactions.

coercive interactions A pattern of dynamic parent–child interactions wherein the aversive behaviours of one individual elicit an equally aversive response from others, resulting in an escalation of dysfunctional behaviours toward one another.

coercive persuasion Forms of social influence that produce significant changes in an individual's behaviour and thought processes.

cognitive-behavioural therapy (CBT) An approach to psychological treatment that focuses on individuals recognizing and changing errors in their thinking as well as developing cognitive skills as a way to avoid problem behaviours.

cognitive dissonance theory A social psychological theory that proposes the experience of inconsistent thoughts (i.e. dissonant cognitions) results in anxiety that people may reduce by changing their attitudes to minimize the inconsistency.

cognitive-interference theories Theories based on the common premise that alcohol intoxication impairs human social cognition in ways that increase the chance of aggressive and violent behaviour.

cognitive psychology The study of the mental processes involved in human perception, thought, memory, and decision-making.

cognitive restructuring A form of cognitive-behavioural therapy that focuses on changing behaviour by altering a person's thought content. It typically involves challenging the person's distorted beliefs and working to replace undesirable thoughts with more appropriate ones.

cognitive skills development A form of cognitive-behavioural therapy that focuses on changing behaviour by altering how a person processes information and decides how to act. It typically involves the use of modelling and role-playing exercises to develop the person's ability to analyze, consider, and respond effectively to different situations.

command hallucination A false auditory perception of being ordered to do something.

co-morbid A mental disorder or condition that presents with another mental disorder or condition.

concordance rate The percentage of two individuals, usually twins, who match one another with respect to the presence of a particular characteristic or condition.

conditionability The degree to which classical conditioning responses can be easily and strongly formed in a person.

conditioned response (CR) A response in classical conditioning that was originally evoked by the unconditioned stimulus but, as a result of repeated pairings between the unconditioned and the conditioned stimuli, is evoked by the conditioned stimulus.

conditioned stimulus (CS) A stimulus in classical conditioning that was originally neutral but, as a result of repeated pairings with an unconditioned stimulus, triggers the response evoked by the unconditioned stimulus.

conduct disorder (CD) A childhood externalizing disorder characterized by aggression toward people and/or animals, deliberate property destruction, deceitfulness or theft, and serious rule violations. This disorder is often viewed as a precursor to antisocial personality disorder.

conflict theory of crime The theory that crime is determined by the powerful and wealthy members of society, who define it in ways that promote and maintain their position of dominance.

confluence model of sexual aggression An integrated theoretical model of sexual violence that proposes the risk for sexually violent behaviour is influenced by two distinct pathways of factors: hostile masculinity and an impersonal sexual orientation. These pathways may work independently or collectively.

congenital adrenal hyperplasia A disorder of the adrenal gland that can result in a failure to produce sufficient levels of certain hormones, such as cortisol, and excessive production of androgens.

consensus theory of crime The theory that crime is defined in a manner that is broadly agreed upon by the members of society.

construction sample The original group of participants studied to develop a new psychological test or assessment tool.

continuous reinforcement Rules specifying that reinforcement should be delivered after every appropriate response.

contrition stage The final stage in Lenore Walker's cycle of abuse theory; characterized by the abusive partner trying to persuade the victim to remain in the relationship by apologizing, promising to change, and, in many cases, lavishing gifts on him or her.

control group The study participants who are not exposed to the variable or condition under investigation and are used for comparison purposes.

control-override symptoms A term used by Bruce Link and colleagues to describe psychotic symptoms that may lead to a diminished sense of control and autonomy over one's body and actions.

conventional moral reasoning The middle of Lawrence Kohlberg's levels of moral development, whereby right and wrong are determined by the expectations of other significant people, such as family members, close friends, or society at large.

corporal punishment A form of discipline that employs physical force to correct or control a child's behaviour. The force is intended to cause the child pain, not injury.

crash The period following a binge on stimulant drugs, when the intoxication effects rapidly diminish and the user experiences feelings of depression, lethargy, and/or hunger.

craving An intense longing or urge for something, such as a drug.

criminal behaviour An act or omission that is legally defined as a crime.

criminalization of mental disorder The processing of individuals with mental disorder through the criminal justice system for committing nuisance or disruptive behaviours instead of treating these individuals as patients in the mental health system.

criminal thinking Cognitive processes and content that facilitate the initiation and continuation of offending behaviour.

cumulative disadvantage An early difficulty that creates subsequent developmental problems for individuals over the life-course.

cycle of abuse theory The theory of intimate partner violence, proposed by Lenore Walker, that abusive relationships exhibit a predictable cycle of behaviour characterized by the following three stages: tension-building, acute-battering, and contrition.

defence mechanisms Unconscious processes employed by the ego to protect the psyche against unacceptable levels of anxiety.

definitions In Edwin Sutherland's differential association theory, the values, attitudes, norms, and beliefs held by people.

dehumanization A moral disengagement mechanism that loosens the perpetrators' connection to their victims by viewing them as devoid of human qualities or as objects deserving mistreatment.

deindividuation A psychological state characterized by a loss of individual identity, self-awareness, and self-evaluation, which is often associated with being immersed in large groups.

deinstitutionalization A policy implemented in many Western jurisdictions that involves transferring psychiatric patients out of large-scale institutions and into community-based care.

delirium tremens (DTs) A pattern of severe symptoms caused by withdrawal from alcohol and characterized by tremors, delusions, hallucinations, and convulsions.

delusional disorder A mental disorder marked by the presence of one or more persistent, non-bizarre delusions, without any other accompanying psychotic symptoms.

delusional distress A sense of fear, anxiety, or sadness experienced as a result of delusions.

delusions A strongly held but false belief.

deoxyribonucleic acid (DNA) A long, coiled, threadlike strand consisting of small segments known as genes, which constitute the blueprints of life.

depressants A class of drugs that dampen certain aspects of central nervous system function.

destructive cult A strictly organized group that has a charismatic leader, uses deceptive means to recruit members, and retains them through manipulative strategies that negate freedom of choice.

deviance-disavowal theory The theory that, when people are intoxicated, the usual social standards of behaviour are temporarily suspended so that they are viewed as less responsible for their actions.

deviant sexual interests Persistent attractions to illegal or highly unusual sexual acts.

deviant sexual preference hypothesis A theory of sexual violence that posits that men who engage in sexually deviant and violent behaviour are motivated by a recurrent and intense pattern of deviant sexual preferences.

diathesis A genetic vulnerability or predisposition to develop a psychopathological condition.

differential association A theory, proposed by Edwin Sutherland, that the behaviour people learn and exhibit varies as a function of their social interactions and relationships.

differential reinforcement The net effect of all reinforcement and punishment received for a certain response.

diffusion of responsibility A moral disengagement mechanism whereby people minimize their responsibility for immoral acts on the grounds that they are merely one among many involved.

direct reinforcement Reinforcement that is personally experienced.

disciple mass killer A type of mass murderer who kills as a result of his or her relationship with a person ordering the murders.

discriminative stimulus In operant conditioning, a stimulus that signals whether a certain response is likely to be reinforced or punished.

disinhibition syndrome An inability to exercise mental control over emotional responses or to consider alternative, socially acceptable responses in stressful situations.

disinhibition theories of alcohol intoxication Theories based on the common premise that alcohol impairs areas of the brain responsible for inhibiting responses and, as a result of intoxication, behaviours normally suppressed are exhibited.

dismissing attachment An adult attachment style that emerges from avoidant attachment in childhood and is characterized by a strong, positive self-image and a poor, mistrusting regard of other people.

disorganized/fearful attachment An adult attachment style that emerges from disorganized attachment in childhood and is characterized by a contradictory desire to be around others while also keeping them at an emotional distance out of a fear of rejection.

disorganized killer The type of serial killer who is typically socially and sexually inept and has below-average intelligence. The disorganized killer's crime scenes reflect spontaneous attacks, suggesting sudden outbursts of anger.

disorganized symptoms A group of symptoms involving bizarre behaviour or confusing speech that reflect a severe underlying disturbance of thought.

displacement A psychodynamic defence mechanism that involves transferring a feeling about an object that causes discomfort onto another, usually less threatening, object or person.

displacement of responsibility A moral disengagement mechanism whereby people avoid responsibility for their immoral acts by attributing them to people in positions of control and authority.

dissocial personality disorder A mental disorder that corresponds to the construct of psychopathy and is recognized in the World Health Organization's International Classification of Diseases.

distal factor Factors that indirectly increase the risk of future violent behaviour by enhancing proximate factors that encourage violence or diminishing proximate factors that disinhibit violence.

dizygotic twins Twins that develop from two eggs that are independently fertilized by different sperm and consequently vary genetically from one another; also known as fraternal twins.

dopamine A major neurotransmitter that operates like a biochemical switch, activating other neurotransmitter systems. Dopamine is also involved in approach-oriented, or exploratory, behaviours and pleasure-seeking actions.

duration In differential association theory, a modality of association that reflects both the length and proportion of time that a person has had a social relationship with a specific individual.

dynamic risk factor A changeable characteristic associated with an increased likelihood of future criminal behaviour.

dysphoria A mental state characterized by a negative mood, such as depression.

dysphoric/borderline assaulter One of three male spousal assaulter types identified by Holtzworth-Munroe and Stuart; an assaulter who engages in moderate to serious forms of abusive behaviour in the domestic sphere and exhibits serious mental health problems (e.g. borderline personality disorder).

economic compulsive crime A form of drug-related crime identified in Paul Goldstein's tripartite model that occurs as a result of drug users engaging in illegal behaviour as a means to support their drug habit.

ego A mental or psychic structure that regulates the id's demands according to the external environment and the limitations of the social context.

emotional lability An emotional instability, wherein an individual's mood or emotional expressions can change rapidly without warning.

encoding The process of perceiving and organizing incoming stimuli such as social cues.

endocrine system A network of glands that secretes hormones into the bloodstream, regulating several essential functions, including growth, metabolism, and sexual development.

environment of evolutionary adaptiveness (EEA) The set of conditions that existed during ancestral times and to which the human body and brain adapted.

epigenetics Processes that raise or lower genes' activity level without altering their genetic sequence.

episodic dyscontrol syndrome (EDS) A pattern of recurrent, generally uncharacteristic outbursts of uncontrollable and unprovoked rage.

erotomania A subtype of delusional disorder characterized by a person's false belief that another person is in love with him or her.

erotomanic stalker A stalker who suffers from erotomania and therefore delusionally believes that a relationship with his or her victim already exists.

erotophonophilia (or lust murder) A paraphilia involving the murder of an unsuspecting sexual partner.

euphemistic labelling A moral disengagement mechanism whereby people apply a positive description to their immoral behaviour to make it sound less offensive.

evolutionary psychology The field of study concerned with understanding how natural selection shapes and influences mental processes and behaviour.

executive control functions (ECF) Housed in the prefontal cortex, a variety of higher-order cognitive skills that include decision-making, planning and predicting, focusing attention, understanding abstraction and logic, and exercising social control.

expectancy theories Theories based on the common premise that the behaviour of people who are intoxicated is strongly influenced by their pre-existing beliefs about how the drug they took is going to affect them.

experimental group The study participants who are exposed to the variable or condition under investigation.

externalizing behaviour disorders A category of mental disorders that is characterized by behavioural indicators such as fighting, impulsivity, lying, or stealing.

extinction In operant conditioning, a process that occurs when reinforcement is discontinued and responding subsequently diminishes until it stops.

extra-familial child molester A person who sexually abuses a child outside his or her family.

extraversion A personality trait, identified by Hans Eysenck, that is generally characterized by thrill-seeking, sociability, and impulsivity.

Eysenck Personality Questionnaire–Revised (EPQ–R) A self-report questionnaire or scale designed by Hans Eysenck to measure the presence or absence of specific personality traits. The scale consists of a series of yes or no questions organized across three personality categories—extraversion, neuroticism, and psychoticism—and a lie scale designed to measure truthfulness in responding.

factor analysis A statistical technique in which correlations among variables, such as personality traits, are analyzed to identify closely related clusters of those variables.

family-only assaulter One of three male spousal assaulter types identified by Holtzworth-Munroe and Stuart; an assaulter who engages in abusive behaviour in the household but generally not outside the domestic sphere and whose abusive behaviour reflects problems with coping skills and cognitions.

fearlessness model A theory postulating that the failure to experience fear increases a person's likelihood of committing criminal behaviour because he or she is unafraid of the consequences, such as being caught and punished.

fight-or-flight response The body's automatic physiological response to anxiety- or fear-inducing situations, which readies a person to flee from danger or respond with aggression to protect one's self.

filicide A general term that refers to the killing of a child by his or her parent.

five-factor model of personality A trait perspective proposing that personalities can be described with five higher-order trait categories: extraversion, neuroticism, openness to experience, agreeableness, and conscientiousness.

fixation A psychodynamic process wherein an individual fails to resolve a conflict at the appropriate stage of development, resulting in later maladaptive personality development.

flashback A spontaneous reoccurrence of a drug-induced perceptual experience that happens during a drug-free state.

flattened affect A lack of appropriate emotion in a person's observable expressions and behaviours (e.g. facial expressions).

foot-in-the-door technique A compliance tactic that involves getting someone to fulfill a more extreme request by first gaining his or her agreement to perform smaller, benign tasks and gradually increasing them.

formal thought disorder A serious disturbance in the organization, process, or flow of a person's thoughts.

frequency In differential association theory, a modality of association that reflects how often a person is in contact with a specific individual.

frequency-dependent strategy In evolutionary theory, a behavioural pattern that produces relatively greater success when its use within a population is rare and relatively lower success when its use within a population is common.

frontal lobes The largest lobes in the cerebral cortex, which govern higher-order thinking, decision-making functions, and aspects of personality.

frustration In the context of the frustration-aggression hypothesis, the state produced when a person is blocked from attaining an expected goal.

gene A small segment of DNA that constitutes the biological instructions for a certain characteristic or part of the body.

generally violent/antisocial assaulter One of three male spousal assaulter types identified by Holtzworth-Munroe and Stuart; an assaulter who is frequently violent in intimate relationships and other contexts.

general responsivity An aspect of the RNR model's responsivity principle stipulating that, for treatment to be effective, it must be structured and delivered within the context of a positive therapeutic environment.

general theory of crime A theory of crime that proposes criminal behaviour is the result of an inability to exercise self-control.

hallucinations A false sensory perception that occurs in the absence of an appropriate external stimulus.

hallucinogens A class of drugs that are chemically unrelated but are all capable of producing hallucinations.

Hare Psychopathy Checklist–Revised (PCL–R) A clinical assessment instrument developed by Robert Hare to evaluate the relative presence of psychopathic symptoms.

hedonistic serial killer The type of serial killer who is motivated by the thrill or enjoyment derived from killing.

hemispheric asymmetry The asymmetrical distribution or lateralization of particular functions, such as language and verbal skills, to one hemisphere of the brain.

homicide The intentional killing of another person.

homophily The tendency of individuals to associate and socialize with similar others (i.e. "birds of a feather flock together").

hormones Chemical messengers secreted by the endocrine system that play a role in the regulation of several vital bodily functions, including growth, metabolism, and sexual development.

hostile attribution bias The tendency to interpret others' neutral or ambiguous conduct as indications of aggressive intent or behaviour.

hostile masculinity One of the pathways of risk factors in the confluence model of sexual aggression; refers to a general cognitive framework characterized by hostile attitudes and beliefs that accept violence against women.

human agency A term that refers to subjective free will and the conscious decision-making activities of an individual.

hydraulic model of aggression The idea that unexpressed innate aggressive tendencies will accumulate over time until the pressure results in an explosion of aggressive behaviour.

hypoemotionality model A theory postulating that psychopaths' emotional deficits increase their likelihood of committing criminal behaviour because they have no feelings for other people and do not experience any distress over causing harm.

id A mental or psychic structure that represents the basic unconscious human drive for food, shelter, and pleasure.

illicit drug A psychoactive substance that is illegal to possess or use.

imitation In observational learning, the process of replicating an observed behaviour.

immediate appraisal A largely automatic, subconscious process in which arousal, affect, and cognition are constantly evaluated to make inferences about a situation. Immediate appraisals may lead to impulsive behavioural responses or a reappraisal.

impersonal sexual orientation pathway One of the pathways of risk factors in the confluence model of sexual aggression. Men high in this pathway do not view sex as a form of emotional intimacy and tend to prefer casual, promiscuous sexual encounters.

implicit theory A set of beliefs or schemas used to explain, predict, and interpret interpersonal phenomenon.

impulsivity A broad personality trait characterized by stimulation-seeking behaviours and an inclination to initiate behaviours without adequate forethought.

incentive instigators Cues in the environment that act as perceived rewards for abusive behaviour.

inclusive fitness The reproductive success of both the individual and his or her close genetic relatives.

infanticide A form of filicide, specifically, the killing of a child older than 24 hours.

insight The appreciation a person has of his or her mental disorder and the need for treatment.

instigators Events or stimuli in the environment that trigger learned behaviours.

intensity In differential association theory, a modality of association that reflects how personally meaningful and respected an individual is to a specific person.

inter-individual differences Variations that exist between two or more individuals.

intermittent reinforcement Rules specifying that reinforcement should be delivered after some but not every appropriate response.

internal working models Mental templates of expectations about other people's trustworthiness and potential helpfulness. These models are developed in childhood as a result of attachment patterns with primary caretakers.

interpersonal symptoms Indicators of a person's characteristic style of interacting with other people.

interrater reliability The extent to which different evaluators' independent assessments of the same person or thing match.

intimate partner violence (IPV) Acts of physical, psychological, and/or sexual violence and other forms of controlling behaviour against a current or former intimate partner.

intoxication A temporary and reversible state induced by the intake of a psychoactive substance and characterized by disturbed cognition, emotion, or behaviour.

intra-familial child molester A person who sexually abuses a biologically related child or a child for whom he or she assumes a parental role.

intra-individual differences Variations occurring within the same person.

intrasexual competition Rivalry among the members of one sex, usually for mates or resources.

lateralization The localization or specialization of particular processes or functions (e.g. language, spatial skills) to a particular hemisphere of the brain.

learned helplessness A psychological condition in which an individual learns to accept his or her current conditions or situation as unchangeable regardless of his or her actions.

learning A process in which experience causes a change in a person's behavioural repertoire.

licit drug A psychoactive substance that is legal to possess or use.

life-course persistent (LCP) pathway The pathway consisting of delinquent offenders who display a persistent, lifelong pattern of serious criminal and/or violent behaviour.

limbic system An intricately connected system of brain structures responsible for primal emotional drives, including fear, aggression, hunger, and sexual arousal.

longitudinal research design A research design that involves making several observations of the same study participants over a period of time, sometimes many years.

loosening of associations A train of thought that seems to shift from one unrelated idea to another.

love bombing A recruitment technique often employed by cults that involves showering potential recruits with unconditional love, affection, flattery, and security.

love obsessional stalker A stalker who has no prior relationship with his or her victim; the parties are strangers or, at most, casual acquaintances (e.g. neighbours, co-workers).

MacDonald triad A set of three behavioural problems—fire-setting, cruelty toward animals, and enuresis (bedwetting)—that emerge early in childhood and may be precursors to serious forms of adult antisocial behaviour.

macro theory A large-scale theory that explains phenomena at a societal or broad group level.

major depression A mental disorder characterized by an extended period of profound sadness and/or anhedonia.

major mental disorders A group of mental disorders characterized by severe and potentially debilitating disturbances of thought and/or emotion. Schizophrenia, major depression, bipolar disorder, and other conditions featuring psychosis are commonly identified as major mental disorders.

manic episode A period featuring unusually elevated mood, thinking, and/or motor activity that is inappropriate for the circumstances.

Massachusetts Treatment Center (MTC) typology An offender typology that categorizes adult male rapists based on observable behavioural and motivational indicators into four broad groups: opportunistic, pervasively angry, sexually motivated, and vindictive.

mass murder A form of multiple murder that involves killing four or more victims as part of one event at a single geographic location.

mating effort The time, energy, and resources dedicated to having sex with others.

mental disorder An abnormal pattern of thoughts, emotions, or behaviours caused by a personal dysfunction and associated with significant personal distress or disability.

meta-analysis A method of data analysis that involves combining the results of many studies on a particular subject to generate a statistical estimate of the overall magnitude of their findings.

micro theory A small-scale theory that explains phenomena at an individual level.

mission-oriented serial killer The type of serial killer who targets victims based on an agenda or mission, selecting people who he or she feels are unworthy and should be systematically eliminated from society.

modalities of association In differential association theory, qualities that impact the degree of social influence a person has over another.

model The person performing a behaviour observed and learned by someone else.

monozygotic twins Twins that develop from a single fertilized egg that, for unknown reasons, has split; also known as identical twins because the offspring are genetically identical.

moral disengagement A process, described by Albert Bandura, in which people employ a variety of psychological mechanisms to avoid the negative feelings they might otherwise experience as a result of violating their moral standards.

moral justification A moral disengagement mechanism whereby people rationalize their immoral behaviour on the grounds that it was necessary to achieve an important goal or avoid a more serious, harmful consequence.

moral reasoning The analytical process used to arrive at decisions about what is right and wrong.

morality The ability to distinguish between right and wrong.

multimodal program An intervention that addresses more than one need.

narcissistic personality disorder A personality disorder characterized by a pervasive pattern of grandiosity (in fantasy or behaviour), need for admiration, and lack of empathy.

natural selection The differential survival and reproduction of individual members of a species and the resulting increase or decrease of the inheritable characteristics associated with those individuals within a population.

need principle A guideline of the RNR model stipulating that, for treatment to be effective, it should be directed at dynamic risk factors.

negative affect A feeling of discomfort or unpleasantness.

negative definitions In differential association-reinforcement theory, the values, attitudes, norms, and beliefs that disapprove of law-breaking behaviour.

negative punishment A type of punishment that reduces the likelihood of a certain response by removing something pleasant or rewarding when that response occurs.

negative reinforcement A type of reinforcement that increases the likelihood of a certain response by removing something unpleasant or aversive when that response occurs.

negative symptoms A group of symptoms characterized by a deficit of psychological functioning.

neonaticide A form of filicide, specifically, the killing of an infant within the first 24 hours of his or her birth.

nervous system The comprehensive network of nerve cells—or neurons, tissue, and organs—that regulates and coordinates all the body's activities.

neuropsychological tests Tests or tasks designed to measure cognitive or motor functions that are believed to be linked to specific brain structures. Poor performance on these tests provides an indirect indication that an area of the brain may be damaged and malfunctioning.

neuropsychology The study of the brain, its functions, and its role in behaviours and psychological processes.

neurotic extravert A category of individuals who score high on both the extraversion and neuroticism scales of the EPQ–R. These individuals seek excitement and thrills and are very emotionally reactive (i.e. easily angered and upset).

neuroticism A personality trait, identified by Hans Eysenck, that is generally characterized by high levels of emotional reactivity, anxiety, anger, guilt, and depressed mood.

neurotic offender An offender who possesses an overactive or strong superego, resulting in oversocialization and a potential tendency to perceive and judge moral transgressions more harshly.

neurotransmitters Electrochemical messengers that transmit information or impulses from neuron to neuron.

neutralizing definitions In differential association-reinforcement theory, the values, attitudes, norms, and beliefs that recognize law-breaking behaviour as normally unacceptable but rationalize or excuse it in the applicable circumstances.

nonsocial cognition The study of how we understand the physical world and other matters unrelated to people and their social interactions.

nonsocial reinforcement Any event that does not depend on social interaction but follows a response and increases the likelihood of it reoccurring. The event may include attaining certain material items or internal physiological and emotional states.

norepinephrine A neurotransmitter and a hormone that is synthesized from dopamine and plays a role in a number of functions governed in the autonomic nervous system, including the fight-or-flight response.

"normal" antisocial offender An offender who is a fully functioning adult with no maladaptive features but whose superego formation includes internalized pro-criminal attitudes and sentiments as a result of being primarily socialized by, and identifying with, a criminal parent.

normative offences Delinquent acts that represent an attempt to gain some symbolic status associated with maturity and adult privilege. These types of offences are less serious in nature than other crimes and might include petty theft, underage drinking, or truancy from school.

obedience The action of complying with the directions of a higher authority.

observational learning A learning process whereby a person acquires a new behaviour after seeing it performed by someone else.

offence cycle The particular sequence of personal and situational factors that led an offender to commit past criminal acts.

offender classification The process of assessing an offender's personal characteristics and circumstances and matching them to appropriate management strategies and services aimed at lowering his or her risk of reoffending.

operant conditioning A learning process whereby anticipated consequences influence voluntary behavioural choices.

opportunistic rapist type The type of adult male rapist who exhibits a general pattern of impulsive behaviour and typically commits his sexual offences in the context of another crime using lower levels of violence. The category can be further distinguished based on levels of social competency.

oppositional defiant disorder (ODD) A childhood externalizing behaviour disorder characterized by angry/irritable mood, argumentative/defiant behaviour, and vindictiveness.

organic brain syndrome (OBS) A general term referring to diseases, usually not psychiatric disorders, that result in decreased mental functioning. Numerous physical conditions can result in organic brain dysfunction, including head trauma or injury, degenerative diseases, strokes, acute infections, or low levels of oxygen to the brain.

organized killer The type of serial killer who is generally intelligent, socially and sexually adept, emotionally controlled, and able to maintain some façade of normalcy. The organized killer's crime scenes reflect elements of planning and premeditation.

outcome expectancy A mental template of the behavioural result anticipated to follow an action such as drug taking; it is theorized that people will behave in a manner consistent with the results they anticipate.

outcome expectations One of the considerations used to evaluate whether to enact a particular script based on a cost–benefit analysis of the possible positive and negative outcomes.

overcontrolled offender A personality type identified by Edwin Megargee and characterized by an individual's extremely rigid behavioural inhibition system against the expression of aggressive impulses. The acts of violence committed by these individuals are typically explosive, occurring after long periods of building anger and frustration.

paraphilia Recurrent and intense sexual urges, fantasies, or behaviours to anomalous or inappropriate stimuli.

paraphilic disorder A paraphilia that causes the person distress or impairment or involves inflicting psychological distress or physical harm on another person.

parental monitoring A process involving several interrelated behaviours, including parents' awareness and knowledge of their children's activities and limit-setting on their behaviour.

parental practices The diverse range of parental behaviours occurring in the family context, including disciplinary approaches, monitoring and supervision strategies, and interactional styles.

parenting effort The time, energy, and resources dedicated to supporting one's mate and raising one's offspring.

parricide The murder of a parent by his or her child. Matricide refers to killing one's mother and patricide to killing one's father.

passive constraint The relatively small conscious and deliberate effort needed to act in a socially acceptable manner in situations where acting violently is perceived to be an ineffective or undesirable course of action.

penile plethysmography (PPG) A psychophysiological measure of penile tumescence, or an erection, used to assess for deviant sexual preferences among sex offenders.

perinatal birth complications Developmental problems experienced immediately before or after birth.

permissive parenting A "hands-off" approach to parenting characterized by warmth, tolerance, and little parental limit-setting on the child's behaviour.

persecutory delusions A strongly held, false belief that others are conspiring against you or wish to cause you harm.

personality The stable and distinct ways in which individuals think, feel, and behave in social interactions.

personality disorder An enduring pattern of thinking and feeling about oneself and others that significantly and adversely affects how one functions in many aspects of life.

personality type The psychological classification of people into discrete categories based on the statistical combination of specific attributes. Personality types reflect qualitative differences between individuals on these characteristics.

pervasively angry rapist type The type of adult male rapist who has a high level of generalized anger and frequently engages in antisocial and violent behaviour that includes sexual violence against women.

physical violence An intentional act that causes physical insult or injury, regardless of how minor, to another nonconsenting person.

pleasure principle The unconscious instinct to satisfy the id's needs and wants with no consideration of environmental demands or limitations.

polygenic A trait or characteristic that is under the influence of multiple genes.

polymorphism A gene that exists in more than one form.

positive definitions In differential association-reinforcement theory, the values, attitudes, norms, and beliefs that approve of law-breaking behaviour.

positive punishment A type of punishment that decreases the likelihood of a certain response by administering something unpleasant or aversive when that response occurs.

positive reinforcement A type of reinforcement that increases the likelihood of a certain response by administering something pleasant or rewarding when that response occurs.

positive symptoms A group of symptoms characterized by an excess or distortion of psychological functioning.

positron emission tomography (PET) An imaging technique that involves injecting the body with a radioactive substance to locate diseases and to evaluate organ function. Procedurally, the patient is injected and performs a task known to activate particular regions of the brain so that the scan, which measures blood flow, can provide an indication of the organ's activity.

postconventional moral reasoning The highest of Lawrence Kohlberg's levels of moral development, whereby right and wrong are determined by an individual's own principles of equality, justice, and respect for human rights.

postpartum psychosis A rare form of depression experienced by some women after childbirth that can cause delusional and/or disorganized thinking, rapid mood shifts, and bizarre behaviour.

power-oriented serial killer The type of serial killer who is motivated by the power and enjoyment derived from exercising an ultimate life-or-death form of control over another person.

preconventional moral reasoning The lowest of Lawrence Kohlberg's levels of moral development, whereby right and wrong are determined by the anticipated rewards or punishments.

prefrontal cortex The part of the brain located in the anterior region of the frontal lobe and which governs higher-ordering thinking, or executive control functions, and aspects of personality.

prenatal birth complications Developmental difficulties experienced prior to birth, caused by such factors as exposure to toxins during gestation.

preoccupied attachment An adult attachment style that emerges from ambivalent/anxious attachment in childhood and is characterized by a negative view of the self and a strong positive view of others.

pressured speech Extremely rapid speech, delivered as though the speaker cannot express his or her ideas fast enough.

primary human goods Personal characteristics, states of mind, and experiences that are intrinsically valued by people and promote their psychological well-being.

priming The process that occurs when recent exposure to stimuli increases the accessibility of associated mental structures such as scripts, raising the possibility of their subsequent activation.

principle of rationality-within-irrationality The theory that violence committed by individuals with psychosis is often a rational response to irrational symptoms that they experience and perceive as real.

priority In differential association theory, a modality of association that reflects the timing of a person's social relationship with a specific individual.

program accreditation A process for assessing and approving offender treatment programs that incorporate best practices.

program audit An inspection of an offender treatment program that assesses whether treatment is being delivered in the intended manner.

protective factor A characteristic associated with a decreased likelihood of future criminal behaviour.

proximate factors Factors that relate to the characteristics of the person or situation and directly impact the risk of violence.

psychoactive drug A substance that acts on the central nervous system and produces changes in a person's cognition, emotion, or behaviour.

psychodynamic perspective A theoretical approach that views personality as the product of a dynamic interaction between conscious and unconscious mental structures and argues that an abnormal or maladaptive personality results from early developmental conflicts.

psychopathy A personality disorder characterized by an absence of emotional attachment to others and a lack of

concern for their rights and welfare, as well as a sense of entitlement and impulsivity.

psychopharmacological crime A form of drug-related crime identified in Paul Goldstein's tripartite model that occurs as a result of the acute and chronic effects produced by a psychoactive substance.

psychopharmacology (or **behavioural pharmacology**) The branch of psychology that studies the effects of drugs on human cognition, emotion, and behaviour.

psychophysiology The study of the relationship between the underlying physical and chemical functions of living organisms and their psychological states.

psychosis A group of symptoms that involve impaired reality testing, whereby a person has difficulty perceiving what is real and what is fantasy. The hallmarks of psychosis are delusions and hallucinations.

psychoticism A personality trait, identified by Hans Eysenck, that is generally characterized by aggression, tough-mindedness, egotism, non-conforming, and coldness.

punishment In operant conditioning, an event following a response that decreases the likelihood of the response being made again.

quasi-experimental group A research design that incorporates some of the features of a true experiment.

random assignment The assignment of participants to different study conditions on the basis of chance.

rape myth An inaccurate and/or stereotypical attitude or belief regarding sexual violence and victims of sexual violence.

reaction formation A psychodynamic defence mechanism that involves substituting unacceptable behaviour, thoughts, or feelings with the direct opposite.

reality principle The way the conscious mind operates by recognizing the external world (i.e. reality) and regulating behaviour in accordance to the constraints of this realm.

reappraisal The process of re-evaluating arousal, affect, and cognition to make inferences about a situation when the initial or immediate appraisal was unsatisfactory and time and cognitive resources permit a further evaluation.

reciprocal cooperation An evolutionary adaptive behaviour that involves providing a non-related individual with a benefit on the basis that he or she will return the favour and thereby increase survival and reproductive success.

regulators Various forms of punishment that potentially inhibit intimate partner violence if present or enacted.

reinforcement In operant conditioning, an event following a response that increases the likelihood of the response being made again.

reinforcement contingency Consequences that increase or decrease the future possibility of a behaviour being repeated in the presence of an antecedent condition.

reinforcement schedules The rules under which appropriate responses are reinforced.

response evaluation One of the considerations used to evaluate whether to enact a particular script based on how closely it fits one's values and moral beliefs.

response modulation model A theory postulating that psychopaths display an impaired ability to monitor and adjust their behaviour, leading them to overlook or disregard factors that would stop most people in the same situation from initiating or continuing a criminal course of conduct.

responsivity principle A guideline of the RNR model stipulating that, for treatment to be effective, it must be delivered in a manner that matches the offender's abilities and learning styles.

reverse psychopharmacological effect The reduced, rather than enhanced, likelihood of criminal behaviour, brought about by the acute and chronic effects of a psychoactive substance.

risk assessment The process of evaluating the likelihood of someone's risk of offending and the reasons that the person poses a risk.

risk factor A characteristic associated with an increased likelihood of future criminal behaviour.

risk management The process of implementing strategies and services intended to mitigate identified risks.

risk of offending The likelihood that a particular person will engage in an act of criminal or violent behaviour, usually within a specified time frame.

risk principle A guideline of the RNR model stipulating that, for treatment to be effective, the intensity level must be matched to the offender's risk of reoffending such that low-risk offenders receive little or no treatment and high-risk offenders receive the most treatment.

rush The sudden and intensely pleasurable feeling users may experience immediately following the administration of a psychoactive drug.

schema A cognitive structure that helps us organize and interpret general information.

schema-based model of sexual assault A theory of sexual assault that proposes sexual offending is precipitated by dysfunctional schemas about sexuality and sexual behaviour interacting with environmental variables.

schizoaffective disorder A mental disorder characterized by symptoms of both schizophrenia and a mood disorder.

schizophrenia A mental disorder characterized by a mixture of psychotic symptoms that are present for a prolonged period.

schizophreniform disorder A mental disorder similar to schizophrenia, except that the symptoms are not present for as long.

script An organized unit of knowledge or mental template that lays out the expected sequence of behaviour for a particular social situation as well as the likely outcome of that behaviour.

secondary traits Personality traits that are related to specific attitudes or preferences and typically appear only in certain situations or under specific circumstances.

secure attachment An adult attachment style that emerges from secure attachment in childhood and is characterized by a positive self-image and positive view of others.

selective disinhibition A theory that the effect of alcohol in disinhibiting violence depends on the perceived effectiveness of acting violently in the particular circumstances.

self-awareness model The theory that people must be actively conscious of what they are doing in order to evaluate their conduct against relevant standards of behaviour; people with an impaired sense of self-awareness are likely to act inappropriately.

self-efficacy One of the considerations used to evaluate whether to enact a particular script based on the likelihood that it can be successfully performed.

self-medication hypothesis A theory proposing that some individuals take psychoactive drugs to suppress pre-existing feelings of anger and aggression; it is thought that, without this suppressing effect, such individuals are prone to act on these feelings.

self-regulation The ability to control our emotional responses and evaluate and select appropriate behavioural responses.

serial murder A form of multiple murder that involves killing two or more victims at different times.

serotonin A neurotransmitter that plays a role in several emotional and behavioural processes, including mood, appetite, and sleep regulation and behavioural inhibition.

sexual fantasy Any mental imagery that an individual experiences as sexually arousing or erotic.

sexually motivated rapist type The type of adult male rapist who is motivated by sexually deviant fantasies. This type can be further distinguished based on levels of social competency and the presence or absence of sadistic expressions of these fantasies.

sexual violence A threatened, attempted, or actual sexual act against another person without his or her consent.

simple obsessional stalker A stalker who has had a relationship with his or her victim (e.g. former intimate partner); the most common type of stalker.

situational (or contextual) factors Features, events, or social interactions that characterize a person's surrounding circumstances.

skin conductance A measure of changes in the skin's resistance to electrical currents, which is closely connected to perspiration levels; it corresponds directly to autonomic nervous system functioning and indirectly to one's emotional state.

social cognition The study of how we understand ourselves and other people.

social construction of crime The process of defining crime is social and political in nature and consequently the definitions of crime embody human values and moral beliefs about right and wrong.

social cues The words, gestures, and actions of other people that provide clues about their feelings, thoughts, and motives.

social dominance A form of non-physical aggression that is characterized by behaviours designed to achieve higher rankings or hierarchical status in social peer groups.

social learning A theory that behaviour is acquired through interaction with other people and the environment.

social mimicry A process in which two species share the same environment and compete for the same resources. When one species is more successful at obtaining resources, the other will mimic or adopt these behaviours to become more competitive and to ensure resource acquisition.

social reinforcement The verbal and non-verbal behaviour and gestures made by others following a response, which increase the likelihood of that response being repeated.

socialization The teaching of values and morals and the setting of limits on behaviour within the family context.

sociometric status A measurement technique in developmental psychology used to gauge the extent that an individual is liked or disliked by his or her peer group.

sociopathy A label previously used to describe the construct of psychopathy. Early editions of the DSM included this term, but it no longer exists as a diagnostic category.

specific responsivity An aspect of the RNR model's responsivity principle stipulating that, for treatment to be effective, the therapeutic approach must be tailored to the offender's particular characteristics and abilities.

spreading activation A process that occurs when activation of one part of an interconnected neural network leads to the activation of the other parts.

spree murder A form of multiple murder that involves killing the victims during one continuous event at two or more geographic locations.

stalking A pattern of repeated contact with a person that is unwanted and causes the person to reasonably fear for his or her safety or the safety of people known to him or her.

static risk factor A permanent, or at least very difficult to change, characteristic associated with an increased likelihood of future criminal behaviour.

stimulants A class of drugs that elevate aspects of central nervous system function.

stimulus generalization In classical conditioning, the capacity of stimuli that are similar to the conditioned stimulus to evoke the same conditioned response.

strange situation An experimental research procedure in which researchers observe childrens' responses to separation from, and reunion with, their mothers or primary caretakers.

structural turning points Significant life events, such as marriage or the birth of a child, that introduce informal social controls to an individual's life.

structured professional judgment (SPJ) method The risk assessment method that prescribes the minimum information that must be gathered and identifies and operationalizes the risk factors that must be considered but gives the evaluator discretion over how to synthesize this information and make the judgment about risk.

subcriminal psychopath An individual who displays the symptoms of psychopathy but whose behaviour has not brought him or her into formal contact with the criminal justice system.

substance misuse The intake of a psychoactive substance in doses or for purposes other than those prescribed or intended.

substance use The consumption of psychoactive drugs in amounts that do not cause significant impairment in a person's functioning.

substance use disorders A pattern of problematic psychoactive drug use that causes significant distress or impairment and is typically associated with impaired control over drug taking and harm to the user.

superego A mental or psychic structure that represents an individual's conscience, or internalized standards of right and wrong.

symptom-based theories of crime Theories that attribute the criminal behaviour of a person with a mental disorder to the altered perceptions, thoughts, and emotions experienced as a result of his or her mental condition.

symptom-consistent behaviour Conduct that appears to reflect the symptoms of a person's mental disorder and therefore makes it reasonable to infer that the disorder contributed to his or her behaviour.

systemic crime A form of drug-related crime identified in Paul Goldstein's tripartite model that occurs because the drug trade is illegal and its participants cannot turn to authorities for assistance.

temperament A person's natural mood state as evidenced by basic emotional and behavioural dispositions.

temporal lobe epilepsy A neurological disorder that originates in the temporal lobes and is characterized by uncontrollable seizures stemming from abnormal electrical activity in the brain.

temptation talk Peer-group discussions that reinforce rule violations and antisocial behaviour.

tense situations A term used by Virginia Hiday to describe incidents of interpersonal distress and/or conflict that result when other people get frustrated or attempt to confront or control a person manifesting psychosis.

tension-building stage The first stage in Lenore Walker's cycle of abuse theory; characterized by the abusive partner becoming increasingly tense, irritable, angry, and psychologically abusive.

testosterone An androgen, or male sex hormone, that is responsible for the development of male sex characteristics.

theory A set of interconnected statements that explain the relationship between two or more events.

third variable An extraneous and uncontrolled factor that may be responsible for changes occurring in a study variable.

thought insertion The perception that ideas or thoughts that do not belong to a person are being put inside his or her mind.

threatened egotism model A model stating that individuals with an inflated sense of themselves may defend against unfavourable feedback that threatens this unrealistic self-appraisal by reacting aggressively against the information source.

threat symptoms A term used by Bruce Link and colleagues to describe psychotic symptoms that cause an individual to feel that he or she is likely to be harmed. These symptoms are equivalent to persecutory delusions.

token economy A structured behaviour modification system that awards tokens or another symbolic reward whenever certain desirable behaviours are exhibited; the accumulated tokens can be exchanged for privileges or prizes.

tolerance A condition caused by regular drug intake, whereby a higher dose is required to produce the same effects previously obtained with a lower dose.

total birth cohort A group of people born in the same jurisdiction during a specific time period.

trait A durable disposition to behave in a particular way across a variety of situations.

trait perspective A theoretical approach that views personality as the combination of various stable dispositional qualities that a person exhibits.

trauma-control model of serial homicide A theory of serial murder that argues that the combination of certain predispositional factors and early traumatic events interact with several other factors (e.g. low self-esteem and abnormal fantasies) over the life-course to create a serial murderer.

trauma reinforcers Events experienced in adulthood that reinforce or trigger responses felt during similar or related traumatic events in childhood.

traumatic events Severely negative events that occur during a person's formative years.

treatment dosage The amount of treatment, usually measured in hours, delivered to participants during the course of a treatment program.

treatment integrity The extent to which a treatment is delivered in the manner intended.

treatment program A highly structured treatment incorporating specific treatment goals and treatment content that is defined and sequenced.

unconditioned response (UCR) A response in classical conditioning that is evoked by a stimulus naturally and without learning.

unconditioned stimulus (UCS) A stimulus in classical conditioning that evokes a response naturally and without learning.

undercontrolled offender A personality type identified by Edwin Megargee and characterized by an individual's quick temper, low tolerance to frustration or provocation, and failure to internalize inhibitions or restraints against behaving aggressively.

underregulation Disinhibited or impulsive behaviour that results from a failure to exert control over one's feelings and subsequent behaviours.

unstructured professional judgment method The risk assessment method that gives the evaluator complete discretion over all aspects of the process, including information gathering, risk factor identification and operationalization, information synthesis, and making the judgment about risk.

vicarious reinforcement Reinforcement that other people are observed experiencing or are known to have experienced.

vindictive rapist type The type of adult male rapist who is a misogynist and whose sexual offences are characterized by a high level of anger specifically intended to humiliate and degrade women. This category can be further distinguished by levels of social competency.

violence An intentional act of threatened, attempted, or actual physical harm directed against a non-consenting person.

violence inhibition mechanism (VIM) A biological system, and part of the fight-or-flight response, that is activated by distress signals and subsequently triggers inhibitory emotional responses from the amygdala.

visionary serial killer The type of serial killer who is motivated by a serious psychotic disorder. These individuals suffer from delusions or hallucinations and often report hearing voices instructing them to target and kill certain people.

weak ego offender An offender who possesses an underdeveloped ego, resulting in an inability to adapt his or her behaviour to the particular demands of the situation.

weak superego offender An offender who possesses a weak or incomplete superego that is unable to control the instincts of the id, resulting in a lack of internalized representations of morality and ethics.

withdrawal A condition characterized by symptoms that emerge when a person who has developed tolerance to a drug abruptly stops taking it. These symptoms are usually the opposite of the effects produced when the drug is taken.

word salad Nonsensical speech characterized by a series of unconnected words and phrases.

References

Ægisdóttir, S., White, M. J., Spengler, P. M., Maugherman, A. S., Anderson, L. A., Cook, R. S., . . . Rush, J. D. (2006). The meta-analysis of clinical judgment project: Fifty-six years of accumulated research on clinical versus statistical prediction. *The Counselling Psychologist, 34,* 341–382.

Abbey, A., Jacques-Tiura, A. J., & LeBreton, J. M. (2011). Risk factors for sexual aggression in young men: An expansion of the Confluence Model. *Aggressive Behavior, 37,* 450–464.

Abramson, M. F. (1972). The criminalization of mentally disordered behaviour: Possible side-effect of a new mental health law. *Hospital and Community Psychiatry, 23,* 101–105.

Adams, G. (2012, June 14). Good night to a goodfella: The death of Henry Hill is the end of a Mafia story. *The Independent.* Retrieved from http://www.independent.co.uk/news/people/news/good-night-to-a-goodfella-the-death-of-henry-hill-is-the-end-of-a-mafia-story-7848862.html

Adorno, T. W., Frenkel-Brunswick, E., Levison, D. J., & Sanford, R. N. (1950). *The authoritarian personality.* New York, NY: Harper.

Advokat, C. D., Comaty, J. E., & Julien, R. M. (2014). *Julien's primer of drug action: A comprehensive guide to the actions, uses, and side effects of psychoactive drugs* (13th ed.). New York, NY: Worth.

Agnew, R., & Brezina, T. (2001). *Juvenile delinquency: Causes and control.* Los Angeles, CA: Roxbury Publishing.

Ahlander, J., & Moskwa, W. (2011, July 27). "There was panic and he was very calm"; Survivors share chilling accounts of Island massacre. *National Post,* p. A1.

Ainsworth, M. D. (1979). Infant–mother attachment. *American Psychologist, 34,* 932–937.

Ainsworth, M. D., Blehar, M. C., Waters, E., & Wall, S. (1979). *Patterns of attachment: A psychological study of the strange situation.* Hillsdale, NJ: Erlbaum.

Akers, R. L. (2009). *Social learning and social structure: A general theory of crime and deviance.* New Brunswick, NJ: Transaction.

Akers, R. L., & Jensen, G. F. (2006). The empirical status of social learning theory of crime and deviance: The past, present, and future. In F. P. Cullen, J. P. Wright, & K. R. Blevins (Eds.), *Taking stock: The status of criminological theory* (pp. 37–76). Piscataway, NJ: Transaction.

Akers, R. L., & Sellers, C. S. (2013). *Criminological theories: Introduction, evaluation, and application.* New York, NY: Oxford University Press.

Akiskal, H. S. (2005a). Mood disorders: Historical introduction and conceptual overview. In B. J. Sadock & V. A. Sadock (Eds.), *Kaplan & Sadock's comprehensive textbook of psychiatry* (8th ed.) (pp. 1559–1575). Philadelphia, PA: Lippincott Williams & Wilkins.

Akiskal, H. S. (2005b). Mood disorders: Clinical features. In B. J. Sadock & V. A. Sadock (Eds.), *Kaplan & Sadock's comprehensive textbook of psychiatry* (8th ed.) (pp. 1611–1652). Philadelphia, PA: Lippincott Williams & Wilkins.

Alcock, J. (2013). *Animal behavior: An evolutionary approach* (10th ed.) Sunderland, MA: Sinauer.

Alexy, E. M., Burgess, A. W., Baker, T., & Smoyak, S. A. (2005). Perceptions of cyberstalking among college students. *Brief Treatment and Crisis Intervention, 5,* 279–289.

Allen, J. P., Hauser, S. T., & Borman-Spurrell, E. (1996). Attachment theory as a framework for understanding sequelae of severe adolescent psychopathology: An 11-year follow-up study. *Journal of Consulting and Clinical Psychology, 64,* 254–263.

Alley, C. S., Minnis, H., Thompson, L., Wilson, P., & Gillberg, C. (2014). Neurodevelopmental and psychosocial risk factors in serial killers and mass murderers. *Aggression and Violent Behavior, 19,* 288–301.

Allport, G. W. (1961). *Pattern and growth in personality.* New York, NY: Holt, Rinehart, and Winston.

Altemeyer, R. A. (1988). *Enemies of freedom: Understanding right-wing authoritarianism.* San Francisco, CA: Jossey-Bass.

Alterman, A. I., & Cacciola, J. S. (1991). The antisocial personality disorder diagnosis in substance abusers: Problems and issues. *Journal of Nervous and Mental Disease, 179,* 401–409.

Alvarez, L., & Buckley, C. (2013, July 13). Zimmerman is acquitted in Trayvon Martin killing. *The New York Times.* Retrieved from http://www.nytimes.com/2013/07/14/us/george-zimmerman-verdict-trayvon-martin.html

Amen, D. G., Stubblefield, M., Carmichael, G., Thisted, R. (1996). Brain SPECT findings and aggressiveness. *Annals of Clinical Psychiatry, 8,* 129–137.

American Psychiatric Association. (2013). *Diagnostic and statistical manual of mental disorders* (5th ed.). Washington, DC: Author.

Anastasio, P. A., & Costa, D. M. (2004). Twice hurt: How newspaper coverage may reduce empathy and engender blame for female victims of crime. *Sex Roles, 51,* 535–542.

Andersen, H. S. (2004). Mental health in prison populations. A review—with special emphasis on a study of Danish prisoners on remand. *Acta Psychiatrica Scandinavica, 110* (Suppl. 424), 5–59.

Anderson, C. A., & Bushman, B. J. (2002). Human aggression. *Annual Review of Psychology, 53,* 27–51.

Anderson, C. A., & Carnagey, N. L. (2004). Violent evil and the general aggression model. In A. G. Miller (Ed.), *The social psychology of good and evil* (pp. 168–192). New York, NY: Guildford.

Anderson, C. A., & Huesmann, L. R. (2003). Human aggression: A social-cognitive view. In M. A. Hogg &

J. Cooper (Eds.), *The Sage handbook of social psychology* (pp. 296–323). Thousand Oaks, CA: Sage.

Anderson, C. A., Shibuya, A., Ihori, N., Swing, E. L., Bushman, B. J., Sakamoto, A., . . . Saleem, M. (2010). Violent video game effects on aggression, empathy, and prosocial behavior in Eastern and Western countries: A meta-analytic review. *Psychological Bulletin, 136*, 151–173.

Anderson, S., Damasio, H., Tranel, D., & Damasio, A. (2000). Long-term sequelae of prefrontal cortex damage acquired in early childhood. *Developmental Neuropsychology, 18*, 281–296.

Andrews, D. A., & Bonta, J. (2006). *The psychology of criminal conduct* (4th ed). Newark, NJ: LexisNexis/Matthew Bender.

Andrews, D. A., & Bonta, J. (2010). Rehabilitating criminal justice policy and practice. *Psychology, Public Policy, and Law, 16*, 39–55.

Andrews, D. A., Bonta, J., & Hoge, R. D. (1990). Classification for effective rehabilitation: Rediscovering psychology. *Criminal Justice and Behavior, 17*, 19–52.

Andrews, D. A., & Dowden, C. (2005). Managing correctional treatment for reduced recidivism: A meta-analytic review of programme integrity. *Legal and Criminological Psychology, 10*, 173–187.

Andrews, D. A., & Dowden, C. (2006). Risk principle of case classification in correctional treatment: A meta-analytic investigation. *International Journal of Offender Therapy and Comparative Criminology, 50*, 88–100.

Andrews, D. A., Zinger, I., Hoge, R. D., Bonta, J., Gendreau, P., & Cullen, F. T. (1990). Does correctional treatment work? A clinically relevant and psychologically informed meta-analysis. *Criminology, 28*, 369–404.

Andrews, T. K, Rose, F. D., & Johnson, D. A. (1998). Social and behavioral effects of traumatic brain injury in children. *Brain Injury, 12*, 133–138.

Ando, K., Tsuchida, S., Imai, Y., Shiomura, K., Murata, K., Watanabe, N., . . . & Genjida, K. I. (1998). College students and religious groups in Japan: How are they influenced and how do they perceive the group members? *Japanese Psychological Research, 40*, 206–220.

Angermeyer, M. C. (2000). Schizophrenia and violence. *Acta Psychiatrica Scandinavia, 102* (Suppl. 407), 63–67.

Anglin, M. D., & Speckart, G. (1988). Narcotics use and crime: A multisample, multimethod analysis. *Criminology, 26*, 197–233.

Appelbaum, P. S., Robbins, P. C., & Monahan, J. (2000). Violence and delusions: Data from the MacArthur violence risk assessment study. *American Journal of Psychiatry, 157*, 566–572.

Arboleda-Florez, J., & Holley, H. L. (1988). Criminalization of the mentally ill: Part II. Initial detention. *Canadian Journal of Psychiatry, 33*, 87–95.

Archer, J. (1991). The influence of testosterone on human aggression. *British Journal of Psychology, 82*, 1–28.

Archer, J. (2006). Testosterone and human aggression: An evaluation of the challenge hypothesis. *Neuroscience and Biobehavioral Reviews, 30*, 319–345.

Arendt, M., Rosenberg, R., Fjordback, L., Brandholdt, J., Foldager, L., Sher, L., & Munk-Jorgensen, P. (2007). Testing the self-medication hypothesis of depression and aggression in cannabis-dependent subjects. *Psychological Medicine, 37*, 935–945.

Arendt, M., Rosenberg, R., Foldager, L., Sher, L., & Munk-Jorgensen, P. (2007). Withdrawal symptoms do not predict relapse among subjects treated for cannabis dependence. *The American Journal on Addictions, 16*, 461–467.

Armstrong, T. A., & Boutwell, B. B. (2012). Low resting heart rate and rational choice: Integrating biological correlates of crime in criminological theories. *Journal of Criminal Justice, 40*, 31–39.

Arrigo, B. A., & Griffin, A. (2004). Serial murder and the case of Aileen Wuornos: Attachment theory, psychopathy, and predatory aggression. *Behavioural Sciences and the Law, 23*, 375–393.

Arrigo, B. A., & Shipley, S. (2001). The confusion over psychopathy (I): Historical considerations. *International Journal of Offender Therapy and Comparative Criminology, 45*, 325–344.

Arseneault, L., Moffitt, T. E., Caspi, A., Taylor, P. J., & Silva, P. A. (2000). Mental disorders and violence in a total birth cohort. *Archives of General Psychiatry, 57*, 979–986.

AuCoin, K., & Beauchamp, D. (2007). *Impacts and consequences of victimization, GSS 2004.* Ottawa, ON: Canadian Centre for Justice Statistics, Statistics Canada.

Azrin, N. H. (1960). Effects of punishment intensity during variable-interval reinforcement. *Journal of the Experimental Analysis of Behavior, 3*, 123–142.

Azrin, N. H., & Holz, W. C. (1966). Punishment. In W. K. Honig (Ed.), *Operant behavior: Areas of research and application* (pp. 380–447). New York, NY: Appleton-Century-Crofts.

Azrin, N. H., Holz, W. C., & Hake, D. F. (1963). Fixed-ratio punishment. *Journal of the Experimental Analysis of Behavior, 6*, 141–148.

Babchishin, K. M., Hanson, R., & Hermann, C. A. (2011). The characteristics of online sex offenders: A meta-analysis. *Sexual Abuse: Journal of Research and Treatment, 23*, 92–123.

Babiak, P. (1995). When psychopaths go to work: A case study of an industrial psychopath. *Applied Psychology: An International Review, 44*, 171–178.

Babiak, P. (2000). Psychopathic manipulation at work. In C. B. Gacono (Ed.), *The clinical and forensic assessment of psychopathy: A practitioner's guide* (pp. 287–312). Mahwah, NJ: Erlbaum.

Babiak, P., & Hare, R. D. (2006). *Snakes in suits: When psychopaths go to work.* New York, NY: HarperCollins.

Bagwell, C. L. (2004). Friendships, peer networks, and antisocial behavior. In J. B. Kupersmidt & K. A. Dodge (Eds.), *Children's peer relations: From development to intervention* (pp. 37–57). Washington, DC: American Psychological Association.

Bailey, D. S., Leonard, K. E., Cranston, J. W., & Taylor, S. P. (1983). Effects of alcohol and self-awareness on human physical aggression. *Personality and Social Psychology Bulletin, 9*, 289–295.

Baker, E., & Beech, A. R. (2004). Dissociation and variability of adult attachment dimensions and early maladaptive schemas in sexual and violent offenders. *Journal of Interpersonal Violence, 19*, 1119–1136.

Bakermans-Kranenburg, M. J., & van Ijzendoorn, M. H. (2006). Gene–environment interaction of the dopamine D4 receptor (DRD4) and observed maternal insensitivity predicting externalizing behavior in preschoolers. *Developmental Psychobiology, 48*, 406–409.

Ball, J. C., Shaffer, J. W., & Nurco, D. (1983). The day-to-day criminality of heroin addicts in Baltimore: A study in the continuity of offence rates. *Drug and Alcohol Dependence, 12*, 119–142.

Bandura, A. (1973). *Aggression: A social learning analysis.* Englewood Cliffs, NJ: Prentice Hall.

Bandura, A. (1977). *Social learning theory.* Englewood Cliffs, NJ: Prentice Hall.

Bandura, A. (1979). The social learning perspective: Mechanisms of aggression. In H. Toch (Ed.), *Psychology of crime and criminal justice* (pp. 198–236). New York, NY: Holt, Rinehart and Winston.

Bandura, A. (1999). Moral disengagement in the perpetration of inhumanities. *Personality and Social Psychology Review, 3*, 193–209.

Bandura, A., Ross, D., & Ross, S. A. (1961). Transmission of aggression through imitation of aggressive models. *Journal of Abnormal and Social Psychology, 63*, 575–582.

Bandura, A., Ross, D., & Ross, S. A. (1963). Vicarious reinforcement and imitative learning. *Journal of Abnormal and Social Psychology, 67*, 601–607.

Bandura, A., Underwood, B., & Fromson, M. E. (1975). Disinhibition of aggression through diffusion of responsibility and dehumanization of victims. *Journal of Research in Personality, 9*, 253–269.

Banks, T., & Dabbs, J. M. (1996). Salivary testosterone and cortisol in a delinquent and violent urban subculture. *Journal of Social Psychology, 136*, 49–56.

Barbaree, H. E., Seto, M. C., Langton, C. M., & Peacock, E. J. (2001). Evaluating the predictive efficiency of six risk instruments for adult sex offenders. *Criminal Justice and Behavior, 28*, 490–521.

Barbaree, H. E., Seto, M. C., Serin, R., Amos, N. L., & Preston, D. L. (1994). Comparisons between sexual and nonsexual rapist subtypes: Sexual arousal to rape, offense precursors, and offense characteristics. *Criminal Justice and Behavior, 21*, 95–114.

Bardone, A. M., Moffitt, T. E., & Caspi, A. (1996). Adult mental health and social outcomes of adolescent girls with depression and conduct disorder. *Development and Psychopathology, 8*, 811–829.

Barlow, D. H., Durand, V. M., & Stewart, S. H. (2009). *Abnormal psychology: An integrative approach* (2nd Canadian ed.). Toronto, ON: Nelson.

Barnes, J. C., & Jacobs, B. A. (2013). Genetic risk for violent behavior and environmental exposure to disadvantage and violent crime: The case for gene–environment interaction. *Journal of Interpersonal Violence, 18*, 92–120.

Baron, R. A., Earhard, B., & Ozier, M. (1998). *Psychology* (2nd Canadian ed.). Scarborough, ON: Prentice Hall.

Barongan, C., & Hall, G. C. (1995). The influence of misogynous rap music on sexual aggression against women. *Psychology of Women Quarterly, 19*, 195–207.

Barratt, E. S. (1994). Impulsiveness and aggression. In J. Monahan and H. Steadman (Eds.), *Violence and mental disorders: Developments in risk assessment* (pp. 61–79). Chicago, IL: University of Chicago Press.

Barrett, L., Dunbar, R., & Lycett, J. (2002). *Human evolutionary psychology.* Princeton, NJ: Princeton University Press.

Barry, C. T., Frick, P. J., DeShazo, T. M., McCoy, M. G., Ellis, M., & Loney, B. R. (2000). The importance of callous-unemotional traits for extending the concept of psychopathy to children. *Journal of Abnormal Psychology, 109*, 335–340.

Barry, D. (2011). Looking behind the mug-shot grin. *The New York Times.* Retrieved from http://www.nytimes.com/2011/01/16/us/16loughner.html?_r=0.

Bartels, R. M., & Gannon, T. A. (2011). Understanding the sexual fantasies of sex offenders and their correlates. *Aggression and Violent Behavior, 16*, 551–561.

Bartels, S. J., Drake, R. E., Wallach, M. A., & Freeman, D. H. (1991). Characteristic hostility in schizophrenic outpatients. *Schizophrenia Bulletin, 17*, 163–171.

Bartholomew, K., & Horowitz, L. M. (1991). Attachment styles among young adults: A test of a four-category model. *Journal Personality and Social Psychology, 61*, 226–244.

Bartol, C. R., & Bartol, A. M. (2012). *Criminal behavior: A psychosocial approach* (10th ed.). Upper Saddle River, NJ: Prentice Hall.

Basile, K. C., Smith, S. G., Breiding, M. J., Black, M. C., & Mahendra, R. (2014). *Sexual violence surveillance: Uniform definitions and recommended data elements. Version 2.0.* Atlanta, GA: Centers for Disease Control and Prevention, National Center for Injury Prevention and Control.

Basinger, K. S., Gibbs, J. C., & Fuller, D. (1995). Context and the measurement of moral judgment. *International Journal of Behavioral Development, 18*, 537–556.

Bates, J. E., Pettit, G. S., Dodge, K. A., & Ridge, B. (1998). Interaction of temperamental resistance to control and restrictive parenting in the development of externalizing behavior. *Developmental Psychology, 34*, 982–995.

Baumeister, R. F. (2001, April). Violent pride: Do people turn violent because of self-hate or self-love? *Scientific American*, 96–101.

Baumeister, R. F., Bushman, B. J., & Campbell, W. K. (2000). Self-esteem, narcissism, and aggression: Does violence result from low self-esteem or from threatened egoism? *Current Directions in Psychological Science, 9*, 26–29.

Baumeister, R. F., Smart, L., & Boden, J. M. (1996). Relation of threatened egotism to violence and aggression: The dark side of high self-esteem. *Psychological Review, 103,* 5–33.

Baumrind, D. (1966). Effects of authoritative parental control on child behavior. *Child Development, 37,* 887–907.

Baumrind, D. (1971). Current patterns of parental authority. *Developmental Psychology Monographs, 4,* 1–103.

Baumrind, D. (1991). Parenting styles and adolescent development. In J. Brook-Gunn, R. Lerner, & A.C. Petersen (Eds.), *The encyclopedia of adolescence.* New York, NY: Garland.

Baumrind, D., Larzelere, R. E., & Cowan, P. A. (2002). Ordinary physical punishment: Is it harmful? *Psychological Bulletin, 138,* 580–589.

Bean, P. (2004). *Drugs and crime* (2nd ed.). Cullompton, UK: Willan.

Beasley, J. O. (2004). Serial murder in America: Case studies of seven offenders. *Behavioral Sciences and the Law, 22,* 395–414.

Beaver, K. M. (2009). Molecular genetics and crime. In A. Walsh & K. M. Beaver (Eds.), *Biosocial criminology: New directions in theory and research* (pp. 50–72). New York, NY: Routledge.

Beaver, K. M. (2013). The familial concentration and transmission of crime. *Criminal Justice and Behavior, 40,* 139–155.

Beaver, K. M., Gibson, C. L., DeLisi, M., Vaughn, M. G., & Wright, J. P. (2012). The interaction between neighborhood disadvantage and genetic factors in the prediction of antisocial outcomes. *Youth Violence and Juvenile Justice, 10,* 25–40.

Beck-Sander, A., Birchwood, M., & Chadwick, P. (1997). Acting on command hallucinations: A cognitive approach. *British Journal of Clinical Psychology, 36,* 139–148.

Bègue, L., Subra, B., Arvers, P., Muller, D., Bricout, V., & Zorman, M. (2009). A message in a bottle: Extrapharmacological effects of alcohol on aggression. *Journal of Experimental Social Psychology, 45,* 137–142.

Beiser, M., Dion, R., & Gotowiec, A. (2000). The structure of attention-deficit and hyperactivity symptoms among Native and non-Native elementary school children. *Journal of Abnormal Child Psychology, 28,* 425–437.

Beitchman, J. H., Baldassarra, L., Mik, H., De Luca, V., King, N., Bender, D., . . . Kennedy, J. L. (2006). Serotonin transporter polymorphisms and persistent, pervasive childhood aggression. *American Journal of Psychiatry, 163,* 1103–1105.

Belfort, J. (2007). *The wolf of Wall Street.* New York, NY: Bantom Dell.

Belfrage, H. (1998). A ten-year follow-up of criminality in Stockholm mental patients: New evidence for a relation between mental disorder and crime. *The British Journal of Criminology, 38,* 145–155.

Belsky, J. (2000). Conditional and alternative reproductive strategies: Individual differences in susceptibility to rearing experiences. In J. L. Rodgers, D. C. Rowe, & W. B. Miller (Eds.), *Genetic influences on human fertility and sexuality: Theoretical and empirical contributions from the biological and behavioral sciences* (pp. 127–146). Boston, MA: Kluwer.

Belsky, J. (2005). Differential susceptibility to rearing influence: An evolutionary hypothesis and some evidence. In B. J. Ellis & D. F. Bjorklund (Eds.), *Origins of the social mind: Evolutionary psychology and child development* (pp. 139–163). New York, NY: Guilford Press.

Belsky, J., Bakermans-Kranenburg, M. J., & van Ijzendoorn, M. H. (2007). For better and for worse: Differential susceptibility to environmental influences. *Current Directions in Psychological Science, 16,* 300–304.

Belsky, J., & Pluess, M. (2009). Beyond diathesis stress: Differential susceptibility to environmental influences. *Psychological Bulletin, 135,* 885–908.

Belsky, J., Steinberg, L., & Draper, P. (1991). Childhood experience, interpersonal development, and reproductive strategy: An evolutionary theory of socialization. *Child Development, 62,* 647–670.

Bengston, S., & Långström, N. (2007). Unguided clinical and actuarial assessment of re-offending risk: A direct comparison with sex offenders in Denmark. *Sex Abuse, 19,* 135–153.

Bennett, T. (2000). *Drugs and crime: The results of the second developmental phase of the NEW-ADAM programme.* Home Office Research Study 205. London, UK: Home Office.

Bennett, T., Holloway, K., & Farrington, D. (2008). The statistical association between drug misuse and crime: A meta-analysis. *Aggression and Violent Behavior, 13,* 107–118.

Berenbaum, S. A., & Resnick, S. M. (1997). Early androgen effects on aggression in children and adults with congenital adrenal hyperplasia. *Psychoneuroendocrinology, 22,* 505–515.

Berkowitz, L. (1965). The concept of aggressive drive: Some additional considerations. In L. Berkowitz (Ed.), *Advances in Experimental Social Psychology* (Vol. 2) (pp. 301–327). New York, NY: Academic Press.

Berkowitz, L. (1968). Impulse, aggression and the gun. *Psychology Today, 2,* 19–22.

Berkowitz, L. (1969). The frustration-aggression hypothesis revisited. In L. Berkowitz (Ed.), *Roots of aggression: A re-examination of the frustration-aggression hypothesis* (pp. 1–28). New York, NY: Atherton Press.

Berkowitz, L. (1978). Whatever happened to the frustration-aggression hypothesis? *American Behavioral Scientist, 21,* 691–708.

Berkowitz, L. (1989). Frustration-aggression hypothesis: Examination and reformulation. *Psychological Bulletin, 106,* 59–72.

Berkowitz, L. (1990). On the formation and regulation of anger and aggression: A cognitive neoassociationistic analysis. *American Psychologist, 45,* 494–503.

Berkowitz, L. (1993). *Aggression: Its causes, consequences, and control.* Philadelphia, PA: Temple University Press.

Berkowitz, L. (2003). Affect, aggression, and antisocial behavior. In R. J. Davidson, K. R. Scherer, & H. H. Goldsmith (Eds.), *Handbook of affective sciences* (pp. 804–823). Oxford, UK: Oxford University Press.

Berkowitz, L., Cochran, S. T., & Embree, M. C. (1981). Physical pain and the goal of aversively stimulated aggression. *Journal of Personality and Social Psychology, 40*, 687–700.

Berkowitz, L., & LePage, A. (1967). Weapons as aggression-eliciting stimuli. *Journal of Personality and Social Psychology, 7*, 202–207.

Berndt, T. J., & Keefe, K. (1995). Friends' influence on adolescents' adjustment to school. *Child Development, 66*, 1312–1329.

Bernstein, D., Cramer, K. M., Fenwick, K. D., & Fraser, I. (2008). *Psychology* (1st Canadian ed.). Boston, MA: Houghton Mifflin.

Berrios, G. E. (1996). *The history of mental symptoms: Descriptive psychopathology since the nineteenth century.* Cambridge, UK: Cambridge University Press.

Bettencourt, B. A., & Kernahan, C. (1997). A meta-analysis of aggression in the presence of violent cues: Effects of gender differences and aversive provocation. *Aggressive Behavior, 23*, 447–456.

Bettencort, B. A., Talley, A., Benjamin, A. J., & Valentine, J. (2006). Personality and aggressive behavior under provoking neutral conditions: A meta-analytic review. *Psychological Bulletin, 132*, 751–777.

Beyer, K., Mack, S. M., & Shelton, J. L. (2008). Investigative analysis of neonaticide: An exploratory study. *Criminal Justice and Behaviour, 35*, 522–535.

Bezchlibnyk-Butler, K. Z., Jeffries, J. J., Procyshyn, R. M., & Virani, A. (2014). *Clinical handbook of psychotropic drugs.* Ashland, OH: Hogrefe.

Bierman, K. L., & Wargo, J.B. (1995). Predicting the longitudinal course associated with aggressive-rejected, aggressive (non-rejected), and rejected (non-aggressive) boys. *Child Development, 64*, 139–151.

Bijleveld, C. C., & Wilkman, M. (2009). Intergenerational continuity in convictions: A five-generation study. *Criminal Behaviour and Mental Health, 19*, 142–155.

Bioulac, B., Benezech, M., Renaud, B., Noel, B., & Roche, D. (1980). Serotonergic function in the 47, XYY syndrome. *Biological Psychiatry, 15*, 917–923.

Bjørkly, S. (2002a). Psychotic symptoms and violence toward others—A literature review of some preliminary findings Part 1. Delusions. *Aggression and Violent Behavior, 7*, 605–616.

Bjørkly, S. (2002b). Psychotic symptoms and violence toward others—A literature review of some preliminary findings Part 2. Hallucinations. *Aggression and Violent Behavior, 7*, 617–631.

Black, D. W., Baumgard, C. H., & Bell, S. E. (1995). A 16- to 45-year follow-up of 71 men with antisocial personality disorder. *Comprehensive Psychiatry, 36*, 130–140.

Black, M. C., Basile, K. C., Breiding, M. J., Smith, S. J., Walters, M. L., Merrick, M. T., . . . Stevens, M. R. (2011). *The national intimate partner and sexual violence survey: 2010 summary report.* Atlanta, GA: National Center for Injury Prevention and Control, Centers for Disease Control and Prevention.

Blackburn, R. (1968). Personality in relation to extreme aggression in psychiatric offenders. *British Journal of Psychiatry, 114*, 821–828.

Blackburn, R. (1993). *The psychology of criminal conduct: Theory, research, and practice.* Toronto, ON: Wiley.

Blackwell, T. (2012, December 15). "Our hearts are broken today": Schoolchildren cower in closets as gunman kills 26. *National Post*, p. A1.

Blair, P. R., Marcus, D. K., & Boccaccini, M. T. (2008). Is there an allegiance effect for assessment instruments? Actuarial risk assessment as an exemplar. *Clinical Psychology: Science and Practice, 15*, 346–360.

Blair, R. J. R. (1995). A cognitive developmental approach to morality: Investigating the psychopath. *Cognition, 57*, 1–29.

Blair, R. J. R. (2001). Neurocognitive models of aggression, the antisocial personality disorders, and psychopathy. *Journal of Neurology, Neurosurgery, and Psychiatry, 71*, 727–732.

Blair, R. J. R., Mitchell, D. G. V., Peschardt, K. S., Colledge, E., Leonard, R. A., Shine, J. H., . . . Perrett, D. I. (2004). Reduced sensitivity to others' fearful expressions in psychopathic individuals. *Personality and Individual Differences, 37*, 1111–1122.

Blair, R. J. R., Mitchell, D. G. V., Richell, R. A., Kelly, S., Leonard, A., Newman, C., & Scott, S. K. (2002). Turning a deaf ear to fear: Impaired recognition of vocal affect in psychopathic individuals. *Journal of Abnormal Psychology, 111*, 682–686.

Blair, R. J. R., Sellars, C., Strickland, I., Clark, F., Williams, A., Smith, M., & Jones, L. (1995). Emotion attributions in the psychopath. *Personality and Individual Differences, 19*, 431–437.

Bland, R. C., Newman, S. C., Dyck, R. J., & Orn, H. (1990). Prevalence of psychiatric disorders and suicide attempts in a prison population. *Canadian Journal of Psychiatry, 35*, 407–413.

Bland, R. C., Orn, H., & Newman, S. C. (1988). Lifetime prevalence of psychiatric disorders in Edmonton. *Acta Psychiatrica Scandinavica, 77* (suppl. 338), 24–32.

Blitstein, J. L., Murray, D. M., Lytle, L. A., Birnbaum, A. S., & Perry, C. L. (2005). Predictors of violent behavior in an early adolescent cohort: Similarities and differences across genders. *Health Education & Behavior, 32*, 175–194.

Bluestein, G. (2010, February 16). Survivor: Alabama professor in slayings shot methodically. *Denver Post.* Retrieved from http://www.denverpost.com/boywonder/ci_14410166

Boardman, J. D., Menard, S., Roettger, M. E., Knight, K. E., Boutwell, B. B., & Smolen, A. (2014). Genes in the dopaminergic system and delinquent behaviors across the life course: The role of social controls and risks. *Criminal Justice and Behavior, 41,* 713–731.

Bocij, P. (2002). Corporate cyberstalking: An invitation to build theory. *First Monday, 7.* Retrieved from http://pear .accc.uic.edu/ojs/index.php/fm/article/view/1002/923

Bocij, P., & McFarlane, L. (2002). Online harassment: Towards a definition of cyberstalking. *Prison Service Journal, 139,* 31–38.

Boer, D. P., Hart, S. D., Kropp, P. R., & Webster, C. D. (1997). *Manual for the Sexual Violence Risk-20: Professional guidelines for assessing risk of sexual violence.* Burnaby, BC: The Mental Health, Law, and Policy Institute, Simon Fraser University.

Bogaert, A. F. (2001). Handedness, criminality, and sexual offending. *Neuropsychologia, 39,* 465–469.

Bogus wife of Letterman ruled unfit to stand trial. (1988, June 19). *Toronto Star,* p. C2.

Bohm, R. M., & Vogel, B. L. (2011). *A primer on crime and delinquency theory* (3rd ed.). Belmont, CA: Wadsworth.

Bohman, M. (1978). Some genetic aspects of alcoholism and crime: A population of adoptees. *Archives of General Psychiatry, 35,* 269–276.

Bohman, M., Cloninger, R., Sigvardsson, S., & von Knorring, A. L. (1982). Predisposition to petty criminality in Swedish adoptees. I. Genetic and environmental heterogeneity. *Archives of General Psychiatry, 39,* 1233–1241.

Boles, S. M., & Miotto, K. (2003). Substance abuse and violence: A review of the literature. *Aggression and Violent Behavior, 8,* 155–172.

Bolt, D., Hare, R. D., Vitale, J. E., & Newman, J. P. (2004). A multigroup item response theory analysis of the Psychopathy Checklist–Revised. *Psychological Assessment, 16,* 155–168.

Bonovitz, J. C., & Bonovitz, J. S. (1981). Diversion of the mentally ill into the criminal justice system: The police intervention perspective. *American Journal of Psychiatry, 138,* 973–976.

Bonta, J. (1996). Risk-needs assessment and treatment. In A. T. Harland (Ed.), *Choosing correctional options that work: Defining the demand and evaluating the supply* (pp. 18–32). Thousand Oaks, CA: Sage.

Bonta, J. (2002). Offender risk assessment: Guidelines for selection and use. *Criminal Justice and Behavior, 29,* 355–379.

Bonta, J., & Andrews, D. A. (2003). A commentary on Ward and Stewart's model of human needs. *Psychology, Crime and Law, 9,* 215–218.

Bonta, J., Law, M., & Hanson, K. (1998). The prediction of criminal and violent recidivism among mentally disordered offenders: A meta-analysis. *Psychological Bulletin, 123,* 123–142.

Book, A. S., Starzyk, K. B., & Quinsey, V. L. (2001). The relationship between testosterone and aggression: A meta-analysis. *Aggression and Violent Behaviour, 6,* 579–599.

Bornewasser, M., & Mummendey, A. (1982). Effects of arbitrary provocation and arousal on aggressive behavior. *Aggressive Behavior, 8,* 229–232.

Borum, R., Swartz, M., & Swanson, J. (1996). Assessing and managing violence risk in clinical practice. *Journal of Practical Psychiatry and Behavioral Health, 4,* 205–215.

Botelho, G. (2013, June 9). Serial killer, rapist Richard Ramirez—known as "Night Stalker"—dead at 53. Retrieved from http://www.cnn.com/2013/06/07/justice/ california-night-stalker-ramirez-dead/

Bourget, D., Gagne, P., & Labelle, M. (2007). Parricide: A comparative study of matricide versus patricide. *The Journal of the American Academy of Psychiatry and the Law, 35,* 306–312.

Bourget, D., Grace, J., & Whitehurst, L. (2007). A review of maternal and paternal filicide. *Journal of the American Academy of Psychiatry and the Law, 35,* 74–82.

Bowden, M. (2001). *Killing Pablo—The hunt for world's greatest outlaw.* New York, NY: Penguin.

Bowlby, J. (1969). *Attachment and loss: Vol. 1. Attachment.* New York, NY: Basic Books.

Boyce, J. (2013). *Adult criminal court statistics in Canada, 2011/2012.* Ottawa, ON: Canadian Centre for Justice Statistics, Statistics Canada.

Boyce, J., Cotter, A., & Perreault, S. (2014). Police reported crime statistics in Canada, 2013. Ottawa, ON: Canadian Centre for Justice Statistics, Statistics Canada.

Boyce, W. T., & Ellis, B. J. (2005). Biological sensitivity to context: I. An evolutionary-developmental theory of the origins and functions of stress reactivity. *Development and Psychopathology, 17,* 271–301.

Braggart, bully, liar, thief, monster: Olson was all of these. (1982, January 15). *The Globe and Mail,* p. 9.

Brands, B., Sproule, B., & Marshman, J. (1998). *Drugs and drug abuse: A reference text* (3rd ed). Toronto, ON: Addiction Research Foundation.

Brandt, J. R., Kennedy, W. A., Patrick, C. J., & Curtin, J. J. (1997). Assessment of psychopathy in a population of incarcerated adolescent offenders. *Psychological Assessment, 9,* 429–435.

Brasic, J. R., Barnett, J. Y., Zelhof, R., & Tarpley, H. (2001). Dopamine antagonists ameliorate the dyskinesias, aggression, and inattention of persons with mental retardation. *German Journal of Psychiatry, 4,* 9–16.

Breiding, M. J., Basile, K. C., Smith, S. G., Black, M. C., & Mahendra, R. (2015). *Intimate partner surveillance: Uniform definitions and recommended data elements.* Atlanta, GA: National Center for Injury Prevention and Control, Centers for Disease Control and Prevention.

Brendgen, M., Bowen, F., Rondeau, N., & Vitaro, F. (1999). Effects of friends' characteristics on children's social cognitions. *Social Development, 8,* 41–51.

Brennan, K. A., & Shaver, P. R. (1995). Dimensions of adult attachment: An integrative overview. In J. A. Simpson

& W. S. Rholes (Eds.), *Attachment theory and close relationships* (pp. 46–76). New York, NY: Guilford Press.

Brennan, P. A., & Mednick, S. A. (1994). Learning theory approach to the deterrence of criminal recidivism. *Journal of Abnormal Psychology, 103*, 430–440.

Brennan, P. A., Mednick, S. A., & Hodgins, S. (2000). Major mental disorder and criminal violence in a Danish birth cohort. *Archives of General Psychiatry, 57*, 494–500.

Brennan, S. (2012). *Police-reported crime statistics in Canada, 2011.* Ottawa, ON: Canadian Centre for Justice Statistics, Statistics Canada.

Bretherton, I. (1992). The origins of attachment theory: John Bowlby and Mary Ainsworth. *Developmental Psychology, 28*, 759–775.

Bridges, A. J., Wosnitzer, R., Scharrer, E., Sun, C., & Liberman, R. (2010). Aggression and sexual behaviour in best-selling pornography videos: A content analysis update. *Violence against Women, 16*, 1065–1085.

Brink, J. (2005). Epidemiology of mental illness in a correctional system. *Current Opinion in Psychiatry, 18*, 536–541.

Brinkley, J. R., Beitman, B. D., & Friedel, R. O. (1979). Low-dose neuroleptic regimens in the treatment of borderline patients. *Archives of General Psychiatry, 36*, 319–326.

Brizer, D. A. (1988). Psychopharmacology and the management of violent patients. *Psychiatric Clinics of North America, 11*, 551–568.

Brochu, S., Cousineau, M.-M., Gillet, M., Cournoyer, L.-G., Pernanen, K., & Motiuk, L. (2001). Drugs, alcohol, and criminal behaviour: A profile of inmates in Canadian federal institutions. *Forum on Corrections Research, 13*, 20–24.

Brockes, E. (2009, January 3). What happens in war happens. *The Guardian.* Retrieved from http://www.theguardian.com/world/2009/jan/03/abu-ghraib-lynndie-england-interview

Brown, P. (1990). The name game: Toward a sociology of diagnosis. *The Journal of Mind and Behavior, 11*, 385–406.

Brown, S. L., & Forth, A. E. (1997). Psychopathy and sexual assault: Static risk factors, emotional precursors, and rapist subtypes. *Journal of Consulting and Clinical Psychology, 65*, 848–857.

Brownfield, D., & Thompson, K. (1991). Attachment to peers and delinquent behaviour. *Canadian Journal of Criminology, 33*, 45–60.

Bruni, F. (1998, November 22). Behind the jokes, a life of pain and delusion; For Letterman stalker, mental illness was family curse and scarring legacy. *The New York Times.* Retrieved from http://www.nytimes.com/1998/11/22/nyregion/behind-jokes-life-pain-delusion-for-letterman-stalker-mental-illness-was-family.html?pagewanted=all

Brunner, H. G. (1996). MAOA deficiency and abnormal behavior. In G. R. Bock & J. A. Goode (Eds.), *CIBA Foundation Symposium 194, Genetics of criminal and antisocial behavior* (pp. 155–167). Chichester, UK: Wiley.

Brunner, H. G., Nelen, M., Breakefield, O., Ropers, H. H., & van Oost, B. A. (1993). Abnormal behavior associated with a point mutation in the structural gene for monoamine oxidase A. *Science, 262*, 578–580.

Brunner, H. G., Nelen, M. R., van Zandvoort, P., Abeling, N. G. G., van Gennip, A. H., Wolters, E. C., . . . van Oost, B. A. (1993). X-linked borderline mental retardation with prominent behavioral disturbance: Phenotype, genetic localization, and evidence for disturbed monoamine metabolism. *American Journal of Human Genetics, 52*, 1032–1039.

Bryant, E. T., Scott, M. L., Golden, C. J., & Tori, C. D. (1984). Neuropsychological deficits, learning disabilities, and violent behaviour. *Journal of Consulting and Clinical Psychology, 52*, 323–324.

Buchanan, A. (1997). The investigation of acting on delusions as a tool for risk assessment in the mentally disordered. *British Journal of Psychiatry, 170*, 12–16.

Buchanan, A., & David, A. (1994). Compliance and the reduction of dangerousness. *Journal of Mental Health, 3*, 427–429.

Buchanan, A., Reed, A., Wessely, S., Gariety, P., Taylor, P., Grubin, D., & Dunn, G. (1993). Acting on delusions. II: The phenomenological correlates of acting on delusions. *British Journal of Psychiatry, 163*, 77–81.

Buchanan, R. W., & Carpenter, W. T. (2005). Concept of schizophrenia. In B. J. Sadock & V. A. Sadock (Eds.), *Kaplan & Sadock's comprehensive textbook of psychiatry* (8th ed.) (pp. 1329–1345). Philadelphia, PA: Lippincott Williams & Wilkins.

Budd, T., & Mattinson, J. (2000). *The extent and nature of stalking: Findings from the 1998 British Crime Survey.* London, UK: Home Office Research, Development and Statistics Directorate.

Budney, A. J., Moore, B. A., Vandrey, R. G., & Hughes, J. R. (2003). The time course and significance of cannabis withdrawal. *Journal of Abnormal Psychology, 112*, 393–402.

Budney, A. J., Vandrey, R. G., Hughes, J. R., Moore, B. A., & Bahrenburg, B. (2007). Oral delta-9-tetrahydrocannabinol suppresses cannabis withdrawal symptoms. *Drug and Alcohol Dependence, 86*, 22–29.

Bufkin, J. L., & Luttrell, V. R. (2005). Neuroimaging studies of aggressive and violent behaviour: Current findings and implications for criminology and criminal justice. *Trauma, Violence, and Abuse, 6*, 176–191.

Bugliosi, V., & Gentry, C. (1974). *Helter Skelter: The true story of the Manson murders.* New York, NY: Norton.

Burger, J. M. (1999). The foot-in-the-door compliance procedure: A multiple-process analysis and review. *Personality and Social Psychology Review, 3*, 303–325.

Burgess, A. W., & Baker, T. (2002). Cyberstalking. In J. Boon & L. Sheridan (Eds.), *Stalking and psychosocial obsession: Psychological perspectives for prevention, policing, and treatment* (pp. 201–219). Chichester, UK: Wiley.

Burgess, A., Hartman, C., Ressler, R., Douglas, J., & McCormack, A. (1986). Sexual homicide: A motivational model. *Journal of Interpersonal Violence, 1*, 251–272.

Burgess, A. W., Nelson, J. A., & Myers, W. C. (1998). Criminal and behavioral aspects of juvenile sexual homicide. *Journal of Forensic Science, 43*, 321–328.

Burgess, R. L., & Akers, R. L. (1966). A differential association reinforcement theory of criminal behavior. *Social Problems, 14*, 128–147.

Burk, L. R., & Burkhart, B. R. (2003). Disorganized attachment as a diathesis for sexual deviance developmental experience and the motivation for sexual offending. *Aggression and Violent Behavior, 8*, 487–511.

Burrough, B. (2007). The Counterfeit Rockefeller. *Vanity Fair*. Retrieved from http://www.vanityfair.com/fame/features/2001/01/rocancourt200101

Burt, M. R. (1980). Cultural myths and supports for rape. *Journal of Personality and Social Psychology, 38*, 217–230.

Bushman, B. J. (1993). Human aggression while under the influence of alcohol and other drugs: An integrative research review. *Current Directions in Psychological Science, 2*, 148–152.

Bushman, B. J. (1997). Effects of alcohol on human aggression: Validity of proposed explanations. In M. Galanter (Ed.), *Recent developments in alcoholism, Volume 13: Alcoholism and violence* (pp. 227–243). New York, NY: Plenum Press.

Bushman, B. J. (2002). Does venting anger feed or extinguish the flame? Catharsis, rumination, distraction, anger and aggressive responding. *Personality and Social Psychology Bulletin, 28*, 724–731.

Bushman, B. J., & Baumeister, R. F. (1998). Threatened egotism, narcissism, self-esteem, and direct and displaced aggression: Does self-love or self-hate lead to violence? *Journal of Personality and Social Psychology, 75*, 219–229.

Bushman, B. J., & Cooper, H. M. (1990). Effects of alcohol on human aggression: An integrative research review. *Psychological Bulletin, 107*, 341–354.

Buss, D. M. (2012). *Evolutionary psychology: The new science of the mind* (4th ed.). Boston, MA: Allyn and Bacon.

Butler, A. C., Chapman, J. E., Forman, E. M., & Beck, A. T. (2006). The empirical status of cognitive-behavioral therapy: A review of meta-analyses. *Clinical Psychology Review, 26*, 17–31.

Byrne, J. M., Bawden, H. N., Beattie, T., & DeWolfe, N. A. (2003). Risk for injury in preschoolers: Relationship to attention deficit hyperactivity disorder. *Child Neuropsychology, 9*, 142–151.

Cadoret, R. J., Cain, C. A., & Crowe, R. R. (1983). Evidence for gene-environment interaction in the development of adolescent antisocial behavior. *Behavior Genetics, 13*, 301–310.

Cadoret, R. J., Yates, W. R., Troughton, E., Woodworth, G., & Stewart, M. A. (1995). Genetic-environmental interaction in the genesis of aggressivity and conduct disorders. *Archives of General Psychiatry, 52*, 916–924.

Cairns, R. B., & Cairns, B. D. (1994). *Pathways of youth in our time*. New York, NY: Harvester Wheatsheaf.

Cairns, R. B., Cairns, B. D., Neckerman, H. J., Ferguson, L. L., & Gariepy, J. (1989). Growth and aggression: 1. Childhood to early adolescence. *Developmental Psychology, 25*, 320–330.

Cairns, R. B., Cairns, B. D., Neckerman, H. J., Gest, S. D., & Gariepy, J. (1988). Social networks and aggressive behavior: Peer support or peer rejection. *Developmental Psychology, 24*, 815–823.

Cale, E. M. (2006). A quantitative review of the relations between the "Big 3" higher order personality dimensions and antisocial behavior. *Journal of Research in Personality, 40*, 250–284.

Cale, E. M., & Lilienfeld, S. O. (2002). Sex differences in psychopathy and antisocial personality disorder: A review and integration. *Clinical Psychology Review, 22*, 1179–1207.

Cale, E. M., & Lilienfeld, S. O. (2006). Psychopathy factors and risk for aggressive behaviour: A test of the "threatened egotism" hypothesis. *Law and Human Behavior, 30*, 51–74.

Camilleri, J. A., & Quinsey, V. L. (2008). Pedophilia: Assessment and treatment. In D. R. Laws & W. O'Donohue (Eds.), *Sexual deviance: Theory, assessment, and treatment, vol. 2* (pp. 183–212). New York, NY: Guilford Press.

Camp, D. S., Raymond, G. A., & Church, R. M. (1967). Temporal relationship between response and punishment. *Journal of Experimental Psychology, 74*, 114–123.

Campbell, A. (1999). Staying alive: Evolution, culture, and women's intrasexual aggression. *Behavioral and Brain Sciences, 22*, 203–252.

Campbell, A. (2002). *A mind of her own: The evolutionary psychology of women*. New York, NY: Oxford University Press.

Campbell, A. (2009). Gender and crime: An evolutionary perspective. In A. Walsh & K. M. Beaver (Eds.), *Biosocial criminology: New directions in theory and research* (pp. 117–136). New York, NY: Routledge.

Campbell, C. (2010, August 25). Gas-and-dash killer sent back to jail. *The Vancouver Sun*, p. A. 9.

Canadian Press. (2015, July 3). Paul Bernardo wants day parole in Toronto area. Retrieved from http://www.cbc.ca/news/canada/toronto/paul-bernardo-wants-day-parole-in-toronto-area-1.3136868

Carabellese, F., Maniglio, R., Greco, O., & Catanesi, R. (2011). The role of fantasy in a serial sexual offender: A brief review of the literature and a case report. *Journal of Forensic Sciences, 56*, 256–260.

Carey, G. (1992). Twin imitation for antisocial behavior: Implications for genetic and family environment research. *Journal of Abnormal Psychology, 101*, 18–25.

Carey, G. (1994). Genetics and violence. In A. J. Reiss, K. A. Miczek, & J. A. Roth (Eds.), *Understanding and Preventing Violence, Volume 2: Biobehavioral Influences* (pp. 21–58). Washington, DC: National Academy Press.

Carey, G. (2003). *Human genetics for the social sciences*. Thousand Oaks, CA: Sage.

Carey, G., & Goldman, D. (1997). The genetics of antisocial behavior. In D. M. Stoff, J. Breiling, & J. D. Maser (Eds.), *Handbook of antisocial behavior* (pp. 243–254). New York, NY: Wiley.

Carlo, P. (1996). *The Night Stalker: The life and crimes of Richard Ramirez.* New York, NY: Kensington.

Carlo, P. (2006). *The ice man: Confessions of a mafia contract killer.* New York, NY: St Martin's Press.

Carlson, M., Marcus-Newhall, A., & Miller, N. (1990). Effects of situational aggression cues: A quantitative review. *Journal of Personality and Social Psychology, 58,* 622–633.

Carrasco, M., Barker, E. D., Tremblay, R. E., & Vitaro, F. (2006). Eysenck's personality dimension as predictors of male adolescent trajectories of physical aggression, theft, and vandalism. *Personality and Individual Differences, 41,* 1309–1320.

Caspi, A., McClay, J., Moffitt, T. E., Mill, J., Martin, J., Craig, I. W., . . . Poulton, R. (2002). Role of genotype in the cycle of violence in maltreated children. *Science, 297,* 851–854.

Caspi, A., & Moffit, T.E. (1995). The continuity of maladaptive behavior: From description to understanding in the study of antisocial behavior. In D. Cicchetti and D. J. Cohen (Eds.), *Developmental psychopathology, Vol. 2: Risk, disorder, and adaptation* (pp. 472–511). Oxford, UK: Wiley.

Cassar, E., Ward, T., & Thakker, J. (2003). A descriptive model of the homicide process. *Behaviour Change, 20,* 76–93.

Catchpole, R. E. H., & Gretton, H. M. (2003). The predictive validity of risk assessment with violent young offenders: A 1-year examination of criminal outcome. *Criminal Justice and Behavior, 30,* 688–708.

Cauffman, E., Monahan, K. C., & Thomas, A. G. (2015). Pathways to persistence: Female offending from 14 to 25. *Journal of Developmental and Life-Course Criminology, 1,* 236–268.

Cavender, G., & Deutsch, S. K. (2007). CSI and moral authority: The police and science. *Crime, Media, Culture, 3,* 67–81.

Chadwick, P., & Birchwood, M. (1994). The omnipotence of voices: A cognitive approach to auditory hallucinations. *British Journal of Psychiatry, 164,* 190–201.

Chambliss, W. (1972). *Boxman: A professional thief's journey.* New York, NY: Harper and Row.

Chan, C. (2010, July 2). Gas-and-dash killer "uncooperative," but given parole. *Edmonton Journal,* p. A6.

Chan, C. (2011, June 29). 800 officers deployed in downtown riot: Police chief. *The Province,* p. A3.

Chaplin, R., Flately, J., & Smith, K. (2011). *Crime in England and Wales, 2010/11: Findings from the British Crime Survey and police recorded crime.* London, UK: Home Office Statistics.

Charles, K. E., & Egan, V. (2005). Mating effort correlates with self-reported delinquency in a normal adolescent sample. *Personality and Individual Differences, 38,* 1035–1045.

Checknita, D., Maussion, G., Labonte, B., Comai, S., Tremblay, R. E., Vitaro, F., . . . Turbecki, G. (2015). Monoamine oxidase A gene promoter methylation and transcriptional downregulation in an offender population with antisocial personality disorder. *The British Journal of Psychiatry, 206,* 216–222.

Chester, B. (2001). Health consequences of criminal victimization. *International Review of Victimology, 8,* 63–73.

Chilcoat, H. D., & Anthony, J. C. (1996). Impact of parental monitoring on initiation of drug use through late childhood. *The Journal of American Academy of Child & Adolescent Psychiatry, 35,* 91–100.

Chivers, T. (2014, April 6). Psychopaths: How can you spot one? *The Telegraph.* Retrieved from http://www.telegraph.co.uk/culture/books/10737827/Psychopaths-how-can-you-spot-one.html

Christian, R. E., Frick, P. J., Hill, N. L., Tyler, L., & Frazer, D. R. (1997). Psychopathy and conduct problems in children: II. Implications for subtyping children with conduct problems. *Journal of the American Academy of Child and Adolescent Psychiatry, 36,* 233–241.

Church, R. M. (1967). Response suppression. In B. A. Campbell & R. M. Church (Eds.), *Punishment and aversive behavior* (pp. 111–156). New York, NY: Appleton-Century-Crofts.

Chyi, H. I., & McCombs, M. (2004). Media salience and the process of framing: Coverage of the Columbine school shootings. *Journalism & Mass Communication Quarterly, 81,* 22–35.

Cillessen, A. H. N., & Mayeux, L. (2004). Sociometric status and peer group behavior: Previous findings and current directions. In J. B. Kupersmidt & K. A. Dodge (Eds.), *Children's peer relations: From development to intervention* (pp. 3–20). Washington, DC: American Psychological Association.

Cima, M., Smeets, T., & Jelicic, M. (2008). Self-reported trauma, cortisol levels, and aggression in psychopathic and non-psychopathic prison inmates. *Biological Psychiatry, 78,* 75–86.

Cleckley, H. (1941/1976). *The mask of sanity* (5th ed.). St Louis, MO: Mosby.

Clements, C. B. (1996). Offender classification: Two decades of progress. *Criminal Justice and Behavior, 23,* 121–143.

Cloninger, C. R., & Gottesman, I. I. (1987). Genetic and environmental factors in antisocial behavior disorders. In S. A. Mednick, T. E. Moffitt, & S. Stack (Eds.), *The causes of crime: New biological approaches* (pp. 92–109). Cambridge, UK: Cambridge University Press.

Cloninger, C. R., Sigvardsson, S., Bohman, M., & von Knorring, A.-L. (1982). Predisposition to petty criminality in Swedish adoptees: II. Cross-fostering analysis of gene–environment interaction. *Archives of General Psychiatry, 39,* 1242–1247.

Coccaro, E. F. (1989). Central serotonin and impulsive aggression. *British Journal of Psychiatry, 155,* 52–62.

Coccaro, E. F., Bergeman, C. S., & McClearn, G. E. (1993). Heritability of irritable impulsiveness: A study of twins reared together and apart. *Psychiatric Research, 48,* 229–242.

Coccaro, E. F., & Murphy, D. L. (1991). *Serotonin in major psychiatric disorders.* Washington, DC: American Psychiatric Press.

Coccaro, E. F., Siever, L., Howard, M., Klar, H., Maurer, G., Cochrane, K., . . . Davis, K. L. (1989). Serotonergic studies in patients with affective and personality disorders. *Archives of General Psychiatry, 46,* 587–599.

Coccaro, E. F., Sripada, C. S., Yanowitch, R. N., & Phan, K. L. (2011). Corticolimbic function in impulsive aggressive behaviour. *Biological Psychiatry, 69,* 1153–1159.

Cochrane, R. (1974). Crime and personality: Theory and evidence. *Bulletin of the British Psychological Society, 27,* 19–22.

Cohen, L. E., & Machalek, R. (1988). A general theory of expropriative crime: An evolutionary ecological approach. *American Journal of Sociology, 94,* 465–501.

Cohen, L. E., & Machalek, R. (1994). The normalcy of crime: From Durkheim to evolutionary ecology. *Rationality and Society, 6,* 286–308.

Coie, J. D. (2004). The impact of negative social experience on the development of antisocial behavior. In J. Kupersmidt & K. A. Dodge (Eds.), *Peer relations in childhood: From development to intervention to public policy* (pp. 243–267). Washington, DC: American Psychological Association.

Coie, J. D., Dodge, K. A., & Kupersmidt, J. B. (1990). Peer group behavior and social status. In S. R. Asher & J. D. Coie (Eds.), *Peer rejection in childhood* (pp. 17–59). New York, NY: Oxford University Press.

Coie, J. D., & Kupersmidt, J. B. (1983). A behavioral analysis of emerging social status in boys' groups. *Child Development, 54,* 1400–1416.

Coie, J., Terry, R., Lenox, K., Lochman, J., & Hyman, C. (1995). Childhood peer rejection and aggression as predictors of stable patterns of adolescent disorder. *Development and Psychopathology, 7,* 697–713.

Coleburn, J. (2011, December 11). Throwing himself on mercy of court; rioter who confessed says he's "very sorry" and ready to "deal with my actions." *The Province,* p. A3.

Coleman, F. L. (1997). Stalking behavior and the cycle of domestic violence. *Journal of Interpersonal Violence, 12,* 420–432.

Coley, R. L., Morris, J. E., & Hernandez, D. (2004). Out-of-school care and problem behavior trajectories among low-income adolescents: Individual, family, and neighborhood characteristics as added risks. *Child Development, 75,* 948–965.

Collins, J. J. (1988). Suggested explanatory frameworks to clarify the alcohol use/violence relationship. *Contemporary Drug Problems, 15,* 107–121.

Conklin, J. E. (2013). *Criminology* (11th ed.). Upper Saddle River, NJ: Pearson.

Cooke, D. J. (1995). Psychopathic disturbance in the Scottish prison population: The cross-cultural generalisability of the Hare Psychopathy Checklist. *Psychology, Crime & Law, 2,* 101–118.

Cooke, D. J. (1998). Psychopathy across cultures. In D. J. Cooke, A. E. Forth, & R. D. Hare (Eds.), *Psychopathy: Theory, research and implications for society* (pp. 13–45). Dordrecht, The Netherlands: Kluwer Academic.

Cooke, D. J., & Michie, C. (2001). Refining the construct of psychopathy: Towards a hierarchical model. *Psychological Assessment, 13,* 171–188.

Cooke, D. J., Michie, C., & Hart, S. D. (2006). Facets of clinical psychopathy: Toward clearer measurement. In C. J. Patrick (Ed.), *Handbook of psychopathy* (pp. 91–106). New York, NY: Guildford Press.

Cooke, D. J., Michie, C., Hart, S. D., & Clark, D. A. (2004). Reconstructing psychopathy: Clarifying the significance of antisocial behaviour in the diagnosis of psychopathic personality disorder. *Journal of Personality Disorders, 18,* 337–356.

Cooper, A., & Smith, E. L. (2011). *Homicide trends in the United States 1980–2008: Annual rates for 2009 and 2010.* Washington, DC: Bureau of Justice Statistics, U.S. Department of Justice.

Cornell, D. G., Warren, J., Hawk, G., Stafford, E., Oram, G., & Pine, D. (1996). Psychopathy in instrumental and reactive violent offenders. *Journal of Consulting and Clinical Psychology, 64,* 783–790.

Corrado, R. R., Cohen, I., Hart, S., & Roesch, R. (2000). Comparative examination of the prevalence of mental disorders among jailed inmates in Canada and in the United States. *International Journal of Law and Psychiatry, 23,* 633–647.

Corrado, R. R., Vincent, G. M., Hart, S. D., & Cohen, I. M. (2004). Predictive validity of the Psychopathy Checklist: Youth Version for general and violent recidivism. *Behavioral Sciences and the Law, 22,* 5–22.

Corrigan, P. W., & Watson, A. C. (2005). Findings from the National Comorbidity Survey on the frequency of violent behaviour in individuals with psychiatric disorder. *Psychiatry Research, 136,* 153–162.

Cortoni, F., & Hanson, R. K. (2005). *A review of the recidivism rates of adult female sexual offenders* (Research Rep. No. R-169). Ottawa, ON: Correctional Service Canada. Retrieved from http://www.csc-scc.gc.ca/research/092/r169_e.pdf

Côté, G., & Hodgins, S. (1992). The prevalence of major mental disorders among homicide offenders. *International Journal of Law and Psychiatry, 15,* 89–99.

Cotter, A. (2014). *Homicide in Canada, 2013.* Ottawa, ON: Canadian Centre for Justice Statistics, Statistics Canada.

Cotter, A., & Beaupré, P. (2014). *Police-reported sexual offences against children and youth in Canada, 2012.* Ottawa, ON: Canadian Centre for Justice Statistics, Statistics Canada.

Cowan, G., & O'Brien, M. (1990). Gender and survival vs. death in slasher films: A content analysis. *Sex Roles, 25,* 187–196.

Cozby, P. C. (2007). *Methods in behavioral research* (9th ed). New York, NY: McGraw-Hill.

Craig, I. W., & Halton, K. E. (2009). Genetics of human aggressive behaviour. *Human Genetics, 126*, 101–113.

Crane, C. A., Easton, C. J., & Devine, S. (2013). The association between phencyclidine use and partner violence: An initial examination. *Journal of Addictive Diseases, 32*, 150–157.

Crawford, C. (1998a). The theory of evolution in the study of human behavior: An introduction and overview. In C. Crawford & D. L. Krebs (Eds.), *Handbook of evolutionary psychology: Ideas, issues and applications* (pp. 3–41). Mahwah, NJ: Erlbaum.

Crawford, C. (1998b). Environments and adaptations: Then and now. In C. Crawford & D. L. Krebs (Eds.), *Handbook of evolutionary psychology: Ideas, issues and applications* (pp. 275–302). Mahwah, NJ: Erlbaum.

Crick, N. R., & Dodge, K. A. (1989). Children's evaluations of peer entry and conflict situations: Social strategies, goals, and outcome expectations. In B. Schneider, J. Nadel, G. Attili, & R. Weissberg (Eds.), *Social competence in developmental perspective* (pp. 369–399). Dordrecht, The Netherlands: Kluwer Academic.

Crick, N. R., & Dodge, K. A. (1994). A review and reformulation of social information-processing mechanisms in children's social adjustment. *Psychological Bulletin, 115*, 75–101.

Crocker, A. G., Mueser, K. T., Drake, R. E., Clark, R. E., McHugo, G. J., Ackerson, T. H., & Alterman, A. I. (2005). Antisocial personality, psychopathy, and violence in persons with dual disorders: A longitudinal analysis. *Criminal Justice and Behavior, 32*, 452–476.

Cullen, D. (2009). *Columbine.* New York, NY: Twelve.

Cullen, F. T., & Agnew, R. (2006). *Criminological theory— past to present: Essential readings* (3rd ed.). Los Angeles, CA: Roxbury.

Curran, D. J., & Renzetti, C. M. (2001). *Theories of crime* (2nd ed.). Needham Heights, MA: Allyn & Bacon.

Curry, C. (2013, November 25). Newton massacre result of mental illness, access to guns, death obsession. Retrieved from http://abcnews.go.com/US/newtown-massacre-result-mental--access-guns-death/story?id=21003690

Daamen, A. P., Penning, R., Brunt, T., & Verster, J. C. (2012). Cocaine. In J. C. Verster, K. Brady, M. Galanter, & P. Conrod (Eds.), *Drug abuse and addiction in medical illness: Causes, consequences, and treatment* (pp. 163–173). New York, NY: Springer.

Dabbs, J. M., & Hargrove, M. F. (1997). Age, testosterone, and behaviour among female prison inmates. *Psychosomatic Medicine, 59*, 477–480.

Dabbs, J. M., Ruback, R. B., Frady, R. L., Hopper, C. H., & Sgoutas, D. S (1988). Saliva testosterone and criminal violence among women. *Personality and Individual Differences, 9*, 269–275.

Dale, P. G. (1980). Lithium therapy in aggressive mentally subnormal patients. *The British Journal of Psychiatry, 137*, 469–474.

Dalgaard, O. S., & Kringlen, E. (1976). A Norwegian twin study of criminality. *British Journal of Criminal Psychology, 16*, 213–232.

Daly, M., & Wilson, M. (1988a). *Homicide.* Hawthorne, NY: Aldine de Gruyter.

Daly, M., & Wilson, M. (1988b). Evolutionary social psychology and family homicide. *Science, 242*, 519–524.

Daly, M., & Wilson, M. (1998). *The truth about Cinderella: A Darwinian view of parental love.* London, UK: Weidenfeld and Nicolson.

Damasio, H., Grabowski, T., Frank, R., Galaburda, A. M., & Damasio, A. R. (1994). The return of Phineas Gage: Clues about the brain from the skull of a famous patient. *Science, 264*, 1102–1104.

Dantas, S., Santos, A., Dias, I., Dinis-Oliveira, R. J., & Magalhaes, T. (2014). *Parricide: A forensic approach. Journal of Forensic and Legal Medicine, 22*, 1–6.

Darwin, C. (1859/1964). *On the origin of species.* Cambridge, MA: Harvard University Press.

Dauvergne, M., & Brennan, S. (2011). *Police-reported hate crime in Canada, 2009.* Canadian Centre for Justice Statistics, Statistics Canada.

Davidson, R. J., Putnam, K. M., & Larson, C. L. (2000). Dysfunction in the neural circuitry of emotion regulation: A possible prelude to violence. *Science, 289*, 591–594.

Davis, K. E., Ace, A., & Andra, M. (2000). Stalking perpetrators and psychological maltreatment of partners: Anger-jealousy, attachment insecurity, need for control, and break-up context. *Violence and Victims, 15*, 407–424.

Davis, K. E., & Mechanic, M. B. (2009). Stalking victimization: The management of its consequences. In C. Mitchell & D. Anglin (Eds.), *Intimate partner violence: A health-based perspective* (pp. 473–488). New York, NY: Oxford University Press.

Davis, S. (1992). Assessing the "criminalization" of the mentally ill in Canada. *Canadian Journal of Psychiatry, 37*, 532–538.

Dawkins, R. (2006). *The selfish gene* (30th anniversary ed.). New York, NY: Oxford University Press.

Day, A., Casey, S., Ward, T., Howells, K., & Vess, J. (2010). *Transitions to better lives: Offender readiness and rehabilitation.* Portland, OR: Willan.

Deckel, A. W., Hesselbrock, V., & Bauer, L. (1996). Antisocial personality disorder, childhood delinquency, and frontal brain functioning: EEG and neuropsychological findings. *Journal of Clinical Psychology, 52*, 639–650.

Decoster, M., Herbert, M., Meyerhoff, J. L., & Potegal, M. (1996). Brief, high-frequency stimulation of the corticomedial amygdala induces a delayed and prolonged increase of aggressiveness in male Syrian golden hamsters. *Behavioural Neuroscience, 110*, 401–412.

DeLisi, M. (2005). *Career criminals in society.* Thousand Oaks, CA: Sage.

DeLisi, M. (2009). Psychopathy is the unified theory of crime. *Youth Violence and Juvenile Justice, 7*, 256–273.

Dempster, R. J., Lyon, D. R., Sullivan L. E., Hart, S. D., Smiley, W. C., & Mulloy, R. (1996, August). *Psychopathy and instrumental aggression in violent offenders.* Paper presented at the annual meeting of the American Psychological Association, Toronto, ON.

Dennison, S. M., & Stewart, A. (2006). Facing rejection: New relationships, broken relationships, shame, and stalking. *International Journal of Offender Therapy and Comparative Criminology, 50*, 324–337.

Deptula, D. P., & Cohen, R. (2004). Aggressive, rejected, and delinquent children and adolescents: A comparison of their friendships. *Aggression and Violent Behavior, 9*, 75–104.

Depue, R. A., & Collins, P. F. (1999). Neurobiology of the structure of personality: Dopamine, facilitation of incentive motivation, and extraversion. *Behavioral and Brain Sciences, 22*, 491–517.

DeRosier, M. E., Cillessen, A. H. N., Coie, J. D., & Dodge, K. A. (1994). Group social context and children's aggressive behavior. *Child Development, 65*, 1068–1079.

Devita, E. L., Forth, A. E., & Hare, R. D. (1990, May). *Family background of male criminal psychopaths.* Paper presented at the annual meeting of the Canadian Psychological Association, Ottawa, ON.

De Waal, F. B. M. (1989). Food sharing and reciprocal obligations among chimpanzees. *Journal of Human Evolution, 18*, 433–459.

DeWall, C. N., & Anderson, C. A. (2011). The general aggression model. In P. R. Shaver & M. Mikulincer (Eds.), *Human aggression and violence: Causes, manifestations, and consequences* (pp. 15–33). Washington, DC: American Psychological Association.

DeWall, C. N., Bushman, B. J., Giancola, P. R., & Webster, G. D. (2009). The big, the bad, and the boozed up: Weight moderates the effect of alcohol on aggression. *Journal of Experimental Social Psychology, 46*, 619–623.

Dewan, S., & Zezima, K. (2010, February 15). After a shooting, colleagues try to regain footing. *The New York Times.* Retrieved from http://www.nytimes.com/2010/02/16/us/16alabama.html?_r=0

Dhillon, S. (2012, February 15). Stanley cup rioter "ashamed" by actions. *The Globe and Mail*, p. S1.

Diamond, P. M., Wang, E. W., Holzer, C. E. III, Thomas, C., & des Anges, C. (2001). The prevalence of mental illness in prison. *Administration and Policy in Mental Health, 29*, 21–40.

Diener, E. (1977). Deindividuation: Causes and consequences. *Social Behavior and Personality, 5*, 143–155.

Diener, E., Fraser, S. C., Beaman, A. L., & Kelem, R. T. (1976). Effects of deindividuation variables on stealing among Halloween trick-or-treaters. *Journal of Personality and Social Psychology, 33*, 178–183.

Dietz, T. L. (1998). An examination of violence and gender role portrayals in video games: Implications for gender socialization and aggressive behaviour. *Sex Roles, 38*, 425–442.

DiLalla, L. F. (2002). Behavior genetics of aggression in children: Review and future directions. *Developmental Review, 22*, 593–622.

Dishion, T. J., & McMahon, R. J. (1998). Parental monitoring and the prevention of child and adolescent problem behavior: A conceptual and empirical formulation. *Clinical Child and Family Psychology Review, 1*, 61–75.

Dishion, T. J., Patterson, G. R., Stoolmiller, M. & Skinner, M. L. (1991). Family, school, and behavioral antecedents to early adolescent involvement with antisocial peers. *Developmental Psychology, 27*, 172–180.

Ditton, P. M. (1999). *Mental health treatment of inmates and probationers.* NCJ 174463. Washington, DC: U.S. Department of Justice, Bureau of Justice Statistics.

Dobson, K. S., & Dozois, D. J. A. (2001). Historical and philosophical bases of the cognitive-behavioral therapies. In K. S. Dobson (Ed.), *Handbook of cognitive-behavioral therapies* (2nd ed.) (pp. 3–39). New York, NY: Guilford Press.

Dobson, V., & Sales, B. (2000). The science of infanticide and mental illness. *Psychology, Public Policy, & Law, 6*, 1098–1112.

Dodd, V. (2014, February 28). Joanna Dennehy: Serial killer becomes first woman told by judge to die in jail. *The Guardian.* Retrieved from http://www.theguardian.com/uk-news/2014/feb/28/joanna-dennehy-serial-killer-first-woman-die-in-jail

Dodge, K. A. (1980). Social cognition and children's aggressive behavior. *Child Development, 51*, 162–170.

Dodge, K. A. (1986). A social information processing model of social competence in children. In M. Perlmutter (Ed.), *Cognitive perspectives on children's social and behavioral development. The Minnesota symposium on child psychology* (pp. 77–125). Hillsdale, NJ: Erlbaum.

Dodge, K. A. (1991). The structure and function of reactive and proactive aggression. In D. J. Pepler & K. H. Rubin (Eds.), *The development and treatment of childhood aggression* (pp. 201–218). Hillsdale, NJ: Erlbaum.

Dodge, K.A. (2003). Do social-information processing patterns mediate aggressive behavior? In B. Lahey, T. E. Moffitt, & A. Caspi (Eds.), *Causes of conduct disorder and juvenile delinquency* (pp. 254–274). New York, NY: Guilford Press.

Dodge, K. A., & Coie, J. D. (1987). Social-information-processing factors in reactive and proactive aggression in children's peer groups. *Journal of Personality and Social Psychology, 53*, 1146–1158.

Dodge, K. A., & Frame, C. L. (1982). Social cognitive biases and deficits in aggressive boys. *Child Development, 53*, 620–635.

Dodge, K. A., Lansford, J. E., Salzer-Burks, V., Bates, J. E., Petit, G. S., Fontaine, R., & Price, J. M. (2003). Peer rejection and social information-processing factors in the development of aggressive behavior problems in children. *Child Development, 74*, 374–393.

Dodge, K. A., Lochman, J. E., Harnish, J. D., Bates, J. E., & Pettit, G. S. (1997). Reactive and proactive aggression in school-children and psychiatrically impaired chronically assaultive youth. *Journal of Abnormal Psychology, 106,* 37–51.

Dodge, K. A., & Petit, G. S. (2003). A biopsychological model of the development of chronic conduct problems in adolescence. *Developmental Psychology, 39,* 349–371.

Dodge, K. A., Price, J. M., Bachorowski, J., & Newman, J. P. (1990). Hostile attribution biases in severely aggressive adolescents. *Journal of Abnormal Psychology, 99,* 385–392.

Dodge, K. A., & Schwartz, D. (1997). Social information processing mechanisms in aggressive behavior. In D. M. Stoff, J. Breiling, & J. D. Maser (Eds.), *Handbook of antisocial behaviour* (pp. 171–180). New York, NY: Wiley.

Dohrenwend, B. P. (1980). *Mental health in the United States: Epidemiological estimates.* New York, NY: Praeger.

Dollard, J., Doob, L. W., Miller, N. E., Mowrer, O. H., & Sears, R. R. (1939). *Frustration-aggression.* New Haven, CT: Yale University Press.

Dollard, J., & Miller, N. E. (1950). *Personality and psychotherapy: An analysis in terms of learning, thinking, and culture.* New York, NY: McGraw-Hill.

Domjan, M. (2005). *The essentials of conditioning and learning* (3rd ed.). Belmont, CA: Wadsworth.

Donnerstein, E. (1980). Aggressive erotica and violence against women. *Journal of Personality and Social Psychology, 39,* 269–277.

Donnerstein, E. (1984). Pornography: Its effect on violence against women. In N. M. Malamute & E. Donnerstein (Eds.), *Pornography and sexual aggression* (pp. 53–81). Toronto, ON: Academic Press.

Donnerstein, E., & Berkowitz, L. (1981). Victim reactions in aggressive erotic films as a factor in violence against women. *Journal of Personality and Social Psychology, 41,* 710.

Doughton, S. (2003, November 3). Why did Ridgway do it? Experts say he's like other serial killers. *Seattle Times.* Retrieved from http://community.seattletimes.nwsource.com/archive/?date=20031110&slug=ridgmind10m

Douglas, J. E., Burgess, A. W., Burgess, A. G., & Ressler, R. K. (1992). *Crime classification manual.* New York: Lexington Books.

Douglas, J. E., Burgess, A. W., Burgess, A. G., & Ressler, R. K. (2013). *Crime classification manual: A standard system for investigating and classifying violent crime* (3rd ed.). Hoboken, NJ: Wiley.

Douglas, K. S., Cox, D. N., & Webster, C. D. (1999). Violence risk assessment: Science and practice. *Legal and Criminological Psychology, 4,* 149–184.

Douglas, K. S., & Dutton, D. G. (2001). Assessing the link between stalking and domestic violence. *Aggression and Violent Behaviour, 6,* 519–546.

Douglas, K. S., Guy, L. S., & Hart, S. D. (2009). Psychosis as a risk factor for violence to others: A meta-analysis. *Psychological Bulletin, 135,* 679–706.

Douglas, K. S., Hart, S. D., Webster, C. D., & Belfrage, H. (2013). *HCR-20 (Version 3): Assessing risk of violence — User guide.* Burnaby, BC: Mental Health, Law, and Policy Institute, Simon Fraser University.

Douglas, K. S., & Reeves, K. A. (2010). Historical-Clinical-Risk Management-20 (HCR-20) violence risk assessment scheme: Rationale, application, and empirical overview. In R. K. Otto & K. S. Douglas (Eds.), *Handbook of violence risk assessment* (pp. 147–185). New York, NY: Routledge.

Douglas, K. S., & Skeem, J. L. (2005). Violence risk assessment: Getting specific about being dynamic. *Psychology, Public Policy, and Law, 11,* 347–383.

Douglas, K. S., Vincent, G. M., & Edens, J. F. (2006). Risk for criminal recidivism: The role of psychopathy. In C. J. Patrick (Ed.), *Handbook of psychopathy* (pp. 533–554). New York, NY: Guilford Press.

Douglas, K. S., & Webster, C. D. (1999). The HCR-20 violence risk assessment scheme: Concurrent validity in a sample of incarcerated offenders. *Criminal Justice and Behavior, 26,* 3–19.

Draine, J., Salzer, M. S., Culhane, D. P., & Hadley, T. R. (2002). Role of social disadvantage in crime, joblessness, and homelessness among persons with serious mental illness. *Psychiatric Services, 53,* 565–573.

Dugdale, R. L. (1887/1970). *"The Jukes": A study in crime, pauperism, disease, and heredity* (4th ed.). New York, NY: Putnam.

Duel, M., & Hall, J. (2014, March 21). "An apology would be pointless": Triple killer Joanna Dennehy shows no remorse in a revealing letter written from her prison cell. *The Daily Mail.* Retrieved from http://www.dailymail.co.uk/news/article-2585923/I-love-Gaz-strong-feelings-Astonishing-letter-sent-serial-killer-Joanna-Dennehy.html

Duke, A. (2009, August 26). Brown sentenced for Rihanna assault; other incidents surface. Retrieved from http://www.cnn.com/2009/CRIME/08/25/chris.brown.sentencing/

Dunford, F. W., & Elliot, D. S. (1984). Identifying career offenders using self-reported data. *Journal of Research in Crime and Delinquency, 21,* 57–86.

Duntley, J. D., & Buss, D. M. (2004). The evolution of evil. In A. G. Arthur (Ed.), *The social psychology of good and evil* (pp. 102–123). New York, NY: Guilford Press.

Durand, V. M., Barlow, D. H., & Stewart, S. H. (2008). *Essentials of abnormal psychology* (1st Canadian Edition). Toronto, ON: Nelson.

Durbin, J. R., Pasewark, R. A., & Albers, D. (1977). Criminality and mental illness: A study of arrest rates in a rural state. *American Journal of Psychiatry, 134,* 80–83.

Dutton, D. G. (1995a). Male abusiveness in intimate relationships. *Clinical Psychology Review, 15,* 567–581.

Dutton, D. G. (1995b). *The domestic assault of women: Psychological and criminal justice perspectives.* Vancouver, BC: University of British Columbia Press.

Dutton, D. G. (1998). *The abusive personality: Violence and control in intimate relationships.* New York, NY: Guilford Press.

Dutton, D. G. (2007). *Rethinking domestic violence.* Vancouver, BC: University of British Columbia Press.

Dutton, D. G., & Aron, A. P. (1974). Some evidence for heightened sexual attraction under conditions of high anxiety. *Journal of Personality and Social Psychology, 30,* 510–517.

Dutton, D. G., Saunders, K., Starzomski, A., & Bartholomew, K. (1994). Intimacy-anger and insecure attachment as precursors of abuse in intimate relationships. *Journal of Applied Social Psychology, 24,* 1367–1386.

Dutton, L. B., & Winstead, B. A. (2006). Predicting unwanted pursuit: Attachment, relationship satisfaction, relationship alternatives, and break-up distress. *Journal of Social and Personal Relationships, 23,* 565–586.

Dvoskin, J. A., & Heilbrun, K. (2001). Risk assessment and release decision-making: Toward resolving the great debate. *The Journal of the American Academy of Psychiatry and the Law, 29,* 6–10.

Dye, M. L., & Davis, K. E. (2003). Stalking and psychological abuse: Common factors and relationship-specific characteristics. *Violence and Victims, 18,* 163–180.

The Economist. (2012, December 22). Evil beyond imagining: The Newtown killing. *The Economist, 405,* 37–38.

Edens, J. F., Buffington-Vollum, J. K., Colwell, K. W., Johnson, D. W., & Johnson, J. K. (2002). Psychopathy and institutional misbehaviour among incarcerated sex offenders: A comparison of the Psychopathy Checklist–Revised and the Personality Assessment Inventory. *International Journal of Forensic Mental Health, 1,* 49–58.

Edens, J. F., Skeem, J. L., Cruise, K. R., Cauffman, E. (2001). Assessment of "juvenile psychopathy" and its association with violence: A critical review. *Behavioral Sciences and the Law, 19,* 53–80.

Egger, S. A. (2002). *The killers among us: An examination of serial murder and its investigation* (2nd ed.). Upper Saddle River, NJ: Prentice Hall.

Ehrensaft, M. K., Cohen, P., Brown, J., Smailes, E., Chen, H., Johnson, J. G. (2003). Intergenerational transmission of partner violence: A 20-year prospective study. *Journal of Consulting and Clinical Psychology, 71,* 741–753.

Eichelman, B. (1983). The limbic system and aggression in humans. *Neuroscience and Biobehavioural Reviews, 7,* 391–394.

Eichelman, B. (1986). The biology and somatic experimental treatment of aggressive disorders. In P. A. Berger and H. K. H. Brodie (Eds.), *The American handbook of psychiatry* (pp. 651–678). New York, NY: Basic Books.

Elbogen, E. B., & Johnson, S. C. (2009). The intricate link between violence and mental disorder: Results from the National Epidemiologic Survey on Alcohol and Related Conditions. *Archives of General Psychiatry, 66,* 152–160.

Elbogen, E. B., Mustillo, S., Van Dorn, R., Swanson, J. W., & Swartz, M. S. (2007). The impact of perceived need for treatment on risk of arrest and violence among people with severe mental illness. *Criminal Justice and Behavior, 34,* 197–210.

Elbogen, E. B., Van Dorn, R., Swanson, J. W., Swartz, M. S., & Monahan, J. (2006). Treatment engagement and violence risk in mental disorders. *British Journal of Psychiatry, 189,* 354–360.

Eley, C., Lichtenstein, P., & Stevenson, J. (1999). Sex differences in the etiology of aggressive and nonaggressive antisocial behavior: Results from two twin studies. *Child Development, 70,* 155–168.

Ellinwood, E. H. (1971). Assault and homicide associated with amphetamine abuse. *American Journal of Psychiatry, 127,* 1170–1175.

Elliot, F. (1977). Propranolol for the control of belligerent behaviour following acute brain damage. *Annals of Neurology, 1,* 489–491.

Elliott, R. (2014). Everything you need to know about the Ray Rice case. *Time.* Retrieved from http://time.com/3329351/ray-rice-timeline/

Ellis, B. J., Boyce, W. T., Belsky, J., Bakermans-Kranenburg, M. J., & van Ijendoorn, M. H. (2011). Differential susceptibility to the environment: An evolutionary-neurodevelopmental model. *Development and Psychopathology, 23,* 7–28.

Ellis, B. J., Essex, M. J., & Boyce, W. T. (2005). Biological sensitivity to context: II. Empirical explorations of an evolutionary-developmental theory. *Development and Psychopathology, 17,* 303–328.

Ellis, L. (1998). Neodarwinian theories of violent criminality and antisocial behavior: Photographic evidence from nonhuman animals and a review of the literature. *Aggression and Violent Behavior, 3,* 61–110.

Ellis, L., & Ames, M. A. (1989). Delinquency, sidedness, and sex. *Journal of General Psychology, 116,* 57–62.

Ellis, L., & Walsh, A. (1997). Gene-based evolutionary theories in criminology. *Criminology, 35,* 229–276.

Ellis, L., & Walsh, A. (2003). Crime, delinquency, and intelligence: A review of the worldwide literature. In H. Nyborg (Ed.), *The scientific study of general intelligence: Tribute to Arthur R. Jensen* (pp. 343–365). Amsterdam, Netherlands: Pergamon.

Engel, R. S., & Silver, E. (2001). Policing mentally disordered suspects: A re-examination of the criminalization hypothesis. *Criminology, 39,* 225–252.

Engler, B. (2009). *Personality theories* (8th ed.). Toronto, ON: Nelson.

Eppright, T. D., Kashani, J. H., Robison, B. D., & Reid, J. C. (1993). Comorbidity of conduct disorder and personality disorders in an incarcerated juvenile population. *American Journal of Psychiatry, 150,* 1233–1236.

Epstein, J. L. (1989). The selection of friends: Changes across the grades and in different school environments. In T. J.

Berndt & G. W. Ladd (Eds.), *Peer relationships in child development* (pp. 158–187). New York, NY: Wiley.

Erford, B. T., Kress, V. E., Giguere, M., Cieri, D., & Erford, B. M. (2015). Meta-analysis: Counseling outcomes for youth with anxiety disorders. *Journal of Mental Health Counseling, 37*, 63–94.

Erhardt, D., & Hinshaw, S. P. (1994). Initial sociometric impressions of attention-deficit hyperactivity disorder and comparison boys: Predictions from social behaviors and from nonbehavioral variables. *Journal of Consulting and Clinical Psychology, 62*, 833–842.

Eronen, M., Angermeyer, M. C., & Schulze, B. (1998). The psychiatric epidemiology of violent behaviour. *Social Psychiatry and Psychiatric Epidemiology, 33*, S13–S23.

Eronen, M., Tiihonen, J., & Hakola, P. (1996). Schizophrenia and homicidal behaviour. *Schizophrenia Bulletin, 22*, 83–89.

Eschholz, S., Mallard, M., & Flynn, S. (2004). Images of prime time justice: A content analysis of "NYPD Blue" and "Law & Order." *Journal of Criminal Justice and Popular Culture, 10*, 161–180.

Escobar, R. (2009). *Escobar. Drugs. Guns. Money. Power. The inside story of Pablo Escobar, the world's most powerful criminal*. London, UK: Hodder.

Estroff, S. E., & Zimmer, C. (1994). Social networks, social support, and violence among persons with severe, persistent mental illness. In J. Monahan & H. Steadman (Eds.), *Violence and mental disorder: Developments in risk assessment* (pp. 259–295). Chicago, IL: University of Chicago Press.

Eysenck, H. J. (1967). *The biological basis of personality*. Springfield, IL: Charles C. Thomas.

Eysenck, H. J. (1977). *Crime and personality*. London, UK: Routledge and Kegan Paul.

Eysenck, H. J. (1983). Personality, conditioning, and antisocial behavior. In W. S. Laufer & J. M. Day (Eds.), *Personality theory, moral development, and criminal behavior* (pp. 51–80). Lexington, MA: Lexington Books.

Eysenck. H. J. (1990). Crime and personality. In N. Z. Hilton, M. A. Jackson, & C. D. Webster (Eds.), *Clinical criminology: Theory, research, and practice* (pp. 85–99). Toronto, ON: Canadian Scholar's Press.

Eysenck, H. J. (1991). Dimensions of personality: 16, 5 or 3?—Criteria for a taxonomic paradigm. *Personality and Individual Differences, 12*, 773–790.

Eysenck, H. J. (1994). Personality: Biological foundations. In P. Version (Ed.), *The neuropsychology of individual differences* (pp. 151–207). San Diego, CA: Academic Press.

Eysenck, H. J. (1996). Personality and crime: Where do we stand? *Psychology, Crime, & Law, 2*, 143–152.

Eysenck, H. J. (1997). Personality and experimental psychology: The unification of psychology and the possibility of a paradigm. *Journal of Personality and Social Psychology, 73*, 1224–1237.

Eysenck, H. J., & Gudjónsson, G. H. (1989). *The causes and cures of criminality*. New York, NY: Plenum Press.

Eysenck, S. B. G., & Eysenck, H. J. (1968). The measurement of psychoticism: A study of factor stability and reliability. *British Journal of Social and Clinical Psychology, 7*, 286–294.

Eysenck, S. B. G., & Eysenck, H. J. (1977). The place of impulsiveness in a dimensional system of personality description. *British Journal of Social and Clinical Psychology, 16*, 57–68.

Eysenck, S. B. G., Eysenck, H. J., & Barrett, P. (1985). A revised version of the psychoticism scale. *Personality and Individual Differences, 6*, 21–29.

Fabian, J. M. (2010). Neuropsychological and neurological correlates in violent and homicidal offenders: A legal and neuroscience perspective. *Aggression and Violence Behaviour, 15*, 209–223.

Fals-Stewart, W., Leonard, K. E., & Birchler, G. R. (2005). The occurrence of male-to-female intimate partner violence on days of men's drinking: The moderating effects of antisocial personality disorder. *Journal of Consulting and Clinical Psychology, 73*, 239–248.

Farabee, D., Shen, H., Hser, Y.-I., Grella, C. E., & Anglin, M. D. (2001). The effect of drug treatment on criminal behavior among adolescents in DATOS-A. *Journal of Adolescent Research, 16*, 679–696.

Farrell, A. L., Keppel, R. D., & Titterington, V. B. (2011). Lethal ladies: Revisiting what we know about female serial murderers. *Homicide Studies, 15*, 228–251.

Farrington, D. P. (1992). Criminal career research in the United Kingdom. *The British Journal of Criminology, 32*, 521–536.

Farrington, D. P. (1995). The development of offending and antisocial behaviour from childhood: Key findings from the Cambridge Study in Delinquent Development. *Journal of Child Psychology and Psychiatry, 360*, 929–964.

Farrington, D. P. (1997). Early prediction of violent and non-violent youthful offending. *European Journal on Criminal Policy and Research, 5*, 51–66.

Fauman, B. J., & Fauman, M. A. (1982). Phencyclinde abuse and crime: A psychiatric perspective. *Bulletin of the American Academy of Psychiatry and the Law, 10*, 171–176.

Faupel, C. E., & Klockars, C. B. (1987). Drugs–crime connections: Elaborations from the life histories of hardcore heroin addicts. *Social Problems, 34*, 54–68.

Fazel, S., & Danesh, J. (2002). Serious mental disorder in 23 000 prisoners: A systematic review of 62 surveys. *The Lancet, 359*, 545–550.

Fazel, S., Gultai, G., Linsell, L., Geddes, J. R., & Grann, M. (2009). Schizophrenia and violence: Systematic review and meta-analysis. *PLoS Medline, 6*: e1000120. doi:10.1371/journal.pmed.1000120

Fazel, S., & Seewald, K. (2012). Severe mental illness in 33 588 prisoners worldwide: Systematic review and meta-regression analysis. *The British Journal of Psychiatry, 200*, 364–373.

Feehan, M., Stanton, W. R., McGee, R., Silva, P. A., & Moffitt, T. E. (1990). Is there an association between lateral preference and delinquent behaviour? *Journal of Abnormal Psychology, 99,* 198–201.

Feeney, J. A., & Noller, P. (1994). Attachment style and romantic love: Relationship dissolution. *Australian Journal of Psychology, 44,* 69–74.

Federal Bureau of Investigation. (2011). *Crime in the United States, 2010: Offenses cleared.* Retrieved from http://www.fbi.gov/about-us/cjis/ucr/crime-in-the-u.s/2010/crime-in-the-u.s.-2010/clearancetopic.pdf

Felson, R. B., & Lane, K. J. (2009). Social learning, sexual and physical abuse, and adult crime. *Aggressive Behavior, 35,* 489–501.

Fennig, S., Fochtmann, L. J., & Bromet, E. J. (2005). Delusional disorder and shared psychotic disorder. In B. J. Sadock & V. A. Sadock (Eds.), *Kaplan & Sadock's comprehensive textbook of psychiatry* (8th ed.) (pp. 1525–1533). Philadelphia, PA: Lippincott Williams & Wilkins.

Ferguson, C. J. (2009, May). The public health risks of media violence: A meta-analytic review. *The Journal of Pediatrics,* 759–763.

Ferguson, C. J., & Beaver, K. M. (2009). Natural born killers: The genetic origins of extreme violence. *Aggression and Violent Behaviour, 14,* 286–294.

Ferguson, C. J., & Ivory, J. D. (2012). A futile game: On the prevalence and causes of misguided speculation about the role of violent video games in mass school shootings. *Studies in Media and Communications, 7,* 47–67.

Ferguson, P. L., & Pickelsimer, E., Corrigan, J. D., Bogner, J. A., & Wald, M. (2012). Prevalence of traumatic brain injury among prisoners in South Carolina. *Journal of Head Trauma Rehabilitation, 27,* E11–E20.

Ferran, L. (2012, September 28). Stink bomb: Underwear Bomber wore explosive undies for weeks, FBI says. Retrieved from http://abcnews.go.com/blogs/headlines/2012/09/stink-bomb-underwear-bomber-wore-explosive-undies-for-weeks-fbi-says/

Ferris, C. F., Herbert, M., Meyerhoff, J., Potegal, M., & Skaredoff, L. (2006). Attack priming in female Syrian golden hamsters is associated with a c-fos-coupled process within the corticomedial amygdala. *Neuroscience, 75,* 869–880.

Festinger, L. (1954). A theory of social comparison processes. *Human Relations, 7,* 117–140.

Festinger, L., Pepitone, A., & Newcomb, T. (1952). Some consequences of de-individuation in a group. *Journal of Abnormal and Social Psychology, 47,* 382–389.

Finkelhor, D., Mitchell, K. J., & Wolak, J. (2000). *Online victimization: A report on the nation's youth.* Alexandria, VA and Durham, NH: National Center for Missing and Exploited Children and Crimes against Children Research Center.

Finn, J. (2004). A survey of online harassment at a university campus. *Journal of Interpersonal Violence, 19,* 468–483.

Finn, J., & Banach, M. (2000). Victimization online: The downside of seeking human services for women on the Internet. *CyberPsychology & Behavior, 3,* 785–796.

Firestone, P., Bradford, J. M., Greenberg, D. M., & Serran, G. A. (2000). The relationship of deviant sexual arousal and psychopathy in incest offenders, extrafamilial child molesters, and rapists. *Journal of the American Academy of Psychiatry and the Law, 28,* 303–308.

Fishbein, D. H. (1992). The psychobiology of female aggression. *Criminal Justice and Behavior, 19,* 99–126.

Fishbein, D. (2000). Sexual preference, crime, and punishment. *Women and Criminal Justice, 11,* 67–84.

Fishbein, D. (2001). *Biobehavioral perspectives in criminology.* Belmont, CA: Wadsworth/Thomson Learning.

Fisher, B. S., Hartman, J. L., Cullen, F. T., & Turner, M. G. (2002). Making campuses safer for students: The Clery Act as a symbolic legal reform. *Stetson Law Review, 32,* 61–89.

Fiske, S. T., & Taylor, S. E. (1991). *Social cognition* (2nd ed.). New York, NY: McGraw-Hill.

Fischman, M. W., Schuster, C. R., Resnekov, L., Shick, J. F. E., Krasnegor, N. A., Fennell, W., & Freedman, D. X. (1976). Cardiovascular and subjective effects of intravenous cocaine administration in humans. *Archives of General Psychiatry, 33,* 983–989.

Flannery, D. J., Modzeleski, W., & Kretschmar, J. M. (2013). Violence and school shootings. *Child and Adolescent Disorders, 15,* 331–338.

Flor-Henry, P. (2003). Lateralized temporal-limbic dysfunction and psychopathology. *Epilepsy and Behaviour, 4,* 578–590.

Foley, D. L., Eaves, L. J., Wormley, B., Silberg, J. L., Maes, H. H., Kuhn, J., & Riley, B. (2004). Childhood adversity, monoamine oxidase A genotype, and risk for conduct disorder. *Archives of General Psychiatry, 61,* 738–744.

Folino, J. O., Marengo, C. M., Marchiano, S. E., & Ascazibar, M. (2004). The risk assessment program and the court of penal execution in the province of Buenos Aires, Argentina. *International Journal of Offender Therapy and Comparative Criminology, 48,* 49–58.

Fontaine, R. G. (2006). Evaluative behavioral judgments and instrumental antisocial behaviors in children and adolescents. *Clinical Psychology Review, 26,* 956–967.

Fontaine, R. G., & Dodge, K. A. (2006). Real-time decision making and aggressive behavior in youth: A heuristic model of response evaluation and decision (RED). *Aggressive Behavior, 32,* 604–624.

Forth, A. E., Brown, S. L., Hart, S. D., & Hare, R. D. (1996). The assessment of psychopathy in male and female non-criminals: Reliability and validity. *Personality and Individual Differences, 20,* 531–543.

Forth, A. E., Hart, S. D., & Hare, R. D. (1990). Assessment of psychopathy in male young offenders. *Psychological Assessment, 2,* 342–344.

Forth, A. E., Kosson, D. S., & Hare, R. D. (2003). *The Psychopathy Checklist: Youth Version manual*. Toronto, ON: Multi-Health Systems.

Fowler, K. A., & Westen, D. (2011). Subtyping male perpetrators of intimate partner violence. *Journal of Interpersonal Violence, 26*, 607–639.

Fowles, D. C. (1988). Psychophysiology and psychopathology: A motivational approach. *Psychophysiology, 25*, 373–391.

Fowles, D. C., & Dindo, L. (2006). A dual-deficit model of psychopathy. In C. J. Patrick (Ed.), *The handbook of psychopathy* (pp. 14–34). New York, NY: Guilford Press.

Fox, J. A., & Levin, J. (1998). Multiple homicide: Patterns of serial and mass murder. In M. Tonry (Ed.), *Crime and justice: A review of research* (Vol. 23) (pp. 407–455). Chicago, IL: University of Chicago Press.

Fox, J. A., & Levin, J. (2005). *Extreme killing: Understanding serial and mass murder*. Thousand Oaks, CA: Sage.

Freedman, J. L., & Fraser, S. C. (1966). Compliance without pressure: The foot-in-the-door technique. *Journal of Personality and Social Psychology, 4*, 195–202.

Freeman, N. J., & Sandler, J. C. (2008). Female and male sex offenders: A comparison of recidivism patterns and risk factors. *Journal of Interpersonal Violence, 23*, 1394–1413.

Freud, S. (1913). The theme of the three caskets. *Standard Edition, 12*, 289–301.

Freud, S. (1920). Beyond the Pleasure Principle. *The Standard Edition of the Complete Psychological Works of Sigmund Freud, Volume XVIII* (1920–1922). London, UK: Vintage Classics.

Frick, P. J. (1994). Family dysfunction and the disruptive behavior disorders: A review of empirical findings. *Advances in Clinical Child Psychology, 16*, 203–206.

Frick, P. J. (2007). Using the construct of psychopathy to understand antisocial and violent youth. In H. Hervé & J. C. Yuille (Eds.), *The psychopath: Theory, research, and practice* (pp. 343–367). Mahwah, NJ: Erlbaum.

Frick, P. J., Kimonis, E. R., Dandreaux, D. M., & Farell, J. M. (2003). The 4-year stability of psychopathic traits in non-referred youth. *Behavioral Sciences and the Law, 21*, 713–736.

Frick, P. J., Stickle, T. R., Dandreaux, D. M., Farell, J. M., & Kimonis, E. R. (2005). Callous-unemotional traits in predicting the severity and stability of conduct problems and delinquency. *Journal of Abnormal Psychology, 33*, 471–487.

Friedman, A. S., Glassman, K., & Terras, A. (2001). Violent behavior as related to use of marijuana and other drugs. *Journal of Addictive Diseases, 20*, 49–72.

Friedman, S. H., Cavney, J., & Resnick, P. J. (2012). Mothers who kill: Evolutionary underpinnings and infanticide law. *Behavioral Sciences & the Law, 30*, 585–597.

Friedman, S. H., & Resnick, P. J. (2009). Neonaticide: Phenomenology and considerations for prevention. *International Journal of Law and Psychiatry, 32*, 43–47.

Friedrich, L. K., & Stein, A. H. (1973). Aggressive and prosocial television programs and the natural behavior of preschool children. *Monographs of the Society for Research in Child Development, 38*, 1–64.

Frisell, T., Lichtenstein, P., & Långström, N. (2011). Violent crime runs in families: A total population study of 12.5 million individuals. *Psychological Medicine, 41*, 97–105.

Gabrielli, W. F., & Mednick, S. A. (1980). Sinistrality and delinquency. *Journal of Abnormal Psychology, 89*, 654–661.

Galanter, H. (1989). *Cults: Faith, healing, and coercion*. New York, NY: Oxford University Press.

Gallagher, C. (1987). The psychologist as psychoanalyst: The proper study of mankind. *The Irish Journal of Psychology, 8*, 111–126.

Gao, Y., Raine, A., Venables, P. H., Dawson, M. E., & Mednick, S. A. (2010). Association of poor childhood fear conditioning and adult crime. *American Journal of Psychiatry, 167*, 56–60.

Gao, Y., Tuvblad, C., Schell, A., Baker, L., & Raine, A. (2015). Skin conductance fear conditioning impairments and aggression: A longitudinal study. *Psychophysiology, 52*, 288–295.

Gardham, D. (2011, October 13). "Underwear bomber" pleads guilty to charges; Nigerian man says Koran backs his jihad. *The Vancouver Sun*, p. B5.

Garrod, A., Ewert, P. W., Field, G., & Warren. G. (1995). *The report of the Criminal Harassment Unit: Part II, The nature and extent of criminal harassment in British Columbia*. Victoria, BC: Ministry of the Attorney General of British Columbia.

Gazzaniga, M. S., & Heatherton, T. F. (2006). *Psychological science* (2nd ed.). New York, NY: Norton.

Geberth, V. J., & Turco, R. N. (1997). Antisocial personality disorder, sexual sadism, malignant narcissism, and serial murders. *Journal of Forensic Sciences, 42*, 49–60.

Gee, D. G., Devilly, G. J., & Ward, T. (2004). The content of sexual fantasies for sexual offenders. *Sexual Abuse: A Journal of Research and Treatment, 16*, 315–331.

Geen, R. G. (1968). Effects of frustration, attack, and prior training in aggressiveness upon aggressive behavior. *Journal of Personality and Social Psychology, 9*, 316–321.

Gendreau, P., Goggin, C., & Smith, P. (2002). Is the PCL–R really the "unparalleled" measure of offender risk? A lesson in knowledge cumulation. *Criminal Justice and Behavior, 29*, 397–426.

Gendreau, P., & Ross, R. R. (1979). Effective correctional treatment: Bibliotherapy for cynics. *Crime and Delinquency, 25*, 463–489.

Gershoff, E. T. (2002). Corporal punishment by parents and associated child behaviors and experiences: A meta-analytic and theoretic review. *Psychological Bulletin, 128*, 539–579.

Giancola, P. R. (1995). Evidence for dorsolateral and orbital prefrontal cortical involvement in the expression of aggressive behaviour. *Aggressive Behaviour, 21*, 431–450.

Giancola, P. R. (2000). Executive functioning: A conceptual framework for alcohol-related aggression. *Experimental and Clinical Psychopharmacology, 8*, 576–597.

Giancola, P. R. (2004). Executive functioning and alcohol-related aggression. *Journal of Abnormal Psychology, 113*, 541–555.

Giancola, P. R., Duke, A. A., & Ritz, K. Z. (2011). Alcohol, violence, and the alcohol myopia model: Preliminary findings and implications for prevention. *Addictive Behaviors, 36*, 1019–1022.

Giancola, P. R., Josephs, R. A., Dewall, C. N., & Gunn, R. L. (2009). Applying the attention-allocation model to the explanation of alcohol-related aggression: Implications for prevention. *Substance Use and Misuse, 44*, 1263–1279.

Giancola, P. R., Parrott, D. J., Silvia, P. J., DeWall, C. N., Bègue, L., Subra, B., . . . Bushman, B. J. (2012). The disguise of sobriety: Unveiled by alcohol in persons with an aggressive personality. *Journal of Personality, 80*, 163–185.

Giancola, P. R., & Zeichner, A. (1994). Neuropsychological performance on tests of frontal lobe functioning and aggressive behaviour in men. *Journal of Abnormal Psychology, 103*, 832–835.

Giancola, P. R., & Zeichner, A. (1997). The biphasic effects of alcohol on human physical aggression. *Journal of Abnormal Psychology, 106*, 598–607.

Gibbs, J. C., Basinger, K. S., & Fuller, D. (1992). *Moral maturity: Measuring the development of sociomoral reflection.* Hillsdale, NJ: Erlbaum.

Gill, R., & Brockman, J. (1996). *A review of section 264 (Criminal Harassment) of the Criminal Code of Canada.* Ottawa, ON: Department of Justice.

Gilligan, D. G., & Lennings, C. J. (2013). Approach-avoidance goals and active-passive self-regulation styles in homicide offending: A pathways analysis. *Psychiatry, Psychology, and Law, 20*, 590–607.

Giovannoni, J. M., & Gurel, L. (1967). Socially disruptive behavior of ex-mental patients. *Archives of General Psychiatry, 17*, 146–153.

Girgis, A. (2006). *Violence from self-love: Narcissism and aggression in the face of ego threat.* (Honors theses). Trinity University, San Antonio, TX. Retrieved from http://digitalcommons.trinity.edu/cgi/viewcontent.cgi?article=1002&context=psych_honors

Glueck, S., & Glueck, E. (1950). *Unraveling juvenile delinquency.* New York, NY: Harper and Row.

Goggin, C., & Gendreau, P. (2006). The implementation and maintenance of quality services in offender rehabilitation programmes. In C. R. Hollin & E. J. Palmer (Eds.), *Offending behaviour programmes: Development, application, and controversies* (pp. 209–246). Chichester, UK: Wiley.

Golde, J. A., Strassberg, D. S., & Turner, C. M. (2000). Psychophysiologic assessment of erectile response and its suppression as a function of stimulus media and previous experience with plethysmography. *Journal of Sex Research, 37*, 53–59.

Golden, C. J., Jackson, M. L., Peterson-Rohne, A., & Gontkovsky, S. T. (1996). Neuropsychological correlates of violence and aggression: A review of the clinical literature. *Aggression and Violent Behaviour, 1*, 3–25.

Goldstein, P. J. (1985). The drugs/violence nexus: A tripartite conceptual framework. *Journal of Drug Issues, 14*, 493–506.

Goldstein, P. J., Brownstein, H. H., & Ryan, P. J. (1992). Drug-related homicide in New York, NY: 1984 and 1988. *Crime and Delinquency, 38*, 459–476.

Goldstein, P. J., Brownstein, H. H., Ryan, P. J., & Bellucci, P. A. (1989). Crack and homicide in New York City, 1988: A conceptually based event analysis. *Contemporary Drug Problems, 16*, 651–687.

Goodwin, C. J., & Goodwin, K. A. (2013). *Research in psychology: Methods and design* (7th ed.). Hoboken, NJ: Wiley.

Gornstein, E. E. (1982). Frontal lobe functions in psychopaths. *Journal of Abnormal Psychology, 91*, 368–379.

Gossop, M., Marsden, J., Stewart, D., & Kidd, T. (2003). The National Treatment Outcome Research Study (NTORS): 4–5 year follow-up results. *Addiction, 98*, 291–303.

Gottfredson, M. R., & Hirschi, T. (1983). Age and the explanation of crime. *American Journal of Sociology, 89*, 552–584.

Gottfredson, M. R., & Hirschi, T. (1990). *A general theory of crime.* Stanford, CT: Stanford University Press.

Gottman, J. M., Jacobson, N. S., Rushe, R. H., & Shortt, J. W. (1995). The relationship between heart rate reactivity, emotionally aggressive behavior, and general violence in batterers. *Journal of Family Psychology, 9*, 227–248.

Gottman, J. M., & Katz, L. (1989). Effects of marital discord on young children's peer interaction and health. *Developmental Psychology, 25*, 373–381.

Goulart, V. D. L. R., & Young, R. J. (2013). Selfish behavior as an antipredator response in schooling fish. *Animal Behaviour, 86*, 443–450.

Gouze, K. R. (1987). Attention and social problem solving correlates of aggression in preschool males. *Journal of Abnormal Child Psychology, 15*, 181–197.

Gover, D. (2014, February 13). Joanna Dennehy: Inside the mind of a female psychopath serial killer. *International Business Times.* Retrieved from http://www.ibtimes.co.uk/joanna-dennehy-inside-mind-female-psychopath-serial-killer-1436317

Grace, W. C. (1987). Strength of handedness as an indicant of delinquent's behaviour. *Journal of Clinical Behaviour, 43*, 151–155.

Grafman, J., Schwab, K., Warden, D., Pridgen, A., Brown, H. R., & Salazar, A. M. (1996). Frontal lobe injuries, violence, and aggression: A report of the Vietnam Head Injury Study. *Neurology, 46*, 1231–1238.

Graham, J., & Bowling, B. (1995). *Young people and crime.* Stanford, CA: Stanford University Press.

Graham, K. (1980). Theories of intoxicated aggression. *Canadian Journal of Behavioural Sciences, 12*, 141–158.

Grann, M. (2000). The PCL–R and gender. *European Journal of Psychological Assessment, 16*, 147–149.

Grann, M., Långström, N., Tengström, A., & Kullgren, G. (1999). Psychopathy (PCL–R) predicts violent recidivism among criminal offenders with personality disorders in Sweden. *Law and Human Behavior, 23*, 205–217.

Gray, J. A. (1981). A critique of Eysenck's theory of personality. In H. J. Eysenck (Ed.), *A model for personality* (pp. 246–276). New York, NY: Springer.

Gray, J. A. (1987). *The psychology of fear and stress.* Cambridge, UK: Cambridge University Press.

Greenfeld, L. A. (1998). *Alcohol and crime.* Washington, DC: Bureau of Justice Statistics, U.S. Department of Justice.

Gretton, H. M., Hare, R. D., & Catchpole, R. E. H. (2004). Psychopathy and offending from adolescence to adulthood: A 10-year follow-up. *Journal of Consulting and Clinical Psychology, 72*, 636–645.

Grigorenko, E. L., DeYoung, C. G., Eastman, M., Getchell, M., Haeffel, G. J., af Klinteberg, B., . . . Yrigollen, C. M. (2010). Aggressive behavior, related conduct problems, and variation in genes affecting dopamine turnover. *Aggressive Behavior, 36*, 158–176.

Grilly, D. M. (2006). *Drugs and human behavior* (5th ed.). Boston, MA: Pearson.

Groth, A. N., Hobson, W. F., & Gary, T. S. (1982). The child molester: Clinical observations. *Journal of Social Work and Human Sexuality, 1*, 129–144.

Grove, W. M., Eckert, E. D., Heston, L., Bouchard, T. J., Segal, N., & Lykken, D. T. (1990). Heritability of substance abuse and antisocial behavior: A study of monozygotic twins reared apart. *Biological Psychiatry, 27*, 1293–1304.

Grove, W. M., & Meehl, P. E. (1996). Comparative efficiency of informal (subjective, impressionistic) and formal (mechanical, algorithmic) prediction procedures: The clinical-statistical controversy. *Psychology, Public Policy, and Law, 2*, 293–323.

Grove, W. M., Zald, D. H., Lebow, B. S., Snitz, B. E., & Nelson, C. (2000). Clinical versus mechanical prediction: A meta-analysis. *Psychological Assessment, 12*, 19–30.

Guo, G., Roettger, M. E., & Cai, T. (2008). The integration of genetic propensities into social-control models of delinquency and violence among male youths. *American Sociological Review, 73*, 543–568.

Guo, G., Roettger, M. E., & Shih, J. C. (2007). Contributions of the DAT1 and DRD2 genes to serious and violent delinquency among adolescents and young adults. *Human Genetics, 121*, 125–136.

Guskiewicz, K. M, Marshall, S. W., Bailes, J., McCrea, M., Cantu, R. C., Randolph, C., & Jordan, B. D. (2005). Association between recurrent concussion and late-life cognitive impairment in retired professional football players. *Neurosurgery, 57*, 719–726.

Guttridge, P., Gabrielli, W. F., Mednick, S. A., & Van Dusen, K. T. (1983). Criminal violence in a birth cohort. In K. T. Van Dusen & S. A. Mednick (Eds.), *Prospective studies of crime and delinquency* (pp. 211–224). Hingham, MA: Kluwer-Nijhoff.

Guy, L. S., Douglas, K. S., & Hart, S. D. (2015). Risk assessment and communication. In B. L. Cutler & P. A. Zapf (Eds.), *APA handbook of forensic psychology* (pp. 35–86). Washington, DC: American Psychological Association.

Guy, L. S., Edens, J. F., Anthony, C., & Douglas, K. S. (2005). Does psychopathy predict institutional misconduct among adults? A meta-analytic investigation. *Journal of Consulting and Clinical Psychology, 73*, 1056–1064.

Haapasalo, J. (1994). Types of offense among the Cleckley psychopath. *International Journal of Offender Therapy and Comparative Criminology, 38*, 59–67.

Haberstick, B. C., Lessem, J. M., Hewitt, J. K., Smolen, A., Hopfer, C. J., Halpern, C. T., . . . Harris, K. M. (2014). MAOA genotype, childhood maltreatment, and their interaction in the etiology of adult antisocial behaviors. *Biological Psychiatry, 75*, 25–30.

Haberstick, B. C., Smolen, A., & Hewitt, J. K. (2006). Family-based association test of the 5HTTLPR and aggressive behavior in a general population sample of children. *Biological Psychiatry, 59*, 836–843.

Hagan, F. E. (2005). *Essentials of research methods in criminal justice and criminology.* Boston, MA: Pearson.

Hagan J. (1991). *The disreputable pleasures: Crime and deviance in Canada* (3rd ed.). Toronto, ON: McGraw-Hill.

Hager, M. (2013, May 27). Abbotsford man pleads guilty in Carly Rae Jepsen hacking case. *The Vancouver Sun.* Retrieved from http://www.vancouversun.com/entertainment/Abbotsford+pleads+guilty+Carly+Jepsen+hacking+case/8441803/story.html

Haines, A. (2005, December 7). Court denies appeal of Homolka decision: Ontario vows to pursue issue. *The National Post*, p. A11.

Hald, G. M., & Malamuth, N. H. (2015). Experimental effects of exposure to pornography: The moderating effect of personality and mediating effect of sexual arousal. *Archives of Sexual Behaviour, 44*, 99–109.

Hamilton, G. (2005, June 3). A killer couple. *National Post*, p. A1.

Hamilton, M. (2016, April 14). Board recommends parole for Charles Manson follower Leslie Van Houten; Victim's daughter vows to oppose. *Los Angeles Times.* Retrieved from http://www.latimes.com/local/lanow/la-me-ln-charles-manson-follower-leslie-van-houten-seeks-parole-for-1969-slaying-20160413-story.html

Hamilton, W. D. (1964). The genetic evolution of social behavior. *Journal of Theoretical Biology, 7*, 1–52.

Haney, C., Banks, C., & Zimbardo, P. (1973). Interpersonal dynamics in a simulated prison. *International Journal of Criminology and Penology, 1*, 69–97.

Hanson, R. K. (1998). What do we know about sex offender risk assessment? *Psychology, Public Policy, and Law, 4*, 50–72.

Hanson, R. K., & Bussiere, M. T. (1998). Predicting relapse: A meta-analysis of sexual offender recidivism studies. *Journal of Consulting and Clinical Psychology, 66*, 348–362.

Hanson, R. K., & Harris, A. (2000). When should we intervene? Dynamic predictors of sexual recidivism. *Criminal Justice and Behavior, 27*, 6–35.

Hanson, R. K., & Morton-Bourgon, K. E. (2005). The characteristics of persistent sexual offenders: A meta-analysis
of recidivism studies. *Journal of Consulting and Clinical
Psychology, 73*, 1154–1163.

Hanson, R. K., & Morton-Bourgon, K. E. (2009). The accu-
racy of recidivism risk assessments for sexual offenders:
A meta-analysis of 118 prediction studies. *Psychological
Assessment, 21*, 1–21.

Harding, C. F. (1983). Hormonal influences on avian aggressive behaviour. In B. Svare (Ed.), *Hormones and aggressive behaviour* (pp. 435–467). New York, NY: Plenum
Press.

Hare, R. D. (1980). A research scale for the assessment of
psychopathy in criminal populations. *Personality and
Individual Differences, 1*, 111–119.

Hare, R. D. (1984). Performance of psychopaths on cognitive
tasks related to frontal lobe function. *Journal of Abnormal Psychology, 93*, 133–140.

Hare, R. D. (1991). *Manual for the Hare Psychopathy Checklist–
Revised*. Toronto, ON: Multi-Health Systems.

Hare, R. D. (1993). *Without conscience: The disturbing world
of the psychopaths among us*. New York, NY: Pocket
Books.

Hare, R. D. (1996). Psychopathy: A clinical construct whose
time has come. *Criminal Justice and Behavior, 23*, 25–54.

Hare, R. D. (1998). Psychopathy, affect and behaviour. In D. J.
Cooke, A. E. Forth, & R. D. Hare (Eds.), *Psychopathy: The-
ory, research and implications for society* (pp. 105–137).
Dordrecht, The Netherlands: Kluwer Academic.

Hare, R. D. (2003). *Manual for the Hare Psychopathy
Checklist–Revised* (2nd ed.). Toronto, ON: Multi-
Health Systems.

Hare, R. D., Clark, D., Grann, M., & Thornton, D. (2000).
Psychopathy and the predictive validity of the PCL–R:
An international perspective. *Behavioral Sciences and
the Law, 18*, 623–645.

Hare, R. D., & Connolly, J. F. (1987). Perceptual asymmetries and information processing in psychopaths. In S.
A. Mednick, T. E. Moffitt, & S. A. Stack (Eds.), *The causes
of crime: New biological approaches* (pp. 218–237). Cambridge, UK: Cambridge University Press.

Hare, R. D., & Forth, A. E. (1985). Psychopathy and lateral
preference. *Journal of Abnormal Psychology, 94*, 541–546.

Hare, R. D., & McPherson, L. M. (1984a). Psychopathy and
perceptual asymmetry during verbal dichotic listening.
Journal of Abnormal Psychology, 93, 141–149.

Hare, R. D., & McPherson, L. M. (1984b). Violent and aggressive behaviour by criminal psychopaths. *International Journal of Law and Psychiatry, 7*, 35–50.

Hare, R. D., McPherson, L. M., & Forth, A. E. (1988). Male
psychopaths and their criminal careers. *Journal of Consulting and Clinical Psychology, 56*, 710–714.

Hare, R. D., & Neumann, C. S. (2006). The PCL–R assessment
of psychopathy: Development, Structural properties, and
new directions. In C. J. Patrick (Ed.), *Handbook of psychopathy* (pp. 58–88). New York, NY: Guilford Press.

Hare, R. D., Williamson, S. E., & Harpur, T. J. (1988). Psychopathy and language. In T. E. Moffitt & S. A. Mednick (Eds.), *Biological contributions to crime casuation*
(pp. 68–92). Dordrecht, The Netherlands: Martinus
Nijhoff.

Harlow, H. F. (1958). The nature of love. *American Psychologist, 13*, 673.

Harlow, J. M. (1868). Recovery from the passage of an iron
bar through the head. *Publication of Massachusetts Medicine and Society, 2*, 327–347.

Harlow, J. M. (1999). Passage of an iron rod through the
head. *Journal of Neuropsychiatry and Clinical Neuroscience, 11*, 281–283.

Harmon, R. B., Rosner, R., & Owens, H. (1995a). Obsessional
harassment and erotomania in a criminal court population. *Journal of Forensic Sciences, 40*, 188–196.

Harmon, R. B., Rosner, R., & Owens, H. (1995b). Sex and violence in a forensic population of obsessional harassers.
Psychology, Public Policy, and Law, 4, 236–249.

Harpending, H., & Draper, P. (1988). Antisocial behavior
and the other side of cultural evolution. In T. E. Moffitt &
S. A. Mednick (Eds.), *Biological contributions to crime
causation* (pp. 293–307). Dordrecht, The Netherlands:
Martinus Nijhoff.

Harpur, T. J., & Hare, R. D. (1994). Assessment of psychopathy as a function of age. *Journal of Abnormal Psychology,
103*, 604–609.

Harpur, T. J., Hare, R. D., & Hakstian, A. R. (1989). Two-
factor conceptualization of psychopathy: Construct
validity and assessment implications. *Psychological Assessment, 1*, 6–17.

Harris, G. T., Rice, M. E., & Cormier, C. A. (1991). Psychopathy and violent recidivism. *Law and Human Behavior,
15*, 625–637.

Harris, G. T., Rice, M. E., & Lalumière, M. (2001). Criminal
violence: The roles of psychopathy, neurodevelopmental
insults, and antisocial parenting. *Criminal Justice and
Behavior, 28*, 402–426.

Harris, G. T., Rice, M. E., & Quinsey, V. L. (1993). Violent
recidivism of mentally disordered offenders: The development of a statistical prediction instrument. *Criminal
Justice and Behavior, 20*, 315–335.

Harris, J. A., Rushton, J. P., Hampson, E., & Jackson, D. N.
(1996). Salivary testosterone and self-report aggressive
and pro-social personality characteristics in men and
women. *Aggressive Behaviour, 22*, 321–331.

Harris, P. (2011, October 12). Al-Qaida "underwear bomber"
stuns Detroit court by changing plea to guilty. *The
Guardian*. Retrieved from http://www.theguardian.com/
world/2011/oct/12/underwear-bomber-abdulmutallab-
pleads-guilty

Hart, S. D. (1998a). Psychopathy and risk for violence. In D. J. Cooke, A. E. Forth, & R. D. Hare (Eds.), *Psychopathy: Theory, research and implications for society* (pp. 355–373). Dordrecht, The Netherlands: Kluwer Academic.

Hart, S. D. (1998b). The role of psychopathy in assessing risk for violence: Conceptual and methodological issues. *Legal and Criminological Psychology, 3*, 121–137.

Hart, S. D. (2001). Assessing and managing violence risk. In K. S. Douglas, C. D. Webster, S. D. Hart, D. Eaves, & J. R. P. Ogloff (Eds.), *HCR-20 Violence risk management companion guide* (pp. 13–25). Burnaby, BC: Mental Health, Law, and Policy Institute, Simon Fraser University.

Hart, S. D., Cox, D. N., & Hare, R. D. (1995). *Manual for the Psychopathy Checklist: Screening Version (PCL:SV)*. Toronto, ON: Multi-Health Systems.

Hart, S. D., & Dempster, R. J. (1997). Impulsivity and psychopathy. In C. D. Webster, & M. A. Jackson (Eds.), *Impulsivity: Theory, assessment, and treatment* (pp. 212–232). New York, NY: Guilford Press.

Hart, S. D., & Hare, R. D. (1996). Psychopathy and risk assessment. *Current Opinion in Psychiatry, 9*, 380–383.

Hart, S. D., & Hare, R. D. (1997). Psychopathy: Assessment and association with criminal conduct. In D. M. Stoff, J. Breiling, & J. D. Maser (Eds.), *Handbook of antisocial behaviour* (pp. 22–35). New York, NY: Wiley.

Hart, S. D., Kropp, P. R., & Hare, R. D. (1988). Performance of psychopaths following conditional release from prison. *Journal of Consulting and Clinical Psychology, 56*, 227–232.

Hart, S. D., Watt, K. A., & Vincent, G. M. (2002). Commentary on Seagrave and Grisso: Impressions of the state of the art. *Law and Human Behavior, 26*, 241–245.

Hartnagel, T. F. (2004). Correlates of criminal behaviour. In R. Linden (Ed.), *Criminology: A Canadian perspective* (5th ed.) (pp. 120–163). Toronto, ON: Nelson.

Hassan, S. (1988). *Combating cult mind control*. Rochester, VT: Park Street Press.

Hathaway, S. R., & McKinley, J. C. (1943). *The Minnesota multiphasic personality inventory* (Rev. Ed.). Minneapolis, MN: University of Minnesota.

Hatters-Friedman, S., Heneghan, A., & Rosenthal, M. (2007). Characteristics of women who deny or conceal pregnancy. *Psychosomatics, 48*, 117–122.

Hatters-Friedman, S., & Resnick, P. J. (2009). Neonaticide: Phenomenology and consideration for prevention. *International Journal of Law and Psychiatry, 32*, 43–47.

Haugen, B. (2010). *The Zodiac Killer: Terror and mystery*. North Mankato, MN: Capstone Press.

Hawkins, K. A., & Trobst, K. K. (2000). Frontal lobe dysfunction and aggression: Conceptual issues and research findings. *Aggression and Violent Behaviour, 5*, 147–157.

Hay, C. (2001). Parenting, self-control, and delinquency: A test of self-control theory. *Criminology, 39*, 707–736.

Hayes, L., Hudson, A., & Matthews, J. (2003). Parental monitoring: A process model of parent–adolescent interaction. *Behavior Change, 20*, 13–24.

Hayes, L., Smart, D., Toumbourou, J., & Sanson. A. (2004). *Parenting influences on adolescent alcohol use*. Melbourne, Australia: Australian Institute of Family Studies.

Hayhurst, K. P., Jones, A., Millar, T., Pierce, M., Davies, L., Weston, S., & Donmall, M. (2013). Drug spend and acquisitive offending by substance misusers. *Drug and Alcohol Dependence, 130*, 24–29.

Hazelwood, R. R., & Douglas, J. D. (1980, April). The lust murderer. *FBI Law Enforcement Bulletin*, 18–22.

Heaven, P. C. L., Newbury, K., & Wilson, V. (2004). The Eysenck psychotocism dimension and delinquent behaviours among non-criminals: Changes across the lifespan? *Personality and Individual Differences, 36*, 1817–1825.

Hebb, D. O. (1955). Drives and the C.N.S. (conceptual nervous system). *Psychological Review, 62*, 243–254.

Heide, K. M., & Petee, T. A. (2007). Parricide: An empirical analysis of 24 years of U.S. data. *Journal of Interpersonal Violence, 22*, 1382–1399.

Heilbrun, K., Yasuhara, K., & Shah, S. (2010). Violence risk assessment tools: Overview and critical analysis. In R. K. Otto & K. S. Douglas (Eds.), *Handbook of violence risk assessment* (pp. 1–17). New York, NY: Routledge.

Hektner, J. M., August, G. J., & Realmuto, G. M. (2000). Patterns and temporal changes in peer affiliation among aggressive and nonaggressive children participating in a summer school program. *Journal of Clinical Child Psychology, 29*, 603–614.

Hellerstein, D., Frosch, W., & Koenigsberg, H. W. (1987). The clinical significance of command hallucinations. *American Journal of Psychiatry, 144*, 219–221.

Hellman, D., & Blackman, N. (1966). Enuresis, firesetting, and cruelty to animals: A triad predictive of adult crime. *American Journal of Psychiatry, 122*, 1431–1435.

Hemphill, J. F., Hare, R. D., & Wong, S. (1998). Psychopathy and recidivism: A review. *Legal and Criminological Psychology, 3*, 141–172.

Hendricks, P. S., Clark, C. B., Johnson, M. W., Fontaine, K. R., & Cropsey, K. L. (2014). Hallucinogen use predicts reduced recidivism among substance-involved offenders under community corrections supervision. *Journal of Psychopharmacology, 28*, 62–66.

Hendricks, S. E., Fitzpatrick, D. F., Hartmann, K., Quaife, M. A., Stratbucker, R. A., & Graber, B. (1988). Brain structure and function in sexual molesters of children and adolescents. *Journal of Clinical Psychiatry, 49*, 108–112.

Henker, B., & Whalen, C. K. (1989). Hyperactivity and attention deficits. *American Psychologist, 44*, 216–244.

Henley, J. (2007, December 13). A glossary of US military torture euphemisms. *The Guardian*. Retrieved from http://www.theguardian.com/world/2007/dec/13/usa.humanrights

Hersh, K., & Borum, R. (1998). Command hallucinations, compliance, and risk assessment. *Journal of the American Academy of Psychiatry and Law, 26*, 353–359.

Hersh, S. M. (2004, May 10). Annals of National Security: Torture at Abu Ghraib. *The New Yorker*. Retrieved from http://www.newyorker.com/archive/2004/05/10/040510fa_fact?currentPage=1

Hervé, H. (2007). Psychopathy across the ages: A history of the Hare psychopath. In H. Hervé & J. C. Yuille (Eds.), *The psychopath: Theory, research, and practice* (pp. 31–55). Mahwah, NJ: Erlbaum.

Hickey, E. W. (2006). *Serial murderers and their victims* (4th ed.). Belmont, CA: Thomson-Wadsworth.

Hickey, E. W. (2013). *Serial murderers and their victims* (6th ed.). Belmont, CA: Wadsworth.

Hiday, V. A. (1995). The social context of mental illness and violence. *Journal of Health and Social Behavior, 26*, 122–137.

Hiday, V. A. (1997). Understanding the connection between mental illness and violence. *International Journal of Law and Psychiatry, 20*, 399–417.

Hiday, V. A., & Burns, P. J. (2010). Mental illness and the criminal justice system. In T. L. Scheid & T. L. Brown (Eds.), *A handbook for the study of mental health: Social contexts, theories, and systems* (2nd ed.) (pp. 478–498). New York, NY: Cambridge University Press.

Hiday, V. A., Swanson, J. W., Swartz, M. S., Borum, R., & Wagner, H. R. (2001). Victimization: A link between mental illness and violence? *International Journal of Law and Psychiatry, 24*, 559–572.

Hiday, V. A., Swartz, M. S., Swanson, J. W., Borum, R., & Wagner, H. R. (1999). Criminal victimization of persons with severe mental illness. *Psychiatric Services, 50*, 62–68.

Hildebrand, M., de Ruiter, C., & de Vogel, V. (2004). Psychopathy and sexual deviance in treated rapists: Association with sexual and nonsexual recidivism. *Sexual Abuse: A Journal of Research and Treatment, 16*, 1–24.

Hirschi, T. (1969). *Causes of delinquency*. Berkeley: University of California Press.

Hirschi, T., & Hindelang, M. J. (1977). Intelligence and delinquency: A revisionst review. *American Sociologist Review, 42*, 571–587.

Hoaken, P. N. S., Alaby, D. B., & Earle, J. (2007). Executive cognitive functioning and the recognition of facial expression of emotion in incarcerated violent offenders and controls. *Aggressive Behaviour, 33*, 412–421.

Hoaken, P. N. S., Hamill, V. L., Ross, E. H., Hancock, M., Lau, M. J., & Tapscott, J. L. (2014). Drug use and abuse and human aggressive behavior. In J. C. Verster, K. Brady, M. Galanter, & P. Conrod (Eds.), *Drug abuse and addiction in medical illness: Causes, consequences, and treatment* (pp. 467–477). New York, NY: Springer.

Hoaken, P. N. S., & Stewart, S. H. (2003). Drugs of abuse and the elicitation of human aggressive behavior. *Addictive Behaviors, 28*, 1533–1554.

Hodgins, S. (1992). Mental disorder, intellectual deficiency, and crime. *Archives of General Psychiatry, 49*, 476–483.

Hodgins, S. (1995). Major mental disorder and crime: An overview. *Psychology, Crime and Law, 2*, 5–17.

Hodgins, S. (2001). The major mental disorders and crime: Stop debating and start treating and preventing. *International Journal of Law and Psychiatry, 24*, 427–446.

Hodgins, S. (2002). Research priorities in forensic mental health. *International Journal of Forensic Mental Health, 1*, 7–23.

Hodgins, S., Alderton, J., Cree, A., Aboud, A., & Mak, T. (2007). Aggressive behaviour, victimisation and crime among severely mentally ill patients requiring hospitalisation. *British Journal of Psychiatry, 191*, 343–350.

Hodgins, S., & Côté, G. (1990). The prevalence of mental disorders among penitentiary inmates. *Canada's Mental Health, 38*, 1–5.

Hodgins, S., & Côté, G. (1993). Major mental disorder and antisocial personality disorder: A criminal combination. *Bulletin of the American Academy of Psychiatry and Law, 21*, 155–160.

Hodgins, S., & Janson, C.-G. (2002). *Criminality and violence among the mentally disordered: The Stockholm Metropolitan Project*. Cambridge, UK: Cambridge University Press.

Hodgins, S., Mednick, S., Brennan, P. A., Schulsinger, F., & Engberg, M. (1996). Mental disorder and crime: Evidence from a Danish birth cohort. *Archives of General Psychiatry, 53*, 489–496.

Hoeve, M., Dubas, J. M, Eichelsheim, V. I., van der Laan, P. H., Smeenk, W., & Gerris, J. R. M. (2009). The relationship between parenting and delinquency: A meta-analysis. *Journal of Abnormal Child Psychology, 37*, 749–775.

Hoeve, M., Dubas, J. M., Gerris, J. R. M., van der Laan, P. H., & Smeenk, W. (2011). Maternal and paternal parenting styles: Unique and combined links to adolescent and early adult delinquency. *Journal of Adolescence, 34*, 813–827.

Hoffman, B. F. (1990). The criminalization of the mentally ill. *Canadian Journal of Psychiatry, 35*, 166–169.

Hogben, M. (1998). Factors moderating the effect of televised aggression on viewer behavior. *Communications Research, 25*, 220–247.

Hohmann, S., Becker, K., Fellinger, J., Banachewski, T., Schmidt, M. H., Esser, G., & Laucht, M. (2009). Evidence for epistasis between the 5-HTTLPR and the dopamine D4 receptor polymorphisms in externalizing behavior among 15-year-olds. *Journal of Neural Transmission, 116*, 1621–1629.

Hollin, C. R. (1995). The meaning and implications of "Programme Integrity." In J. McGuire (Ed.), *What works: Reducing re-offending* (pp. 195–208). Chichester, UK: Wiley.

Hollin, C. R., & Palmer, E. J. (2006). Offending behaviour programmes: History and development. In C. R. Hollin & E. J. Palmer (Eds.), *Offending behaviour programmes: Development, application, and controversies* (pp. 1–32). Chichester, UK: Wiley.

Hollister-Wagner, G. H., Foshee, V. A., & Jackson, C. (2001). Adolescent aggression: Models of resilience. *Journal of Applied Social Psychology, 31*, 445–466.

Holmes, C., Smith, H., Ganderton, R., Arranz, M., Collier, D., Powell, J., & Lovestone, S. (2001). Psychosis and aggression in Alzheimer's disease: The effect of dopamine receptor gene variation. *The Journal of Neurology and Neurosurgical Psychiatry, 71,* 777–779.

Holmes, R. M., & DeBurger, J. (1988). *Serial murder.* Newbury Park, CA: Sage.

Holmes, R. M., & Holmes, S. T. (1998). *Serial murder* (2nd ed.). Thousand Oaks, CA: Sage.

Holmes, R. M., & Holmes, S. T. (2001). *Mass murder in the United States.* Upper Saddle River, NJ: Prentice Hall.

Holmes, R. M., & Holmes, S. T. (2002). *Current perspectives on sex crimes.* Upper Saddle River, NJ: Sage.

Holmqvist, R. (2008). Psychopathy and affect consciousness in young criminal offenders. *Journal of Interpersonal Violence, 23,* 209–224.

Holt, R. R. (1970). Yet another look at clinical and statistical prediction: Or, is clinical psychology worthwhile? *American Psychologist, 25,* 337–349.

Holtzworth-Munroe, A., & Stuart, G. L. (1994). Typologies of male batterers: Three subtypes and the differences among them. *Psychological Bulletin, 116,* 476–497.

Home Office. (1993). *Digest 2: Information on the criminal justice system in England and Wales.* London, UK: Home Office Research and Statistics Department.

Homolka moved from psych hospital to maximum security prison. (2001, April 4). *Sudbury Star,* p. A8.

Hoptman, M. J., & Antonius, D. (2011). Neuroimaging correlates of aggression in schizophrenia: An update. *Current Opinion in Psychiatry, 24,* 100–106.

Hotton Mahony, T., & Turner, J. (2012). *Police-reported clearance rates in Canada, 2010.* Ottawa, ON: Canadian Centre for Justice Statistics, Statistics Canada.

Hucker, S., Langevin, R., Wortzman, G., Bain, J., Handy, L., Chambers, J., & Wright, S. (1986). Neuropsychological impairment in pedophiles. *Canadian Journal of Behavioural Science, 18,* 440–448.

Hucker, S., Langevin, R., Wortzman, G., Dickey, R., Bain, J., Handy, L., . . . & Wright, S. (1988). Cerebral damage and dysfunction in sexually aggressive men. *Annals of Sex Research, 1,* 33–47.

Hudgins, W., & Prentice, N. M. (1973). Moral judgment in delinquent and nondelinquent adolescents and their mothers. *Journal of Abnormal Psychology, 82,* 145–152.

Hudson, C. G. (1988). Socioeconomic status and mental illness: Implications of the research for policy and practice. *Journal of Sociology and Social Welfare, 15,* 27–54.

Hudson, C. G. (2005). Socioeconomic status and mental illness: Tests of the social causation and selection hypotheses. *American Journal of Orthopsychiatry, 75,* 3–18.

Huesmann, L. R. (1988). An information processing model for the development of aggression. *Aggressive Behavior, 14,* 13–24.

Huesmann, L. R. (1998). The role of social information processing and cognitive schema in the acquisition and maintenance of habitual aggressive behavior. In R. G. Geen & E. Donnerstein (Eds.), *Human aggression: Theories, research, and implications for social policy* (pp. 73–109). New York, NY: Academic Press.

Huesmann, L. R. (2007). The impact of electronic media violence: Scientific theory and research. *Journal of Adolescent Health, 41,* S6–S13.

Huesmann, L. R., & Eron, L. D. (1992). Childhood aggression and adult criminality. In J. McCord (Eds.), *Facts, frameworks, and forecasts: Advances in criminological theory* (pp. 137–156). New Brunswick, NJ: Transaction Publishers.

Huesmann, L. R., Moise-Titus, J., Podolski, C.-L., & Eron, L. D. (2003). Longitudinal relations between children's exposure to TV violence and their aggressive and violent behavior in young adulthood: 1977–1992. *Developmental Psychology, 39,* 201–221.

Huesmann, L. R. & Podolski, C.-L. (2003). Punishment: A psychological perspective. In S. McConville (Ed.), *The use of punishment* (pp. 55–88). Devon, UK: Willan.

Huizinga, D., Haberstick, B. C., Smolen, A., Menard, S., Young, S. E., Corey, R. P., . . . Hewitt, J. K. (2006). Childhood maltreatment, subsequent antisocial behavior, and the role of monoamine oxidase A genotype. *Biological Psychiatry, 60,* 677–683.

Hull, J. G. (1981). A self-awareness model of the causes and effects of alcohol consumption. *Journal of Abnormal Psychology, 90,* 586–600.

Hull, J. G., & Bond, C. F. (1986). Social and behavioral consequences of alcohol consumption and expectancy: A meta-analysis. *Psychological Bulletin, 99,* 347–360.

Hunt, D., Lipton, D. S., & Spunt, B. (1984). Patterns of criminality among methadone clients and current narcotics users not in treatment. *Journal of Drug Issues, 14,* 687–702.

Hunter, M. (2013, June 18). JPSO: 13-year-old Terrytown boy booked with murder of his 5-year-old sister. *The Times-Picayune.* Retrieved from http://www.nola.com/crime/index.ssf/2013/06/jpso_13-year-old_boy_booked_wi.html?utm

Huttenlocher, P. R., & Dabholkar, A. S. (1997). Regional differences in synaptogensis in human cerebral cortex. *The Journal of Comparative Neurology, 387,* 167–178.

"I'm sorry but no regrets—Zidane" (2006, July 12). Retrieved from http://news.bbc.co.uk/sport2/hi/football/world_cup_2006/5169342.stm

Ingram, R. E., & Luxton, D. D. (2005). Vulnerability-stress models. In B. L. Hankin, & J. R. Z. Abela (Eds.), *Development of psychopathology: A vulnerability-stress perspective* (pp. 32–46). Thousand Oaks, CA: Sage.

"In Trayvon Martin shooting, background of George Zimmerman can confound, confuse." (2012, March 23). *Washington Post.* Retrieved from http://www.tampabay.com/news/publicsafety/crime/in-trayvon-martin-shooting-background-of-george-zimmerman-can-confound/1221662

Irons, M. E. (2010, February 17). Alabama slaying defendant is related to novelist John Irving. *The Boston Globe*. Retrieved from http://archive.boston.com/news/local/massachusetts/articles/2010/02/18/bishops_novel_offers_insight_into_her_thoughts/

Ishikawa, S. S., & Raine, A. (2002). Behavioral genetics and crime. In J. Glicksohn (Ed.), *The neurobiology of criminal behavior* (pp. 81–109). Boston, MA: Kluwer Academic.

Ito, T. A., Miller, N., & Pollock, V. E. (1996). Alcohol and aggression: A meta-analysis on the moderating effects of inhibitory cues, triggering events, and self-focused attention. *Psychological Bulletin, 120*, 60–82.

Jackson, C., & Henriksen, L. (1996). Do as I say: Parent smoking, antismoking socialization, and smoking onset among children. *Addictive Behaviors, 22*, 107–114.

Jackson, R., & Richards, H. (2007). Psychopathy in women: A valid construct with clear implications. In H. Hervé & J. C. Yuille (Eds.), *The psychopath: Theory, research, and practice* (pp. 389–410). Mahwah, NJ: Erlbaum.

Jared Fogle, ex-Subway pitchman, paid kids for sex on New York trips, prosecutor says. (2015, August 20). Retrieved from http://www.foxnews.com/us/2015/08/20/prosecutor-ex-subway-pitchman-paid-kids-for-sex-on-new-york-trips/

Jeffery, C. R. (1965). Criminal behavior and learning theory. *The Journal of Criminal Law, Criminology and Police Science, 56*, 294–300.

Jenkins, P. (1989). Serial murder in the United States 1900–1940: A historical perspective. *Journal of Criminal Justice, 17*, 377–392.

Jennings, W. G., Piquero, A. R., & Farrington, D. P. (2013). Does resting heart rate at age 18 distinguish general and violent offending up to age 50? Findings from the Cambridge Study in Delinquent Development. *Journal in Criminal Justice, 4*, 213–219.

Jennings, W. S., Kilkenny, R., & Kohlberg, L. (1983). Moral-development theory and practice for youthful and adult offenders. In W. S. Laufer & J. M. Day (Eds.), *Personality theory, moral development, and criminal behavior* (pp. 281–355). Lexington, MA: Lexington Books.

Jennissen, R. (2014). On the deviant age-crime curve of Afro- Caribbean populations: The case of Antilleans living in the Netherlands. *American Journal of Criminal Justice, 39*, 571–594.

Jensen, G. F. (2007). Social learning and violent behavior. In D. J. Flannery, A. T. Vazsonyi, & I. D. Waldman (Eds.), *The Cambridge handbook of violent behavior and aggression* (pp. 636–646). Cambridge, UK: Cambridge University Press.

Joanna Dennehy was a "classic psychopath." (2014, February 12). Retrieved from http://www.itv.com/news/update/2014-02-12/joanna-dennehy-was-a-classic-psychopath/

Johnson, B. D., Goldstein, P. J., Preble, E., Schmeidler, J., Lipton, D. S., Spunt, B., & Miller, T. (1985). *Taking care of business: The economics of crime by heroin abusers.* Lexington, MA: Lexington Books.

Johnson, B. D., Williams, T., Dei, K. A., & Sanabria, H. (1990). Drug abuse in the inner city: Impact on hard-drug users and the community. In M. Tonry & J. Q. Wilson (Eds.), *Drugs and crime* (pp. 9–67). Chicago, IL: University of Chicago Press.

Johnson, G. (1997, August 24). He's very pleased with the way he is right now. *The Province*, p. A41.

Johnson, J. D., Adams, M. S., Ashburn, L., & Reed, W. (1995). Differential gender effects of exposure to rap music on African American adolescents' acceptance of teen dating violence. *Sex Roles, 33*, 597–605.

Johnston, J. M. (1972). Punishment of human behavior. *American Psychologist, 27*, 1033–1054.

Jones, B. T., Cobrin, W., & Fromme, K. (2001). A review of expectancy theory and alcohol consumption. *Addiction, 96*, 57–72.

Josephson, W. L. (1987). Television violence and children's aggression: Testing the priming, social script, and disinhibition predictions. *Journal of Personality and Social Psychology, 53*, 882–890.

Joy, L. A., Kimball, M. M., & Zabrack, M. L. (1986). Television and children's aggressive behavior. In T. M. Williams (Ed.), *The impact of television: A natural experiment in three communities* (pp. 303–360). Orlando, FL: Academic Press.

Joyal, C. C., Dubreucq, J.-L., Gendron, C., & Millaud, F. (2007). Major mental disorders and violence: A critical update. *Current Psychiatry Review, 3*, 33–50.

Junginger, J. (1990). Predicting compliance with command hallucinations. *American Journal of Psychiatry, 147*, 245–247.

Junginger, J. (1995). Command hallucinations and the prediction of dangerousness. *Psychiatric Services, 46*, 911–914.

Junginger, J., Claypoole, K., Laygo, R., & Crisanti, A. (2006). Effects of serious mental illness and substance abuse on criminal offenses. *Psychiatric Services, 57*, 879–882.

Junginger, J., Parks-Levy, J., & McGuire, L. (1998). Delusions and symptom-consistent violence. *Psychiatric Services, 49*, 218–220.

Jurkovic, G. J., & Prentice, N. M. (1977). Relation of moral and cognitive development to dimensions of juvenile delinquency. *Journal of Abnormal Psychology, 86*, 414–420.

Kanazawa, S. (2003). A general evolutionary psychological theory of criminality and related male-typical behavior. In A. Walsh & L. Ellis (Eds.), *Biosocial criminology: Challenging environmentalism's supremacy* (pp. 37–60). Hauppauge, NY: Nova Science Publishers.

Kanazawa, S. (2005). Is "discrimination" necessary to explain the sex gap in earnings? *Journal of Economic Psychology, 26*, 269–287.

Kanazawa, S. (2008). Theft. In J. D. Duntley & T. K. Shackelford (Eds.), *Evolutionary forensic psychology: Darwinian foundations of crime and law* (pp. 160–175). New York, NY: Oxford University Press.

Kanazawa, S., & Still, M. C. (2000). Why men commit crimes (and why they desist). *Sociological Theory, 18*, 434–447.

Kandel, D. B. (1978). Homophily, selection, and socialization in adolescent friendships. *American Journal of Sociology, 84*, 427–436.

Kandel, E., & Mednick, S. A. (1991). Perinatal complications predict violent offending. *Criminology, 29*, 519–530.

Kantor, J. (2014). Seeing abuse, and a pattern too familiar: Janay Palmer, Ray Rice's wife, implied the assault was taken out of context. *The New York Times*. Retrieved from http://www.nytimes.com/2014/09/10/us/seeing-abuse-and-a-pattern-too-familiar.html?_r=0

Kasper, M. E., Rogers, R., & Adams, P. A. (1996). Dangerousness and command hallucinations: An investigation of psychotic inpatients. *Bulletin of the American Academy of Psychiatry and Law, 24*, 219–224.

Kasperkevic, J. (2015, December 30). "Affluenza teen" and mother traced in Mexico after ordering takeaway pizza. *The Guardian*. Retrieved from http://www.theguardian.com/us-news/2015/dec/29/texas-affluenza-teen-arrested-mexico-ethan-couch

Kasperkevic, J. (2016, April 13). "Affluenza" teen Ethan Couch sentenced to 720 days in jail. *The Guardian*. Retrieved from http://www.theguardian.com/us-news/2016/apr/13/affluenz-teen-ethan-couch-sentenced-jail

Kazdin, A. E., & Bootzin, R. R. (1972). The token economy: An evaluative review. *Journal of Applied Behavior Analysis, 5*, 343–372.

Keane, C., Maxim, P. S., & Teevan, J. S. (1993). Drinking and driving, self-control, and gender: Testing a General Theory of Crime. *Journal of Research in Crime and Delinquency, 30*, 30–46.

Kellert, S. R., & Felthous, A. R. (1985). Childhood cruelty toward animals among criminals and noncriminals. *Human Relations, 38*, 1113–1129.

Kelly, S. (1995). *The Boston Stranglers: The public conviction of Albert Desalvo and the true story of eleven shocking murders*. New York, NY: Citadel.

Kemp, D. E., & Center, D. B. (2003). An investigation of Eysenck's antisocial behavior hypothesis in general education students and students with behavior disorders. *Personality and Individual Differences, 35*, 1359–1371.

Kenny, P. J. (2007). Brain reward systems and compulsive drug use. *Trends in Pharmacological Studies, 28*, 135–141.

Kernis, M. H., & Sun, C. R. (1994). Narcissism and reactions to interpersonal feedback. *Journal of Research in Personality, 28*, 4–13.

Kessler, R., Crum, R., Warner, L., Nelson, C., Schulenberg, J., & Anthony, J. (1997). Lifetime co-occurrence of *DSM-III-R* alcohol abuse and dependence with other psychiatric disorders in the National Comorbidity Survey. *Archives of General Psychiatry, 54*, 313–321.

Keune, P. M., van der Heiden, L., Varkuti, B., Konicar, L., Veit, R., & Birbaumer, N. (2012). Prefrontal brain asymmetry and aggression in imprisoned violent offenders. *Neuroscience Letters, 515*, 191–195.

Khajawall, A. M., Erickson, T. B., & Simpson, G. M. (1982). Chronic phencyclidine abuse and physical assault. *The American Journal of Psychiatry, 139*, 1604–1606.

Khantzian, E. J. (1985). The self-medication hypothesis of addictive disorders: Focus on heroin and cocaine dependence. *American Journal of Psychiatry, 142*, 1259–1264.

Kiefer, M. (2010, October 25). Judge to question whether Arizona illegally obtained lethal-injection drug. *The Arizona Republic*. Retrieved from http://www.azcentral.com/arizonarepublic/news/articles/2010/10/25/20101025arizona-jeffrey-landrigan.html

Kiehl, K. A. (2006). A cognitive neuroscience perspective on psychopathy: Evidence for paralimbic system dysfunction. *Psychiatry Research, 142*, 107–128.

Kiehl, K. A., Hare, R. D., McDonald, J. J., & Brink, J. (1999). Semantic and affective processing in psychopaths: An event related potential (ERP) study. *Psychophysiology, 36*, 765–774.

Kiehl, K. A., Smith, A. M., Hare, R. D., Mendrek, A., Forster, B. B., Brink J., & Liddle, P. F. (2001). Limbic abnormalities in affective processing by criminal psychopaths as revealed by functional magnetic resonance imaging. *Biological Psychiatry, 50*, 677–684.

Kienlen, K. K. (1998). Developmental and social antecedents of stalking. In J. R. Meloy (Ed.), *The psychology of stalking: Clinical and forensic perspectives* (pp. 51–67). San Diego, CA: Academic Press, Harcourt Brace.

Kienlen, K. K., Birmingham, D. L., Solberg, K. B., O'Regan, J. T., & Meloy, J. R. (1997). A comparative study of psychotic and nonpsychotic stalking. *Journal of the American Academy of Psychiatry and Law, 25*, 317–334.

Kilgore, K., Snyder, J., & Lentz, C. (2000). The contribution of parental discipline, parental monitoring, and school risk to early-onset conduct problems in African American boys and girls. *Developmental Psychology, 36*, 835–845.

Killer of actress stabbed in prison. (2007, July 28). *USA Today*. Retrieved from http://usatoday30.usatoday.com/life/television/2007-07-28-2301673642_x.htm

Kim, E. (2002). Agitation, aggression, and disinhibition syndromes after traumatic brain injuries. *NeuroRehabilitation, 17*, 297–310.

Kim-Cohen, J., Caspi, A., Taylor, A., Williams, B., Newcombe, R., Craig, I. W., & Moffitt, T. E. (2006). MAOA, maltreatment, and gene–environment interaction predicting children's mental health: New evidence and a meta-analysis. *Molecular Psychiatriy, 11*, 903–913.

Kinlock, T. W., O'Grady, K. E., & Hanlon, T. E. (2003). Prediction of the criminal activity of incarcerated drug-abusing offenders. *Journal of Drug Issues, 33*, 897–920.

Kirigin, K. A., Braukmann, C. J., Atwater, J. D., & Wolf, M. M. (1982). An evaluation of teaching-family (Achievement

Place) group homes for juvenile offenders. *Journal of Applied Behavior Analysis, 15,* 1–16.

Kirk, S. A., & Kutchins, H. (1994). The myth of the reliability of *DSM. The Journal of Mind and Behavior, 15,* 71–86.

Kirkpatrick, B., & Tek, C. (2005). Schizophrenia: Clinical features and psychopathology concepts. In B. J. Sadock & V. A. Sadock (Eds.), *Kaplan & Sadock's comprehensive textbook of psychiatry* (8th ed.) (pp. 1416–1436). Philadelphia, PA: Lippincott Williams & Wilkins.

Klockars, C. B. (1974). *The professional fence.* New York, NY: Free Press.

Knight, R. A., & Prentky, R. A. (1990). Classifying sexual offenders: The development and corroboration of taxonomic models. In W. L. Marshall & D. R. Laws (Eds.), *Handbook of psychopathy* (pp. 23–52). New York, NY: Plenum Press.

Knight, R. A., Prentky, R. A., & Cerce, D. D. (1994). The development, reliability, and validity of an inventory for the multidimensional assessment of sex and aggression. *Criminal Justice and Behaviour, 21,* 72–94.

Koenig, D., & Linden, R. (2004). Conventional or street crime. In R. Linden (Ed.), *Criminology: A Canadian perspective* (pp. 408–433). Toronto, ON: Nelson.

Kohlberg, L. (1969). Stage and sequence: The cognitive-developmental approach to socialization. In D. A. Goslin (Ed.), *Handbook of socialization theory and research* (pp. 347–480). Chicago, IL: Rand McNally.

Kohlberg, L. (1976). Moral stages and moralization: Cognitive-developmental approach. In T. Lickona (Ed.), *Moral development and behavior: Theory, research and social issues* (pp. 31–53). New York, NY: Holt, Rinehart and Winston.

Kolb, B., Gibb, R., & Gorny, G. (2001). Cortical plasticity and the development of behaviour after early frontal cortical injury. *Developmental Neuropsychology, 18,* 423–444.

Kolb, B., & Whishaw, I. Q. (1998). Brain plasticity and behaviour. *Annual Review of Psychology, 49,* 43–64.

Kong, R., Johnson, H., Beattie, S., & Cardillo, A. (2003). *Sexual offences in Canada.* Ottawa, ON: Canadian Centre for Justice Statistics, Statistics Canada.

Koob, G. F. & Le Moal, M. (2008). Addiction and the brain antireward system. *Annual Review of Psychology, 59,* 29–53.

Kosson, D. S. (1998). Divided visual attention in psychopathic and nonpsychopathic offenders. *Personality and Individual Differences, 24,* 373–391.

Kosson, D. S., Cyterski, T. D., Steuerwald, B. L., Neumann, C., & Walker-Matthews, S. (2002). The reliability and validity of the Psychopathy Checklist: Youth Version in non-incarcerated adolescent males. *Psychological Assessment, 14,* 97–109.

Kosson, D. S., Smith, S. S., & Newman, J. P. (1990). Evaluating the construct validity of psychopathy in Black and White male inmates: Three preliminary studies. *Journal of Abnormal Psychology, 99,* 250–259.

Kouri, E. M., Lukas, S. E., Pope, H. G., & Oliva, P. S. (1995). Increased aggressive responding in male volunteers following the administration of gradually increasing doses of testosterone cypionate. *Drug and Alcohol Dependence, 40,* 73–79.

Kouri, E. M., Pope, H. G., & Lukas, S. E. (1999). Changes in aggressive behavior during withdrawal from long-term marijuana use. *Psychopharmacology, 143,* 302–308.

Kraemer, G. W., Lord, D. W., & Heilbrun, K. (2004). Comparing single and serial homicide offenses. *Behavioral Sciences and the Law, 22,* 325–343.

Kraemer, H. C., Kazdin, A. E., Offord, D. R., Kessler, R. C., Jensen, P. S., & Kupfer, D. J. (1997). Coming to terms with the terms of risk. *Archives of General Psychiatry, 54,* 337–343.

Krafka, C., Linz, D., Donnerstein, E., & Penrod, S. (1997). Women's reactions to sexually aggressive mass media depictions. *Violence Against Women, 3,* 149–181.

Kramp, P. (2004). Schizophrenia and crime in Denmark. *Criminal Behaviour and Mental Health, 14,* 231–237.

Kretschmar, J. M., & Flannery, D. J. (2007). Substance use and behavior. In D. J. Flannery, A. T. Vazsonyi, & I. D. Waldman (Eds.), *The Cambridge handbook of violent behavior and aggression* (pp. 647–663). Cambridge, UK: Cambridge University Press.

Kropp, P. R., Hart, S. D., & Lyon, D. R. (2002). Risk assessment of stalkers: Some problems and possible solutions. *Criminal Justice and Behaviour, 29,* 590–616.

Kruesi, M. J. P. (2007). Psychopharmacology of violence. In D. J. Flannery, A. T. Vazsonyi, & I. D. Waldman (Eds.), *The Cambridge handbook of violent behavior and aggression* (pp. 618–635). Cambridge, UK: Cambridge University Press.

Kruesi, M. J. P., Hibbs, E., Zahn, T., Keysor, C. S., Hanburger, S. D., Bartko, J. J., & Rapaport, J. L. (1992). A 2-year prospective follow-up study of children and adolescents with disruptive behaviour disorders: Prediction by CSF 5HIAA, HVA, and autonomic measures? *Archives of General Psychiatry, 49,* 429–435.

Kruesi, M. J. P., Rapoport, J. L,. Hamburger, S., Hibbs, E., Potter, W. Z., Lenane, M., & Brown, G. I. (1990). Cerebrospinal fluid monoamine metabolites, aggression and impulsivity in disruptive behaviour disorders of children and adolescents. *Archives of General Psychiatry, 47,* 419–426.

Ksir, C., Hart, C. L., & Ray, O. (2006). *Drugs, society, and human behavior* (11th ed.). Boston, MA: McGraw-Hill.

Kuhns, J. B., Exum, M. L., Clodfelter, T. A., & Bottia, M. C. (2013). The prevalence of alcohol-involved homicide offending: A meta-analytic review. *Homicide Studies, 18,* 1–20.

Kumari, V., Aasen, I., Taylor, P., Ffytche, D. H., Das, M., Barkataki, I., . . . Sharma, T. (2006). Neural dysfunction and violence in schizophrenia: An fMRI investigation. *Schizophrenia Research, 84,* 144–164.

Kumari, V., Barkataki, I., Goswami, S., Flora, S., Das, M., & Taylor, P. (2009). Dysfunctional, but not functional, impulsivity is associated with a history of seriously violent behaviour and reduced orbitofrontal and hippocampal volumes in schizophrenia. *Psychiatry Research: Neuroimaging, 173*, 39–44.

Kupersmidt, J. B, & Patterson, C. J. (1991). Childhood peer rejection, aggression, withdrawal, and perceived competence as predictors of self-reported behavior problems in preadolescence. *Journal of Abnormal Child Psychology, 19*, 427–449.

Kushel, M. B., Hahn, J. A., Evans, J. L., Bangsberg, D. R., & Moss, A. R. (2005). Revolving doors: Imprisonment among the homeless and marginally housed population. *American Journal of Public Health, 95*, 1747–1752.

Kuzawa, C. W., Gettler, L., Muller, M. N., McDade, T. W., Feranil, A. B. (2009). Fatherhood, pairbonding and testosterone in the Philippines. *Hormones and Behavior, 56*, 429–435.

Kyckelhahn, T. (2011). *Justice expenditures and employment, FY 1982-2007—Statistical tables*. Washington, DC: Bureau of Justice Statistics, U.S. Department of Justice.

LaGrange, T. C., & Silverman, R. A. (1999). Low self-control and opportunity: Testing the general theory of crime as an explanation for gender differences in delinquency. *Criminology, 37*, 41–72.

Lahey, B. B., Van Hulle, C. A., D'Onofrio, B. M., Rodgers, J. L., & Waldman, I. D. (2008). Is parental knowledge of their adolescent offspring's whereabouts and peer associations spuriously associated with offspring delinquency? *Journal of Abnormal Child Psychology, 36*, 807–823.

Laird, R. D., Pettit, G. S., Dodge, K. A., & Bates, J. E. (2005). Peer relationship antecedents of delinquent behavior in late adolescence: Is there evidence of demographic group differences in developmental processes. *Development and Psychopathology, 17*, 127–144.

Lalumière, M. L., Harris, G. T., Quinsey, V. L., & Rice, M. E. (2005). *The causes of rape*. Washington, DC: American Psychological Association.

Lamb, H. R. (2001). Deinstitutionalization at the beginning of the new millennium. In H. R. Lamb & L. E. Weinberger (Eds.), *Deinstitutionalization: Promise and problems* (pp. 3–20). San Francisco, CA: Josey-Bass.

Lamb, H. R., & Grant, R. W. (1982). The mentally ill in an urban county jail. *Archives of General Psychiatry, 39*, 17–22.

Lamb, H. R., Shaner, R., Elliot, D. M., DeCuir, W. J., & Foltz, J. T. (1995). Outcome for psychiatric emergency patients seen by an outreach police–mental health team. *Psychiatric Services, 46*, 1267–1271.

Lamb, H. R., & Weinberger, L. E. (1998). Persons with severe mental illness in jails and prisons: A review. *Psychiatric Services, 49*, 483–492.

Lamb, H. R., & Weinberger, L. E. (2005). The shift of psychiatric inpatient care from hospitals to jails and prisons. *Journal of the American Academy of Psychiatry and Law, 33*, 529–533.

Landenberger, N. A., & Lipsey, M. W. (2005). The positive effects of cognitive-behavioral programs for offenders: A meta-analysis of factors associated with effective treatment. *Journal of Experimental Criminology, 1*, 451–476.

Langevin, R., Wortzman, G., Dickey, R., Wright, P., & Handy, L. (1988). Neuropsychological impairment in incest offenders. *Annals of Sex Research, 1*, 401–415.

Langman, P. (2009). Rampage school shooters: A typology. *Aggression and Violent Behavior, 14*, 79–86.

Långström, N., & Grann, M. (2000). Risk for criminal recidivism among young sex offenders. *Journal of Interpersonal Violence, 15*, 856–872.

Lanning, K. (1992). *Child molesters: A behavioral analysis* (3rd ed.). Alexandria, VA: National Center for Missing and Exploited Children.

Lapierre, D., Braun, C. M. J., & Hodgins, S. (1995). Ventral frontal deficits in psychopathy: Neuropsychological test findings. *Neuropsycholigica, 33*, 139–151.

Larzelere, R. (2000). Child outcomes of nonabusive and customary physical punishment by parents: An updated literature review. *Clinical Child and Family Psychology Review, 3*, 199–221.

Lau, M. A., Pihl, R. O., & Peterson, J. B. (1995). Provocation, acute alcohol intoxication, cognitive performance, and aggression. *Journal of Abnormal Psychology, 104*, 150–155.

Laub, J. H., & Sampson, R. J. (2003). *Shared beginnings, divergent lives: Delinquent boys to age 70*. Cambridge, MA: Harvard University Press.

Lavine, R. (1997). Psychopharmacological treatment of aggression and violence in the substance using population. *Journal of Psychoactive Drugs, 29*, 321–329.

Lavoie, J. A. A., Guy, L. S., & Douglas, K. S. (2009). Violence risk assessment: Principles and models of bridging prediction to management. In J. L. Ireland, C. A. Ireland, & P. Birch (Eds.), *Violent and sexual offenders* (pp. 3–26). Portland, OR: Willan.

Lawrence, J. (2013, September 6). Jepsen's hacker used inactive email to download "sensitive" photos, court hears. Retrieved from http://bc.ctvnews.ca/jepsen-s-hacker-used-inactive-email-to-download-sensitive-photos-court-hears-1.1443211

Laws, D. R., & Marshall, W. L. (1990). A conditioning theory of the etiology and maintenance of deviant sexual preferences and behavior. In W. L. Marshall, D. R. Laws, & H. E. Barbaree (Eds.), *Handbook of sexual assault: Issues, theories, and treatment of the offender* (pp. 209–230). New York, NY: Plenum Press.

Leary, M. R., Kowalski, R. M., Smith, L., & Phillips, S. (2003). Teasing, rejection, and violence: Case studies of the school shootings. *Aggressive Behavior, 29*, 202–214.

LeBlanc, A. E., Kalant, H., & Gibbins, R. J. (1975). Acute tolerance to ethanol in the rat. *Psychopharmacologia, 41*, 43–46.

LeDoux, J. (1996). *The emotional brain*. New York, NY: Simon & Schuster.

LeFever, G. B., Dawson, K. V., & Morrow, A. L. (1999). The extent of drug therapy for attention deficit-hyperactivity disorder among children in public schools. *American Journal of Public Health, 89*, 1359–1364.

Lee, M., & Prentice, N. M. (1988). Interrelations of empathy, cognition, and moral reasoning with dimensions of juvenile delinquency. *Journal of Abnormal Child Psychology, 16*, 127–139.

Lee, Z., Klaver, J. R., Hart, S. D., Moretti, M. M., & Douglas, K. S. (2009). Short-term stability of psychopathic traits in adolescent offenders. *Journal of Clinical Child & Adolescent Psychology, 38*, 595–605.

Leitenberg, H., & Henning, K. (1995). Sexual fantasy. *Psychological Bulletin, 117*, 469–496.

Lett, D. (2009, March 6). Gradual descent into mental illness; Vincent Li and his wife, Ana, struggled to make new life in Canada. *The Vancouver Sun*, p. B3.

Letterman gets stalker's visit. (1993, May 5). *The Vancouver Sun*, p. C5.

Letterman stalker picks a new target. (1997, September 27). *Star-Phoenix*, p. D19.

Leung, R. (2003, April 18). The counterfeit Rockefeller. Retrieved from http://www.cbsnews.com/news/the-counterfeit-rockefeller/

Lewis, D. O., Pincus, H. J., Feldman, M., Jackson, L., & Bard, B. (1986). Psychiatric, neurological, and psychoeducational characteristics of 15 death row inmates in the United States. *American Journal of Psychiatry, 143*, 838–845.

Lewis, S. (2012, September 27). FBI agents reveal underwear bomber Abdulmutallab wore explosive underwear for three weeks. Retrieved from http://www.wxyz.com/dpp/news/local_news/investigations/fbi-agents-underwear-bomber-abdulmutallab-wore-underwear-for-3-weeks#ixzz27mGLVwIk

Lezak, M. D., & O'Brien, K. P. (1988). Longitudinal study of emotional, social, and physical changes after traumatic brain injury. *Journal of Learning Disabilities, 21*, 456–463.

Lieberman, D. A. (2000). *Learning: behavior and cognition* (5th ed.). Belmont, CA: Wadsworth.

Lindert, J. (2015). *Violence and mental health: Its manifold faces*. New York, NY: Springer.

Lindqvist, P. (1986). Criminal homicide in Northern Sweden 1970–1981: Alcohol intoxication, alcohol abuse and mental disease. *International Journal of Law and Psychiatry, 8*, 19–37.

Lindqvist, P., & Allebeck, P. (1990). Schizophrenia and crime: A longitudinal follow-up of 644 schizophrenics in Stockholm. *British Journal of Psychiatry, 157*, 345–350.

Link, B. G., Andrews, H. A., & Cullen, F. T. (1992). The violent and illegal behavior of mental patients reconsidered. *American Sociological Review, 57*, 275–292.

Link, B. G., Monahan, J., Stueve, A., & Cullen, F. T. (1999). Real in their consequences: A sociological approach to understanding the association between psychotic symptoms and violence. *American Sociological Review, 64*, 316–332.

Link, B. G., & Stueve, A. (1994). Psychotic symptoms and the violent/illegal behavior of mental patients compared to community controls. In J. Monahan & H. Steadman (Eds.), *Violence and mental disorder: Developments in risk assessment* (pp. 137–159). Chicago, IL: University of Chicago Press.

Linnoila, M., Virkkunen, M., Scheinin, M., Nuutila, A., Rimon, R., & Goodwin, F. K. (1983). Low cerebrospinal fluid 5-hydroxyindoleacetic acid concentration differentiates impulsive from nonimpulsive violent behaviour. *Life Sciences, 33*, 2609–2614.

Linz, D., Donnerstein, E., & Adams, S. M. (1989). Physiological desensitization and judgments about female victims of violence. *Human Communication Research, 15*, 509–522.

Linz, D., Donnerstein, E., & Penrod, S. (1984). The effects of multiple exposures to filmed violence against women. *Journal of Communication, 34*, 130–147.

Linz, D., Donnerstein, E., & Penrod, S. (1988). The effects of long-term exposure to violent and sexually degrading depictions of women. *Journal of Personality and Social Psychology, 55*, 758–768.

Lipsey, M. W. (1992). Juvenile delinquency treatment: A meta-analytic inquiry into the variability of effects. In T. D. Cook, H. Cooper, D. S. Cordray, H. Hartmann, L. V. Hedges, R. J. Light, T. A. Louis, & F. Mosteller (Eds.), *Meta-analysis for explanation: A casebook* (pp. 83–127). New York, NY: Russell Sage Foundation.

Lipsey, M. W. (1995). What do we learn from 400 research studies on the effectiveness of treatment with juvenile delinquents? In J. McGuire (Ed.), *What works: Reducing reoffending—Guidelines from research and practice* (pp. 63–78). Chichester, UK: Wiley.

Lipsey, M. W. (1999). Can rehabilitative programs reduce the recidivism of juvenile offenders? An inquiry into the effectiveness of practical programs. *Virginia Journal of Social Policy & the Law, 6*, 611–641.

Lipsey, M. W. (2009). The primary factors that characterize effective interventions with juvenile offenders: A meta-analytic overview. *Victims and Offenders, 4*, 124–147.

Lipsey, M. W., Chapman, G. L., & Landenberger, N. A. (2001). Cognitive-behavioral programs for offenders. *Annals of the American Academy of Political and Social Science, 578*, 144–157.

Lipsey, M. W., & Cullen, F. T. (2007). The effectiveness of correctional rehabilitation: A review of systematic reviews. *Annual Review of Law and Social Science, 3*, 297–320.

Lipsey, M. W., & Wilson, D. B. (1998). Effective intervention for serious juvenile offenders: A synthesis of research. In R. Loeber & D. P. Farrington (Eds.), *Serious and violent juvenile offenders: Risk factors and successful interventions* (pp. 313–345). Thousand Oaks, CA: Sage.

Lipton, D., Martinson, R., & Wilks, J. (1975). *The effectiveness of correctional treatment: A survey of treatment evaluation studies*. New York, NY: Praeger.

Litwack, T. R. (2001). Actuarial versus clinical assessments of dangerousness. *Psychology, Public Policy, and Law, 7,* 409–443.

Litwack, T. R., Zapf, P. A., Groscup, J. L., & Hart, S. D. (2006). Violence risk assessment: Research, legal, and clinical considerations. In I. B. Weiner & A. K. Hess (Eds.), *The handbook of forensic psychology* (3rd ed.) (pp. 487–533). Hoboken, NJ: Wiley.

Lochman, J. E., & Dodge, K. A. (1994). Social-cognitive processes of severely violent, moderately aggressive and nonaggressive boys. *Journal of Consulting and Clinical Psychology, 62,* 366–374.

Loeber, R. (1982). The stability of antisocial and delinquent child behavior: A review. *Child Development, 53,* 1431–1446.

Loeber, R. (1988). Natural histories of conduct problems, delinquency, and associated substance use. In B. B. Lahey & A. E. Kazdin (Eds.), *Advances in clinical child psychology, Vol I* (pp. 73–124). New York, NY: Plenum Press.

Loeber, R. (1990). Development and risk factors of juvenile antisocial behavior and delinquency. *Clinical Psychology Review, 10,* 1–41.

Loeber, R., Burke, J. D., Lahey, B. B., Winters, A., & Zera, M. (2000). Oppositional defiant and conduct disorder: A review of the past 10 years, Part I. *Journal of the American Academy of Child and Adolescent Psychiatry, 39,* 1468–1484.

Loeber, R., & Farrington, D. P. (2000). Young children who commit crime: Epidemiology and developmental origins, risk factors, early interventions and policy implications. *Development and Psychopathology, 12,* 737–762.

Loeber, R., Farrington, D. P., & Petechuk, D. (2003). Child delinquency: Early intervention and prevention. *Child Delinquency Bulletin Series.*

Loeber, R., & Stouthmaer-Loeber, M. (1986). Family factors as correlates and predictors of juvenile conduct problems and delinquency. In N. Morris & M. Tonry (Eds.), *Crime and justice: An annual review of research* (Vol. 7). Chicago, IL: University of Chicago Press.

Loeber, R., & Stouthamer-Loeber, M. (1998). Development of juvenile aggression and violence: Some common misconceptions and controversies. *American Psychologist, 53,* 242–259.

Loeber, R., Stouthamer-Loeber, M., van Kammen, W., & Farrington, D. P. (1991). Initiation, escalation, and desistance in juvenile offending and their correlates. *The Journal of Criminal Law and Criminology, 82,* 36.

Logan, T. K., Leukefeld, C., & Walker, B. (2000). Stalking as a variant of intimate violence: Implications from a young adult sample. *Violence and Victims, 15,* 91–111.

Loney, B. R., Taylor, J., Butler, M. A., & Iacono, W. G. (2007). Adolescent psychopathy features: 6-year temporal stability and the prediction of externalizing symptoms during the transition to adulthood. *Aggressive Behavior, 33,* 242–252.

Lorenz, A. R., & Newman, J. P. (2002). Deficient response modulation and emotional processing in low anxious Caucasian psychopathic offenders: Results from a lexical decision task. *Emotion, 2,* 91–104.

Lorenz, K. Z. (1966/2002). *On aggression.* London: Routledge.

Lösel, F. (1995). The efficacy of correctional treatment: A review and synthesis of meta-evaluations. In J. McGuire (Ed.), *What works: Reducing reoffending—Guidelines from research and practice* (pp. 79–111). Chichester, UK: Wiley.

Lowenkamp, C. T., Latessa, E. J., & Holsinger, A. M. (2006). The risk principle in action: What have we learned from 13,676 offenders and 97 correctional programs? *Crime and Delinquency, 52,* 77–93.

Lucks, B. D. (2004). *Cyberstalking: Identifying and examining electronic crime in cyberspace.* (Unpublished doctoral dissertation). San Diego, CA: Alliant International University.

Lykken, D. T. (1957). A study of anxiety in the sociopathic personality. *The Journal of Abnormal and Social Psychology, 55,* 6–10.

Lykken, D. T. (1995). *The antisocial personalities.* Hillsdale, NJ: Erlbaum.

Lynam, D. R. (1996). Early identification of chronic offenders: Who is the fledgling psychopath? *Psychological Bulletin, 120,* 209–234.

Lynam, D. R., Caspi, A., Moffitt, T. E., Loeber, R., & Stouthamer-Loeber, M. (2007). Longitudinal evidence that psychopathy scores in early adolescence predict adult psychopathy. *Journal of Abnormal Psychology, 116,* 155–165.

Lynam, D. R., Caspi, A., Moffitt, T. E., Wikstrom, P. O., Loeber, R., & Novak, S. (2000). The interaction between impulsivity and neighbourhood context on offending: The effects of impulsivity are stronger in poorer neighbourhoods. *Journal of Abnormal Psychology, 109,* 563–574.

Lynam, D. R., Charnigo, R., Moffitt, T. E., Raine, A., Loeber, R., & Stouthamer-Loeber, M. (2009). The stability of psychopathy across adolescence. *Development and Psychopathology, 21,* 1133–1153.

Lynam, D. R., & Miller, J. D. (2004). Personality pathways to impulsive behavior and their relations to deviance: Results from three samples. *Journal of Quantitative Criminology, 20,* 319–341.

Lynam, D., Moffitt, T., & Stouthamer-Loeber, M. (1993). Explaining the relation between IQ and delinquency: Class, race, test motivation, school failure or self-control. *Journal of Abnormal Psychology, 102,* 187–196.

Lynn, D. D., & Donovan, J. M. (1980). Medical versus surgical treatment of coronary artery disease. *Evaluation in Education, 4,* 98–99.

Lynndie England still haunted by Abu Ghraib scandal. (2009, June 29). Associated Press. Retrieved from http://www.foxnews.com/story/2009/06/29/lynndie-england-still-haunted-by-abu-ghraib-scandal/

Lyon, D. R. (1997). *The characteristics of stalkers in British Columbia: A statistical comparison of persons charged with criminal harassment and persons charged with other Criminal Code offences* (Master's thesis). Simon Fraser University, Burnaby, BC.

Lyon, D. R., Hart, S. D., & Webster, C. D. (2001). Violence and the assessment of risk. In R. Schuller & J. R. P. Ogloff (Eds.), *Law and psychology: Canadian perspectives* (pp. 314–350). Toronto, ON: University of Toronto Press.

Lytton, H., Maunula, S. R., & Watts, D. (1987). Moral judgments and reported moral actions: A tenuous relationship. *The Alberta Journal of Education Research, 3*, 150–162.

MacCoon, D. G., Wallace, J. F., & Newman, J. P. (2004). Self-regulation: Context-appropriate balanced attention. In R. F. Baumeister & K. D. Vohs (Eds.), *Handbook of self-regulation: Research, theory, and applications* (pp. 422–444). New York, NY: Guilford Press.

MacDonald, J. M. (1963). The threat to kill. *American Journal of Psychiatry, 120*, 125–130.

MacHovec, F. J. (1989). *Cults and personality.* Springfield, IL: Charles C. Thomas.

Mack, T. D., Hackney, A. A., & Pyle, M. (2011). The relationship between psychopathic traits and attachment behavior in a non-clinical population. *Personality and Individual Differences, 51*, 584–588.

MacKenzie, R. D., Mullen, P. E., Ogloff, J. R. P., McEwan, T. E., & James, D. V. (2008). Parental bonding and adult attachment styles in different types of stalker. *Journal of Forensic Sciences, 53*, 1443–1449.

MacKenzie, D. L. (2006). *What works in corrections: Reducing the criminal activities of offenders and delinquents.* New York, NY: Cambridge University Press.

Maddux, J. E. (2004). The mythology of psychopathology: A social cognitive view of deviance, difference, and disorder. In R. M. Kowalski & M. R. Leary (Eds.), *The interface of social and clinical psychology* (pp. 240–257). New York, NY: Psychology Press.

Main, M., & Solomon, J. (1986). Discovery of a new, insecure-disorganized/disoriented attachment pattern. In T. B. Brazelton & M. Yogman (Eds.), *Affective development in infancy* (pp. 95–124). Norwood, NJ: Ablex.

Main, M., & Solomon, J. (1990). Procedures for identifying disorganized/disoriented infants during the Ainsworth Strange Situation. In M. Greenberg, D. Cicchetti, & M. Cummings (Eds.), *Attachment in the preschool years* (pp. 121–160). Chicago, IL: University of Chicago Press.

Malamuth, N. M. (2003). Criminal and non-criminal sexual aggressors: Integrating psychopathy into a hierarchical-mediational confluence model. In R. A. Prentky, E. Janus, & M. Seto (Eds.), *Understanding and managing sexually coercive behavior. Annals of the New York Academy of Sciences, Vol. 989* (pp. 33–58). New York, NY: New York Academy of Sciences.

Malamuth, N. M., Addison, T., & Koss, M. (2000). Pornography and sexual aggression: Are there reliable effects and can we understand them? *Annual Review of Sex Research, 11*, 26–91.

Malamuth, N., & Donnerstein, E. (1982). The effects of aggressive-pornographic mass media stimuli. In L. Berkowitz (Ed.), *Advances in experimental social psychology, Vol. 15* (pp. 103–136). New York, NY: Academic Press.

Malamuth, N. M., Hald, G. M., & Koss, M. (2012). Pornography, individual differences in risk and men's acceptance of violence against women in a representative sample. *Sex Roles, 66*, 427–439.

Malone, D., & Swindle, H. (2013). *America's condemned: Death row inmates in their own words.* Kansas City, MO: Andrews McMeel.

Mangino, M. T. (2014). *The executioner's toll, 2010: The crimes, arrests, trials, appeals, last meals, final words, and executions of 46 people in the United States.* Jefferson, NC: McFarland and Company.

Maniglio, R. (2009). Severe mental illness and criminal victimization: A systematic review. *Acta Psychiatrica Scandinavica, 119*, 180–191.

Maniglio, R. (2010). The role of deviant sexual fantasy in the etiopathogenesis of sexual homicide: A systematic review. *Aggression and Violent Behavior, 15*, 294–302.

Mann, R. E., & Beech, A. R. (2003). Cognitive distortions, schemas, and implicit theories. In T. Ward, D. R. Laws, & S. M. Hudson (Eds.), *Sexual deviance: Issues and controversies* (p. 146). Thousand Oaks, CA: Sage.

Mann, R. E., Hanson, R. K., & Thornton, D. (2010). Assessing risk for sexual recidivism: Some proposals on the nature of psychologically meaningful risk factors. *Sexual Abuse: A Journal of Research and Treatment, 22*, 191–217.

Manuck, S. B., Flory, J. D., Ferrell, R. E., Mann, J. J., & Muldoon, M. F. (2000). A regulatory polymorphism of the monoamine oxidase-A gene may be associated with variability in aggression, impulsivity, and central nervous system serotonergic responsivity. *Psychiatry Research, 95*, 9–23.

Marleau, J. D., Auclair, N., & Millaud, F. (2006). Comparison of factors associated with parricide in adults and adolescents. *Journal of Family Violence, 21*, 321–325.

Marshall, W. L. (2000). Revisiting the use of pornography by sexual offenders: Implications for theory and practice. *Journal of Sexual Aggression, 6*, 67–77.

Marshall, W. L., Marshall, L. E., Serran, G. A., & O'Brien, M. D. (2013). What works in reducing sexual offending. In L. A. Craig, L. Dixon, & T. A. Gannon (Eds.), *What works in offender rehabilitation: An evidence-based approach to assessment and treatment* (pp. 173–191). New York, NY: Wiley.

Marshall, W. L., Serran, G. A., & Cortoni, F. A. (2000). Childhood attachments, sexual abuse, and their relationship to adult coping in child molesters. *Sexual Abuse: A Journal of Research and Treatment, 12*, 17–26.

Martell, D. A. (1991). Mentally disordered offenders and violent crimes: Preliminary research findings. *Law and Human Behavior, 15,* 333–347.

Martell, D. A. (1992). Estimating the prevalence of organic brain dysfunction in maximum-security forensic psychiatric patients. *Journal of Forensic Sciences, 37,* 878–893.

Martell, D. A. (2007). Organic brain dysfunctions and criminality. In L. B. Schlesinger (Ed.), *Explorations in criminal psychopathology: Clinical syndromes with forensic implications* (2nd ed.). Springfield, IL: Charles C. Thomas.

Martell, D. A., Rosner, R., & Harmon, R. B. (1995). Base-rate estimates of criminal behavior by homeless mentally ill persons in New York City. *Psychiatric Services, 46,* 596–601.

Martin, C. S., & Earleywine, M. (1990). Ascending and descending rates of change in blood alcohol concentrations and subjective intoxication ratings. *Journal of Substance Abuse, 2,* 345–352.

Martin, D. (2013, June 13). Richard Ramirez, the "Night Stalker" killer, dies at 53. *The New York Times,* p. D8.

Martinson, R. (1974). What works?—Questions and answers about prison reform. *The Public Interest, 35,* 22–54.

Martinson, R. (1979). New findings, new views: A note of caution regarding prison reform. *Hofstra Law Review, 7,* 243–258.

Matthews, R., Matthews, J. K., & Speltz, K. (1989). *Female sexual offenders: An empirical study.* Orwell, VT: The Safer Society Press.

Maxwell, S. E., Lau, M. Y., & Howard, G. S. (2015). Is psychology suffering from a replication crisis? *American Psychologist, 70,* 487–498.

Mazur, D. A., & Booth, A. (1998). Testosterone and dominance in men. *Behavioral and Brain Sciences, 21,* 353–363.

Mazur, D. A., Booth, A., & Dabbs, J. M. (1992). Testosterone and chess competition. *Social Psychology Quarterly, 55,* 70–77.

Mazur, J. E. (2013). *Learning and behavior* (7th ed.). Upper Saddle River, NJ: Pearson.

McBurnett, K., Lahey, B. B., Frick, P. J., Risch, C., Loeber, R., Hart, E. L., . . . Hanson, K. S. (1991). Anxiety, inhibition, and conduct disorder in children: Relation to salivary cortisol. *Journal of the American Academy of Child and Adolescent Psychiatry, 30,* 192–196.

McBurnett, K., Lahey, B. B., Rathouz, P. J., & Loeber, R. (2000). Low salivary cortisol and persistent aggression in boys referred for disruptive behaviour. *Archives of General Psychiatry, 57,* 38–43.

McCardle, L., & Fishbein, D. H. (1989). The self-reported effects of PCP on human aggression. *Addictive Behaviors, 14,* 465–472.

McCarthy, B., & Hagan, J. (1991). Homelessness: A criminogenic situation? *British Journal of Criminology, 31,* 393–410.

McClellan, J. (2006). Case study: Ted Bundy, an offender-based comparison of murder typologies. *Journal of Security Education, 2,* 19–37.

McConaghy, N. (1970). Penile response conditioning and its relationship to aversion therapy in homosexuals. *Behavior Therapy, 1,* 213–221.

McCord, J., Widom, C. S., & Crowell, N. A. (2001). *Juvenile crime, juvenile justice, panel on juvenile crime: Prevention, Treatment, and Control.* Washington, DC: National Academy Press.

McCord, W. M., & McCord, J. (1959). *Origins of crime: A new evaluation of the Cambridge-Somerville youth study.* New York, NY: Columbia University Press.

McCrae, R. R., & Costa Jr, P. T. (1997). Personality trait structure as a human universal. *American Psychologist, 52,* 509–516.

McCrae, R. R., & Costa Jr, P. T. (1999). A five-factor theory of personality. In O. P. John, R. W. Robins, & L. A. Pervin (Eds.), *Handbook of personality: Theory and research* (pp.139–153). New York, NY: Guilford Press.

McCrae, R. R., & Costa Jr, P. T. (2004). A contemplated revision of the NEO Five-Factor Inventory. *Personality and Individual Differences, 36,* 587–59.

McFarlane, J., Campbell, J. C., & Watson, K. (2002). Intimate partner stalking and femicide: Urgent implications for women's safety. *Behavioral Sciences and the Law, 20,* 51–68.

McFarlane, J. M., Campbell, J. C., Wilt, S., Sachs, C. J., Ulrich, Y., & Xu, X. (1999). Stalking and intimate partner femicide. *Homicide Studies, 3,* 300–316.

McGrath, M. G., & Casey, E. (2002). Forensic psychiatry and the Internet: Practical perspectives on sexual predators and obsessional harassers in cyberspace. *Journal of the American Academy of Psychiatry and the Law, 30,* 81–94.

McGregor, I. (2003). Defensive zeal: Compensatory conviction about attitudes, values, goals, groups, and self-definitions in the face of personal uncertainty. In S. J. Spencer, S. Fein, M. P. Zanna, & J. M. Olson (Eds.), *Motivated social perception: The Ontario symposium* (Vol. 9) (pp. 73–92). Mahwah, NJ: Erlbaum.

McGregor, I., & Marigold, D. C. (2003). Defensive zeal and the uncertain self: What makes you so sure? *Journal of Personality and Social Psychology, 85,* 838–852.

McGregor, I., Zanna, M. P., Holmes, J. G., & Spencer, S. J. (2001). Compensatory conviction in the face of personal uncertainty: Going to extremes and being oneself. *Journal of Personality and Social Psychology, 80,* 472–488.

McGuire, J. (2000). *Cognitive-behavioural approaches: An introduction to theory and research.* London, UK: Home Office.

McGuire, J. (2002a). Integrating findings from research reviews. In J. McGuire (Ed.), *Offender rehabilitation and treatment: Effective programmes and policies to reduce re-offending* (pp. 3–38). Chichester, UK: Wiley.

McGuire, J. (2002b). Criminal sanctions versus psychologically-based interventions with offenders: A comparative empirical analysis. *Psychology, Crime and Law, 8,* 183–208.

McGuire, J. (2004). *Understanding psychology and crime: Perspectives on theory and action.* Maidenhead, UK: Open University Press.

McGuire, J. (2006). General offending behaviour programmes: Concept, theory, and practice. In C. R. Hollin & E. J. Palmer (Eds.), *Offending behaviour programmes: Development, application, and controversies* (pp. 69–111). Chichester, UK: Wiley.

McGuire, J., & Priestley, P. (1995). Reviewing "What works": Past, present and future. In J. McGuire (Ed.), *What works: Reducing reoffending—Guidelines from research and practice* (pp. 3–34). Chichester, UK: Wiley.

McGuire, R. J., Carlisle, J. M., & Young, B. G. (1965). Sexual deviations as conditioned behaviour: A hypothesis. *Behavior Research and Therapy, 2*, 185–190.

McIntyre, M. (2009, March 4). Killer believed he was "acting on God's order"; Beheading trial. *National Post*, p. A9.

McKee, G. R., & Shea, S. J. (1998). Matricide: A cross-national comparision. *Journal of Clinical Psychology, 54*, 679–687.

McKeown, B. (Writer), & Karp, M. (Director). (2008). A fight to the death [Television series episode]. In M. Karp (Producer), *The Fifth Estate*. Toronto, ON: Canadian Broadcasting Corporation.

McKim, W. A., & Hancock, S. D. (2013). *Drugs and behavior: An introduction to behavioral pharmacology*. Boston, MA: Pearson.

McLaughlin, K. A., Green, J. G., Gruber, M. J., Sampson, N. A., Zaslavsky, A. M., & Kessler, R. C. (2010). Childhood adversities and adult psychopathology in the National Comorbidity Survey Replication (NCS–R) III: Associations with functional impairment related to *DSM-IV* disorders. *Psychological Medicine, 40*, 847–859.

McMurran, M. (2012). Treatments for offenders in prison and the community. In M. McMurran (Ed.), *Alcohol-related violence: Prevention and treatment* (pp. 205–225). Chichester, UK: Wiley-Blackwell.

McNiel, D. E., Eisner, J. P., & Binder, R. L. (2000). The relationship between command hallucinations and violence. *Psychiatric Services, 51*, 1288–1292.

MacQueen, K., & Hall, N. (1997, August 23). Inside the mind of a monster. *The Ottawa Citizen*, p. A5.

Meadows, R. J., & Kuehnel, J. (2005). *Evil minds: Understanding and responding to violent predators*. Upper Saddle River, NJ: Pearson/Prentice Hall.

Mealey, L. (1995). The sociobiology of sociopathy: An integrated evolutionary model. *Behavioral and Brain Sciences, 18*, 523–599.

Mears, D. P., & Cochran, J. C. (2013). What is the effect of IQ on offending? *Criminal Justice and Behavior, 40*, 1280–1300.

Mednick, S. A., Gabrielli, W. F., & Hutchings, B. (1983). Genetic influences in criminal behavior: Evidence from an adoption cohort. In K. T. Van Dusen & S. A. Mednick (Eds.), *Prospective studies of crime and delinquency* (pp. 39–56). Hingham, MA: Kluwer-Nijhoff.

Mednick, S. A., Gabrielli, W. F., & Hutchings, B. (1984). Genetic influences in criminal convictions: Evidence from an adoption cohort. *Science, 224*, 891–894.

Meehl, P. E. (1954). *Clinical versus statistical prediction*. Minneapolis: University of Minnesota Press.

Megargee, E. I. (1966). Undercontrolled and overcontrolled personalty types in extreme antisocial aggression. *Psychological Monographs: General and Applied, 80*, 1–29.

Megargee, E. I., Cook, P. E., & Mendelsohn, G. A. (1967). Development and validation of an MMPI scale of assaultiveness in overcontrolled individuals. *Journal of Abnormal Psychology, 72*, 519–528.

Meloy, J. R. (1988). *The psychopathic mind: Origins, dynamics, and treatment*. New York, NY: Jason Aronson.

Meloy, J. R. (1992). *Violent attachments*. Northvale, NJ: Jason Aronson.

Meloy, J. R. (1996). Stalking (obsessional following): A review of some preliminary studies. *Aggression and Violent Behavior, 1*, 147–162.

Meloy, J. R. (1998). *The psychology of stalking: Clinical and forensic perspectives*. San Diego, CA: Academic Press.

Meloy, J. R. (1999). Stalking: An old behavior, a new crime. *The Psychiatric Clinics of North America, 22*, 85–99.

Meloy, J. R., & Gacono, C. B. (1992). The aggression response and the Rorschach. *Journal of Clinical Psychology, 48*, 104–114.

Meloy, J. R., & Gothard, S. (1995). Demographic and clinical comparison of obsessional followers and offenders with mental disorders. *American Journal of Psychiatry, 152*, 258–263.

Melton, G. B., Petrila, J., Poythress, N. G., & Slobogin, C. (2007). *Psychological evaluations for the courts: A handbook for mental health professionals and lawyers* (3rd ed.). New York, NY: Guilford Press.

Menard, S., & Mihalic, S. (2001). The tripartite conceptual framework in adolescence and adulthood: Evidence from a national sample. *Journal of Drug Issues, 31*, 905–940.

Meuer, T., Seymour, A., & Wallace, H. (2002, June). Domestic violence. In A. Seymour, M. Murray, J. Sigmon, M. Hook, C. Edwards, M. Gaboury, & G. Coleman (Eds.), *National Victim Assistance Academy textbook*. Washington, DC: U.S. Department of Justice, Office for Victims of Crimes.

Meyer, C., & Oberman, M. (2001). Mothers who kill their children: Understanding the acts of moms from Susan Smith to the "prom mom." New York, NY: New York University Press.

Meyers, W. C., & Vo, E. J. (2012). Adolescent parricide and psychopathy. *International Journal of Offender Therapy and Comparative Criminology, 56*, 715–729.

Miladinovic, Z., & Mulligan, L. (2015). *Homicide in Canada, 2014*. Ottawa, ON: Canadian Centre for Justice Statistics, Statistics Canada.

Milgram, A. (2000). My personal view of Stanley Milgram. In T. Blass (Ed.), *Obedience to authority: Current perspectives on the Milgram paradigm* (pp. 1–7). Mahwah, NJ: Erlbaum.

Milgram, S. (1963). Behavioral study of obedience. *Journal of Abnormal and Social Psychology, 67*, 371–378.

Milgram, S. (1965). Some conditions of obedience and disobedience to authority. *Human Relations, 18*, 57–76.

Miles, D. R., & Carey, G. (1997). Genetic and environmental architecture of human aggression. *Journal of Personality and Social Psychology, 72*, 207–217.

Milkie, M. A. (1994). Social world approach to cultural studies: Mass media and gender in the adolescent peer group. *Journal of Contemporary Ethnography, 23*, 354–380.

Miller-Johnson, S., Coie, J., Maumary-Gremaud, A., Lochman, J., & Terry, R. (1999). Relationship between childhood peer rejection and aggression and adolescent delinquency severity and type among African American youth. *Journal of Emotional and Behavioral Disorders, 7*, 137–146.

Miller, L. (2014a). Serial killers: I, Subtypes, patterns, and motives. *Aggression and Violent Behavior, 19*, 1–11.

Miller, L. (2014b). Serial killers: II, Development, dynamics, and forensics. *Aggression and Violent Behavior, 19*, 12–22.

Miller, M., & Morris, N. (1988). Predictions of dangerousness: An argument for limited use. *Violence and Victims, 3*, 263–283.

Miller, N. E. (1960). Learning resistance to pain and fear: Effects of overlearning, exposure, and rewarded exposure in context. *Journal of Experimental Psychology, 60*, 137–145.

Milton, T., Simonsen, E., Birket-Smith, M., & Davis, R. D. (1998). *Psychopathy: Antisocial, criminal, and violent behavior.* New York, NY: Guilford Press.

Ministy of Justice, Home Office and the Office for National Statistics. (2013). *An overview of sexual offending in England and Wales.* Retrieved from http://webarchive.nationalarchives.gov.uk/20160105160709/https://www.gov.uk/government/uploads/system/uploads/attachment_data/file/214970/sexual-offending-overview-jan-2013.pdf

Mischkowitz, R. (1994). Desistance from a delinquent way of life? In E. G. M. Weitekamp & H. J. Kerner (Eds.), *Cross-national longitudinal research on human development and criminal behavior* (pp. 303–327). Dordrecht, The Netherlands: Kluwer Academic.

Modestin, J., & Ammann, R. (1995). Mental disorders and criminal behaviour. *British Journal of Psychiatry, 166*, 667–675.

Modestin, J., Hug, A., & Ammann, R. (1997). Criminal behaviour in males with affective disorders. *Journal of Affective Disorders, 42*, 29–38.

Modestin, J., & Wuermle, O. (2005). Criminality in men with major mental disorder with and without comorbid substance abuse. *Psychiatry and Clinical Neurosciences, 59*, 25–29.

Modzeleski, W., Feucht, T., Rand, M., Hall, J. E., Simon, T. R., Butler, L., . . . Hertz., M. (2008). School-associated student homicides—United States, 1992–2006. *Morbidity and Mortality Weekly Report, 57*, 33–36.

Moeller, F. G., Dougherty, D. M., Barratt, E. S., Oderinde, V., Mathias, C. W., Harper, R. A., & Swann, A. C. (2002). Increased impulsivity in cocaine dependent subjects independent of antisocial personality disorder and aggression. *Drug and Alcohol Dependence, 68*, 105–111.

Moeller, F. G., Dougherty, D. M., Rustin, T., Swann, A. C., Allen, T. J., Shah, N., & Cherek, D. R. (1997). Antisocial personality disorder and aggression in recently abstinent cocaine dependent subjects. *Drug and Alcohol Dependence, 44*, 175–182.

Moffitt, T. E. (1983). The learning theory model of punishment: Implications for delinquency deterrence. *Criminal Justice and Behavior, 10*, 131–158.

Moffitt, T. E. (1990). Juvenile delinquency and attention deficit disorder: Boys' developmental trajectories from age 13 to age 15. *Child Development, 61*, 893–910.

Moffitt, T. E. (1993a). Adolescence-limited and life-course persistent antisocial behavior: A developmental taxonomy. *Psychological Review, 100*, 674–701.

Moffitt, T. E. (1993b). The neuropsychology of conduct disorder. *Development and Psychopathology, 5*, 135–151.

Moffitt, T. E. (2003). Life-course persistent and adolescent-limited antisocial behavior: A 10-year research review and research agenda. In B. B. Lahey, T. E. Moffitt, & A. Caspi (Eds.), *Causes of conduct disorder and juvenile delinquency* (pp. 49–75). New York, NY: Guilford Press.

Moffitt, T. E. (2005). The new look of behavioral genetics in developmental psychopathology: Gene–environment interplay in antisocial behaviors. *Psychological Bulletin, 131*, 533–554.

Moffitt, T. E., Caspi, A., Dickson, N., Silva, P. A., & Stanton, W. (1996). Childhood-onset versus adolescent-onset antisocial conduct problems in males: Natural history from ages 3 to 18 years. *Development and Psychopathology, 8*, 399–424.

Moffitt, T. E., Caspi, A., Harrington, H., & Milne, B. J. (2002). Males on the life-course persistent and adolescence-limited antisocial pathways: Follow-up at age 26 years. *Development and Psychopathology, 14*, 179–207.

Moffitt, T. E., Lynam, D. R., & Silva, M. A. (1994). Neuropsychological tests predicting persistent male delinquency. *Criminology, 32*, 277–300.

Moffitt, T. E., & Silva, P. A. (1988). Self-reported delinquency, neuropsychological deficit, and history of attention deficit disorder. *Journal of Abnormal Child Psychology, 16*, 553–569.

Mofina, R., & Aubry, J. (2001, March 9). Homolka likely to kill again if released, parole board rules: Convicted in sex slayings, she must stay in jail until 2005. *The Vancouver Sun*, p. A9.

Mojtabai, R. (2006). Psychotic-like experiences and interpersonal violence in the general population. *Social Psychiatry and Psychiatric Epidemiology, 41*, 183–190.

Molitor, F., & Sapolsky, B. S. (1993). Sex, violence, and victimization in slasher films. *Journal of Broadcasting and Electronic Media, 37*, 233–242.

Moltó, J., Poy, R., & Torrubia, R. (2000). Standardization of the Hare Psychopathy Checklist–Revised in a Spanish prison sample. *Journal of Personality Disorders, 14*, 84–96.

Monahan, J. (1992). Mental disorder and violent behavior. *American Psychologist, 47*, 511–521.

Monahan, J. (2008). Structured risk assessment of violence. In R. I. Simon & K. Tardiff (Eds.), *Violence assessment and management* (pp. 17–33). Washington, DC: American Psychiatric Publishing.

Monahan, J., Steadman, H. J., Silver, E., Appelbaum, P. S., Robbins, P. C., Mulvey, E. P., . . . Banks, S. (2001). *Rethinking risk assessment: The MacArthur study of mental disorder and violence.* Oxford, UK: Oxford University Press.

Monnat, S. M., & Chandler, R. F. (2015). Long-term health consequences of adverse childhood experiences. *The Sociological Quarterly, 56*, 723–752.

Monroe, R. R. (1970). *Episodic behavioral disorders: A psychodynamic and neurophysiologic analysis.* Cambridge, MA: Harvard University Press.

Moore, A., & Gibbons, D. (1986). *Watchmen.* New York, NY: DC Comics.

Moore, T. M., & Stuart, G. L. (2005). A review of the literature on marijuana and interpersonal violence. *Aggression and Violent Behavior, 10*, 171–192.

Moore, T. M., Stuart, G. L., Meehan, J. C., Rhatigan, D. L., Hellmuth, J. C., & Keen, S. M. (2008). Drug abuse and aggression between intimate partners: A meta-analytic review. *Clinical Psychology Review, 28*, 247–274.

Morley, K. I., & Hall, W. D. (2006). Is there a genetic susceptibility to engage in criminal acts? *Trends and Issues in Crime and Criminal Justice, 263*, 1–6.

Morris, S. (2014, February 12). From netball team to psychopath: The strange descent of Joanna Dennehy. *The Guardian.* Retrieved from http://www.theguardian.com/uk-news/2014/feb/12/joanna-dennehy-psychology-sadomasochism-murder

Moss, H., Yao, J., & Panzak, G. (1990). Serotonergic reactivity and behavioural dimensions in antisocial personality disorder with substance abuse. *Biological Psychiatry, 28*, 325–338.

Mossman, D. (1994). Assessing predictions of violence: Being accurate about accuracy. *Journal of Consulting and Clinical Psychology, 62*, 783–792.

Motiuk, L. L., & Porporino, F. J. (1992). *The prevalence, nature, and severity of mental health problems among federal male inmates in Canadian penitentiaries.* Ottawa, ON: Correctional Service of Canada.

Muhlbauer, H. D. (1985). Human aggression and the role of central serotonin. *Pharmacopsychiatry, 18*, 218–221.

Mulac, A., Jansma, L. L., & Linz, D. G. (2002). Men's behavior toward women after viewing sexually-explicit films: Degradation makes a difference. *Communication Monographs, 69*, 311–328.

Mulgrew, I. (2011, October 3). Clifford Olson—Canada's national monster—dead at 71. *The Vancouver Sun.* Retrieved from http://www.vancouversun.com/news/Clifford+Olson+Canada+national+monster+dead/5484826/story.html

Mullen, P. E., Burgess, P., Wallace, C., Palmer, S., & Ruschena, D. (2000). Community care and criminal offending in schizophrenia. *Lancet, 355*, 614–617.

Mullen, P. E., Pathé, M., & Purcell, R. (2001). Stalking: New constructions of human behaviour. *Australian and New Zealand Journal of Psychiatry, 35*, 9–16.

Mullen, P. E., Pathé, M., Purcell, R., & Stuart, W. (1999). Study of stalkers. *American Journal of Psychiatry, 156*, 1244–1249.

Muller, J., Wagner, V., Lange, K., & Taschler, H. (2003). Abnormalities in emotion processing within cortical and subcortical regions in criminal psychopaths: Evidence from a functional magnetic resonance imaging study using pictures with emotional content. *Biological Psychiatry, 54*, 152–162.

Mulvey, E. P. (1994). Assessing the evidence of a link between mental illness and violence. *Hospital and Community Psychiatry, 45*, 663–668.

Mumola, C. J., & Karberg, J. C. (2006). *Drug use and dependence, state and federal prisoners, 2004.* Washington, DC: U.S. Department of Justice, Bureau of Justice Statistics.

Murphy, J. (1976). Psychiatric labelling in cross-cultural perspective: Similar kinds of disturbed behaviour appear to be labelled abnormal in diverse cultures. *Science, 191*, 1019–1027.

Murrie, D. C., Cornell, D. G., Kaplan, S., McConville, D., & Levy-Elkon, A. (2004). Psychopathy scores and violence among juvenile offenders: A multi-measure study. *Behavioral Sciences and the Law, 22*, 49–67.

Muschert, G. W. (2007). Research in school shootings. *Sociology Compass, 1*, 60–80.

Myers, W. C., Gooch, E., & Meloy, J. R. (2005). The role of psychopathy and sexuality in a female serial killer. *Journal of Forensic Sciences, 50*, 1–6.

Nachshon, I. (1983). Hemisphere dysfunction in psychopathy and behaviour disorders. In M. Myslobodsky (Ed.), *Hemisyndromes: Psychobiology, neurology, psychiatry.* New York, NY: Academic Press.

Nachschon, I., & Denno, D. (1987). Violent behaviour and cerebral hemisphere function. In S. A. Mednick, T. E. Moffitt, & S. A. Stack (Eds.), *The causes of crime: New biological approaches* (pp. 185–217). Cambridge, UK: Cambridge University Press.

Nasby, W., Hayden, B., & DePaulo, B. M. (1980). Attributional bias among aggressive boys to interpret unambiguous social stimuli as displays of hostility. *Journal of Abnormal Psychology, 89*, 459–468.

National Center on Addiction and Substance Abuse at Columbia University. (2010). *Behind bars II: Substance abuse and America's prison population.* New York, NY: Author.

Newcomb, A. F., Bukowski, W. M., & Bagwell, C. L. (1999). Knowing the sounds: Friendship as a developmental content. In W. A. Collins & B. Laursen (Eds.), *Relationship as developmental contexts: The Minnesota Symposia on Child Psychology* (Vol. 30, pp. 63–84). Mahwah, NJ: Erlbaum.

Newman, G. R. (1976). *Comparative deviance: Perceptions and law in six cultures*. New York, NY: Elsevier.

Newman, J. P., Patterson, C. M., & Kosson, D. S. (1987). Response perseveration in psychopaths. *Journal of Abnormal Psychology, 96*, 145–8.

Newman, K. (2004). *Rampage: The social roots of school shootings*. New York, NY: Basic Books.

New Shorter Oxford English Dictionary. (1993). Oxford, UK: Clarendon Press.

Neylan, T. C. (1999). Frontal lobe function: Mr. Phineas Gage's famous injury. *Journal of Neuropsychiatry and Clinical Neuroscience, 11*, 281–283.

Nicolaidis, C., & Liebschutz, J. (2009). Chronic physical symptoms in survivors of intimate partner violence. In C. Mitchell & D. Anglin (Eds.), *Intimate partner violence: A health-based perspective* (pp. 133–145). New York, NY: Oxford University Press.

Nilsson, K. W., Sjöberg, R. L., Damberg, M., Leppert, J., öhrvik, J., Alm, P. O., . . . Oreland, L. (2006). Role of monoamine oxidase A genotype and psychosocial factors in male adolescent criminal activity. *Biological Psychiatry, 59*, 121–127.

Nolan, J. (2004, October 14). Ohio killer executed for shotgun murder. *The Vancouver Sun*, p. A11.

Norris, J. (1988). *Serial killers*. New York, NY: Doubleday.

Novak, K. J., & Engel, R. S. (2005). Disentangling the influence of suspects' demeanor and mental disorder on arrest. *Policing: An International Journal of Police Strategies and Management, 28*, 493–512.

Nunberg, H. (1955). *Principles of psychoanalysis: Their application to the neuroses*. New York, NY: International Universities Press.

Nurco, D. N., Hanlon, T. E., Kinlock, T. W., & Duszynski, K. R. (1988). Differential criminal patterns of narcotic addicts over an addiction career. *Criminology, 26*, 407–423.

Nurco, D. N., Kinlock, T., & Hanlon, T. (1990). The drugs–crime connection. In J. A. Inciardi (Ed.), *Handbook of drug control in the United States* (pp. 71–90). Westport, CT: Greenwood Press.

O'Connor, E. (2006a, September 10). Car thief drives toward publication. *The Province*, p. A3.

O'Connor, E. (2006b, December 18). Ex-thief wants to steal time for family. *The Province*, p. A4.

O'Connor, E. (2008, November 24). If I can do it, so can you. *The Province*, p. A4.

Office of National Drug Control Policy (ONDCP). (2014a). *What America's users spend on illegal drugs: 2000–2010*. Washington, DC: Author.

Office of National Drug Control Policy (ONDCP). (2014b). *National drug control policy: Data supplement, 2014*. Washington, DC: Author.

Office for National Statistics. (2014, Feb 13). *Chapter 4 – Intimate personal violence and partner abuse*. Retrieved from http://www.ons.gov.uk/ons/dcp171776_352362.pdf

Offord, D. R., Boyle, M. H., & Racine, Y. A. (1991). The epidemiology of antisocial behavior in childhood and adolescence. In D. J. Pepler & K. H. Rubin (Eds.), *The development and treatment of childhood aggression* (pp. 31–54). Hillsdale, NJ: Erlbaum.

Ofshe, R., & Watters, E. (1994). *Making monsters: False memories, psychotherapy, and sexual hysteria*. New York, NY: Charles Scribner's Sons.

Ogilvie, E. (2000, December). *The Internet and cyberstalking* (pp. 1–7). Paper presented at the Stalking: Criminal Justice Responses Conference. Sydney: Australian Institute of Criminology.

Ohan, J. L., & Johnston, C. (2007). What is the social impact of ADHD in girls? A multi-method assessment. *Journal of Abnormal Child Psychology, 35*, 239–250.

O'Leary, M. M., Loney, B. R., & Eckel, L. A. (2007). Gender differences in the association between psychopathic personality traits and cortisol response to induced stress. *Psychoendocrinology, 32*, 183–191.

Oleson, J. C. (2005). King of killers: The criminological theories of Hannibal Lecter, Part One. *Journal of Criminal Justice and Popular Culture, 12*, 186–210.

Oleson, J. C. (2006). King of killers: The criminological theories of Hannibal Lecter, Part Two. *Journal of Criminal Justice and Popular Culture, 13*, 29–45.

Olson, J. M., Breckler, S. J., & Wiggins, E. C. (2008). *Social psychology alive* (1st Canadian ed.). Toronto, ON: Nelson.

Omalu, B. I., DeKosky, S. T., Minster, R. L., Kamboh, M. I., Hamilton, R. L., & Wecht, C. H. (2005). Chronic traumatic encephalopathy in a National Football League player. *Neurosurgery, 57*, 128–134.

Open Science Collaboration. (2015). Estimating the reproducibility of psychological science. *Science, 349*, aac4716–aac4716-8.

Ostrom, B. J., & Kauder, N. B. (1998). *Examining the work of state courts, 1998: A national perspective from the court statistics project*. Williamsburg, VA: National Center for State Courts.

Osumi, T., Nakao, T., Kasuya, Y., Shinoda, J., Yamada, J., & Ohira, H. (2012). Amygdala dysfunction attenuates frustration-induced aggression in psychopathic individuals in a non-criminal population. *Journal of Affective Disorders, 142*, 331–338.

Otto, R. K. (2000). Assessing and managing violence risk in outpatient settings. *Journal of Clinical Psychology, 56*, 1239–1262.

Page, M. M., & Scheidt, R. J. (1971). The elusive weapons effect: Demand awareness, evaluation apprehension, and slightly sophisticated subjects. *Journal of Personality and Social Psychology, 20*, 304–318.

Paik, H., & Comstock, G. (1994). The effects of television violence on antisocial behavior: A meta-analysis. *Communication Research, 21*, 516–546.

Palermo, G. B., Smith, M. B., & Liska, F. J. (1991). Jails versus mental hospitals: A social dilemma. *International Journal of Offender Therapy and Comparative Criminology, 35*, 97–106.

Palmer, C. T., & Tilley, C. F. (1995). Sexual access to females as a motivation for joining gangs: An evolutionary approach. *The Journal of Sex Research, 32*, 213–217.

Palmer, E. J. (2003). An overview of the relationship between moral reasoning and offending. *Australian Psychologist, 38*, 165–174.

Palmer, E. J., & Hollin, C. R. (1998). A comparison of patterns of moral development in young offenders and non-offenders. *Legal and Criminological Psychology, 3*, 225–235.

Palmer, T. (1975). Martinson revisited. *Journal of Research in Crime and Delinquency, 12*, 133–152.

Palmero, G. B. (2004). *The faces of violence* (2nd ed.). Springfield, IL: Charles C. Thomas.

Pandiani, J. A., Banks, S. M., Carroll, B. B., & Schlueter, M. R. (2007). Crime victims and criminal offenders among adults with serious mental illness. *Psychiatric Services, 58*, 1483–1485.

Pardini, D. A., Raine, A., Erickson, K., & Loeber, R. (2013). Lower amygdala volume in men is associated with childhood aggression, early psychopathic traits, and future violence. *Biological Psychiatry, 75*, 73–80.

Parent, G., Guay, J. P., & Knight, R. A. (2011). An assessment of long-term risk of recidivism by adult sex offenders: One size doesn't fit all. *Criminal Justice and Behavior, 38*, 188–109.

Parker, J. G., & Asher, S. R. (1987). Peer relations and later personal adjustment: Are low-accepted children at risk? *Psychological Bulletin, 102*, 357–389.

Parker, R. N., & Auerhahn, K. (1998). Alcohol, drugs, and violence. *Annual Review of Sociology, 24*, 291–311.

Parker, R. N., & Rebhun, L.-A. (1995). *Alcohol and homicide: A deadly combination of two American traditions.* Albany, NY: State University of New York Press.

Passingham, R. E. (1972). Crime and personality: A review of Eysenck's theory. In V. D. Nebylitsin & J. A. Gray (Eds.), *Biological bases of individual behaviour* (pp. 342–371). New York, NY: Academic Press.

Patrick, C. J. (2006). *Handbook of psychopathy.* New York, NY: Guilford Press.

Patterson, C. M., & Newman, J. P. (1993). Reflectivity and learning from aversive events: Toward a psychological mechanism for the syndromes of disinhibition. *Psychological Review, 100*, 716–736.

Patterson, G. R. (1982). *Coercive family processes.* Eugene, OR: Castalia Press.

Patterson, G. R. (1986). Performance models for antisocial boys. *American Psychologist, 41*, 432–444.

Patterson, G. R. (1995). Coercion as a basis for early age of onset for arrest. In J. McCord (Ed.), *Coercion and punishment in long-term perspectives* (pp. 81–105). New York, NY: Cambridge University Press.

Patterson, G. R., DeBaryshe, B. D., & Ramsey, E. (1989). A developmental perspective on antisocial behavior. *American Psychologist, 44*, 329–335.

Patterson, G. R., & Dishion, T. J. (1998). Multilevel family precess models: Traits, interactions, and relationships. In R. Hinde & J. Stevenson-Hinde (Eds.), *Relationships within families: Mutual influences* (pp. 283–310). Oxford, UK: Clarendon.

Patterson, G. R., Reid, J. B., & Dishion, T. J. (1992). *Antisocial boys: A social interactional approach* (4th ed.). Eugene, OR: Castalia.

Patterson, G. R., & Southamer-Loeber, M. (1984). The correlation of family management practices and delinquency. *Child Development, 55*, 1299–1307.

Patterson, G. R., & Yoerger, K. (1995). Two different models for adolescent physical trauma and for early arrest. *Criminal Behavior & Mental Health, 5*, 411–423.

Patton, C. L., Nobles, M. R., & Fox, K. A. (2010). Look who's stalking: Obsessive pursuit and attachment theory. *Journal of Criminal Justice, 38*, 282–290.

Paulhus, D. L. & Williams, K. M. (2002). The Dark Triad of personality: Narcissism, Machiavellianism, and psychopathy. *Journal of Research in Personality, 36*, 556–563.

Peachey, P. (2014, February 13). Joanna Dennehy: The girl from a loving home who became a serial killer. *The Independent.* Retrieved from http://www.independent.co.uk/news/uk/crime/joanna-dennehy-the-girl-from-a-loving-home-who-turned-into-a-serial-killer-9124128.html

Penrose, L. S. (1939). Mental disease and crime: Outline of a comparative study of European statistics. *British Journal of Medical Psychology, 18*, 1–15.

Perez, P. R. (2012). The etiology of psychopathy: A neuropsychological perspective. *Aggression and Violent Behaviour, 17*, 519–522.

Perreault, S. (2015). *Criminal victimization in Canada, 2014.* Ottawa, ON: Canadian Centre for Justice Statistics, Statistics Canada.

Perreault, S., & Brennan, S. (2010). *Criminal victimization in Canada, 2009.* Ottawa, ON: Canadian Centre for Justice Statistics, Statistics Canada.

Pérusse, D. (1993). Cultural and reproductive success in industrial societies: Testing the relationship at the proximate and ultimate levels. *Behavioral and Brain Sciences, 16*, 267–322.

Peterson, D. L., & Pfost, K. S. (1989). Influence of rock videos on attitudes of violence against women. *Psychological Reports, 64*, 319–322.

Pétursson, H., & Gudjónsson, G. H. (1981). Psychiatric aspects of homicide. *Acta Psychiatrica Scandinavica, 64*, 363–372.

Pfiffner, L. J., McBurnett, K., Rathouz, P. J., & Judice, S. (2005). Family correlates of oppositional and conduct disorders in children with attention deficit/hyperactivity disorder. *Journal of Abnormal Child Psychology, 33*, 551–563.

Pileggi, N. (1985). *Wiseguy.* New York, NY: Pocket Books.

Pillmann, F., Rohde, A., Ullrich, S., Draba, S., Sannemuller, U., & Marneros, A. (1999). Violence, criminal behaviour, and the EEG: Significance of left hemispheric focal abnormalities. *Journal of Neuropsychiatry and Clinical Neuroscience, 11*, 454–457.

Planty, M., Langton, L., Krebs, C., Berzofsky, M., & Smiley-McDonald, H. (2013). *Female victims of sexual violence, 1994–2010.* Washington, DC: Bureau of Justice Statistics, U.S. Department of Justice.

Plea deal in case of Letterman plot. (2005, July 12). *Kingston Whig—Standard*, p. 20.

Plomin, R., DeFries, J. C., McClearn, G. E., & McGuffin, P. (2008). *Behavioral genetics* (5th ed.). New York, NY: Worth.

Polman, H., Orbio de Castro, B., & van Aken, M. A. G. (2008). Experimental study of the differential effects of playing versus watching violent video games on children's aggressive behavior. *Aggressive Behavior, 34*, 256–264.

Ponizovsky, A. M., Nechamkin, Y., & Rosca, P. (2007). Attachment patterns are associated with symptomatology and course of schizophrenia in male patients. *American Journal of Orthopsychiatry, 77*, 324–331.

Popper, C. W., Gammon, G. D., West, S. A., & Bailey, C. E. (2003). Disorders usually first diagnosed in infancy, childhood, or adolescence. In R. E. Hales & S. C. Yudofsky (Eds.), *The American Psychiatric Publishing textbook of clinical psychiatry* (4th ed.) (pp. 833–974). Arlington, VA: American Psychiatric Publishing.

Porac, C., & Coren, S. (1981). *Lateral preferences and human behaviour.* New York, NY: Springer-Verlag.

Porter, S. (1996). Without conscience or without active conscience? The etiology of psychopathy revisited. *Aggression and Violent Behavior, 1*, 179–189.

Porter, S., Birt, A. R., & Boer, D. P. (2001). Investigation of the criminal and conditional release profiles of Canadian federal offenders as a function of psychopathy and age. *Law and Human Behavior, 25*, 647–661.

Porter, S., & Woodworth, M. (2007). "I'm sorry I did it . . . but he started it." A comparison of the official and self-reported homicide descriptions of psychopaths and non-psychopaths. *Law and Human Behavior, 31*, 91–107.

Porter, S., Woodworth, M., Earle, J., Drugge, J., & Boer, D. (2003). Characteristics of sexual homicides committed by psychopathic and nonpsychopathic offenders. *Law and Human Behavior, 27*, 459–470.

Porter, T., & Gavin, H. (2010). Infanticide and neonaticide: A review of 40 years of research literature on incidence and causes. *Trauma, Violence, & Abuse, 11*, 99–122.

Portnoy, J., & Farrington, D. P. (2015). Resting heart rate and antisocial behavior: An updated systematic review and meta-analysis. *Aggression and Violent Behavior, 22*, 33–45.

Postmes, T., & Spears, R. (1998). Deindividuation and antinormative behavior: A meta-analysis. *Psychological Bulletin, 123*, 238–259.

Potegal, M. (2012). Temporal and frontal lobe initiation and regulation of the top-down escalation of anger and aggression. *Behavioural Brain Research, 231*, 386–395.

Potegal, M., Ferris, C. F., Herbert, M., Meyerhoff, J., & Skaredoff, L. (1996). Attack priming in female Syrian golden hamsters is associated with a c-fos-coupled process within the corticomedial amygdala. *Neuroscience, 75*, 869–880.

Powell, T. A., Holt, J. C., & Fondacaro, K. M. (1997). The prevalence of mental illness among inmates in a rural sate. *Law and Human Behavior, 21*, 427–438.

Pratt, T. C., Cullen, F., Blevins, K. R., Daigle, L., & Unnever, J. D. (2002). The relationship of attention deficit hyperactivity disorder to crime and delinquency: A meta-analysis. *International Journal of Police Science and Management, 4*, 344–360.

Prentky, R. A, Burgess, A. W., Rokous, F., Lee, A., Hartman, C., Ressler, R., & Douglas, J. (1989). The presumptive role of fantasy in serial sexual homicide. *American Journal of Psychiatry, 146*, 887–891.

Prentky, R. A., & Knight, R. A. (1991). Identifying critical dimensions for discriminating among rapists. *Journal of Consulting and Clinical Psychology, 59*, 643–661.

Pressly, L. (2014, December 2). Pablo Escobar: Atoning for the sins of a brother. Retrieved from http://www.bbc.com/news/magazine-30278303

Pristach, C. A., & Smith, C. M. (1996). Self-reported effects of alcohol use on symptoms of schizophrenia. *Psychiatric Services, 47*, 421–423.

Pruden, J. G. (2010, July 23). Sex offender begs for prison time. *Leader Post*, p. A1.

Purcell, C. E., & Arrigo, B. A. (2006). *The psychology of lust murder: Paraphilia, sexual killing, and serial homicide.* London, UK: Academic Press.

Purpura, P. (2013, December 10). Terrytown teen who killed sister with wrestling moves must have known he was hurting her, judge says. *The Times-Picayune.* Retrieved from http://www.nola.com/crime/index.ssf/2013/12/terrytown_teen_who_killed_half_1.html

Putkonen, A., Ryynänen, O.-P., Eronen, M., & Tiihonen, J. (2007). Transmission of violent offending and crime across three generations. *Social Psychiatry and Psychiatric Epidemiology, 42*, 94–99.

Putkonen, H., Amon, S., Eronen, M., Klier, C. M., Almiron, M. P, Cedarwall, J. Y., & Weizmann-Henelius, G. (2011). Gender differences in filicide offense characteristics—A comprehensive register-based study of child murder in two European countries. *Child Abuse & Neglect, 35*, 319–328.

Putkonen, H., Collander, J., Weizmann-Henelius, G., & Eronen, M. (2007). Legal outcomes of all suspected neonaticides in Finland 1980–2000. *International Journal of Law and Psychiatry, 30*, 248–254.

Quay, H. C. (1987). Intelligence. In H. C. Quay (Ed.), *Handbook of juvenile delinquency* (pp. 106–117). Oxford, UK: Wiley.

Quigley, B. M., & Leonard, K. E. (2006). Alcohol expectancies and intoxicated aggression. *Aggression and Violent Behavior, 11*, 484–496.

Quinet, K. (2007). Victimization in the United States: The missing missing—Toward a quantification of serial murder. *Homicide Studies, 11*, 319–339.

Quinsey, V. L. (2002). Evolutionary theory and criminal behaviour. *Legal and Criminological Psychology, 7*, 1–13.

Quinsey, V. L., Harris, G. T., Rice, M. E., & Cormier, C. A. (2006). *Violent offenders: Appraising and managing risk* (2nd ed.). Washington, DC: American Psychological Association.

Quinsey, V. L., Rice, M. E., & Harris, G. T. (1995). Actuarial prediction of sexual recidivism. *Journal of Interpersonal Violence, 10*, 85–105.

Quinsey, V. L., Skilling, T. A., Lalumière, M. L., & Craig, W. (2003). *Juvenile delinquency: Understanding the origins of individual differences*. Washington, DC: American Psychological Association.

R. v. Swain (1986), 24 C.C.C. (3d) 385 (Ont. C.A.), reversed [1991] 1 S.C.R. 933.

Rabkin, J. G. (1979). Criminal behavior of discharged mental patients: A critical appraisal of the research. *Psychological Bulletin, 86*, 1–27.

Rachman, S. (1966). Sexual fetishisms: An experimental analogue. *Psychological Record, 16*, 293–296.

Rachman, S., & Hodgson, R. J. (1968). Experimentally induced "sexual fetishism": Replication and development. *Psychological Record, 18*, 25–27.

Rada, R. T., Kellner, R., & Winslow, W. W. (1976). Plasma testosterone and aggressive behaviour. *Psychosomatics, 17*, 138–142.

Raine, A. (1993). *The psychopathology of crime: Criminal behavior as a clinical disorder*. San Diego, CA: Academic Press.

Raine, A. (2013). *The anatomy of violence: The biological roots of crime*. New York, NY: Pantheon.

Raine, A., Brennan, P. A., Farrington, D. P., & Mednick, S. A. (1997). *Biosocial bases of violence*. New York, NY: Plenum Press.

Raine, A., Brennan, P., & Mednick, S. A. (1997). Interaction between birth complications and early maternal rejection in predisposing individuals to adult violence: Specificity to serious, early-onset violence. *American Journal of Psychiatry, 154*, 1265–1271.

Raine, A., & Buchsbaum, M. S. (1996). Violence and brain imaging. In D. M. Stoff & R. B. Cairns (Eds.), *Neurobiological approaches to clinical aggression research* (pp. 195–218). Mahwah, NJ: Erlbaum.

Raine, A., Buchsbaum, M., LaCasse, L. (1997). Brain abnormalities in murderers indicated by Positron Emission Tomography. *Biological Psychiatry, 42*, 495–508.

Raine, A., Buchsbaum, M. S., Stanley, J., Lottenberg, S., Abel, L., & Stoddard, J. (1994). Selective reductions in pre-frontal glucose metabolism assessed with positron emission tomography in accused murderers pleading not guilty by reason of insanity. *Biological Psychiatry, 36*, 365–373.

Raine, A., Lencz, T., Birhle, S., LaCasse, L., & Colletti, P. (2000). Reduced prefrontal grey matter volume and reduced autonomic activity in antisocial personality. *Archives of General Psychiatry, 57*, 119–127.

Raine, A., Meloy, J. R., Bihrle, S., Stoddard, J., Lacasse, L., & Buchsbaum, M. S. (1998). Reduced prefrontal and increased subcortical brain functioning assessed using positron emission tomography in predatory and affective murderers. *Behavioural Sciences and the Law, 16*, 319–332.

Raine, A., O'Brien, M., Smiley, N., Scerbo, A., & Chan, C. J. (1990). Reduced lateralization in verbal dichotic listening in adolescent psychopaths. *Journal of Abnormal Psychology, 99*, 272–277.

Raine, A., Venables, P. E., & Medick, S. A. (1997). Low resting heart rate at age 3 years predisposes to aggression at age 11 years: Evidence from the Mauritius Child Health Project. *Journal of the American Academy of Child and Adolescent Psychiatry, 36*, 1457–1464.

Rampling, D. (1978). Aggression: A paradoxical response to tricyclic antidepressants. *American Journal of Psychiatry, 135*, 117–118.

Rappeport, J. R., & Lassen, G. (1966). Dangerousness—Arrest rate comparisons of discharged patients and the general population. *American Journal of Psychiatry, 121*, 776–783.

Raskin, R., & Terry, H. (1988). A principal-components analysis of the Narcissistic Personality Inventory and further evidence of its construct validity. *Journal of Personality and Social Psychology, 54*, 890–902.

Rasmussen, K., Storsaeter, O., & Levander, S. (1999). Personality disorders, psychopathy, and crime in a Norwegian prison population. *International Journal of Law and Psychiatry, 22*, 91–97.

Ratey, J. J., Mikkelsen, E. J., Smith, G. B., Upadhyaya, A., Zuckerman, H. S., Martell, D., . . . & Bemporad, J. (1986). Beta-blockers in the severely and profoundly mentally retarded. *Journal of Psychopharmacology, 6*, 103–107.

Ratey, J. J., Mikkelsen, E. J., Sorgi, P., Zuckerman, H. S., Polakoff, S., Bemporad, J., . . . Kadish, W. (1987). Autism: The treatment of aggressive behaviours. *Journal of Clinical Psychopharmacology, 7*, 35–41.

Raynor, G., Bingham, J., & Whitehead, T. (2011, July 25). Christian extremist seeks white European "jihad"; Anders Behring Breivik acknowledges he will be considered a monster in 1,500-page document emailed to friends before attacks. *Vancouver Sun*, p. B2.

Redondo, S., Sánchez-Meca, J., & Garrido, V. (1999). The influence of treatment programmes on the recidivism of juvenile and adult offenders: An European meta-analytic review. *Psychology, Crime & Law, 5*, 251–278.

Rehm, J., Steinleitner, M., & Lilli, W. (1987). Wearing uniforms and aggression—A field experiment. *European Journal of Social Psychology, 17*, 357–360.

Reicher, S. D., Spears, R., & Postmes, T. (1995). A social identity model of deindividuation phenomena. *European Review of Social Psychology, 6,* 161–198.

Reid, W. H. (2003). Risk assessment, prediction, and foreseeability. *Journal of Psychiatric Practice, 9,* 82–86.

Reif, A., Rösler, M., Freitag, C. M., Schneider, M., Eujen, A., Kissling, C., . . . Retz, W. (2007). Nature and nurture predispose to violent behavior: Serotonergic genes and adverse childhood environment. *Neuropsychopharmacology, 32,* 2375–2383.

Reiss, A. J., & Roth, J. A. (1993). *Understanding and preventing violence.* Washington, DC: National Academies Press.

Resnick, P. (1970). Murder of the newborn: A psychiatric review of neonaticide. *American Journal of Psychiatry, 126,* 1414–1420.

Ressler, R., Burgess, A., & Douglas, J. (1988). *Sexual homicide.* Lexington, MA: Lexington Books.

Ressler, R. K., Burgess, A. W., Douglas, J. E., Hartman, C. R., & D'Agostino, R. B. (1986). Sexual killers and their victims: Identifying patterns through crime scene analysis. *Journal of Interpersonal Violence, 1,* 288–308.

Ressler, R. K., Burgess, A., & Goulas, J. E. (1988). *Sexual homicide: Patterns and motives.* Lexington, MA: Lexington Books.

Ressler, R. K., Burgess, A., Hartman, C. R., Douglas, J. E., & McCormick, A. (1986). Murderers who rape and mutilate. *Journal of Interpersonal Violence, 1,* 273–287.

Ressler, R. K., & Schactman, T. (1992). *Whoever fights monsters: My twenty years of hunting serial killers for the FBI.* New York, NY: St Martin's.

Retz, W., Retz-Junginger, P., Supprian, T., Thome, J., & Rösler, M. (2004). Association of serotonin transporter promoter gene polymorphism with violence: Relation with personality disorders, impulsivity, and childhood ADHD psychopathology. *Behavioral Sciences and the Law, 22,* 415–425.

Rhee, S. H., & Waldman, I. D. (2002). Genetic and environmental influences on antisocial behavior: A meta-analysis of twin and adoption studies. *Psychological Bulletin, 128,* 490–529.

Rhee, S. H., & Waldman, I. D. (2007). Behavior-genetics of criminality and aggression. In D. J. Flannery, A. T. Vazsonyi, & I. D. Waldman (Eds.), *The Cambridge Handbook of Violent Behavior and Aggression* (pp. 77–90). New York, NY: Cambridge University Press.

Rhodewalt, F., & Morf, C. C. (1998). On self-aggrandizement and anger: A temporal analysis of narcissism and affective reactions to success and failure. *Journal of Personality and Social Psychology, 74,* 672–685.

Rice, M. E., & Harris, G. T. (1997). Cross-validation and extension of the Violence Risk Appraisal Guide for child molesters and rapists. *Law and Human Behavior, 21,* 231–241.

Rice, M. E., Harris, G. T., & Hilton, N. Z. (2010). The Violence Risk Appraisal Guide and Sex Offender Risk Appraisal Guide for violence risk assessment and the Ontario Domestic Assault Risk Assessment and Domestic Violence Risk Appraisal Guide for wife assault risk assessment. In R. K. Otto & K. S. Douglas (Eds.), *Handbook of violence risk assessment* (pp. 99–119). New York, NY: Routledge.

Richard, B. A., & Dodge, K. A. (1982). Social maladjustment and problem-solving in school-aged children. *Journal of Consulting and Clinical Psychology, 50,* 226–233.

Richards, J. E., & Hawley, R. S. (2011). *The human genome: A user's guide* (3rd ed.). London, UK: Academic Press.

Rihmer, A., & Angst, J. (2005). Mood disorders: Epidemiology. In B. J. Sadock & V. A. Sadock (Eds.), *Kaplan & Sadock's comprehensive textbook of psychiatry* (8th ed.) (pp. 1575–1582). Philadelphia, PA: Lippincott Williams & Wilkins.

Robertiello, G., & Terry, K. J. (2007). Can we profile sex offenders? A review of sex offender typologies. *Aggression and Violent Behavior, 12,* 508–518.

Roberts, J. E., Gotlib, I. H., & Kassel, J. D. (1996). Adult attachment security and symptoms of depression: The mediating roles of dysfunctional attitudes and low self-esteem. *Journal of Personality and Social Psychology, 70,* 310–320.

Robertson, G. (1988). Arrest patterns among mentally disordered offenders. *British Journal of Psychiatry, 153,* 313–316.

Robertson, G., Pearson, R., & Gibb, R. (1996). The entry of mentally disordered people to the criminal justice system. *British Journal of Psychiatry, 169,* 172–180.

Robins, L. N., & Regier, D. A. (1991). *Psychiatric disorders in America: The Epidemiologic Catchment Area study.* New York, NY: free press.

Robinson, J. P., & Bachman, J. G. (1972). Television viewing habits and aggression. In G. A. Comstock & E. A. Rubinstein (Eds.), *Television and social behavior: Television and adolescent aggressiveness,* Vol. 3 (pp. 372–382). Rockville, MD: National Institute of Mental Health.

Robinson, T. E., & Berridge, K. C. (2001). Incentive-sensitization and addiction. *Addiction, 96,* 103–114.

Robles, F. (2012, March 21). Shooter of Trayvon Martin a habitual caller to cops. *Miami Herald.* Retrieved from http://www.miamiherald.com/2012/03/17/v-fullstory/2700249/trayvon-martin-shooter-a-habitual.html

Roche, K. M., Ensminger, M. E., & Cherlin, A. J. (2007). Variations in parenting and adolescent outcomes among African American and Latino families living in low-income, urban areas. *Journal of Family Issues, 28,* 882–909.

Rodriguez, J. (2009, November 7). Rihanna details Chris Brown assault in *20/20* interview. Retrieved from http://www.mtv.com/news/1625783/rihanna-details-chris-brown-assault-in-2020-interview/

Rogers, R. (2000). The uncritical acceptance of risk assessment in forensic practice. *Law and Human Behavior, 24,* 595–605.

Rogers, R., Gillis, J. R., Turner, R. E., & Frise-Smith, T. (1990). The clinical presentation of command hallucinations in a forensic population. *American Journal of Psychiatry, 147*, 1304–1307.

Roman, K. (2001, February 9). Homolka refuses treatment. *Sudbury Star*, p. A9.

Rose, A. J., Swenson, L. P., & Waller, E. M. (2004). Overt and relational aggression and perceived popularity: Developmental differences in concurrent and prospective relations. *Developmental Psychology, 40*, 378–387.

Rosenbaum, A., & Hoge, S. K. (1989). Head injury and marital aggression. *American Journal of Psychiatry, 146*, 1048–1051.

Rosenfeld, B. (2004). Violence risk factors in stalking and obsessional harassment: A review and preliminary meta-analysis. *Criminal Justice and Behavior, 31*, 9–36.

Rosenfeld, B., & Harmon, R. (2002). Factors associated with violence in stalking and obsessional harassment cases. *Criminal Justice and Behavior, 29*, 671–691.

Rosenfield, M. (2011, October 11). Accused "underwear bomber" Umar Farouk Abdulmutallab pleads guilty to all 8 counts. Retrieved from http://www.wxyz.com/dpp/news/region/detroit/live-blog%3A-%27underwear-bomber%27-trial-begins

Rosenthal, R. (1991). Meta-analysis: A review. *Psychosomatic Medicine, 53*, 247–271.

Ross, J., Teesson, M., Darke, S., Lynskey, M., Ali, R., Ritter, A., & Cooke, R. (2006). Short-term outcomes for the treatment of heroin dependence. *Addictive Disorder and Their Treatment, 5*, 133–143.

Ross, J. M, & Babcock, J. C. (2009). Proactive and reactive violence among intimate partner violent men diagnosed with antisocial and borderline personality disorder. *Journal of Family Violence, 24*, 607–617.

Ross, R. R., & Fabiano, E. (1981). *Time to think. Cognition and crime: Link and remediation.* Ottawa, ON: University of Ottawa, Department of Criminology.

Rotenberg, M., & Diamond, B. L. (1971). The biblical conception of the psychopath: The law of the stubborn and rebellious son. *Journal of History of Behavioral Sciences, 7*, 29–38.

Roth, J. A. (1994). *Psychoactive substances and violence.* Washington, DC: National Institute of Justice, U.S. Department of Justice.

Roth, R., Koven, N., & Pendergrass, J. (2008). An introduction to structural and functional neuroimaging. In A. Horton & D. Wedding (Eds.), *The neuropsychology handbook* (pp. 217–250). New York, NY: Springer.

Rotton, J., Frey, J., Barry, T., Milligan, M., & Fitzpatrick, M. (1979). The air pollution experience and physical aggression. *Journal of Applied Social Psychology, 9*, 397–412.

Rowe, D. C. (1996). An adaptive strategy theory of crime and delinquency. In J. D. Hawkins (Ed.), *Delinquency and crime: Current theories* (pp. 268–314). Cambridge, UK: Cambridge University Press.

Rowe, D. C. (2002). *Biology and crime.* Los Angeles, CA: Roxbury.

Rowe, R., Maughan, B., Worthman, C. M., Costello, E. J., & Angold, A. (2004). Testosterone, antisocial behaviour, and social dominance in boys: Pubertal development and biosocial interaction. *Biological Psychiatry, 55*, 546–552.

Rowlands, M. (1990). Multiple murder: A review of the international literature. *Journal of the College of Prison Medicine, 1*, 3–7.

Rubin, K. H., Burgess, K. B., Dwyer, K. M., & Hasting, P. D. (2003). Predicting preschoolers' externalizing behaviors from toddler temperament, conflict, and maternal negativity. *Developmental Psychology, 39*, 164–176.

Rubin, K. H., Bukowski, W., & Parker, J. G. (1998). Peer interactions, relationships, and groups. In W. Damon & N. Eisenberg (Eds.), *Handbook of child psychology Vol. 3—Social, emotional, and personality development* (pp. 571–645). New York, NY: Wiley.

Rubin, R. T. (1987). The neuroendocrinology and neurochemistry of antisocial behavior. In S. A. Mednick, T. E. Moffitt, & S. A. Stack (Eds.), *The causes of crime: New biological approaches* (pp. 239–262). Cambridge, UK: Cambridge University Press.

Rubinow, D. R., & Schmidt, P. J. (1996). Androgens, brain, and behaviour. *American Journal of Psychiatry, 153*, 974–984.

Ruchkin, V. (2002). Family impact on violent youth. In R. R. Corradio, R. Roesch, S. D. Hart, & J. K. Gierowski (Eds.), *Multi-problem violent youth: A foundation for comparative research on needs, interventions, and outcomes* (pp. 105–115). Amsterdam, The Netherlands: IOS Press.

Rudnick, A. (1999). Relation between command hallucinations and dangerous behaviour. *Journal of the American Academy of Psychiatry and Law, 27*, 253–257.

Rutherford, M. J., Alterman, A. I., Cacciola, J. S., & McKay, J. R. (1997). Validity of the Psychopathy Checklist–Revised in male methadone patients. *Drugs & Alcohol Dependence, 44*, 143–149.

Rutherford, M. J., Cacciola, J. S., Alterman, A. I., & McKay, J. R. (1996). Reliability and validity of the Revised Psychopathy Checklist in women methadone patients. *Assessment, 3*, 145–156.

Ryan, A. M. (2001). The peer group as a context for the development of young adolescent motivation and achievement. *Child Development, 72*, 1135–1150.

Ryan, K. M. (2011). The relationship between rape myths and sexual scripts: The social construction of rape. *Sex Roles, 65*, 774–782.

Sadock, B. J. (2005). Signs and symptoms in psychiatry. In B. J. Sadock & V. A. Sadock (Eds.), *Kaplan & Sadock's comprehensive textbook of psychiatry* (8th ed.) (pp. 847–859). Philadelphia, PA: Lippincott Williams & Wilkins.

Salekin, K. L., Ogloff, J. R. P., Ley, R. B., & Salekin, R. T. (2002). The overcontrolled hostility scale: An evaluation of its applicability with an adolescent population. *Criminal Justice and Behavior, 29*, 718–733.

Salekin, R. T. (2006). Psychopathy in children and adolescents: Key issues in conceptualization and assessment. In C. J. Patrick (Ed.), *Handbook of psychopathy* (pp. 389–414). New York, NY: Guilford Press.

Salekin, R. T., Rogers, R., & Sewell, K. W. (1996). A review and meta-analysis of the Psychopathy Checklist and Psychopathy Checklist–Revised: Predictive validity of dangerousness. *Clinical Psychology: Science and Practice, 3*, 203–215.

Salekin, R. T., Rogers, R., & Sewell, K. W. (1997). Construct validity of psychopathy in a female offender sample: A multitrait-multimethod evaluation. *Journal of Abnormal Psychology, 106*, 576–585.

Salekin, R. T., Rosenbaum, J., Lee, Z., & Lester, W. S. (2009). Child and adolescent psychopathy: Like a painting by Monet. *Youth Violence and Juvenile Justice, 7*, 239–255.

Saltaris, C. (2002). Psychopathy in juvenile offenders: Can temperament and attachment be considered as robust developmental precursors? *Clinical Psychology Review, 22*, 729–752.

Sampson, R. J., & Laub, J. H. (1990). Crime and deviance over the life course: The salience of adult social bonds. *American Sociological Review, 55*, 609–627.

Sampson, R. J., & Laub, J. H. (1993). *Crime in the making: Pathways and turning points through life*. Cambridge, MA: Harvard University Press.

Sapolsky, B. S., Molitor, F., & Luque, S. (2003). Sex and violence in slasher films: Re-examining the assumptions. *Journalism and Mass Communication Quarterly, 80*, 28–38.

Satterfield, J. H., Swanson, J., Schell, A., & Lee, F. (1994) Prediction of antisocial behavior in attention-deficit hyperactivity disorder boys from aggression/defiance scores. *Journal of the American Academy of Child and Adolescent Psychiatry, 33*, 185–191.

Saunders, D. (1992). A typology of men who batter women: Three types derived from cluster analysis. *American Journal of Orthopsychiatry, 62*, 264–275.

Saunders, R. (1998). The legal perspective on stalking. In J. R. Meloy (Ed.), *The psychology of stalking: Clinical and forensic perspectives* (pp. 25–49). San Diego, CA: Academic Press.

Sawle, G. A., & Kear-Colwell, J. (2001). Adult attachment pedophilia: A developmental perspective. *International Journal of Offender Therapy and Comparative Criminology, 45*, 32–50.

Savage, J. (2004). Does viewing violent media really cause criminal violence? A methodological review. *Aggression and Violent Behavior, 10*, 99–129.

Savage, J. (2008). The role of exposure to media violence in the etiology of violent behavior: A criminologist weighs in. *American Behavioral Scientist, 51*, 1123–1136.

Savage, J., & Yancey, C. (2008). The effects of media violence exposure on criminal aggression. *Criminal Justice and Behavior, 35*, 772–791.

Sayette, M. A. (1993). An appraisal-disruption model of alcohol's effects on stress responses in social drinkers. *Psychological Bulletin, 114*, 459–476.

Schalling, D. (1993). Neurochemical correlates of personality, impulsivity, and disinhibitory suicidality. In S. Hodgins (Ed.), *Mental disorder and crime* (pp. 208–226). Newbury, CA: Sage.

Schein, E. (1961). *Coercive persuasion: A socio-psychological analysis of the "brainwashing" of American civilian prisoners by the Chinese Communists*. New York, NY: Norton.

Schmid, D. (2005). *Natural born celebrities: Serial killers in American culture*. Chicago, IL: University of Chicago Press.

Schmidt, S., Morrongiello, B. A., & Colwell, S. R. (2014). Evaluating a model linking assessed parent factors to four domains of youth risky driving. *Accident Analysis and Prevention, 69*, 40–50.

Schoenfeld, R. (1971). A psychoanalytic theory of juvenile delinquency. *Crime and Delinquency, 19*, 469–480.

Schroeder, R. D., Bulanda, R. E., Giordano, P. C., & Cernkovich, S. A. (2010). Parenting and adult criminality: An examination of direct and indirect effects by race. *Journal of Adolescent Research, 25*, 64–98.

Schroeder, R. D., & Mowen, T. J. (2014). Parenting style transitions and delinquency. *Youth & Society, 46*, 228–254.

Schultz, D. P., & Schultz, S. E. (2009). *Theories of personality* (9th ed.). Toronto, ON: Nelson.

Schwartz, B., Wasserman, E. A., & Robbins, S. J. (2001). *Psychology of learning and behavior* (5th ed.). New York, NY: Norton.

Schwartz, D., Dodge, K. A., Coie, J. D., Hubbard, J. A., Cillessen, A. H. N., Lemerise, E. A., & Bateman, H. (1998). Social-cognitive and behavioral correlates of aggression and victimization in boys' play groups. *Journal of Abnormal Child Psychology, 26*, 431–440.

Scott, B. M., Schwartz, M. A., & VanderPlaat, M. (2000). *Sociology: Making sense of the social world* (Canadian ed.). Toronto, ON: Pearson.

Seagrave, D., & Grisso, T. (2002). Adolescent development and the measurement of juvenile psychopathy. *Law and Human Behavior, 26*, 219–239.

Sealy, P., & Whitehead, P. C. (2004). Forty years of deinstitutionalization of psychiatric services in Canada: An empirical assessment. *Canadian Journal of Psychiatry, 49*, 249–257.

Seguin, J. R., Pihl, R. O., Haden, P. W., Tremblay, R. E., & Boulerice, B. (1995). Cognitive and neuropsychological characteristics of physically aggressive boys. *Journal of Abnormal Psychology, 104*, 614–624.

Seligman, M. E. (1975). *Helplessness: On depression, development, and death*. San Francisco, CA: Freeman.

Seligman, M. E., & Maier, S. F. (1967). Failure to escape traumatic shock. *Journal of Experimental Psychology, 74*, 1–9.

Semple, S. J., Zians, J., Grant, I., & Patterson, T. L. (2005). Impulsivity and methamphetamine use. *Journal of Substance Abuse Treatment, 29*, 85–93.

Serin, R. C. (1991). Psychopathy and violence in criminals. *Journal of Interpersonal Violence, 6*, 423–431.

Serin, R. C. (1996). Violent recidivism in criminal psychopaths. *Law and Human Behavior, 20*, 207–217.

Serin, R. C., & Amos, N. L. (1995). The role of psychopathy in the assessment of dangerousness. *International Journal of Law and Psychiatry, 18*, 231–238.

Serin, R. C., Peters, R. D., & Barbaree, H. E. (1990). Predictors of psychopath and release outcome in a criminal population. *Psychological Assessment, 2*, 419–422.

Seto, M. C. (2008). *Pedophilia and sexual offending against children: Theory, assessment, and intervention.* Washington, DC: American Psychological Association.

Seto, M. C., Maric, A., Barbaree, H. E. (2001). The role of pornography in the etiology of sexual aggression. *Aggression and Violent Behavior, 6*, 35–53.

Shanahan, M. J., & Boardman, J. D. (2009). Genetics and behavior in the life course: A promising frontier. In G. H. Elder & J. Z. Giele (Eds.), *The craft of life course research* (pp. 215–235). New York, NY: Guilford Press.

Sheard, M. H. (1975). Lithium in the treatment of aggression. *The Journal of Nervous and Mental Disease, 160*, 108–118.

Sheard, M. H., Marini, J. L., Bridges, C. I., & Wagner, E. (1976). The effect of lithium on impulsive aggressive behavior in man. *American Journal of Psychiatry, 133*, 1409–1413.

Sheldon, K., & Howitt, D. (2008). Sexual fantasy in paedophile offenders: Can any model explain satisfactorily new findings from a study of Internet and contact sexual offenders? *Legal and Criminological Psychology, 13*, 137–158.

Shephard, M. (1999, November 3). Karla fights for a taste of freedom; Convicted killer asks the courts for escorted temporary releases. *Toronto Star*, p. 1.

Sheridan, L. P., & Grant, T. (2007). Is cyberstalking different? *Psychology, Crime & Law, 13*, 627–640.

Shia Labeouf gives rambling apology after headbutting man in pub. (2014, January 17). *Toronto Sun*. Retrieved from http://www.torontosun.com/2014/01/17/shia-labeouf-gives-rambling-apology-after-headbutting-man-in-pub

Shimamura, A.P. (1996). Unraveling the mystery of the frontal lobes: Explorations in cognitive neuroscience. *Psychological Science Agenda, September–October*, 8–9.

Shipley, S.L., & Arrigo, B.A. (2004). *The female homicide offender: Serial murder and the case of Aileen Wuornos.* Upper Saddle River, NJ: Prentice Hall.

Shiroma, E.J., Ferguson, P.L., & Pickelsimer, E.E. (2010). Prevalence of traumatic brain injury in an offender population: A meta-analysis. *Journal of Head Trauma Rehabilitation, 27*, E1–E10.

Siassi, I. (1982). Lithium treatment of impulsive behaviour in children. *Journal of Clinical Psychiatry, 43*, 482–484.

Siegel, L. J., & McCormick, C. (2003). *Criminology in Canada: Theories, patterns, and typologies* (2nd ed). Scarborough, ON: Nelson.

Siegel, S. (2005). Drug tolerance, drug addiction, and drug anticipation. *Current Directions in Psychological Science, 14*, 296–300.

Siegel, S., Hinson, R. E., Krank, M. D., & McCully, J. (1982). Heroin "overdose" death: Contribution of drug-associated environmental cues. *Science, 216*, 436–437.

Siegel, S., & Ramos, B. M. C. (2002). Applying laboratory research: Drug anticipation and the treatment of drug addiction. *Experimental and Clinical Psychopharmacology, 10*, 162–183.

Siegel, A., Roeling, T. A., Gregg, T. R., & Kruk, M. R. (1999). Neuropharmacology of brain-stimulation-evoked aggression. *Neuroscience & Biobehavioral Reviews, 23*, 359–389.

Silva, J. A., Leong, G. B., & Ferrari, G. G. (2004). A neuropsychiatric developmental model of serial homicidal behavior. *Behavioral Sciences & the Law, 22*, 787–799.

Silver, E. (2000). Extending social disorganization theory: A multilevel approach to the study of violence among persons with mental illnesses. *Criminology, 38*, 1043–1074.

Silver, E. (2002). Mental disorder and violent victimization: The mediating role of involvement in conflicted social relationships. *Criminology, 40*, 191–212.

Silver, E. (2006). Understanding the relationship between mental disorder and violence: The need for a criminological perspective. *Law and Human Behavior, 30*, 685–706.

Silver, E., Arsenault, L., Langley, J., Caspi, A., & Moffitt, T. E. (2005). Mental disorder and violent victimization in a total birth cohort. *American Journal of Public Health, 95*, 2015–2021.

Silver, E., Mulvey, E. P., & Monahan, J. (1999). Assessing violence risk among discharged psychiatric patients: Toward an ecological approach. *Law and Human Behavior, 23*, 237–255.

Silver, E., & Teasdale, B. (2005). Mental disorder and violence: An examination of stressful life events and impaired social support. *Social Problems, 52*, 62–78.

Simon, R. I. (1996). *Bad men do what good men dream: A forensic psychiatrist illuminates the darker side of human behavior.* Washington, DC: American Psychiatric Press.

Simons, J. S., Oliver, M. N. I., Gaher, R. M., Ebel, G., & Brummels, P. (2005). Methamphetamine and alcohol abuse and dependence symptoms: Associations with affect lability and impulsivity in a rural treatment population. *Addictive Behaviors, 30*, 1370–1381.

Simons, R. L., Johnson, C., Conger, R. D., & Elder, G. (1998). A test of latent trait versus life-course perspectives on the stability of adolescent antisocial behavior. *Criminology, 36,* 901–927.

Simons, R. L., Lei, M. K., Stewart, E. A., Beach, S. R. H., Brody, G. H., Philibert, R. A., & Gibbons, F. X. (2012). Social adversity, genetic variation, street code, and aggression: A genetically informed model of violent behavior. *Youth Violence and Juvenile Justice, 10,* 3–24.

Simons, R. L., Wu, C., Conger, R., & Lorenz, F. O. (2006). Two routes to delinquency: Differences between early and late starters in the impact of parenting and deviant peers. *Criminology, 32,* 247–276.

Simourd, D. J., & Hoge, R. D. (2000). Criminal psychopathy: A risk-and-need perspective. *Criminal Justice and Behavior, 27,* 256–272.

Singer, M. T. (1996). *Cults in our midst: The continuing fight against their hidden menace.* San Francisco, CA: Jossey-Bass.

Sinoski, K. (2010, March 23). Family, 2 children sought for DVD, Blu-ray theft. *The Vancouver Sun,* p. A6.

Sin, L., Cooper, S., & Mercer, K. (2010, February 19). Parties earn gold medal from visitors. *The Province,* p. A5.

Sinha, M. (Ed.). (2013). *Measuring violence against women: Statistical trends.* Ottawa, ON: Canadian Centre for Justice Statistics, Statistics Canada.

Slack, D., & Rezendes, M. (2010, February 17). She held shotgun on police after killing brother, report says. Retrieved from http://archive.boston.com/news/local/massachusetts/articles/2010/02/17/bishop_held_shotgun_on_police_after_killing_brother_report_says/

Slaymaker, V. J. (2014). Occupational impact of drug abuse and addiction. In J. C. Verster, K. Brady, M. Galanter, & P. Conrod (Eds.), *Drug abuse and addiction in medical illness: Causes, consequences, and treatment* (pp. 511–521). New York, NY: Springer.

Skrapec, C. A. (1996). The sexual component of serial murder. In T. O'Reilly-Fleming (Ed.), *Serial and mass murder: Theory, research, and policy* (pp. 155–179). Toronto, ON: Canadian Scholars' Press.

Smallbone, S. W., & Dadds, M. R. (2001). Further evidence for a relationship between attachment insecurity and coercive sexual behaviour in non-sexual offenders. *Journal of Interpersonal Violence, 16,* 23–35.

Smith, P., Gendreau, P., & Swartz, K. (2009). Validating the principles of effective intervention: A systematic review of the contributions of meta-analysis in the field of corrections. *Victims & Offenders, 4,* 148–169.

Smith, S. L., Lachlan, K., & Tamborini, R. (2003). Popular video games: Quantifying the presentation of violence and its context. *Journal of Broadcasting and Electronic Media, 47,* 58–76.

Snowden, P. (1997). Practical aspects of clinical risk assessment and management. *British Journal of Psychiatry, 170* (Suppl. 32), 32–34.

Snyder, J., Horsch, E., & Childs, J. (1997). Peer relationships of young children: Affiliative choices and the shaping of aggressive behavior. *Journal of Clinical Child Psychology, 26,* 145–156.

Snyder, J., & Patterson, G. (1987). Family interaction and delinquent behavior. In H. C. Quay (Ed.), *Handbook of juvenile delinquency* (pp. 216–243). New York, NY: Wiley.

Socolar, R. R. S. (1997). A classification scheme for discipline: Type, mode of administration, context. *Aggression and Violent Behavior, 2,* 355–364.

Solomon, R. L., Turner, L. H., & Lessac, M. S. (1968). Some effects of delay of punishment on resistance to temptation in dogs. *Journal of Personality and Social Psychology, 8,* 233–238.

Sorenson, A. M., & Brownfield, D. (1995). Adolescent drug use and a general theory of crime: An analysis of a theoretical integration. *Canadian Journal of Criminology, 37,* 19–37.

Sosowsky, L. (1978). Crime and violence among mental patients reconsidered in view of the new legal relationship between the state and the mentally ill. *American Journal of Psychiatry, 135,* 33–42.

Soubrie, P. (1986). Reconciling the role of central serotonin neurons in human and animal behaviour. *The Behavioral and Brain Sciences, 9,* 319–365.

Soyka, M. (2011). Neurobiology of aggression and violence in schizophrenia. *Schizophrenia Bulletin, 37,* 913–920.

Spears, R., Postmes, T., Lea, M., & Watt, S. A. (2001). A SIDE view of social influence. In J. P. Forgas & K. D. Williams (Eds.), *Social influence: Direct and indirect processes* (pp. 331–350). Philadelphia, PA: Psychology Press.

Spitzberg, B. H., & Cupach, W. R. (2007). The state of the art of stalking: Taking stock of the emerging literature. *Aggression and Violent Behavior, 12,* 64–86.

Spitzberg, B. H., & Hoobler, G. (2002). Cyberstalking and the technologies of interpersonal terrorism. *New Media & Society, 4,* 71–92.

Spitzberg, B. H., Marshall, L., & Cupach, W. R. (2001). Obsessive relational intrusion, coping, and sexual coercion victimization. *Communication Reports, 14,* 19–30.

Spitzberg, B. H., & Rhea, J. (1999). Obsessive relational intrusion and sexual coercion victimization. *Journal of Interpersonal Violence, 14,* 3–20.

Staller, J. A. (2006). Diagnostic profiles in outpatient child psychiatry. *American Journal of Orthopsychiatry, 76,* 98–102.

Stams, G. J., Brugman, D., Deković, M., van Rosmalen, L., van der Laan, P., & Gibbs, J. C. (2006). The moral judgment of juvenile delinquents: A meta-analysis. *Journal of Abnormal Child Psychology, 34,* 697–713.

Stangor, C. (2011). *Research methods for the behavioural sciences* (4th ed.). Belmont, CA: Wadsworth.

Starkstein, E. E., & Robinson, R. (1997). Mechanisms of disinhibition after brain lesions. *The Journal of Nervous and Mental Disease, 185,* 108–114.

Steadman, H. J., Cocozza, J. J., & Melick, M. E. (1978). Explaining the increased arrest rate among mental patients: The changing clientele of state hospitals. *American Journal of Psychiatry, 135,* 816–820.

Steadman, H. J., & Felson, R. B. (1984). Self-reports of violence: Ex-mental patients, ex-offenders, and the general population. *Criminology, 22,* 321–342.

Steadman, H. J., Monahan, J., Duffee, B., Hartstone, E., & Robbins, P. C. (1984). The impact of state mental hospital deinstitutionalization on United States prison populations, 1968–1978. *Journal of Criminal Law and Criminology, 75,* 474–490.

Steadman, H. J., Mulvey, E. P., Monahan, J., Robbins, P. C., Appelbaum, P. S., Grisso, T., . . . Silver, E. (1998). Violence by people discharged from acute psychiatric inpatient facilities and others in the same neighborhoods. *Archives of General Psychiatry, 55,* 391–401.

Steadman, H. J., & Ribner, S. (1980). Changing perceptions of the mental health needs of inmates in local jails. *American Journal of Psychiatry, 137,* 1115–1116.

Steele, C. M., & Josephs, R. A. (1990). Alcohol myopia: Its prized and dangerous effects. *American Psychologist, 45,* 921–933.

Steinberg, L., Blatt-Eisengart, I., & Cauffman, E. (2006). Patterns of competence and adjustment among adolescents from authoritative, authoritarian, indulgent, and neglectful homes: A replication in a sample of serious juvenile offenders. *Journal of Research on Adolescence, 16,* 47–58.

Steinberg, L., Lamborn, S. D., Darling, N., Mounts, N. S., & Dornbusch, S. M. (1994). Over-time changes in adjustment and competence among adolescents from authoritative, authoritarian, indulgent, and neglectful families. *Child Development, 65,* 754–770.

Steinberg, M. D., & Dodge, K. A. (1983). Attributional bias in aggressive adolescent boys and girls. *Journal of Social and Clinical Psychology, 1,* 312–321.

Stevens, D., Charman, T., & Blair, R. J. R. (2001). Recognition of emotion in facial expression and vocal tones in children with psychopathic tendencies. *Journal of Genetic Psychology, 162,* 201–211.

Stewart, D., Gossop, M., Marsden, J., & Rolfe, A. (2000). Drug misuse and acquisitive crime among clients recruited to the National Treatment Outcome Research Study (NTORS). *Criminal Behaviour and Mental Health, 10,* 10–20.

Stoff, D., Breiling, J., & Maser, J. (1997). *Handbook of antisocial behavior.* New York, NY: Wiley.

Stoller, G. (2013, November 26). The mystery of Adam Lanza, the Sandy Hook school gunman. *USA Today.* Retrieved from http://www.usatoday.com/story/news/nation/2013/11/25/newtown-shooting-investigation/3696425/

Stompe, T., Ortwein-Swoboda, G., & Schanda, H. (2004). Schizophrenia, delusional symptoms, and violence: The threat/control-override concept reexamined. *Schizophrenia Bulletin, 30,* 31–44.

Stone, M. H. (1998). Sadistic personality in murderers. In T. Millon, E. Simonsen, M. Birket-Smith, & R. D. Davis (Eds.), *Psychopathy: Antisocial, criminal and violent behaviour* (pp. 346–355). New York, NY: Guilford Press.

Stone, M. H. (2007). Violent crimes and their relationship to personality disorders. *Personality and Mental Health, 1,* 138–153.

Storey, J. E., Hart, S. D., Meloy, J., & Reavis, J. A. (2009). Psychopathy and stalking. *Journal of Law and Human Behavior, 33,* 237–246.

Stouthamer-Loeber, M., & Wei, E. H. (1998). The precursors of young fatherhood and its effect on delinquency of teenage males. *Journal of Adolescent Health, 22,* 56–65.

Straus, M. A. (1994). *Beating the devil out of them: Corporal punishment in American families.* New York, NY: Lexington Books.

Stucke, T. S., & Sporer, S. L. (2002). When a grandiose self-image is threatened: Narcissism and self-concept clarity as predictors of negative emotions and aggression following ego threat. *Journal of Personality, 70,* 509–532.

Studer, L. H., Aylwin, A. S., & Reddon, J. R. (2005). Testosterone, sexual offense recidivism, and treatment effect among adult male sex offenders. *Sexual Abuse: A Journal of Research and Treatment, 17,* 171–181.

Stueck, W., Tait, C., & Blaze-Baum, K. (2016). A familiar pain, a persistent hope. *The Globe and Mail.* Retrieved from http://www.theglobeandmail.com/news/a-familiar-heartache-for-the-isolated-community-of-laloche/article28470923/

Stueve, A., & Link, B. G. (1997). Violence and psychiatric disorders: Results from an epidemiological study of young adults in Israel. *Psychiatric Quarterly, 68,* 327–342.

Suarez, E., & Gadailla, T. M. (2010). Stop blaming the victim: A meta-analysis on rape myths. *Journal of Interpersonal Violence, 25,* 2010–2035.

Suavé, J., & Hung, K. (2008). *An international perspective on criminal victimisation.* Ottawa, ON: Canadian Centre for Justice Statistics, Statistics Canada.

Suay, F., Salvador, A., Gonzalez-Bono, E., Sanchis, C., Martinez, M., Martinez-Sanchis, S., . . . & Montoro, J. B. (1999). Effects of competition and its outcome on serum testosterone, cortisol, and prolactin. *Psychoneuroendocrinology, 24,* 551–566.

Sullivan, E. A., & Kosson, D. S. (2006). Ethnic and cultural variations in psychopathy. In C. J. Patrick (Ed.), *Handbook of psychopathy* (pp. 437–458). New York, NY: Guilford Press.

Sullivan, C. J. (2008). Childhood emotional and behavioral problems and prediction of delinquency: A longitudinal assessment of an empirically-identified latent profile. *Applied Psychology in Criminal Justice, 4,* 45–80.

Sundel, S. S., & Sundel, M. (1993). *Behavior modification in human in the human services: A systematic introduction to concepts and applications* (3rd ed.). Newbury Park, CA: Sage.

Sun Hong, J., Cho, H., Allen-Meares, P., & Espelage, D. L. (2011). The social ecology of the Columbine High School shootings. *Children and Youth Services Review, 33,* 861–868.

Surette, R. (2011). *Media, crime, and criminal justice: Images, realities, and policies.* Belmont, CA: Wadsworth.

Sutherland, E. H. (1937). *The professional thief.* Chicago, IL: University of Chicago Press.

Sutherland, E. H. (1947). *Principles of criminology* (4th ed.). Chicago, IL: Lippincourt.

Susman, E. J., Dorn, L. D., & Chrousos, G. P. (1991). Negative affect and hormone levels in young adolescents: Concurrent and predictive perspectives. *Journal of Youth and Adolescence, 20,* 167–190.

Susman, E. J., & Ponirakis, A. (1997). Hormones—Context interactions and antisocial behavior in youth. In A. Raine, P. A. Brennan, D. P. Farrington, and S. A. Mednick (Eds.), *Biosocial bases of violence* (pp. 251–269). New York, NY: Plenum Press.

Swanson, J. W. (1994). Mental disorder, substance abuse, and community violence: An epidemiological approach. In J. Monahan & H. Steadman (Eds.), *Violence and mental disorder: Developments in risk assessment* (pp. 101–136). Chicago, IL: University of Chicago Press.

Swanson, J. W., Borum, R., Swartz, M. S., & Monahan, J. (1996). Psychotic symptoms and disorders and the risk of violent behaviour in the community. *Criminal Behaviour and Mental Health, 6,* 309–329.

Swanson, J. W., Estroff, S., Swartz, M., Borum, R., Lachiotte, W., Zimmer, C., & Wagner, R. (1997). Violence and severe mental disorder in clinical and community populations: The effects of psychotic symptoms, comorbidity, and lack of treatment. *Psychiatry, 60,* 1–22.

Swanson, J. W., & Holzer, C. E. (1991). Violence and the ECA data. *Hospital and Community Psychiatry, 42,* 79–80.

Swanson, J. W., Holzer, C. E., Ganju, V. K., & Jono, R. T. (1990). Violence and psychiatric disorder in the community: Evidence from the Epidemiologic Catchment Area surveys. *Hospital and Community Psychiatry, 41,* 761–770.

Swanson, J. W., Swartz, M. S., & Elbogen, E. B. (2004). Effectiveness of atypical antipsychotic medications in reducing violent behavior among persons with schizophrenia in community-based treatment. *Schizophrenia Bulletin, 30,* 3–20.

Swanson, J. W., Swartz, M. S., Essock, S. M., Osher, F. C., Wagner, H. R., Goodman, L. A., . . . Meador, K. G. (2002). The social-environmental context of violent behaviour in persons treated for severe mental illness. *American Journal of Public Health, 92,* 1523–1532.

Swanson, J. W., Swartz, M. S., Estroff, S., Borum, R., Wagner, R., & Hiday, V. (1998). Psychiatric impairment, social contact, and violent behaviour: Evidence from a study of outpatient-committed persons with severe mental disorder. *Social Psychiatry and Psychiatric Epidemiology, 33,* 86–94.

Swanson, J. W., Swartz, M. S., van Dorn, R. A., Elbogen, E. B., Wagner, H. R., Rosenheck, R. A., . . . Lieberman, J. A. (2006). A national study of violent behaviour in persons with schizophrenia. *Archives of General Psychiatry, 63,* 490–499.

Swartz, J. A., & Lurigio, A. J. (2007). Serious mental illness and arrest: The generalized mediating effect of substance use. *Crime & Delinquency, 53,* 581–602.

Swartz, M. S., Swanson, J. W., Hiday, V. A., Borum, R., Wagner, H. R., & Burns, B. J. (1998). Violence and severe mental illness: The effects of substance abuse and nonadherence to medication. *American Journal of Psychiatry, 155,* 226–231.

Sweet, R. A., Nimgaonkar, V. L., Kamboh, M. I., Lopez, O. L., Zhang, F., & DeKosky, S. T. (1998). Dopamine receptor genetic variation, psychosis, and aggression in Alzheimer Disease. *Archives of Neurology, 55,* 1335–1340.

Taibbi, M. (2006, March 12). Catch him if you can. How did the phony French "Rockefeller" con Americans? Retrieved from http://www.nbcnews.com/id/11770944/ns/dateline_nbc/t/catch-him-if-you-can/

Tao, S., Dong, Q., Pratt, M. W., Hunsberger, B., & Pancer, S. M. (2000). Social support relations to coping and adjustment during the transition to university in the People's Republic of China. *Journal of Adolescent Research, 15,* 123–144.

Tappan, P. W. (1947). Who is the criminal? *American Sociological Review, 12,* 96–102.

Taylor, P. J. (1985). Motives for offending among violent and psychotic men. *British Journal of Psychiatry, 147,* 491–498.

Taylor, P. J. (1998). When symptoms of psychosis drive serious violence. *Social Psychiatry and Psychiatric Epidemiology, 33,* S47–S54.

Taylor, P. J. (2008). Psychosis and violence: Stories, fears, and reality. *The Canadian Journal of Psychiatry, 53,* 647–659.

Taylor, P. J., & Gunn, J. (1984). Violence and psychosis: I-risk of violence among psychotic men. *British Medical Journal, 288,* 1945–1949.

Taylor, P. J., Leese, M., Williams, D., Butwell, M., Daly, R., & Larkin, E. (1998). Mental disorder and violence: A special (high security) hospital study. *British Journal of Psychiatry, 172,* 218–226.

Taylor, S. P., & Leonard, K. E. (1983). Alcohol and human aggression. In R. G. Geen & E. I. Donnerstein (Eds.), *Aggression: Theoretical and empirical reviews, Volume 2: Issues in research* (pp. 77–101). New York, NY: Academic Press.

Temrin, H., Buchmayer, S., & Enquist, M. (2000). Step-parents and infanticide: New data contradict evolutionary predictions. *Proceedings of the Royal Society, London, B, 267,* 943–945.

Tennes, K., & Kreye, M. (1985). Children's adrenocortical response to classroom activities in elementary school. *Psychosomatic Medicine, 47,* 451–460.

Teplin, L. A. (1983). The criminalization of the mentally ill: Speculation in search of data. *Psychological Bulletin, 94,* 54–67.

Teplin, L. A. (1984). Criminalizing mental disorder: The comparative arrest rate of the mentally ill. *American Psychologist, 39,* 794–803.

Teplin, L. A. (1990). The prevalence of severe mental disorder among male urban jail detainees: Comparison with the Epidemiological Catchment Area program. *American Journal of Public Health, 80,* 663–668.

Teplin, L. A., McClelland, G. M., Abram, K. M., & Weiner, D. A. (2005). Crime victimization in adults with severe mental illness: Comparison with the national crime victimization survey. *Archives of General Psychiatry, 62*, 911–921.

The madman in the tower [Electronic Version]. (1966, August 12). *Time.* Retrieved from http://content.time.com/time/magazine/article/0,9171,842584,00.html

Thomas, A., Chess, S., & Birch, H. G. (1968). *Temperament and behavior disorders in children.* New York, NY: New York University Press.

Thompson, A., Hollis, C., & Richards, D. (2003). Authoritarian parenting attitudes as a risk for conduct problems: Results from a British national cohort study. *European Child & Adolescent Psychiatry, 12*, 84–91.

Thompson, R. H., Iwata, B. A., Conners, J., & Roscoe, E. M. (1999). Effects of reinforcement for alternative behavior during punishment of self-injury. *Journal of Applied Behavior Analysis, 32*, 317–328.

Thornhill, T. (2013, November 7). Brother pleads guilty to killing his step-sister trying out moves he'd seen on TV wrestling show. *The Daily Mail.* Retrieved from http://www.dailymail.co.uk/news/article-2490032/Devalon-Armstrong-Teenage-boy-pleads-guilty-killing-sister-Viloude-Louis-5.html

Thornhill, T., & Farberov, S. (2013, 11 December). Louisiana boy, 13, sentenced to three years for beating five-year-old stepsister to death by practicing wrestling-style moves on her. Retrieved from http://www.dailymail.co.uk/news/article-2522257/Armstrong-Desvallons-13-sentenced-years-killing-year-old-stepsister.html

Tibbetts, S. G. (2003). Selfishness, social control, and emotions: An integrated perspective on criminality. In A. Walsh & L. Ellis (Eds.), *Biosocial criminology: Challenging environmentalism's supremacy* (pp. 83–101). Hauppauge, NY: Nova Science Publishers.

Tiihonen, J., Hakola, P., Eronen, M., Vartiainen, H., & Ryynänen, O.-P. (1996). Risk of homicidal behavior among discharged forensic psychiatric patients. *Forensic Science International, 79*, 123–129.

Tiihonen, J., Isohanni, M., Räsänen, P., Koiranen, M., & Moring, J. (1997). Specific major mental disorders and criminality: A 26-year prospective study of the 1966 Northern Finland birth cohort. *American Journal of Psychiatry, 154*, 840–845.

Tinsley, B. R., & Parke, R. D. (1983). The person–environment relationship: Lessons from families with preterm infants. In D. Magnusson & V. L. Allen (Eds.), *Human development: An interactional perspective* (pp. 93–110). San Diego, CA: Academic Press.

Tjaden, P., & Thoennes, N. (2000). *Full report of the prevalence, incidence, and consequences of violence against women: Research report. Findings from the National Violence Against Women Survey. Washington,* DC: National Institute of Justice, U.S. Department of Justice.

Tonin, E. (2004). The attachment styles of stalkers. *Journal of Forensic Psychiatry and Psychology, 15*, 584–590.

Tong, L. S. J., & Farrington, D. P. (2006). How effective is the "Reasoning and Rehabilitation" programme in reducing re-offending? A meta-analysis of evaluations in four countries. *Psychology, Crime and Law, 12*, 3–24.

Tranel, D. (2000). Nerual correlates of violent behavior. In J. Bogousslavsky and J. Cummings (Eds.), *Behavior and mood disorders in focal brain lesions.* Cambridge, UK: Cambridge University Press.

Tranel, D., & Eslinger, P. (2000). Effects of early onset brain injury on the development of cognition and behavior: Introduction to the special issue. *Developmental Neuropsychology, 18*, 273–280.

Tremblay, R. E. (2015). Developmental origins of chronic physical aggression: An international perspective on using singletons, twins and epigenetics. *European Journal of Criminology, 12*, 551–561.

Trevethan, S. D., & Walker, L. J. (1989). Hypothetical versus real-life moral reasoning among psychopathic and delinquent youth. *Development and Psychopathology, 1/2*, 91–103.

Trivers, R. L. (1971). The evolution of reciprocal altruism. *The Quarterly Review of Biology, 46*, 35–57.

Trivers, R. L. (1972). Parental investment and sexual selection. In B. Campbell (Ed.), *Sexual selection and the descent of man: 1871-1971* (pp. 136–179). Chicago, IL: Aldine.

Trivers, R. L. (1985). *Social evolution.* Menlo Park, CA: Benjamin/Cummings.

Truman, J. L., & Langton, L. (2014). *Criminal victimization, 2013.* Washington, DC: Bureau of Justice Statistics, U.S. Department of Justice, Bureau of Justice Statistics.

Truman, J. L., & Langton, L. (2015). *Criminal victimization, 2014.* Washington, DC: Bureau of Justice Statistics, U.S. Department of Justice.

Tupper, K. W. (2012). Psychoactive substances and the English language: "Drugs," discourses, and public policy. *Contemporary Drug Problems, 39*, 461–492.

Turner, C. W., & Simons, L. S. (1974). Effects of subject sophistication and evaluation apprehension on aggressive responses to weapons. *Journal of Personality and Social Psychology, 30*, 341–348.

Twelve years of life behind bars. (2005, May 31). *The Montreal Gazette*, p. A2.

Twenge, J. M., & Campbell, W. K. (2003). "Isn't it fun to get the respect that we're going to deserve?" Narcissism, social rejection, and aggression. *Personality and Social Psychology Bulletin, 29*, 261–272.

Uggen, C. (2000). Work as a turning point in the life course of criminals: A duration model of age, employment, and recidivism. *American Sociological Review, 65*, 529–546.

Uggen, C., & Shannon, S. C. S. (2014). Productive addicts and harm reduction: How work reduces crime—but not drug use. *Social Problems, 61*, 105–130.

UK Ministry of Justice, Home Office & the Office for National Statistics. (2013). An overview of sexual offending in England and Wales. Retrieved from https://www.gov.uk/government/uploads/system/uploads/attachment_data/file/214970/sexual-offending-overview-jan-2013.pdf

Urberg, K. A., Degirmencioglu, S. M., & Tolson, J. M. (1998). Adolescent friendship selection and termination: The role of similarity. *Journal of Social and Personal Relationships, 15,* 703–710.

Usher, A. M., Stewart, L. A., & Wilton, G. (2013). Attention deficit hyperactivity disorder in a Canadian prison population. *International Journal of Law and Psychiatry, 36,* 311–315.

Van Dam, C., Janssens, J. M. A. M., & De Bruyn, E. E. J. (2006). PEN, Big Five, juvenile delinquency, and criminal recidivism. *Personality and Individual Differences, 39,* 7–19.

Vandiver, D. M., & Kercher, G. (2004). Offender and victim characteristic of registered female sexual offenders in Texas: A proposed typology of female sexual offenders. *Sexual Abuse: Journal of Research and Treatment, 16,* 121–137.

Van Goozen, S. H., Matthys, W., Cohen-Kettenis, P. T., Thijssen, J. H., & van Engeland H. (1998). Adrenal androgens and aggression in conduct disorder prepubertal boys and normal controls. *Biological Psychiatry, 43,* 156–158.

Van Houten, R. (1983). Punishment from the animal laboratory to the applied setting. In S. Axelrod & J. Apsche (Eds.), *The effects of punishment on human behavior* (pp. 13–44). New York, NY: Academic Press.

Van Ijzendoorn, M. H. (1997). Attachment, emergent morality, and aggression: Toward a developmental socioemotional model of antisocial behaviour. *International Journal of Behavioral Development, 21,* 703–727.

Van Ijzendoorn, M. H., Feldbrugge, J. T. T. M., Derks, F. C. H., de Ruiter, C., Verhagen, M. F. M., Philipse, M. W. G., . . . Riksen-Walraven, J. M. A. (1997). Attachment representations of personality-disordered criminal offenders. *American Journal of Orthopsychiatry, 67,* 449–459.

Van Ijzendoorn, M. H., Schuengel, C., & Bakermans-Kranenburg, M. J. (1999). Disorganized attachment in early childhood: Meta-analysis of precursors, concomitants, and sequelae. *Development and Psychopathology, 11,* 225–250.

Van Langen, M. A. M., Wissink, I. B., van Vugt, E. S., Van der Stouwe, T., & Stams, G. J. J. M. (2014). The relation between empathy and offending: A meta-analysis. *Aggression and Violent Behavior, 19,* 179–189.

Van Voorhis, P., & Lester, D. (2009). Cognitive therapies. In P. Van Voorhis, M. Braswell, & D. Lester (Eds.), *Correctional counselling and rehabilitation* (7th ed.) (pp. 185–211). New Providence, NJ: Matthew Bender.

Van Voorhis, P., & Salisbury, E. J. (2014). *Correctional counselling and rehabilitation* (8th ed.). Waltham, MA: Anderson.

Van Vugt, E., Gibbs, J., Stams, G. J., Bijleveld, C., Hendriks, J., & van der Laan, P. (2011). Moral development and recidivism: A meta-analysis. *International Journal of Offender Therapy and Comparative Criminology, 55,* 1234–1250.

Vaughn, M. G., DeLisi, M., Beaver, K. M., & Wright, J. P. (2009). DAT1 and 5HTT are associated with pathological criminal behavior in a nationally representative sample of youth. *Criminal Justice and Behavior, 36,* 1113–1124.

Vega, V., & Malamuth, N. M. (2007). Predicting sexual aggression: The role of pornography in the context of general and specific risk factors. *Aggressive Behavior, 33,* 104–107.

Verhulst, F. C., Eussen, M. L., Berden, G. F., Sanders-Woudstra, J., & Van Der Ende, J. (1993). Pathways of problem behaviors from childhood to adolescence. *Journal of the American Academy of Child Adolescent Psychiatry, 32,* 388–396.

Verlinden, S., Hersen, M., & Thomas, J. (2000). Risk factors in school shootings. *Clinical Psychology Review, 20,* 3–56.

Verona, E., & Vitale, J. (2006). Psychopathy in women: Assessment, manifestations, and etiology. In C. J. Patrick (Ed.), *Handbook of psychopathy* (pp. 415–436). New York, NY: Guilford Press.

Vila, B. (1994). A general paradigm for understanding criminal behavior: Extending evolutionary ecological theory. *Criminology, 32,* 311–359.

Vincent, G. M., & Hart, S. D. (2002). Psychopathy in childhood and adolescence: Implications for the assessment and management of multi-problem youths. In R. R. Corrado, R. Roesch, S. D. Hart, & J. K. Gierowski (Eds.), *Multi-problem violent youth: A foundation for comparative research on needs, interventions and outcomes* (pp. 150–168). Washington, DC: IOS Press.

Vincent, G. M., Vitacco, M. J., Grisso, T., & Corrado, R. R. (2003). Subtypes of adolescent offenders: Affective traits and antisocial behaviour patterns. *Behavioral Sciences and the Law, 21,* 695–712.

Virkkunen, M. (1985). Urinary free cortisol secretion in habitually violent offenders. *Acta Psychiatrica Scandanavia, 72,* 40–44.

Virkkunen, M., Goldman, D., & Linnoila, M. (1996). Serotonin in alcoholic violent offenders. *Ciba Foundation Symposium, 194,* 168–77.

Virkkunen, M., & Linnoila, M. (1993a). Brain serotonin, type II alcoholism, and impulsive violence. *Journal of Studies on Alcohol and Drugs, 11,* 163–169.

Virkkunen, M., & Linnoila, M. (1993b). Serotonin in personality disorders with habitual violence and impulsivity. In S. Hodgins (Ed.), *Mental disorder and crime* (pp. 227–243). Newbury Park, CA: Sage.

Virkkunen, M., Nuutila, A., & Huusko, S. (1976). Effect of brain injury on social adaptability, *Acta Psychiatica Scandinavica, 53,* 168–172.

Visser, T. A. W., Ohan, J. L., Whittle, S., Yucuel, M., Simmons, J. G., & Allen, N. B. (2013). Sex differences in structural brain asymmetry predict overt aggression in early adolescents. *Social Cognitive and Affective Neuroscience, 8*, 1–8.

Vitacco, M. J., Neumann, C. S., & Jackson, R. L. (2005). Testing a four-factor model of psychopathy and its association with ethnicity, gender, intelligence, and violence. *Journal of Consulting and Clinical Psychology, 73*, 466–476.

Vitale, J. E., & Newman, J. P. (2001). Using the Psychopathy Checklist–Revised with female samples: Reliability, validity, and implications for clinical utility. *Clinical Psychology: Science and Practice, 8*, 117–132.

Vitale, J. E., & Newman, J. P. (2009). Psychopathic violence: A cognitive-attention perspective. In M. McMurran & R. C. Howard (Eds.), *Personality, personality disorder and violence* (pp. 247–263). Chichester, UK: Wiley.

Vitale, J. E., Serin, R. C., Bolt, D., & Newman, J. P. (2005). Hostile attributions in incarcerated adult male offenders: An exploration of two pathways. *Aggressive Behavior, 31*, 99–115.

Vitale, J. E., Smith, S. S., Brinkley, C. A., & Newman, J. P. (2002). The reliability and validity of the Psychopathy Checklist–Revised in a sample of female offenders. *Criminal Justice and Behavior, 29*, 202–231.

Vitaro, F., Brendgen, M., & Barker, E. D. (2006). Subtypes of aggressive behaviors: A developmental perspective. *International Journal of Behavioral Development, 30*, 12–19.

Vogel-Sprott, M. (1992). *Alcohol tolerance and social drinking: Learning the consequences.* New York, NY: Guilford Press.

Vogel-Sprott, M., & Fillmore, M. T. (1993). Impairment and recovery under repeated doses of alcohol: Effects of response outcomes. *Pharmacology, Biochemistry and Behavior, 45*, 59–63.

Volkow, N. D., & Tancredi, L. (1987). Neural substrates of violent behavior: A preliminary study with positron emission tomography. *British Journal of Psychiatry, 151*, 668–673.

Vossekuil, B., Fein, R., Reddy, M., Borum, R., & Modzeleski, W. (2004). *The final report and findings of the Safe School Initiative: Implications of the prevention of school attacks in the United States.* Retrieved from https://www2.ed.gov/admins/lead/safety/preventingattacksreport.pdf

Wahl, O. F. (2003). News media portrayal of mental illness: Implications for public policy. *American Behavioral Scientist, 46*, 1594–1600.

Wahlund, K., & Kristiansson, M. (2009). Aggression, psychopathy and brain imaging—Review and future recommendations. *International Journal of Law and Psychiatry, 32*, 266–271.

Wakefield, J. C. (1992). Disorder as harmful dysfunction: A conceptual critique of *DSM-III-R*'s definition of mental disorder. *Psychological Review, 99*, 232–247.

Walker, L. E. (1984). *The battered woman syndrome.* New York, NY: Springer.

Wallace, C., Mullen, P., & Burgess, P. (2004). Criminal offending in schizophrenia over a 25-year period marked by deinstitutionalization and increasing prevalence of comorbid substance use disorders. *American Journal of Psychiatry, 161*, 716–727.

Wallace, C., Mullen, P., Burgess, P., Palmer, S., Ruschena, D., & Browne, C. (1998). Serious criminal offending and mental disorder. *British Journal of Psychiatry, 172*, 477–484.

Wallace, H. (2004). *Family violence: Legal, medical, and social perspectives.* Boston, MA: Allyn & Bacon.

Walling, S. M., Meehan, J. C., Marshall, A. D., Holtzworth-Munroe, A. H., & Taft, C. T. (2012). The relationship of intimate partner aggression to head injury, executive functioning, and intelligence. *Journal of Marital & Family Therapy, 38*, 471–485.

Walsh, A. (2002). *Biosocial criminology: Introduction and integration.* Cincinatti, OH: Anderson.

Walsh, A. (2009). *Biology and criminology: The biosocial synthesis.* New York, NY: Routledge.

Walsh, A., & Ellis, L. (2007). *Criminology: An interdisciplinary approach.* Thousand Oaks, CA: Sage.

Walsh, E., Buchanan, A., & Fahy, T. (2002). Violence and schizophrenia: Examining the evidence. *British Journal of Psychiatry, 180*, 490–495.

Walsh, E., Moran, P., Scott, C., McKenzie, K., Burns, T., Creed, F., . . . Fahy, T. (2003). Prevalence of violent victimisation in severe mental illness. *British Journal of Psychiatry, 183*, 233–238.

Walsh, J. A., Krienert, J. L., & Crowder, D. (2008). Innocence lost: A gender-based study of parricide offender, victim, and incident characteristics in a national sample, 1976–2003. *Journal of Aggression, Maltreatment, & Trauma, 16*, 202–227.

Walters, G. D. (1990). *The criminal lifestyle: Patterns of serious criminal conduct.* Newbury Park, CA: Sage.

Walters, G. D. (1995). The Psychological Inventory of Criminal Thinking Styles. Part I: Reliability and preliminary validity. *Criminal Justice and Behavior, 22*, 307–325.

Walters, G. D. (2002). The Psychological Inventory of Criminal Thinking Styles (PICTS): A review and meta-analysis. *Assessment, 9*, 278–291.

Walters, G. D. (2003). Predicting institutional adjustment and recidivism with the Psychopathy Checklist Factor scores: A meta-analysis. *Law and Human Behavior, 27*, 541–558.

Walters, G. D. (2006). Appraising, researching and conceptualizing criminal thinking: A personal view. *Criminal Behaviour and Mental Health, 16*, 87–99.

Walters, G. D. (2012). Criminal thinking and recidivism: Meta-analytic evidence on the predictive and incremental validity of the Psychological Inventory of Criminal Thinking Styles (PICTS). *Aggression and Violent Behavior, 17*, 272–278.

Walters, G. D., & Elliot, W. N. (1999). Predicting release and disciplinary outcome with the Psychological Inventory of Criminal Thinking Styles: Female data. *Legal and Criminological Psychology, 4,* 15–21.

Walters, G. D., Elliot, W. N., & Miscoll, D. (1998). Use of the Psychological Inventory of Criminal Thinking Styles in a group of female offenders. *Criminal Justice and Behavior, 25,* 125–134.

Walters, G. D., & White, T. W. (1989). The thinking criminal: A cognitive model of lifestyle criminality. *Criminal Justice Research Bulletin, 4,* 1–10.

Ward, T. (2000). Sexual offenders' cognitive distortions as implicit theories. *Aggression and Violent Behavior, 5,* 491–507.

Ward, T. (2002). Good lives and the rehabilitation of offenders: Promises and problems. *Aggression and Violent Behavior, 7,* 513–528.

Ward, T., & Beech, A. (2006). An integrated theory of sexual offending. *Aggression and Violent Behavior, 11,* 44–63.

Ward, T., & Gagnon, T. A. (2006). Rehabilitation, etiology, and self-regulation: The comprehensive good lives model of treatment for sexual offenders. *Aggression and Violent Behavior, 11,* 77–94.

Ward, T., Hudson, S. M., Johnston, L., & Marshall, W. L. (1997). Cognitive distortions in sex offenders: An integrative review. *Clinical Psychology Review, 17,* 479–507.

Ward, T., Hudson, S. M., & Marshall, W. L. (1996). Attachment style in sex offenders: A preliminary study. *Journal of Sex Research, 33,* 17–26.

Ward, T., & Keenan, T. (1999). Child molesters' implicit theories. *Journal of Interpersonal Violence, 14,* 821–838.

Ward, T., Keenan, T., & Hudson, S. M. (2000). Understanding cognitive, affective, and intimacy deficits in sexual offenders: A developmental perspective. *Aggression and Violent Behavior, 5,* 41–62.

Ward, T., Mann, R. E., & Gagnon, T. A. (2007). The good lives model of offender rehabilitation: Clinical implications. *Aggression and Violent Behavior, 12,* 87–107.

Ward, T., & Marshall, W. L. (2004). Good lives, etiology, and the rehabilitation of sex offenders: A bridging theory. *Journal of Sexual Aggression, 10,* 153–169.

Ward, T., & Maruna, S. (2007). *Rehabilitation: Beyond the risk assessment paradigm.* London, UK: Routledge.

Ward, T., Polaschek, D. L. L., & Beech, A. R. (Eds.) (2006). *Theories of sexual offending.* Hoboken, NJ: Wiley.

Warren, J., Hazelwood, R., & Dietz, P. (1996). The sexually sadistic serial killer. *Journal of Forensic Sciences, 41,* 970–974.

Warshaw, C., Brasher, P., & Gil, J. (2009). Mental health consequences of intimate partner violence. In C. Mitchell & D. Anglin (Eds.), *Intimate partner violence: A health-based perspective* (pp. 147–171). New York, NY: Oxford University Press.

Waschbusch, D. A. (2002). A meta-analytic examination of comorbid hyperactive-impulsive attention problems and conduct problems. *Psychological Bulletin, 128,* 118–150.

Watson, R. I. (1973). Investigation into deindividuation using a cross-cultural survey technique. *Journal of Personality and Social Psychology, 25,* 342–345.

Weaver, I. C. G., Cervoni, N., Champagne, F. A., D'Alessio, A. C., Sharma, S., Seckl, J. R., . . . Meaney, M. J. (2004). Epigenetic programming by maternal behavior. *Nature Neuroscience, 7,* 847–854.

Weaver, J. B. (1991). Are "slasher" horror films sexually violent? A content analysis. *Journal of Broadcasting and Electronic Media, 35,* 385–393.

Webster, C. D., Douglas, K. S., Eaves, D., & Hart, S. D. (1997). *HCR-20: Assessing risk for violence, Version 2.* Burnaby, BC: Mental Health, Law and Policy Institute, Simon Fraser University.

Webster, C. D., Harris, G. T., Rice, M. E., Cormier, C., & Quinsey, V. L. (1994). *The violence prediction scheme: Assessing dangerousness in high risk men.* Toronto, Canada: Centre of Criminology, University of Toronto.

Webster, C. D., Hucker, S. J., & Bloom, H. (2002). Transcending the actuarial versus clinical polemic in assessing risk for violence. *Criminal Justice and Behavior, 29,* 659–665.

Weerman, F. M. (2011). Delinquent peers in context: A longitudinal network analysis of selection and influence effects. *Criminology, 49,* 253–286.

Weiler, B. L., & Widom, C. S. (1996). Psychopathy and violent behaviour in abused and neglected young adults. *Criminal Behavior and Mental Health, 6,* 253–271.

Welsh, A. (2009). On the perils of living dangerously in the slasher horror film: Gender differences in the association between sexual activity and survival. *Sex Roles, 62,* 762–773.

Welsh, A. (2010). Sex and violence in the slasher horror film: A content analysis of gender differences in the depiction of violence. *Journal of Criminal Justice and Popular Culture, 16,* 1–25.

Wessely, S. C., Castle, D., Douglas, A. J., & Taylor, P. J. (1994). The criminal careers of incident cases of schizophrenia. *Psychological Medicine, 24,* 483–502.

West, R. (2001). Theories of addiction. *Addiction, 96,* 3–15.

West, S. A., Griffin, A. S., & Gardner, A. (2007). Evolutionary explanations for cooperation. *Current Biology, 17,* R661–R672.

West, S. G., Hatters-Friedman, S., & Resnick, P. J. (2009). Fathers who kill their children: An analysis of the literature. *Journal of Forensic Science, 54,* 463–468.

Westrup, D., & Fremouw, W. J. (1998). Stalking behavior: A literature review and suggested functional analytic assessment technology. *Aggression and Violent Behavior, 3,* 255–274.

"What are you saying about my girl's mom?" Shia LaBeouf headbutts drinker in London bar brawl as girlfriend screams to stop. (2014, January 17). *Daily Mail Reporter.* Retrieved from http://www.dailymail.co.uk/tvshowbiz/article-2540990/Shia-LaBeouf-headbutts-patron-South-London-pub-girlfriend-screams-stop.html

White, E. (2012, February 16). "Underwear bomber," Abdulmutallab faces life sentence. Retrieved from http://www.wxyz.com/dpp/news/region/detroit/underwear-bomber-abdulmutallab-faces-life-sentence

White, J. L., Moffitt, T. E., Caspi, A., Bartusch, D. J., Needles, D. J., & Stouthamer-Loeber, M. (1994). Measuring impulsivity and examining its relationship to delinquency. *Journal of Abnormal Psychology, 103*, 192–205.

White, J. L., Moffitt, T. E., Earls, F., Robins, L., & Silva, P. A. (1990). How early can we tell? Predictors of childhood conduct disorder and adolescent delinquency. *Criminology, 28*, 507–533.

White, J. L., Moffitt, T. E., & Silva, P. A. (1989). A prospective replication of the protective effects of IQ in subjects at high risk for juvenile delinquency. *Journal of Consulting and Clinical Psychology, 57*, 719–724.

White, M. C., Chafetz, L., Collins-Bride, G., & Nickens, J. (2006). History of arrest, incarceration and victimization in community-based severely mentally ill. *Journal of Community Health, 31*, 123–135.

Whiteside, S. P., & Lynam, D. R. (2001). The five factor model and impulsivity: Using a structural model of personality to understand impulsivity. *Personality and Individual Differences, 30*, 669–689.

Widom, C. S. (1989). Child abuse, neglect, and adult behavior: Research design and findings on criminality, violence, and child abuse. *American Journal of Orthopsychiatry, 59*, 355–367.

Wiebe, R. P. (2012). Integrating criminology through adaptive strategy and life history theory. *Journal of Contemporary Criminal Justice, 28*, 346–365.

Wikie, T. L., & Fraser, M. W. (2009). School shootings: Making sense of the senseless. *Aggression and Violent Behavior, 14*, 162–169.

Wilkinson, G. S. (1990). Food sharing in vampire bats. *Scientific American, 262*, 76–82.

Williams, C., South Richardson, D., Hammock, G. S., & Janit, A. S. (2012). Perceptions of physical and psychological aggression in close relationships: A review. *Aggression and Violent Behavior, 17*, 489–494.

Williams, F. P., & McShane, M. D. (2010). *Criminological theory* (5th ed.). Upper Saddle River, NJ: Pearson.

Williams, S. (1999). *Invisible darkness: The strange case of Paul Bernardo and Karla Homolka*. Toronto, ON: McArthur.

Williams, T. M. (1986). Background and overview. In T. M. Williams (Ed.), *The impact of television: A natural experiment in three communities* (pp. 1–38). Orlando, FL: Academic Press.

Williamson, S. E., Hare, R. D., & Wong, S. (1987). Violence: Criminal psychopaths and their victims. *Canadian Journal of Behavioural Science, 19*, 454–462.

Williamson, S., Harpur, T. J., & Hare, R. D. (1991). Abnormal processing of affective words by psychopaths. *Psychophysiology, 28*, 260–273.

Willis, G. M., & Ward, T. (2013). The good lives model: Does it work? Preliminary evidence. In L. A. Craig, L. Dixon, & T. A. Gagnon (Eds.), *What works in offender rehabilitation: An evidence-based approach to assessment and treatment* (pp. 305–317). New York, NY: Wiley.

Wilper, A. P., Woolhandler, S., Boyd, J. W., Lasser, K. E., McCormick, B., Bor, D. H., Himmelstein, D. U. (2009). The health and health care of US prisoners: Results of a nationwide survey. *American Journal of Public Health, 99*, 666–672.

Wilson, C. M., Douglas, K. S., & Lyon, D. R. (2011). Violence against teachers: Prevalence and consequences. *Journal of Interpersonal Violence, 26*, 2353–2371.

Wilson, D. B., Bouffard, L. A., & MacKenzie, D. L. (2005). A quantitative review of structured, group-oriented, cognitive-behavioral programs for offenders. *Criminal Justice and Behavior, 32*, 172–204.

Wilson, D. B., Gallagher, C. A., & MacKenzie, D. L. (2000). A meta-analysis of corrections-based education, vocation and work programs for adult offenders. *Journal of Research in Crime and Delinquency, 37*, 568–581.

Wilson-Bates, F. (2008). *Lost in transitions: How a lack of capacity in the mental health system is failing Vancouver's mentally ill and draining police resources*. Vancouver, BC: Vancouver Police Department.

Wilton, K. (2016, April 21). Homolka's presence irks neighbours. *The Vancouver Sun*, p. NP5.

Wintre, M. G., & Yaffe, M. (2000). First-year students' adjustment to university life as a function of relationships with parents. *Journal of Adolescent Research, 15*, 9–37.

Wolfgang, M. E. (1983). Delinquency in two birth cohorts. In K. T. Van Dusen & S. A. Mednick (Eds.), *Prospective studies in crime and delinquency* (pp. 7–16). Hingham, MA: Kluwer-Nijhoff.

Wolfgang, M. E., Figlio, R., & Selling. T. (1972/1987). *Delinquency in a birth cohort*. Chicago, IL: University of Chicago Press.

Wong, S. (1984). *Criminal and institutional behaviours of psychopaths*. Ottawa, ON: Programs Branch Users Report, Ministry of the Solicitor General of Canada.

Wood, W., Wong, F. Y., & Chachere, J. G. (1991). Effects of media violence on viewers' aggression in unconstrained social interaction. *Psychological Bulletin, 109*, 371–383.

Woodworth, M., Freimuth, T., Hutton, E. L., Carpenter, T., Agar, A. D., & Logan, M. (2013). High-risk sexual offenders: An examination of sexual fantasy, sexual paraphilia, psychopathy, and offence characteristics. *International Journal of Law and Psychiatry, 36*, 144–156.

Woodworth, M., & Porter, S. (2002). In cold blood: Characteristics of criminal homicides as a function of psychopathy. *Journal of Abnormal Psychology, 111*, 436–445.

World Health Organization. (1990). *International Classification of Diseases and Related Health Problems, 10th Revision*. Geneva: Author.

World Health Organization. (1992). *The ICD-10 classification of mental and behavioural disorders: Clinical descriptions and diagnostic guidelines.* Geneva, Switzerland: Author.

World Health Organization (2002). *Intimate partner violence: Facts.* Retrieved from: http://www.who.int/violence_injury_prevention/violence/world_report/factsheets/en/ipvfacts.pdf

Worthington, P. (1993, July/August). The journalist and the killer. *Saturday Night Magazine, 108,* 30–55.

Wortley, R. (2011). *Psychological criminology: An integrative approach.* New York, NY: Routledge.

Wright, P., Nobrega, J., Langevin, R., & Wortzman, G. (1990). Brain density and symmetry in pedophilic and sexually aggressive offenders. *Annals of Sex Research, 3,* 319–328.

WWE Canadian wrestler Benoit, wife and son found dead: Police treating case as murder-suicide. (2007, June 25). *Toronto Star,* p. A2.

Yarvis, R. M. (1990). Axis I and axis II diagnostic parameters of homicide. *Bulletin of the American Academy of Psychiatry and the Law, 18,* 249–269.

Yesavage, J. A. (1984). Correlates of dangerous behavior by schizophrenics in hospital. *Journal of Psychiatric Research, 18,* 225–231.

Yeudall, L. T., & Fromm-Auch, D. (1979). Neuropsychological impairments in various psychopathological populations. In J. Gruzelier & P. Flor-Henry (Eds.), *Hemisphere asymmetries of function and psychopathology* (pp. 5–13). New York, NY: Elesvier.

Yeudall, L. T., Fromm-Auch, D., & Davis, P. (1982). Neuropsychological impairment in persistent criminal/antisocial behavior. *Journal of Nervous and Mental Disease, 170,* 257–265.

Yochelson, S., & Samenow, S. E. (1976). *The criminal personality: A profile for change.* New York, NY: Jason Aronson.

Yoon, J. S., Hughes, J. N., Cavell, T. A., & Thompson, B. (2000). Social cognitive differences between aggressive-rejected and aggressive-nonrejected children. *Journal of School Psychology, 38,* 551–570.

Young, J. E., Klosko, M. E., & Weishaar, M. E. (2003). *Schema therapy: A practitioner's guide.* New York, NY: Guilford Press.

Young, S. E., Smolen, A., Hewitt, J. K., Haberstick, B. C., Stallings, M. C., Corely, R. P., & Crowley, T. J. (2005). Interaction between MAO-A genotype and maltreatment in risk for conduct disorder: Failure to confirm in adolescent patients. *American Journal of Psychiatry, 163,* 1019–1025.

Zhang, L., Welte, J. W., & Wieczorek, W. W. (2002). The role of aggression-related alcohol expectancies in explaining the link between alcohol and violent behavior. *Substance Use and Misuse, 37,* 457–471.

Zhang, T. (2008). *Costs of crime in Canada, 2008.* Ottawa, ON: Department of Justice Canada. Retrieved from http://www.justice.gc.ca/eng/rp-pr/csj-sjc/crime/rr10_5/rr10_5.pdf

Zillman, D., Katcher, A. H., & Milavsky, B. (1972). Excitation transfer from physical exercise to subsequent aggressive behavior. *Journal of Experimental Social Psychology, 8,* 247–259.

Zimbardo, P. G. (1970). The human choice: Individuation, reason, and order versus deindividuation, impulse, and chaos. In W. J. Arnold & D. Levine (Eds.), *Nebraska Symposium on Motivation, 1969* (pp. 237–307). Lincoln: University of Nebraska Press.

Zimbardo, P. G., & Leippe, M. R. (1991). *The psychology of attitude change and social influence.* New York, NY: Mcgraw-Hill.

Zimbardo, P. G., Maslach, C., & Haney, C. (2000). Reflections on the Stanford prison experiment: Genesis, transformations, consequences. In T. Blass (Ed.), *Obedience to authority: Current perspectives on the Milgram paradigm* (pp. 193–237). Mahwah, NJ: Erlbaum.

Zitrin, A., Hardesty, A. S., Burdock, E. I., & Drossman, A. K. (1976). Crime and violence among mental patients. *American Journal of Psychiatry, 133,* 142–149.

Zona, M. A., Sharma, K. K., & Lane, J. C. (1993). A comparative study of erotomanic and obsessional subjects in a forensic sample. *Journal of Forensic Sciences, 38,* 894–903.

Zuckerman, M. (1999). *Vulnerability to psychopathology: A biosocial model.* Washington, DC: American Psychological Association.

Index